Big Data and Artificial Intelligence for Healthcare Applications

Big Data for Industry 4.0: Challenges and Applications

Series Editors

Sandhya Makkar, K. Martin Sagayam, and Rohail Hassan

Industry 4.0 or fourth industrial revolution refers to interconnectivity, automation and real time data exchange between machines and processes. There is a tremendous growth in big data from internet of things (IoT) and information services which drives the industry to develop new models and distributed tools to handle big data. Cutting-edge digital technologies are being harnessed to optimize and automate production including upstream supply-chain processes, warehouse management systems, automated guided vehicles, drones etc. The ultimate goal of industry 4.0 is to drive manufacturing or services in a progressive way to be faster, effective and efficient that can only be achieved by embedding modern day technology in machines, components, and parts that will transmit real-time data to networked IT systems. These, in turn, apply advanced soft computing paradigms such as machine learning algorithms to run the process automatically without any manual operations.

The new book series will provide readers with an overview of the state-of-the-art in the field of Industry 4.0 and related research advancements. The respective books will identify and discuss new dimensions of both risk factors and success factors, along with performance metrics that can be employed in future research work. The series will also discuss a number of real-time issues, problems and applications with corresponding solutions and suggestions. Sharing new theoretical findings, tools and techniques for Industry 4.0, and covering both theoretical and application-oriented approaches. The book series will offer a valuable asset for newcomers to the field and practicing professionals alike. The focus is to collate the recent advances in the field, so that undergraduate and postgraduate students, researchers, academicians, and Industry people can easily understand the implications and applications of the field.

Industry 4.0 Interoperability, Analytics, Security, and Case Studies
Edited by G. Rajesh, X. Mercilin Raajini, and Hien Dang

Big Data and Artificial Intelligence for Healthcare Applications
Edited by Ankur Saxena, Nicolas Brault, and Shazia Rashid

For more information on this series, please visit: https://www.routledge.com/Big-Data-for-Industry-4.0-Challenges-and-Applications/book-series/CRCBDICA

Big Data and Artificial Intelligence for Healthcare Applications

Edited by
Ankur Saxena, Nicolas Brault, and Shazia Rashid

CRC Press
Taylor & Francis Group
Boca Raton London New York

CRC Press is an imprint of the
Taylor & Francis Group, an **informa** business

First edition published 2021
by CRC Press
6000 Broken Sound Parkway NW, Suite 300, Boca Raton, FL 33487-2742

and by CRC Press
2 Park Square, Milton Park, Abingdon, Oxon, OX14 4RN

CRC Press is an imprint of Taylor & Francis Group, LLC

Library of Congress Cataloging-in-Publication Data

Names: Saxena, Ankur, editor. | Brault, Nicolas, editor. | Rashid, Shazia, editor.
Title: Big data and artificial intelligence for healthcare applications / edited by Ankur Saxena, Nicolas Brault, and Shazia Rashid.
Description: First edition. | Boca Raton : CRC Press, 2021. | Includes bibliographical references and index.
Identifiers: LCCN 2020056220 (print) | LCCN 2020056221 (ebook) | ISBN 9780367554958 (hardback) | ISBN 9781003093770 (ebook)
Subjects: LCSH: Medical informatics--Technological innovations. | Medical telematics--Technological innovations. | Big data. | Data mining. | Artificial intelligence--Medical applications.
Classification: LCC R858.A3 B54 2021 (print) | LCC R858.A3 (ebook) | DDC 610.285--dc23
LC record available at https://lccn.loc.gov/2020056220
LC ebook record available at https://lccn.loc.gov/2020056221

ISBN: 978-0-367-55495-8 (hbk)
ISBN: 978-0-367-55497-2 (pbk)
ISBN: 978-1-003-09377-0 (ebk)

Typeset in Times
by Deanta Global Publishing Services, Chennai, India

Contents

Preface

The word Artificial Intelligence (AI) was coined by John McCarthy in 1956. However, the possibility of machines being able to mimic human actions and think was posed earlier by Alan Turing who created the Turing test to distinguish humans from machines. Since then the power of computation has evolved to the point of instant calculations and the ability to analyze new data, in real-time. Over the years AI has grown to be overused and misused to include all kinds of computerized automated systems, including logical programming, probability algorithms and remote-controlled surgical robotics. Machine Learning (ML) is a branch of AI, where the system is trained by introducing data to its learning algorithms, from which it uncovers patterns, builds models, and makes predictions based on the best fit model. Big data is another branch of AI involved in managing extremely large data sets that are too big and complex to be dealt by traditional data-processing application software and maybe analyzed effectively using computational tools to reveal patterns, trends, and associations, especially relating to human behavior and interactions.

Health care is a dynamic research field that is continually confronted by issues with the acquisition, distribution, and utilization of a vast volume of information. These struggles partially emerged as a consequence of the incorporation and use of methods which create big data. Furthermore, there are persistent demands, such as improving access to medical care, reducing operational costs and improving outcomes of treatment. Instead of concentrating on patient safety, the stress of adjusting the workflow to ever-evolving requirements and protocols raises the dissatisfaction of healthcare professionals and causes professionally qualified experts to waste more and more hours on paperwork. The extreme shortage of healthcare practitioners is also attributed to the tremendous growth in indicated medical treatments and exams. With such burden on healthcare systems, AI, ML, and Big Data have been incorporated into healthcare services to improve patient care by speeding up procedures and ensuring greater accuracy, paving the door to provide improved overall healthcare. ML is evaluating radiological images, pathology slides, and patients' electronic medical records (EMR), assisting in the process of diagnosis and treatment of patients and increasing the skills of physicians. ML and AI have varied applications and healthcare has come up as a major area that has benefited from these advanced tools and techniques. Some of the areas where AI is predicted to have a major influence are in the prediction of population health outcomes for formulating smart personalized health plans, Clinical decision support (CDS) which will provide a framework for precision medicine, medical imagining, and diagnostics, drug discovery and digital patient engagement platforms to promote preventive care practices for chronic disease management. AI has the potential to ease the human resources crisis in healthcare by facilitating diagnostics, decision-making, big data analytics, and administration, among others. Big data analysis in medicine and healthcare includes the integration and analysis of large volumes of complex heterogeneous data, such as omics data (genomics, epigenomics, transcriptomics, proteomics, metabolomics, pharmacogenomics, interactomics, diseasomics), biomedical data, and data from electronic health records. Coupled with related technologies, the use of mobile health devices (mobile health/mHealth) promises to transform global health delivery by creating new delivery models that can be integrated with existing health services. These delivery models could facilitate the delivery of health care to rural areas where access to high-quality care is limited.

Despite the great potential of AI and ML research and development in the field of healthcare, new governance requirements have been raised by the ethical challenges induced by its applications. The establishment of an ethical global governance structure and functionality, as well as special guidelines for AI applications in health care, is needed to ensure "trustworthy" AI systems. The roles of governments in ethical auditing and the roles of participants in the framework of ethical governance are the most significant elements.

With a multi-disciplinary approach, this book focuses on the principles and applications of AI, ML, and Big Data in different areas of health care and highlights the current research in these areas. This book also covers the associated ethical issues and concerns in using these technologies in healthcare. This book will be useful for programmers, clinicians, healthcare professionals, policymakers, scientists, young researchers, and students and can provide information to each stakeholder in their areas to develop, implement, and regulate these modern revolutionary technologies.

Editors

Ankur Saxena is currently working as Assistant Professor in Amity University Uttar Pradesh (AUUP), Noida. He has 14 years of wide teaching experience at graduation and post-graduation levels and 3 years of industrial experience in the field of Software Development. He has published 10 books with international reputed publication. He has published 40 research papers in reputed national and international journals. He is Editorial Board Member and Reviewer for a number of journals. His research interests are Cloud Computing, Big Data, Artificial Intelligence, Machine Learning evolutionary algorithms, software framework, design and analysis of algorithms, and Biometric identification.

Nicolas Brault is Associate Professor in History and Philosophy of Science, Institute Polytechnique UniLaSalle, France. He is Research Associate at SPHERE Research Unit, and Part-time lecturer for Data science and Biotechnology in Society at various Schools in Paris Metropolitan. He obtained his PhD in Epistemology from SPHERE Research Unit, University Paris.

Shazia Rashid is working as Assistant Professor in Amity Institute of Biotechnology (AIB) and Adjunct faculty at Amity Institute of Molecular Medicine and Stem Cells (AIMMSCR), Amity University Uttar Pradesh, Noida, India. Dr. Rashid has 10 years of teaching and research experience in the area of Cancer biology and Drug Discovery. She received her PhD in Biomedical Sciences from University of Ulster, United Kingdom, after which she worked as a post-doctoral fellow at University of Ulster and later at University of Oxford, United Kingdom. She later joined Amity University Uttar Pradesh, Noida, India, and has since been involved in teaching undergraduate, postgraduate, and PhD students and carrying out research in the areas of women-associated cancers, specifically HPV infection and cervical cancer. She has published a number of research papers and book chapters in reputed international and national journals. She is a strong advocate of women's health and is involved in various outreach activities such as spreading awareness about HPV infection in women.

Contributors

Isha Agarwal
Bioinformatics
Amity University
Noida, India

Vandana Bhatia
Department of Computer Science and Engineering
Amity University
Noida, India

Nicolas Brault
Interact Research Unit
UniLaSalle Polytechnic Institute
Beauvais, France

Anveshita Deo
University of Glasgow
Glasgow, United Kingdom

Benoit Duchemann
Sphere Research Unit
University of Paris
Paris, France

Rajiv Janardhanan
Amity Institute of Public Health (AIPH)
Amity University
Noida, India

Rajesh Jangade
Amity University
Noida, India

Neha Kathuria
Amity Institute of Biotechnology
Amity University
Noida, India

Alejandra Rodríguez Llerena
Institut Supérieur Des Biotechnologies De Paris
Paris, France

Jai Prakash Mehta
SEQOME Limited
Ireland

Nita Parekh
IIIT
Hyderabad, India

Urvija Rani
Netaji Subhas University of Technology
New Delhi, India

Priya Ranjan
Department of Electronics and Communication Engineering
SRM University
Guntur, India

Shazia Rashid
Amity Institute of Biotechnology (AIB) and Adjunct faculty at Amity Institute of Molecular Medicine and Stem Cells (AIMMSCR)
Amity University
Noida, India

Bhawna Rathi
Amity University
Noida, India

Suba Suseela
International Institute of Information Technology
Hyderabad, India

Aditya Narayan Sarangi
Computational Genomics Lab
CSIR-Indian Institute of Chemical Biology
Kolkata, India

Ankur Saxena
Amity Institute of Biotechnology
Amity University
Noida, India

Mohit Saxena
Institut Pasteur
Paris, France

Harpreet Singh
Indian Council of Medical Research (ICMR)
New Delhi, India

Smitha Mony Sreedharan
Amity Institute of Microbial Technology
Amity University
Noida, India

Arti Taneja
Amity Institute of Information Technology
Amity University
Noida, India

Neha Taneja
Amity Institute of Public Health (AIPH)
Amity University
Noida, India

Amit Ujlayan
Gautam Buddha University
Noida, India

Part I

Conceptual

1 Introduction to Big Data

Ankur Saxena, Urvija Rani,
Isha Agarwal, and Rajesh Jangade

CONTENTS

1.1 BIG DATA: INTRODUCTION

The current scenario in the world tells us the importance of data that is collected in our daily lives in various forms. The data is collected in unimaginable size every minute of the day. When one half of the earth sleeps, the other half starts their morning with web surfing. So, one can say that data never sleeps. A 2018 article from Forbes tells us that 2.5 quintillion bytes of data are created each day, and the number is increasing with every year ahead. All this data is being collected from Netflix, Amazon, Google, office meetings and messages and emails, hospital records or health records, financial firms, the entertainment world, government sector, social networking sites, shopping sites, etc. The amount of data helps in making personalized experiences for humans, and all this is because of big data [1, 26].

"Big data" is a term that covers large and complex datasets that cannot be processed using traditional methods of data management. All this vast data can be stored, processed, and analyzed computationally to get useful results. There is no exact range of which data can be considered as big data, but the more data one has, the more meaningful and resourceful it is. But according to a few, any data that cannot be treated with traditional management models can be treated as big data. This big data concept gathered momentum in the early 2000s. Big data has brought major changes in the information management industry. So, one needs to know how to make this data informative and knowledgeable [2, 27].

Big data undergoes various stages, the last one of which is the analysis of the data, which gives all the information that one can extract from that dataset. Traditional data analysis methods included exploratory paths that consider the past and the current form of data, but big data analysis is a predictive analysis that tends to focus on the current phase and future outcome of the data; earlier, analytics was a model-driven process, but now it is a data-driven process [3, 28]. Another difference between traditional and new management methods is that nowadays data analysts tend to use structured and clean data for building a model, but they want to try that model on unstructured data, which is not possible using traditional data management methods. Models are built using statistical and probabilistic methods while analyzing big data, which help effectively in making real-time predictions and detecting anomalies that were not possible before. Real-time data found around us in our day-to-day lives can be in any form such as finance or government records, research or biological data, and many more. All this data is useless unless it is filtered and a conclusion is made out of it. I have dealt with healthcare data to understand how big data can be used to gain knowledge and derive conclusions [4, 29].

1.2 BIG DATA: 5 VS

Big data was first defined using 3 Vs, but with the expansion of the term, it is now defined with 5 Vs. These Vs are Volume, Velocity, Variety, Veracity, and Value. These are all the characteristics of big data, or we can say that these are the parameters that are used to define whether data is big data or not [5, 30].

1.2.1 Volume

As the name suggests, big data comprises large chunks of data, which ultimately defines the word "volume." These large chunks of data can be of any volume. It plays an important role in interpreting the worthiness of data, which means to consider a chunk of data as big data volume plays a very important role. In the case of the healthcare sector, a huge amount of data concerning an individual is generated on a daily basis. This huge amount of data is needed to be handled properly. So, here big data comes into use.

1.2.2 Velocity

Since the amount of data is very large, it is necessary that the rate of collection of data should also increase. That's why the term "velocity" is introduced in the context of big data. Velocity in big data is very important because there is continuous circulation as well as building up of data, so it is necessary to process and analyze these data at the same rate so that we can gain valuable information from these chunks of data.

Suppose a survey is being held to know the actual cause of malnutrition among children below the age of 5. This data is collected as well as interpreted simultaneously to know about each and every reason which is responsible for causing malnutrition.

1.2.3 Variety

It defines the diverseness of the huge amount of data that is being collected. In the context of big data, "variety" tells us about characteristics of data, that is whether the data is sorted, which means data of the same category are in the same group, or unsorted, which means data are not arranged at all—there is no relationship that can be established between them.

1.2.4 Veracity

It is related to the affirmation of data. It tells us about the reliability of the chunk of data, which means whether the collected data can be useful for the establishment of any useful relation or not and whether any useful interpretation can be made or not. Veracity is very helpful in checking the credibility of data as well as in ensuring that the interpreted information does not have any error. In the case of healthcare, multiple examinations are done on an individual so that the diagnosis of a disease has no room for error and treatment can be provided accordingly.

1.2.5 Value

It is the most important among the five Vs. This is so because the other four Vs are dependent on it. Without value, there is no interpretation, no analysis of data, and no affirmation of data. There would be no use of volume also because volume shows how huge a chunk of data is and if this chunk of data can't be processed further, then there is no use in collecting it either (Figure 1.1).

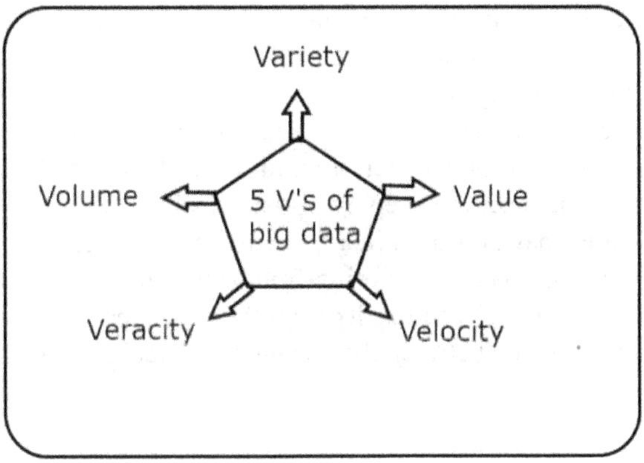

FIGURE 1.1 Five V's of Big Data.

1.3 BIG DATA: TYPES OF DATA

Variety, which is one of the Vs, is the cause of the emergence of the different types of big data, as variety itself defines the diverseness of the huge amount of collected data in the context of big data. There are three different types of big data: structured data, semi structured data, and unstructured data. These three types of big data are defined below.

1.3.1 Structured Data

Structured data is one of the types of data that comes under the "variety" category of big data. As the name suggests, it comprises a group of data that are assembled in such a way that they belong to some criteria and show some meaningful relationship among them. These types of data show a particular pattern among themselves. They are easy to be retrieved and analyzed by any individual or any type of computer program. The structured data is arranged in a tabular manner, i.e. in rows and columns, to define the characteristic feature of the dataset. In big data, structure query language, i.e. SQL, plays a crucial role in the arrangement of the structured data. This tabular arrangement of data leads to the generation of a database. This type of data is very helpful in affirming the security of the data. It also helps in modifying the data easily if it is required. In the case of the healthcare sector, structured data is very valuable in maintaining the clinical records of an individual for the treatment of disease [7, 31].

1.3.2 Semi structured Data

Semi structured data is the second type of data that comes under the "variety" category of big data. As the name suggests, it comprises a particular group of data which shows a particular arrangement but fails to define a relationship between them. This type of data does not show the arrangement of data in a tabular manner, which helps in defining the attributes. The relation type of database can be generated from the given semi structured datasets. This type of data comprises tags and elements which are being used to gather data of one type and also explain the way in which data is being kept. The same type of data belongs to a certain group that is assembled and arranged in a hierarchical manner. Since there is no sure and certain relationship among the datasets, it causes difficulty for a computer program to work efficiently. Due to the semi structured nature of the data, the keeping of data has become tough. The size of the characteristic features may be varied in a particular criterion. It can be understood in situations such as when a person suffering from stomach pain is prescribed to do a blood test and X-ray of bone. The results from these two tests are well structured in their criteria, but the relation between them cannot be established at all [8, 32].

1.3.3 Unstructured Data

Unstructured data is the third and last type of data that comes under the "variety" category of big data. As the name suggests, it comprises a group of data which cannot be arranged, nor can any type of relationship be established between them. Unlike structured data, the dataset belonging to this type cannot be arranged in a tabular manner. So, there is no generation of a database. Due to the lack of a well-defined structure of data, a computer program is restricted to access it. This type of data lacks a particular type of pattern in its datasets. Since there is no well-established relationship, the processing and analysis of this type of data is very difficult. It is a very time-consuming process if we want to infer any kind of information from it. This type of data is very helpful in handling the diverseness of data present in a group of datasets. But this type of data does not guarantee the security of data. The process of modification of the dataset is also restricted due to its nature. Generally, this type of data can be handled with the help of extensible markup language, i.e. XML [6].

1.4 BIG DATA ANALYSIS: TOOLS AND THEIR INSTALLATIONS

The processing and analysis of big data can be done with the help of tools such as Apache Hadoop, Hive, and HBase.

I. **Hadoop** is an open-source platform provided by Apache. It provides a platform on which a huge chunk of data can be processed and interpreted. It is written in Java and the processing and analysis of data are done in offline mode. Hadoop has its architecture based on the data being processed and analyzed, which is composed of Hadoop Distributed File System, i.e., HDFS and MapReduce. Hadoop mainly focuses its work on nodes that consist of one master node and several slave nodes. HDFS mainly focuses on the master-slave framework. It has a name node, which acts as a master node that plays a role in controlling each step of the task processing, and a data node, which acts as a slave node that follows the commands given by the name node [9].

MapReduce is also a part of the Hadoop architecture that has a role in making a large amount of data concise to get valuable information as there may be many redundancies in the datasets. Thus, MapReduce takes the input, maps the input, reduces the mapped input, and finally gives the accurate and concise output [10].

Hadoop Installation

Hadoop generally supports Linux/Unix environment, but it can also work on Windows using Cygwin. The following are the steps for Hadoop installation [11]:

Step 1: Check whether Java is installed or not using "java-version." If not, then it can be downloaded from www.oracle.com. A tar file is downloaded.

Step 2: Extract the tar file using the following command:

```
#tar zxf jdk-7u71-linux x64.tar.gz
```

Step 3: Make Java available to all users using the following command:

```
# mv jdk1.7.0_71 /usr/lib/
```

Step 4: In ~/.bashrc use the following command for setting up the path:

```
# export JAVA_HOME=/usr/lib/jdk1.7.0_71
# export PATH=PATH:$JAVA_HOME/bin
```

For confirming the installation, use the "java-version" command.

Step 5: Create Hadoop user for the further purpose of SSH installation using the following command:

```
# useradd hadoop
# passwd Hadoop
```

Step 6: Map nodes by putting the IP address and their names (Master-Slave architecture of Hadoop) with the help of the following commands:

```
# vi /etc/hosts
```

After executing the above command, enter the following lines:

```
190.12.1.114 hadoop-master
190.12.1.121 hadoop-salve-one
190.12.1.143 hadoop-slave-two
```

Step 7: Set up an SSH key in master and slave nodes so that they can interact smoothly with the help of the following commands:

```
# su hadoop
$ ssh-keygen -t rsa
$ ssh-copy-id -i ~/.ssh/id_rsa.pub tutorialspoint@
hadoop-master
$ ssh-copy-id -i ~/.ssh/id_rsa.pub hadoop_tp1@
hadoop-slave-1
$ ssh-copy-id -i ~/.ssh/id_rsa.pub hadoop_tp2@
hadoop-slave-2
$ chmod 0600 ~/.ssh/authorized_keys
$ exit
```

Now, our main focus is to install Hadoop.

Step 8: Download the latest version of Hadoop from "hadoop.apache.org". A tar file will be downloaded. Now, extract this tar file to a particular location with the help of the following command:

```
$ mkdir /usr/hadoop
$ sudo tar vxzf hadoop-2.2.0.tar.gz ?c /usr/hadoop
```

Step 9: Edit the ownership of Hadoop with the help of the following command:

```
$sudo chown -R hadoop usr/hadoop
```

Step 10: Make changes to the configuration file of Hadoop in the following way:

Files required for the configuration are available in the path "/usr/local/Hadoop/etc/Hadoop".
In hadoop-env.sh file, execute the following command:

```
export JAVA_HOME=/usr/lib/jvm/jdk/jdk1.7.0_71
```

At core-site.xml, execute the following commands:

```
<configuration>
<property>
<name>fs.default.name</name>
<value>hdfs://hadoop-master:9000</value>
</property>
<property>
<name>dfs.permissions</name>
<value>false</value>
</property>
</configuration>
```

In hdfs-site.xml, execute the following command:

```
<configuration>
<property>
<name>dfs.data.dir</name>
<value>usr/hadoop/dfs/name/data</value>
<final>true</final>
</property>
<property>
<name>dfs.name.dir</name>
<value>usr/hadoop/dfs/name</value>
<final>true</final>
```

```
</property>
<property>
<name>dfs.replication</name>
<value>1</value>
</property>
</configuration>
```

Make changes to Mapred-site.xml in the following way:

```
<configuration>
<property>
<name>mapred.job.tracker</name>
<value>hadoop-master:9001</value>
</property>
</configuration>
```

Finally, update $HOME/.bahsrc with the help of the following commands:

```
cd $HOME
vi .bashrc
Append following lines in the end and save and exit
#Hadoop variables
export JAVA_HOME=/usr/lib/jvm/jdk/jdk1.7.0_71
export HADOOP_INSTALL=/usr/hadoop
export PATH=$PATH:$HADOOP_INSTALL/bin
export PATH=$PATH:$HADOOP_INSTALL/sbin
export HADOOP_MAPRED_HOME=$HADOOP_INSTALL
export HADOOP_COMMON_HOME=$HADOOP_INSTALL
export HADOOP_HDFS_HOME=$HADOOP_INSTALL
export YARN_HOME=$HADOOP_INSTALL
```

Step 11: Now install Hadoop on the machine that will act as a slave with the help of the following commands:

```
# su hadoop
$ cd /opt/hadoop
$ scp -r hadoop hadoop-slave-one:/usr/hadoop
$ scp -r hadoop hadoop-slave-two:/usr/Hadoop
```

Step 12: Configure the master node and slave nodes with the help of the following commands:

```
$ vi etc/hadoop/masters
hadoop-master

$ vi etc/hadoop/slaves
hadoop-slave-one
hadoop-slave-two
```

Step 13: Finally, format the data nodes and initialize the daemons in the following way:

```
# su hadoop
$ cd /usr/hadoop
$ bin/hadoop namenode -format

$ cd $HADOOP_HOME/sbin
$ start-all.sh
```

II. **Hive** is one of the tools that come under the Hadoop environment. It acts as a data repository for the structured type of datasets. As structured data support structure query language (SQL), in which data can be stored in a tabular form, in which there is room for retrieval, addition, and removal of data to establish valuable relationships among data, these features are also available in Hive. The analyzing process is very fast. It can also function in a compressed file that is present in the Apache Hadoop environment. But it is not suitable for performing the analysis of real-time data [12].

Hive Installation

The following are the steps of installation of Hive [13]:

Step 1: Before proceeding with the installation of Hive, install Java and Hadoop beforehand. To check whether they are already installed or not, we can execute "java-version" and "Hadoop version." If they are not installed, we can follow the steps that have been mentioned previously.
Step 2: Download the latest version of Hive from "hive.apache.org".
Step 3: Extract the files using the following command:

```
tar -xvf apache-hive-2.3.7-bin.tar.gz
```

Step 4: Now, open the bashrc file using the following command:

```
$ sudo nano ~/.bashrc
```

Step 5: Provide the path to Hive using the following command:

```
export HIVE_HOME=/home/codegyani/apache-hive-2.3.7-bin
export PATH=$PATH:/home/codegyani/apache-hive-2.3.7-bin/bin
```

Step 6: Update an environment variable:

```
$ source ~/.bashrc
```

Step 7: To work with Hive, just type "hive" in the command line.

```
$ hive
```

III. **HBase** is also a very useful tool that comes under the Hadoop environment. It is mainly a column-based type of database. It also has a feature of adding any number of columns to it at any span of time while processing. It is more suitable for scattered types of datasets, which means it is very useful in datasets that have multiple null values to an attribute. It provides a very good platform for saving and providing data without any restriction to its access. It only allows read and write operations on datasets, with the option of updating or modifying it. It has an important characteristic of automatic failover in which whenever the system faces any problem while performing the task, it puts the computation on hold [14].

HBase Installation

The following are the steps of HBase installation [1515]:

Step 1: Before proceeding with the installation of HBase, install Java and Hadoop beforehand. To check whether they are already installed or not, we can execute "java-version" and "Hadoop version." If they are not installed, we can follow the steps that have been mentioned previously.

Step 2: Download the latest version of HBase from "hbase.apache.org". A tar file will be downloaded.

Step 3: Extract the files using the following command:

```
$tar -zxvf hbase-2.3.1-hadoop2-bin.tar.gz
```

Step 4: Now, login as a super user:

```
$su
$password: enter your password here
```

```
mv hbase-2.3.1/* Hbase/
```

Step 5: Configure HBase in stand-alone mode with the help of the following commands:

```
cd /usr/local/Hbase/conf
gedit hbase-env.sh
```

Substitute the already present JAVA_HOME value with the latest one.

```
export JAVA_HOME=/usr/lib/jvm/java-1.7.0
```

Within /usr/local/Hbase, get hbase-site.xml. For this we need to add the following code in between configuration.

```
<configuration>
//Here you have to set the path where you want HBase
to store its files.
<property>
<name>hbase.rootdir</name>
<value>file:/home/hadoop/HBase/HFiles</value>
</property>

//Here you have to set the path where you want HBase
to store its built in zookeeper files.
<property>
<name>hbase.zookeeper.property.dataDir</name>
<value>/home/hadoop/zookeeper</value>
</property>
</configuration>
```

Step 6: Initialize HBase using the following command:

```
$cd /usr/local/HBase/bin
$./start-hbase.sh
```

IV. **Apache Pig** is also a component of the Hadoop environment. It acts as a possible alternative to the MapReduce tool in case of highly complex structured data. It has the advantage of handling all three types of big data: structured, semi structured, and unstructured. It also provides an option of built-in operators such as sort, filter, and joins. It allows access for creating a user-defined function in which the user is free to use his logic to solve the problem. It also provides nested data types, i.e., tuple, bag, and map [16].

Pig Installation

The following are the steps of Pig installation [17]:

Step 1: Before proceeding with the installation of Pig, install Java and Hadoop beforehand. To check whether they are already installed or not, we can execute "java-version" and "Hadoop version." If they are not installed, we can follow the steps that have been mentioned previously.

Step 2: Download the latest version of Pig from "pig.apache.org". A tar file will be downloaded.

Step 3: Extract the files using the following command:

```
$ tar -xvf pig-0.17.0.tar.gz
```

Step 4: Open the bashrc file using the following command:

```
$ sudo nano ~/.bashrc
```

Step 5: Give the path to PIG_HOME in the following way:

```
export PIG_HOME=/home/hduser/pig-0.16.0
export PATH=$PATH:$PIG_HOME/bin
```

Step 6: Use the following command for updating the variable of environment:

```
$ source ~/.bashrc
```

Step 7: Finally, check whether the Pig has been successfully installed or not using the following command:

```
$ pig -h
```

1.5 BIG DATA: COMMANDS

There are several commands that are frequently being used in big data. Some of these commands are as follows:

HDFS Commands

- **ls:** This command is used to show all the files present in the folder or all the folders present in the directory.

  Syntax:

  ```
  bin/hdfs dfs -ls <path>
  ```

- **mkdir:** This command is used to make a new directory.

  Syntax:

  ```
  bin/hdfs dfs -mkdir <folder name>

  creating home directory:

  hdfs/bin -mkdir /user
  hdfs/bin -mkdir /user/username -> write the username of your
  computer
  ```

- **touchz:** It is used to make an empty file.

  Syntax:

  ```
  bin/hdfs dfs -touchz <file_path>
  ```

- **cat:** This command is used to show what is written in the file.

  Syntax:

  ```
  bin/hdfs dfs -cat <path>
  ```

- **mv:** This command is used to shift the files in between HDFS.

  Syntax:

  ```
  bin/hdfs dfs -mv <src(on hdfs)> <src(on hdfs)>
  ```

- **cp:** This command is used for copying the content of file in between HDFS.

  Syntax:

  ```
  bin/hdfs dfs -cp <src(on hdfs)> <dest(on hdfs)>
  ```

- **du:** This command helps in giving the size of a particular directory that is mentioned.

  Syntax:

```
bin/hdfs dfs -du <dirName>
```

- **stat:** This command is used to provide us the time at which the changes can be made in a file or a directory.

  Syntax:

```
bin/hdfs dfs -stat <hdfs file>
```

Hive Commands

- For generating a database:

```
hive>create the database emp
>WITH DBPROPERTIES ('name' = 'XYZ', 'id' = '101');
```

- For checking if there is any new database:

```
hive> show databases;
```

- For getting required information from database:

```
hive> describe database extended emp;
```

- For deleting database:

```
hive> drop database emp;
```

- For making an internal table:

```
hive> create table emp (Id int, Name string, Salary float)
row format delimited
fields terminated by ',';
```

- For making an external table:

```
hdfs dfs -mkdir /HiveDirectory
hdfs dfs -put hive/emp_details /HiveDirectory

hive> create external table emplist (Id int, Name string, Salary float)
row format delimited
fields terminated by ','
location '/HiveDirectory';
```

- USE statement in Hive: The USE statement in Hive is used to select the specific database:

  Hive >USE Employee;

- DROP DATABASE in Hive:

  Hive> DROP Employee;

- ALTER DATABASE in Hive: This is used to change the metadata associated with the database in Hive:

  Hive> alter database Employee set OWNER ROLE admin;

  - ALTER TABLE in Hive:

hive> ALTER TABLE college. Student RENAME TO college.college_students;

hive> ALTER TABLE collge. college_students SET TBLPROPERTIES ('creator'='Emp');

hive> ALTER TABLE college.college_students SET TBLPROPERTIES ('comment'='this table is created by Student');

HBase Commands

- **Create:** This command is used to generate a new table.

  hbase(main):002:0> create 'emp', 'personal data', 'professional data'

- **Put:** This command is used for inputting the data.

  hbase(main):002:0> put '<table name>' ,'rowl', '<colfamily:colname>', '<value>'

  hbase(main):005:0> put 'emp','1','personal data:name','Nitin'

  hbase(main):006:0> put 'emp','1','personal data:city','Delhi'

  hbase(main):007:0> put 'emp','1','professional data: designation','manager'

  hbase(main):007:0> put 'emp','1','professional data:salary','70000'

- **Scan:** This command is used to show the data that are already present in the table.

  hbase(main):003:0> scan 'emp'

- **Get:** This command is used to show the data that is asked in the query.

  hbase(main):012:0>Get '<table name>' ,'row1'

  hbase(main):012:0> get 'emp', '1'

1.6 BIG DATA: APPLICATIONS

In our daily life, zillions of data are being generated constantly. Every minute there is a constant need to handle these data carefully for further processing. These data can be generated in any sector of our daily life such as marketing, healthcare, research, banking, and many more. Therefore, big data has a very responsible job for performing the task of handling, processing, and analyzing the data that are constantly being produced over a period of time very precisely. Let's focus on the healthcare sector to know what are the tasks which are needed to be taken care of with the help of big data, which ultimately shows the divergence of application of big data in the case of healthcare management:

- An enormous number of images are being generated every second in the healthcare sector, whether they are in the form of CT scan, MRI, X-ray, ultrasound, and many more. These images are constantly being stored and updated for a particular individual who is being diagnosed with some disease in a database of healthcare centers. The storage of this kind of data is very helpful in keeping the records of a patient so that the history of his disease can be understood carefully and also ease the way of his/her treatment [18].
- Apart from the continuous generation of various healthcare images, there is a constant generation of vital signals of a patient too. These vital signals comprise heart rate, pulse rate, level of oxygen in the blood, and many more. These data are very crucial in constantly monitoring the seriousness of a patient. Since at a time in a hospital many patients are there, so here the task of big data is to not only collect the information regarding these vital signals but also assign them to the correct patient record [19].
- There is a lot of research work happening around the world. These research works generate a large amount of desirable or undesirable outcomes. These outcomes are generally stored in a repository called the database. Thus, big data performs the task of regularly maintaining and storing these data so that if some other person wants to refer to a particular work that has already been performed, then he can have easy access to it [20].
- Another role of big data can be seen during the clinical trial. A clinical trial is a process where a drug is tested on an individual to know about its efficacy and efficiency. There is a lot of documentation work done during

a clinical trial as a record of each and every step of it must be recorded for analyzing the drug. Therefore, big data has a very important role in handling these records [21].

- Another big data application that helps in managing the big data and giving useful outputs is Cloudera. It provides a flexible, scalable, and integrated platform to store and get a reasonable output for a variety of big data. Cloudera products and solutions enable us to deploy and manage Apache Hadoop and related projects, manipulate and analyze data, and keep the data secure [24]. Cloudera provides a number of tools form, a few of which are listed below [25]:
    1. *CDH:* Cloudera Distribution Hadoop is an Apache Hadoop Distribution. It also includes Cloudera Impala and Cloudera Search with many other related projects. Cloudera Impala is a parallel processing SQL engine, while Cloudera search provides real-time text exploration, indexing, and other search operations.
    2. *Cloudera Manager:* While CDH is busy with deployments, Cloudera manager keeps a check on all the deployments performed by CDH. It manages, deploys, monitors, and diagnoses various issues encountered in CDH deployment.
    3. *Cloudera Navigator:* It works from end to end to manage and secure CDH platform. This tool helps in robust auditing, data management, lineage management, life cycle management, and encryption key management in Cloudera Navigator.

All this helps in big data analytic, the most modern tool used for big data analytic is Cloudera's Enterprise data hub.

Not only the healthcare sector has a requirement of big data but other sectors are also in need of it. For example, in the banking sector, big data is being used to track the record of the account of a customer; in companies, big data is being used to track the record of the employees, projects as well as profit and loss; in the stock market, big data has a role in tracking the price of stocks that are available in the market and whether there is an increment in price or not, and many more.

1.7 BIG DATA: CHALLENGES

Even though big data many uses and advantages, there are still some problems related to it which are needed to be solved carefully. Some of the challenges of big data are as follows [22, 23]:

- One of the most basic problems related to big data is continuously growing up in its volume. A very large amount of data are regularly being generated. So, there is a constant question of which tool is the best one to handle this.
- Even after so much development in the field of big data, there is a constant question being raised related to handling real-time data. As mentioned earlier, the data is increasing every second in multiple folds, so the tool

includes the features of velocity and veracity because not only the rate of collection of data but also the type of data that is collected is important.
- Data security is one of the most important challenges related to big data. Not only data handling and processing but also its security is important. If the tool used for big data does not focus on the security aspect, then the user's information is sacrificed and some unauthorized users can take advantage of it.
- Since this field of big data is still in progress, there is a scarcity of skilled individuals who know how to use tools for big data handling.

REFERENCES

1. Fernández-Manzano, Eva-Patricia, Neira, Elena & Gavilán, Judith (2016). Data management in audiovisual business: Netflix as a case study. *El Profesional de la Información* 25: 568. 10.3145/epi.2016.jul.06.
2. Mehta, Tripti, Mangla, Neha & Guragon, Gitm (2016). *A Survey Paper on Big Data Analytics using Map-Reduce and Hive on Hadoop Framework.*
3. Oguntimilehin, Abiodun & Ademola, Ojo (2014). A review of big data management, benefits and challenges. *Journal of Emerging Trends in Computing and Information Sciences* 5: 433–438.
4. Adam, Khalid, Adam, Mohammed, Fakharaldien, Ibrahim, Mohamad Zain, Jasni, & Majid, Mazlina. (2014). Big Data Management and Analysis. In International Conference on Computer Engineering & Mathematical Sciences (ICCEMS 2014).
5. Ishwarappa, Anuradha J. (2015). A brief introduction on big data 5Vs characteristics and Hadoop technology. *Procedia Computer Science* 48: 319–324.
6. Eberendu, Adanma (2016). Unstructured data: An overview of the data of Big Data. *International Journal of Computer Trends and Technology* 38: 46–50. doi: 10.14445/22312803/IJCTT-V38P109.
7. Acharjya, D. P. and Ahmed, P. Kauser (2016). A survey on big data analytics: Challenges, open research issues and tools. *International Journal of Advanced Computer Science and Applications(IJACSA)* 7 (2): 511–518.
8. Adnan, K. and Akbar, R. (2019). An analytical study of information extraction from unstructured and multidimensional big data. *Journal of Big Data* 6: 91.
9. Beakta, Rahul. (2015). Big data and hadoop: A review paper. *International Journal of Computer Science & Information Technology* (2) e-ISSN: 1694–2329 | p-ISSN: 1694–2345.
10. Buono, D., Danelutto, M., and Lametti, S. (2012). Map, reduce and MapReduce, the skeleton way. In *Proceedings of International Conference on Computational Science, ICCS 2010, Procedia Computer Science* 1: 2095–2103.
11. Shah, Ankit & Dr. Padole, Mamta (2019). Apache Hadoop: A guide for cluster configuration & testing. *International Journal of Computer Sciences and Engineering* 7: 792–796. doi: 10.26438/ijcse/v7i4.792796.
12. Chandra, Shireesha, Varde, Aparna & Wang, Jiayin. (2019). A Hive and SQL Case Study in Cloud Data Analytics. doi: 10.1109/UEMCON47517.2019.8992925.
13. Available at: https://www.javatpoint.com/hive-installation.
14. Patel, Hiren (2017). HBase: A NoSQL Database. doi: 10.13140/RG.2.2.22974.28480.
15. Available at: https://www.javatpoint.com/hive-installation.
16. Swa, Cdsa & Ansari, Zahid. (2017). Apache Pig–A data flow framework based on Hadoop Map reduce. *International Journal of Engineering Trends and Technology* 50: 271–275. doi: 10.14445/22315381/IJETT-V50P244.

17. Available at: https://www.javatpoint.com/pig-installation.
18. Dash, S., Shakyawar, S. K., Sharma, M. et al. (2019). Big data in healthcare: Management, analysis and future prospects. *Journal of Big Data* 6: 54.
19. Belle, A., Thiagarajan, R., Soroushmehr, S.M., Navidi, F., Beard, D.A., & Najarian, K. (2015). Big data analytics in healthcare. *BioMed Research International* 2015: 370194. doi: 10.1155/2015/370194. Epub 2015 Jul 2. PMID: 26229957; PMCID: PMC4503556.
20. Belle, Ashwin, Thiagarajan, Raghuram, Soroushmehr, S.M. Reza, Navidi, Fatemeh, Beard, Daniel, & Najarian, Kayvan. (2015). Review article big data analytics in healthcare. *Biomed Res Int.* 370194. doi: 10.1155/2015/370194.
21. Ristevski, B. & Chen M. (2018). Big data analytics in medicine and healthcare. *Journal of Integrative Bioinformatics* 15 (3): 20170030. doi: 10.1515/jib-2017-0030.
22. Patgiri, Ripon. (2018). Issues and challenges in big data: A survey. 10.1007/978-3-319-72344-0_25.
23. Hariri, R. H., Fredericks, E. M. & Bowers, K. M. (2019). Uncertainty in big data analytics: survey, opportunities, and challenges. *Journal of Big Data* 6: 44.
24. Pol, Urmila. (2014). Big data and Hadoop technology solutions with Cloudera Manager. *International Journal of Advanced Research in Computer Science and Software Engineering* 4: 1028–1034.
25. Available at: https://docs.cloudera.com/documentation/enterprise/5-10-x/PDF/cloudera-introduction.pdf.
26. Jain, S. & Saxena A. (2016). Analysis of Hadoop and MapReduce tectonics through Hive Big Data. *International Journal of Control Theory and Applications* 9 (14): 3811–3911.
27. Saxena, A., Kaushik, N., Kaushik, N. & Dwivedi, A. (2016). Implementation of cloud computing and big data with Java based web application. *2016* 3rd International Conference on Computing for Sustainable Global Development (INDIACom), New Delhi, 1289–1293.
28. Saxena, A., Kaushik, N. & Kaushik, N. (2016). Implementing and analyzing big data techniques with spring framework in Java & J2EE. Second International Conference on Information and Communication Technology for Competitive Strategies (ICTCS) ACM Digital Library.
29. Saxena, A., Chaurasia, A., Kaushik, N., Dwivedi, A. & Kaushik, N. (2018). Handling big data using Map-Reduce over hybrid cloud. International Conference on Innovative Computing and Communications Springer, 135–144.
30. Nagpal, D., Sood, S., Mohagaonkar, S., Sharma, H. & Saxena, A. (2019). Analyzing Viral Genomic Data Using Hadoop Framework in Big Data. *2019* 6th International Conference on Computing for Sustainable Global Development (INDIACom), New Delhi, India, 680–685.
31. Saluja, M. K., Agarwal, I., Rani, U. & Saxena, A. (2020). Analysis of diabetes and heart disease in big data using MapReduce framework. In D. Gupta, A. Khanna, S. Bhattacharyya, A. E. Hassanien, S. Anand, & A. Jaiswal (eds.), International Conference on Innovative Computing and Communications. *Advances in Intelligent Systems and Computing*, vol. 1165 (Springer: Singapore). doi: 10.1007/978-981-15-5113-0_3.
32. Saxena, Ankur, Chand, Monika, Shakya, Chetna, Singh Gagandeep Singh Saggu, Gagandeep, Saha, Deepesh, & Shreshtha, Inish Krishna. (2020). Analysis of big data using Apache Spark (April 4, 2020). Available at SSRN: https://ssrn.com/abstract=3568360.

2 Introduction to Machine Learning

Ankur Saxena, Urvija Rani, Isha Agarwal, and Smitha Mony Sreedharan

CONTENTS

2.1 INTRODUCTION TO MACHINE LEARNING

In today's world, everyone wants quick and effective solutions to every problem in every field. All that humans want is computers that work like the human brain. The desired accuracy and speed intended for all human activities is achieved with the help of machine learning (ML).

The term Machine Learning was coined in 1959 by Arthur Samuel, an American pioneer in the fields of computer gaming and Artificial Intelligence (AI). He said, "It gives computers the ability to learn without being explicitly programmed." In 1997, Tom Mitchell gave a "well-posed" definition that "A computer program is said to learn from experience E concerning some task T and some performance measure P, if its performance on T, as measured by P, improves with experience E" [1].

Machine Learning (ML) is nothing but a set of methods that contain models that work and learn like the human brain. It is a branch of Artificial Intelligence that requires minimal human interventions to give predictions of complex datasets [2]. Earlier, Machine Learning made use of pattern matching, but with advancements in computer functions and configurations, this technique has found applications in various fields. The input data can be of any type, for example, biological data involving gene sequences, or measurements of various attributes of a disease, or information on how different chemical reactions occur. The data can also be of various origins, such as financial or banking service sectors, retail market, government data, transportation, and entertainment. In all these fields, one can find a trend of a particular thing and such a trend can help in further research, provide ways to save expenditure, assist government in making improvements in providing public services and amending in rules and regulations(e.g., Traffic rules), or show personalized suggestions or recommendations based on previous data (e.g., Netflix or Amazon). These data are nowadays collected using different sensors put everywhere in the form of fitness bands and cameras or tracking devices or different applications that humans use in their day-to-day life.

All these data collected are in large quantities and cannot be handled using the basic programming language. And this enormous amount of data is called big data. Machine learning assists in deriving meaning out of big data [3].

2.2 ARTIFICIAL INTELLIGENCE

Artificial Intelligence is a science of how computers mimic the human brain, while deep learning, Machine Learning, and natural language processing are the methods of how to implement this science [6]. Artificial Intelligence, which was introduced in the 1950s, works on large datasets and has been the world's most popular branch of computer science for many years. There are a lot of examples of AI present in our daily life like navigations, robotics, automatic cars, and Siri on iPhone. Artificial Intelligence is a science that implements and can be understood using topics like Machine Learning, deep learning, and neural networks. The term Artificial Intelligence implies that it is the intelligence exhibited by a machine artificially. This science deals with building machines that can simulate the human brain; also, this term can be given to any machine that functions like the human brain in solving problems and making tasks easier. With AI, a machine first learns and reasons the topic and then it helps in problem-solving, giving a new perception to the topic [4].

There are two ways by which Artificial Intelligence works: the symbolic/ top-down approach and the connectionist/bottom-up approach. In the top-down approach, symbols are given to a machine and then data is given to the machine to predict the output; but in the bottom-up approach, the reverse is done; that is, the machine is fed with each attribute first, and it learns automatically, and then the test is performed to predict the output [5].

AI is of three types:

a. *Strong AI:* It is used to build a machine that can think for itself[8].
b. *Cognitive AI:* It is for information processing. It aims to build smart systems and applications [7].

c. *Applied AI:* This is applied on computers to test theories defined by humans and also which are based on the human brain [9].

All these theories are applied in various fields of medical science, banking and finance, gaming, cars, mobiles and systems, and government surveillance, and also on advancing technologies to ease human efforts.

Machine Learning models are made using Python language. They can also be built using SAS which is Statistical Analysis Software. Python language is used because it facilitates easy importing of libraries and various datasets using Jupyter Notebook. Python language also provides easy and comprehensive programming. Python is a general-purpose interpreted, interactive, object-oriented, and high-level programming language created by Guido van Rossum during 1985–1990 [10]. Like Perl, Python's source code is also available under the GNU General Public License (GPL). Python is a scripting language, that can be easily read because it uses frequent English conversions and has less punctuation and syntactical constructions than other languages.

2.3 PYTHON LIBRARIES USED IN MACHINE LEARNING

Python has made it easy to perform complex programming in Machine Learning with a vast collection of libraries that the program code uses to manage the dataset. Various libraries and uses are described below [11]:

i. ***NumPy***
NumPy is a very popular library in Python. It is used for large multidimensional matrices and arrays because it contains high-level mathematical functions. It is imported when scientific calculations are performed in arrays or matrices in Machine Learning. It makes calculations faster and efficient. NumPy assists in sorting, selecting, random selection, manipulation, data cleaning, and many other functions. It works on the Object-oriented Programming Concept and can integrate many other languages like C and C++.

ii. ***TensorFlow***
It is widely used in many fields as it is an open-source library developed by Google. It defines and performs computations on tensors as the name suggests. It is the best library in Python to make models in Machine Learning as TensorFlow makes model building easier and faster. TensorFlow helps in natural language processing, deep neural network building, image search, speech and text recognition, etc.

iii. ***Pandas***
It is also one of the most used libraries in Python, but it is not directly related to building Machine Learning algorithms however, it helps in tasks related to data preprocessing like data extraction, manipulation, and processing, which can include handling missing data, encoding data, merging and joining data, data alignment, and a few others.

iv. ***Scikit-Learn***
It is also a widely used library because it has algorithms related to classification, regression, model selection, and clustering, and these algorithms

help to build models using different methods. It is simple to use because it can be integrated with NumPy and Pandas very easily.

v. ***Theano***

This library is used to optimize and define mathematical expressions, which is done by optimizing the usage of GPU instead of CPU. It is a robust library in Python and is very powerful to perform mathematical functions related to a multidimensional array. It helps in the rapid and efficient development of several algorithms due to its strong incorporation of NumPy, as well as many other libraries like Keras and Blocks.

vi. ***Matplotlib***

This library, as the name suggests, is used for plotting graphs and output visualizations. Like Pandas, this library is also not directly related to Machine Learning but helps to visualize different patterns in the form of plots and graphs in Machine Learning. A library named Pyplot is among the most used under Matplotlib.

vii. ***Keras***

It is used in neural network programming and works on top of Theano and TensorFlow. It is a popular open-source library that provides open-source prototyping. Keras was also developed by Google.

viii. ***PyTorch***

It was developed by Facebook, and is in close competition with TensorFlow as it is also used to compute tensors but with GPU, which makes it more enhanced in speed and accuracy. PyTorch is an open-source library that also helps to build graphs and is based on Torch, which works on C and C++ interfaces.

Apart from these, many libraries come in handy while building Machine Learning models.

2.4 CLASSIFICATION OF MACHINE LEARNING BASED ON SIGNALS AND FEEDBACK

Machine Learning works on the system of signals and feedback.Signals are are sent to a machine which happens after machine haslearned the statistics from a set of data, and feedback is the response which machine gives to the signalprovided. Based on signals and feedback, Machine Learning implementations can be classified as follows [1].

2.4.1 Supervised Learning

In supervised learning, the algorithm learns from the data provided and the responses are given to it in the form of labels or tags or values to predict the correct response when new data is provided, i.e., provide all the necessary patterns to the machine that needs to be matched instead of it determining. The approach is similar to how the human brain processes new information received from a teacher or an expert and applies that knowledge to a related field. This is also referred to as providing trained datasets to the machine. The method finds various applications such as detecting fraudulent transactions. [12].

2.4.2 Unsupervised Learning

In this algorithm, the machine is provided with datasets but not the labels that define the pattern to be matched; i.e., they are provided with untrained datasets. This type of learning helps humans to get a new perspective on the datasets, which may not be possible through a visual search alone. The datasets used in this do not have any historical background and so no tags are known. The human brain learns to identify different objects by detecting their various features. This feature can be applied to machine learning, which can find different patterns in a dataset; for example in biological data, it can help categorize genes sharing similar structures under one class. [13].

2.4.3 Reinforcement Learning

In this type, the algorithm is provided with unlabeled datasets as in unsupervised learning, but certain outcomes are provided ranked. This way the algorithm has no or little room for errors and provides maximum output. This method learns by trial and error. Reinforcement Learning has three components—agent, environment, and actions—where the agent is the learner who learns and makes the decision, the environment is the component with which the agent interacts to give accurate predictions, and actions are the different paths that the agent takes to get the maximum score. This type of learning is used in robotics, gaming, and navigation, where each path to a single destination is first analyzed and then the best one is selected [14].

2.4.4 Semisupervised Learning

In this type, some part of the data is labeled while the rest of the data is unlabeled. This method is transduction where the whole learning is done first, but few of the unique cases are missing from labeled data set. The simplest example of this is of labeled and unlabeled files in a folder, where prediction is made using only the labeled files in a step-by-step manner; i.e., first the unlabeled data is labeled and then the algorithm is applied to other files [15].

2.5 DATA PREPROCESSING USING PYTHON IN MACHINE LEARNING

Data preprocessing is the first step in building a good Machine Learning model. The data imported is first refined, because the raw data collected is a bit messed up and can't be directly fed to the algorithm in further processes. This process is performed to achieve better results in the proper format, and also one dataset can be used in any of the three algorithms of ML, NLP, or DL.

Collection sources of the raw data must be authentic for accurate and efficient data processing. The data can then be imported to the Jupyter Notebook. Next, data preparation steps follows, such as filling all the missing spaces, encoding the data in a machine-readable format, splitting the dataset into two parts, feature scaling, and refining the data for further processing. All these steps are discussed in detail below.

The data thus processed can be applied to make various predictions, such as whether a person of a certain age and income group and living in a particular country would purchase a product or not.

1) **Importing the Libraries**
This step is the most important as in this the libraries are imported with initials for easy identification and processing. The initials are added following the "as" keyword.

▾ Importing the libraries

```
[ ] import numpy as np
    import matplotlib.pyplot as plt
    import pandas as pd
```

In these commands, NumPy, Pandas, and Matplotlib.pyplot are imported.

2) **Importing the Dataset**
In this step, the file that contains data is imported in a tabular form. Here the file has an extension of .csv.

```
[ ] dataset = pd.read_csv('Data.csv')
    x = dataset.iloc[:, :-1].values
    y = dataset.iloc[:, -1].values
```

pd.read_csv = helps to read the csv file present in the working directory folder.

x = variable is used to store the independent variables (these are the ones which one inputs to predict something out of them).

y = variable is used to store the dependent variable (they contain the value that is dependent on independent variable).

iloc, values = method that helps to index columns in a given table and values helps to get the data present in the table.

After this print x and y to check if the data is imported correctly.

```
[ ] print(x)

[['France' 44.0 72000.0]
 ['Spain' 27.0 48000.0]
 ['Germany' 30.0 54000.0]
 ['Spain' 38.0 61000.0]
 ['Germany' 40.0 nan]
 ['France' 35.0 58000.0]
 ['Spain' nan 52000.0]
 ['France' 48.0 79000.0]
 ['Germany' 50.0 83000.0]
 ['France' 37.0 67000.0]]
```

```
[ ] print(y)

['No' 'Yes' 'No' 'No' 'Yes' 'Yes' 'No' 'Yes' 'No' 'Yes']
```

3) **Taking Care of Missing Data**

As in x, two values have nan as their values, which means there is no data in the Data.csv in those cells. This is the missing data that needs to be treated because any of the dependent columns having the missing data can create a great difference in the output predictions.

This missing data can be replaced using many methods like the mean, the median value of the column, or the most frequent value from the column. Below the mean method is used.

```
[ ] from sklearn.impute import SimpleImputer
    imputer = SimpleImputer(missing_values=np.nan, strategy='mean')
    imputer.fit(x[:, 1:3])
    x[:, 1:3] = imputer.transform(x[:, 1:3])

[ ] print(x)

    [['France' 44.0 72000.0]
     ['Spain' 27.0 48000.0]
     ['Germany' 30.0 54000.0]
     ['Spain' 38.0 61000.0]
     ['Germany' 40.0 63777.77777777778]
     ['France' 35.0 58000.0]
     ['Spain' 38.77777777777778 52000.0]
     ['France' 48.0 79000.0]
     ['Germany' 50.0 83000.0]
     ['France' 37.0 67000.0]]
```

In the above commands, SimpleImputer is used and where it is defined which all values need to be replaced by what value. Then the "fit" method is used to retrieve the missing value cells from the table and also the mean for each of the columns of age and salary. Further "transform" method is used to make changes in the table. Print(x) command shows the output after missing values are replaced in both the columns.

4) **Encoding Categorical Data**

This is a step where the data is made in machine-readable forms, like country and purchase columns.

a.) **Encoding the Independent Variable**

The country column has three countries—France, Spain, and Germany—and each country is given a particular code of 0,1,2 and made in a machine-readable form.

```
[ ] from sklearn.compose import ColumnTransformer
    from sklearn.preprocessing import OneHotEncoder
    ct = ColumnTransformer(transformers =[('encoder' , OneHotEncoder(), [0])], remainder ='passthrough')
    x = np.array(ct.fit_transform(x))

[ ] print(x)

    [[0.0 1.0 0.0 0.0 44.0 72000.0]
     [1.0 0.0 0.0 1.0 27.0 48000.0]
     [1.0 0.0 1.0 0.0 30.0 54000.0]
     [1.0 0.0 0.0 1.0 38.0 61000.0]
     [1.0 0.0 1.0 0.0 40.0 63777.77777777778]
     [0.0 1.0 0.0 0.0 35.0 58000.0]
     [1.0 0.0 0.0 1.0 38.77777777777778 52000.0]
     [0.0 1.0 0.0 0.0 48.0 79000.0]
     [1.0 0.0 1.0 0.0 50.0 83000.0]
     [0.0 1.0 0.0 0.0 37.0 67000.0]]
```

In the above code, the fit_transform method is called from OneHotEncoder class. It transforms all the strings to integers and assigns them to separate columns in the binary format of 0 and 1.

b.) **Encoding the Dependent Variable**

The purchase column has the value as yes and no and so the machine-readable format will be in 0,1.

```
[ ] from sklearn.preprocessing import LabelEncoder
    le = LabelEncoder()
    y = le.fit_transform(y)

[ ] print(y)

[0 1 0 0 1 1 0 1 0 1]
```

In the above code, the fit_transform method is called from LabelEncode class. It transforms all the strings to integers, thus assigning the value of 1 and 0 to yes and no, respectively.

5) **Splitting the Dataset into Test and Training Sets**

The step to split the dataset into the training set and the test set is almost the same in all the model-building techniques.

```
[ ] from sklearn.model_selection import train_test_split
    x_train, x_test, y_train, y_test = train_test_split(x, y, test_size = 0.2, random_state = 1)

[ ] print(x_train)

[[0.0 0.0 1.0 38.77777777777778 52000.0]
 [0.0 1.0 0.0 40.0 63777.77777777778]
 [1.0 0.0 0.0 44.0 72000.0]
 [0.0 0.0 1.0 38.0 61000.0]
 [0.0 0.0 1.0 27.0 48000.0]
 [1.0 0.0 0.0 48.0 79000.0]
 [0.0 1.0 0.0 50.0 83000.0]
 [1.0 0.0 0.0 35.0 58000.0]]

[ ] print(x_test)

[[0.0 1.0 0.0 30.0 54000.0]
 [1.0 0.0 0.0 37.0 67000.0]]

[ ] print(y_train)

[0 1 0 0 1 1 0 1]

[ ] print(y_test)

[0 1]
```

In the above command, the train_test_split method is used that takes into account four arguments, namely dependent and independent variables, test_size, and random_state

Dependent and independent variables are already defined.

Test_size is the size that one wants to use; the suggested size is 20% of the total data.

Random_state is by which one defines whether they want to split data sequentially or in random manner; 1 means true and 0 means false.

x_test, x_train, y_test, and y_train are the variables where the value obtained after train_test_split is stored in the form of matrices.

6) **Feature Scaling of the Data**

Feature scaling is the method to define a range for each and every attribute in a dataset, mostly training set is defined which is why splitting of data must be done before feature scaling of data. The range is usually between –3 to +3. This can be done using normalization, or standardization which is used mostly.

In our data, age and salary are the attributes that need to undergo this step. We do not do feature scaling of encoded attributes unless they are in the range of 0–3 or unless they are in the form of 0 and 1, so the country column does not need to undergo this process.

```
[28] from sklearn.preprocessing import StandardScaler
     sc = StandardScaler()
     x_train = sc.fit_transform(x_train[:, 3:])
     x_test = sc.transform(x_test[:, 3:])

[29] print(x_train)

     [[-0.19159184 -1.07812594]
      [-0.01411729 -0.07013168]
      [ 0.56670851  0.63356243]
      [-0.30453019 -0.30786617]
      [-1.90180114 -1.42046362]
      [ 1.14753431  1.23265336]
      [ 1.43794721  1.57499104]
      [-0.74014954 -0.56461943]]

     print(x_test)

     [[-1.46618179 -0.9069571 ]
      [-0.44973664  0.20564034]]
```

In the above code, StandardScaler is used to perform standardization on the indexed column of x_train and y_test data. Using fit_transform, we can convert the values to the desired range and transform them in our actual dataset.

2.6 TYPES OF MACHINE LEARNING ON THE BASIS OF OUTPUT TO BE PREDICTED

2.6.1 Regression

This is also a type of supervised learning. In this, the output predicted are in a continuous form rather than in a discrete form [16]. The graph formed is linear. Further, regression is divided into many methods such as decision tree, Bayesian tree, and random forest.

This method has a real-world and continuous numerical value as its output such as salary, age, and stock price. The method uses linear and nonlinear datasets and consists of many ways:

I. **Simple Linear Regression [17]**

- This is a method that performs regression, where a target variable is predicted using an independent variable.
- The equation for a simple linear regression model is as follows:

$$\mathbf{y = b_0 + b_1 * x_1}$$

where

y is the dependent variable
b_0 is the constant
b_1 is the coefficient of x
x_1 is the independent variable which is input as training data

- In the above equation, x_1 has power 1, indicating that the prediction of the dependent variable is made using only one variable.
- In Figure 2.1, the grey crosses indicate the numeric values present in the x_1 variable and the black line is drawn using the simple linear equation on the y-axis, where the dependent variable is indicated.
- The more the points on the black line, the more accurate the prediction of the test data.
- The following is the code block with the output for the simple linear regression model.

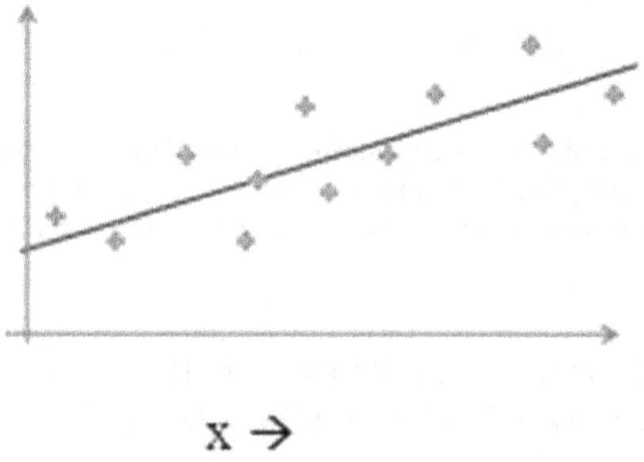

FIGURE 2.1 This figure represents the linear regression between x and y.

Importing the libraries

```
[ ] import numpy as np
    import matplotlib.pyplot as plt
    import pandas as pd
```

Importing the dataset

```
[ ] dataset = pd.read_csv('Salary_Data.csv')
    X = dataset.iloc[:, :-1].values
    y = dataset.iloc[:, -1].values
```

Splitting the dataset into the Training set and Test set

```
[ ] from sklearn.model_selection import train_test_split
    X_train, X_test, y_train, y_test = train_test_split(X, y, test_size = 1/3, random_state = 0)
```

This block will remain the same as that in data preprocessing, except that the output file is now Salary_Data.csv, which contains 30 samples of salary based on years of experience. In this test, the data size is 30% of the total dataset.

Training the Simple Linear Regression model on the Training set

```
[ ] from sklearn.linear_model import LinearRegression
    regressor = LinearRegression()
    regressor.fit(X_train, y_train)

LinearRegression(copy_X=True, fit_intercept=True, n_jobs=None, normalize=False)
```

Predicting the Test set results

```
[ ] y_pred = regressor.predict(X_test)
```

In this code, the LinearRegression method is used on training data to train it in a model.

After that the prediction of test results is done using predict method in the regressor variable.

Visualising the Training set results

```
[ ] plt.scatter(X_train, y_train, color = 'red')
    plt.plot(X_train, regressor.predict(X_train), color = 'blue')
    plt.title('Salary vs Experience (Training set)')
    plt.xlabel('Years of Experience')
    plt.ylabel('Salary')
    plt.show()
```

First, visualization of the training data is made to get an idea of whether the model is applied correctly or not. For this, Matplotlib is used with scatter, plot, show, and label methods (Figure 2.2).

▾ Visualising the Test set results

```
[ ] plt.scatter(X_test, y_test, color = 'red')
    plt.plot(X_train, regressor.predict(X_train), color = 'blue')
    plt.title('Salary vs Experience (Test set)')
    plt.xlabel('Years of Experience')
    plt.ylabel('Salary')
    plt.show()
```

Finally the test set is visualized using the Matplotlib library alone.

- Both the graphs having almost similar lines show that the simple linear regression model is formed successfully and is now predicting the data accurately. In this way, by using the LinearRegression method, one can easily make a simple linear regression model using a single variable (Figure 2.3).

II. **Multiple Linear Regression [18]**

- The second type of the linear regression model is the multiple linear model where one target value is predicted using two or more variables.
- The equation for this model is as follows:

$$\mathbf{y = b_0 + b_1 * x_1 + b_2 * x_2 + b_3 * x_3 + \cdots + b_n * x_n}$$

FIGURE 2.2 This figure represents the straight line between Salary vs Experience in Training set.

FIGURE 2.3 This figure represents the straight line between salary vs experience in testing set.

where y is the target variable that depends on all the feature variables, x_1, x_2, x_3, …, x_n, and b_0 is the constant while all the others are coefficients.

- The x or the dependent variable can be anything—a numeric value or a categorical data. If it is a categorical data, then it should be encoded beforehand by the steps shown in data preprocessing. But once the data is encoded, it cannot be considered as a single unit; therefore each category must be considered as a separate unit and then must be computed using the equation.
- Multiple linear regression is performed in the same manner as that of simple linear regression with the LinearRegression method having training and test data.
- There are a few things that need to be checked or assumed beforehand while performing MLR, such as whether a linear relationship exists between the response variable and the feature variable, whether the residuals follow normal distributions, and whether least or no correlation exists between all the dependent variables.
- This method is used in the stock market to predict the profit or loss percentage; it can also be used in detecting pollutants from vehicles and in many other real-world situations where the output is a numeric value and is dependent on many changing, continuous, or categorical variables.

III. **Polynomial Linear Regression [19]**

- This is a type of nonlinear regression where the graph obtained is curvilinear instead of a straight line. It is because the line obtained is based on the data type and not on the mean of the data points.

- The equation for PLM is

$$\mathbf{y = b_0 + b_1 * x_1 + b_2 * x_1^2 + b_3 * x_1^3 + \cdots + b_n * x_1^n}$$

where y is the dependent variable that depends on x_1 having power that shows the increasing exponentially and not in the same format.
- The graph for polynomial linear regression is as shown in Figure 2.4: The graph in Figure 2.4 shows that the line passes through all the data points of a single feature variable following the equation of PLM.
- It is still called linear because this is considered as an advanced model of multiple linear regression which gives the prediction more accuracy. This similarity exists due to similarity in the equation of both the models where x has a different exponent values but have the same coefficients. So, it is a type of linear model that implements a nonlinear dataset.
- Therefore, one can say that in a polynomial model, the features or the independent variables are first converted into polynomial features with certain change in degree and then linear regression is used to model this dataset.
- This model is created using the same code as that of simple linear regression using the LinearRegression method and then the output is predicted again in the same way by the predict method.
- Finally, this method can increase the accuracy and efficiency of nonlinear data in regression, and can decrease errors.

IV. **Decision Tree Regression [20]**
- This is again a regression model that deals with a nonlinear dataset. It can be a part of both regression and classification, but here it only involves regression.
- It is also called CART (Classification and Regression Tree).

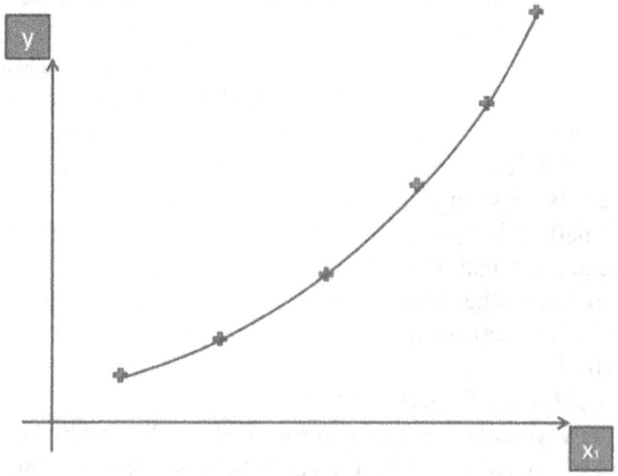

FIGURE 2.4 This figure represents the line between data points.

- In DecisionTreeRegression (DTR), there is no equation involved in forming a model; instead, all the datapoints of variables are marked on a 3D graph, with the dependent variables on the z-coordinate.
- Once all the data points are marked, using certain random parameters the graph is then spilt into various sections where each section's mean is calculated and assigned to that split block.
- Following this, one tree is formed where each node is a test condition and after passing all the nodes, the test value is assigned a split. The result of that prediction is the mean of that particular block where its data point lies.
- Figure 2.5 shows the graph of decision tree regression:

  In the graph of Figure 2.5, x_1 and x_2 are the two features or independent variables whose data points are marked on the graph in black. On one side of the graph is the three-dimensional graph showing y or the dependent variable coming out of the plane.

  There are four split blocks that are formed one by one on the graph. And the mean for each split is written inside the block.
- Figure 2.6 shows the graph of the tree based on the test condition fulfilling the split markings.
  If value is passed in test variable then first it will go to the root node; which will be considered as a yes, then another node in one direction or if the value is not passes that is no will stem in another direction the value is checked further below at every condition in the same pattern until it reaches the final prediction value.
- The code for building a decision tree regression model is as follows:

  First the import commands are executed using steps similar to those applied for data preprocessing, which helps us to import all the required libraries and dataset files whose data is saved using different variables as dependent and independent variables.

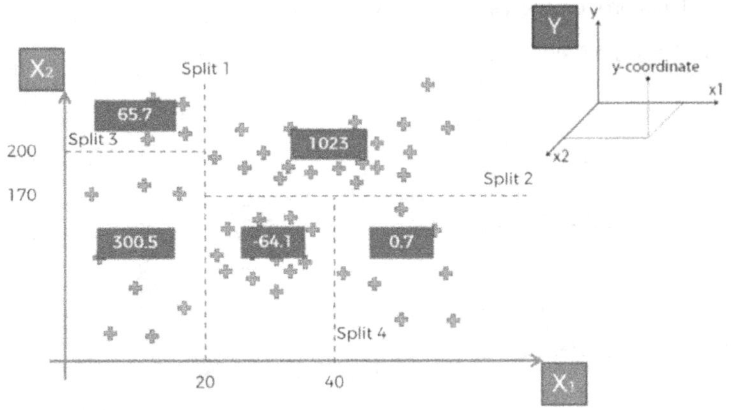

FIGURE 2.5 This figure represents the relation between dependent and independent variables.

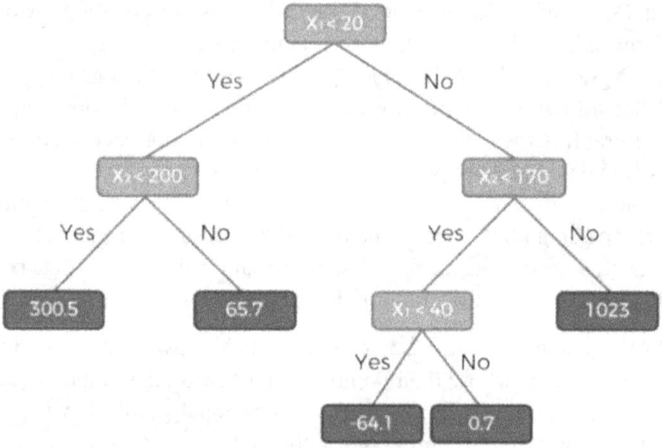

FIGURE 2.6 This figure represents the decision tree of test conditions.

Training the Decision Tree Regression model on the whole dataset

```
from sklearn.tree import DecisionTreeRegressor
regressor = DecisionTreeRegressor(random_state = 0)
regressor.fit(X, y)
```

```
DecisionTreeRegressor(ccp_alpha=0.0, criterion='mse', max_depth=None,
                      max_features=None, max_leaf_nodes=None,
                      min_impurity_decrease=0.0, min_impurity_split=None,
                      min_samples_leaf=1, min_samples_split=2,
                      min_weight_fraction_leaf=0.0, presort='deprecated',
                      random_state=0, splitter='best')
```

As no categorical data is taken into consideration, there is no need to run the encoding block. So, the model is directly made using the DecisionTreeRegression class with two variables.

Predicting a new result

```
[ ] regressor.predict([[6.5]])
```

```
array([150000.])
```

Visualising the Decision Tree Regression results (higher resolution)

```
[ ] X_grid = np.arange(min(X), max(X), 0.01)
    X_grid = X_grid.reshape((len(X_grid), 1))
    plt.scatter(X, y, color = 'red')
    plt.plot(X_grid, regressor.predict(X_grid), color = 'blue')
    plt.title('Truth or Bluff (Decision Tree Regression)')
    plt.xlabel('Position level')
    plt.ylabel('Salary')
    plt.show()
```

In DTR, one does not need to perform the splitting of training and test datasets because their value can be input manually. If more than one feature variable is involved or more than one value is to be predicted, then the input can be easily fed into the predict method.

Prediction is made using the predict method, while visualization is done using the Matplotlib library. In the above block of code, visualization must be performed in high resolution, meaning a grid is used to visualize the output; otherwise, the graph would not be accurate, so one cannot know the range of each test condition Figure 2.7 shows a high-resolution graph for easy visualization.

- This is how a decision tree regression model works. It is efficient and easy to use when the data has a precise and clearly defined range.
- Real-world examples are flight selection for travel, ordering food online, etc.

V. **Random Forest Regression (RFR) [21]**

- This type of model is present in both regression and classification and works on nonlinear data.
- This technique is a simple yet efficient one as it combines n number of decision tree to give one output and so is called the ensemble model.
- The ensemble model that is used to perform RFR is bagging.
- RFR is required because one decision tree is good for one particular type of data having a particular range; if the range varies by a large percentage or if the attributes change, then decision tree gives garbage output. So, one can achieve accuracy and efficiency in predictions using

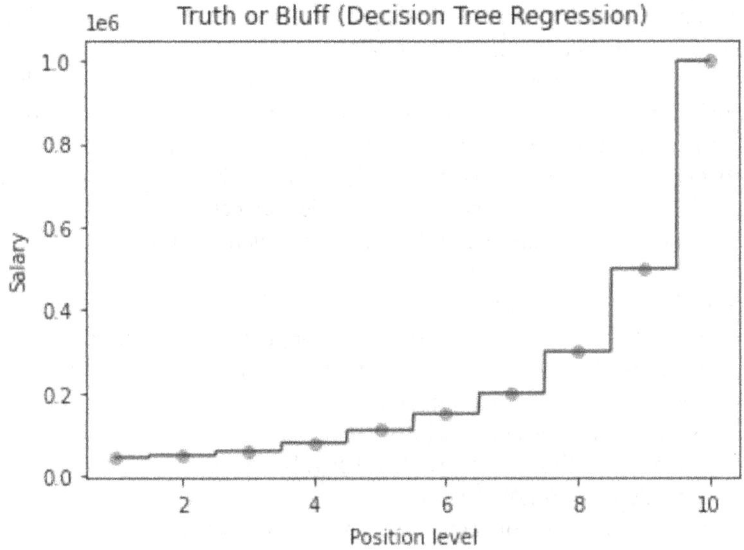

FIGURE 2.7 This graph represents the decision tree regression between x and y variables.

RFR, which combines *n* trees, and then the test case has to pass each decision tree, and every tree gives a separate mean value. Then the aggregate average of these values is calculated and finally one output is predicted.

- All the steps in RFR are similar to those of decision tree, except the class used is RandomForestRegressor that contains the code for building the model. This class is part of the ensemble package in the sklearn library. It also takes input of few arguments. After the model is made, one can again visualize the predicted data by Matplotlib and the prediction is done using the predict method only.
- RFR can handle a large number of inputs without any deletion and it also gives unbiased results, which makes it one of the best algorithms to be used. It is highly accurate as it can handle missing data very effectively.
- One of the drawbacks of RFR is that it causes overfitting of the data, giving noisy results.

These are the available regression models that help one to create a model for continuous data. These models can be further checked and evaluated based on their error rates. Also, score is calculated using the score method available in the sklearn. metrices package.

2.6.2 Classification

In this type of ML, the input data is used to divide the dataset into different classes. This is a type of supervised learning because it uses trained datasets. An example of classification is categorizing mails into spam and not spam. Further classifications include various parts such as Logistic, KNN, SVM.

Classification is a type of algorithm used to build Machine Learning models. It uses finite and discrete values for predicting a category of data and gives one of two outputs: positive or negative. For example, it shows two aspects of a prediction such as pass/fail or yes/no, or it predicts gender based on the handwriting, house price, etc. The dependent variable need not be a real-world value while using classification [22]. There are many different algorithms present in classification, which are discussed below.

I. **Logistic Regression [28]**

- The first algorithm of classification is logistic regression. As the name suggests, it uses the equation of regression with different functions to give probability of any test value.
- But as LR is a part of classification, it works to predict a category of the value, so it gives the value either 0 or 1. If the condition is fulfilled, then the value is 1; if it is not, then 0.
- LR follows a sigmoid equation to predict its output.

$$1/(1+e^{-\text{value}})$$

This equation gives a sigmoid line, which is similar to a simple regression line, but its value is restricted only between 0 and 1, meaning the range coverage is between 0 and 1 for any attribute.

- The final equation of LR is:

$$y = e^{(b0+b1*x)} / (1 + e^{(b0+b1*x)})$$

where y is the dependent variable and x is the independent variable; b is a constant.

- This equation predicts the probability of any value and then it defines a mid-range for a particular factor. Once the mid-range of this factor is defined, the probability value above that range is considered to be 1 i.e., yes, and the value below that range is treated as 0, i.e., no.
- Now implementation of logistic regression is shown below.

▾ Importing the libraries

```
[14] import numpy as np
     import matplotlib.pyplot as plt
     import pandas as pd
```

▾ Importing the dataset

```
[15] dataset = pd.read_csv('Social_Network_Ads.csv')
     X = dataset.iloc[:, [2, 3]].values
     y = dataset.iloc[:, 4].values
```

▾ Splitting the dataset into the Training set and Test set

```
[16] from sklearn.model_selection import train_test_split
     X_train, X_test, y_train, y_test = train_test_split(X, y, test_size = 0.25, random_state = 0)
```

▾ Feature Scaling

```
[21] from sklearn.preprocessing import StandardScaler
     sc = StandardScaler()
     X_train = sc.fit_transform(X_train)
     X_test = sc.transform(X_test)
```

```
[22] print(X_train)

     [ 0.08648817  1.05583366]
     [-0.11157634 -0.3648304 ]
     [-1.20093113  0.07006676]
     [-0.30964085 -1.3505973 ]
```

This code shows the basic import of libraries and dataset. And once the data is imported, it is split into test and training data. Thereafter, all the four components will be printed using the print function, which shows all the columns separately. Then feature scaling is also performed.

Training the Logistic Regression model on the Training set

```
[24] from sklearn.linear_model import LogisticRegression
     classifier = LogisticRegression(random_state = 0)
     classifier.fit(X_train, y_train)
```

```
LogisticRegression(C=1.0, class_weight=None, dual=False, fit_intercept=True,
                   intercept_scaling=1, l1_ratio=None, max_iter=100,
                   multi_class='auto', n_jobs=None, penalty='l2',
                   random_state=0, solver='lbfgs', tol=0.0001, verbose=0,
                   warm_start=False)
```

This block of code shows how the data is trained using LogisticRegression class and how the model is formed. This class is present in the sklearn. linear_model package.

Predicting a new result

```
[25] print(classifier.predict(sc.transform([[30,87000]])))
```

```
[0]
```

Predicting the Test set results

```
[26] y_pred = classifier.predict(X_test)
     print(np.concatenate((y_pred.reshape(len(y_pred),1), y_test.reshape(len(y_test),1)),1))
```

```
[0 1]
[1 1]
[0 0]
[0 0]
```

This block shows the predict method by which the value is predicted. The first shows the prediction of a new value, and the next shows the prediction of the test result.

Making the Confusion Matrix

```
[27] from sklearn.metrics import confusion_matrix, accuracy_score
     cm = confusion_matrix(y_test, y_pred)
     print(cm)
     accuracy_score(y_test, y_pred)
```

```
[[65  3]
 [ 8 24]]
0.89
```

This block is used to create a confusion matrix, which is built using confusion_metrices of the sklearn.metrices package. This is performed to determine which of the prediction is correct and which one incorrect.

- Visualising the Training set results

```
[28] from matplotlib.colors import ListedColormap
     X_set, y_set = sc.inverse_transform(X_train), y_train
     X1, X2 = np.meshgrid(np.arange(start = X_set[:, 0].min() - 10, stop = X_set[:, 0].max() + 10, step = 0.25),
                          np.arange(start = X_set[:, 1].min() - 1000, stop = X_set[:, 1].max() + 1000, step = 0.25))
     plt.contourf(X1, X2, classifier.predict(sc.transform(np.array([X1.ravel(), X2.ravel()]).T)).reshape(X1.shape),
                  alpha = 0.75, cmap = ListedColormap(('red', 'green')))
     plt.xlim(X1.min(), X1.max())
     plt.ylim(X2.min(), X2.max())
     for i, j in enumerate(np.unique(y_set)):
         plt.scatter(X_set[y_set == j, 0], X_set[y_set == j, 1], c = ListedColormap(('red', 'green'))(i), label = j)
     plt.title('Logistic Regression (Training set)')
     plt.xlabel('Age')
     plt.ylabel('Estimated Salary')
     plt.legend()
     plt.show()

'c' argument looks like a single numeric RGB or RGBA sequence, which should be avoided as value-mapping will have
'c' argument looks like a single numeric RGB or RGBA sequence, which should be avoided as value-mapping will have
```

Then one can visualize the output for the training dataset and the test dataset. The graph shows a light grey zone indicating people belonging to a certain age and income group will not buy an SUV and the dark grey zone shows that they will buy. There is a distinct line between these two zones formed using sigmoid function, but we also see that a few points lie on this line and are not clear as to which region they belong. These are the points which we can identify using the confusion matrix as incorrect values. A few points are also present between the zones that can help us in calculating the error rate of this method (Figure 2.8).

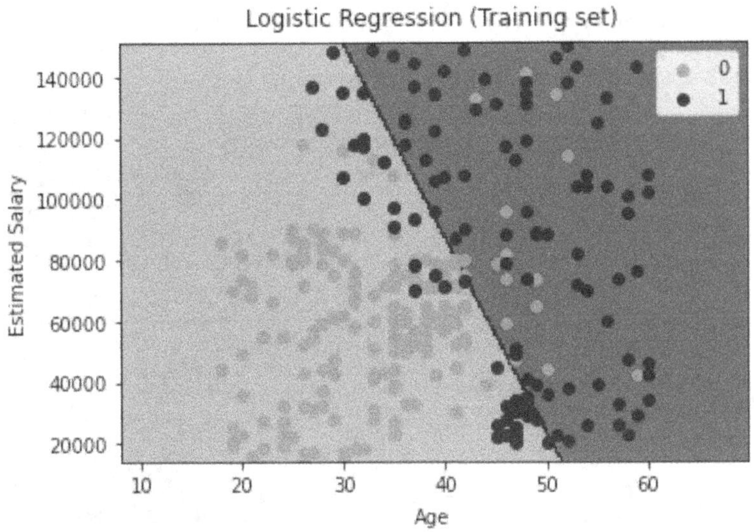

FIGURE 2.8 This picture represents the logistics regression beween age and salary in training set.

▾ Visualising the Test set results

```
[29] from matplotlib.colors import ListedColormap
     X_set, y_set = sc.inverse_transform(X_test), y_test
     X1, X2 = np.meshgrid(np.arange(start = X_set[:, 0].min() - 10, stop = X_set[:, 0].max() + 10, step = 0.25),
                          np.arange(start = X_set[:, 1].min() - 1000, stop = X_set[:, 1].max() + 1000, step = 0.25))
     plt.contourf(X1, X2, classifier.predict(sc.transform(np.array([X1.ravel(), X2.ravel()]).T)).reshape(X1.shape),
                  alpha = 0.75, cmap = ListedColormap(('red', 'green')))
     plt.xlim(X1.min(), X1.max())
     plt.ylim(X2.min(), X2.max())
     for i, j in enumerate(np.unique(y_set)):
         plt.scatter(X_set[y_set == j, 0], X_set[y_set == j, 1], c = ListedColormap(('red', 'green'))(i), label = j)
     plt.title('Logistic Regression (Test set)')
     plt.xlabel('Age')
     plt.ylabel('Estimated Salary')
     plt.legend()
     plt.show()

'c' argument looks like a single numeric RGB or RGBA sequence, which should be avoided as value-mapping will hav
'c' argument looks like a single numeric RGB or RGBA sequence, which should be avoided as value-mapping will hav
```

Then a graph obtained using the test dataset can help to determine if the result is correct. The starting point and the ending point of the line dividing the zones can be different, but this graph should contain a less number of incorrect values than the training data as machine has learned to identify almost everything. So, using this, one can get the desired result in a presentable manner (Figure 2.9).

- This is how a logistic regression model works. It is efficient and accurate because it does not require scaling and uses least amount of resources. Its simplicity makes it easy to use and so this algorithm is used widely.

II. **K-Nearest Neighbor (KNN) [24]**

- This is another type of classification for supervised learning.
- According to KNN, similar things tend to be in close proximity; i.e., it finds similarity between cases to predict the output.

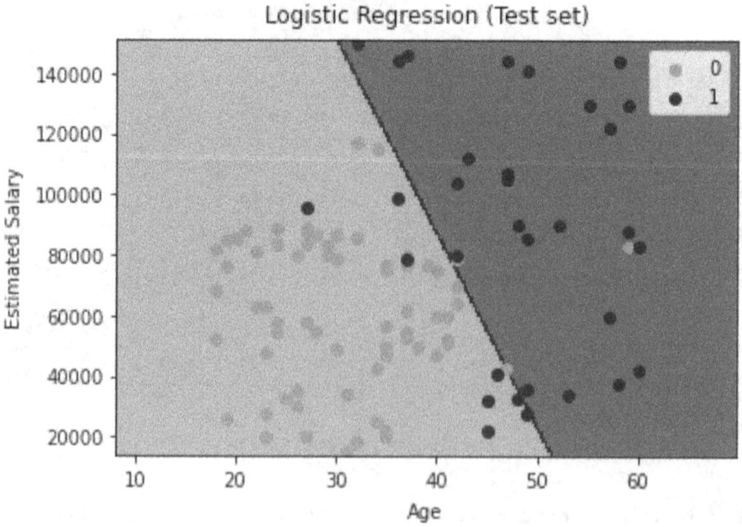

FIGURE 2.9 This picture represents the logistics regression beween age and salary in testing set.

- KNN works on the Euclidean distance equation.
  Figure 2.10 shows the distance between two points A and B.
- In KNN also, two or more categories are made, as shown in Figure 2.11. Then a place for the test data value is selected by following the below steps.
- In KNN, first a K value is assigned, which indicates the number of neighbors, and then Euclidean distance of these K numbers of points is calculated for each of the test data value. Thereafter, the total number of data points nearest to the test value is checked in both the categories. Once this is done, the category which has the maximum number of data points is selected as the predicted output.
- Code for K-nearest neighbor is pretty much similar to logistic regression except that feature scaling is done before the training data is trained by

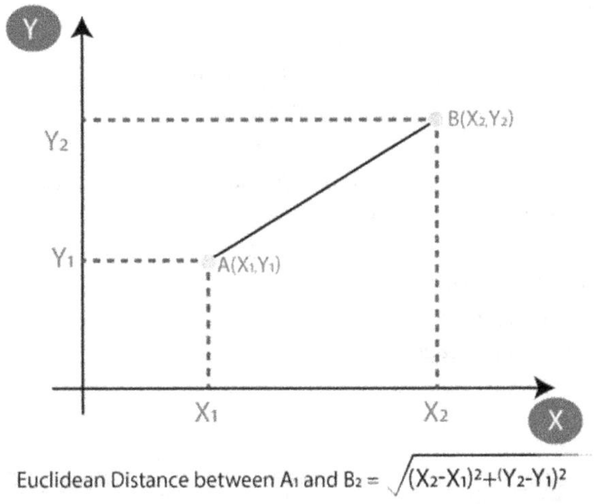

FIGURE 2.10 The graph shows the distance between two points A and B through a straight line.

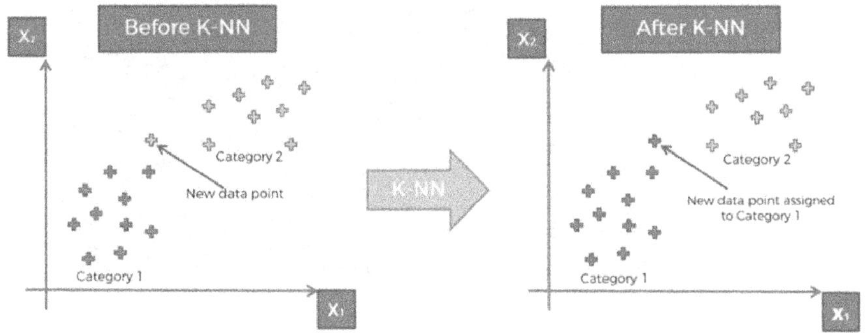

FIGURE 2.11 The figure shows how a data point is assigned to a cluster after KNN is done.

the K-nearest classifier method. This method takes the value of K as one of its argument. Once this is done, one can visualize the output in the graphical form similar to that of logistic regression.

- Feature scaling is an important step in this model if the values of an attribute are in a wide range, because later it will be difficult to judge the minimum distance between them.
- The graph visualized in KNN is different from that of logistic regression as this graph does not contain a straight line between the light grey and the dark grey zones, but it contains a random yet distinct line separating the two zones (Figure 2.12).
- This way KNN is an important algorithm because it is easy to implement and very effective on large training data. But it is difficult to decide a K-value beforehand, and calculating Euclidean distance is very costly. On the other hand, KNN's robustness makes it efficient to use for noisy data.

III. **Naive Bayes [25]**

- It is another algorithm of classification based on supervised Machine Learning that works on Bayes' theorem.
- In this algorithm, several methods are combined together. It is a probabilistic model which calculates probability from Bayes' theorem and then classifies the data based on each probability.
- Unlike other classification algorithms, Naive Bayes gives equal importance to each quality and predicts the output.
- The model is made using the GaussianNB method of the sklearn. Naive_Bayes package.

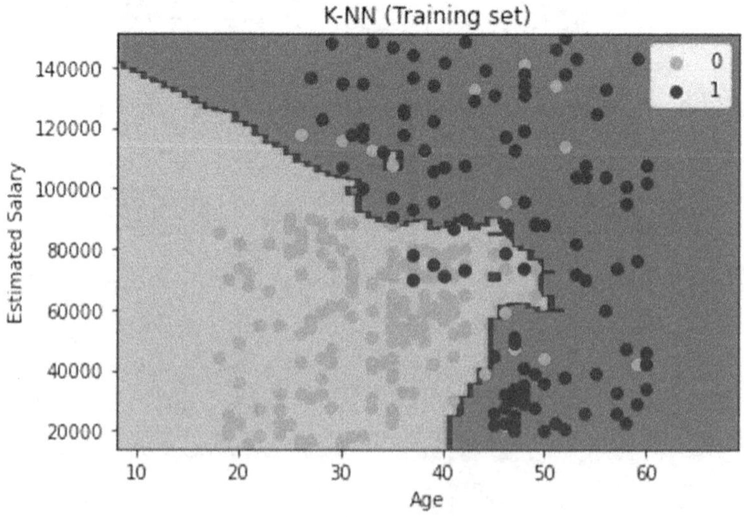

FIGURE 2.12 This picture represents K-NN effects on age and salary with training set.

▾ Training the Naive Bayes model on the Training set

```
[ ] from sklearn.naive_bayes import GaussianNB
    classifier = GaussianNB()
    classifier.fit(X_train, y_train)
```

- The graph obtained shows a distinct line, but it is made by vertical and horizontal groups, thus making it different from the other two classification techniques.
- All the steps are similar to those of other classification techniques.

IV. **Decision Tree Classification [26]**

- This algorithm is a supervised algorithm part of classification.
- As described previously, decision tree is also a part of regression; the difference between the two is that in classification the end node represents a category instead of a mean numeric value.
- In decision tree, there are two types of nodes: decision node and leaf node. Decision nodes are those where test cases are assigned a category and passed on further to be identified in another split; leaf node is the last node on each decision node that tells us the final category a test value belongs to.
- Splits formed in decision tree classification is not done randomly; instead, it is done on the basis of category: in one split only one type of data attribute is present and can be dark grey or light grey.
- As seen in the graph, all splits are categorized before only (Figure 2.13).
- This way a decision tree is made using the DecisionTreeClassifier (DTC) method in which certain arguments are taken to build an accurate model. The rest of the steps are similar to those of other classification models (Figure 2.14).

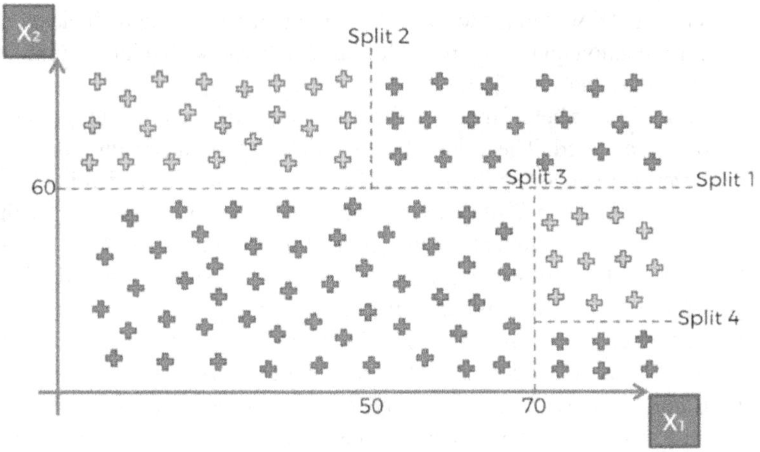

FIGURE 2.13 Splits are distinct for 2*2 cases.

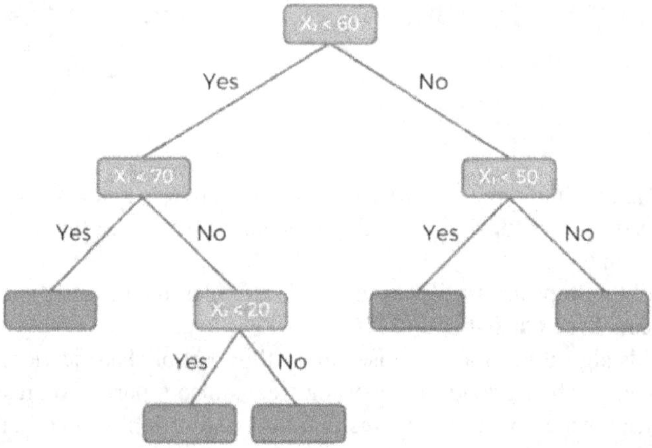

FIGURE 2.14 This figure represents the decision tree of the dataset.

- Visualization is also done in a similar way but the graph formed does not have a clear line between the light grey and the dark grey zone. Rather, it is spread unevenly between the two zones. This is because in DTC, overfitting is done and the model tries to include each and every dataset possible. But one should also notice that the graph below has only horizontal and vertical lines that separate the light grey and dark grey boxes, showing how splitting is done in DTC.
- Therefore, this model works similarly to how a human takes a decision and is very useful to take decisions that can have a lot of outcomes. It also needs lesser cleaning of data than other models (Figure 2.15).

V. **Random Forest Classification[27]**

- This model was made to resolve the issue of overfitting in decision tree classification and to be useful for large datasets with a large number of attributes and variations.
- In this, *n* number of trees are first identified and then the output of each tree is counted. The value of 0 or 1 that occurs maximum number of times is taken as the final output for random forest classification.
- Random forest classification uses the RandomForestClassifier method with certain arguments as no_estimator, random_state, etc., to build the model based on the training dataset. The rest of the functioning is similar to other classification implementations.
- The visualization in this model is clearer and shows the reduction is overfitting to that compared to decision tree classification.
- Random forest classification and random forest regression work similarly, except that the former's data is continuous, while that of the latter is discrete (Figure 2.16).
- It is efficient for high-dimensional large datasets and is used widely.

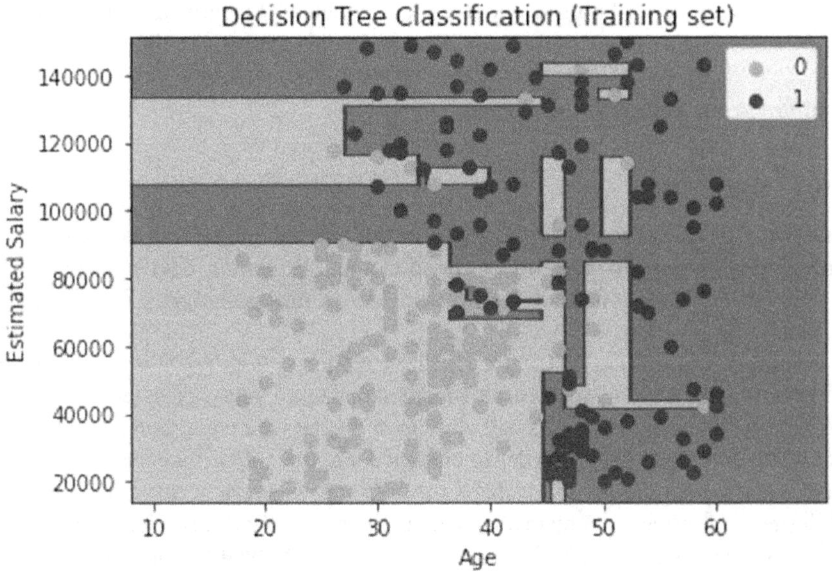

FIGURE 2.15 Decision tree classification of training set between age and salary.

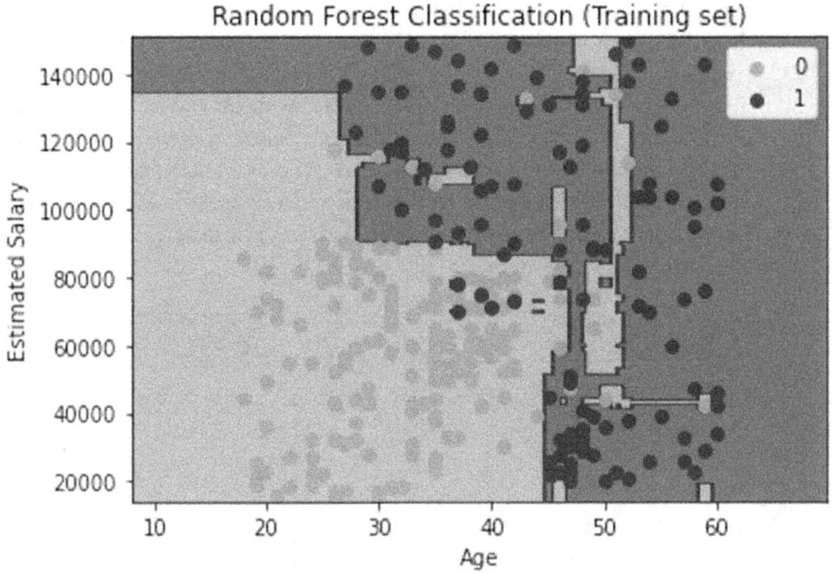

FIGURE 2.16 Random forest classification of training set between age and salary.

All these methods for building classification models of Machine Learning use discrete data to give a categorized output. That's why this method is called classification because it classifies any amount of data into particular parts, thus making it easy to identify the characteristics of a group.

2.6.3 Clustering

This is a type of unsupervised learning. In this, the data used is unlabeled but the final prediction is similar to that of classification, i.e., similar data is grouped into one cluster by keeping in mind a few parameters. K-means clustering and hierarchical clustering are its types.

Another method to build Machine Learning model is clustering. It is a model based on the unsupervised Machine Learning method that takes unlabeled data as input from the user. As the name implies, small clusters of datasets are made using certain common features. Clustering is similar to classification, the only difference being that in classification, prior groups are made by the user only, whereas in clustering *n* number of clusters are formed automatically. This is the reason why clustering is used, as it reveals all the possible outcomes that cannot be identified by the human brain [29].

I. **K-Means Clustering [30]**
- It is a method of clustering that is similar to K-nearest neighbor.
- In this method clusters are made using Euclidean distance and the features that are already known to the user.
- First, the dataset is taken and is placed alongside similar data points, and then the mean of these two is calculated and a centroid is formed for a particular cluster. Similarly, each dataset is placed near its similar cluster and then the mean is calculated. Next, this new mean will be the centroid of this circle or cluster. This way all the datasets are arranged and trained into various clusters. Once this is done, a test point is taken and kept to the mean or centroid that is most similar to it and a category is assigned to it.
- Figure 2.17 shows the graph of how clusters are formed.

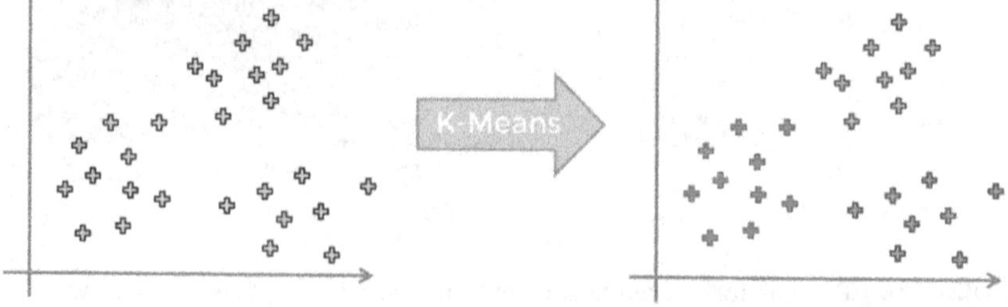

FIGURE 2.17 This picture represents the K-NN effect on various points.

- Now the code for K-means clustering is as follows:

Importing the libraries

```
[4] import numpy as np
    import matplotlib.pyplot as plt
    import pandas as pd
```

Importing the dataset

```
[5] dataset = pd.read_csv('Mall_Customers.csv')
    X = dataset.iloc[:, [2, 3]].values
```

First the data and libraries are imported as usual.

Using the elbow method to find the optimal number of clusters

```
[6] from sklearn.cluster import KMeans
    wcss = []
    for i in range(1, 11):
        kmeans = KMeans(n_clusters = i, init = 'k-means++', random_state = 42)
        kmeans.fit(X)
        wcss.append(kmeans.inertia_)
    plt.plot(range(1, 11), wcss)
    plt.title('The Elbow Method')
    plt.xlabel('Number of clusters')
    plt.ylabel('WCSS')
    plt.show()
```

Then using the K-means method and the append method, the optimal number of clusters is calculated and the dataset is trained using the same method. The elbow method is used, which means a point where an elbow or knee shape is formed is taken as the optimum number of K (Figure 2.18).

Training the K-Means model on the dataset

```
[ ] kmeans = KMeans(n_clusters = 5, init = 'k-means++', random_state = 42)
    y_kmeans = kmeans.fit_predict(X)
```

In this one need not split the data in training and test data as it is a part of unsupervised learning.

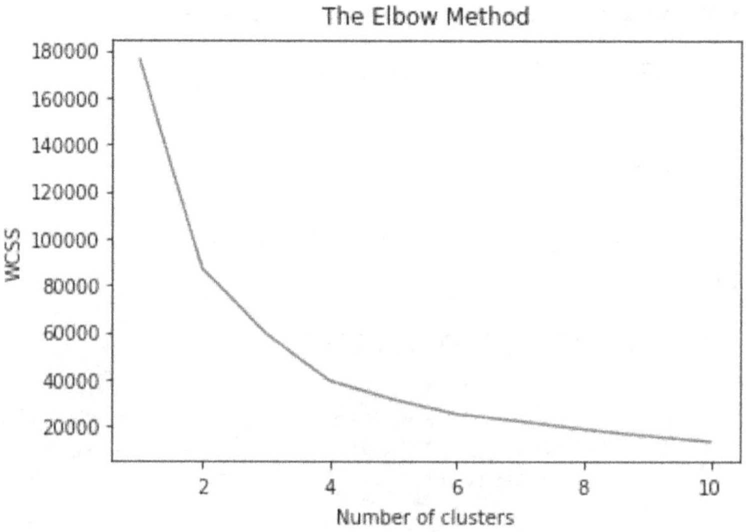

FIGURE 2.18 This graph represents the Elbow method of two points.

▾ Visualising the clusters

```
[ ] plt.scatter(X[y_kmeans == 0, 0], X[y_kmeans == 0, 1], s = 100, c = 'red', label = 'Cluster 1')
    plt.scatter(X[y_kmeans == 1, 0], X[y_kmeans == 1, 1], s = 100, c = 'blue', label = 'Cluster 2')
    plt.scatter(X[y_kmeans == 2, 0], X[y_kmeans == 2, 1], s = 100, c = 'green', label = 'Cluster 3')
    plt.scatter(X[y_kmeans == 3, 0], X[y_kmeans == 3, 1], s = 100, c = 'cyan', label = 'Cluster 4')
    plt.scatter(X[y_kmeans == 4, 0], X[y_kmeans == 4, 1], s = 100, c = 'magenta', label = 'Cluster 5')
    plt.scatter(kmeans.cluster_centers_[:, 0], kmeans.cluster_centers_[:, 1], s = 300, c = 'yellow', label = 'Centroids')
    plt.title('Clusters of customers')
    plt.xlabel('Annual Income (k$)')
    plt.ylabel('Spending Score (1-100)')
    plt.legend()
    plt.show()
```

Finally, the dataset is visualized in the form of clusters showing the centroid value of each cluster. This is done using the Matplotlib library (Figure 2.19).

- This way K-means is a very important algorithm that helps in building a model for unsupervised learning and it can categorize data into several categories more than a human brain can see.
- As the clusters formed in K-means clustering are not spherical, the result cannot be trusted to be accurate and a slight variation in the dataset can create a huge difference in the clusters. So it is not so much efficient to use.

II. **Hierarchical Clustering [31]**

- Another type of clustering is hierarchical clustering. It works just like a hierarchy tree that has many nodes with one root node.
- This clustering is divided into two parts:
  1. *Agglomerative:* In this, each data point is treated as separate unit in starting and then all separate units are combined into a single unit.

FIGURE 2.19 This figure represents the clusters of customers.

2. *Divisive:* In this, first the whole data is considered as a single data point and then the values are broken down one by one.

- As divisive clustering is not used much in the real world, one has to focus more on agglomerative clustering. And the steps are as follows:
  First two data points are taken and the mean is calculated.
  Then another data point is taken and this forms a cluster again with the nearest mean present to the cluster.
  This way, each cluster starts from two points and addition of a similar data point changes its mean and the clusters with similar properties are formed.
- This method uses a dendrogram to make the number of clusters. A dendrogram is made from a big cluster. It separates the big cluster into two parts and a point value is considered in graph above in which 22 clusters are considered. Similarly, as the line moves below the dendrogram, clusters are defined and each data point is part of any one cluster. The graph in Figure 2.20 can be used to explain how a line is drawn to decide a cluster.
- Code for hierarchical clustering is again similar to that of K-means clustering, except that instead of k-means, first dendrogram class is used to decide the optimal number of clusters. The dendrogram formed is shown in Figure 2.21.

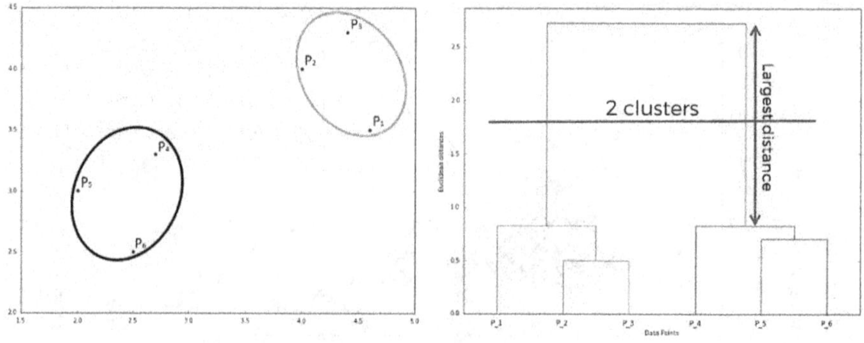

FIGURE 2.20 This figure represents the clustering of two data points.

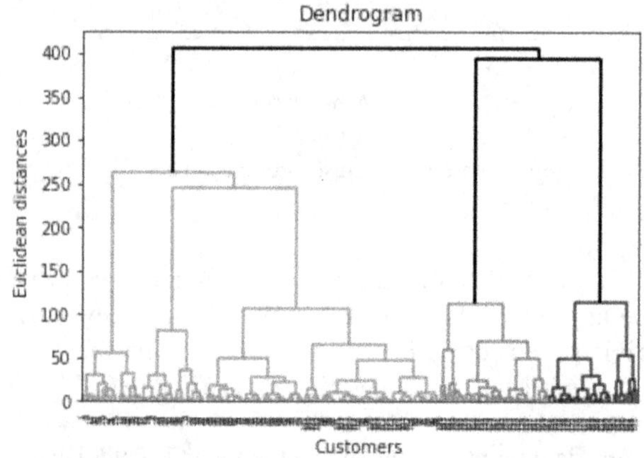

FIGURE 2.21 This figure represents the Euclidian distances between x and y axis..

▾ Using the dendrogram to find the optimal number of clusters

```
[3] import scipy.cluster.hierarchy as sch
    dendrogram = sch.dendrogram(sch.linkage(X, method = 'ward'))
    plt.title('Dendrogram')
    plt.xlabel('Customers')
    plt.ylabel('Euclidean distances')
    plt.show()
```

- Then the agglomerative clustering method is used to train the dataset.

▾ Training the Hierarchical Clustering model on the dataset

```
[4] from sklearn.cluster import AgglomerativeClustering
    hc = AgglomerativeClustering(n_clusters = 5, affinity = 'euclidean', linkage = 'ward')
    y_hc = hc.fit_predict(X)
```

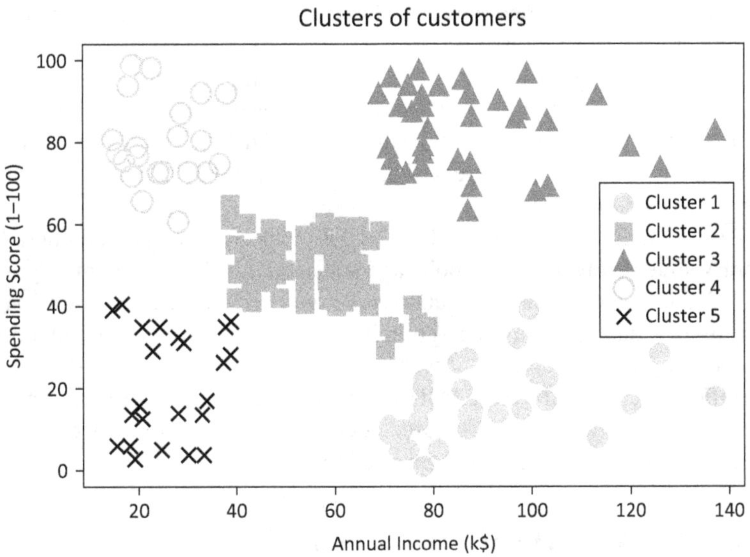

FIGURE 2.22 This figure represents the cluster of customers based on annual income..

- Visualization of clusters in the graphical form is shown in Figure 2.22.
- This is how hierarchical clustering works. It is a popular and easy way to cluster data.

These two methods make clustering an efficient method to categorize discrete unlabeled data. These two methods are the only ones which can help in training unsupervised data efficiently because clustering involves minimal human interventions once the data is fed to the machine (Figure 2.22).

This way Machine Learning is used to make different models to make it easy and fast to use a huge amount of data. These topics will help further to train real-world data and make it useful in one way or the other.

2.7 NATURAL LANGUAGE PROCESSING FOR BIG DATA

It is a form of Artificial Intelligence that helps machines in reading text data just the way a human reads it. It aids in several domains like statistics, linguistics, semantics and machine learning by helping to define relationships between entities and to understand texts that are either verbal or written. Tasks such as automatic summary, translation, named entity recognition, relationship extraction, sentiment analysis, speech recognition, and topic segmentation can be performed using NLP [32].

Natural language processing is in trend nowadays because every field has a large amount of text data that have to be interpreted for useful reports and analyses. All this humongous data is big data and NLP deals with it in a very smooth and subtle manner. NLP finds application in various biomedical domains including pharmaceutics and healthcare.

Using advanced algorithms and Machine Learning, NLP can change the way a patient is treated, by digitizing every word used by the doctor, by making fixed plans for the patients, and by using the whole unstructured data to predict results and provide treatment. Rest assured, there will be a great usage of NLP in the near future in the healthcare industry [33].

NLP uses Natural Language Toolkit (NLTK) to perform text recognition. NLTK is a library suite that helps in symbolic and statistical NLP. It is used mostly in NLP. NLTK helps in tokenization (punctuations are removed and sentences are converted into words or clauses), stemming (grouping of related words to a common stem), removal of stop words (removal of words that are commonly used and do not have any significance), and many more. All the functions help in converting verbal reports from doctors and patients into structured documents for quick reference and in making such reports more effective and generic [34].

2.8 BIG DATA WITH DEEP LEARNING

Deep learning is a subfield of Machine Learning; it helps machines mimic the human brain in performing tasks such as speech recognition, processing data, detecting entities and their relationships, and analyses and making decisions. But we know that Machine Learning does the same kind of work, so why do we need deep learning? Unlike Machine Learning where the machine learns on its own using algorithms, deep learning performs these tasks by structuring algorithms and making artificial neural networks. Deep learning has a major impact on big data as it helps to extract relevant information from huge amounts of unstructured, unlabeled big data [35].

Deep learning uses artificial neural networks to do the programming. Artificial neural networks are a web-like structure which has nodes equivalent to synapses of the human brain. These neural networks work in a hierarchical pattern while in Machine Learning the algorithms are run in a linear fashion; hence it is said that deep learning is an advancement of Machine Learning. There are three components of a neural network: input layer, output layer, and middle layer that undergo entire processing to make the raw data provided in the input layer into relevant output. Neural networks are built in Python language and use libraries like Tensorflow and pyTorch to build the model. The advantage of neural networks over Machine Learning algorithm is that it helps to get the data as a whole without the need to remove the undesired data or consider the missing data. They also provide a solution to the problem of overfitting as it processes the data in a stepwise manner [36].

In the healthcare industry, deep learning is used in image recognition and chatbots that interact with patients in an easy manner. Medical imaging feature is the one that is most used in treating patients with cancer as it recognizes the patterns that are developed and also compares the cancer data with the already present data. It can also easily inform us of the unusual pattern or the new one, thus making the job easy for doctors and efficient for the medical system. This is just the starting stage of deep learning and AI in the healthcare field. According to experts, deep learning has great potential in making medical systems more relevant and easy for doctors. More and more clinical functions can be performed by deep learning that helps in patient analysis, e.g., in radiology or administration interference to review patients' details, etc. [37].

2.9 HOW MACHINE LEARNING CAN BE APPLIED TO BIG DATA

So far we have looked at all the algorithms that can be performed in Machine Learning. Let us see how big data can be applied to these algorithms to predict a pattern or a solution from unorganized data [38].

1. **Applying K-Nearest Neighbors to Data**
   - Classification, which is a supervised form of Machine Learning, explains the intuition of K-nearest neighbors algorithm. In this section, we're going to apply a simple example of the algorithm using Scikit-Learn, and then in the subsequent sections we'll build our own algorithm to learn more about how it works under the hood.
   - To exemplify classification, we're going to use a Breast Cancer Dataset, which is a dataset donated to the University of California, Irvine (UCI) collection from the University of Wisconsin-Madison. UCI has a large Machine Learning repository. The datasets present are organized by types of Machine Learning often used for them, such as data types, attribute types, topic areas, and a few others. It is very useful for both educational uses and development of Machine Learning algorithms. From the Breast Cancer Dataset page, choose the Data Folder link. From there, grab breast-cancer-wisconsin.data and breast-cancerwisconsin.names. These may not download automatically, but may instead display in the browser. Right click to save, if this is the case for you.
   - After downloading, open the breast-cancer-wisconsin.names file. Scrolling down the file just after line 100, we can get the names of the attributes (columns). With this information, we can manually add these labels to the breast-cancer-wisconsin.data file.

     Open that, and enter a new first line:
     - Id,
     - clump_thickness,
     - uniform_cell_size,
     - uniform_cell_shape,
     - marginal_adhesion,
     - single_epi_cell_size,
     - bare_nuclei,
     - bland_chromation,
     - normal_nucleoli,
     - mitoses,
     - class.

You might wonder what these features and labels are. What we're attempting is to classify things so that we have a list of attributes indicating either a benign or a malignant tumor. Also, most of these columns appear to be of use, but the question is whether they are similar to the others or they might be useless? Absolutely, this ID column is not something we actually want to feed into the classifier.

- *Missing/bad data*

  This dataset also has some missing data in it, which we're going to need to clean! Let's start off with our imports, pulling in the data, and do some cleaning:

```
import numpy as np
from sklearn import preprocessing, cross_validation, neighbors
import pandas as pd

df = pd.read_csv('breast-cancer-wisconsin.data.txt')
df.replace('?',-99999, inplace=True)
df.drop(['id'], 1, inplace=True)
```

  After feeding in the data, we take note that there are some columns with missing data. These columns have a "?" filled in. The .names file informed us of this, but we would have discovered this eventually via an error if we attempted to feed this information to a classifier. In this case, we're choosing to fill in a –99,999 value for any missing data. You can choose how you want to handle missing data, but, in the real world, you may find that 50% or more of your rows contain missing data in one of the columns, especially if you are collecting data with extensive attributes. The value –99999 isn't perfect, but it works well enough. Next, we're dropping the IDcolumn. When we are done, we'll comment out the dropping of the id column just to see what sort of impact it might have to include it.

- Next, we define our features (X) and labels (y):

```
X = np.array(df.drop(['class'], 1))
y = np.array(df['class'])
```

  The features X are everything except for the class. Doing df.drop returns a new dataframe with our chosen column(s) dropped. The label y is just the class column.

- Now we create training and testing samples using Scikit-Learn Learns cross_validation.train_test_split:

```
X_train, X_test, y_train, y_test =
cross_validation.train_test_split(X, y, test_size=0.2)
```

- Define the classifier:

```
clf = neighbors.KNeighborsClassifier()
```

In this case, we're using the K-nearest neighbors classifier from Sklearn.

- Train the classifier:

```
clf.fit(X_train, y_train)
```

- Test:

```
accuracy = clf.score(X_test, y_test)
print(accuracy)
```

The result should be about 95%, and that's out of the box without any tweaking. Very cool! Let's show what happens when we do indeed include truly meaningless and misleading data by commenting out the dropping of the id column:

```
import numpy as np
from sklearn import preprocessing, cross_validation, neighbors
import pandas as pd

df = pd.read_csv('breast-cancer-wisconsin.data.txt')
df.replace('?',-99999, inplace=True)
```

```
#df.drop(['id'], 1, inplace=True)

X = np.array(df.drop(['class'], 1))
y = np.array(df['class'])

X_train, X_test, y_train, y_test =
cross_validation.train_test_split(X, y, test_size=0.2)

clf = neighbors.KNeighborsClassifier()
clf.fit(X_train, y_train)
accuracy = clf.score(X_test, y_test)
print(accuracy)
```

The impact is staggering, where accuracy drops from ~95% to ~60% on average. In the future, when AI rules the planet, note that you just need to feed it meaningless attributes to outsmart it! Interestingly enough, adding noise can be a way to help or hurt your algorithm. When combatting your robot overlords, being able to distinguish between helpful noise and malicious noise may save your life!

- Next, you can probably guess how we'll be predicting if you followed the regression tutorial that used Scikit-Learn. First, we need some sample data. We can just make it up. For example, I will look at one of the lines in the sample file and make something similar by merely shifting some of the values. You can also just add noise to do further testing, provided the standard deviation is not outrageous. Doing this is relatively safe as well, since you're not actually training on the falsified data but merely testing. I will just manually do this by making up a line:

```
example_measures = np.array([4,2,1,1,1,2,3,2,1])
```

Feel free to search the document for that list of features. It doesn't exist. Now you can do:

```
prediction = clf.predict(example_measures)
print(prediction)
```

... or depending on when you are watching this, you might not be able to! When doing that, I get a warning:

```
DeprecationWarning: Passing 1d arrays as data is deprecated in
0.17 and will raise ValueError in 0.19. Reshape your data
either using X.reshape(-1, 1) if your data has a single
feature or X.reshape(1, -1) if it contains a single sample.
```

Okay, no problem. Do we have a single feature? Nope. Do we have a single example? Yes! So we will use X.reshape(1, –1):

```
example_measures = np.array([4,2,1,1,1,2,3,2,1])
example_measures = example_measures.reshape(1, -1)
prediction = clf.predict(example_measures)
```

```
print(prediction)
```

Output:

```
0.95
[2]
```

The output here is first the accuracy (95%) and then the prediction (2), and this is what we expected to model from our fake data.

- What if we had two samples?

```
example_measures =
np.array([[4,2,1,1,1,2,3,2,1],[4,2,1,1,1,2,3,2,1]])
example_measures = example_measures.reshape(2, -1)
prediction = clf.predict(example_measures)
print(prediction)
```

- What if we don't know how many samples?!

```
example_measures =
np.array([[4,2,1,1,1,2,3,2,1],[4,2,1,1,1,2,3,2,1]])
example_measures =
example_measures.reshape(len(example_measures), -1)
prediction = clf.predict(example_measures)
print(prediction)
```

As you can see, implementing K-nearest neighbors is not only easy but also extremely accurate in this case. In the next section, we're going to build our own K-nearest neighbors algorithm from scratch, rather than using Scikit-Learn, in an attempt to learn more about the algorithm, understand how it works, and, most importantly, learn one of its pitfalls.

2. **The CART Training Algorithm**
   Scikit-Learn uses the *Classification And Regression Tree* (CART) algorithm to train decision trees (also called "growing" trees). The idea is really quite simple: the algorithm first splits the training set into two subsets using a single feature *k* and a threshold *tk* (e.g., "petal length ≤ 2.45 cm"). How does it choose *k* and *tk*? It searches for the pair (*k*, *tk*) that produces the purest subsets (weighted by their size). The cost function that the algorithm tries to minimize is given by the following equation:

$$J(k,t_k) = \frac{m_{\text{left}}}{m} G_{\text{left}} + \frac{m_{\text{right}}}{m} G_{\text{right}}$$

$$\text{where} \begin{cases} G_{\text{left/right}} \text{ measures the impurity of the left/right subset} \\ m_{\text{left/right}} \text{ is the number of instances of the left/right subset} \end{cases}$$

   Once it has successfully split the training set into two, it splits the subsets using the same logic into sub-subsets, and so on, recursively. It stops recursing once it reaches the maximum depth (defined by the max_depth hyperparameter), or if it cannot find a split that will reduce impurity. A few other hyperparameters (described in a moment) control additional stopping conditions (min_samples_split, min_samples_leaf, min_weight_fraction_leaf, and max_leaf_nodes).
   Algorithm

   We will use the Scikit-Learn library to build the decision tree model. We will be using the iris dataset to build a DecisionTreeClassifier. The dataset contains information of three classes—Iris Setosa, Iris Versicolour, and Iris Virginica—of the iris plant with the following attributes:

   - Sepal length
   - Sepal width
   - Petal length
   - Petal width

The task is to predict which class do the iris plant belong to based on the attributes.

```
#Importing required libraries
import pandas as pd
import numpy as np
from sklearn.datasets import load_iris
from sklearn.tree import DecisionTreeClassifier
from sklearn.model_selection import train_test_split

#Loading the iris data
data = load_iris()
print('Classes to predict: ', data.target_names)
```

```
#Extracting data attributes
X = data.data
### Extracting target/ class labels
y = data.target

print('Number of examples in the data:', X.shape[0])
```

```
#First four rows in the variable 'X'
X[:4]

#Output
Out: array([[5.1, 3.5, 1.4, 0.2],
       [4.9, 3. , 1.4, 0.2],
       [4.7, 3.2, 1.3, 0.2],
       [4.6, 3.1, 1.5, 0.2]])
```

```
#Using the train_test_split to create train and test sets.
X_train, X_test, y_train, y_test = train_test_split(X, y, random_state = 47,
 test_size = 0.25)
```

```
#Importing the Decision tree classifier from the sklearn library.
from sklearn.tree import DecisionTreeClassifier
clf = DecisionTreeClassifier(criterion = 'entropy')
```

```
#Training the decision tree classifier.
clf.fit(X_train, y_train)

#Output:
Out:DecisionTreeClassifier(class_weight=None, criterion='entropy', max_depth=None,
            max_features=None, max_leaf_nodes=None,
            min_impurity_decrease=0.0, min_impurity_split=None,
            min_samples_leaf=1, min_samples_split=2,
            min_weight_fraction_leaf=0.0, presort=False, random_state=None,
            splitter='best')
```

```
#Predicting labels on the test set.
y_pred =  clf.predict(X_test)
```

```
#Importing the accuracy metric from sklearn.metrics library

from sklearn.metrics import accuracy_score
print('Accuracy Score on train data: ', accuracy_score(y_true=y_train,
y_pred=clf.predict(X_train)))
print('Accuracy Score on test data: ', accuracy_score(y_true=y_test, y_pred=y_pred))

#Output:
Out: Accuracy Score on train data:  1.0
   Accuracy Score on test data:  0.9473684210526315
```

```
clf = DecisionTreeClassifier(criterion='entropy', min_samples_split=50)
clf.fit(X_train, y_train)
print('Accuracy Score on train data: ', accuracy_score(y_true=y_train,
y_pred=clf.predict(X_train)))
print('Accuracy Score on the test data: ', accuracy_score(y_true=y_test,
y_pred=clf.predict(X_test)))

#Output:
Out: Accuracy Score on train data:  0.9553571428571429
   Accuracy Score on test data:  0.9736842105263158
```

```
from sklearn.externals.six import StringIO
from IPython.display import Image
from sklearn.tree import export_graphviz
import pydotplus
dot_data =StringIO()
export_graphviz(dtree, out_file=dot_data, filled=True, rounded=True)
graph = pydotplus.graph_from_dot_data(dot_data.getvalue())
Image(graph.create_png())
```

Decision Tree (Figure 2.23).

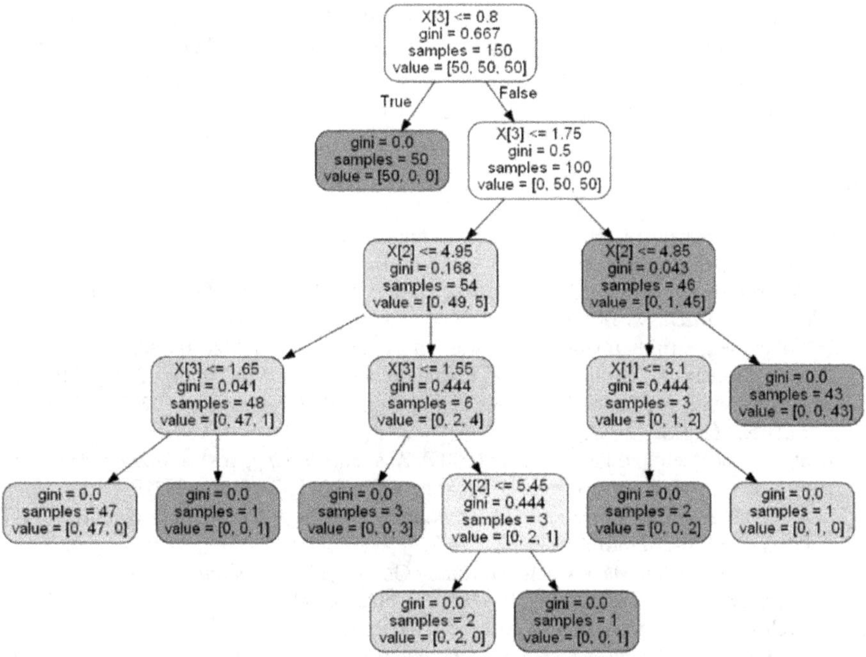

FIGURE 2.23 This figure represents the decision tree of the dataset.

2.10 MACHINE LEARNING IN HEALTHCARE

We now know what Machine Learning means and how it works on big data and biological data. Let us see in brief what its uses are in today's world. In healthcare, Machine Learning and Artificial Intelligence have played a great role as they have made it easy for patients to interact with the system as well as for doctors to diagnose patients and analyze their medical profiles. Not only this, Machine Learning has made it easy and fast to do researches on biological data as it is always large in amount and is always present in an unstructured form [39].

The collaboration between big data and artificial intelligence had helped in analyzing and deriving conclusions out of humongous data available. Currently, a large number of companies are able to understand their customers better using machine learning.

Not only this, Machine Learning helps in cost-reduction for research work and medicinal formulation and also helps in detecting the root cause of disease in large numbers of patients at a time. With reduction in paper work and manual input of data, Machine Learning has helped in saving time as well, and also diagnostics results can be generated faster than it used to be. Better treatment plans can be made on a more generic level. Interaction between community and doctors can be made easy and fast. All this tells us that usage of Machine Learning, Artificial Intelligence, deep learning, and natural language processing is going to increase in future as the amount of data collected day to day is increasing

In future the usage of machine learning, artificial intelligence, deep learning and natural language processing is going to enhance exponentially keeping abreast with the enormous amount of data generated on a daily basis due to the ease of easy-to-use algorithms and no human interference. [40, 41]

REFERENCES

1. John R. Koza, Forrest H. Bennett, David Andre and Martin A. Keane (1996). *Automated Design of Both the Topology and Sizing of Analog Electrical Circuits Using Genetic Programming. Artificial Intelligence in Design '96* (Dordrecht: Springer), pp. 151–170. doi: 10.1007/978-94-009-0279-4_9.
2. "Machine Learning textbook". www.cs.cmu.edu. Retrieved 2020-05-28.
3. A. L'Heureux, K. Grolinger, H. F. Elyamany and M. A. M. Capretz (2017). Machine learning with big data: Challenges and approaches. *IEEE Access* 5: 7776–7797. doi: 10.1109/ACCESS.2017.2696365.
4. Stuart J. Russell and Peter Norvig (2009). *Artificial Intelligence: A Modern Approach* (3rd ed.). Upper Saddle River, NJ: Prentice Hall. ISBN 978-0-13-604259-4.
5. John Haugeland (1985). *Artificial Intelligence: The Very Idea*, Cambridge, MA: MIT Press. ISBN 0-262-08153-9.
6. David Poole, Alan Mackworth and Randy Goebel (1998). *Computational Intelligence: A Logical Approach*. New York: Oxford University Press. ISBN 978-0-19-510270-3. Archived from the original on 26 July 2020. Retrieved 22 August 2020.
7. Dr. John Kelly III (2015). "Computing, cognition and the future of knowing" (PDF). *IBM Research: Cognitive Computing*. IBM Corporation. Retrieved February 9, 2016.
8. MIT Encyclopedia of Cognitive Science Archived 19 July 2008 at the Wayback Machine (quoted in "AITopics").

9. Sergio Alejandro Gómez, Carlos Iván Chesñevar and Guillermo Ricardo Simari (2010). Reasoning with inconsistent ontologies through argumentation. *Applied Artificial Intelligence* 24 (1–2): 102–148. doi: 10.1080/08839510903448692.
10. Y. C. Huei (2014). "Benefits and introduction to python programming for freshmore students using inexpensive robots," *2014* IEEE International Conference on Teaching, Assessment and Learning for Engineering (TALE), *Wellington*, 12–17. doi: 10.1109/TALE.2014.7062611.
11. Sebastian Raschka, Joshua Patterson and Corey Nolet (2020). Machine learning in python: Main developments and technology trends in data science, machine learning, and artificial intelligence. *Information* 11: 193. doi: 10.3390/info11040193.
12. Stuart J. Russell and Peter Norvig (2010). *Artificial Intelligence: A Modern Approach* (3rd ed.). Upper Saddle River, NJ: Prentice Hall.
13. Victor Roman (2019). Unsupervised machine learning: Clustering analysis. *Medium*. Retrieved: 2019–10-01.
14. Leslie P. Kaelbling, Michael L. Littman and Andrew W. Moore (1996). Reinforcement learning: A survey. *Journal of Artificial Intelligence Research* 4: 237–285. arXiv:cs/9605103. doi: 10.1613/jair.301.
15. Y. Reddy, Viswanath Pulabaigari and B. Eswara (2018). Semi-supervised learning: A brief review. *International Journal of Engineering & Technology* 7: 81. doi: 10.14419/ijet.v7i1.8.9977.
16. David A. Freedman (2009). *Statistical Models: Theory and Practice*. Cambridge University Press.
17. Naomi Altman and Martin Krzywinski (2015). Simple linear regression. *Nature Methods* 12 (11): 999–1000. doi: 10.1038/nmeth.3627.
18. https://www.investopedia.com/terms/m/mlr.asp.
19. Yin-Wen Chang, Cho-Jui Hsieh, Kai-Wei Chang, Michael Ringgaard, Chih-Jen Lin (2010). Training and testing low-degree polynomial data mappings via linear SVM. *Journal of Machine Learning Research* 11: 1471–1490.
20. Lingjian Yang, Songsong Liu, Sophia Tsoka and Lazaros Papageorgiou (2017). A regression tree approach using mathematical programming. *Expert Systems with Applications* 78: 347–357. doi: 10.1016/j.eswa.2017.02.013.
21. Adele Cutler, David Cutler and John Stevens (2011). "Random Forests," in Zhang, C. and Ma, Y.Q. (eds.), *Ensemble Machine Learning*, Springer, New York, 157–175. http://dx.doi.org/10.1007/978-1-4419-9326-7_5.
22. Sotiris Kotsiantis, I. Zaharakis and P. Pintelas (2006). Machine learning: A review of classification and combining techniques. *Artificial Intelligence Review* 26: 159–190. Doi: 10.1007/s10462-007-9052-3.
23. Maher Maalouf (2011). Logistic regression in data analysis: An overview. *International Journal of Data Analysis Techniques and Strategies* 3: 281–299. doi: 10.1504/IJDATS.2011.041335.
24. Youguo Li and Haiyan Wu (2012). A clustering method based on K-Means algorithm. *Physics Procedia* 25: 1104–1109. doi: 10.1016/j.phpro.2012.03.206.
25. Irina Rish (2001). "An empirical study of the Naïve Bayes Classifier," in IJCAI 2001 Workshop on Empirical Methods in Artificial Intelligence, vol. 3.
26. Harsh Patel and Purvi Prajapati (2018). Study and analysis of decision tree based classification algorithms. *International Journal of Computer Sciences and Engineering* 6: 74–78. doi: 10.26438/ijcse/v6i10.7478.
27. Qiong Ren, Hui Cheng and Hai Han (2017). Research on machine learning framework based on random forest algorithm. *AIP Conference Proceedings* 1820: 080020. doi: 10.1063/1.4977376.

28. O. Simeone (2018). "A Very Brief Introduction to Machine Learning With Applications to Communication Systems," in *IEEE Transactions on Cognitive Communications and Networking* (vol. 4, no. 4, pp. 648–664). doi: 10.1109/TCCN.2018.2881442.
29. Alauddin Al-Omary and Mohammad Jamil (2006). A new approach of clustering based machine-learning algorithm. *Knowledge-Based Systems* 19: 248–258. doi: 10.1016/j.knosys.2005.10.011.
30. Youguo Li and Haiyan Wu (2012). A clustering method based on K-Means algorithm. *Physics Procedia* 25: 1104–1109. doi: 10.1016/j.phpro.2012.03.206.
31. Fionn Murtagh and Pedro Contreras (2011). Methods of hierarchical clustering. Computing Research Repository - CORR. doi: 10.1007/978-3-642-04898-2_288.
32. Diksha Khurana, Aditya Koli, Kiran Khatter and Sukhdev Singh (2017). Natural Language Processing: State of The Art, Current Trends and Challenges. Cornell University.
33. Sumithra Velupillai, Hanna Suominen, Maria Liakata, Angus Roberts, Anoop Shah, Katherine Morley, David Osborn, Joseph Hayes, Robert Stewart, Johnny Downs, Wendy Chapman and Rina Dutta (2018). Using clinical natural language processing for health outcomes research: Overview and actionable Suggestions for future advances. *Journal of Biomedical Informatics* 88: 11–19. doi: 10.1016/j.jbi.2018.10.005.
34. S. Mohagaonkar, A. Rawlani and A. Saxena (2019). "Efficient decision tree using machine learning tools for acute ailments," in *2019* 6th International Conference on Computing for Sustainable Global Development (INDIACom), New Delhi, India, pp. 691–697.
35. A. Saxena, N. Kushik, A. Chaurasia and N. Kaushik (2020). "Predicting the outcome of an election results using sentiment analysis of machine learning," in *International Conference on Innovative Computing and Communications. Advances in Intelligent Systems and Computing*, vol. 1087 (Singapore: Springer), pp. 503–516.
36. S. Mohanty, A. Mishra and A. Saxena (2020). "Medical data analysis using machine learning with KNN," in Gupta D., Khanna A., Bhattacharyya S., Hassanien A., Anand S. and Jaiswal A. (eds.), International Conference on Innovative Computing and Communications. *Advances in Intelligent Systems and Computing*, vol 1166 (Singapore: Springer). doi: 10.1007/978-981-15-5148-2_42.
37. Riccardo Miotto, Fei Wang, Shuang Wang and Xiaoqian Jiang (2017). Deep learning for healthcare: Review, opportunities and challenges. *Briefings in Bioinformatics* 19, pp. 1236–1246. doi: 10.1093/bib/bbx044.
38. A. Agarwal and A. Saxena (2018). Malignant tumor detection using machine learning through Scikit-learn. *International Journal of Pure and Applied Mathematics* 119(15): 2863–2874.
39. K. Shailaja, B. Seetharamulu and M. A. Jabbar (2018). "Machine learning in health-care: A review," *2018* Second International Conference on Electronics, Communication and Aerospace Technology (ICECA), *Coimbatore*, pp. 910–914. doi: 10.1109/ICECA.2018.8474918.
40. A. Agarwal and A. Saxena (2020). "Comparing machine learning algorithms to predict diabetes in women and visualize factors affecting it the most—A step toward better health care for women," in *International Conference on Innovative Computing and Communications. Advances in Intelligent Systems and Computing*, vol 1087. (Singapore: Springer), pp. 339–350.
41. A. Agarwal and A. Saxena (2019). "Analysis of Machine Learning Algorithms and Obtaining Highest Accuracy for Prediction of Diabetes in Women," in *2019* 6th International Conference on Computing for Sustainable Global Development (INDIACom), New Delhi, India, pp. 686–690.

Part II

Application

3 Machine Learning in Clinical Trials

A New Era

Shazia Rashid and Neha Kathuria

CONTENTS

3.1 INTRODUCTION

Artificial Intelligence (AI) and Machine Learning (ML) have been the most important technological innovations of the modern world. AI generally infers the use of a computer to ideal intelligent behavior with minor human interference (Hamet and Tremblay 2017). AI uses specific algorithms that help the computer system to think in terms of human intelligent behavior (Park et al. 2019). The term "Artificial Intelligence" was first coined by John McCarthy in 1956 during a computer science conference held at Dartmouth College (Shortliffe 2019). ML is a branch of AI that utilizes computer calculations to recognize designs in enormous informational collections and can consistently improve with extra information (Waljee 2010). AI has a wide range of applications in the healthcare sector and has revolutionized several patient management programs. The first clinical experiment using computer research and artificial neural networks (ANN) was carried out by Nathanial Rochester at International Business Machines (IBM) and by Bernard Widrow and Marcian Hoff at Stanford in 1950 (Miller and Brown 2017). ANN are simple mathematical designs which comprise various algorithms that help in determining the relationships within large analytical datasets (Miller and Brown 2017). The ANN used in the brain model is one of the most interesting areas in AI. ANN operate on the principle of the biological neural network, where the neurons are interconnected to and coordinate with each other (Renganathan 2019). Hence, the application of AI is very useful in the area of medicine and healthcare. For example, AI-based programs, methods, and algorithms are used in cardiology to examine advanced imaging technologies, EHR (electronic health records), biobanks, clinical trials, clinical sensors, genomics, and other molecular profiling techniques (Shameer et al. 2018). The simple repetitive task of maintaining clinical records can be quickly performed using AI applications (Park et al. 2019). ML is based on a simple process of making computer programs access data followed by learning from it, which can also be incorporated through deep learning algorithms and simple decision-making trees such as if-then, for-while, do-while, etc. (Dhillon et al. 2019). Algorithms like ANN, support vector machines (SVM), and decision trees are the most used in ML (Waljee and Higgins 2010). The ML algorithm methods are of two types: the supervised method and the unsupervised method (Sidey-Gibbons et al. 2019). Both the algorithms of ML have been used for developing different devices and for examining clinical results. As of late, managed learning was utilized to build up a psychological ML-based classifier machine to recognize the constrictive pericarditis and prohibitive cardiomyopathy (Shameer et al. 2018), where both unsupervised learning and supervised learning are used in ANN (Lavrač 1999). Apart from AI and ML, big data, which is an extension of these technologies, has also played an important part in the healthcare industry. Big data is referred to as managing enormous collections of data which cannot be managed through traditional ways. The basic application of big data analytics is associated with functions like improving patient-based services, detecting the spread of disease, analyzing the mode of action of certain diseases, providing better healthcare services as well as maintenance and monitoring the quality of treatment of medical institutions (Ristevski and Chen 2018).

3.2 ML-BASED ALGORITHMS AND METHODS

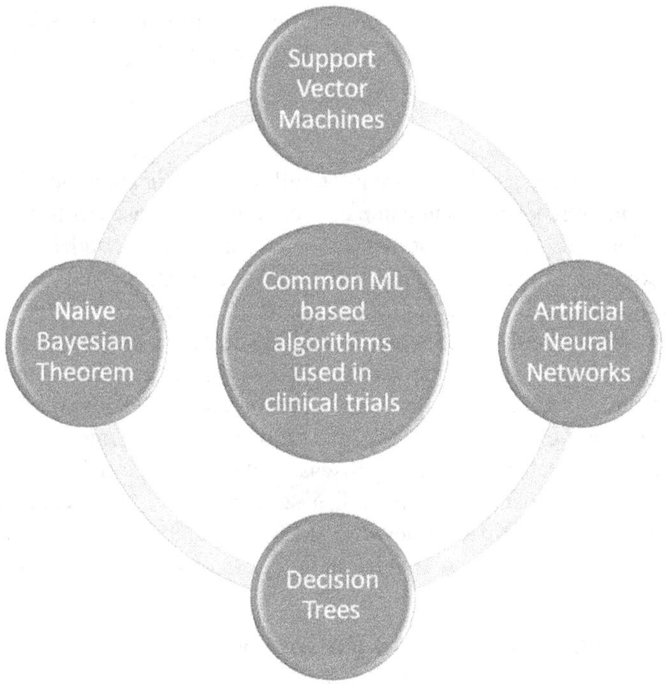

FIGURE 3.1 Some common ML-based algorithms used in clinical trials.

An algorithm is defined as the set of well-defined sequences and mathematical equations put together to resolve a problem that applies to the computer. Machine learning algorithms in the medical sector are designed in such a way that they can predict results after reading the data entries. So far, various algorithms like SVM, supervised, unsupervised, ANN, decision trees, K-means, and Naive Bayes' theorem have been developed and implemented successfully. Here some of these algorithms will be discussed in detail (Figure 3.1).

3.2.1 Support Vector Machine

In 1992, Boser, Guyon, and Vapnik introduced SVMs in COLT-92 (Weston 2013). Starting from 1962, SVMs have gained pace, and the first SVM algorithm and method was published in 1996 with the "Generalised Portrait" method for pattern recognition. Further, methods like "The Kuhn–Tucker Theorem," "Searching for Coefficients Instead of Coordinates," "Optimum (Largest Margin) Hyperplane," and "Lagrangian Dual Function" came into existence and are used till date in almost all the algorithms (Chervonenkis 1970). SVMs to date have shown enormous uses in the medical sector and have always been up to the mark in their performance. The major areas of the SVM application are chemistry, biotechnology, molecular biology, and further ahead to bioinformatics (Liang et al. 2011). For example, Battineni et al. (2019) experimented on validating SVM algorithm performance in determining dementia through a statistical approach and reported reliable results for predicting dementia. SVM is considered as one of the most important algorithms in ML.

3.2.2 Decision Trees

Decision trees are known to be common for building classification models that easily understand human reasoning and can easily combine sequences of tests (Kotsiantis 2011). Decision tree, as the name suggests, uses a tree-like model to predict the probable outcomes and chances of events. These models are formed based on conditional statements like do-while, for, and do-until used while coding the algorithms. In medical sciences, decision trees help in making decisions based on the probability of managing and organizing many patient data on the system. Decision trees often help in the classification and diagnosis of certain diseases (Podgorelec 2002). For instance, Shouman et al. (2011) concluded through an experiment the usefulness of decision trees in determining heart disease risks with specificity, reliability, and efficiency. Since early detection of liver diseases is not easy, Abdar et al. (2017) used the multilayer perceptron neural network (MLPNN) algorithm, which is based on decision trees, and was successful in the early detection of liver diseases.

3.3 ML-BASED DEVICES IN CLINICAL TRIALS

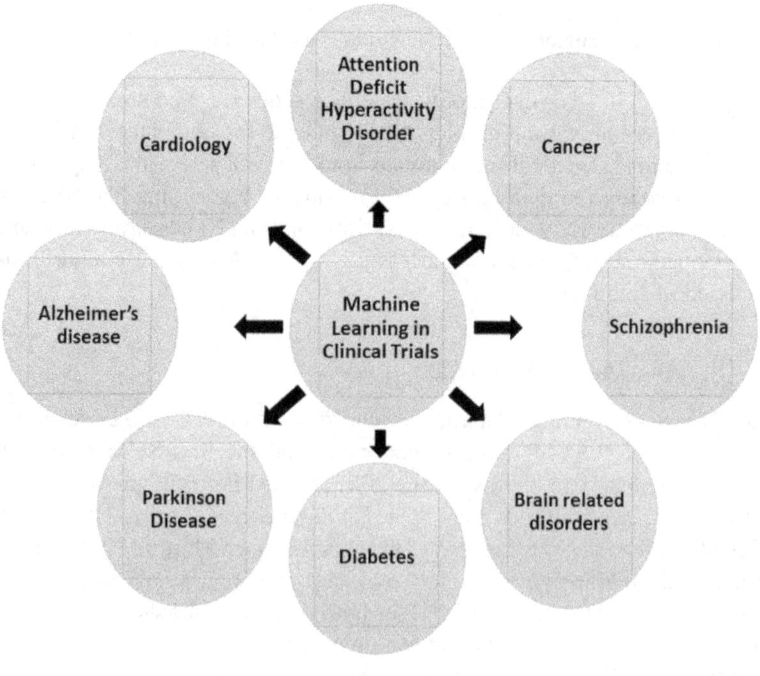

FIGURE 3.2 Applications of Machine Learning in clinical trial.

The evolution of ML-based algorithms and methods have further given rise to healthcare devices. ML-based devices are used for either detection of a disease or analyzing its status followed by monitoring its transmission. Their main applications are in clinical trials, imaging and radiology laboratories, protein engineering, genetic engineering, pharmaceuticals, bioinformatics, and biotechnology. Below are some recently developed ML-based devices along with their uses in different clinical trials.

3.3.1 ML-Based Classifiers and Sensor Data to Diagnose Neurological Issues in Stroke Patients

The most common issue that arises after brain-related strokes in patients is that of motor movements. The brain, which is the controller of all activities, alters the muscles and results in motor weakness or their complete loss. Thus, to test this weakness in patients, a pronator drift test (PDT) is performed by the neurological examiners. Park et al. (2017) used the ML-based classifiers and successfully identified the causes of the stroke using sensors and signaling based on proximal arm weakness. Thus, ML-based classifiers could help in monitoring stroke patients in the future.

3.3.2 Detection of Severe Wounds and the Risk of Infection

The maintenance of chronic wounds after surgery is a tedious task and requires proper treatment, care, and changing bandages from time to time to avoid any type of infection. Hsu et al. (2019) developed an ML-based hands-on app for automatically detecting any type of wound-related infection, which could help in immediate response to infection and prevent complications in diagnosis and treatment.

3.3.3 Bone Age Analysis

The study of bone age and its assessment is important especially for older people and orthopedics to identify different types of diseases and bone-related disorders. But it is a time-consuming task and is mostly carried out through wrist and hand radiographs. Dallora et al. (2019) presented the research studies on bone age analysis using machine learning techniques and included a total of 26 studies that all discussed on the use of ML-based techniques for diagnosis.

3.3.4 Smart Watch and Shoulder Physiotherapy

One of the friendliest and widely used ML applications in gadgets has been in a smart watch. Smart watches, being extremely handy and easy to carry, have gained attention all over the world. Burns et al. (2018) developed a home-performing shoulder physiotherapy monitoring system using the easily available smart watch. Algorithms like activity recognition chain (ARC) framework, supervised learning, k-nearest neighbor (k-NN), random forest (RF), support vector machine classifier (SVC), and a convolutional recurrent neural network (CRNN) were used to develop this system. Thus, the smart watch and SVM algorithm are efficient tools that could help manage home-adherent physiotherapy.

3.4 MACHINE LEARNING IN THE HEALTHCARE SECTOR

Healthcare is the system that is involved in providing better medical services and treatment facilities to patients (Dhillon et al. 2018). The development of vaccines, antibiotics, and advanced devices for monitoring and management of patients in the healthcare sector is one of the fastest-growing sectors in AI (Bhardwaj et al. 2017). In broad terms, ML is the ability of the computer system to learn from experience, which means the processing of the current acquired information (Mintz 2019). ML in healthcare helps to determine the patient's existing medical condition and then predict the future needs and requirements of the patient for the improvement of the health along with proper management of medical records in the technical system (Dhillon et al. 2018). For instance, a recent study indicated the role of ML in diagnosing various types of cancers, along with suggesting the type of symptoms as well as causes for each type (Hafeez and Ahmed 2019). The most common algorithm used in ML is the one used in the Naive Bayesian Classifier (Kononenko 2001). The Naive Bayesian Classifier works on the simple Bayle's Theorem, named after the Reverend Thomas Bayes. This is a collection of algorithms that works on the principle of probability and treating each entry as independent of another (Kononenko 2001). For example, if we feed the data as patient "A" having flu with symptoms like fever, cold, cough, and tiredness, the algorithm will process each of these entries independent of the probability that the disease is flu, regardless of any relation between symptoms. ML has also helped in developing techniques for biologists and scientists. For example, Benevolent Bio is used for applying technology in biosciences industries, and was discovered by Ken Mulvany (founder of Proximagen) in 2013 (Bhardwaj et al. 2017). Technologies like Butterfly Network, Flatiron Health, iCarbonX, Pathway Genomics, and AliveCor are currently changing the face of medicine (Bhardwaj et al. 2017). ML applications have also been used in diagnostic, imaging and radiology laboratories and have revolutionized patient care (Lynch and Liston 2018).

3.5 MACHINE LEARNING IN CLINICAL TRIALS

The application of ML algorithms and their methods has given rise to advances in clinical trials and associated research areas. ML-based techniques have proved reliable as well as efficient. Dhungana et al. experimented on validating supervised machine learning methods for producing fast, reliable, and efficient results in data abstraction of sepsis and septic shock alternative to manual chart review. The results revealed that the sensitivity-specificity was 100%–100% for the validation cohort for both sepsis and septic shock (Dhungana et al. 2019). ML has also been applied in biotechnology companies and associated research laboratories (Shah et al. 2019). Some of these sectors include pharmaceutical industries for advancement in drug development, imagining, and diagnostic laboratories using pattern recognition and segmentation techniques and in deep learning techniques for analysis of genomic and clinical data. ML in clinical trials has gained pace and is showing promising results. Various clinical trials have succeeded in improving the treatment outcome of patients. DNA profiling, RNA sequencing, proteomics, and preclinical datasets are also emerging through various ML applications (Shah et al. 2019). The application of ML in clinical trials for some of the diseases is explained in more detail below (Figure 3.2).

3.5.1 Alzheimer's Disease (AD)

AD is a very common disease in elderly people that distorts the memory and mental functions of an individual. Thus, AD requires the diagnosis of the mild cognitive impairment (MCI) stage in the brain that is associated with impairment in the brain resulting in a memory loss which is different from dementia. The need to identify the MCI stage is important for the development of a disease-modifying drug for AD. However, conducting AD clinical trials is a tedious task and requires a lot of attention. ML can help to identify biomarkers and data patterns for fast monitoring using ML-based CT scans and analysis of the disease by reducing the need for a larger sample size for analysis. A study carried out by Escudero applied four ML classifiers that decreased the sample size of CT by using SVM as well as for MCI subjects (Escudero et al. 2011). Mirzaei et al. reviewed various imaging techniques for AD; however, the sensitivity of images depends on the specificity of biomarkers detection. ML-based methods and algorithms like ANN, logistic regression classification, probabilistic methods, K-means clustering (hard clustering), fuzzy clustering, and atlas-guided approaches have been successfully used for AD (Mirzaei et al. 2016).

3.5.2 Parkinson's Disease (PD)

PD is the disorder of the central nervous system which affects bodily movement, often resulting in tremors. Zhan et al. used ML in smartphones to determine PD severity, symptom fluctuations, and response to dopaminergic therapy (Zhan et al. 2018). This study evaluated individuals suffering from PD for five tasks such as voice, finger tapping, gait, balance, and reaction time and developed an ML-based mobile Parkinson score (mPDS) derived from smartphones. The mPDS could detect symptom fluctuations and compare them with the PD symptoms and respond to the dopaminergic medication. Another innovation of ML is the recent large-scale "wearable, sensor-based, quantitative, objective, and easy-to-use systems for quantifying PD signs for large numbers of participants over extended durations" (Kubota et al. 2016). This technology is ML based that can improve clinical diagnosis as well as management in PD for conducting clinical trials.

3.5.3 Attention-Deficit Hyperactivity Disorder (ADHD)

ADHD is a very common neurodevelopment disorder, which is marked by an ongoing pattern of inattention, hyperactivity, and impulsiveness. An 8-week open-laboratory trial was carried out in 83 ADHD youths to predict methylphenidate response using ML (Kim et al. 2015). The results reported 84.6% accuracy of SVMs for analyzing methylphenidate response, supporting the development of SVMs, which could help estimate treatment response in ADHD. Yasumura et al. reported an independent biomarker for ADHD using ML algorithms (Yasumura et al. 2017). The use of SVM showed results with 88.7% sensitivity and 83.78% specificity while the result of the discrimination rate was 86.25%, establishing the importance of SVM for diagnosing ADHD among children.

3.5.4 Cancer

Cancer is the abnormal and uncontrollable spread of cells and tissues in the body and one of the leading causes of death in the world, with the prevalence of >10 million mortalities annually. ML-based solutions have the potential to revolutionize medicine by performing complex tasks that are currently assigned to specialists to improve diagnostic accuracy, increase the efficiency of throughputs, improve clinical work process, decline human asset costs, and improve treatment decisions. A clinical trial was reported to identify the status of genetic lesions in the tumor of cancer patients. The ML method used consisted of two steps: first was to distinguish gene entities from that of non-gene entities, and second was to identify and analyze the genetic lesion associated with the identified gene entity. The results were reported with 83.7% accuracy, while the results for real-world cancer trial annotation showed 89.8% accuracy, establishing the role of ML-based methods in gene-associated clinical trials (Wu et al. 2012). ML was also applied to predict the possibility of prostate cancer among the patients (Jovic et al. 2017). ML can be used to carry out probability-based experiments and three different ML-based methods were used in this study, out of which the ELM model showed the most accurate results, and can be used in the future for carrying out predictions related to different cancers.

3.5.5 Heart and the Circulatory System Disorders

The most common heart-related problems are cardiac arrest, atrial fibrillation, acute myocardial infarction, and cardiovascular diseases. The major limitation in the treatment of heart-related disease is that most of the time it remains undiagnosed unless complications arise. Since the ML-based approaches and methods are not restricted, they provide a wide scope for understanding cardiology better. Than et al. (2019) performed a clinical trial using an ML algorithm (myocardial-ischemic-injury-index [MI^3]) incorporating their age, sex, and concentrations of cardiac troponin I. The algorithm provided detailed and elaborated information about diagnosing the risks of myocardial infarction along with a profile of low-risk and high-risk patients. Kartal and Balaban (2018) conducted an experiment to identify the cardiac risk assessment on patients' pre- or postsurgery, which would predict the mortality rates in patients. A C4.5 tree decision model was used for the same process, which showed the highest performance. The use of ML-based models and algorithms for predicting and diagnosing various diseases could be beneficial to both doctors and patients.

3.6 CHALLENGES AND FUTURE SCOPE IN CLINICAL TRIALS WITH MACHINE LEARNING

Although ML has modernized the area of clinical trials, some major challenges need to be addressed. The major issues with ML are the complexity of the methods and complicated language to be learned and applied. ML algorithms are completely independent systems and require no manual assistance, which could lead to the replacement of clinical staff and technicians and hence could be responsible for seizing several jobs (Weins et al. 2020). The second problem is that most clinical reasoning for different diseases is collected from various institutions, while, contrary to this, ML-based models are developed using data from a single institute, which creates the problem of limited data generalization (Sendak et al. 2019). Third, biologists and scientists interested in ML-based research in medicine should be ready to spend a large amount of money in setting up an ML-based environment which is both expensive and time-consuming (Sendak et al. 2019). The fourth issue reported on ML is the lack of privacy, confidentiality, and misuse of data. However, it is nearly challenging to protect this data due to the "black box" approach in most of the algorithms. "Black Box" is a direct approach where data is created directly from ML-based algorithms. Since data is linked to the electronic systems, the threat to the personal information of patients as well as doctors increases as many medical identity thefts have been reported (Mothkur and Poornima 2018). Thus, access permission to this data should be assigned to the concerned authorities.

3.6.1 Future Scope

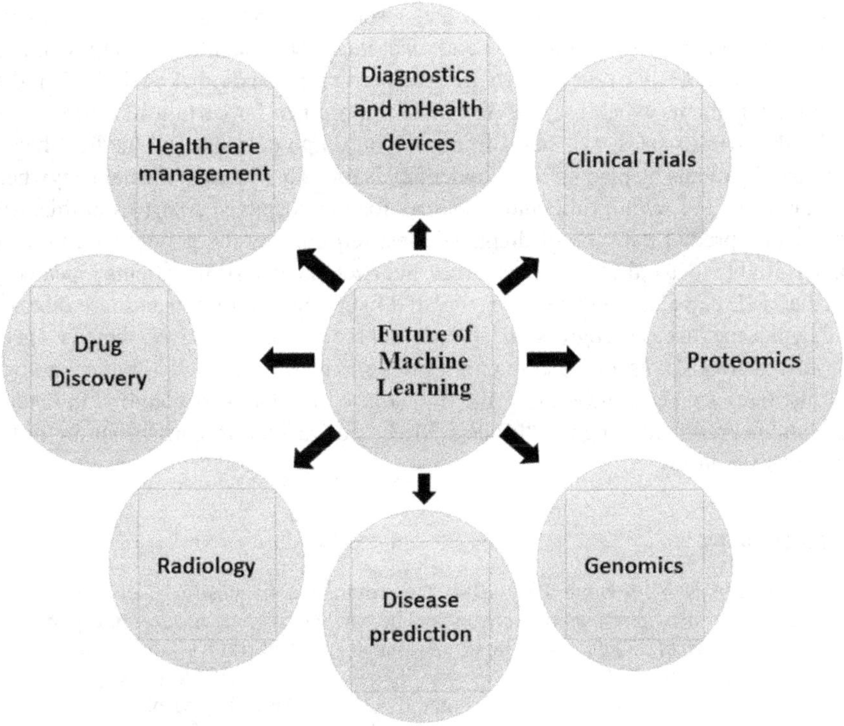

FIGURE 3.3 Applications of Machine Learning in various fields of health science.

The clinical development of drug innovation has not changed much for the past 30 years due to unknown and unproved technologies of AI and ML (Shah et al. 2019). The need to improve the efficiency of clinical trials is also increasing as carrying out these trials is expensive in terms of both time and money (Zhang et al. 2018). ML-based application has a huge potential for advancement not only in clinical trials which involve identifying meaningful clinical patterns but also in the diagnosis of diseases, radiology, and imaging in healthcare along with providing a strong basis for the healthcare system (Handelman 2018). ML is potentially a technology of choice for future that can help to improve the prognosis system, automate image analysis which should reduce the time considerably compared to manual interpretation, and quicker patient test result prediction, thus reducing the overuse of testing and wasting of resources (Obermeyer and Emanuel 2016). ML has scope for the development of next-generation antibiotics and personalized medicine (Shah et al. 2019). The power of prediction in ML-based algorithms could help to understand and predict the pathways of disease development and response to drugs, which can be very useful for their clinical trials (Savage 2012) (Figure 3.3).

3.7 CONCLUSION

ML offers algorithms, methods, and models with valuable characteristics, which can provide long-term solutions and assist scientists and researchers around the globe. Developing mHealth devices and machines in the healthcare sector can help decrease the mortality rate by early disease predictions and quick and efficient disease management, which may be of utmost importance for certain life-threatening and unknown diseases. ML helps in organizing large datasets and medical health records of patients by placing them under labels for easy access to the data anywhere and anytime and saving time and resources for the hospitals. Apart from this, ML has helped predict the type of diagnostic test required by the patient based on the data available to avoid waste of resources and overuse by testing patients repeatedly. Further, ML can also produce a consolidated list of most common and rare diseases and depict the disease progression, spread, and recurrence. However, there is a need for introducing ML as a subject in universities and medical as well as biotechnological institutes for better awareness and knowledge. ML has vast potential in healthcare and is predicted to be the "Modern Medicine" revolutionizing the future of the healthcare industry.

REFERENCES

Abdar, M., Yen, N. Y., & Hung, J. C. (2017). "Improving the diagnosis of liver disease using multilayer perceptron neural network and boosted decision trees". *Journal of Medical and Biological Engineering*, 38 (3). Available from: https://www.researchgate.net/publication/321653455.

Battineni, G., Chintalapudi, N., & Amenta, F. (2019). "Machine learning in medicine: Performance calculation of dementia prediction by support vector machines (SVM)". *Informatics in Medicine Unlocked*, 16, 100200. doi: 10.1016/j.imu.2019.100200.

Bhardwaj, R., et al. (2017). "A Study of Machine Learning in Healthcare". Available from https://www.researchgate.net/publication/319634446_A_Study_of_Machine_Learning_in_Healthcare.

Burns, D., Leung, N., Hardisty, M., Whyne, C., Henry, P., & McLachlin, S. (2018, July 23). "Shoulder physiotherapy exercise recognition: Machine learning the inertial signals from a smartwatch". *Physiological Measurement*, 39 (7), 075007. Available from https://www.ncbi.nlm.nih.gov/pubmed/29952759.

Chervonenkis, A. (1970). "Early history of support vector machines". In *Empirical Inference 2013* (pp. 13–20). Berlin, Heidelberg: Springer. Available from https://link.springer.com/chapter/10.1007/978-3-642-41136-6_3.

Dhillon, A. (2019). "Machine learning for Internet of Things data analysis". *Journal of Biology and Today,s World*, 2018 Jan; 8 (2), 1–10. Available from https://www.researchgate.net/publication/320393191_Machine_learning_for_Internet_of_Things_data_analysis_A_survey.

Dhungana, P., Serafim, L. P., Ruiz, A. L., Bruns, D., Weister, T. J., Smichney, N. J., & Kashyap, R. (2019). "Machine learning in data abstraction: A computable phenotype for sepsis and septic shock diagnosis in the intensive care unit". *World Journal of Critical Care Medicine*, 8 (7), 120–126. doi:10.5492/wjccm.v8.i7.120.

Escudero, J., Zajicek, J. P., & Ifeachor, E. (2011). "Machine Learning classification of MRI features of Alzheimer's disease and mild cognitive impairment subjects to reduce the sample size in clinical trials", in Annual International Conference of the IEEE Engineering in Medicine and Biology Society. doi:10.1109/iembs.2011.6091962.

Hafeez, K., & Ahmed, Q. (2019). "Applications of machine learning in education and health sector: An empirical study". *Journal of Software Engineering and Intelligent Systems*, 3. Journal of Software Engineering & Intelligent Systems ISSN 2518-8739 31st December 2019, Volume 4, Issue 3, JSEIS, CAOMEI

Handelman, G., Kok, H., Chandra, R., Razavi, A., Lee, M., & Asadi, H. (2018, December). *Edoctor: Machine learning and the future of medicine*. Retrieved from https://www.ncbi.nlm.nih.gov/pubmed/30102808

Hamet, P., & Tremblay, J. (2017). "Artificial intelligence in medicine". *Metabolism*, 69. doi: 10.1016/j.metabol.2017.01.011.

Hsu, J., Chen, Y., Ho, T., Tai, H., Wu, J., Sun, H., Lai, F. (2019). "Chronic Wound Assessment and Infection Detection Method". *BMC Medical Informatics and Decision Making*, 19 (1), 99. Available from: https://www.ncbi.nlm.nih.gov/pubmed/31126274.

Jović, S., Miljković, M., Ivanović, M., Šaranović, M., & Arsić, M. (2017). "Prostate cancer probability prediction by machine learning technique". *Cancer Investigation*, 35 (10), 647–651. doi: 10.1080/07357907.2017.1406496.

Kartal, E., & Balaban, M. E. (2018). "Machine learning techniques in cardiac risk assessment". *The Turkish Journal of Thoracic and Cardiovascular Surgery*, 26 (3), 394–401. doi: 10.5606/tgkdc.dergisi.2018.15559.

Kim, J., Sharma, V., & Ryan, N. D. (2015). "Predicting methylphenidate response in ADHD using machine learning approaches". *International Journal of Neuropsychopharmacology*, 18 (11), 1–7. doi: 10.1093/ijnp/pyv052.

Kononenko, I. (2001). "Machine learning for medical diagnosis: History, state of the art and perspective". *Artificial Intelligence in Medicine*, 23 (1), 89–109. doi: 10.1016/s0933-3657(01)00077-x.

Kotsiantis, S. B. (2011). "Decision trees: A recent overview." *Artificial Intelligence Review*, 39 (4), 261–283. doi: 10.1007/s10462-011-9272-4.

Kubota, K. J., Chen, J. A., & Little, M. A. (2016). "Machine learning for large-scale wearable sensor data in Parkinson's disease: Concepts, promises, pitfalls, and futures". *Movement Disorders*, 31 (9), 1314–1326. doi: 10.1002/mds.26693.

Lavrač, N. (1999). "Machine Learning for Data Mining in Medicine", 47–62. doi: 10.1007/3-540-48720-4_4.

Liang, Y., Xu, Q., Li, H., & Cao, D. (2011). "Support Vector Machines and Their Application in Chemistry and Biotechnology". Available from https://www.worldcat.org/title/support-vector-machines-and-their-application-in-chemistry-and-biotechnology/oclc/729371391.

Lynch, C. J., & Liston, C. (2018). "New machine-learning technologies for computer-aided diagnosis". *Nature Medicine*, 24 (9), 1304–1305. doi: 10.1038/s41591-018-0178-4.

Miller, D. D., & Brown, E. W. (2018). "Artificial intelligence in medical practice: The question to the answer?" *The American Journal of Medicine*, 131 (2), 129–133. doi: 10.1016/j.amjmed.2017.10.035.

Mirzaei, G., Adeli, A., & Adeli, H. (2016). "Imaging and machine learning techniques for diagnosis of Alzheimer's disease". *Reviews in the Neurosciences*, 27 (8), 857–870. doi: 10.1515/revneuro-2016-0029.

Mintz, Y., & Brodie, R. (2019). *Introduction to artificial intelligence in medicine*. Retrieved from https://www.tandfonline.com/doi/abs/10.1080/13645706.2019.1575882

Mothkur, R., & Poornima, K. (2018). "Machine Learning will Transfigure Medical Sector: A Survey", in International Conference on Current Trends towards Converging Technologies (ICCTCT). doi:10.1109/icctct.2018.8551134.

Obermeyer, Z., & Emanuel, E. J. (2016). "Predicting the future — Big data, machine learning, and clinical medicine". *New England Journal of Medicine*, 375 (13), 1216–1219. doi: 10.1056/nejmp1606181.

Park, E., Chang, H., & Nam, H. (2017, April 18). "Use of Machine Learning Classifiers and Sensor Data to Detect Neurological Deficit in Stroke Patients". Available from https://www.ncbi.nlm.nih.gov/pubmed/28420599.

Park, S. H., Do, K., Kim, S., Park, J. H., & Lim, Y. (2019). "What should medical students know about artificial intelligence in medicine?" *Journal of Educational Evaluation for Health Professions*, 16, 18. doi:10.3352/jeehp.2019.16.18.

Podgorelec, V., Kokol, P., Stiglic, B., & Rozman, I. (2002). *(PDF) decision Trees: An overview and their use in medicine*. Retrieved from https://www.researchgate.net/publication/11205595_Decision_Trees_An_Overview_and_Their_Use_in_Medicine

Renganathan, V. (2019). "Overview of artificial neural network models in the biomedical domain". *Bratislava Medical Journal*, 120 (07), 536–540. doi: 10.4149/bll_2019_087.

Ristevski, B., & Chen, M. (2018). "Big data analytics in medicine and healthcare". *Journal of Integrative Bioinformatics*, 15 (3). doi: 10.1515/jib-2017-0030.

Savage, N. (2012). "Better medicine through machine learning". *Communications of the ACM*, 55 (1), 17–19. doi: 10.1145/2063176.206182.

Sendak, M., Gao, M., Nichols, M., Lin, A., & Balu, S. (2019). "Machine learning in health care: A critical appraisal of challenges and opportunities". *EGEMs (Generating Evidence & Methods to Improve Patient Outcomes)*, 7 (1), 1. doi:10.5334/egems.287.

Shah, P., Kendall, F., Khozin, S., Goosen, R., Hu, J., Laramie, J., & Schork, N. (2019). "Artificial intelligence and machine learning in clinical development: A translational perspective". *NPJ Digital Medicine*, 2 (1). doi: 10.1038/s41746-019-0148-3.

Shameer, K., Johnson, K. W., Glicksberg, B. S., Dudley, J. T., & Sengupta, P. P. (2018). "Machine learning in cardiovascular medicine: Are we there yet?" *Heart*, 104 (14): 1156–1164. doi: 10.1136/heartjnl-2017-311198.

Shortliffe, E. (2019). "Artificial intelligence in medicine: Weighing the accomplishments, hype, and promise". *Yearbook of Medical Informatics*, 28 (01), 257–262. doi: 10.1055/s-0039-1677891.

Shouman, M., Turner, T., & Stocker, R. (2011). "Using Decision Tree for Diagnosing Heart Disease". Available from: https://www.researchgate.net/publication/262321354.

Sidey-Gibbons, J., & Sidey-Gibbons, C. (2019). "Machine learning in medicine: A practical introduction". *BMC Medical Research Methodology*, 19 (1).

Than, M., Pickering, J., Sandoval, Y., Shah, A., Tsanas, A., & Apple, F. (2019). "Machine learning to predict the likelihood of acute myocardial infarction". *MI3 Collaborative*. Available from https://www.ncbi.nlm.nih.gov/pmc/articles/PMC6749969/.

Waljee, A. K., & Higgins, P. D. (2010). "Machine learning in medicine: A primer for physicians". *American Journal of Gastroenterology*, 105 (6), 1224–1226. doi: 10.1038/ajg.2010.173.

Weston, J. (2013). "Support Vector Machine - Columbia University". Available from http://www.cs.columbia.edu/~kathy/cs4701/documents/jason_svm_tutorial.pdf.

Wiens, J., Saria, S., Sendak, M., Ghassemi, M., Liu, V. X., Doshi-Velez, F., & Goldenberg, A. (2019). "Do no harm: A roadmap for responsible machine learning for health care". *Nature Medicine*, 25 (9), 1337–1340. doi:10.1038/s41591-019-0548-6.

Wu, Y., Levy, M. A., Micheel, C. M., Yeh, P., Tang, B., Cantrell, M. J., & Xu, H (2012). "Identifying the status of genetic lesions in cancer clinical trial documents using machine learning". *BMC Genomics*, 13 (Suppl 8). doi:10.1186/1471-2164-13-s8-s21.

Yasumura, A., Omori, M., Fukuda, A., Takahashi, J., Yasumura, Y., Nakagawa, E., & Inagaki, M. (2017). "Applied machine learning method to predict children with ADHD using prefrontal cortex activity: A multicenter study in Japan". *Journal of Attention Disorders*, 108705471774063. doi: 10.1177/1087054717740632.

Zhan, A., Mohan, S., Tarolli, C., Schneider, R. B., Adams, J. L., Sharma, S., & Saria, S. (2018). "Using smartphones and machine learning to quantify Parkinson disease severity". *JAMA Neurology*, 75 (7), 876. doi: 10.1001/jamaneurol.2018.0809.

4 Deep Learning and Its Biological and Biomedical Applications

Bhawna Rathi and Aditya Narayan Sarangi

CONTENTS

4.1 INTRODUCTION

Advancement in newer-generation sequencing technology led to the increased availability of omics data in the public domain at a brisk pace. These voluminous and highly divergent omics data (genomics, transcriptomics, proteomics, epigenomic, metagenomics, metabolomics, etc.) directed biological and biomedical research toward the big data era. The data generated post sequencing requires efficient analysis as it addresses various biological queries and paves the way for revolutionizing health and medical sciences. The memory usage and execution times of the algorithms used to analyze the big data scale linearly with the depth of the reads demand high-computing power in terms of memory, which is actually challenging for a small-scale research lab. Biological and bio-medical big data analytics demands development of advanced and efficient computational algorithms to gain insights into these data not only to get detailed information regarding diseases but also to improve diagnosis and develop personalized medicines. Machine Learning (ML) algorithms have become one of the most promising methods to address such issues.

Machine Learning methods can broadly be divided into two categories: supervised learning and unsupervised learning. Supervised learning algorithms are based on the theory of inductive inference, i.e., prediction based on prior observation. Examples of supervised Machine Learning approaches are decision tree, support vector machine (SVM), and neural network. Unsupervised learning algorithms help to deduce previously undetected patterns from data without any preexisting labels. Two popular unsupervised methods that are used to detect patterns in high-dimensional biological and bio-medical data are clustering and principal component analysis. Methods and algorithm in the ML do classification, regression, and clustering, which have been proven beneficial for solving biological research questions related to gene patterns, functional genomics, genotype-phenotype associations, and gene-protein interactions. A major constraint of ML methods is that they cannot handle proficiently natural data in their raw form.

Deep learning (DL), a subcategory of the Machine Learning method, can be both supervised and unsupervised, and uses reinforcement learning models to train a class of large neural networks. Deep learning has been successfully applied to create predictive models and deduce information from much complex and heterogeneous omics and clinical data. Deep learning has been widely used in big data analytics these days (Najafabadi et al., 2015). DL has enormous uses in voice, signal processing, machine vision, text and sequence prediction, and computational biology areas, altogether shaping the productive Artificial Intelligence (AI) fields (Bengio and LeCun, 2007; Zhang et al., 2016; Esteva et al., 2017; Ching et al., 2018). Deep learning has several application models such as artificial neural network, hierarchical learning, and deep structured learning, which generally apply a class of structured networks (Ditzler et al., 2015; Liang et al., 2015; Xu et al., 2016; Giorgi and Bader, 2018).

DL has also proven to provide models with higher precision that are efficient at discovering patterns in high-dimensional data, making them applicable to a variety of areas (Koumakis, 2020). In the case of DL, the amount of training data is more demanding as compared to ML, because there are many parameters in a deep learning algorithm which can drastically affect the predicting value of the trained model.

The graph in Figure 4.1 reflects the number of published papers in Pubmed in the last decade, which clearly depicts an exponential growth of the usage of these techniques in biological research.

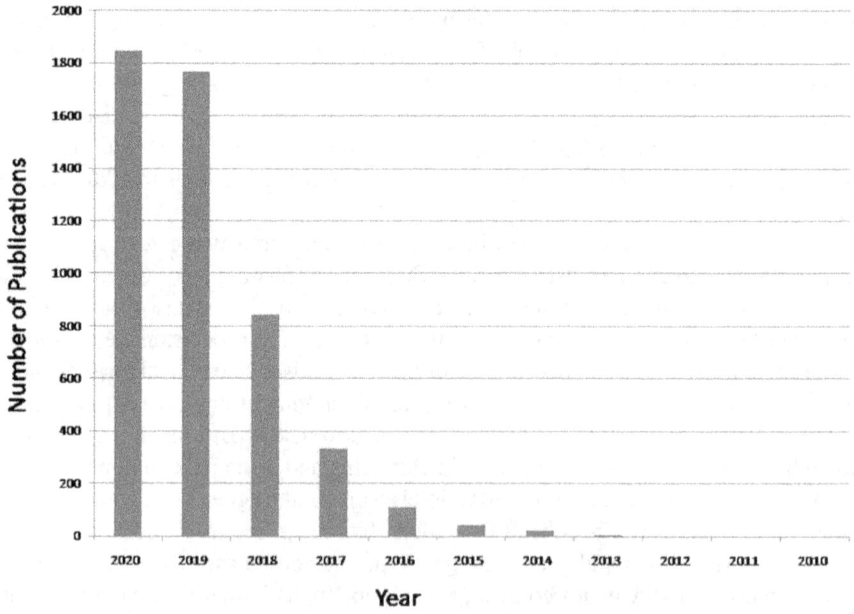

FIGURE 4.1 Deep learning searches by years in PubMed.

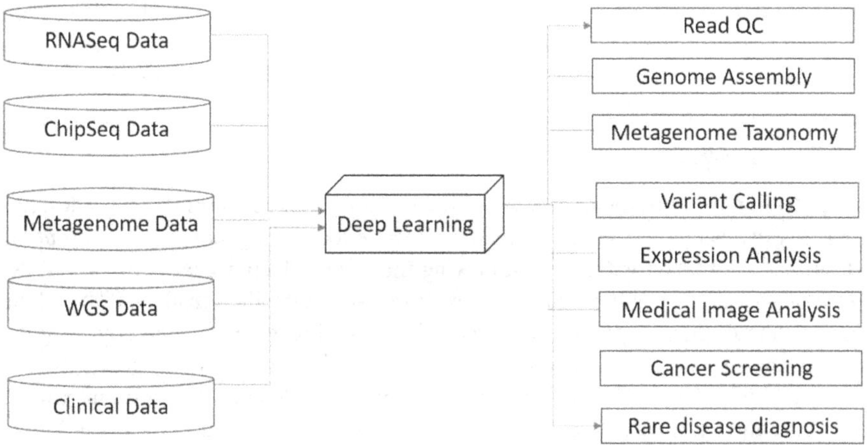

FIGURE 4.2 Biological and biomedical application of deep learning.

This chapter depicts various methods and tools to discuss Machine Learning and deep learning, a subfield that emerged from Machine Learning, for the NGS data analytics.

4.1.1 (I) Application of Deep Learning in Biological Data Analysis

The overview of the potential biological and biomedical applications of deep learning is shown in Figure 4.2.

4.2 READ QUALITY CONTROL ANALYSIS

In the NGS data, the read specifies a single uninterrupted series of nucleotides representing the sequence of the template. Advanced sequencing technologies can generate an enormous number of sequence reads in a single experiment. However, no sequencing technology is flawless, and each instrument may generate different types and numbers of errors. Therefore, it is necessary to understand, identify, and exclude the errors that may impact the interpretation of experiment. Sequence quality control is therefore an essential first step in the NGS analysis. Catching errors early saves time later on. Mentioned below are the methods developed using deep learning for read quality control analysis.

4.2.1 MiniScrub: De Novo Nanopore Read Quality Improvement Using Deep Learning

Oxford Nanopore long read sequencing technology significantly reduces the complexity of de novo assembly. The tool MiniScrub is developed on a convolutional neural network (CNN) based method, which identifies and subsequently removes low-quality Nanopore read segments to minimize their interference in the downstream assembly process. MiniScrub is found to robustly improve read quality of Oxford Nanopore reads, especially in the metagenome setting. MiniScrub is an open-source software and is available at https://bitbucket.org/berkeleylab/jgi-miniscrub.

4.2.2 Deepbinner

Multiplexing, the simultaneous sequencing of multiple barcoded DNA samples, has made Oxford Nanopore sequencing cost-effective for small genomes. Deepbinner is a tool for Oxford Nanopore demultiplexing that uses a deep neural network (DNN) to classify reads. Deepbinner had the lowest rate of unclassified reads (7.8%) and the highest demultiplexing precision (98.5% of classified reads were correctly assigned in comparison with Albacore and Porechop). It can be used alone (to maximize the number of classified reads) or in conjunction with other demultiplexers (to maximize precision and minimize false positive classifications). Deepbinner is open source (GPLv3) and available at https://github.com/rrwick/Deepbinner.

4.3 GENOME ASSEMBLY

Genome assembly refers to the process of putting nucleotide sequences into the correct order. To assemble the read obtained by the sequencing experiment, various methods and programs are used. This segment refers to the deep learning method used for genome assembly.

4.3.1 CONNET: Accurate Genome Consensus in Assembling Nanopore Sequencing Data via Deep Learning

To have a high-quality consensus from long reads is important and can be achieved by spatial relationship of alignment pileup. CONNET is a deep-learning-based consensus tool based on partial order alignment. It has been tested using a 90× dataset of *E. coli* and a 37× human dataset. The tool has the capability of delivering phased diploid genome consensus.

4.4 APPLICATION IN METAGENOMICS

Metagenomics is the technique of retrieving microbial genome directly from the environmental samples regardless of the nature of the sample and abundance of microbial entities (Oulas et al., 2015). The analysis explores the entire genetic composition of the microbial communities by sequencing and subsequently doing data analysis. It also plays a role in understanding the biochemical part of the microbes in the atypical environments as well as their interactions with other environmental factors (Thomas et al., 2012). A metagenomic analysis comprises the isolation of metagenomic DNA from the samples, followed by 16S rRNA gene amplification and shotgun metagenome sequencing, analysis of amplicon reads, analysis of metagenomic reads, and finally the determination of microbial community diversity using the databases (Sarangi et al., 2019). This section reviews some tools developed on the basis of the deep learning algorithms for metagenome analysis.

4.4.1 DeepARG: A Deep Learning Approach for Predicting Antibiotic Resistance Genes (ARGs) from Metagenomic Data

Due to the increasing antibiotic resistance, there is a need to identify the antibiotic-resistant genes, their hot spots or gene hubs, and the several pathways where these genes are playing a pivotal role. ARGs can be predicted by considering the similarity search of the whole metagenomic gene pool with the databases, but the approach leads to a lot of false negatives. To address this limitation, deep learning approach takes into account a dissimilarity matrix created using all known categories and parameters of ARGs. Evaluation of the deep learning models over 30 antibiotic resistance categories demonstrates that the DeepARG models can predict ARGs with both high precision (>0.97) and recall (>0.90).

4.4.2 NanoARG: A Web Service for Detecting and Contextualizing Antimicrobial Resistance Genes from Nanopore-Derived Metagenomes

Indirect and direct pressures enforced by antibiotics, along with horizontal gene transfer and co-selective agents, are the primary reasons for evolution as well as spread of antibiotic resistance. The various tools in existence just help to identify the ARGs, but this information is limited to the mobile genetic elements (MGEs) and the co-selective pressure; for example, metal-resistant genes have not been identified. Second, various methods and web servers consider the short reads in assembling the NGS data, whereas NanoARG takes advantage of the long reads produced by nanopore sequencing technology. These long nanopore reads help to identify not only the ARGs but also the genes in the vicinity with the mobile genetic elements as well as other co-selectives. NanoARG is publicly available and freely accessible at https://bench.cs.vt.edu/nanoarg.

4.4.3 DeepBGC: A Deep Learning Genome-Mining Strategy for Biosynthetic Gene Cluster (BGC) Prediction

Natural products represent a rich pool of small-molecule drug candidates. These molecules are microbial secondary metabolites synthesized by co-localized genes termed Biosynthetic Gene Clusters (BGCs). A deep learning strategy—DeepBGC—proposes reduced false positive rates in BGC identification and an enhanced ability to extrapolate and identify novel BGC classes compared to present Machine Learning tools. DeepBGC has been supplemented with random forest classifiers that accurately predict BGC product classes and potential chemical activity. Application of DeepBGC to bacterial genomes uncovered earlier untraceable putative BGCs that may code for natural products with novel biologic activities.

4.4.4 MetaPheno: A Critical Evaluation of Deep Learning and Machine Learning in Metagenome-Based Disease Prediction

Revolutions in sequencing technology have led to a swift surge in publicly available sequencing data. This leads to growing efforts to predict disease status from metagenomic sequencing data, with utilization of new approaches. Deeper analysis of type 2 diabetes and obesity datasets that have eluded improved results was performed using a variety of Machine Learning and feature extraction methods. This study concluded by offering perspectives on study design considerations that may impact results and future. The scripts and extracted features for the analyses conducted in this chapter are available at GitHub:https://github.com/nlapier2/metapheno.

4.4.5 MetagenomicDC

Metagenomic Data Classifier based on deep learning models uses a deep learning approach for taxonomic classification of metagenomic data, which can be employed for both whole genome shotgun (WGS) and amplicon (AMP). The data from both WGS and AMP short reads were simulated using the tool called Grinder (Angly et al., 2012). k-mer representation was adopted to map sequences as vectors into a numerical space. Finally, two different deep learning architectures, i.e., convolutional neural network and deep belief network (DBN), were used to train models for each taxon. MetagenomicDC pipeline was found to outperform the RDP classifier at each taxonomic level with both architectures. For instance, at the genus level, both CNN and DBN reached 91.3% of accuracy with AMP short reads, whereas RDP classifier obtained 83.8% with the same data.

4.4.6 DEEPre: Sequence-Based Enzyme Commission (EC) Number Prediction by Deep Learning

Annotation of enzyme function has a broad range of applications, from metagenomics to diagnosis to industrial biotechnology. Computational enzyme function prediction has become quite important. This approach determines the enzyme function by predicting the Enzyme Commission number. The method proposes an end-to-end feature selection and classification model training approach, as well as an automatic and robust feature dimensionality uniformization method. In spite of extracting the enzyme sequence manually, the model takes the raw sequence encoding as inputs, extracting convolutional and sequential features from the raw encoding based on the classification result to directly improve the prediction performance. In addition, the server is shown to outperform the other programs in determining the main class of enzymes on a separate low-homology dataset. Two case studies demonstrate DEEPre's ability to capture the functional difference of enzyme isoforms. The server could be accessed freely at http://www.cbrc.kaust.edu.sa/DEEPre.

4.4.7 DeepMAsED: Evaluating the Quality of Metagenomic Assemblies

DeepMAsED is a deep learning approach for identifying misassembled contigs without the need for reference genomes. Moreover, the tool provides an in silico pipeline for generating large-scale, realistic metagenome assemblies for comprehensive model training and testing. DeepMAsED accuracy substantially exceeds the state of the art when applied to large and complex metagenome assemblies. DeepMAsED accurately identifies misassemblies in metagenome-assembled contigs from a broad diversity of bacteria and archaea without the need for reference genomes or strong modeling assumptions. DeepMAsED is available from GitHub at https://github.com/leylabmpi/DeepMAsED.

4.4.8 DeepMicrobes: Taxonomic Classification for Metagenomics with Deep Learning

DeepMicrobes trained on genomes reconstructed from gut microbiomes has helped discover potential novel signatures in inflammatory bowel diseases. DeepMicrobes facilitates effective investigations into the uncharacterized roles of metagenomic species.

4.4.9 Meta-MFDL: Gene Prediction in Metagenomic Fragments with Deep Learning

Accurately identifying genes from metagenomics fragments is one of the most fundamental challenges in metagenomics. This tool combines multifeatures (i.e., monocodon usage, monoamino acid usage, ORF length coverage, and Z-curve features) and, using deep stacking networks learning model, presents a novel method (called Meta-MFDL) to predict the metagenomic genes. Meta-MFDL is a powerful tool for identifying genes from metagenomic fragments.

4.4.10 IDMIL

The tool articulates the problem of predicting human disease from whole-metagenomic data using multiple instance learning (MIL), a popular supervised learning technique. This method proposes an alignment-free approach that provides higher accuracy in prediction by harnessing the capability of deep CNN within a MIL framework and provides interpretability via neural attention mechanism. The approach does not rely on alignment, assembly, and reference sequence databases, thus making it fast and scalable for large-scale metagenomic data. IDMIL is available at https://github.com/mrahma23/IDMIL.

4.5 VARIANT CALLING FROM NGS DATA

Variant calling is the process by which we identify variants from sequence data. Variant analysis is the study of the genetic differences (variants) between healthy and diseased tissue, between individuals of a population, or between strains of an organism. It can provide mechanistic insight into disease processes and the natural function of affected genes. This section specifies the various models of deep learning employed for variant calling.

4.5.1 GARFIELD-NGS: Genomic vARiants FIltering by dEep Learning moDels in NGS

Exome sequencing is a widely used approach in clinical research as it helps identify the genomic variants. However, a substantial number of genomic variants identified may be false positive. This new tool GARFIELD-NGS relies on deep learning models to predict false and true variants in exome sequencing experiments performed with the help of Illumina or ION platforms. GARFIELD-NGS depicted strong performances for both SNP (single-nucleotide polymorphism) and INDEL variants (AUC 0.71-0.98). Thus, it can be easily integrated into existing analysis pipeline. GARFIELD-NGS is available at https://github.com/gedoardo83/GARFIELD-NGS.

4.5.2 DeepSVR: A Deep Learning Approach to Automate Refinement of Somatic Variant Calling from Cancer Sequencing Data

Cancer sequencing data requires in-depth analysis to accurately identify the somatic variations. After the automatic processing of the data, manual review of the data is required, though this is time-consuming, more expensive, non-reproducible, and even standardization is required. DeepSVR (https://github.com/griffithlab/DeepSVR) has been developed using the Machine Learning approach for standardizing the somatic variation refinement. The final model incorporates 41,000 variants from 440 sequencing cases. The model improves on manual somatic refinement by reducing bias on calls otherwise subject to high inter-reviewer variability.

4.5.3 DeepVariant: A Universal SNP and Small-Indel Variant Caller Using Deep Neural Networks

In spite of the high-end sequencing technologies, calling the genomic variants accurately still remains a big challenge. A deep convolutional neural network can call genetic variation in aligned next-generation sequencing read data by learning statistical relationships between images of read pileups around putative variant and true genotype calls. DeepVariant can learn to call variants in a variety of sequencing technologies and experimental designs, including deep whole genomes from 10X Genomics and Ion Ampliseq exomes, highlighting the benefits of using more automated and generalizable techniques for variant calling.

4.5.4 Clairvoyante: A Multi-Task Convolutional Deep Neural Network for Variant Calling in Single-Molecule Sequencing

For a single-molecule sequencing, it is a challenging task to identify DNA sequence variants. Clairvoyante is a multitask five-layer convolutional neural network model for predicting variant type (SNP or indel), alternative allele, zygosity, and indel length from aligned reads. Clairvoyante finds variants in less than 2 hours on a standard server. Clairvoyante is available open-source (https://github.com/aquaskyline/Clairvoyante), with modules to train, utilize, and visualize the model.

4.6 SNP EFFECT PREDICTION

Single-nucleotide polymorphisms, frequently called SNPs (pronounced "snips"), are the most general type of genetic variation among individuals. These can act as biological markers, helping researchers to locate genes that are associated with disease. When SNPs occur within a gene or in any regulatory region near a gene, they might play a more important role in disease by affecting the gene's function. The methods below states the deep learning methods used for SNP predictions.

4.6.1 DeepSEA: Predicting Effects of Non-Coding Variants with Deep-Learning-Based Sequence Model

In human genetics, it is a challenging task to identify the functional effect in the non-coding region. A deep-learning-based algorithmic framework, DeepSEA (http://deepsea.princeton.edu/), directly learns a regulatory sequence code from large-scale chromatin-profiling data, enabling prediction of chromatin effects of sequence alterations with single-nucleotide sensitivity. This approach is further used to improve the identification of the functional variants.

4.6.2 DANN: A Deep Learning Approach for Annotating the Pathogenicity of Genetic Variants

Combined annotation-dependent depletion (CADD) is an algorithm designed to annotate both coding and non-coding variants. CADD trains a linear kernel support vector machine to differentiate evolutionarily derived, likely benign alleles from simulated, likely deleterious variants. However, SVMs cannot capture non-linear relationships among the features, which can be captured by a deep learning approach. DANN uses the same feature set and training data as CADD to train a deep neural network. DNNs can capture non-linear relationships among features and are better suited than SVMs for problems with a large number of samples and features. All data and source code are available at https://cbcl.ics.uci.edu/public_data/DANN/.

4.6.3 DeepMAsED

Functional interpretation of genetic variants using deep learning predicts impact on chromatin accessibility and histone modification.

DeepMAsED is a deep learning approach for identifying misassembled contigs without the requirement for any reference genomes. It provides an in silico pipeline for generating large-scale, realistic metagenome assemblies for comprehensive model training and testing. Executing DeepMAsED is simple. DeepMAsED is a flexible misassembly classifier that can be applied to a wide range of metagenome assembly projects.

DeepMAsED is available from GitHub at https://github.com/leylabmpi/DeepMAsED.

4.6.4 DeFine

Deep convolutional neural networks accurately quantify intensities of transcription factor (TF)-DNA binding and facilitate evaluation of functional non-coding variants.

The tool DeFine (deep-learning-based functional impact of non-coding variants evaluator) has improved performance of assessing the functional impact of non-coding variants, including SNPs and indels. DeFine accurately identifies the causal functional non-coding variants from disease-associated variants in Genome Wide Association Studies (GWAS). DeFine is an effective and easy-to-use tool that facilitates systematic prioritization of functional non-coding variants.

4.7 GENE EXPRESSION ANALYSIS (BULK RNASEQ, SINGLE-CELL RNASEQ)

Gene expression analyses study the formation of a gene product from its coding gene. It is an important indicator of biological activity wherein changes in gene expression patterns are reflected in changes in biological processes. Gene expression profiling goes beyond the information of the genome sequence into a functional view of an organism's biology and is a widely used approach in research, clinical, and pharmaceutical settings to better understand individual genes, gene pathways, or greater gene activity profiles. This section states the various deep learning approaches used for gene expression analyses with huge precision and accuracy.

4.7.1 Decode

Deep learning decodes the principles of differential gene expression (DE).

Differential gene expression analysis is a very important way to study the molecular mechanism. These studies are quite popular in health as well as diagnostics. A model called Decode utilizes the deep learning approach to predict differential gene expression based on genome-wide binding sites on RNAs and promoters. To identify influential molecular mechanisms for any human expression data, researchers can freely utilize Decode available at www.differentialexpression.org.

4.7.2 DESC

Deep learning enables accurate clustering with batch effect removal in single-cell RNA-seq analysis.

DESC is an unsupervised deep embedding algorithm that clusters single-cell RNA-seq data by iteratively optimizing a clustering function. Comprehensive evaluations show that DESC offers a proper balance of clustering accuracy and stability both. DESC is an important tool for the researchers to solve the complex cellular problems.

4.7.3 scAnCluster: Integrating Deep-Supervised, Self-Supervised, and Unsupervised Learning for Single-Cell RNA-seq Clustering and Annotation

scAnCluster combines deep-supervised learning, self-supervised learning, and unsupervised learning techniques together, and it outperforms other customized scRNA-seq annotation methods (CellAssign, Garnett, SingleR, scANVI-semi-supervised deep generative model) in both simulation and real data. The method performs efficiently on the challenging task of discovering novel cell types that are absent in the reference data.

4.7.4 Digitaldlsorter: Deep-Learning on scRNA-Seq to Deconvolute Gene Expression Data

The approach makes use of a Deep Neural Network model that allows quantification of lymphocytes and also of specific CD8+, CD4Tmem, CD4Th, and CD4Tregs subpopulations, as well as B-cells and stromal content. This method was applied to synthetic bulk RNA-Seq and to samples from the TCGA project, yielding very accurate results in terms of quantification and survival prediction.

4.8 TRANSCRIPTION FACTOR/ENHANCER (CHIPSEQ)

Transcription factor (or sequence-specific DNA-binding factor) is a protein that controls the rate of transcription of genetic information from DNA to messenger RNA, by binding to a specific DNA sequence. The method below discusses the various deep learning models to identify the transcription factors/enhancers.

4.8.1 Enhancer Recognition and Prediction during Spermatogenesis Based on Deep Convolutional Neural Networks

The development of ChIP-Chip and ChIP-Seq sequencing technology has enabled the researchers to focus on the relationship between enhancers and DNA sequences and histone protein modifications. This study proposed a convolutional neural network model to predict enhancers that can regulate gene expression during spermatogenesis. Finally, it compared the CNN algorithm with the gkmSVM algorithm.

It is well proven that CNN has better performance than the gkmSVM algorithm, especially in the generalization ability. The work demonstrated their strong learning ability and the low CPU requirements for the experiment, with a small number of convolution layers and simple network structure, while avoiding overfitting the training data.

4.8.2 DeepEnhancer: Predicting enhancers with deep convolutional neural networks

Experimental methods are both time-consuming and expensive for the large-scale identification of enhancers. DeepEnhancer is a tool to distinguish enhancers from background genomic sequences. The method purely relies on DNA sequences to predict enhancers in an end-to-end manner by using a deep convolutional neural network. The method proves to be quite efficient in the classification of the enhancers against the random sequences.

4.8.3 DeepHistone: A Deep Learning Approach to Predict Histone Modifications

Identification of the histone modification has proved to be very successful in understanding the biological processes such as DNA damage and chromosome packing. DeepHistone demonstrated the possibility of using a deep learning framework to link DNA sequence and experimental data for predicting epigenomic signals. With the state-of-the-art performance, DeepHistone was expected to ease out the study of epigenomic. DeepHistone is freely available at https://github.com/QijinYin/DeepHistone.

4.8.4 An Integrative Framework for Combining Sequence and Epigenomic Data to Predict Transcription Factor Binding Sites (TFBSs) Using Deep Learning

TFBS is essential for understanding the underlying binding mechanisms and follow-up cellular functions. Convolutional neural networks have outperformed the traditional methods in predicting TFBSs from the primary DNA sequence. This CNN model integrates data like histone modifications and chromatin accessibility for predicting TFBSs. Moreover, the integrative CNN framework is superior to traditional Machine Learning methods with significant improvements.

4.9 RNA PROTEIN INTERACTION PREDICTION

RNA-protein interactions (RPIs) play important roles in an extensive variety of cellular processes, ranging from transcriptional and posttranscriptional regulation of gene expression to host defense against pathogens. High-throughput experiments to identify RNA-protein interactions are beginning to provide valuable information about the complexity of RNA-protein interaction networks, but are expensive and time-consuming. Hence, there is a need for reliable computational methods for predicting RNA-protein interactions. The following section states few deep learning methods for RNA-protein interactions.

4.9.1 Recent Methodology Progress of Deep Learning for RNA-Protein Interaction Prediction

Interactions between RNAs and proteins play a pivotal role in many important biological processes. The advances in next-generation sequencing technologies have hugely benefitted researchers to identify hundreds of RNA-binding proteins (RBP) and their associated RNAs, which enables the large-scale prediction of RNA-protein interactions using Machine Learning approaches. This chapter provides an overview of the successful implementation of various deep learning approaches for predicting RNA-protein interactions, mainly focusing on the prediction of RNA-protein interaction pairs and RBP-binding sites on RNAs. It also discusses the advantages and disadvantages of these approaches, and highlights future perspectives on how to design better deep learning models. Finally, it provides deep insights into the future directions of computational tasks in the study of RNA-protein interactions, especially the interactions between non-coding RNAs and proteins.

4.9.2 iDEEP: RNA-Protein Binding Motifs Mining with a New Hybrid Deep-Learning-Based Cross-Domain Knowledge Integration Approach

RNA-binding proteins and their binding motifs enable crucial understanding of the posttranscriptional regulation of RNAs. Machine-Learning-based algorithms are widely acknowledged to be capable of speeding up this process. We propose a deep learning-based framework (iDeep) by using a novel hybrid convolutional neural network and deep belief network to predict the RBP interaction sites and motifs on RNAs. This new protocol transforms the original observed data into a high-level abstraction feature space using multiple layers of learning blocks. The iDeep framework can not only achieve promising performance than the state-of-the-art predictors, but also easily capture interpretable binding motifs. iDeep is available at http://www.csbio.sjtu.edu.cn/bioinf/iDeep.

4.9.3 iDEEPS: Prediction of RNA-Protein Sequence and Structure Binding Preferences Using Deep Convolutional and Recurrent Neural Networks

A deep-learning-based method, iDeepS simultaneously identifies the binding sequence and structure motifs from RNA sequences using convolutional neural networks and a bidirectional long short-term memory network (BLSTM). It first performs encoding for both the sequence and predicted secondary structure. CNNs are applied to reveal the hidden binding knowledge from the observed sequences. Considering the close relationship between sequence and predicted structures, the BLSTM is used to capture possible long-range dependencies between binding sequence and structure motifs identified by the CNNs. Finally, the learned weighted representations are fed into a classification layer to predict the RBP-binding sites. It has been evaluated on verified RBP-binding sites derived from large-scale representative CLIP-seq datasets. The iDeepS method identifies the sequence and structure motifs to accurately predict

RBP-binding sites. iDeepS is available at https://github.com/xypan1232/iDeepS.

4.9.4 Applications of Deep Learning in Biomedical Research

An overview of applications of deep learning in biomedical research is shown in Figure 4.3.

Advances in biological and medical areas are resulting in explosive volumes of biological data like genomic and proteomic sequences, medical images, and lots of physiological data. Learning from these data simplifies the understanding of human

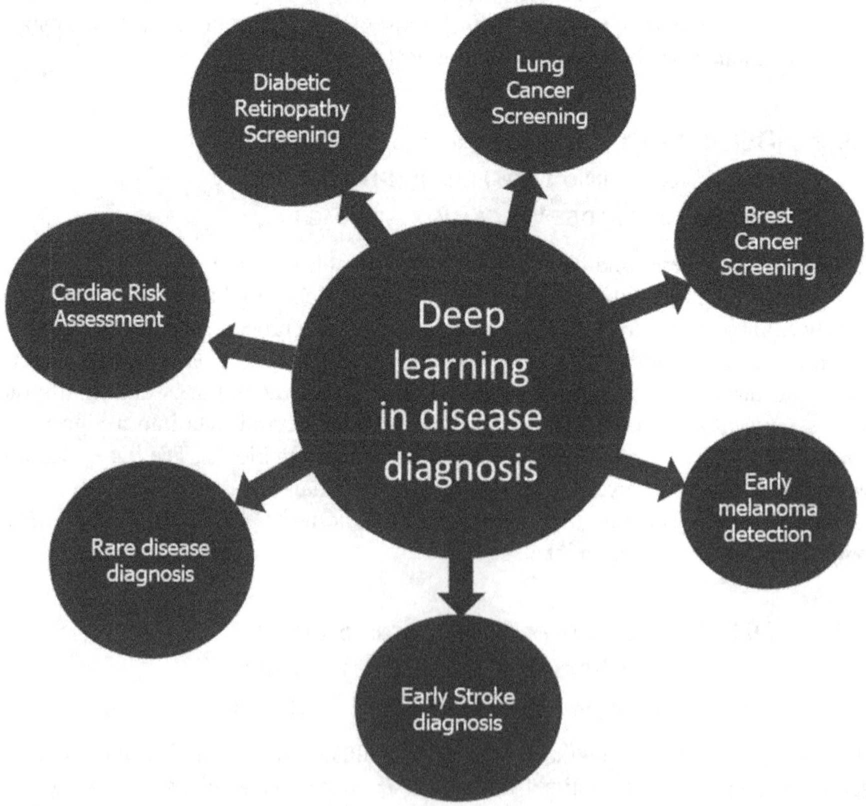

FIGURE 4.3 Deep learning in disease diagnosis.

health and diagnosis of disease. Deep-learning-based algorithms show revolutionary results in fetching features and learning patterns from complex datasets. This section aims to provide an insight into deep learning techniques and some of the state-of-the-art applications in the biomedical field.

4.10 DEEP LEARNING IN DISEASE DIAGNOSIS

Deep learning has largely been employed in radiology as well as in other diagnosis practices because of the sustained growth of computing power and storage technologies, decreasing cost of hardware, increasing cost of healthcare, the scarcity of healthcare workers, and a plenty of medical datasets to train the models.

4.10.1 Breast Cancer Screening

According to the World Health Organization (WHO) survey analysis, breast cancer is the most common cancer among women that leads to around 627,000 deaths annually. To save lives, many countries have introduced screening programs targeting to spot the cancer at an early stage. In the very beginning of 2020, Google's Artificial Intelligence division DeepMind introduced a deep learning model that reportedly improved results of an average radiologist by 11.5%.

Commercially Available Solutions

Breast Health Solutions by iCAD (based in New Hampshire, USA, FDA-cleared, CE-marked)*:* The AI suite applies deep learning algorithms to 2D mammography, 3D mammography (digital breast tomosynthesis or DBT), and breast density assessment. Its ProFound AI technology became the first Artificial Intelligence solution for 3D mammography approved by the FDA.

Transpara by ScreenPoint Medical (based in the Netherlands, FDA-cleared, CE-marked)*:* Trained on over a million mammograms, Transpara deep learning algorithm helps radiologists analyze both 2D and 3D mammograms. The solution is already in use in many countries.

4.10.2 Early Melanoma Detection

Skin diseases are the fourth most frequent cause of disability worldwide, while skin cancer is the world's most common malignancy, hitting 20% of people by age 70. At this place, AI can play a promising role. Similar to radiologists, dermatologists largely rely on visual pattern identification. In 2017, computer scientists from Stanford University created a convolutional neural network model that was trained on over 130,000 clinical images of skin pathologies to spot cancer. The algorithm reached the accuracy demonstrated by dermatologists. Finally, in March 2020, the *Journal of Investigative Dermatology* published the study by researchers from Seoul National University. Their CNN model learned from over 220,000 images to predict malignancy and classify 134 skin disorders.

Commercially Available Solutions

SkinVision (based in the Netherlands, CE-marked): The app is designed for assessing the risk of cancer based on photos of suspicious moles or other marks. Its AI algorithm was trained to spot warning signs on 3.5 million pictures. SkinVision has already contributed to the diagnosing of over 40,000 cases of skin cancer.

skinScan by TeleSkin ApS (based in Denmark, CE-marked): The iOS app available for downloading in Scandinavia, New Zealand, and Australia uses an AI algorithm for distinguishing a typical mole from an atypical one.

4.10.3 Lung Cancer Screening

Lung cancer is one of the world's deadliest cancers. It leads the list of cancer-related mortality and is second only to skin cancer in the prevalence rate. As with other malignancies, early detection may always be lifesaving.

The 2019 research by Google showed a promising result: a deep learning model created in collaboration with Northwestern Medicine and trained on 42,000 chest CT scans was way better at diagnosing lung cancer than radiologists with eight years of expertise. The algorithm was able to find malignant lung modes 5–9.5% more often than human specialists. Earlier, another CNN model proved its ability to spot chronic obstructive pulmonary disease (COPD) which often develops into cancer.

Commercially Available Solutions

Veye Chest by Aidense (based in the Netherlands, CE-marked): The AI solution automatically detects suspicious nodules in the lungs from low-dose CT scans, measures them, and compares them with previous images to identify the growth rate.

Veye Chest by ClariPi (based in South Korea, FDA-cleared): This solution does not detect cancer, but denoises low-dose and ultra-low-dose CT scans, thus improving the confidence of radiologists. The CNN model was trained on over a million images of different parts of the body, but ClariPi accentuates lung cancer screening as a key application of their algorithm.

4.10.4 Diabetic Retinopathy Screening

In the field of ophthalmology, AI is mostly used for retina image analysis—and specifically for diabetic retinopathy (DR) detection. This eye complication can cause blindness and strikes one in three patients with diabetes, amounting to 422 million globally. Early detection prevents the risk of vision loss.

IBM's deep learning technology launched in 2017 reached an accuracy score of 86% in detecting DR and classifying its severity—from mild to proliferative.

This result was outperformed by Google. In collaboration with its sister organization, Verily, the tech giant had been training a deep neural network for three years, using a dataset of 128,000 retinal images. In 2018, Google's AI Eye Doctor demonstrated 98.6% accuracy, on par with human experts. Now the algorithm serves to help doctors at Aravind Eye Hospital in India.

Commercially Available Solutions

IDx-DR by IDx (based in Iowa, USA, FDA-cleared, CE-marked): Known as the first AI system for DR diagnosis approved by FDA, IDx-DR software can be paired only with a particular retinal camera called Topcon. The deep learning algorithm provides one of two results:

1) Visit an ophthalmologist (for more than mild DR spotted)
2) Rescreen in 12 months (for mild and negative results)

IRIS (based in Florida, USA, FDA-cleared): Intelligent Retinal Imaging Systems can work with different cameras as it automatically enhances the quality of original images. The company benefits from Microsoft's Azure Machine Learning Package for Computer Vision.

4.10.5 Cardiac Risk Assessment from Electrocardiograms (ECGs)

Heart disease is the number one cause of death among men and women in the United States and worldwide. Timely risk assessment based on ECGs—the quickest and simplest test of heart activity—may significantly decrease mortality and prevent heart attacks.

With more than 300 million ECGs preformed globally each year, algorithms obtain a huge data pool for learning. Multiple studies show that AI already not only spots current abnormalities from ECGs but predicts future risks as well. For example, RiskCardio technology developed in 2019 at MIT assesses the likelihood of cardiovascular death within 30–365 days for patients who have already survived acute coronary syndrome (ACS).

Commercially Available Solution

KardiaMobile by AliveCor (based in California, USA, FDA-cleared, CE-marked): The personal ECG solution consists of a small recording device that captures an ECG in 30 seconds and a mobile app that utilizes a deep neural network to detect slow and fast heart rhythms (bradycardia and tachycardia), atrial fibrillation (AF), and normal rhythms. Once taken, ECG recording can be sent to a clinician for further analysis.

4.10.6 Early Stroke Diagnosis from Head CT Scans

Stroke or the sudden death of brain cells due to lack of oxygen is the second major cause of death and the third leading cause of long-term disability globally. This dangerous condition requires immediate diagnosis and treatment. Statistics show that patients who receive professional help within 3 hours after the first symptoms typically make a better and faster recovery.

Commercially Available Solutions

Viz LVO and Viz-ICH by Viz.ai (based in California, USA, and Israel, FDA-cleared, CE-marked): The deep learning algorithms analyze CT scans to detect suspected ICH and LVO strokes. The system automatically alerts specialists, saving precious time and brain cells.

AI Stroke by Aidoc (based in Israel, FDA-cleared, CE-marked): AI Stroke package covers two types of stroke—ICH and LVO. The system automatically flags suspected cases, enabling radiologists to quickly decide on the course of action.

e-Stroke suite by Brainomix (based in UK, CE-marked): This AI-driven imaging software automatically assesses CT scans of stroke patients. Currently, the algorithm identifies only the ischemic stroke that amounts to 85% of all cases.

4.11 DEEP LEARNING IN DIAGNOSIS OF RARE DISEASES

Diseases that affect fewer than 5 patients per 10,000 are defined as rare in Europe. With more than 6000 known rare diseases, their joint global health burden is large, and recent estimates report a population occurrence of at least 3.5–5.9%. According to a study from 2013, it takes, on average, more than five years, eight physicians, and two to three misdiagnoses until a rare disease patient obtains the correct diagnosis. Once appropriately diagnosed, the challenges remain: due to the small patient numbers, commercials for developing medications are often low. Furthermore, the pathophysiological mechanisms underlying rare diseases are often not well understood. As a consequence, many rare diseases lack adequate treatment options.

One of the most extensive knowledge bases for rare diseases is Orphanet, which provides data about disease epidemiology, linked genes, inheritance types, disease onsets, or bibliography to terminologies, as well as links to expert centers, patient organizations, and other resources. Another European ventures include RD-Connect, which combines archives, biobanks, and genetic datasets with bioinformatics tools to provide a central resource for research on rare diseases; the European Reference Networks (ERNs), which also provides an IT infrastructure that allows healthcare professionals to collaborate on virtual panels to exchange knowledge and decide on optimal treatments; and the European Joint Programme on Rare Diseases (EJP RD), a multinational cooperation aiming to create an ecosystem that facilitates research, care, and medical innovation in the field of rare diseases. In the United States, the Undiagnosed Diseases Network (UDN) brings together experts to diagnose and treat patients with rare conditions.

In addition to these collaborative efforts and international platforms, another important factor that can improve the condition for rare disease patients are improvements in information technology—particularly in the field of deep learning and Artificial Intelligence. DL and AI classically use large, multivariate datasets to "train" models and algorithms, which are then used to make predictions on new data (for example, by classifying tumors in radiological images as benign or malignant). Importantly, the computations by which these models generate their output are not explicitly coded by a programmer, but instead they are implicitly "learned" by the algorithm from example data (hence the term "Machine Learning" or "deep learning"). DL and AI and are progressively applied in medicine and healthcare and, in some areas, are beginning to achieve (and sometimes even surpass) human-level performance and precisions.

4.12 CONCLUSIONS

In this chapter, we have comprehensively summarized all the fundamental but essential concepts, methods, and tools of deep learning extensively used for the processing and analysis of the next-generation sequencing data. By reviewing these deep learning and Machine Learning methods—from quality control analysis of the reads to their assembly, followed by metagenomics analysis, variant analysis, SNP detection, gene expression analysis, identification of transcriptomics factors, RNA-protein interaction predictions—we highlighted and explored all the important analysis parameters of next-generation sequencing data which would help to gain knowledge from the biological data.

Second, the successful application of deep learning and Artificial Intelligence in the field of medical research and diagnostics has been discussed. Deep learning algorithms, in particular convolutional networks, have rapidly become a methodology of choice for analyzing medical images. Concise overviews are provided for studies per application area: neuro, retinal, pulmonary, melanoma detection, breast, cardiac, stroke, and rare disease diagnosis. We have ended with a summary of the current state-of-the-art approach and open challenges and directions for future research.

Deep learning is a big-data-driven approach, which has made it unique from conventional statistical approaches, as statistical methods rely on the assumptions of the generated data, deep learning. Statistics can deliver clear interpretations through fitting a definite probability model when adequate data are collected from well-designed studies, whereas deep learning is involved with the creation of questions and application of algorithms which improvise with training datasets. Many deep learning approaches can derive models for pattern recognition, classification, and prediction from existing data and do not rely on strict assumptions about the data-generating systems, which makes them more efficient in some complicated applications. Finally, deep learning can be integrated with the existing conventional methods and algorithms to tackle the complicated biological data analysis.

BIBLIOGRAPHY

Ainscough, B.J., Barnell, E.K., Ronning, P., Campbell, K.M., Wagner, A.H., Fehniger, T.A., Dunn, G.P., Uppaluri, R., Govindan, R., Rohan, T.E., and Griffith, M. "A deep learning approach to automate refinement of somatic variant calling from cancer sequencing data." *Nature Genetics* 50 (12): 1735–1743.

Angly, F.E., Willner, D., Rohwer, F., Hugenholtz, P., Tyson, G.W. (2012) "Grinder: A versatile amplicon and shotgun sequence simulator." *Nucleic Acids Research* 40 (12): e94.

Arango-Argoty, G., Garner, E., Pruden, A., Heath, L.S., Vikesland, P., and Zhang, L. (2018) "DeepARG: A deep learning approach for predicting antibiotic resistance genes from metagenomic data." *Microbiome* 6 (1): 23.

Arango-Argoty, G.A., Dai, D., Pruden, A., Vikesland, P., Heath, L.S., and Zhang, L. (2019) "NanoARG: A web service for detecting and contextualizing antimicrobial resistance genes from nanopore-derived metagenomes." *Microbiome* 7 (1): 88.

Bengio, Y. and LeCun, Y. (2007) "Scaling learning algorithms toward AI," in *Large-Scale Kernel Machines*, edited by L. Bottou, O. Chapelle, D. DeCoste, and J. Weston (Cambridge, MA: The MIT Press).

Chen, L., Zhai, Y., He, Q., Wang, W., and Deng, M. (2020) "Integrating deep supervised, self-supervised and unsupervised learning for single-cell RNA-seq clustering and annotation." *Genes (Basel)* 11 (7): 792.

Ching, T., Himmelstein, D. S., Beaulieu-Jones, B. K., Kalinin, A. A., Do, B. T., Way, G. P., et al. (2018) "Opportunities and obstacles for deep learning in biology and medicine". *Journal of the Royal Society Interface* 15: 20170387. doi: 10.1098/rsif.2017.0387.

Ditzler, G., Polikar, R., Member, S., Rosen G., and Member, S. (2015) "Multi-layer and recursive neural networks for metagenomic classification". *IEEE* Transactions *on NanoBioscience* 14: 608. doi: 10.1109/TNB.2015.2461219.

Esteva, A., Kuprel, B., Novoa, R.A., Ko, J., Swetter, S.M., Blau, H.M., and Thrun, S. (2017) "Dermatologist-level classification of skin cancer with deep neural networks". *Nature* 542: 115–118. doi: 10.1038/nature21056.

European Commission. (n.d.) https://ec.europa.eu/info/research-and-innovation/research-area/health-research-and-innovation/rare-diseases_en. Accessed 16 Apr 2020.

European Joint Programme on Rare Diseases. (n.d.) https://www.ejprarediseases.org. Accessed 16 Apr 2020.

European Reference Networks. (n.d.) https://ec.europa.eu/health/ern_en. Accessed 16 Apr 2020.

EURORDIS. (n.d.) https://www.eurordis.org/about-rare-diseases. Accessed 16 Apr 2020.

Fiannaca, A., La Paglia, L., La Rosa, M., Renda, G., Rizzo, R., Gaglio, S., and Urso, A. (2018) "Deep learning models for bacteria taxonomic classification of metagenomic data." *BMC Bioinformatics* 19 (Suppl 7): 198.

Giorgi, J.M. and Bader, G.D. (2018) "Transfer learning for biomedical named entity recognition with neural networks". *Bioinformatics* 34: 4087–4094. doi: 10.1093/bioinformatics/bty449.

Hannigan, G.D., Prihoda, D., Palicka, A., Soukup, J., Klempir, O., Rampula, L., Durcak, J., Wurst, M., Kotowski, J., Chang, D., and Wang, R. (2019) "A deep learning genome-mining strategy for biosynthetic gene cluster prediction." *Nucleic Acids Research* 47 (18): e110.

Jing, F., Zhang, S., Cao, Z., and Zhang, S.. (2019) "An integrative framework for combining sequence and epigenomic data to predict transcription factor binding sites using deep learning." *IEEE/ACM Transactions on Computational Biology Bioinformatics* (18): 355–364.

Korvigo, I., Afanasyev, A., Romashchenko, N., and Skoblov, M. (2018) "Generalising better: Applying deep learning to integrate deleteriousness prediction scores for whole-exome SNV studies." *PLoS One* 13 (3): e0192829.

Koumakis, L. (2020) "Deep learning models in genomics; are we there yet?" *Computational and Structural Biotechnology Journal* 18: 1466–1473.

LaPierre, N., Egan, R., Wang, W., and Wang, Z. (2019) "De novo Nanopore read quality improvement using deep learning". *BMC Bioinformatics* 20 (1): 552.

LaPierre, N., Ju, C.J.T., Zhou, G., and Wang, W. (2019) "MetaPheno: A critical evaluation of deep learning and machine learning in metagenome-based disease prediction." *Methods* 166: 74–82.

Li, X., Wang, K., Lyu, Y., Pan, H., Zhang, J., Stambolian, D., Susztak, K., Reilly, M.P., Hu, G., and Li, M. (2020) "Deep learning enables accurate clustering with batch effect removal in single-cell RNA-seq analysis." *Nature Communications* 11 (1): 2338.

Li, Y., Wang, S., Umarov, R., Xie, B., Fan, M., Li, L., and Gao, X. (2018) "DEEPre: Sequence-based enzyme EC number prediction by deep learning." *Bioinformatics* 34 (5): 760–769.

Liang, M., Li, Z., Chen, T., and Zeng, J. (2015) "Integrative data analysis of multi-platform cancer data with a multimodal deep learning approach". *IEEE/ACM Transactions on Computational Biology and Bioinformatics* 12: 928–937. doi: 10.1109/TCBB.2014.2377729.

Liang, Q., Bible, P.W., Liu, Y., Zou, B., and Wei, L. (2020) "DeepMicrobes: Taxonomic classification for metagenomics with deep learning." *NAR Genomics and Bioinformatics* 2 (1): lqaa009.

Libbrecht, M.W. and Noble, W.S. (2015) "Machine learning applications in genetics and genomics". Nature Reviews Genetics 16: 321–322. doi: 10.1038/nrg3920.

Luo, R., Sedlazeck, F.J., Lam, T.W. and Schatz, M.C. (2019) "A multi-task convolutional deep neural network for variant calling in single molecule sequencing." *Nature Communications* 10 (1): 998.

Min, X., Zeng, W., Chen, S., Chen, N., Chen, T., and Jiang, R. (2017) "Predicting enhancers with deep convolutional neural networks." *BMC Bioinformatics* 18 (Suppl 13): 478.

Mineeva, O., Rojas-Carulla, M., Ley, R.E., Schölkopf, B., and Youngblut, N.D. (2020) "DeepMAsED: Evaluating the quality of metagenomic assemblies." *Bioinformatics* 36 (10): 3011–3017.

Mineeva, O., Rojas-Carulla, M., Ley, R.E., Schölkopf, B., and Youngblut, N.D. (2020) "DeepMAsED: Evaluating the quality of metagenomic assemblies." *Bioinformatics* 36 (10): 3011–3017.

Najafabadi, M.M., Villanustre, F., Khoshgoftaar, T.M., Seliya, N., Wald, R., and Muharemagic, E. (2015) "Deep learning applications and challenges in big data analytics". *Journal of Big Data* 2: 1. doi: 10.1186/s40537-014-0007-7.

Orphanet. (n.d.) http://www.orpha.net. Accessed 16 Apr 2020.

Pan, X. and Shen, H. (2017) "RNA-protein binding motifs mining with a new hybrid deep learning based cross-domain knowledge integration approach." *BMC Bioinformatics* 18 (1): 136.

Pan, X., Rijnbeek, P., Yan, J., and Shen, H.B. (2018) "Prediction of RNA-protein sequence and structure binding preferences using deep convolutional and recurrent neural networks." *BMC Genomics* 19 (1): 511.

Pan, X., Yang, Y., Xia, C.Q., Mirza, A.H., and Shen, H.B. (2019) "Recent methodology progress of deep learning for RNA-protein interaction prediction." *Wiley Interdisciplinary Reviews: RNA* 10 (6): e1544.

Poplin, R., Chang, P.C., Alexander, D., Schwartz, S., Colthurst, T., Ku, A., Newburger, D., Dijamco, J., Nguyen, N., Afshar, P.T., and Gross, S.S. (2018) "A universal SNP and small-indel variant caller using deep neural networks." *Nature Biotechnology* 36 (10): 983–987.

Quang, D., Chen, Y., and Xie, X. (2015) "DANN: A deep learning approach for annotating the pathogenicity of genetic variants." *Bioinformatics* 31 (5): 761.

Rahman, M.A., and Rangwala, H. (2020) "IDMIL: An alignment-free Interpretable Deep Multiple Instance Learning (MIL) for predicting disease from whole-metagenomic data." *Bioinformatics* 36 (Supplement_1): i39–i47.

Ramoni, R.B., Mulvihill, J.J., Adams, D.R., Allard, P., Ashley, E.A., Bernstein, J.A., et al. (2017) "The undiagnosed diseases network: Accelerating discovery about health and disease." *American Journal of Human Genetics* 100: 185–192.

Ravasio, V., Ritelli, M., Legati, A., and Giacopuzzi, E. (2018) "GARFIELD-NGS: Genomic vARiants FIltering by dEep Learning moDels in NGS." *Bioinformatics* 34 (17): 3038–3040.

Sarangi, A.N., Goel, A., and Aggarwal, R. (2019) "Methods for studying gut microbiota: A primer for physicians." *Journal of Clinical and Experimental Hepatology* 9 (1): 62–73. doi: 10.1016/j.jceh.2018.04.016.

Shire, Rare Disease Impact Report. (n.d.) https://globalgenes.org/wp-content/uploads/2013/04/ShireReport-1.pdf. Accessed 16 Apr 2020.

Sun, C., Zhang, N., Yu, P., Wu, X., Li, Q., Li, T., Li, H., Xiao, X., Shalmani, A., Li, L., and Che, D. (2020) "Enhancer recognition and prediction during spermatogenesis based on deep convolutional neural networks." *Molecular Omics* 16: 308–321.

Tasaki, S., Gaiteri, C., Mostafavi, S., and Wang, Y. (2020) "Deep learning decodes the principles of differential gene expression." *Nature Machine Intelligence* 2 (7): 376–386.

Telenti, A., Lippert, C., Chang, P.C., and DePristo, M. (2018) "Deep learning of genomic variation and regulatory network data." *Human Molecular Genetics* 27 (R1): R63–R71.

Thompson, R., Johnston, L., Taruscio, D., Monaco, L., Béroud, C., Gut, I.G., et al. (2014) "RD-connect: An integrated platform connecting databases, registries, biobanks and clinical bioinformatics for rare disease research." *Journal of General Internal Medicine* 29 (Suppl 3): S780– S787.

Torroja, C., and Sanchez-Cabo, F. (2019) "Digitaldlsorter: Deep-learning on scRNA-Seq to deconvolute gene expression data." *Frontiers in Genetics* 10: 978.

Wakap, S.N., Lambert, D.M., Olry, A., Rodwell, C., Gueydan, C., Lanneau, V., et al. (2020) "Estimating cumulative point prevalence of rare diseases: Analysis of the Orphanet database." *European Journal of Human Genetics* 28: 165–173.

Wang, M., Tai, C., Weinan, E., and Wei, L. (2018) "DeFine: Deep convolutional neural networks accurately quantify intensities of transcription factor-DNA binding and facilitate evaluation of functional non-coding variants." *Nucleic Acids Research* 46 (11): e69.

Wick, R.R., Judd, L.M., and Holt, K.E. (2018) "Deepbinner: Demultiplexing barcoded Oxford Nanopore reads with deep convolutional neural networks." *PLOS Computational Biology* 14 (11): e1006583.

Xu, J., Xiang, L., Liu, Q., Gilmore, H., Wu, J., Tang, J., and Madabhushi, A. (2016) "Stacked sparse autoencoder (SSAE) for nuclei detection on breast cancer histopathology images". *IEEE Transactions on Medical Imaging* 35: 119–130. doi: 10.1109/TMI.2015.2458702.

Yin, Q., Wu, M., Liu, Q., Lv, H., and Jiang, R.. (2019) "DeepHistone: A deep learning approach to predicting histone modifications." *BMC Genomics* 20 (Suppl 2): 193.

Zhang, S., Zhou, J., Hu, H., Gong, H., Chen, L., Cheng, C., and Zeng, J. (2016) "A deep learning framework for modeling structural features of RNA-binding protein targets". *Nucleic Acids Research* 44: e32. doi: 10.1093/nar/gkv1025.

Zhang, S.W., Jin, X.Y., and Zhang, T. (2017) "Gene prediction in metagenomic fragments with deep learning". *BioMed Research International* (9).

Zhang, Y., Liu, C.M., Leung, H.C., Luo, R., and Lam, T.W. (2020) "Nanopore sequencing data via deep learning." *iScience* 23 (5): 101128.

Zhou, J. and Troyanskaya, O.G. (2015) "Predicting effects of noncoding variants with deep learning-based sequence model." *Nature Methods* 12 (10): 931–934.

5 Applications of Machine Learning Algorithms to Cancer Data

Suba Suseela, Nita Parekh

CONTENTS

5.1 INTRODUCTION

Classification of cancer types/subtypes has become more important with increasing incidence rates, and cancer remains the leading cause of death globally. Identification of novel classes (subtypes) in cancer can help in planning more effective treatment strategies, reduce toxicity, and improve survival rates of patients. Traditionally, tumors have been classified based on tissue types, primary sites of occurrence, and/or their morphology, which can often be very subjective. Moreover, treatment therapies based on tumor histology alone are not very effective as different tumors may respond differently to the same drug therapy. A promising alternative approach is the classification of tumors based on expression levels of multiple genes involved in the disease. Even though the human genome has approximately 20,000 protein coding genes, all of them would not be active/expressed in any single biological process, including cell growth, metabolism, tumorigenesis, etc. This requires identifying relevant genes that may be responsible for the proliferation of malignant cells. Most research in this area has focused on selecting a subset of genes in cancer samples for classification purposes using expression data. The advances in gene profiling technologies like high-throughput sequencing have generated huge amounts of genomic data. Large-scale cancer studies initiated by various consortia, viz., TCGA, ICGC, ENCODE project, etc., have generated thousands of samples from over hundreds of different types of cancer. However, the scale of data generation has made it highly challenging to integrate and model this complex, noisy, high-dimensional data. Classification approaches based on supervised/unsupervised learning, viz., support vector machines (SVM), decision trees, or neural networks for identifying genetic features for binary or multi-class classification of tumors and tumor subtypes have been proposed. These approaches help in revealing relationships between the features in the data and exhibit improved performance compared to other alternative approaches.

In this chapter, an attempt has been made to provide an overview of the evolution of Machine Learning (ML) algorithms in analyzing gene expression data over the past two decades. A brief review of some widely used algorithms for feature selection and subtype classification is also provided. Cancer datasets are of different types based on the data type (e.g., gene expression, copy number variation [CNV], DNA methylation), experimental techniques (e.g., microarray, RNASeq), microarray platforms (e.g., Agilent, Affymetrix, Illumina), data formats (e.g., text, XML, JSON, TSV), etc. The two most common platforms generating gene expression data are microarrays and RNA sequencing. The data types are very different in the two cases and require very different preprocessing and analysis pipelines; in microarray data, it is intensity values while in RNASeq data it is represented as read counts. Typically, in any experiment, the number of features (genes) is considerably higher than the number of samples available. This makes it difficult to select the optimal number of features for classifying various cancers and subtypes. Machine Learning algorithms can be useful to some extent in dealing with such problems and can be broadly classified as supervised, unsupervised, and semisupervised approaches (Ang et al., 2016). Numerous methods have been proposed in each category based on how the model is generated. In this chapter, some of these algorithms for gene selection in prediction/classification of binary/multiclass cancers, classification of benign/malign tumor cells, different grades of cancers, prognosis/survival of cancer patients, etc., are reviewed. Graph-based algorithms to associate the features selected with various pathways involved in cancer are also briefly discussed.

Feature selection is a major preprocessing step in ML applications to gene expression data analysis of tumor samples. Other challenges include limited access to data, integration of data from different experimental platforms/techniques, and lack of reproducibility in modeling high-dimensional data in the case of limited samples. A raw gene expression file may contain expression values of more than 20,000 genes. Majority of these genes are irrelevant in tumor progression and many others, though relevant, are redundant, resulting in noisy signals or in overfitting of data when used for training in an ML algorithm. Thus, there clearly is a need for feature selection in reducing dimensionality of the data. With reduced sets of features, ML algorithms have been successfully applied to classify samples into appropriate categories (Zhang and Deng, 2007), predict the prognosis of patients (Gevaert et al., 2006), or identify suitable therapy (Tabl et al., 2018). Various methods proposed for feature selection or feature transformation are principal component analysis, linear discriminant analysis, singular value decomposition (SVD), information gain, chi-square test, fisher score, etc. The objective in the classification problem is to identify genes that are significant to a particular type/subtype of cancer. Numerous classes of ML approaches have been used for this purpose, e.g., random forests, support vector machines, regression, and neural networks.

5.2 OVERVIEW OF FEATURE SELECTION APPROACHES

Methods for feature selection have been applied in various domains over the past 50 years. These are categorized into filter, wrapper, and embedded methods based on the evaluation metrics used to score the feature subsets. In filter-based methods, feature selection is based on the score of a feature in a statistical test for their correlation with the outcome variable, e.g., Pearson's correlation, chi-square test, or linear discriminant analysis. These methods are independent of the ML algorithm used and easy to implement. In wrapper methods, a model is built on a subset of features and its performance evaluated. For optimal performance of the model, features are either added or removed from the subset. It is basically a search problem for identifying the best set of features for classification. Some examples of this approach include forward selection, backward selection, and recursive feature elimination methods. This approach is computationally more intensive compared to filter-based approach. Embedded methods combine features of both filter and wrapper methods and are generally included in ML algorithms with built-in methods such as LASSO, RIDGE regression, etc., to penalize overfitting.

In biological data analysis, the feature selection method helps in identifying features that would help in determining the disease class or differentiate between disease and normal cells. Typically, only a few genes are directly linked to the disease, while the majority only exhibit a weak or indirect association. The goal of the selection algorithm is to be able to distinguish between relevant and noisy/redundant ones. Most importantly, the result of the algorithm should be interpretable and feasible for clinical use. However, in most cases, the number of features returned by ML algorithms is too large, making it impractical to be used in a clinical setting and/or give non-interpretable results. Some of the algorithms claim to achieve both small and interpretable set of features, but may not be always accurate as desired. Major steps in feature selection in any ML approach are discussed below.

5.2.1 MAIN STEPS IN FEATURE SELECTION

The objective of any feature selection process is to identify a relevant set of features that are strongly correlated to the traits of interest and few features that are weakly correlated but still important for the classification of samples and for avoiding noisy features.

5.2.1.1 Preprocessing Step

Genome-wide analysis results in thousands of genes (features), which poses a major hurdle in the learning phase of ML algorithms when the number of samples is few. This is generally handled by subjecting raw datasets to some initial level of filtering based on statistical relevance of the features and/or removal of noisy signals—for example, filtering genes based on signal-to-noise ratio (Golub et al., 1999), differential expression of genes with respect to control (Xiao et al., 2018), correlation of genes to the trait of interest (Tabl et al., 2018), etc. The resultant dataset with a reduced number of features may include many correlated and redundant features. Selection of an optimal set of features from this resultant set involves some of the steps discussed below.

5.2.1.2 Determining the Direction of Selection

The selection algorithm may start with an empty set, a complete set, or a random selection of genes. That is, genes are either added one by one to a set of candidate genes or removed one by one from the initial set of genes, or a hybrid approach of adding and removing genes simultaneously is applied based on some criteria that improve the classification capability of candidate genes.

5.2.1.3 Determining the Stopping Criteria

The above process of adding/removing genes needs to be terminated to obtain an optimal set of relevant genes and reduce redundancy. This is done by defining a stopping criterion that requires the candidate genes to have some attributes that differentiate them from others. This step can be done either separately or combined with the next step of feature selection, for example, setting a threshold for the error rate in the performance of the model. Naively, this can be achieved by predeciding the number of features/iterations the algorithm must run.

5.2.1.4 Evaluating the Selection

Feature selection algorithms are categorized as filter-based, wrapper, or embedded methods. Filter-based methods evaluate the performance of candidate genes after the selection process with evaluation methods such as LOOCV, *k*-fold CV, etc. The wrapper method does the performance evaluation during the selection process and the stopping criterion in such cases is to continue adding or removing of genes till the performance improves. But with a change in the classification algorithm, the gene selection process may also change in this case. Embedded methods integrate classification and gene selection algorithms such that the performance of classification accuracy decides the selection of features.

5.2.1.5 Validation Methods

Cross-validation, use of confusion matrix, or various methods evaluating the similarity of selected genes, error rates, etc., are some of the validation methods commonly used.

5.2.2 Challenges in Feature Selection

The set of features selected can affect the performance of classification algorithms, and hence care should be taken when choosing feature selection methods that are robust and provide stable results. That is, change in the dataset or methods for feature selection should not affect the selected set of features. However, several factors are observed to affect the stability of the result. "Curse of dimensionality" is one major factor when the sample size is significantly small compared to the size of a feature set. This may result in problems such as missing important features or undue emphasis given to irrelevant features, leading to reduction in the performance of classifiers. Class imbalance is another important problem that causes prediction of classifier to be biased when some classes dominate others, i.e., when the number of samples in one or more classes outnumber the samples in other classes in a dataset. For example, in breast cancer datasets, Luminal A subtype is the most common subtype of breast cancer, while Normal-like subtype is observed with least frequency, resulting in class imbalance. Different standards followed by different microarray platforms, such as Agilent, Affymetrix, etc., and sequencing platforms in gene expression profiling incur difficulties in the analysis of cross-platform data, making it difficult to merge datasets across different platforms for increasing the sample size.

5.3 OVERVIEW OF CLASSIFICATION METHODS

Machine Learning is slowly replacing traditional classification approaches for the analysis of cancer samples due to high volumes of data resulting from next-generation sequencing technologies and the complexities involved in data interpretation. The classification algorithms are broadly categorized into three categories: supervised, semisupervised, and unsupervised algorithms. Supervised methods use labeled data for classification purposes, e.g., linear regression (Seber and Lee, 2012), random forest (Breiman, 2001), and support vector machine (Cortes and Vapnik, 1995). Unsupervised algorithms do not require labeled data, e.g., clustering algorithms ("Unsupervised Learning: Clustering," n.d.), self-organizing feature maps (Marsland, 2011), etc. Semisupervised algorithms are a mixture of both the techniques wherein prediction is improved with labeled data and using some discriminant methods to classify/predict. These methods generally depend on the techniques, such as eigenvector expressions of the datasets, probabilistic modeling, distance metrics, hierarchical/agglomerative techniques, etc. Supervised learning methods are the most common learning methods used in the classification of disease/control or subtyping of microarray datasets. Unsupervised and semisupervised methods are less studied but appear to be promising and more suitable for gene expression profiles where labeling of data is very costly and availability of a large number of samples is not common.

5.3.1 Overview of Popular ML Algorithms

In this section, some of the most widely used ML methods are discussed followed by those combining ML with other non-ML methods in this domain. The well-accepted

ML methods in the domain of gene expression data analysis are SVM and its variants, regression-based methods, random forest, clustering approaches, and neural networks. Commonly used non-ML methods for gene selection are statistical models. Many studies consider a combined strategy to improve the results. Other methods, among many, proposed for classification include genetic algorithm for preselection of genes for multiclass classification using a maximum likelihood (MLHD) classifier (Ooi and Tan, 2003), *t*-statistic for gene pair scoring and feature selection for a binary class problem (Bø and Jonassen, 2002), and maximum relevance minimum redundancy (mRMR) approach using an entropy-based method for assessing relevance (Liu et al., 2005).

Support Vector Machine: SVM and its variants are supervised ML algorithms widely used because of their robustness and performance (Cortes and Vapnik, 1995). The first application of SVM in cancer classification dates back to 2000. Linear and non-linear SVMs are the most primitive categories of SVMs. Other variants include soft margin SVMs and hard margin SVMs (based on regularization penalty), support vector regression (SVR) (based on objective function), and binary and multiclass SVMs (based on number of classes). Depending on the loss function and kernels used, SVMs are of many types. Limitations of SVM are difficulty in parameter selection and extensive memory and time requirements. Non-interpretability of the features used for classification is another major drawback of SVMs in medical applications.

Support vector machine finds a maximum margin hyperplane (linear or non-linear) to split the data points into separate classes. A hyperplane is defined as set of points, *X*, satisfying the following equation:

$$\vec{W} \cdot \vec{X} - b = 0 \tag{1}$$

where $\vec{W}$ is a vector normal to the hyperplane. For linearly separable data, the two hyperplanes that would segregate the data into two different groups with a maximum margin between them are defined by the following equations:

$$\vec{W} \cdot \vec{X} - b \geq 1 \quad \text{and} \quad \vec{W} \cdot \vec{X} - b \leq -1 \tag{2}$$

where all points on or above the first inequality are labeled "1," and those on or below the second inequality are labeled "–1." Thus, the classifier is determined by parameters $\vec{W}$ and *b*, and $\vec{X}$ that lie near the hyperplanes form the support vectors. When an additional parameter λ is introduced, the hyperplanes have soft margins to separate non-linear data points, with loss function given by

$$\max\left(0, 1 - Y_i\left(\vec{W} \cdot \vec{X} - b\right)\right) + \lambda \left\|\vec{W}\right\|^2 \tag{3}$$

where Y_i is the *i*th target and $\vec{W} \cdot \vec{X} - b$ is the current output. For smaller values of λ, the hyperplane behaves as a hard margin. Further, if instead of simple dot product, non-linear kernel functions are used, the SVM becomes a non-linear classifier. In the study by Huang et al. (Huang et al., 2017), SVM ensembles with linear kernels and bagging method are shown to perform well on a preprocessed set of genes (a small-scale dataset) for predicting breast cancer, whereas an SVM ensemble with radial basis function (RBF) kernels with boosting method shows better performance on a large-scale dataset.

Regression: These models estimate conditional probability of a class label given the observations and are widely used for prediction tasks. Regression predicts continuous values of the dependent variable, whereas in classification a categorical value is predicted. For high-dimensional data, regression models can also be used to understand which among the independent variables are more related to the label and thereby help in dimensionality reduction. In linear regression, the dependent variable is defined as follows:

$$\widehat{y_i} = \beta_1 x_{i1} + \beta_2 x_{i2} + \cdots + \beta_p x_{ip} + \varepsilon_i \tag{4}$$

where x_{ij} is the ith observation of the pth independent variable β_i, the parameters, and ε_i is an error term. In non-linear regression, the function of independent variables is non-linear in nature, viz., power functions, Gaussian, etc. For fitting a model to data, the parameters are learned by minimizing sum of squared residuals (SSR):

$$SSR = \sum_{i=1}^{n} e_i^2 \tag{5}$$

where $e_i = y_i - \hat{y}_i$, y_i is the true value of the dependent variable, $\hat{y}_i$ is the predicted value, and n is the sample size, or by mean squared error (MSE):

$$MSE = \frac{SSR}{n-p} \tag{6}$$

After model construction, the goodness-of-fit measure of the model and statistical significance of the parameters are estimated using R-squared analysis, F-test, or t-test. Logistic regression is a classification algorithm where the dependent variable can take only discrete values. The categories are binomial or multinomial (based on the number of values the dependent variable takes), or ordinal if the values are ordered. Model fitting is done by maximum likelihood estimation. Other types of regressions based on penalty terms include LASSO, RIDGE, elastic net regression, etc. An elastic net penalized logistic regression was used for classifying breast cancer samples as normal versus tumor with aberrant RAS pathway activity (Tabl et al., 2018). Advantages of the regression model are that it identifies relative importance of variables which influence the decision and its ability to identify the outliers. These models are not suitable in case of incomplete data as then all the variables that contribute to the prediction may not be captured, or when the correlation is interpreted falsely as causation, as then the algorithm returns a higher number of features which would be misleading. To overcome these disadvantages, a structured penalized logistic regression method was recently proposed (Liu and Wong, 2019). Here, a modification to the regularization term in the penalized regression equation is proposed:

$$F(\beta) = \lambda\alpha \sum_{j=1}^{p} \theta_j |\beta_j| + \lambda(1-\alpha) \sum_{i=1}^{p} \sum_{j=1}^{p} w_{ij} \left(\mu_i \beta_i - \mu_j \beta_j \right)^2 \tag{7}$$

where the weight w_{ij} measures similarity between the pair of variables X_i and X_j. It controls the second regularization term in the above equation by penalizing the coefficients based on the structure of the data. The parameter θ_{ij} in the first regularization term selects features that correlate strongly and β_j introduced into the pairwise structured regularization term reduces the number of relevant features.

Random Forest (RF): It is another supervised learning algorithm and is used for classification or regression tasks (Breiman, 2001). It constructs multiple decision trees during the training phase and reports the mean or majority prediction of the individual decision trees as the algorithm's output. As shown in Figure 5.1, decision tree has a directed graph structure wherein each internal node represents an evaluation of an attribute, each branch denotes the outcome of that evaluation, and the terminal or leaf node represents a class label. The ensemble of decision trees is built using bagging method and the samples are selected with replacement. The features are selected randomly, and the best feature is used for splitting the node in a tree. The algorithm is widely used because of its good accuracy and ease of measuring the importance of features used for prediction, which helps in identifying and ranking

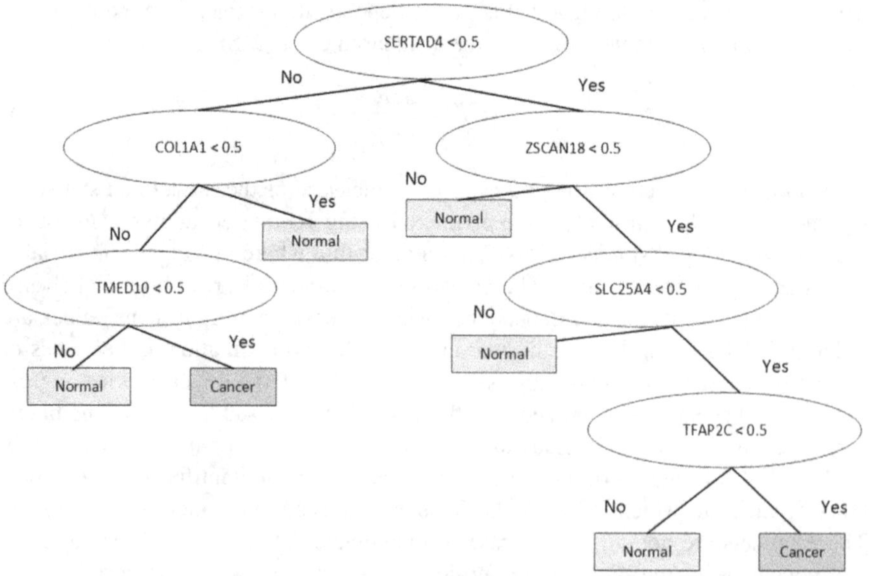

FIGURE 5.1 A representative decision tree.

the genes for classification purposes. In the study by Díaz-Uriarte and Alvarez de Andrés (2006), RF was used to select the minimum number of genes for classification. The disadvantage of decision tree is that it overfits, but random forests do not overfit the data if the number of trees in the forest is sufficiently large. Though with the increase in the number of decision trees the accuracy of the model improves, the algorithm becomes slower. The model is a predictive tool and not a descriptive one as it lacks interpretability. To improve its interpretability, various methods have been proposed. For example, the advantages of RFs have been combined with those of a generalized linear model to achieve interpretability of results by Song et al. (2013).

Neural Networks: These are non-linear, statistical, decision-making tools based on the working principle of biological neurons. It involves a set of processing elements connected to each other either densely or sparsely. The network may consist of a single layer or multiple layers of such connections, called hidden layers, apart from input and output layers. Neural networks can be used in supervised as well as unsupervised learning approaches. The learning here happens by updating the model parameters in iterations based on backpropagation of the error using techniques like stochastic gradient descent.

Neural networks propagate the input via hidden layers to the output layer such that the input to neuron j (successor) from neuron i (predecessor) is given by the propagation function:

$$p_j(t) = \sum_i o_i(t) \cdot w_{ij} + w_{0j} \tag{8}$$

where w_{ij} is the weight assigned to the connection between node i and node j and w_{0j} is the bias. Learning in neural network happens by minimizing a cost function, backpropagating the error, and updating the weights of the network. The cost function depends on the task to solve, for example, $C = E\left[\left(f(x) - y\right)^2\right]$ minimizes the cost over the sample data by minimizing $\hat{C} = \frac{1}{N}\sum_{i=1}^{N} f\left(x_{(i)} - y_i\right)^2$, thus solving the task in an optimal way by learning from the individual samples.

Neural networks were proposed in the early 1990s and its first application on gene expression microarray analysis was in a study conducted by Khan et al. in 2001 for classifying small round blue cell tumor (SRBCT) samples into four different tumor categories (Khan et al., 2001). Neural networks combined with various other gene selection strategies have been proposed in subsequent years, with the most recent being application of deep learning networks. As the number of layers increases, the neural network is called a deep neural network. With deeper layers, the network is able to capture better subtle features within the data and the deep learning concepts are widely used in genomics, proteomics, drug discovery, etc.

Deep learning networks are a category of artificial neural networks that make use of error backpropagation technique to automatically learn relevant patterns in the data. It is essentially a neural network with several layers of nodes (approximately hundreds) built according to the depths required by the problem. Automatic feature extraction is done within the layers of the network. Figure 5.2 shows a typical deep learning network's architecture extracting features of a handwritten digit and classifying it. It learns higher levels of features from the compositions of lower level features in a hierarchical fashion. Thus, it is a representation learning method with representations of data at multiple levels, obtained by non-linear transformations of the representations at one level to a higher level of abstraction in the next level. There are different types of deep learning networks based on the architecture of the network, e.g., convolutional neural networks (CNN) (Fukushima, 1980), deep belief networks (DBN) (Hinton et al., 2006), deep stacking networks (DSN) (Deng and Yu, 2011), and AutoEncoders (AE) (Bengio and Lecun, 2007).

Clustering: An unsupervised learning method, clustering has been widely used in gene expression analysis. In clustering approaches, set of objects are grouped such that objects within a group are more similar than those between groups, with similarity being defined in terms of distance between objects, distribution of the objects, density of objects, clique in the case of graph-based models, etc. These algorithms can be broadly classified as connectivity-based (hierarchical), density-based, centroid-based, and distance-based approaches. Connectivity-based clustering requires the user to specify the distance to consider two objects to be in a cluster and the linkage criterion between objects, while hierarchical clustering forms clusters at various distances which can be represented using a dendrogram. In centroid-based clustering, distance of objects is computed from the centroid of a cluster to place the objects in appropriate clusters. Distribution-based clustering models make use of distribution models so that the objects belonging to the same cluster are more likely from the same distribution. In density-based clustering, clusters are identified as regions with higher density of objects and have been applied for feature selection in the classification of various cancer types (Loscalzo et al., 2009). Figure 5.3 presents examples of the different clustering techniques.

Probabilistic graphical models: Probabilistic graphical models, as the name suggests, bring together graph theory and probability theory and provide a framework for modeling high-dimensional data and the interactions between them (Koller and Friedman, 2009; Hartemink et al., 2000). In such a model, uncertainties associated with the data are represented using the probability values and the interactions

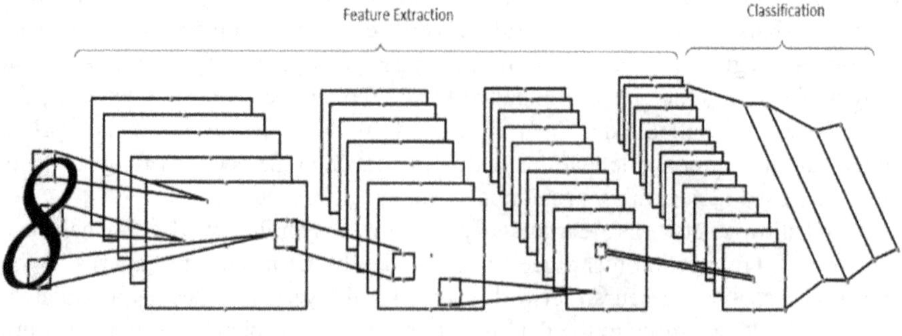

FIGURE 5.2 Representative deep learning network architecture.

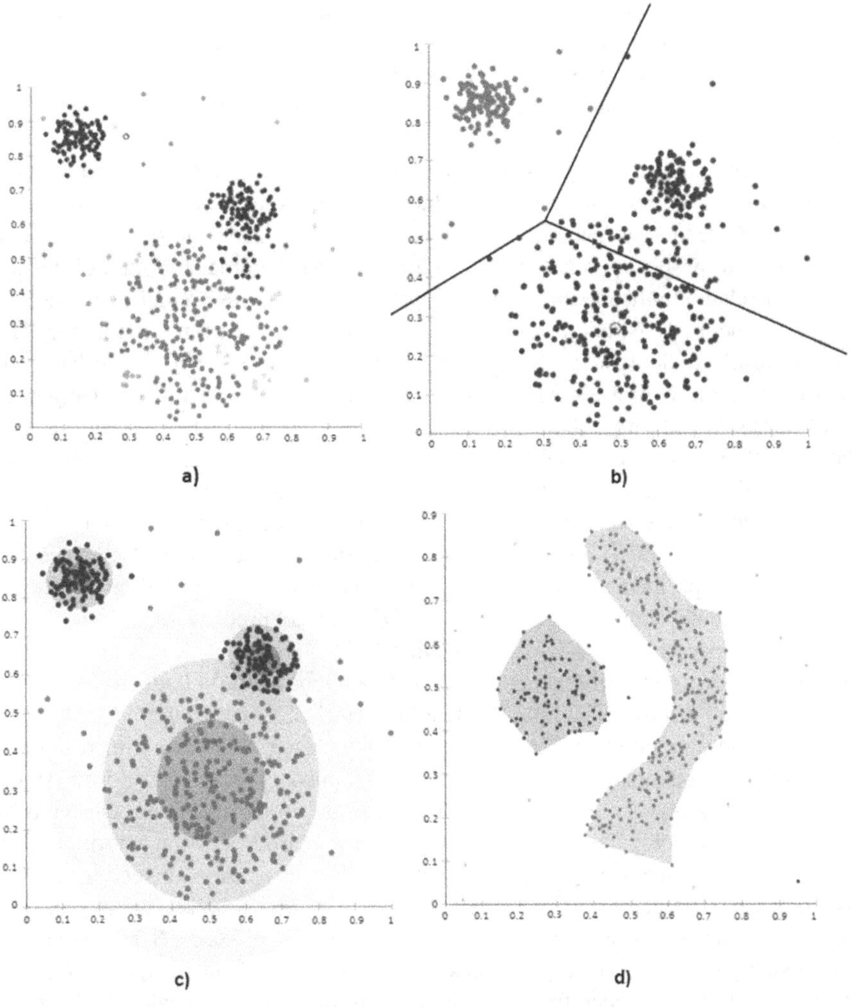

FIGURE 5.3 Clustering approaches: a) connectivity-based, b) centroid-based, c) distribution-based, d) density-based. (*Source:* https://en.wikipedia.org/wiki/Cluster_analysis.

among the variables are represented in a graph. The probabilities of the model are learned from the data and predictions made from the conditional probability calculations for the variable of interest given the observed variables. This is based on conditional independence assumption among variables.

5.4 RECENT APPLICATIONS OF ML IN CANCER DIAGNOSIS/CLASSIFICATION

Over the past two decades, various machine learning approaches have been proposed in the analysis of cancer samples. The methods vary from the analysis of gene expression data from microarrays and RNA sequencing to sequence and structural variation data such as single-nucleotide variations, insertion-deletions, and copy number variations to pathway enrichment. Below we give a brief review of these studies to give insight into the direction of research in cancer subtype classification and class discovery.

One of the pioneering works in cancer classification and discovery is the study by Golub et al. (1999) on a leukemia dataset comprising 27 acute lymphoblastic leukemia (ALL) and 11 acute myeloid leukemia (AML) samples. In this work two methods were proposed, one for class prediction and the other for class discovery. Genes correlated to the phenotype were identified by the class prediction method by neighborhood analysis that looks for genes exhibiting higher expression in one class and uniformly underexpressed in the other class. The genes were sorted based on their correlation to ALL or AML class and a small subset of "informative genes" (~50) were selected for prediction. Each informative gene then votes for a class with the strength of vote determined by the magnitude of its expression and its correlation with a particular class. Prediction strength (PS) is then determined from the sum of votes and provides confidence to the prediction. Assignment of samples to the predicted class is done if PS is above a predetermined value (~0.3), else considered uncertain. The performance of the 50-gene predictor was then tested on a different set of 34 leukemia samples and resulted in 29/34 correct predictions.

For class discovery, Self-Organizing Map (SOM) was used. It was proposed by Teuvo Kohonen as an artificial neural network (Kohonen, 1990). It identifies a specified number of "centroids" within the data to form clusters with centroid as the cluster center and data points around it as part of the cluster. SOM is a dimensionality reduction technique that uses an ANN and maps input data on to a lower dimensional space, typically two-dimensional. This results in the input data being clustered by preserving the topological properties of data. SOM is different from a normal ANN in its learning process, which is competitive rather than error correcting. It consists of a visualizable map space made up of interconnected nodes like a grid, each initialized with a random weight that represents the input space. The weights are continuously updated to bring it as close as possible to the input space, as depicted in Figure 5.4. The distance from each node to an input vector is calculated using a distance function, usually Euclidean distance, to identify most similar node to input

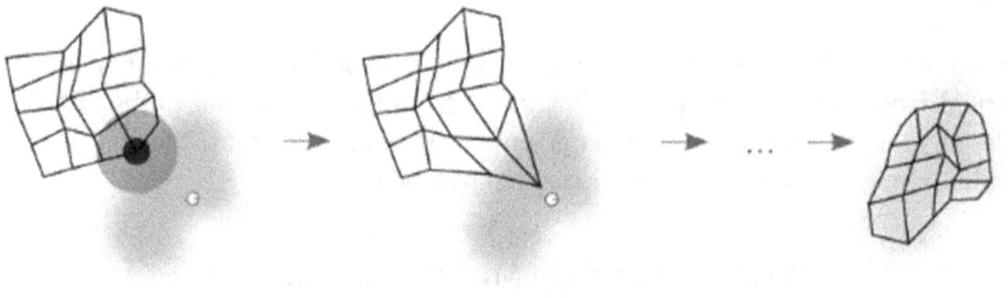

FIGURE 5.4 Illustration of training of self-organizing map. (*Source:* https://en.wikipedia.org/wiki/Self-organizing_map

vector, called a best matching unit (BMU). The neighboring nodes are identified with a neighborhood function based on the distance between BMU and a node. The process is repeated for each input for a number of iterations. As training proceeds, the magnitude of change in weights decreases and finally the output nodes unwind the pattern in the input data. SOM was applied to the same leukemia dataset of 38 samples and resulted in correctly grouping 24/25 samples of ALL and 10/13 samples of AML. The class discovery method was also applied to discover novel classes and evaluated using class prediction technique. The cross-validation of both the techniques, the neighborhood analysis and SOM, reported high accuracies.

In the study by Liu et al. (2004), various methods, namely, feature selection by Wilcoxon rank-sum test, clustering, and principal component analysis, followed by *t*-test and classification using three neural network models were carried out. In PCA, orthogonal linear transformation of the data matrix to a new coordinate system is done such that maximum variance is observed on the first coordinate, next higher variance on the second coordinate, and so on. By using multiple feature selection methods, the authors attempted to obtain a hypothesis that is closer to the true hypothesis by averaging over multiple hypotheses. Wilcoxon rank-sum test helped in identifying the top correlated genes, while PCA captured most of the variations in the samples and provided clustering information. This was followed by *t*-test for identifying lower ranked genes that may be associated with important biological pathways. An ensemble neural network was then chosen to classify the samples with the selected features and provided improved accuracy over a unitary network. The individual networks built using bagging method of resampling exhibited better performance over boosting approach in microarray data which are typically noisy. The results from multiple networks were combined using majority voting approach with confidence of each network output as voting value, instead of zero-one voting scheme. In this analysis, performance of the approach was evaluated on three categories of datasets: binary class with and without testing samples and multiclass. Seven cancer datasets were used for the analysis, viz., leukemia (binary class), lung, prostate, ovarian, DLBCL, colon, and leukemia (multiclass). The proposed method exhibited better or similar performance with other methods such as SVM, decision trees, etc., using LOOCV and 10-fold cross-validation methods.

In the study by Gevaert et al. (2006), a probabilistic model with a dependency structure was used to integrate microarray expression data and clinical data to extract relevant genes and other clinical characteristics contributing to the prognosis of breast cancer. The dependency structure captures the interdependency between the variables and is represented by directed edges, with no closed loops allowed. The probability distribution of how the variables depend on their parent variables is captured by using conditional probability tables (CPT). Probability of the variables is given by

$$p\left(x_1,\ldots,x_n\right)=\prod_{i=1}^{n} p\left(x_i | Pa\left(x_i\right)\right) \tag{9}$$

where $Pa(x_i)$ are the parents of x_i. The model building in this case involves learning the dependency structure and the parameters for CPTs as described below.

Structure Learning: In this case, the variables of interest are first arranged in a random order and model building is done by iterating the process with different permutations of ordering. The structure learning is through a greedy-based search strategy with the search space restricted by the order of variables, i.e., a variable is considered a parent only if it precedes the current variable in the ordered set. The searching algorithm starts with an empty set, iterates over the variables for finding the structure of the network by adding parents to a variable if the score of the structure, computed using Bayesian Dirichlet (BD) scoring metric (given by Equation (10)), improves on adding the parent variable to the structure. If not, the algorithm continues to the next variable in the ordered set. Once the entire list is exhausted, the algorithm terminates and the network with maximum score is selected.

$$p(S \mid D) \propto p(S) \prod_{i=1}^{n} \prod_{j=1}^{q_i} \left[\frac{(\Gamma(N'_{ij})}{\Gamma(N'_{ij} + N_{ij})} \prod_{k=1}^{r_i} \frac{\Gamma(N'_{ijk} + N_{ijk})}{\Gamma(N'_{ijk})} \right] \tag{10}$$

where N_{ijk} denotes number of samples that have variable i in state k with parent having jth instantiation in structure S. N_{ij} corresponds to samples with variable i summed over all states, N'_{ij}, similar to N_{ij}, requires prior knowledge for assertion of parameters. In the absence of prior knowledge, it is given by N/r_iq_i, where N is the sample size, r_i is the number of states the variable can assume, q_i is the number of instantiations of its parents, and $p(S)$ gives prior probability of structure S.

Parameter Learning: The next step in the model building process involves parameter estimation in CPTs corresponding to the structure learned in the previous step. Considering the outcome variable as "Prognosis" that takes two values: "poor" (recurrence of disease within 5 years after treatment) and "good" (5-year disease-free period), parent variables could be a gene expression (overexpressed [on]/under-expressed [off]) or a clinical characteristic (age ≥50 or <50). The Dirichlet score of the parameters which is initialized with a uniform prior value is updated during the parameter learning process. This is done by taking the maximum a posteriori (MAP) parameterization of Dirichlet distribution given by

$$p(\theta \mid D,S) = Dir(\theta_{ij} \mid N'_{ij1} + N_{ij1}, \ldots, N'_{ijk} + N_{ijk}, \ldots, N'_{ijr_i} + N_{ijr_i}) \tag{11}$$

Integration of microarray and clinical data involves full, partial, or decision-based integration. Of these, decision and partial integration methods are identified to be equally good. After integration from different orderings of training data,100 models were trained and one with maximum area under the curve was chosen. Given the Markov blanket, defined as the parents of a variable, children, and their other parents in a Bayesian network, a variable becomes conditionally independent of other variables. So, the Markov blanket of the outcome variable, prognosis in this case, is only required for classification purposes. Based on their analysis, age, grade, and angioinvasion, 13 genes were identified to fall under the Markov blanket.

There are very few unsupervised or semisupervised approaches applied to the analysis of gene expression data. One such study by Liu et al. (2006) is based on

SVD and seeded region growing clustering approach, a semisupervised algorithm. Singular value decomposition is an important concept in ML wherein a matrix is factorized into its components such that the resultant components are easy to handle. A real/complex matrix A can be decomposed as $U \sum V^T$, where the columns of matrices U and V are called left and right singular vectors of A, respectively, and $\sum$ is a diagonal matrix with non-negative real numbers representing the singular values of A. Orthonormal eigenvectors of AA^T and A^TA are the left and right singular vectors, respectively, and the non-negative singular values are the square roots of non-negative eigenvalues of AA^T and A^TA. By doing the conversion into factors, principal components of the matrix A are identified which can be further used for reducing the dimensions in the original matrix.

Spectral biclustering involves data normalization, bi-stochastization, and seeded region growing clustering. In data normalization step, logarithm of gene expression matrix A is obtained. Few cycles (5–10) of subtracting mean (or median) of rows and columns (i.e., genes and conditions) is performed followed by few cycles of row-column normalization. For bi-stochastization, first a matrix of interactions, K_{ij}, is defined by taking mean of rows (A_i), mean of columns (A_j), and mean of the matrix ($A_{..}$) as

$$K_{ij} = A_{ij} - A_i - A_j + A.. \tag{12}$$

Then SVD of the matrix is performed and eigenvalues determined. The eigenvectors corresponding to the largest s eigenvalues are also determined. The similarity measure between eigenvector and the genes is found using cosine similarity and for each eigenvector a set of genes which exhibit high similarity is chosen. The combination of genes chosen for each selected eigenvector is considered for evaluating their performance in classification using SVM and the set giving highest accuracy is chosen. Two datasets, lymphoma and liver cancer, were used to demonstrate the performance of the algorithm. Two pairs of genes from two eigenvectors were able to divide the samples into three types of lymphoid malignancies: chronic lymphocytic leukemia (CLL), follicular lymphoma (FL), and diffuse large B-cell lymphoma (DLBCL). One gene from two eigenvectors gave highest accuracy in classifying the samples into non-tumor and hepatocellular carcinoma (HCC).

A novel approach proposed by Zhang and Deng (2007) is based on Bayes error results in very few genes for classification. In this work, Based Bayes error Filter (BBF) method is implemented, which uses Bhattacharyya distance to identify genes that exhibit highest joined significance to the cancer class and simultaneously minimizes redundancy in the selected genes. The redundant genes thus identified by Bhattacharyya distance minimizes the Bayes error, known to be the lowest error probability achievable using a classifier according to Bayesian decision theory. It depends only on the features (genes) selected and not on the model used, which is the motivation behind this method. The classification error in this case is indirectly controlled by the Bhattacharyya distance as it gives an approximation to Bayes error. A preselected gene set with their individual relevance to cancer classes is used as input to the BBF method.

The algorithm comprises two steps. In the gene preselection step, relevant candidate genes are selected based on Wilcoxon rank-sum test with family-wise error rate (FWER ≤ 0.05) to evaluate the discriminative power of each gene in classifying a sample into one of the target classes. The second step applies redundancy filter using Bayes error to the preselected genes for removing redundancy. Starting with a single gene, the algorithm computes Bhattacharyya distance of every other gene from this gene. If the error exceeds a predefined cutoff, the gene is selected along with the first gene to the final list. The process is iteratively applied to the remaining genes till the required number of genes is selected, or the threshold on Bayes error is not met. The algorithm is evaluated using two classifiers, KNN and SVM with LOOCV, with error rate as the metric. In comparison to other methods such as minimum redundancy maximum relevance, simulated annealing, normalized mutual information, signal to noise ratio, information gain, etc., the proposed method chooses very small number of genes for attaining lowest error rates. The cancer datasets used in the study were colon, DLBCL, leukemia, prostate, and lymphoma. The number of genes identified with lowest error rate using KNN was 12, 6, 3, 11, and 8, respectively, and using SVM it was 20, 5, 2, 13, and 3, respectively, for the five cancer datasets.

Loscalzo et al. (2009) use dense group feature selection algorithm to identify group of features from a user-specified number of subsamples of the dataset. It finds core groups in the gene set with Kernel density estimation and iterative mean shift process. When the mean shift procedure converges, the nearby features of the mean will be grouped and returned by the algorithm. For every pair of genes, the algorithm computes a weight based on how often they were grouped together per subsample. With these weights, a hierarchical clustering of features is performed to form consensus groups. For every consensus group, a representative feature is selected and its relevance computed. On ordering the features based on relevance measure, k features are selected. A pairwise similarity comparison is done for calculating the similarity between features from different subsamples. Performance is evaluated using the genes selected for classification with SVM and KNN. Consensus group stable (CGS) feature selection is shown to have higher stability and accuracy than features selected by the algorithm DRAGS (dense relevant attribute group selector) and SVM-RFE.

Several methods proposed for cancer classification involves integration of more than one method for improving the performance. One such approach proposed by Song et al. (2013) has attempted to incorporate the advantages of RF algorithm and a generalized linear model (GLM). Random forest, even though highly accurate, is not interpretable, whereas a GLM can be used as a multipurpose model for binary/multiclass outcome prediction. The interpretability is better compared to RF because of forward variable selection of the features in the proposed approach. The method initially generates a number of equal-sized datasets, "nbags," from the original data using a bootstrap method by sampling with replacement. A random set of features chosen from each bag are sorted based on their correlation to outcome variable, considering absolute value of correlation coefficient to the output variable. The high ranked features were selected based on an input parameter "nCandidateCovariates" (default value 50) for each bag on which the forward variable selection method was applied to build a multivariable generalized linear model for each bag. The predictions from each model were then aggregated to give the final ensemble prediction. Results carried out on 20 disease-related and synthetic expression datasets and other UCI ML benchmark datasets showed better prediction accuracies with their method compared to SVM, KNN, and LDA.

Apart from expression data, mutation profiles of patients have also been used for cancer classification. In the study by Hofree et al. (2013), gene interaction networks for stratifying somatic mutation profiles of patients into biologically and clinically relevant subtypes have been proposed. The somatic mutation profiles are digital signals representing whether a gene is mutated or not while all other data types like gene expression provide continuous values for a measurement. Hence, the somatic mutation profiles give more precise results and are robust to noise. These profiles were projected onto gene interaction network and the mutations propagated to its network neighborhood using network propagation technique. The clustering of network-smoothed matrix of patient profiles was performed using non-negative matrix factorization method. Clustering result was further improved using consensus clustering technique. STRING, HumanNet, and PathwayCommons were the network data resources used for the analysis. Performance analysis of network-based stratification (NBS) to assign correct subtypes was carried out on ovarian tumor mutation data from TCGA, full exome sequence data of uterine, and ovarian and lung cancers from TCGA with standard consensus clustering without any network knowledge. The testing was also carried out on other data types, including copy number variations, mRNA expressions, methylation data, and protein profiles. The NBS subtypes were shown to give better performance and overlapped with results from other types of datasets.

Another clustering approach, a bottom-up hierarchical multiclass tree model, proposed by Tabl et al. (2018) uses Ward's linkage to discriminate different classes of samples by minimizing the within-cluster variance. In each branch of the tree, classifiers such as Naive Bayes and random forests were used to determine biomarker genes with most discriminative power for separating the classes and SVM was used to optimize the classifier's parameters. In this study, 347 out of 2433 breast cancer samples were categorized into six classes based on the available information about treatment given (hormone therapy, radiotherapy, or surgery) and the patient's status (alive or dead). Initial feature selection was done using chi-square, Info-Gain, and mRMR (minimum redundancy maximum relevance) methods. The class imbalance problem was addressed with methods such as SMOTE and resampling. The small set of genes selected by the algorithm for predicting the therapy was confirmed by enrichment analysis as the most responsive ones.

It is expected that different types of tumors may share some common features and this concept can be used to address the problem of limited data. The work of Liu et al. (2018) is one such study which integrates data from multiple domains to infer common functional modules, e.g., gene expression data across multiple types of tumors. It proposes considering association among domains by spectral clustering method to identify different clustering structures across multiple domains. It then computes consistency of the clustering structure to determine how associated domains may influence the clustering results. The approach makes use of domain relevance to build better clusters in each individual domain with the help of block Laplacian matrices B. The optimization problem in this case is to minimize the trace (U^TBU) subject to $U^TU = I_k$, where matrix U gives the assignment of objects to clusters. The eigenvector associated with smallest eigenvalue of Block signed Laplacian matrix is used to identify the initial candidate cluster. If the intracluster variance of the initial cluster is larger than a given threshold, it is split into more candidate clusters. When all intracluster variances are within a predefined cutoff, the algorithm proceeds to find intracluster variances based on the next eigenvector. In each iteration, adjacency matrix between domains is updated based on the clustering structure of the respective domain. Performance of the algorithm was evaluated on datasets of neural activity, gene expression data from colon, two types of kidney tumors, and another cohort of data from two types of lung, ovarian, and uterine cancers. The algorithm was able to find strongly and weakly correlated domains and overlapping genes from these domains along with better clustering in each domain. Gene ontology enrichment analysis and pathway enrichment analysis were carried out to confirm the correctness of results.

Another approach in classification studies is to apply ML algorithms at multiple levels such that input of the classifier at one level is fed as input to the second level and so on to improve the accuracy of classification. Xiao et al. (2018) proposed an ensemble of Machine Learning models in which prediction from models in the first stage form input to the models in the second stage. Five different classifiers were used in the first level: KNN, SVM, RFs, decision trees, and gradient-boosting decision trees. An ANN was used in the second stage to capture non-linear patterns for improving the prediction accuracy. In this study, DESeq (Anders and Huber, 2010) was used to identify differentially expressed genes (DEGs) and fed as input to the first-level model for classification. The second-level model was then trained on the predictions from the previous level for final classification.

In the first level, the dataset was divided into five subgroups D_1 to D_5 containing labeled points drawn independently and identically from the same distribution. In the first iteration, four subgroups D_1 to D_4 were combined to form training set and the remaining fifth group formed test set, where $D_i = \{x_i y_i\}$, x_i represents gene expression and y_i the corresponding label. For a given input x_1, five different models perform the classification and propose the corresponding hypotheses, $h_1(x_1)$, $h_2(x_2)$, …, $h_5(x_5)$, where $h_i(x_1)$ is a binary variable. Predictions of each model were assembled into $H_1 = [h_1(x_1), h_2(x_2), \ldots, h_5(x_5)]$ along with corresponding label y_1, which forms the input dataset D_{10} for the second level. The fivefold cross-validation was performed by repeating the procedure five times to generate five new datasets, $D_{i0} = \{H_i, y_i\}$, $i = 1, 2, \ldots, 5$.

In the second level, a five-layer ANN is used to classify the samples into normal/tumor. Five models obtained in the first stage are given as input to this model. Each hidden layer consists of different number of nodes and the output layer consists of a single node that predicts 0/1 for normal/tumor samples, respectively. A fivefold cross-validation is employed at this level also and the mean value is taken as the outcome. This ensemble approach of multiple models with a deep neural network reduces generalization error by considering the predictions from the first level as features in the second level compared to independently training the model using the data. The relationships among the first-level classifier's outcomes are learned automatically, resulting in improved prediction. Experiments were conducted on breast, stomach, and lung cancer RNASeq data from TCGA. Raw read counts were used for identifying differentially expressed genes and FPKM values for classification. The proposed deep learning method exhibited higher accuracies compared to the first-stage models and majority voting algorithm.

Under the assumption that there exist common features among different tumor types, Sevakula et al. proposed a transfer learning approach to train an autoencoder to learn its initial parameters and later fine-tune the parameters to specific problems (Sevakula et al., 2018). These methods make use of (general) solutions of similar problems in improving solutions for new (specific) problems. Autoencoders are multilayered neural networks that reconstruct the input data by generating an intermediate representation of the input features with fewer nodes in hidden layers. Since input is required to be reconstructed at output with minimal loss, the autoencoders learn the best possible latent space with a fewer number of features in the intermediate layers.

Initial feature selection in this case was done to rank features using the individual training error reduction (ITER) ranking method. A linear classifier was trained independently for each feature in the input data resulting in as many trained classifiers. The features were sorted based on training error and those with least training errors selected. Selected feature values were then normalized using zero-one normalization method or mean-variance normalization method. The weights in each layer of the neural network were initialized using autoencoders. For each layer, the autoencoder has a structure matching the corresponding layer. After the weights were learned, the weighted input was propagated to the next layer. This data serves as input to another autoencoder, having the same architecture for the next layer, to learn the weights for the next layer. This process of initialization of weights was continued till the last hidden layer. After initialization, weights of the deep neural network (DNN) were fine-tuned (median-based method) based on the target problem. The data when sent through the DNN was transformed to a more appropriate representation for classification. The newly constructed features were then fed to three classifiers: Softmax classifier, RF, and kernel SVM. In this study, unlabeled data from seven different types of tumor were considered for learning the abstract similarities of gene expression pattern, and two other types of tumor data for binary classification problem. The DNN used in the study had three hidden layers with respective dimensions of 900, 800, and 750. The dimension of the input layer was 1024, equal to the features selected based on ITER ranking. Using this DNN, the proposed algorithm statistically outperformed several classification approaches such as SVM, RF, PCA, and sequential forward selection.

5.5 WEB-BASED TOOLS

Various web-based tools based on Machine Learning approaches are available for analysis of gene expression and variation profiles and pathway enrichment (Lim and Wong, 2014). Few popular and recent tools are briefly discussed in this section.

A web-based tool, gene-set activity toolbox (GAT), to integrate gene expression data with gene networks to identify biomarkers of various cancers and classification of samples has been developed (Engchuan et al., 2016). It provides gene expression analysis and performance assessment of selected features with *k*-fold cross-validation. Functional analysis of the selected features and network visualization can also be performed. The classification of samples can be done using SVM, RF, or logistic regression.

The role of sequence and structural variants is well known in tumorigenesis. A decision support tool for variant reporting that makes use of RF and logistic regression models has been developed by Zomnir et al. (2018) to address the problem of understanding the output of complex bioinformatics pipeline for next-generation sequencing data. It provides a score in the range of 0–1 that represents the variant calling from no to yes, which can be verified by a pathologist and help to understand the reason behind the model's decision. That is, the model selection also takes into consideration the interpretability factor of the results.

The ML approach to predict *Ras* activity in solid tumors has been proposed by Way et al. (2018) and the code is available at https://github.com/greenelab/pancancer. It helps in categorizing abnormal pathway activities in tumors and the analysis of transcriptomes of patients who fail to respond to treatments. It has integrated RNASeq data, copy number variations, and small-sequence variations in 9075 tumors from 33 forms of cancers from PanCanAtlas project from TCGA. A supervised classifier, logistic regression with stochastic gradient descent, was trained on this data to predict whether the gene is activated or wild type. Only non-silent genic mutations and mutations at splice sites are considered. Additionally, data from oncogenes (*KRAS*, *NRAS*, and *HRAS*) for functional gain (by mutation or copy gain) and tumor suppressor *NF1* (copy loss) are integrated.

Numerous methods have been proposed for cancer subtype classification. A representative list of different categories of approaches is given in Table 5.1.

5.6 CONCLUSION

There is considerable research going on in applying Machine Learning and deep learning approaches for classification and feature selection of cancer samples. Major studies covered in this chapter discuss the analysis of microarray gene expression data and also few recent studies on RNA sequencing data and variation data. Most studies use some feature selection algorithm before applying a classification algorithm, of which filter-based approaches are most common. Few studies that consider wrapper, embedded, or hybrid methods are also discussed along with their advantages and limitations. The application and development of embedded methods in gene expression data analysis would provide a direction for future research.

It is observed that SVMs are most popular compared to other classification methods in gene expression analysis. This is probably because compared to other methods such as KNN, hierarchical clustering, etc., SVMs use distance functions that can operate in high-dimensional feature space. Because of this property, SVMs can accommodate the high correlations among genes and still find a hyperplane to

TABLE 5.1
A Representative List of Feature Selection and Classification Methods

Feature Selection Methods	Classifier	Validation Method	Datasets	Performance Metrics	Reference
SNR	Weighted voting SOM	CV	Leukemia	Accuracy	Golub et al., 1999
Wilcoxon rank-sum test, PCA, clustering followed by *t*-test	NN	LOOCV, 10-fold CV	Leukemia, lung, prostate, ovarian, DLBCL, colon	Accuracy	Liu et al., 2004
Bayesian network with K2 algorithm	Bayesian network with K2 algorithm	–	Breast	AUC Standard deviation	Gevaert et al., 2006
SVD	SVM	10-fold CV	Lymphoma, liver	Accuracy	Bing Liu et al., 2006
Wilcoxon rank-sum test	KNN, SVM	LOOCV	Leukemia, prostate, lymphoma, DLBCL, colon	Error rate	Zhang and Deng, 2007
CGS	SVM, KNN	10-fold CV	Leukemia, colon, lung, lymphoma, prostate, SRBCT	Accuracy, stability	Loscalzo et al., 2009
–	RGLM predictor	3-fold CV	Adenocarcinoma, brain, breast, lung, leukemia, colon, lymphoma, NCI60, prostate, DLBCL, SRBCT, multiple, sclerosis, psoriasis	Accuracy	Song et al., 2013
–	Negative matrix factorization, clustering	–	Ovarian, uterine, lung	–	Hofree et al. 2013
Chi-square, information gain, mRMR	Hierarchical bottom-up agglomerative clustering, Naive Bayes, RF	–	Breast	Accuracy, sensitivity, specificity, F-measure	Tabl et al., 2018

(Continued)

TABLE 5.1 (CONTINUED)
A Representative List of Feature Selection and Classification Methods

Feature Selection Methods	Classifier	Validation Method	Datasets	Performance Metrics	Reference
Graph clustering	K-means	–	Lung, kidney, ovarian, uterine, colon	Number of overlapped genes, enrichment analysis	Liu et al., 2018
–	KNN, SVM, DT, GBDT, RF, NN	Fivefold CV	Lung, stomach, breast	Precision, recall, accuracy	Xiao et al., 2018
Individual training error reduction ranking	SVM-linear, SVM-RBF, NN, RF	10-fold CV	Breast, lung, ovary, prostate, omentum, kidney, colon, endometrium, uterus	AUC, Friedman test, Bonferroni-Dunn test	Sevakula et al., 2018
Two sample *t*-statistic	DLD, FLDA, KNN	LOOCV, LKOCV	Colon, leukemia	Accuracy	Bø and Jonassen, 2002
Based on genetic algorithm	Maximum likelihood estimator	LOOCV	NCI60, GCM	Accuracy	Ooi and Tan, 2003
mRMR	K-means	LOOCV	SRBCT, breast, colon	Error rate	Liu et al., 2005
Structured penalized logistic regression	Structured penalized logistic regression	–	Leukemia, Lung, Colon, DLBCL, prostate	Youden Index, F1-score	Liu and Wong, 2019
RF	RF	OOB	Adenocarcinoma, brain, breast, leukemia, colon, lymphoma, NCI60, prostate, SRBCT	Accuracy, error rate	Díaz-Uriarte and Alvarez de Andrés, 2006
PCA, Relief-F, gain ratio, information gain	SVM, RF, logistic regression, multilayer perceptron	*k*-fold cross-validation	Breast, lung, colorectal	AUC, recall	Engchuan et al., 2016

SNR: signal-to-noise ratio, SOM: self-organizing map, CV: cross-validation, PCA: principal component analysis, NN: neural network, LOOCV: leave-one-out cross-validation, DLBCL: diffuse large B-cell lymphoma, AUC: area under ROC curve, SVD: singular value decomposition, SVM: support vector machine, KNN: K-nearest neighbor, CGS: consensus group stable, RF: random forest, RGLM: random generalized linear model, SRBCT: small-round-blue-cell tumor, mRMR: minimum redundancy maximum relevancy, DT: decision tree, GBDT: gradient boosting decision tree, SVM-RBF: SVM-radial basis function, DLD: diagonal linear discriminant, FLDA: Fisher's linear discriminant analysis, LKOCV: leave-K-out cross-validation.

distinguish between classes in the dataset. Further, its ability to rank features based on their distance from the hyperplane helps in selecting best features for discrimination. However, the results of SVM are not interpretable; it behaves like a black box and does not reveal much on why the decision was made for a particular non-linear kernel function chosen. Due to the properties like interpretability and ability to measure importance of variable, RFs are equally widely used in gene expression analysis. The random sampling and ensemble strategies applied in RFs are observed to result in better accuracies and generalizations. KNN is another classification method that has been used for over two decades in this field due to its simplicity. It is the simplest Machine Learning algorithm to use if the number of classes in a dataset is known a priori. Clustering approaches are popular in gene expression data analysis due to the ease of understandability. Neural networks and deep learning networks are finding a fresh and unmatchable application in many domains, including gene expression analysis. The power of deep learning networks to capture the relationships among genes and high accuracies in decision-making are the reasons behind their acceptance. These networks are capable of handling high-dimensional data and give intermediate feature representations with much lesser dimensions. There definitely is lot of scope in exploring these models for interpretability of results which would make them more suitable for use in cancer detection and subtype classification in clinical settings.

Majority of the classification methods reviewed here fall under the supervised category and require a huge number of labeled samples for training the model. The limited availability of cancer datasets makes the application of these methods difficult because of the problem of overfitting. Data merging is a possible solution to this problem, but integrating data from multiple platforms and from different technologies is a tedious task. Research can be directed toward the area of data integration which can be a breakthrough in gene expression data analysis and related fields. Unsupervised and semisupervised algorithms may be further explored as most available gene expression data are unlabeled.

REFERENCES

Anders, S., & Huber, W. (2010). Differential expression analysis for sequence count data. *Genome Biology*, *11*(10), R106. doi: 10.1186/gb-2010-11-10-r106

Ang, J. C., Mirzal, A., Haron, H., & Hamed, H. N. A. (2016). Supervised, unsupervised, and semi-supervised feature selection: A review on gene selection. *IEEE/ACM Transactions on Computational Biology and Bioinformatics*, *13*(5), 971–989. doi: 10.1109/TCBB.2015.2478454.

Bengio, Y., & Lecun, Y. (2007). Scaling learning algorithms towards AI. *Large-Scale Kernel Machines*. Retrieved from https://nyuscholars.nyu.edu/en/publications/scaling-learning-algorithms-towards-ai.

Bing Liu, Wan, C., & Lipo Wang. (2006). An efficient semi-unsupervised gene selection method via spectral biclustering. *IEEE Transactions on NanoBioscience*, *5*(2), 110–114. doi: 10.1109/TNB.2006.875040.

Bø, T., & Jonassen, I. (2002). New feature subset selection procedures for classification of expression profiles. *Genome Biology*, *3*(4), RESEARCH0017.

Breiman, L. (2001). Random forests. *Machine Learning, 45*(1), 5–32. doi: 10.1023/A:1010933404324.

Cortes, C., & Vapnik, V. (1995). Support-vector networks. *Machine Learning, 20*(3), 273–297. doi: 10.1007/BF00994018.

Deng, L., & Yu, D. (2011). *Deep Convex Network: A Scalable Architecture for Speech Pattern Classification.* Retrieved from https://www.microsoft.com/en-us/research/publication/deep-convex-network-a-scalable-architecture-for-speech-pattern-classification/.

Díaz-Uriarte, R., & Alvarez de Andrés, S. (2006). Gene selection and classification of microarray data using random forest. *BMC Bioinformatics, 7*, 3. doi: 10.1186/1471-2105-7-3.

Engchuan, W., Meechai, A., Tongsima, S., Doungpan, N., & Chan, J. H. (2016). Gene-set activity toolbox (GAT): A platform for microarray-based cancer diagnosis using an integrative gene-set analysis approach. *Journal of Bioinformatics and Computational Biology, 14*(4), 1650015. doi: 10.1142/S0219720016500153.

Fukushima, K. (1980). Neocognitron: A self-organizing neural network model for a mechanism of pattern recognition unaffected by shift in position. *Biological Cybernetics, 36*(4), 193–202. doi: 10.1007/BF00344251.

Gevaert, O., De Smet, F., Timmerman, D., Moreau, Y., & De Moor, B. (2006). Predicting the prognosis of breast cancer by integrating clinical and microarray data with Bayesian networks. *Bioinformatics (Oxford, England), 22*(14), e184–e190. doi: 10.1093/bioinformatics/btl230.

Golub, T. R., Slonim, D. K., Tamayo, P., Huard, C., Gaasenbeek, M., Mesirov, J. P., … Lander, E. S. (1999). Molecular classification of cancer: Class discovery and class prediction by gene expression monitoring. *Science (New York, N.Y.), 286*(5439), 531–537.

Hartemink, A. J., Gifford, D. K., Jaakkola, T. S., & Young, R. A. (2000). Using graphical models and genomic expression data to statistically validate models of genetic regulatory networks. *Biocomputing, 2001*, 422–433. doi: 10.1142/9789814447362_0042.

Hinton, G. E., Osindero, S., & Teh, Y.-W. (2006). A fast learning algorithm for deep belief nets. *Neural Computation, 18*(7), 1527–1554. doi: 10.1162/neco.2006.18.7.1527.

Hofree, M., Shen, J. P., Carter, H., Gross, A., & Ideker, T. (2013). Network-based stratification of tumor mutations. *Nature Methods, 10*(11), 1108–1115. doi: 10.1038/nmeth.2651.

Huang, M.-W., Chen, C.-W., Lin, W.-C., Ke, S.-W., & Tsai, C.-F. (2017). SVM and SVM ensembles in breast cancer prediction. *PLOS ONE, 12*(1), e0161501. doi: 10.1371/journal.pone.0161501.

Khan, J., Wei, J. S., Ringnér, M., Saal, L. H., Ladanyi, M., Westermann, F., … Meltzer, P. S. (2001). Classification and diagnostic prediction of cancers using gene expression profiling and artificial neural networks. *Nature Medicine, 7*(6), 673–679. doi: 10.1038/89044.

Kohonen, T. (1990). The self-organizing map. *Proceedings of the IEEE, 78*(9), 1464–1480. doi: 10.1109/5.58325.

Koller, D., & Friedman, N. (2009). *Probabilistic Graphical Models: Principles and Techniques.* MIT Press.

Lim, K., & Wong, L. (2014). Finding consistent disease subnetworks using PFSNet. *Bioinformatics (Oxford, England), 30*(2), 189–196. doi: 10.1093/bioinformatics/btt625.

Liu, B., Cui, Q., Jiang, T., & Ma, S. (2004). A combinational feature selection and ensemble neural network method for classification of gene expression data. *BMC Bioinformatics, 5*, 136. doi: 10.1186/1471-2105-5-136.

Liu, C., & Wong, H. S. (2019). Structured penalized logistic regression for gene selection in gene expression data analysis. *IEEE/ACM Transactions on Computational Biology and Bioinformatics, 16*(1), 312–321. doi: 10.1109/TCBB.2017.2767589.

Liu, X., Krishnan, A., & Mondry, A. (2005). An entropy-based gene selection method for cancer classification using microarray data. *BMC Bioinformatics, 6*, 76. doi: 10.1186/1471-2105-6-76.

Liu, Y., Ng, M. K., & Wu, S. (2018). Multi-domain networks association for biological data using block signed graph clustering. *IEEE/ACM Transactions on Computational Biology and Bioinformatics*, *17*(2), 1–1. doi: 10.1109/TCBB.2018.2848904.

Loscalzo, S., Yu, L., & Ding, C. (2009). Consensus group stable feature selection. In *Proceedings of the 15th ACM SIGKDD International Conference on Knowledge Discovery and Data Mining*, 567–576. doi: 10.1145/1557019.1557084.

Marsland, S. (2011). *Machine Learning: An Algorithmic Perspective* (1st ed.), Chapman and Hall/CRC. doi: 10.1201/9781420067194.

Network-based stratification of tumor mutations | Nature Methods. (n.d.). Retrieved March 22, 2019, from https://www.nature.com/articles/nmeth.2651.

Ooi, C. H., & Tan, P. (2003). Genetic algorithms applied to multi-class prediction for the analysis of gene expression data. *Bioinformatics (Oxford, England)*, *19*(1), 37–44.

Seber, G. A. F., & Lee, A. J. (2012). *Linear Regression Analysis*. John Wiley & Sons.

Sevakula, R. K., Singh, V., Verma, N. K., Kumar, C., & Cui, Y. (2018). Transfer learning for molecular cancer classification using deep neural networks. *IEEE/ACM Transactions on Computational Biology and Bioinformatics*, *16*(6), 1–1. doi: 10.1109/TCBB.2018.2822803.

Song, L., Langfelder, P., & Horvath, S. (2013). Random generalized linear model: A highly accurate and interpretable ensemble predictor. *BMC Bioinformatics*, *14*, 5. doi: 10.1186/1471-2105-14-5

Tabl, A. A., Alkhateeb, A., Pham, H. Q., Rueda, L., ElMaraghy, W., & Ngom, A. (2018). A novel approach for identifying relevant genes for breast cancer survivability on specific therapies. *Evolutionary Bioinformatics Online*, *14*, 1176934318790266. doi: 10.1177/1176934318790266

Unsupervised Learning: Clustering. (n.d.). 54.

Way, G. P., Sanchez-Vega, F., La, K., Armenia, J., Chatila, W. K., Luna, A., … Greene, C. S. (2018). Machine learning detects Pan-cancer Ras pathway activation in the cancer genome atlas. *Cell Reports*, *23*(1), 172–180.e3. doi: 10.1016/j.celrep.2018.03.046

Xiao, Y., Wu, J., Lin, Z., & Zhao, X. (2018). A deep learning-based multi-model ensemble method for cancer prediction. *Computer Methods and Programs in Biomedicine*, *153*, 1–9. doi: 10.1016/j.cmpb.2017.09.005.

Zhang, J.-G., & Deng, H.-W. (2007). Gene selection for classification of microarray data based on the Bayes error. *BMC Bioinformatics*, *8*(1), 370. doi: 10.1186/1471-2105-8-370.

Zomnir, M. G., Lipkin, L., Pacula, M., Dominguez Meneses, E., MacLeay, A., Duraisamy, S., … Lennerz, J. K. (2018). Artificial intelligence approach for variant reporting. *JCO Clinical Cancer Informatics*, (2) 1–13. doi: 10.1200/CCI.16.00079.

6 Pancreatic Cancer Detection by an Integrated Level Set-Based Deep Learning Model

Arti Taneja, Priya Ranjan, Amit Ujlayan, and Rajiv Janardhanan

CONTENTS

6.1 INTRODUCTION

On the basis of the patient history and clinically apparent symptoms, the diagnosis of the pancreatic pseudocysts has become difficult in recent medical scenarios. The basic diagnostics requires computed tomography (CT) images of the round, fluid-filled structures of cysts [1]. The pseudocysts and the pancreatic mucinous cysts are hard to discriminate in some images. Pancreas segmentation is an essential step in the early computer-aided diagnosis for quantitative analysis. But an accurate segmentation of pancreatic images is a challenging task due to its shape, size, and location in the abdominal region [2]. Pancreas is an anatomical variable organ within which the abdominal cavity varies from patient to patient [3]. The boundary contrast may vary due to the quantity of visceral fat in the proximity of the pancreas. This makes segmentation of the pancreas a challenging task. Hence, the pancreas segmentation becomes more difficult than other segmentation tasks with the statistical models [4]. The application of Convnets shows good promising results with the progressive pruning.

The factors which have a great impact on classification are features, edges, and appearance consistency and inconsistency. Hence, the important visual cues for the segmentation process are in obtaining hierarchical features corresponding to the boundary and interior [5]. Achieving accuracy and pixel-level labeling consistency requires these important visual cues. Image segmentation, object detection, and localization are generalized with the neural network formulation due to their flexibility and limited modifications. Recently, various research studies have shown that computed tomography [6, 7] is an efficient method to estimate pancreatic atrophy in patients. The review of image features such as mass size, location, shape, wall thickness, cyst configuration, and signal intensity of the lesions with heterogeneity is performed. The cystic fibrosis–related diabetes (CFRD) [8] is a different form of diabetes mellitus (DM) and hence improvement in care and treatment is required. CFRD hypothesizes that there are differences in the size and morphology of the pancreas of patients with cystic fibrosis (CF). It projects two objectives such as the comparison of the volume and features of patients with and without CFRD, and The correlation between the pancreas volume with age-matched non-CF patients as well as long-standing type 1 diabetes mellitus (T1DM) with healthy controls. The cystic pancreatic lesions are majorly non-malignant lesions consisting of pseudocysts, mucinous cystic neoplasms, intraductal papillary mucinous neoplasms (IPMN), solid pseudo-papillary tumor (SPT), and lymph epithelial cysts. Among these, the IPMN, mucinous cyst adenomas, and SPT have malignant potential but less frequent. Also, the malignant lesions of the pancreas are comprised of cystic variants like endocrine tumors, metastases, and ductal adenocarcinomas. Conversely, cystic variations in large pancreatic lesions generally exist in adenocarcinomas and endocrine tumors [9]. The pancreatic cancer patients have poor diagnosis in which most of the patients affected with pancreatic cancers are diagnosed at advanced stages. This poor diagnosis causes difficulty in diagnosing pancreatic cancer early. Most of these pancreatic cancers arise from the branches of the pancreatic duct. Generally, the diameter of the pancreatic duct is 2–3 mm. If small duct cell pancreatic carcinoma is presented in the branch, the lesion can be detected due to the obstruction [10]. The ultimate objective of the proposed work is to efficiently segment the pancreas from the abdominal images irrespective of the probable map variations and to improve the accuracy and Dice coefficients effectively. An integrated framework of Gaussian formulation with the double-well level set function predicts the region of interest (ROI) effectively. The multi-angular n-ternary pattern extraction predicts the features that describe the edge information clearly. Diverse patterns based on multi-directions efficiently support the clear image analysis. The integration of level set formulation with the convolution neural network (CNN)-based classification increases the classification performance, which highly contributes towards the early detection applications. The rest of the chapter is organized as follows: Section 6.2 describes the related work available for the pancreas segmentation. Section 6.3

discusses the implementation process of the proposed integrated framework of level set function with the convolution Neural network (IF-CNN) to segment the pancreas in the input images. Section 6.4 describes the performance analysis of the proposed work. This chapter concludes with Section 6.9.

6.2 RELATED WORK

Roth et al. [11] presented the fully automated bottom approach to segment the pancreas in CT abdominal images. Based on the coarse to fine classification of local image regions, the extraction of superpixels was carried out by a method called simple linear iterative clustering (SLIC) [12]. The assignment of distinct probabilities was the prior stage in SLIC to state whether the region was pancreas or not. Roth et al. [13] extended their approach by applying the dense labeling of local image patches by integration of SLIC with the nearest neighbor fusion. The application of these integrated methods improved the Dice similarity coefficient in both training and testing stages. Besides, Roth et al. [14] utilized holistic learning through the integration of semantic midlevel cues with the interior and boundary maps. The generation of boundary preserving pixel-wise labels was the necessary stage for pancreas segmentation. An analysis of statistical differences of the CT features was performed with two different tests: Student's test and Fisher's test. Age, size, and the total number of locules in tumors in two groups were compared in Student's test. The shape, location, wall thickness, and cyst configuration were analyzed using Fisher's test. Farag et al. [15] presented the fully automated bottom-up approach to segment the pancreas into four stages: (i) decomposition of image slices into the disjoint boundary-preserving superpixels, (ii) probability estimation through the dense patch labeling, (iii) pooling of intensity and probability features for cascaded random forest, and (iv) connectivity-based postprocessing. The segmentation through the deep patch labeling confidences was the stable approach against the small deviations in parameter variations. Moeskops et al. [16] investigated the issues of single CNN training to segment the MRI brain images, pectoral images, and the coronary arteries in the heart through the learning of image modalities and their visual anatomical structures. The single system utilization to perform the diverse segmentation tasks without any training was achieved. Cai et al. [17] formulated the pancreas segmentation as the graph-based decision fusion, which was integrated with the deep CNN models in the MRI scans. Two models—tissue detection and boundary detection—were employed with the spatial intensity context and semantic boundaries allocation, respectively. The final segmented output was generated through the initialization of conditional random field (CRF) [18] framework with the fusion of results obtained from the above processes. Wang et al. [19] presented the novel-patch-based label propagation approach, which uses the relative geodesic distances to define the patient-specific systems as spatial context to overcome the issues in the existing methods. Wolz et al. [20] applied the automatic intensity learning model with the incorporation of high-level spatial knowledge to handle the inter-subject variation. They evaluated the segmentation performance on 150 manually segmented images against the various existing methods. The generation of target-specific priors was a major issue in an automatic segmentation method. Tong et al. [21] applied the postprocessing step based on graph-cut (GC) methods. Besides, the voxel-wise local atlas selection strategy was proposed to handle the intersubject variations effectively. Lucchi et al. [22] proposed the automated graph-partitioning methods that incorporate the shape and distinctive shape learning for better recognition. They demonstrated better computational efficiency and segmentation quality. Lucchi et al. [22] concluded that a suitable weight estimation and a multilevel set formulation are required to provide the optimal trade-off between the accuracy improvement and clear image analysis. The automated assisted reading (AAR) technique used in the cervical screening process has less error rates and maximum productivity, depending on the accurate segmentation of abnormal cells. Zhang et al. [23] proposed the global/local scheme with the graph-cut approaches that utilized the combination of normal and abnormal cells. The tumor histopathology characterization defined the nuclear regions from the hematoxylin and eosin stained tissue sections. Chang et al. [24] performed the automated analysis by using the nuclear segmentation formulation within the graph framework. They presented the multi-reference graph cut (MRGC) with the prior knowledge regarding the reference and local image features. Zhang et al. [25] introduced the autofocusing method that rejected the coverslip and the actual focal plan was extracted. The hybrid global and local schemes segmented the normal and abnormal cells by CNN-based approach with three-dimensional filters. The existing CNN approaches on medical image segmentation allowed full access to three-dimensional structures. But they had some challenges such as high-class imbalance in the ground truth, high memory requirement, and shortage of labeled data. To overcome the above-mentioned issues, two modifications in CNN were incorporated and discussed in this work. Here a network architecture related to the U-net architecture was used. The two modifications in this architecture were that the multiple segmentation maps created at various scales were combined and the feature maps were forwarded from one stage to the other stage of the network by using element-wise summation. Litjens et al. [27] reviewed the major deep learning concepts related to medical imaging analysis. Various methods such as CNN, fCNN, RNN, and auto-encoders and stacked auto-encoders such as U-net and V-net were discussed in this survey. Their performance analyses were evaluated and compared. Milletari et al. [28] proposed an approach to 3D image segmentation based on the volumetric, fully conventional neural network. Here a novel objective function was introduced to optimize the system based on the Dice coefficient. The histogram matching and random non-linear transformations were applied to manage with the limited number of annotated volumes in training. The major drawback was the segmentation of volumes with multiple regions and higher resolutions. Sudre et al. [29] investigated the behavior of loss functions and sensitivity of rate tuning due to the presence of various label imbalance rates in the 2D and 3D segmentation processes. Also, a known metric for assessing the segmentation was proposed by using class rebalancing properties of generalized Dice overlap.

6.3 INTEGRATED LEVEL SET-BASED DEEP LEARNING

The proposed work comprises four new methods to segment the pancreas from the abdominal images. First, the Laplacian-based filtering is used to remove the noise present in the image and enhance the quality level. Then, the Gaussian operator is integrated with the level set formulation to segment the pancreas among other organs from the abdominal images due to high anatomical variability across patients from diverse genetic makeup. Second, the weight update with the level set estimates the region of interest (ROI-pancreas). Here, the N-ternary pattern extracts the texture pattern features of the pancreas in the form of angle variations. Finally, the CNN model predicts the classes of normal and abnormal effectively. The periodical weight update by level set, N-ternary patterns, and CNN improved the performance effectively.

6.4 LAPLACIAN-BASED PREPROCESSING

Noise removal is the initial stage in a proposed algorithm which includes the Laplacian of Gaussian (LoG) function for noise filtering in images. The Laplacian operator is considered as the 2D isotropic model, which measures the second spatial derivative of the input image $I(x,y)$. The rapid changes in the pixel intensity values are highlighted with this operator. Traditionally, the Gaussian filter is used to remove the noise present in the images. But its sensitivity to the noise variations is high and hence an approximation is required. The Laplacian operator is applied to provide such a smoothening effect on the images. The Laplacian $L(x,y)$ of the input image $I(x,y)$ is expressed as follows:

$$L(x,y) = \frac{\partial^2 I}{\partial x^2} + \frac{\partial^2 I}{\partial y^2} \tag{1}$$

Due to the image representation in a discrete set of pixels, an approximation of second-order derivatives was obtained by computing the discrete set of kernels, as shown in Figure 6.1. With these kernels, the LoG function is estimated by the standard convolution methods. Prior to the differentiation step, the reduction of high-frequency noise components was performed using the Laplacian operator. The convolving of Gaussian with the Laplacian operator followed by convolving of this hybrid filter with the image provides the required noise-free image effectively.

The two-dimensional LoG function with the zero mean and standard deviation σ is expressed as follows:

$$\log(x,y) = \frac{-1}{\pi\sigma^4}\left[1 - \frac{x^2+y^2}{2\sigma^2}\right] e^{\frac{-x^2+y^2}{2\sigma^2}} \tag{2}$$

The calculation of the second spatial derivative of the image means that the LoG response is zero for the regions having constant intensity. If there are any changes in pixel intensities, then the Laplacian response is positive for the darker side and it

0	-1	0
-1	4	-1
0	-1	0

(a)

-1	-1	-1
-1	8	-1
-1	-1	-1

(b)

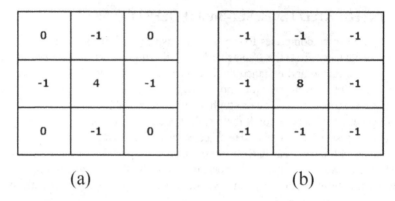

FIGURE 6.1 Kernels matrix for Laplacian of Gaussian preprocessing of the image.

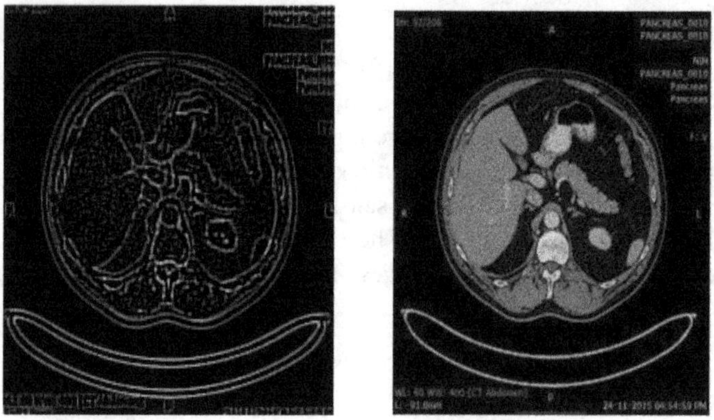

(a) (b)

FIGURE 6.2 CT images before and after preprocessing step to make segmentation step more accurate.

is negative for the brighter side. The edge extracted from the Laplacian operator is sharp across the different pixel intensities. Figure 6.2 (a) and (b) show the Gaussian-filtered and Laplacian-smoothened images, respectively.

After obtaining the preprocessed images, the ROI (the pancreatic region) in the abdominal image is necessitated. In order to accomplish such a refined delineation of the original abdominal image, the integrated level set segmentation procedure is employed.

6.5 INTEGRATED LEVEL SET-BASED SEGMENTATION

The proposed workflow comprises four new methods to segment the pancreas from the abdominal images. First and foremost, the Laplacian-based filtering has been used to remove the noise present in the image and enhance its quality (Figure 6.3).

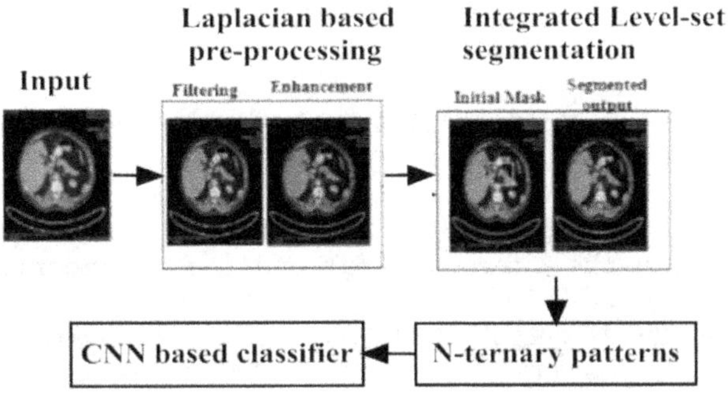

FIGURE 6.3 Operational steps of the designed system: (i) original image, (ii) filtered and enhanced image, (iii) initial mask as an input to the level set algorithm and ROI segmentation using level sets, (iv) feature extraction, and (v) convolutional neural networks for classification into categories benign and malignant.

6.6 N-TERNARY PATTERNS

The traditional N-ternary pattern described in Reference [30] is considered as the base for the proposed pattern extraction. The modeling of lower and upper ternary patterns corresponding to the 5 × 5 pixel to represent the image highly contributes to the clear information extraction by using the comparison among the center and neighborhood pixels. Initially, the enhanced image set is processed through our proposed LNTP algorithm and the major difference that lies between the existing N-ternary patterns and our algorithm is the pixel value selection for comparison. In the traditional approach, the center pixel value is selected for comparison. Alternatively, the median value is selected in proposed LNTP (median value 2). Then, the row (R) and column (C) values corresponding to the pixel values of (3, 4), (2, 4), (2, 3), (2, 2), (3, 2), (4, 2), (4, 3), and (4, 4) are updated by subtracting the median value (*med*). The algorithm to extract the patterns for the enhanced image set is listed as follows.

```
Local N-ternary pattern
Input: Segmented image (seg_i)
Output: Output patterns for categorized images

Procedure:
Initialize I (m,n)=size(seg_i) // Consider image size (m,n)=
(256x256)
Let D= [0°,45°, 90°,135°,180°,225°,270°,315°,360°]
For R= 3,C=3 to m-2,n-2
Select the 5x5 pixel window from I, img=I(R-2:R+2, C-2:C+2)
Med= Min C(Min R(img)) //median value
Let k=2;
//For 0° angle :

If(abs _dif(img(R,C+2)-img(R,C+1) ) > abs_dif(img(R,C+1)-med))
Set Low (R, C+1)=1; Up(R, C+1)=0;
```

```
Else if ( abs_dif(img(R,C+2)-img(R,C+1) ) <
abs_dif(img(R,C+1)-med+k))

Set Low(R, C+1)=0; Up(R, C+1)=1;
Else Set Low(R, C+1)=0; Up(R, C+1)=0;
End if;
// simil Early compute in 45°, 90°, 135°,180°, 225°, 270°,315°,
360° considering the current pixel and the neighboring pixel.

LowPattern(R,C)= Low(360°)*2^8+Low(315°)*2^7+ Low(270°)*2^6+
Low (225°)*2^5+ Low (180°)*2^4+ Low (135°)*2^3+ Low (90°)*2^2+
Low (45°)*2^1+ Low (0°)*2^0;
UpPattern(R,C)= Up (360°)*2^8+Up (315°)*2^7+ Up (270°)*2^6+ Up
(225°)*2^5+ Up (180°)*2^4+ Up (135°)*2^3+ Up (95°)*2^2+ Up
(45°)*2^1+ Up (0°)*2^0;
End for R,C;
```

6.7 CNN-BASED DEEP LEARNING

The output patterns from N-ternary are passed to the CNN, as shown in Figure 6.4. The CNN in machine learning is a deep, feedforward artificial neural network which can be used for analyzing the visual imagery. Generally, it uses a variety of multilayer perceptron, which is designed for the requirement of minimal preprocessing. It comprises an input layer, an output layer, and three hidden layers. These hidden layers mainly contain convolution layers, pooling layers, normalized layers, and fully connected layers. In the convolution layer, a sliding window is running through the image. The subimages are convolved with the size and number of kernel/filters used in each layer at each step of the convolution layer, which produces a new layer while increasing the depth. The volume down-sampling is done by the pooling layer by using some aspects along with the spatial dimensions. This makes the model more efficient by reducing the size of the representations and the number of parameters. It also helps to avoid overfitting. The max-pooling layer is the most used pooling layer

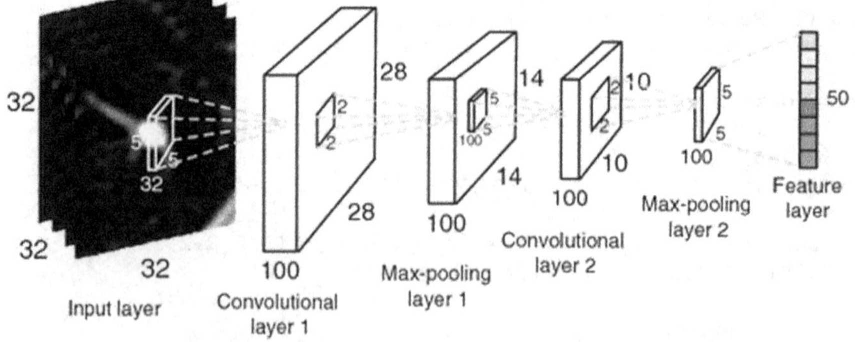

FIGURE 6.4 CNN classification.

which uses the maximum value of the cluster of neurons from the previous layer of each down-sampled block.

A non-linearity which mapped the score at each neuron can be applied after each layer in CNN. It helps to improve the speed, accuracy, and training time of the system. Generally, the sigmoid function is used in this non-linearity function, but here the *tanh* function is used which maps the real numbers in the interval of [–1, –1] and this can be represented as

$$\tanh(x) = \frac{\left(e^{x} - e^{-x}\right)}{e^{x} + e^{-x}} \tag{15}$$

In this work, the *tanh* function is integrated with the most popular non-linearity function, which is termed as rectified linear unit (ReLU). In this, *tanh* is computed after the convolution and therefore a non-linear activation functions like a sigmoid. Due to its simple and linear form, this ReLU function has become more popular in activation function, which also helps to improve the speed of stochastic gradient descent (SGD). Moreover, it does not involve any experimental validations, so it is easy to evaluate. Even though these ReLUs are fragile, they can die permanently while training. In order to overcome the above-mentioned problem, leaky ReLU is used which contains a small negative slope for negative inputs. But the ReLU helps to enhance the accuracy and training time. The definition of ReLU function is described as

$$f(x) = \max(0, x) \qquad 16)$$

Initially, the labels are initialized as n and $L = 1$. The patterns corresponding to the edge are assigned as P. The maximum and the mean of patterns are computed, and they can be regarded as M and N, respectively. The limit of subdivided intervals for the classification process lies in the range $(1 < \frac{1}{n} < N)$. Then, the rules necessary to perform the classification process are extracted as follows:

$$R = SF\left(M - N\right)* \tag{17}$$

where SF is the selected feature of a matrix.

The neighbor link parameter (ρ_t) and the kernel function (K) are necessary for accurate classification:

$$\rho_t = SF^{-1}\, TS(t) \tag{18}$$

$$K = R^{-1}\varnothing(t) \tag{19}$$

where SF^{-1} is the selected feature of the inverse matrix.

TS is the tested feature set.

The training feature set with the neighbor link and the kernel parameter for the mapping process is constructed by

$$P_i = K_i + \rho_i = R^{-1}\varnothing(i) + \rho_i \tag{20}$$

The probability distribution on feature set for neighboring features to update the kernel function is computed as follows:

$$\varnothing(t) = \frac{1}{(2\pi)^{\frac{n}{2}}} \frac{1}{N_i} \sum_{i=1}^{N_i} e^{\left[\frac{-(Tr_i - p_t)^{-1}(Tr_i - R_j)}{2\sigma^2}\right]} \tag{21}$$

Finally, the kernel function checks whether the value of patterns is compared with the probability distribution for each column (t) ($p_t > \varnothing(t)$) defined in Equation (25). The kernel function formulation for the class labels are listed as follows:

$$V_t(TP) = \sum_{n=1}^{N} \sum_{m=1}^{M} \left(\frac{\partial P_{p,m}}{\partial t_i} TP_{p,m} \right) \tag{22}$$

where *TP* is the testing pattern.

If the probability distribution function is greater than the count of patterns *P*, then the corresponding label is ($C=L(\varnothing(t))$).

6.8 PERFORMANCE ANALYSIS

The authors collected the images to validate the effectiveness of proposed IF-CNN. The input dataset contains 256 training points and Table 6.1 presents the comparative analysis of proposed IF-CNN with the SVM [16] on the basic performance parameters for pancreas images.

Figure 6.5 shows the comparative analysis between Machine Learning methods IF-CNN and SVM in terms of sensitivity, specificity measures, precision recall, and various other performance metrics for both normal and abnormal cases of pancreatic cancer. The optimal weight update by the integrated level set formulation and the N-ternary patterns improves specificity values. The numerical values of sensitivity and specificity for SVM are 100% and 52.0833%, respectively. But the proposed IF-CNN provides 97.2222% and 98.0392%, respectively. Compared to SVM, the IF-CNN offers 46.87% improvement specificity values.

Figure 6.6 shows the comparative analysis of accuracy, precision, and recall values for IF-CNN and SVM formulation. The SVM offers 85.2564%, 82.4427%, and 100%, respectively. The proposed IF-CNN offers 96.7949%, 96.3303%, and 97.2222%, respectively. The IF-CNN formulation and novel pattern extraction methods improve accuracy and precision by 11.92% and 14.42%, respectively.

Figure 6.7 shows the comparative analysis of Jaccard, Dice, and kappa coefficient for IF-CNN and SVM formulation. The SVM offers 85.2564%, 92.0415%, and

TABLE 6.1
Comparative Performance Analysis of IF-CNN with SVM for Images of Pancreas

Parameters	IF-CNN	SVM
True Positive (TP)	108	105
True Negative (TN)	42	23
False Positive (FP)	3	23
False Negative (FN)	3	5
Sensitivity (%)	97.2222	100
Specificity (%)	98.0392	52.0833
Precision (%)	96.3303	82.4427
Recall (%)	97.2222	100
Jaccard coefficient (%)	97.7564	85.2564
Dice overlap (%)	98.8655	92.0415
Kappa coefficient	99.04	60.08
Accuracy (%)	96.7949	85.2564

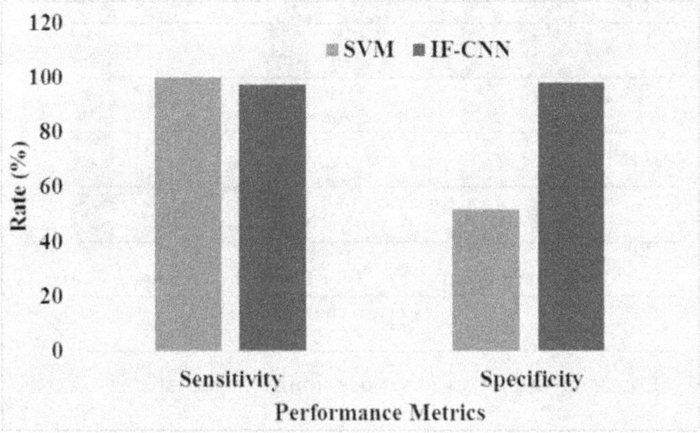

FIGURE 6.5 Sensitivity/specificity analysis.

60.08% and the IF-CNN offers 97.7564%, 98.8655%, and 99.04%, respectively. The integrated level set formulation with the IF-CNN improves the accuracy, precision, and recall by 12.79%, 6.92%, and 39.34%, respectively.

Figure 6.8 shows the loss over time of the proposed work; this represents the validation loss and training loss. By considering the time, the validation loss and training loss reduce with respect to the increasing time.

Table 6.2 shows the performance of the proposed system using various algorithms. Here various algorithms such as U-Net, Deformed U-Net, V-Net, Holistically Nested Network (HNN), Holistically Nested Network-Random forest (HNN-RF) are used to evaluate the performance of the proposed system. The V-net algorithm is analyzed

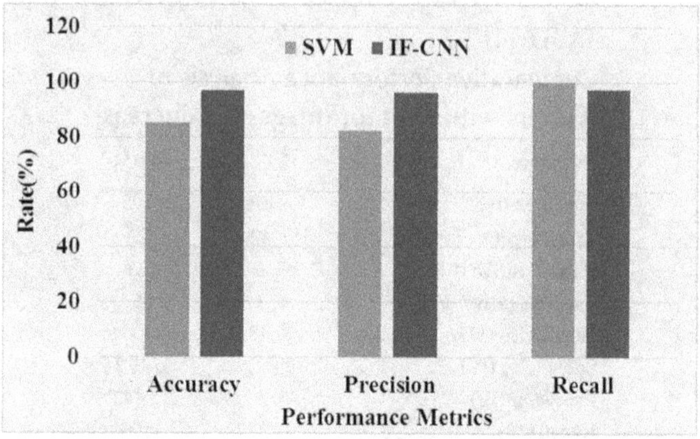

FIGURE 6.6 Analysis of accuracy, precision, and recall.

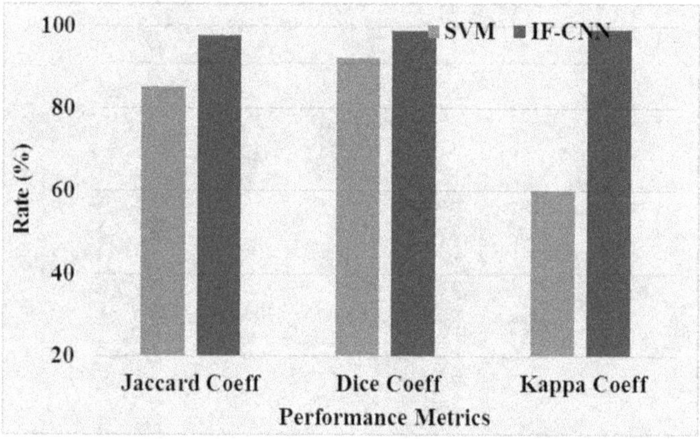

FIGURE 6.7 Comparative analysis of various similarity measures.

with this proposed system by the evaluation of parameters such as average Dice coefficients and average Hausdorff distances of the predicted delineation to the ground truth annotation. The performance of the U-Net model is evaluated by using the measures such as inducing loss, false positive rate, and false negative rate. Also, the error rates 1 and 2 are estimated.

6.9 CONCLUSION

A high-anatomical variation in the pancreas region resulted in the reduced performance of traditional segmentation approaches to demarcate/differentiate the pancreas region from the other organs in the CT abdominal imagery. The state-of-the-art image processing and computer vision techniques like segmentation and filtering classification already witnessed (e.g., **K-means clustering, level set Segmentation,**

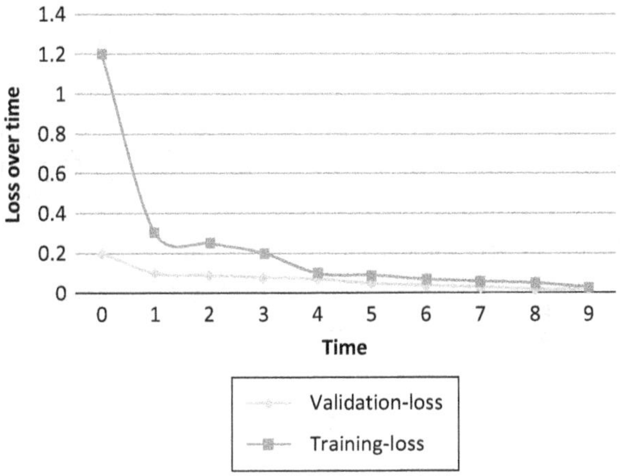

FIGURE 6.8 Loss over time.

region growing, Otsu segmentation, Fuzzy C-means clustering, Bilateral filtering, Angular Texture pattern etc.) have successfully eradicated some of the above-mentioned issues. However, image segmentation algorithms rarely adapt well to the changes in the imaging system or to a different image analysis problem, so there is a demand for solutions that can be easily modified to analyze different image modalities, which are more accurate than the existing ones. To overcome these demerits faced by the above-mentioned customized segmentation approaches and to enhance segmentation precision, we need to design a model that gives us more finer segmentations and that clearly demarcates the location of the pancreas. Initially, the proposed work employed the Laplacian formula to filter the noisy regions from the images and the second-order formulation to sharpen the edges of images. The multi directional angle-based feature extraction methodology extracts the different patterns in the images. We propose a novel integrated segmentation approach that joins both level sets and deep neural networks to significantly improve the more accuracy of the segmentation and correctly distinguish between pancreatic and non-pancreatic imagery via assigning exact labels. The main idea behind this dual approach is to improve the segmentation accuracy by first utilizing level sets which comprise the following steps to gauge the initial boundary of the pancreas region. The initial level contour grows and shrinks based on the principle of energy minimization to finally surround the pancreatic region. Subsequently, the post-segmentation results can be further fine-tuned by providing the correct hyperparameters for the training of our proposed level-set-based CNN model (IFCNN) and by giving abundance of examples to our learning algorithm to depict the exact labels for classification. Hence, customized image processing solutions for pancreas segmentation can be replaced by a trainable method which can be applicable to a large variety of image data instead of solving only one specific problem. The comparative analysis between the proposed CNN-based learning models and the various methods like SVM, V-Net, and U-NET are then performed and extracted performance parameters such as Jaccard, Dice, and

TABLE 6.2
Performance Analysis of the Proposed System Using Various Machine Learning Algorithms

			Algorithm	**Average Dice**	**Average Hausdorff**			
			V-Net	0.872$^{+}_{-}$0.034	0.547$^{+}_{-}$1.20			
		Algorithm	**Loss**	**FN**	**FP**	**Error1**	**Error2**	
		U-Net	0.1456	5	10	70	43	
		Deformed U-Net	0.1001	2	4	60	9	
	$HNN_{meanmax}$	**HNN-RF**	$HNN_{meanmax}$	**HNN-RF**	$HNN_{meanmax}$	**HNN-RF**	$HNN_{meanmax}$	**HNN-RF**
Mean	80.15	81.54	65.21	69.21	25.25	16.21	0.54	0.41
Standard	7.5	6.21	9.5	8.21	12.62	10.5	0.35	0.32
Median	83.54	82.57	70.54	70.57	17.8	15.2	0.32	0.31
Min	45.26	50.65	28.95	33.54	5.84	5.30	0.20	0.21
Max	90.98	89.25	78.53	80.24	78.51	70.54	1.2	2.12

Average Hausdorff ensure the effectiveness of the early diagnosis by the proposed model. Furthermore, we can improve our segmentation by introducing end-to-end training architecture CNN, e.g., semantic segmentation, for dense pixel classification and generate segmentation maps independent of any size of the image. This could be extrapolated to other organs of high anatomical variability along with improved performance of the segmentation task.

REFERENCES

1. Clores, M. J., Thosani, A., & Buscaglia, J. M. (2014). Multidisciplinary diagnostic and therapeutic approaches to pancreatic cystic lesions. *Journal of Multidisciplinary Healthcare*, 7, 81.
2. Fritz, S., Bergmann, F., Grenacher, L., Sgroi, M., Hinz, U., Hackert, T., ... & Werner, J. (2014). Diagnosis and treatment of autoimmune pancreatitis types 1 and 2. *British Journal of Surgery*, 101(10), 1257–1265.
3. Rosenberger, I., Strauss, A., Dobiasch, S., Weis, C., Szanyi, S., Gil-Iceta, L., ... & Plaza-García, S. (2015). Targeted diagnostic magnetic nanoparticles for medical imaging of pancreatic cancer. *Journal of Controlled Release*, 214, 76–84.
4. Trikudanathan, G., Walker, S. P., Munigala, S., Spilseth, B., Malli, A., Han, Y., ... & Beilman, G. J. (2015). Diagnostic performance of contrast-enhanced MRI with secretin-stimulated MRCP for non-calcific chronic pancreatitis: A comparison with histopathology. American Journal of Gastroenterology, 110(11), 1598–1606.
5. Brugge, W. R. (2015), Diagnosis and management of cystic lesions of the pancreas. *Journal of Gastrointestinal Oncology*, 6, 375.
6. Lee, J. H., Kim, J. K., Kim, T. H., Park, M. S., Yu, J. S., Choi, J. Y., ... & Kim, K. W. (2012). MRI features of serous oligocystic adenoma of the pancreas: differentiation from mucinous cystic neoplasm of the pancreas. *The British Journal of Radiology*, 85(1013), 571–576.
7. Legrand, L., Duchatelle, V., Molinié, V., Boulay-Coletta, I., Sibileau, E., & Zins, M. (2015). Pancreatic adenocarcinoma: MRI conspicuity and pathologic correlations. *Abdominal Imaging*, 40(1), 85–94.
8. Sequeiros, I. M., Hester, K., Callaway, M., Williams, A., Garland, Z., Powell, T., ... & Bristol Cystic Fibrosis Diabetes Group. (2010). MRI appearance of the pancreas in patients with cystic fibrosis: a comparison of pancreas volume in diabetic and non-diabetic patients. *The British Journal of Radiology*, 83(995), 921–926.
9. Barral, M., Soyer, P., Dohan, A., Laurent, V., Hoeffel, C., Fishman, E. K., & Boudiaf, M. (2014). Magnetic resonance imaging of cystic pancreatic lesions in adults: An update in current diagnostic features and management. *Abdominal Imaging*, 39(1), 48–65.
10. Hanada, K., Okazaki, A., Hirano, N., Izumi, Y., Teraoka, Y., Ikemoto, J., ... & Yonehara, S. (2015). Diagnostic strategies for early pancreatic cancer. *Journal of Gastroenterology*, 50(2), 147–154.
11. Roth, H. R., Lu, L., Farag, A., Shin, H. C., Liu, J., Turkbey, E. B., & Summers, R. M. (2015, October). Deeporgan: Multi-level deep convolutional networks for automated pancreas segmentation. In International conference on medical image computing and computer-assisted intervention (pp. 556–564). Cham: Springer.
12. Achanta, R., Shaji, A., Smith, K., Lucchi, A., Fua, P., & Süsstrunk, S. (2012). SLIC superpixels compared to state-of-the-art superpixel methods. *IEEE Transactions on Pattern Analysis and Machine Intelligence*, 34(11), 2274–2282.

13. Roth, H. R., Farag, A., Lu, L., Turkbey, E. B., & Summers, R. M. (2015, March). Deep convolutional networks for pancreas segmentation in CT imaging. In *Medical Imaging 2015: Image Processing* (Vol. 9413, p. 94131G). International Society for Optics and Photonics.
14. Roth, H. R., Lu, L., Farag, A., Sohn, A., & Summers, R. M. (2016, October). Spatial aggregation of holistically-nested networks for automated pancreas segmentation. In International Conference on Medical Image Computing and Computer-Assisted Intervention (pp. 451–459). Cham: Springer.
15. Farag, A., Lu, L., Roth, H. R., Liu, J., Turkbey, E., & Summers, R. M. (2016). A bottom-up approach for pancreas segmentation using cascaded superpixels and (deep) image patch labeling. *IEEE Transactions on Image Processing*, 26(1), 386–399.
16. Moeskops, P., Wolterink, J. M., van der Velden, B. H., Gilhuijs, K. G., Leiner, T., Viergever, M. A., & Išgum, I. (2016, October). Deep learning for multi-task medical image segmentation in multiple modalities. In International Conference on Medical Image Computing and Computer-Assisted Intervention (pp. 478–486). Cham: Springer.
17. Cai, J., Lu, L., Zhang, Z., Xing, F., Yang, L., & Yin, Q. (2016, October). Pancreas segmentation in MRI using graph-based decision fusion on convolutional neural networks. In International Conference on Medical Image Computing and Computer-Assisted Intervention (pp. 442–450). Cham: Springer.
18. Zheng, S., Jayasumana, S., Romera-Paredes, B., Vineet, V., Su, Z., Du, D., ... & Torr, P. H. (2015). Conditional random fields as recurrent neural networks. In *Proceedings of the IEEE International Conference on Computer Vision* (pp. 1529–1537).
19. Wang, Z., Bhatia, K. K., Glocker, B., Marvao, A., Dawes, T., Misawa, K., ... & Rueckert, D. (2014, September). Geodesic patch-based segmentation. In International Conference on Medical Image Computing and Computer-Assisted Intervention (pp. 666–673). Cham: Springer.
20. Wolz, R., Chu, C., Misawa, K., Fujiwara, M., Mori, K., & Rueckert, D. (2013). Automated abdominal multi-organ segmentation with subject-specific atlas generation. *IEEE Transactions on Medical Imaging*, 32(9), 1723–1730.
21. Tong, T., Wolz, R., Wang, Z., Gao, Q., Misawa, K., Fujiwara, M., ... & Rueckert, D. (2015). Discriminative dictionary learning for abdominal multi-organ segmentation. *Medical Image Analysis*, 23(1), 92–104.
22. Lucchi, A., Smith, K., Achanta, R., Knott, G., & Fua, P. (2011). Supervoxel-based segmentation of mitochondria in em image stacks with learned shape features. *IEEE Transactions on Medical Imaging*, 31(2), 474–486.
23. Zhang, L., Kong, H., Chin, C. T., Liu, S., Chen, Z., Wang, T., & Chen, S. (2014). Segmentation of cytoplasm and nuclei of abnormal cells in cervical cytology using global and local graph cuts. *Computerized Medical Imaging and Graphics*, 38(5), 369–380.
24. Chang, H., Han, J., Borowsky, A., Loss, L., Gray, J. W., Spellman, P. T., & Parvin, B. (2012). Invariant delineation of nuclear architecture in glioblastoma multiforme for clinical and molecular association. *IEEE Transactions on Medical Imaging*, 32(4), 670–682.
25. Zhang, L., Kong, H., Ting Chin, C., Liu, S., Fan, X., Wang, T., & Chen, S. (2014). Automation-assisted cervical cancer screening in manual liquid-based cytology with hematoxylin and eosin staining. *Cytometry Part A*, 85(3), 214–230.
26. Kayalibay, B., Jensen, G., & van der Smagt, P. (2017). CNN-based segmentation of medical imaging data. arXiv preprint arXiv:1701.03056.
27. G. Litjens, T. Kooi, B. E. Bejnordi, A. A. A. Setio, F. Ciompi, M. Ghafoorian, et al. (2017). A survey on deep learning in medical image analysis. *Medical Image Analysis* 42, 60–88.

28. F. Milletari, N. Navab, and S.-A. Ahmadi. (2016). V-net: Fully convolutional neural networks for volumetric medical image segmentation. In *3D Vision (3DV), 2016* Fourth International Conference on, pp. 565–571
29. Sudre, C. H., Li, W., Vercauteren, T., Ourselin, S., & Cardoso, M. J. (2017). Generalised Dice overlap as a deep learning loss function for highly unbalanced segmentations. In *Deep Learning in Medical Image Analysis and Multimodal Learning for Clinical Decision Support* (pp. 240–248). Cham: Springer.
30. Wang, S., Wu, Q., He, X., Yang, J., & Wang, Y. (2015). Local N-Ary pattern and its extension for texture classification. *IEEE Transactions on Circuits and Systems for Video Technology*, 25(9), 1495–1506.

7 Early and Precision-Oriented Detection of Cervical Cancer

A Deep-Learning-Based Framework

Vandana Bhatia, Priya Ranjan, Neha Taneja, Harpreet Singh, and Rajiv Janardhanan

CONTENTS

7.1 INTRODUCTION

The abnormal growth of cells of any organ in the human body can be the effect of cancer. The abnormal growth of cells of different body organs can affect both males and females. Some types of cancers are very frequent in women such as breast cancer and cervical cancer. A significant proportion of these cancers are burdened with poor clinical outcomes due to delay in detection as well as misdiagnosis. For example, breast cancer impacts 2.1 million women worldwide every year and is the major cause of mortality among women. In 2018, it was estimated that breast cancer took the lives of around 627,000 women—approximately 15% of all cancer-associated deaths taken together (Wang, Khosla, Gargeya, Irshad, & Beck, 2016).

Similarly, cervical cancer is the fourth most common cancer among women, with an estimation of around 570,000 new cases in 2018, i.e., 6.6% of all female cancers. Roughly 90% of deaths take place due to cervical cancer in low- and middle-income countries (Kessler, 2017; Kumar & Tanya, 2014; Srivastava, Misra, Srivastava, Das, & Gupta, 2018). It is the second most prominent cause of female cancer among women in the age group 15–44 years in India. Annually, around 96,922 new cervical cancer cases are detected in India (Bobdey, Sathwara, Jain, & Balasubramaniam, 2016; Bray et al., 2018). While cervical cancer cases are declining in the developed countries, they pose a heavy burden on developing countries, where the risk of developing cervical cancer is 35% greater compared to developed countries (Bray et al., 2018). India accounts for approximately 25% of the mortality globally because of cervical cancer (Kumar & Tanya, 2014).

Early detection of solid tumors is critical for improving the clinical outcomes in patients afflicted with reproductive cancers such as breast cancer and cervical cancer. For example, early detection has been shown to correlate with more than 80% five-year survival rate; however, this rate decreases quickly in patients with advanced stages, reaching 15–20% population at stage IV (Meiquan et al., 2018).

Fortunately, cervical and breast cancers have an adequate premalignant time, which provides an opportunity for treating and screening before it turns to be aggressive cervical cancer. Pap smear or cytology-based population screening is a crucial secondary preventive measure that precedes a high-cure rate among patients suffering from cervical cancer. Early detection and treatment via screening can prevent nearly 80% of the cases of cervical cancers in developed countries, where efficient screening programs are in place (Srivastava et al., 2018). In developing countries, however, there is limited access to wide-scale and effective screening, leading to increased deaths due to cervical and breast cancers (Srivastava et al., 2018).

For providing context, the first step of any cancer diagnosis is the visual examination, in which a specialized doctor examines a lesion of interest with the assistance of devices. If the doctor considers the lesion to be cancerous in nature, or the initial opinion is unpersuasive, the primary healthcare physician will recommend a follow-up with a biopsy, which is indeed invasive and uncomfortable for the patients. The Institute of Medicine at the National Academies of Science, Engineering and Medicine has discoursed that "diagnostic errors account for approximately 10 percent of patient deaths," and also reports for 6–17% of complications at hospitals (Kessler, 2017). It is worthwhile to mention here that a general physician's performance cannot be calculated by false prediction of cancer. Researchers worldwide have attributed a variety of factors to a wrong diagnosis:

- Ineffective collaboration and integration of technology for efficient diagnostics.

- Disparities in communication among clinicians, patients, and their caretakers.
- Inadequate support provided to the diagnostic process by the healthcare work system.

The amalgamation of digital colposcopy for cervical cancer screening in the place of manual diagnosis can significantly strengthen the precision. Applications of Artificial Intelligence (AI) in medical diagnostics in both low- and middle-income countries (LMICs) are in the early adoption phase across healthcare settings (Kessler, 2017). These applications have the potential to revolutionize the provisioning of not only healthcare but also the clinical outcomes of patients affected with reproductive cancers such as breast cancer and cervical cancer in a real-time frame.

Artificial Intelligence along with Machine Learning has proved to be very efficient as classifier for the early detection of both cervical cancer (Menezes, Vazquez, Mohan, & Somboonwit, 2019) and breast cancer. AI-based approaches have been used widely in literature for the diagnosis of many deadly cancers (Anagnostou, Remzi, Lykourinas, & Djavan, 2003; Lisboa & Taktak, 2006). The accuracy and efficiency depend predominantly on the experience and in this case for training an AI-based model: the more the data, the better the experience. It might be pertinent to mention here that AI-based deep learning models, in vogue since the beginning of the 21st century, have been extensively used for image-analytics-based detection of anomalous tumors (Hu et al., 2018; Razzak, Naz, & Zaib, 2018).

Deep learning is a neural-network-based model which exploits multiple layers for efficient processing (Zhang & Chen, 2014) and has been extensively used for the detection of breast cancer (Hu et al., 2018; Togaçar & Ergen, 2018) and cervigram image analysis-based diagnosis of cervical cancer (Alyafeai & Ghouti, 2020; Hu et al., 2018; Togaçar & Ergen, 2018). It has proved to be very efficient when the data are very large. In literature, deep learning models such as convolutional neural networks (CNNs) were broadly used for cervical cancer classification (Alyafeai & Ghouti, 2020). In this chapter, the efficiency of CNN for the classification of cervical cancer has been discussed at length. It will be interesting to observe the capability of an AI-based approach for early detection of cervical cancer.

This chapter is organized as follows: deep learning models will be discussed in Section 7.2. In Section 7.3, related work done for detection of cancer with the help of deep learning has been discussed. Section 7.4 provides a deep-learning-based framework for cervical cancer classification. Section 7.5 provides results and observations of classification. Section 7.6 discusses the limitation of deep learning models for cancer prediction. Section 7.7 concludes the chapter and focuses on the way forward.

7.2 DEEP LEARNING NETWORKS AND CERVICAL CANCER

Intelligent diagnosis of cervical cancer is the need of the current time. Generally, five types of cervical precancerous data (i.e., cytology, fluorescence in situ hybridization [FISH], electromagnetic spectra, cervicography, and colposcopy) can be utilized for an intelligent screening of cervical cancer. However, the computer system based on cytology data and electromagnetic spectra data attained improved accuracy than the other data (Taneja, Ranjan, & Ujlayan, 2018). For example, by using the pap smear in neural networking system (PAPNET), equipped with neural network, cancer cells can be identified in repeatedly misdiagnosed pap smears (Lisboa & Taktak, 2006). The last two decades have witnessed an increasing use of computer-based intelligent techniques for solving complicated problems in the medical science domain such as perinatology, cardiology, urology, liver pathology, oncology, gynecology, and thyroid disorders (Anagnostou et al., 2003; Fein, Wong, Rosa-Cunha, Slomovitz, & Potter, 2018; Meiquan et al., 2018; Palefsky, 2009). The main aim of using Artificial Intelligence tools in medical science is to enable the development of intelligent decision support systems that can act as adjunct clinical aids in improving the diagnosis of cervical cancer.

In literature, AI-based approaches have been observed to be very popular among researchers for helping healthcare professionals toward the timely diagnosis of cancer. Wen et al. (2016) predicted prostate cancer patient survivability using four different Machine Learning techniques—decision tree, support vector machine, k-nearest neighbor and Naive Bayes—and achieved a satisfactory 85.67% accuracy (Wen et al., 2016). AI-based approaches have been extensively used for the diagnosis and classification of cancer. Wu and Zhou (Wu & Zhou, 2017) used support vector machine for the diagnosis of cervical cancer. They considered 32 risk factors that help in categorization into four target diagnosis methods.

Deep-learning-based approaches have also been proposed in literature for the classification of cervical cancer. A fully automated approach was proposed by Alyafeai and Ghouti (2020) for cervical cancer classification using deep learning. Mesut et al. (Togaçar & Ergen, 2018) have used a deep learning approach for breast cancer detection (Togaçar & Ergen, 2018). However, most of the proposed approaches have been tested on a relatively small dataset consisting of less than 100 images. Deep learning models provide better results in the presence of larger sample data. In this chapter, more than 1000 images are considered for training deep learning models.

7.3 DEEP LEARNING MODELS

Deep learning is a special kind of Machine Learning technique that utilizes the "learning by example" approach for training of the computer model. It has been used in many domains such as network clustering (Bhatia & Rani, 2019), image classification (Arel, Rose, & Coop, 1988), and recommendation systems (Fu, Qu, & Yi, 2019), to name but a few examples. This kind of technique is similar to how humans learn. Deep learning models are trained to directly perform classification tasks on images, text, sound, and so on and so forth. Some of the deep learning models are known to achieve very high accuracy levels, even exceeding that of humans. The key features of deep-learning-based models are that they are trained over very large datasets of labeled data and are designed using neural networks with several layers.

Deep learning models use artificial neural networks to train, which is why they are often called deep neural networks also. Deep learning is called "deep" because

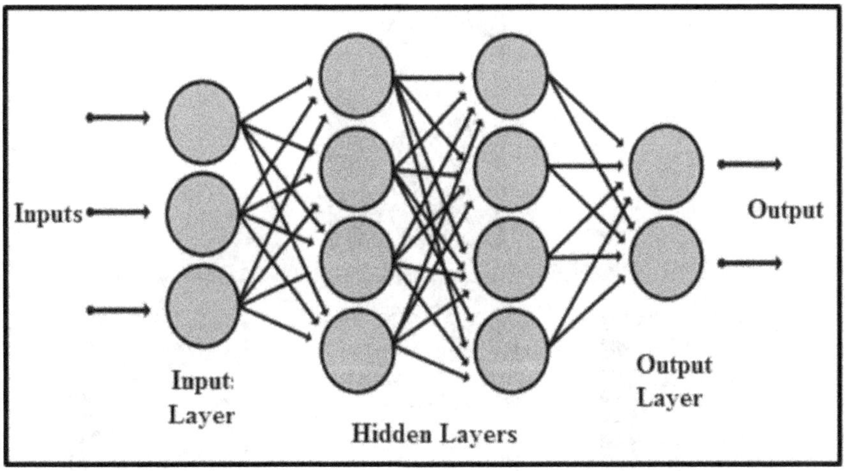

FIGURE 7.1 Neural network with two hidden layers and binary output.

of the various hidden layers that are present in the neural network. While most neural networks consist of around two to three hidden layers, deep neural networks can contain much more, about 150 hidden layers, as shown in Figure 7.1.

It will be interesting to observe the performance of deep learning for the identification of cervical cancer lesions. There are various challenges like image segmentation, efficient feature extraction from cervigrams that can be solved using Artificial Intelligence approaches such as deep learning and EMD if used together.

7.4 DEEP-LEARNING-BASED CLASSIFICATION OF CERVICAL CANCER

A deep-learning-based CNN model is used for the classification task. First, data augmentation is performed. Then the region of interest (ROI) is extracted so that features can be extracted efficiently. Further classification is performed using CNN. The main steps that are performed are as follows.

7.4.1 Image Preprocessing and Data Augmentation

Images are rarely gathered without any noise in them. Often, the dataset contains images with noise and corrupted data. Thus, image preprocessing is required so that any neural network can have increased effectiveness in classifying the images. In the case of the cervical cancer dataset, the noise which can be seen pertains to human error, similarities between various classes as well as specular reflection. First, image normalization was performed. An image is nothing but a matrix of numbers, and

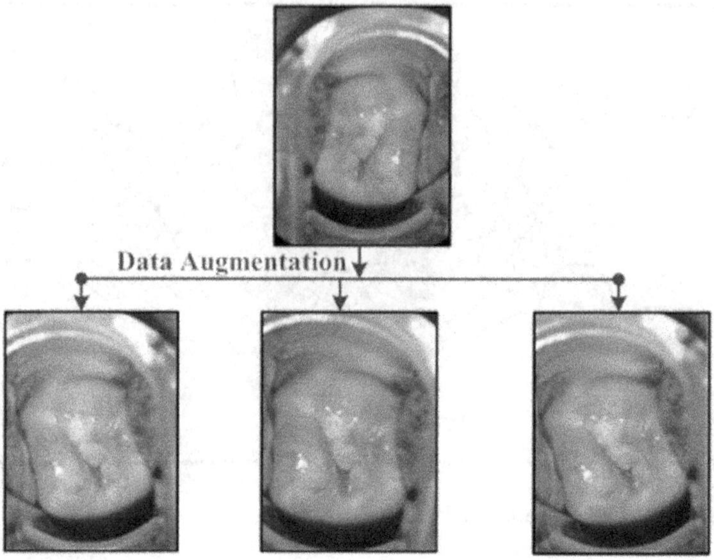

FIGURE 7.2 Augmentation of cervigrams using scaling, cropping and flipping.

these numbers are generally in the range of 0–255, which can be disruptive to the learning of the neural network, and thus the values of every pixel are normalized to fall between 0 and 1. Further, to avoid any outliers in the dataset, blurred images were manually removed.

After preprocessing, data augmentation was performed, as shown in Figure 7.2. Deep learning requires a lot of data to perform well and thus a larger dataset is required than that available in the Intel and MobileODT repository. Image augmentation is therefore used to create new images from the existing dataset to feed the network with adequate images; we augmented the images based on random rotations of the datasets based on the rotation angles.

7.4.2 Region of Interest Extraction

Instead of handling images, the first step involved the extraction of the region of interest. ROI was the designated region from which the subsequent images would be analyzed for performing classification. The images in themselves are very large in size and thus make training a very long and time-consuming process along with a lot of noise in them, causing the accuracy of the neural network to drop, thereby significantly compromising the quality of the images.

We used UNET to resolve the issue. UNET is essentially a convolutional neural network developed (Wen et al., 2016) for the application in biomedical image segmentation.

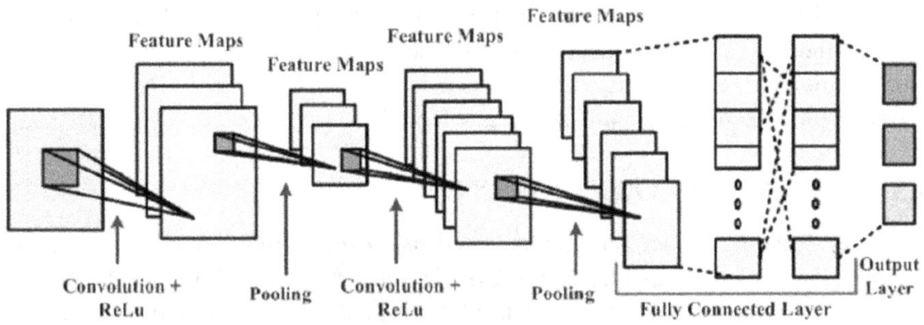

FIGURE 7.3 Architecture of convolutional neural network for classification of cervical cancer.

7.4.3 Feature Extraction and Mapping

Convolutional neural networks are among popular deep learning models used for many tasks like image classification, object recognition, etc. CNN can be used on any device and are proven to be computationally efficient by many researchers. CNN performs parameter sharing by using special convolution and pooling operations for feature extraction and mapping. In this work, the CNN model was used by performing multiple convolutional and pooling operations that were followed by a number of fully connected layers. The building block of CNN is the convolutional layer.

In it, mathematical operations were performed to merge two sets of information such as an image matrix and a filter or kernel. Rectified linear unit (ReLU) activation function was used for a non-linear operation. The output of ReLU was calculated as follows:

$$f(x) = \max(0, x) \quad (1)$$

The purpose of ReLU's activation function was to add the non-linearity in the proposed approach. As the real-world data had many non-negative linear values, the deep-learning-based model should be able to learn from them.

In the proposed model, the activation function in the output layer was SoftMax, as multiclass classification needed to be performed. The detailed model is shown in Figure 7.3. The deep learning model will consist of several convolutional layers combined with non-linear and pooling layers. When the images are passed through one convolution layer, the output of the first layer is passed as the input for the next layer. The same process was continued for further convolutional layers as well.

7.4.4 Cervical Cancer Classification

After the completion of series of convolutional, pooling, and non-linear layers, using a fully connected layer was necessary. The fully connected layer took the output information from convolutional networks and provided the final classification. Connecting a fully connected layer in the end of the convolutional neural network results in a vector with *N* dimensions, where *N* can be defined as the number of classes from which the desired class was selected.

7.5 RESULTS AND OBSERVATIONS

The deep learning model was implemented using the Python-3-based deep learning package named Keras along with Google TensorFlow. For implementation, the Google Collaboratory platform was used by exploiting various features available such as GPU processing.

7.5.1 Cervical Cancer Dataset

Intel and MobileODT jointly have provided the cervical cancer screening dataset. The dataset of screening is available publicly on Kaggle portal ("Kaggle, Intel& Mobile ODT cervical cancer screening dataset," 2020). The Intel & MobileODT dataset was used mainly for training the machine and deep learning models so that they can perform classification for the cervix types correctly. All the images of cervigram that were used for training are gathered from women who have no history of cervical cancer. Such images were used for extracting the region of interest. These images are not expected to train for the object detection using deep-learning-based models; thus, the cervical region of interest must be annotated manually first. A subset of physically annotated data by a human expert is considered ("Kaggle, Manual annotation of intel&mobileodt cervical cancer screening dataset," 2020).

The type of the cervix is closely related to the transformation zone location ("Kaggle, Intel&MobileODT cervical cancer screening dataset," 2020). Table 7.1 provides a summary on cervix type classification across the Intel & MobileODT dataset. It should be observed that 1500 images were accurately annotated only in the aforementioned dataset ("Kaggle, Manual annotation of intel&MobileODT cervical cancer screening dataset," 2020).

7.5.2 Model Validation

The UNET was used to segment the images and acquire the region of interest from the images. This is done by applying a CNN over the images. Train error and test error metrics are considered for the model validation. Train loss is the value of

TABLE 7.1
Dataset Characteristics

Cervigram Type	Type 1	Type 2	Type 3
Number of images	1241	4348	2426
Train data	992	3478	1940
Test data	243	870	486

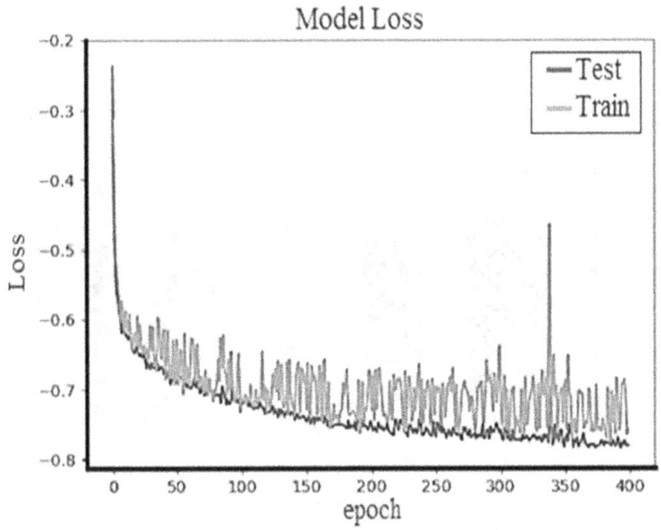

FIGURE 7.4 Image segmentation and classification using UNET: Lower test loss indicates good performance.

objective function which is being optimized by the model. Test loss is calculated over the unseen data. When the training loss is smaller than the testing loss, there are chances that the model is suffering from overfitting; and when the training loss is much higher than the testing loss, the model may have the problem of underfitting.

The goal of any good model is to minimize the loss. Loss can be considered as a penalty for wrong prediction. Lower loss values are an indication of a better model. For perfect prediction, loss should be equal to zero. The results acquired from the CNN model are shown in Figure 7.4. As it can be observed, the testing loss decreases when the number of epochs increases. There is a noticeable reduction in testing errors.

This is essential as the risk cannot be taken when the model is making predictions for a very sensitive problem such as cervical cancer prediction. In such problems, patients may have different characteristics. However, the train error is fluctuating between −0.6 and −0.7. It indicates that the model is neither overfitted nor underfitted (Figure 7.5).

7.5.3 Classification Results

A fully connected layer in a convolutional neural network will perform the final classification. The results are analyzed based on accuracy. In classification, accuracy can be given as follows:

$$\text{Accurancy} = \frac{\text{Number of correctly classified target}}{\text{Total number of classification}} \tag{2}$$

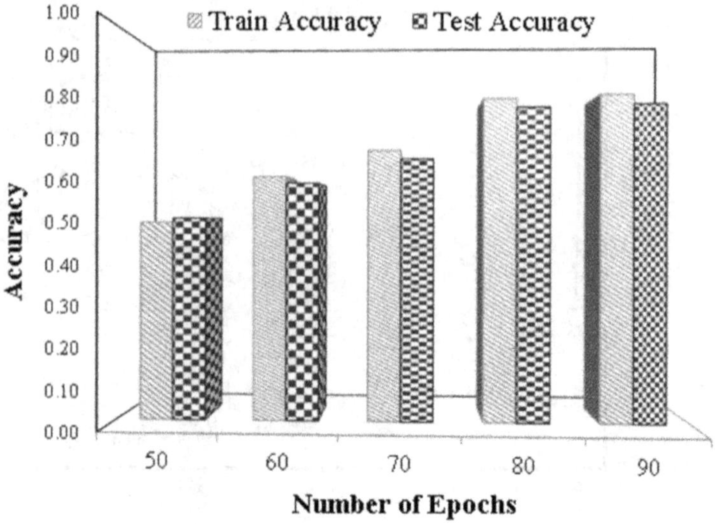

FIGURE 7.5 Train and test accuracy trade of the proposed solution indicating better performance in terms of train and test accuracy.

The test accuracy and training accuracy are illustrated in Figure 7.5. Training accuracy is computed based on the data; the model was trained on. Test accuracy is computed over the data that is unseen to the model. For a perfect blend, training accuracy should not be much higher than the test accuracy as the larger difference signifies that the model is suffering from the problem of overfitting. As shown in figure, we have tested the model on a different number of epochs of CNN. As the number of epochs increases, the complexity of the model will also increase. As observed, there is not much difference in accuracy received when we run the model for 80 epochs and when we run the model for 90 epochs. As healthcare professionals expect a prompt and timely reply from an AI-based prediction model, we have considered 80 epochs because it will save a significant amount of time. It can be observed from the figure that the proposed model is not suffering from overfitting as the training accuracy and test accuracy are almost the same in the case of all the epochs.

7.6 LIMITATIONS OF DEEP LEARNING FOR CANCER PREDICTION AND FUTURE POSSIBILITIES

Despite all the work done in literature involving deep learning for cervical cancer diagnosis, it is frequently treated as a black box approach. For critical applications like cancer detection, the algorithmic relevance is as important as algorithmic performance. And, the model interpretability is vital for convincing medical professionals to use deep-learning-based models for recommendations, which does not even provide the basis of the prediction (Razzak et al., 2018).

Another challenge in using a deep-learning-based model for cancer detection lies in its complexity. The power required by a system machinery for training the deep learning model can be the major reason for not using it in handy devices. If healthcare professionals rely on deep learning for cancer prediction or classification, they expect to get the result in a shorter span of time. However, due to the complexity of deep learning models, it is also a big challenge.

The data storage is also an issue as deep learning models require large amounts of data for maintaining precision. Although this problem can be resolved by training deep learning models on the top of cloud and edge processing so that they can learn using all the available data centrally. But healthcare professionals will not prefer to pass their data on the cloud due to security concerns. It also requires affirmation from patients, which in most cases is denied (Razzak et al., 2018).

However, the recent burst in the growth of the medical device sector has witnessed companies making several attempts to diagnose solid tumors in an accurate and reliable manner, as development of niche-specific and reliable diagnostic tools might capture a percentage of this profitable market. Better infrastructure in healthcare will play a vital role in implementation of deep learning approaches for assisting the specialized professional in diagnosis and making critical decisions.

7.7 CONCLUSION

In this chapter, the cervical classification model was performed using deep learning. Convolutional neural network, a popular deep-learning-based model, was used for image classification. The use of CNN for cervical cancer classification was done by providing cervigrams as input. Data augmentation was performed on the images to provide input to the CNN model. The images were then processed to get the region of interest. Further feature mapping was performed to extract desired features from images. Further, images are classified as normal and abnormal. Deep learning is observed to provide 0.79 training accuracy and 0.72 test accuracy. In the end, the limitations and challenges of using CNN for cervical cancer prediction have been discussed.

The results of this research have shown a strong capability of foreseeing data. More specific usage of the variants of deep-learning-based models will be very much helpful to people with high risk by providing timely screening and positive precaution measures.

ACKNOWLEDGMENTS

We acknowledge the Indian Council of Medical Research, New Delhi, for support as grant-in-aid to Dr Rajiv Janardhanan and Dr Priya Ranjan (Grant Id No. 2029-0416-No. ISRM/12(23)/2019).

REFERENCES

Alyafeai, Z., & Ghouti, L. (2020). A fully-automated deep learning pipeline for cervical cancer classification. *Expert Systems with Applications*, *141*, 112951. doi: 10.1016/j.eswa.2019.112951.

Anagnostou, T., Remzi, M., Lykourinas, M., & Djavan, B. (2003). Artificial neural networks for decision-making in urologic oncology. *European Urology*, *43*(6), 596–603.

Arel, I., Rose, D., & Coop, R. (1988). DeSTIN : A scalable deep learning architecture with application to high-dimensional robust pattern recognition. *Biologically Inspired Cognitive Architectures*, 11–15.

Bhatia, V., & Rani, R. (2019). A distributed overlapping community detection model for large graphs using autoencoder. *Future Generation Computer Systems*, *94*, 16–26. doi: 10.1016/j.future.2018.10.045.

Bobdey, S., Sathwara, J., Jain, A., & Balasubramaniam, G. (2016). Burden of cervical cancer and role of screening in India. *Indian Journal of Medical and Paediatric Oncology: Official Journal of Indian Society of Medical \& Paediatric Oncology*, *37*(4), 278.

Bray, F., Ferlay, J., Soerjomataram, I., Siegel, R. L., Torre, L. A., & Jemal, A. (2018). Global cancer statistics 2018: GLOBOCAN estimates of incidence and mortality worldwide for 36 cancers in 185 countries. *CA: A Cancer Journal for Clinicians*, *68*(6), 394–424.

Fein, L. A., Wong, A., Rosa-Cunha, I., Slomovitz, B., & Potter, J. (2018). Anal cancer risk factors and utilization of anal pap smear screening among transgender persons. *Papillomavirus Research*, *5*, S4.

Fu, M., Qu, H., & Yi, Z. (2019). A novel deep learning-based collaborative filtering model for recommendation system. *IEEE Transactions On Cybernetics*, *49*(3), 1084–1096.

Hu, Z., Tang, J., Wang, Z., Zhang, K., Zhang, L., & Sun, Q. (2018). Deep learning for image-based cancer detection and diagnosis- A survey. *Pattern Recognition*, *83*, 134–149.

Kaggle, Intel & mobileodt cervical cancer screening dataset. (2020, May).

Kaggle, Manual annotation of intel&mobileodt cervical cancer screening dataset. (2020, May).

Kessler, T. A. (2017). Cervical cancer: Prevention and early detection. In *Seminars in Oncology Nursing* (Vol. 33, pp. 172–183). WB Saunders, 2017.

Kumar, H. H. N., & Tanya, S. (2014). A study on knowledge and screening for cervical cancer among women in Mangalore city. *Annals of Medical and Health Sciences Research*, *4*(5), 751–756.

Lisboa, P. J., & Taktak, A. F. G. (2006). The use of artificial neural networks in decision support in cancer: A systematic review. *Neural Networks*, *19*(4), 408–415.

Meiquan, X., Weixiu, Z., Yanhua, S., Junhui, W., Tingting, W., Yajie, Y., … Longsen, C. (2018). Cervical cytology intelligent diagnosis based on object detection technology.

Menezes LJ, Vazquez L, Mohan CK, Somboonwit C. (2019). Eliminating cervical cancer: A role for artificial intelligence. In *Global Virology III*: *Virology in the 21st Century*, 405–422. doi: 10.1007/978-3-030-29022-1_13.

Palefsky, J. (2009). Human papillomavirus-related disease in people with HIV. *Current Opinion in HIV and AIDS*, *4*(1), 52.

Razzak, M. I., Naz, S., & Zaib, A. (2018). Deep learning for medical image processing: Overview, challenges and the future. In *Classification in BioApps* (pp. 323–350). Springer.

Srivastava, A. N., Misra, J. S., Srivastava, S., Das, B. C., & Gupta, S. (2018). Cervical cancer screening in rural India: Status & current concepts. *The Indian Journal of Medical Research*, *148*(6), 687.

Taneja, A., Ranjan, P., & Ujlayan, A. (2018). Multi-cell nuclei segmentation in cervical cancer images by integrated feature vectors. *Multimedia Tools and Applications*, *77*(8), 9271–9290.

Togaçar, M., & Ergen, B. (2018). Deep learning approach for classification of breast cancer. In *2018* International Conference on Artificial Intelligence and Data Processing (IDAP) (pp. 1–5).

Wang D, Khosla A, Gargeya R, Irshad H, Beck AH. (2016). Deep learning for identifying metastatic breast cancer. *ArXiv Preprint ArXiv:1606.05718*. Retrieved from https://arxiv.org/abs/1606.05718 Last accessed on 14-01-2020

Wen, H., Li, S., Li, W., Li, J., and Yin, C. (2016). Comparison of Four Machine Learning Techniques for the Prediction of Prostate Cancer Survivability. In *2018* 15th International Computer Conference on Wavelet Active Media Technology and Information Processing (ICCWAMTIP) (pp. 112–116).

Wu, W., & Zhou, H. (2017). Data-driven diagnosis of cervical cancer with support vector machine-based approaches. *IEEE Access*, *5*, 25189–25195.

Zhang, K., & Chen, X. W. (2014). Large-scale deep belief nets with mapreduce. *IEEE Access*, *2*, 395–403. doi: 10.1109/ACCESS.2014.2319813.

8 Transformation of mHealth in Society

Ankur Saxena, Mohit Saxena, Anveshita Deo, and Alejandra Rodríguez Llerena

CONTENTS

8.1 WHAT IS mHEALTH?

mHealth refers to mobile health. mHealth can share data continuously, not for a limited time but for longer duration in order to see the difference between statistics and the behavioral patterns of an individual [1]. It is a constituent of eHealth, which is concerned with the electronic processes and communication in the field of healthcare. It deals not only with Internet medicine but also with virtual examination, diagnosis, and telemedicine. Mobile health thus greatly emphasizes the usage of different mobile devices such as smartphones, smart clothing, smart chips, wireless devices, personal digital assistants (PDAs) and other patient monitoring devices, as shown in Figure 8.1, which are easily accessible for users, professional medical practitioners, and healthcare advisors [2]. This new digital healthcare system makes healthcare more attainable for the rising population and more manageable for the healthcare providers, by having a steady data storage system and tracking of the significant changes in the user for better diagnosis and treatment. mHealth can be a great asset to track physical health as well as mental health [3].

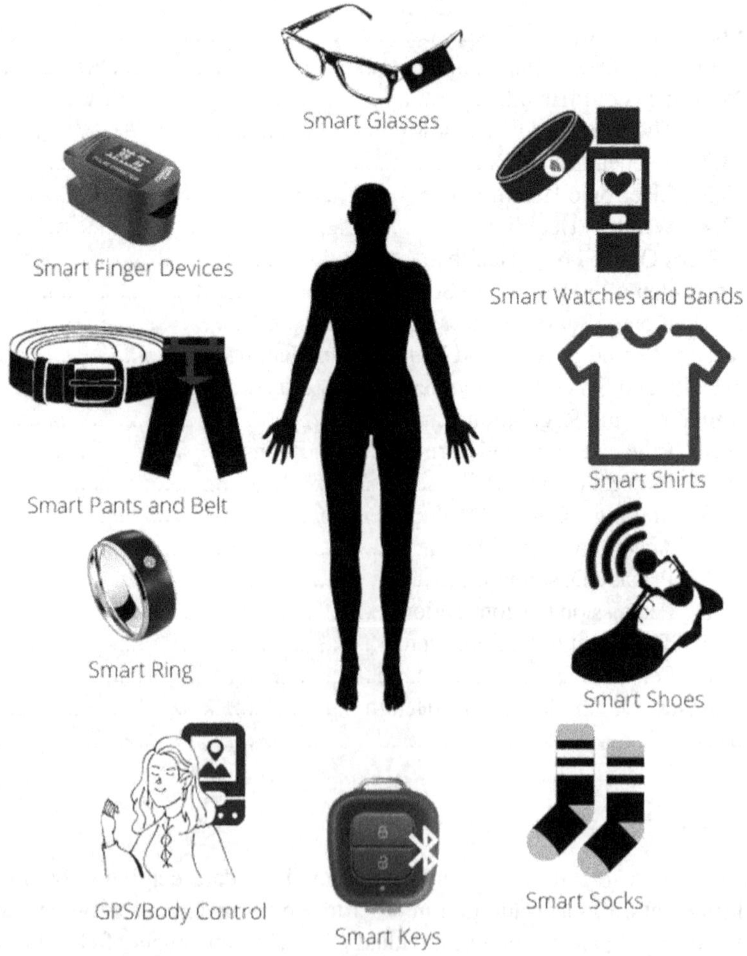

FIGURE 8.1 Patient monitoring with smart devices.

There are numerous sensory devices available on the market today—smart watches, smartphones, smart jewelry (e.g., band, ring, etc.), and other smart wearable devices (e.g., shirts, pants, belt, shoes, socks, etc.)—that aim to keep a check on physical health. Recent advancements and adaptability in technology have proven that this technology could also keep a check on mental and emotional well-being[4].

mHealth technology, being user-friendly, has integrated deep into our daily lives, enabling us to easily store data in real time. The monitoring of daily activities constantly gives a lot of meaningful data related to heart rate, pulse, oxygen saturation, perspiration, geo-location, physical exercise, etc. These data help both the users and their healthcare professionals to better diagnose if there are some serious fluctuations in the vital physiological cycle of an individual. Such healthcare databases when compiled together can give a pictorial or graphical representation of the medical history as well as the present health state of a person along with special cases like chronic diseases and the body's reaction to a certain kind of medications. It can thus help physicians in better monitoring the medical situation in real time, leading to early diagnosis and prediction of disease and a better understanding of disease progression and effect of medication [5].

On the contrary, mental health is the state of mind where a person can cope with day-to-day normal stresses and find solutions to the problems faced by any individual. This is also considered as the "mental sanity" of an individual, where a person recognizes their potential to encounter a situation or circumstance before them. There are several factors that might hamper the mental health of an individual. This may include emotional trauma, corporate load, problems in personal lives, accidents, and senescence, which impact the mental health in a massive manner leading to conditions like psychosis, dementia, attention-deficit hyperactivity disorder (ADHD), posttraumatic stress disorder (PTSD), schizophrenia, and depression, the last of which is one of the most neglected mental disorders [6].

mHealth uses and works on the basic utility of mobile phones, which involves short messaging service (SMS) and voice clips from the voice calls, nexus of functions and applications like Bluetooth technology, general packet radio service (GPRS), global positioning systems (GPS), and third- and fourth-generation mobile telecommunications (3G and 4G systems). These applications when working in a collaborative manner produce a personalized health data of the user which can be easily stored and accessed with the users' consent. These data can be relayed or shared to the medical practitioners and healthcare professionals for the detailed analysis of one's medical condition [7].

Smartphones are one of the most common mobile devices used by the general population all around the globe. These smartphones are equipped with a number of sensors, as shown in Figure 8.2, which help in the collection of essential data constituting the healthcare database. A few sensors that are ubiquitously available in smartphones and wearable sensory devices are microphones, GPS sensors, gyroscopes, and accelerometers. With the assistance of such sensors, the calculation

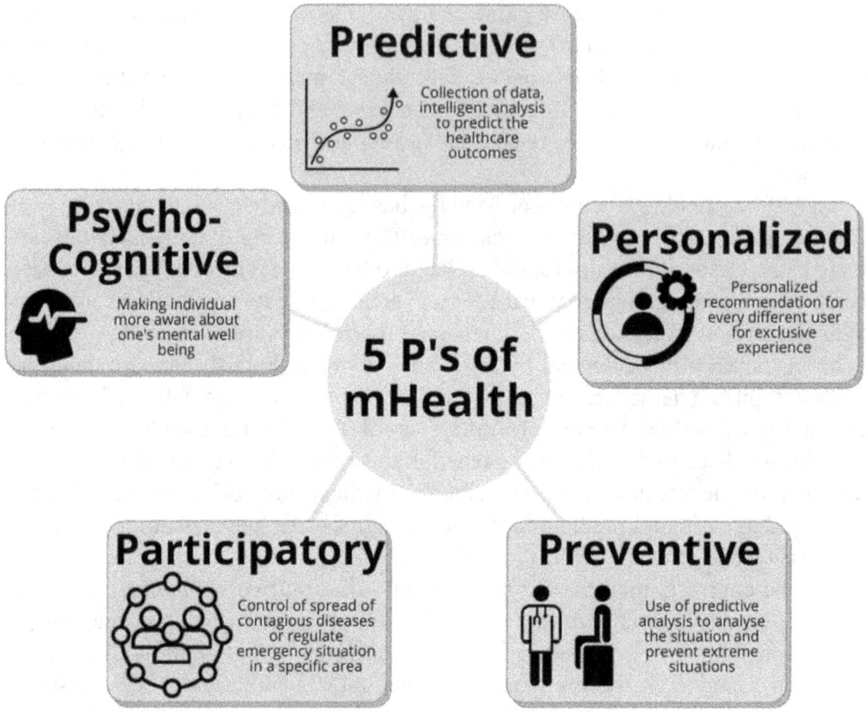

FIGURE 8.2 Five P's of mHealth.

and monitoring of sleeping pattern, pulse, heart rate, blood pressure, oxygen and hydration level, etc., can be enabled. They cumulatively give rise to the real-time data regarding the health information of the user. Any sudden shift from the normal pattern and medical condition will immediately send the "alert notification" to the user and the emergency contact information provided by the user, before the unnoticed symptoms transform into a serious cause of illness physically or mentally [7, 8].

Such advances in the applications of the healthcare system have given us some well-renowned health platforms in mHealth: Apple HealthKit, Google Fit, WHOOP, Shealth, and many more. These applications can be used by both iOS and android users. mHealth also has an advantage when it comes to data processing and storage. The smartphones and smart devices have cloud computing platforms such as Google cloud and Amazon Web Services; however, when big data processing is involved, Hadoop is more conveyable. These progressions are possible due to the advancement in Artificial Intelligence (AI), Machine Learning (ML), and natural language processing (NLP). These revolutionary changes make mHealth more compatible with the population [5, 8–11].

8.2 P'S OF mHEALTH

With the global rise in population, advancement in technology, and improvement in living standard, the demand for better healthcare facilities has increased drastically, which means that healthcare professionals are now overwhelmed with work in order to meet the public healthcare demand. In this scenario, mHealth offers exactly what is the need of the hour. By incorporating information technology (IT) along with medicines and healthcare, the channel between the medical professionals and the mHealth users has become more accessible, making the availability of medical care for the user as well as the healthcare professionals at convenience.

With the real-time analysis of this acquired data retrieved from smartphones, smart devices, and other sensory devices, mHealth can be regarded as a tool to narrow the gap between the mHealth user and healthcare system. The mHealth sensory system works on the principle of 5 potential P's (Predictive, Personalized, Preventive, Participatory, and Psychocognitive), by which it assesses the real-time data of an individual [1, 2, 12]

a. *Predictive mHealth*

The predictive nature of mHealth collects the user's data from their day-to-day life and analyzes the pattern in their everyday routine. Different sensors of smart devices fetch mHealth a large amount of information about the user, their habits, and day-to-day activities, which results in the accumulation of data in a healthcare database that includes a predictive nature of the user for a better understanding of their normal routine. For instance, if the user is a swimmer and he trains himself daily in the evening, the predictive nature of mHealth automatically gets used to his active vitals for a specific duration during the day by taking into account the geo-location, which means that the increased heart rate and the pulse recorded by the sensors is a normal routine for that individual during active hour; however, if a person leading a sedentary lifestyle happens to have a shooting heart rate and pulse at a specific time period, mHealth will regard it as an anomaly until it happens in a repetitive cycle.

b. *Personalized mHealth*

The personalized factor of mHealth focuses on treating every individual in a specific manner, which is totally customized according to the individual's own needs. Every person has a different demand for their body and mHealth provides that personalized monitoring by recommending the mHealth apps that suits the requirement of the individual according to the bio-psycho-social characteristics to provide non-redundant data. For instance, a user belonging to an athletic background will need mHealth apps with advanced accelerometer to record his efficiency to perform better; however, a person engaged with indoor work can achieve desired monitoring with the basic mHealth apps to track their daily heart rate, pulse, and caloric intake.

c. *Preventive mHealth*

The preventive factor aims at excluding the possibility of a serious ailment by monitoring every single detail of an individual's vitals and comparing it with the database formed so far to notice any significant difference or fluctuation which may indicate the proper consultation with the medical professionals for a thorough diagnosis. For instance, if the data achieved from the athlete shows the oxygen saturation of the individual in the range of 96–99, but a sudden drop in the oxygen saturation is recorded for consecutive days, the individual will be alerted to consult a doctor to get himself checked for any underlying reasons behind the situation. Thus, by closely monitoring one's physical activity in real time, many serious diseases or medically important conditions can be detected before it transforms into a chronic disease or a life-threatening situation.

d. *Participatory mHealth*

The participatory mHealth factor recognizes the individuals who are active participants toward their physical and mental health. Users who make active decisions for health will be given feedback and suggestions according to their demands and, on the contrary, the inactive users will be notified to push themselves to achieve their targeted goal. For instance, an individual who has routine checkups scheduled all by himself in his calendar, that person might not be sent multiple alert notifications for the doctor consultations. However, an individual who has not got himself under medical inspection for a significant period might be asked to visit the doctor to update their medical database, especially when a certain anomaly is detected in their routine according to the statistics achieved from the daily vitals database.

e. *Psychocognitive Strategy of mHealth*

The psychocognitive strategy of mHealth focuses on making an individual self-sufficient and more liable toward their health and well-being. This involves the individual actively with their self-statistics and vitals, propelling them toward making an active choice for choosing healthier and better lifestyle for their well-being. For instance, when an individual with a fondness for sugar discovers his increased blood sugar levels and heart rate at regular intervals, he will start cutting down his sugar intake in an active manner. This shift may or may not be drastic, but it will definitely be the initiation toward a healthier life choice.

8.3 CONSTITUENTS OF mHEALTH

mHealth functionality depends on the basic four pillars that enable it to perform, providing the users and the medical professionals the easiest and hassle-free experience without hindering their routine activities. The four essentials that constitute mHealth are mobile health sensory devices, telehealth (teleconsultation

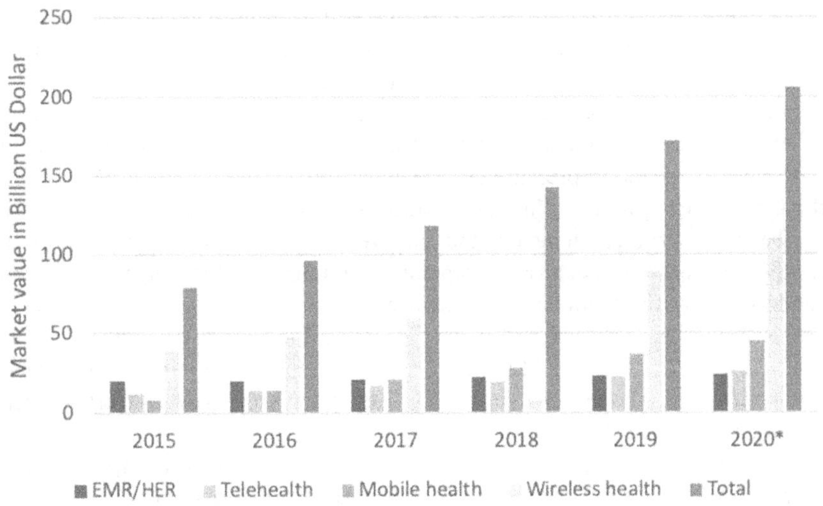

FIGURE 8.3 Constituents of mHealth.

or robo-consultation), electronic health record (EHR)/electronic medical record (EMR), and wireless health. The data processing of these constituents combined gives a better user-specific data that makes it more personalized toward physical and mental healthcare. Figure 8.3 shows the progressive growth of mHealth during recent years and suggests it as a promising tool for improved healthcare outcomes in the coming future.

8.3.1 The Sensory Device or Mobile Health

Sensory devices perform detection based on external stimuli from the user. They are readily available on the market in recent times. They are cost-effective as well as user-friendly. Every stratum of the population needs some kind of monitoring toward their health—it can be physical health or the mental health. The only thing that can monitor this in real time without intervening with the routine of the modern and busy user are the sensors which are available in smartphone and other mobile devices. These sensors may not be restricted just to smartphones or smart watches; even fitness trackers, implants, smart jewelry, head accessories, patches, clips, etc., can also be used to track minute to minute activities of an individual. When the smart sensor technology of smartphones is combined with the biosensor technology in smart wearable sensors, the accuracy of data is greater than that of data obtained from a professional, single sensory device.

Smartphones and smart watches are some of the most common sensory devices that are majorly preferred across the globe. They are equipped with multiple sensors that monitor multiple health statistics, as mentioned in the previous sections.

Certain sensors are available in both the devices; however, there are also some sensors that are exclusively available in a certain device. A few common sensors that are present in both smartphones and smartwatches are accelerometer (measures body movements to track steps and sleep patterns), gyroscope sensor (measures rotation), magnetometer sensor (compass assists in the accuracy while motion tracking), GPS sensor (detects location), pressure sensor (measures altitudes, which helps cyclists and runners during uphill climbing), hydration or humidity sensor (measures the intensity of a workout, skin health, and toxin release), and temperature sensor (measures the difference between skin temperature and the ambient temperature for better understanding of the intensity of exercise).

Smartphones have an edge over smartwatches due to their use, size, complexity and presence of various additionl sensors. The sensors that are present solely in smartphones are light sensors, proximity sensors, microphones, fingerprint scanners, cameras, and CMOS image scanners.

There are more serviceable sensors that are incorporated in a smartphone than in a smartwatch. There are certain sensors which are available and are more utilitarian for smart watches such as oximetric sensor, skin temperature sensor, skin conductance sensor, and heart rate monitor. Since a smartwatch is closer to the wrist and in direct contact with the skin and the pulse, the statistics obtained by these sensors are relatively more accurate.

8.3.2 Telehealth

Telehealth refers to receiving healthcare services remotely via telecommunication or digital communication. It has become one of the most accepted health consultation techniques in recent years. Due to its 24/7 availability to the user and the emergency services it provides, it is possible for the user to record and consult on the telephone and avoid the hassles of traveling, except in case of emergency. Teleconsultation/robo-consultation help people with long term medical conditions as well as healthy individuals, especially those in remote and rural areas, in self-managing their health. The user needs to record their vitals and the teleconsultation techniques tell the self-care measures that should be implicated by the individual, except for such medical conditions when self-care precautions are not enough and the user has to reach out for expert medical help. It not only makes the user self-aware of their own conditions, but also makes them self-dependent for minor health ailments which can be treated by adaptation of certain healthy habits. Even in emergency situations when there is no expert doctor available, primary healthcare providers and nurses can seek necessary advice of the senior doctor through telephone or other digital devices and thus can help the patient stabilize and get relief from immediate stress until the patient reaches the hospital. The advancement in telehealth skyrocketed when the first shoulder surgery was performed in Avicenne Hospital (AP-HP) on December 5, 2017, with the virtual assistance. The surgery took place on the HoloPortal platform from TeraRecon and Microsoft developed HoloLens holographic computer. During the surgery, 3D patient's internal anatomical images could be modeled and visualized in real time by the expert doctor panel. The relevant data about the surgery could also be shared and stored. The HoloLens enabled the proper accurate imagery, assisting the doctor in placement of the prosthesis. This ground-breaking experience of the mixed reality connected the external world to the live medical surgery.

8.3.3 Electronic Health Records

EHR and EMR both go hand in hand to deal with the patients' data, which medical professionals can share for a better understanding of any ailment faced by an individual. The data that are stored in these databases are comparatively more secure than any other means of data storage software systems.

The difference between EHR and EMR is that EMR is the patient's chart that is retrieved from one consultation session only. It is generally present in the doctor's office and is not followed up if the patient changes the doctor. So, it is more likely for the doctor's reference. EHR on the other hand comprises a chart with details of several consultation sessions, test reports, and follow-up records, giving a more vivid picture about the patient's medical condition, especially of chronic diseases. If a patient has to refer to a different doctor for further treatment, this record can be further shared for a better understanding of the patient's medical history and medication that the patient undertook.

8.3.4 Wireless Health

Wireless health is the integration of sensors or wireless technology into the trivial medicinal practice. In other words, any health record or data that is shared wirelessly, by means of Internet, comes under wireless health. The mobile devices and the sensory devices are supposed to monitor, store, and share the data with proper access to Internet connectivity. This will not only help ensure the proper storage of data but also eliminate any possibility of the redundancy of the data. Since all the data are collected and stored by cloud syncing, the real-time data become more accurate for the doctors to follow up.

8.4 SERVICES OFFERED BY mHEALTH

The acceptance of mHealth in society has been possible due to services it provides and advancement that is made in the existing technologies over the years. It has its ramifications in almost all the fields and has been developing personalized services for individual's personal requirements. The data collection and data analysis of distinct fields require a different and specific approach, which is managed by mHealth in a very simplified manner for the general population. Apart from this, the data collected from the users are stored according to the necessity of the target demand of the user. Some of the major services offered by mHealth that will be discussed in further sections are shown in Figure 8.4; these services include health, productivity, sports, geo-tracking, meditation, quantified self, sleep, brain training, period tracking, and nutrition.

FIGURE 8.4 Services offered by mHealth applications.

One of the most highlighted and prominent services provided by mHealth is healthcare. There are numerous mHealth apps, as shown in Figure 8.5, which are developed solely for tracking the health of an individual. A few popular mHealth apps for healthcare are Fitbit, Apple Heart Study, Google Fit, Samsung Health, BlueStar, and AliveCor's KardiaMobile. These apps aim towards monitoring the general health of an individual. Apart from this, the patients who have undergone major surgery or are suffering from any chronic disease are recorded in the database of these apps, which enables monitoring of medications and treatment. Patient rehabilitation costs are reduced dramatically as the mHealth app guides the patients or the user on self-care and self-maintenance unless professional medical help is the need of the hour. In addition, the patients can also be sent medication reminders and instructions for speedy recovery postsurgery. In this way, the patient stays under constant supervision because the statistics and the instructions are provided to the patient by the medical professionals through this mobile channel (Figure 8.12).

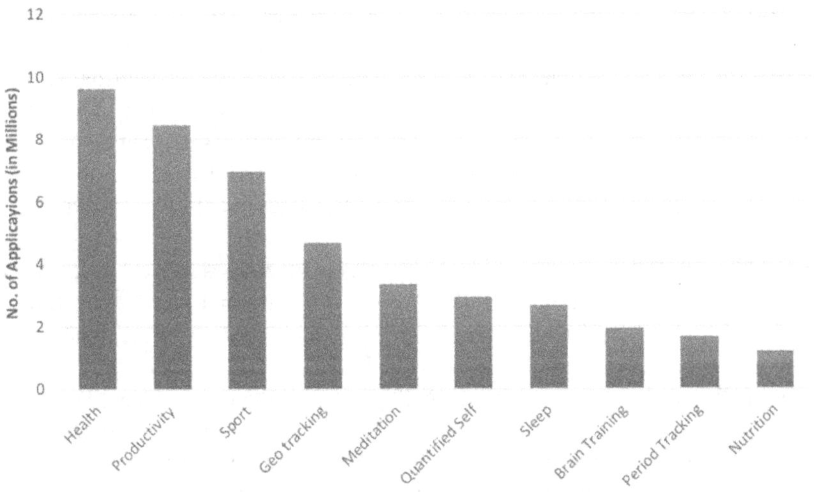

FIGURE 8.5 Graph showing people's interest in mHealth services.

In today's busy lifestyle and hectic schedule, mHealth applications also provide platforms that enhance the productivity of an individual. Due to industrialization, workforce has increased. The growing network also has its impact on a person's life. It has been seen that Internet and social media has a huge traffic, with the majority of the population being youth, who keep themselves busy on social media and the web. There are certain mHealth applications that keep a check on the hourly indulgence of an individual on the internet. The user can customize their needs accordingly. For instance, if the user feels that being active on social media is consuming a lot of time, the mHealth application responsible for productivity can help in customizing the daily hours of social media usage. In this manner, the user is obligated to get back to the immediate and pressing concerns for which he/she has customized the mHealth application settings. In a way, this also helps the user in self-restraining from excessive screen time and ultimately gets better at time management. Artificial Intelligence used in these applications enables them to be active in the background monitoring the activity of other applications used by the user and it sends an alert if the daily usage limit which is set by the user is crossed.

Sports has been one of the largest industries as people have started becoming more aware and cautious about their health. Not only the athletes but also all those who aspire to maintain good health and are inclined toward fitness need to keep a check on their vitals to track their performance and progress. mHealth applications provide them with a platform that is sports specific, which means these applications are specifically designed to monitor vigorous training and intense workouts.

A normal health application may just calculate the vitals, but the applications designed specifically for sports activities calculate and compare to provide the performance statistics based on the previous and the current performance of an individual. Cardiorespiratory fitness (CRF) is one such factor on which mHealth applications for sports mainly focus. The cardiorespiratory assessment when done in sports settings provides information about an athlete's performance on the basis of the training program chosen by the user. The CRF assessment can be used for both sports and clinical purposes [13].

mHealth also has its ramifications in the geo-tracking services. Geo-trackers inform an individual about their location as well as the destination. The geo-tracking service provided by mHealth is the base where certain data are calculated, for instance, the number of steps of an individual, distance covered during sports, and vigorous activity like running, hiking, and cycling. In addition, it also gives an idea about the distance to be covered if the user has set up a destination location. Taxi and food delivery services are some of the popular examples of the services where geo-tracking is extensively used in our daily lives. We are able to track the driver and the estimated time of arrival. Similarly, by use of such services, similar kinds of data could be provided by mHealth applications. The geo-tracking services are not just confined to taxis, food, and calculation of physical steps. It can also be helpful in the state of emergencies. Multiple user-friendly applications aim to provide safety services in the state of emergencies. These apps work on the principle of sharing location. If a user is in danger, they can send location-specific details to the police authorities as well as their emergency contacts for immediate help. This revolutionary advancement has made help readily available by immediate reinforcement from concerned authorities for appropriate action.

People with vivid interests are inclined toward different forms of health and fitness programs. One such program is meditation. It not only builds physical strength but also has a strong effect on mental strength, which is why people all around the world prefer meditation. Since it hardly requires any heavy weights and equipment, it is user-friendly with respect to time and space.

mHealth services not only focuses on being instrumental to the user in every possible means; it also extends its help to enable users to build self-care programs. These applications form meditation plans according to the person's need. Some people adopt meditation as a daily practice in their routine; however, others require it as a break from their daily stressful lives. These applications help in building programs according to the state of an individual's mind. It also guides people in the progressive format which assists them in understanding how to follow instructions.

In 2017, the mobile application "Calm" was awarded "2017 app of the year" by Apple. This was followed by apps "Aura" and "Headspace." These apps help people suffering from conditions like insomnia and daily stress to attain mental peace. For instance, playing of nature sounds in a relaxing tone helps the user sleep [14].

It has become difficult to have a regular sleep cycle in today's life, especially in metropolitan regions. The growing stress levels and work anxiety are the major reasons for such issues. Recent studies show that almost 30% of the population from all age groups are suffering from insomnia. Since their brain is loaded with multiple thoughts and stress, it is nearly impossible to get mental peace, which results in overworking of the brain [15].

Mental stress can not only lead to insomnia; it might also cause extra hours of sleep. It is clinically proven that a person suffering from mental stress may sleep for unusual extra hours to avoid the feeling of depression. To help prevent people falling into such vicious cycles, mHealth has brought applications that help people attain mental peace and have adequate amount of sleep in order to keep their brains healthy. A few examples of such applications are Calm, Headspace, Noisli, Sleep Cycle, etc. These applications are not necessarily used to encounter mentally stressful problems; they can also be used by people facing temporary issues like jet lag after intercontinental travel. In order to set up a proper circadian rhythm, people tend to require some extra help which can lead them toward a proper sleep cycle. These are some of the concerns addressed by the mHealth app with respect to the sleep cycle of an individual.

Extensive studies about the brain have led to the conclusion that with today's lifestyle and old age, people are more prone to suffering from memory disorders like dementia and Alzheimer's disease. These disorders are escalating at an alarming rate each year and are affecting a large number of population. People who are entering old age are comparatively at a higher risk of suffering with these disorders than it was a few decades earlier. This happens due to weak cognitive functioning of the brain. Increased stress levels in society have led people toward poor development of the cognitive functioning of their brains. The symptoms are often small when compared to the humongous effects of the poorly developed cognitive functioning of the brain.

mHealth introduces Assistive Technology (AT) which involves therapeutic training of the brain, making it more efficient to conduct tasks and memorize the details in their daily lives. The application designed to assist in the cognitive training of the brain mainly focuses on (a) activities of daily living (ADL) based cognitive training, (b) monitoring, (c) dementia screening, (d) reminiscence and socialization, (e) tracking, and (f) caregiver support.

With these measures, the application assists the individual with the daily monitoring of the cognitive fitness of the individual's brain. Constant training of the brain helps individuals to understand their brain health and to take actions accordingly with respect to their mental fitness [16].

Menstrual cycle trackers have been introduced in society in a recent couple of years, making the hormonal cycle tracking easier for millions of women all around the world. This might not be the most accurate way to track menstruation, but it has certainly proven to calculate the approximate time that different events take place in the menstruation cycle, including the ovulation period, bleeding phase, and the hormonal mood fluctuations experienced by women.

Since the menstrual cycle is considered an indication of women's health, it is important to ensure that reproductive health is also monitored like the overall health of an individual. Monitoring the menstrual health also tells a lot about a woman's mental health and the stress levels influencing the cycle. It helps women to be aware of their own fertility and also assists the couples who are planning to conceive. For such activities, it is important to track the ovulation period for the better understanding of their own body [17].

Furthermore, it helps in practicing contraception and maintaining an overall healthy reproductive system. This application enables the women toward self-care and symptom management. The behavioral change patterns, irregular menstruation cycle, and other symptoms can be some of the primary symptoms of chronic hormonal disorders like PCOD (polycystic ovarian disease) and PCOS (polycystic ovarian syndrome). These disorders not only affect the reproductive health of a woman but also affects physical health, which is marked by sudden weight gain or weight loss, mood swings, and discomfort [18].

Food nutrition can be tricky when it comes to consuming a balanced diet with all the macronutrients, micronutrients, vitamins, and minerals. We all know proteins, carbohydrates, fats, and essential elements are required by our body, but keeping track of them can be a tedious job. Since everybody is different with different body compositions, it is crucial to keep in mind that the nutrient requirements will also vary from individual to individual.

The mHealth services enable people to calculate the amount of nutrients required by the body against the nutrients actually consumed. The mHealth application related to monitoring the nutrition makes sure that the food consumed and the nutrients acquired by it by the body is according to the BMI (Body Mass Index) of an individual, which varies in males and females. When such calculations are put on the algorithms, it becomes easier for the user to keep track of everything consumed by the body. These applications can be set up in order to achieve the fitness goals that are desired by the user. The applications can be manually set to the desired plans like weight loss, muscle gain, and even maintaining a toned muscle. In this way, the mHealth applications provide services as a weight tracker, calculator, weight loss assistant, nutritionist, and food tracker [19]. Different subcategories of mHealth are shown in Figure 8.5.

8.5 PENETRATION OF mHEALTH INTO SOCIETY

Technology has become an integral part of our life. It is practically impossible to imagine our day-to-day life without a smartphone and smart devices. Integration of Artificial Intelligence and Machine Learning into smart sensing technology has led to the vivid range and increased potential of smart technology in our daily lives.

By the time you will be reading this book, there will be over 3.5 billion smartphone users (most of them coming from urban and suburban areas) in the world, which constitutes approximately 44.9% of the total world population; however, there are over 5.2 billion smart feature phones in the world, which constitutes over 66.8% of the world population who owns a mobile phone with over 10 billion active mobile connections, which accounts to approximately 128.9% of total world population, among which 5.23 billion are the unique mobile subscribers according to GSMA real-time intelligence survey and UN digital analyst estimate.

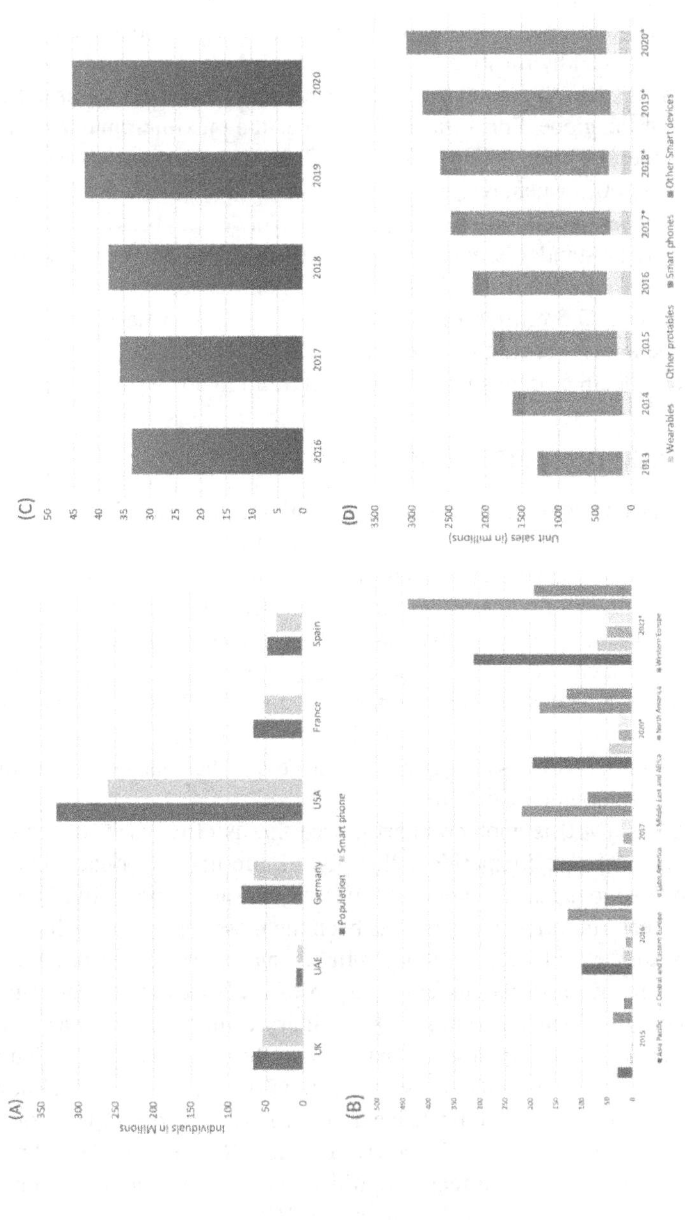

FIGURE 8.6 Distribution of mHealth in society.

These figures clearly state that the number of smartphone users has increased drastically, with over a 40% increase between 2016 and 2020. This increase could be the result of globalization and digitalization policies adopted by most of the countries across the world, reduced smartphone costs due to advancement in technology, and improved living standards. More and more people are connecting to the smart technology and a bigger proportion of youth and elderly population are getting inclined toward a healthy lifestyle.

Penetration of smartphone, smart devices, and other mobile devices is not same in every corner of the globe. For instance, China has the maximum number of smartphone users (due to its population). However, China's smart device penetration rate is approximately 60% when, on the contrary, Switzerland has the lowest number of smartphone devices in a country but the penetration of devices is as high as 73%. This is due to high living standards, awareness about the features, and better affordability.

The United Kingdom has the highest smartphone penetration with about 83% of population, i.e., 55.5 million people, having at least one smart device, whereas Nigeria has the lowest penetration rate of about 14.9% or 30 million users, as shown in Figure 8.6, reflecting promising growth of mHealth in upcoming years.

8.6 DISTRIBUTION OF SMART DEVICES

The sale of smart devices has been increasing with the addition of new technologies into smart devices. People do not restrict themselves to the usage of smartphones and smart watches. Smart homes have also become one of the trendsetters in using smart devices and making our daily work to our convenience, where all the commands can be accessed with just the voice activation of an individual. The smart STB is one of the applications which allows user to access "anything on anything." This means that this application can be installed on any device like smart TV, smartphones, or computers where it allows the user to open their own portal to the world of IPTV. This also takes care of the wireless and remote-less access to these services, provided that there is a stable Internet connection.

Virtual reality (VR) is another smart device that is often used for recreational activities. It is a simulated experience that gives a life-like experience that may or may not be related to the actual world. It can serve various purposes like educational purposes. The entertainment platform has been the most popular one which enables an individual to play videogames along with having an experience of being in the game. Virtual reality also has its contribution to the educational platform where it provides certain beneficial training like military training and medical training. The virtual reality enables the user to place themselves in a scenario which allows them to picture themselves in the training situations, giving them a vivid knowledge comparative to just theoretical knowledge. Furthermore, with mixed technology and augmented reality, they can also be referred to as XR, which is the abbreviation of extended reality. The virtual reality ramifications into text-based network VR is often termed as cyberspace and the immersive VR. The only difference between these two is that in immersive VR, when an individual moves or tilts their head, the view of the individual also changes. However, cyberspace is more concerned with calibrating the distance.

The other most popular smart device that is available on the market is the omnidirectional (360 degrees) camera. It is supposed to capture approximately a sphere from its front view on a horizontal plane. The concept of omnidirectional cameras arose from the pictures that needed wide visual coverage like panoramic photography. These cameras are also used in scientific labs in the field of robotics, due to its wide-angle visual coverage.

Smart TV, on the other hand, has been another advancement in smart devices. It is often known as connected TV (CTV). It works on the principle of integration of the normal set-top box with the Internet connectivity along with the interactive Web 2.0 features. This makes the TV accessible to the users through the Internet so that they can access and stream videos and music even on their television. The smart TV, besides performing the traditional tasks of broadcasting media, can also provide the connectivity needed to stream Internet content and home networking access.

The number of wearable sensor devices all over the world has been increasing with time, as seen in Figure 8.7. Smartphones and smart watches are some of the common wearable smart devices that are available with the maximum population. Between 2015 and 2020, an upward trend in the usage of wearable smart devices has been observed. These devices have also been cost-effective and easily accessible, which means that people are more prone to buying them. Wearable devices have been trending in different regions of the world in the past five years. A combination

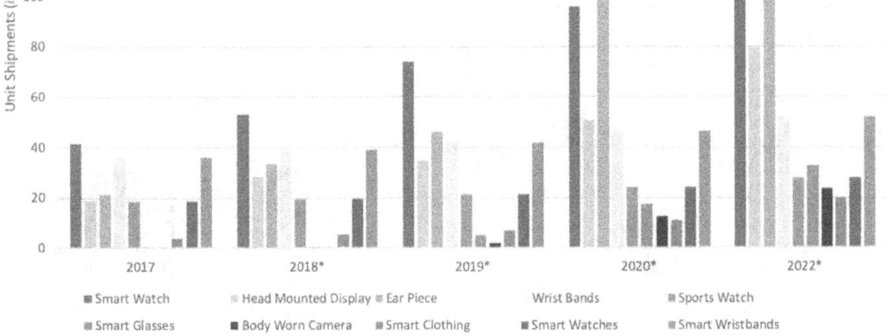

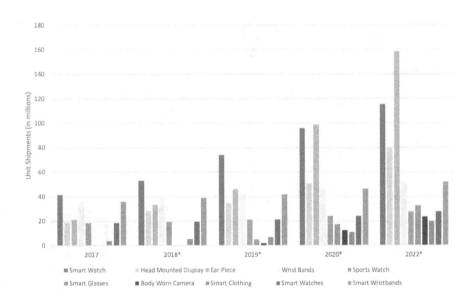

FIGURE 8.7 Global interest of people towards mHealth smart devices.

of different sensors from different mHealth devices could lead to reliable data and productive outcomes when shared using technology, could result into a mHealth network where user's information could be captured via different sensors, could be stored in real time in the portable smart device (smartphones usually), and could also be permanently stored in a medical database. This database could be accessed by physicians, healthcare providers, emergency services, and users themselves when necessary, as shown in Figure 8.8.

The North American region has been the highest consumer of wearable smart devices. In 2015, the number of connected wearable devices was approximately 36.65 million, which escalated to 217 million in 2017. It was followed by the Asia-Pacific region, which estimated around 30.4 million wearable devices in 2015, and 99.8 million and 155 million devices in 2016 and 2017, respectively, as shown in Figure 8.6b.

This rising pattern was also observed in the regions like Western Europe, Central and Eastern Europe, Middle East, and Africa and Latin America. In 2015 and 2016, the Asia-Pacific region accepted the wearable smart devices with open arms, which resulted in a high number of sales in such devices—30.4 million devices in 2015 and

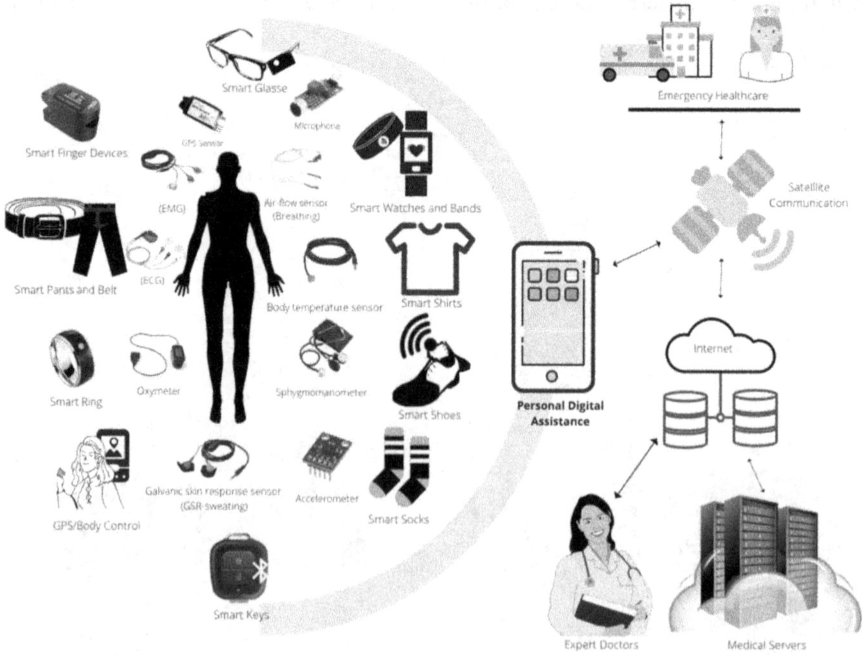

FIGURE 8.8 mHealth network architecture.

99.8 million devices in 2016. This statistical growth was followed in the regions like Western Europe, Middle East, and Africa and Latin America.

8.7 REASONS BEHIND SUCCESS AND FAILURES OF mHEALTH

mHealth has been a fast growing industry, providing services all across the globe with its new invention each day. It strives toward making the lives of the people more reliable toward themselves and stimulates the discipline and self-care required to keep oneself in a healthy state of mind and body. With the rising empire of mHealth, it has had numerous milestones in the journey with both success and failures. Where the industry of mHealth aims for higher goals after every successful invention and technological growth, it has also been careful about the failures and the reasons behind those failures. The setbacks help the mHealth industry to know their scope of growth. In this section, we will look into various reasons behind the success and failures of mHealth as an industry.

For an industry like mHealth to be successful, there are three factors that are highly essential: access, quality, and cost-containment. The acceptance of mHealth by society has mainly taken place due to these pillars of mHealth, which define the innovation's success in the society.

The accessibility of the mHealth devices makes it user-friendly. The user is able to easily understand the working of the device: how to operate and read the statistics and the steps to be taken with respect to the instructions provided by the device. The accessibility of the device is followed by the quality of the device. A technical device like mHealth device has to be built with good quality products as it has to monitor the day-to-day life activity in real time, which indicates that the device will be in constant use. The probability of wear and tear should be as low as possible, which will add to its usage life. Lastly, cost-containment plays a vital role in the triumph of the industry. Since these devices are so technologically advanced and user-friendly, they should also be cost-effective for the population to actually afford it and use it in their daily lives. It should not be merely a luxury device, rather an assistance to everyone.

The increasing demographic population and the increased number of elderly people put the industry in the position to produce more and more new innovative mHealth devices to assist people all around the world. However, in recent years, vast amounts of mHealth and eHealth interventions have failed in clinical implementations. All the industries around the globe have been developing, all incorporating mHealth in almost all the sectors. Due to this, with increasing industrialization, the demand for new innovation and technologies has been more than ever. This results in more and more failed prototypes of the inventions and the breach in mHealth promise toward providing good quality and services. There is still a huge stratum of population that finds the cost of mHealth devices expensive to be incorporated into their daily lives. Considering these setbacks, the mHealth industry has been working to overcome these odds [20]. The graph in Figure 8.9 shows a rough sketch about the reasons behind lagging of mHealth despite being a promising technology.

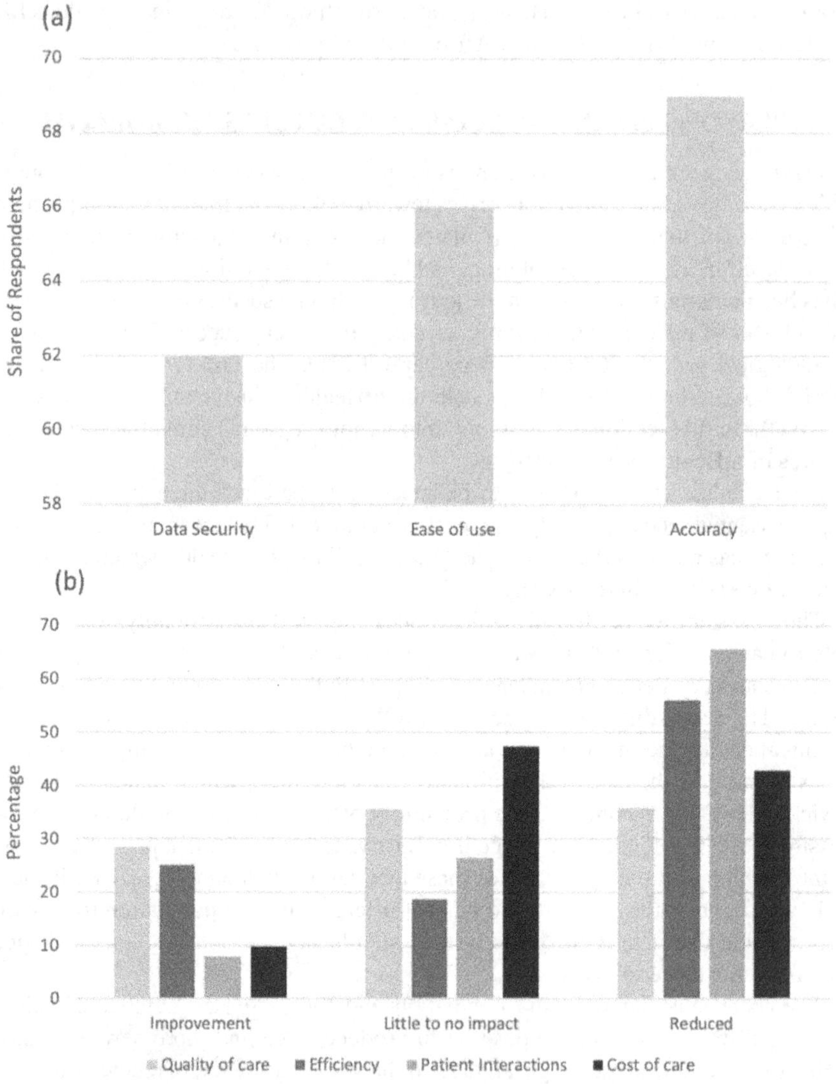

FIGURE 8.9 Acceptance and rejection of smart mHealth devices.

8.8 mHEALTH AND SISTER TECHNOLOGIES

The sister technology of mHealth includes not only the technologies that are available on our smartphones, smart watches, and wearables, but also the devices that are designed to monitor health statistics and data on a mobile platform. Certain devices may not be completely travel-friendly but they work on the principle of mHealth, which is monitoring health data for an individual. Unlike smart devices, these devices are specifically designed to monitor a specific variable of health. In this section, we will talk about the sister technologies of mHealth like sphygmomanometer, pulse oximeter, body temperature sensor, electromyography sensor (EMG), electrocardiogram sensor (ECG), airflow sensor, accelerometer, galvanic skin response sensor (GSR-sweating) [7].

Blood pressure monitor or sphygmomanometer is the device which is used to monitor blood pressure. It comprises an inflatable cuff which works on the artery by creating controlled pressure while collapsing and releasing pressure. The blood pressure in the artery is calculated by the mercury which indicates the systolic and the diastolic pressure. The manual sphygmomanometer is generally coupled with a stethoscope in order to calculate the blood pressure. There are also many automated sphygmomanometers available on the market, which show the readings in the digital format.

The pulse oximeter is a device used for clinical use and is user-friendly. The device is non-invasive in nature and calculates the blood oxygen saturation levels in the artery. The readings that are obtained from it are generally peripheral oxygen saturation. The sensor part of the device is placed on the earlobes or the fingertips, provided that the nails are not coated with any nail enamel paint for the sensor to provide an accurate reading. The device works by sending two wavelengths of light passing through the body part to the photodetector. The changing absorbance of the light is measured, which gives the absorbance due to pulsatile arterial blood.

As the name suggests, the body temperature sensor is used to measure the temperature of the body. It is also known as the thermometer. The thermometer has two parts. One is the temperature sensor, which is used to measure the temperature of the body, and the other is the device or a scale that can convert the reading into numeric form, which is easily accessible and understood by the user. The temperature sensor in the glass sensor is the bulb of the mercury; however, in the infrared sensor, it is the polymeric sensor. Similarly, in glass thermometers, the readings can be seen on the visible scale and in infrared thermometers, it is visible on the digital readouts.

Electromyography sensor (EMG) is another technology which can be used to calculate health statistics with the help of sensors. These sensors are used in the device electromyograph and the record is known as electromyogram. It is used to evaluate the electric potential that is produced by the skeletal cells. These cells are generally electrically or neurologically activated. With the help of this device, physical abnormalities or anomalies can be detected. In addition, EMG can also be used in the computer gestures to understand the human and computer interactions.

An ECG or the electrocardiograph is the device that works on the principle of electrical changes. The electrodes present in the device can detect even small significant electrical changes that are the result of the polarization and the repolarization of the cardiac muscles with each heartbeat. If there is a cardiac abnormality present in an individual, it will be recorded on the electrocardiogram, as the electric changes will differ from the normal pattern of the ECG.

An accelerometer is a sensor that senses the acceleration of a body. With the help of this device, an individual can calculate their acceleration rate with respect to their rest frame. Fitness enthusiasts can use this device to calculate their acceleration and velocity while training and keeping track of their daily fitness goals. Accelerometer sensors can be installed in multiple devices like smartphones, tablets, and smart watches.

Galvanic skin response (GSR) sensors work on the ectodermal activity and conductance. It can be used to measure the sweating and perspiration of an individual. Hence, this sensor can be used in the calculation of the physical health and the activity done by the user. It works on the electrical characteristics of the skin allowing the sensor to measure the reading consequential to the impulses.

Collectively, these microsensors inbuilt in smartphone and other smart devices monitor changes in the body's physiology and keep a track via mobile application or standard portable device. This data can be stored in the healthcare server and cloud storage and can be accessed anywhere using Internet. This could help in timely detection, better monitoring, and quick access to emergency healthcare as shown in Figure 8.10.

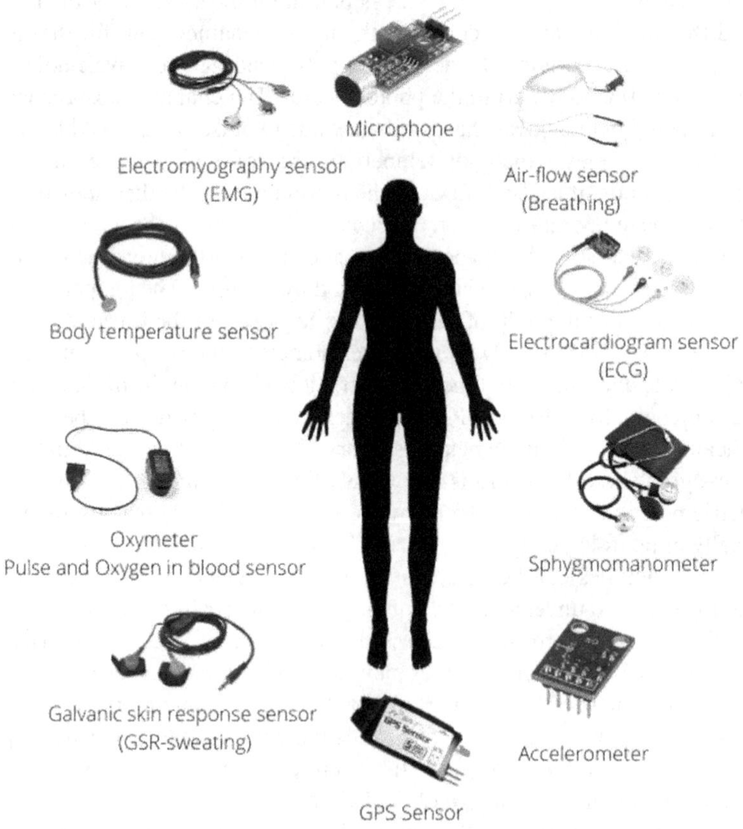

FIGURE 8.10 Sensors for mHealth smart devices.

8.9 LIMITATIONS AND REGULATIONS

The mHealth platform makes the electronic health medium available to people anywhere and everywhere. It mainly functions on the availability of Internet connectivity and database systems. To manage such intensive data, it is also important to keep in my mind that the data stored can always be misled and be compromised [21, 22]. In order to ensure that the confidentiality of the data is always safe and secured, several limitations, legislations, and regulations have been laid down, as shown in Figure 8.11.

8.9.1 Privacy Policy and Terms and Conditions

The privacy policy and the terms and conditions should be easily accessible to the user. It should be documented in simple and plain language which can be understood by the user. The section of "terms and conditions" should contain a link or a logo so that it is easily visible to the user (Figure 8.12).

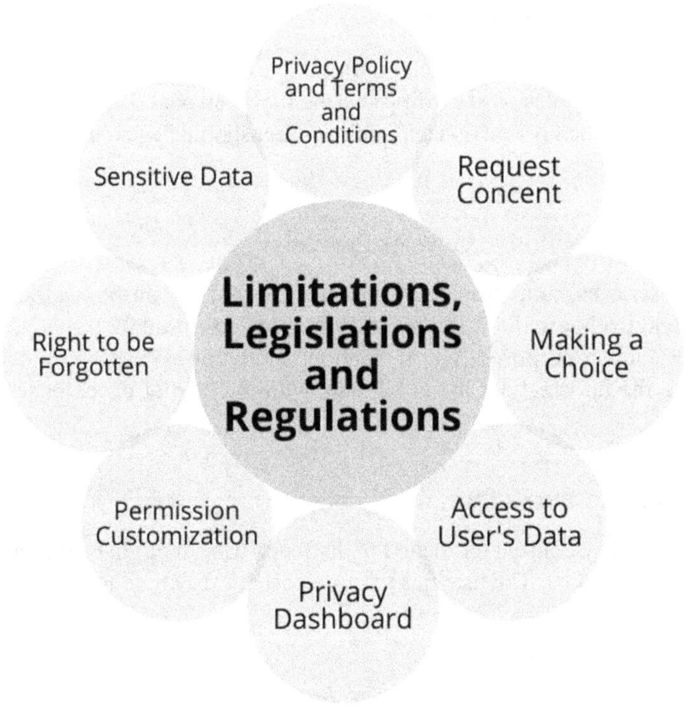

FIGURE 8.11 Legislations of mHealth.

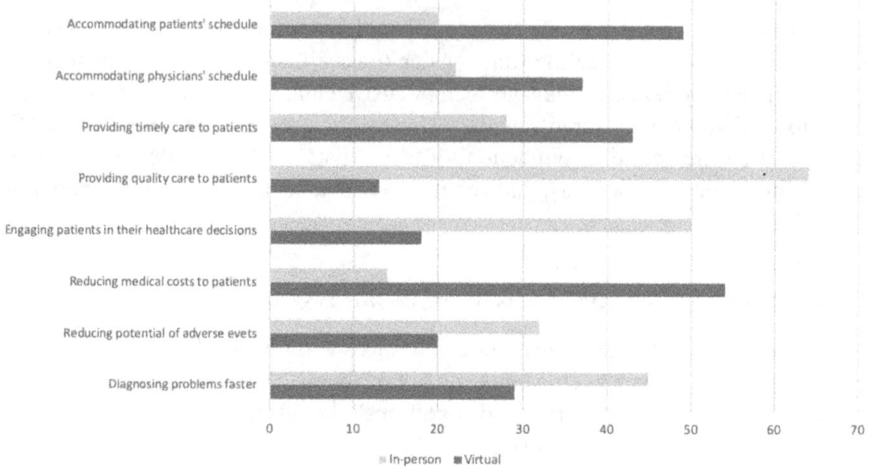

FIGURE 8.12 Face to face vs virtual acceptance of mHealth.

8.9.2 Request (Explicit) Consent

The specifications about the personal information should be very clear. Whenever a user is asked for permission regarding sharing their personal details, they should be provided with all the information and their consent should be taken through targeted and clear guidelines.

8.9.3 Making a Choice (Multiple Purposes)

When the user is asked to provide information for multiple purposes, the user must have the right to choose their personal information to be used for a specific purpose and not for another purpose. Clear indications should be given toward the specificity of using the information. It can be done with the help of check boxes and tick boxes.

8.9.4 Access to User's Data

The user has to give consent for the use of data each time. It might be for one purpose or for several purposes. The user has to give consent every time for each purpose.

8.9.5 Privacy Dashboard

The user should be provided with a privacy dashboard, where they can alter the usage of their privacy settings. Clear instructions should be provided stating the consequences of changing the settings and confirmation from the user should be asked before making any changes.

8.9.6 Permission Customization

All the permissions should be visible to the users. The users should also have the right to edit these permissions. The applications should be very descriptive with the permissions and the data access that will be granted.

8.9.7 The Right to be Forgotten

The user should be able to edit the setting of their privacy and if needed to delete the data sharing options of certain data.

8.9.8 Sensitive Data

The sensitive data, like biometric data, should be included in the special categories. The applications should be very particular about the user's consent if it requires data on such a personal category.

8.10 PROMISES AND CHALLENGES OF mHEALTH

mHealth is the provision for healthcare by which information is shared and stored through mobile technologies and personal digital assistants (PDAs). With the help of wearable sensors and smart devices, these services can reach people to influence them toward a better lifestyle and a better version of themselves. This has changed the society and the mindset of people toward healthcare in a drastic manner. It has revolutionized the conceptualization of the orthodox methods of healthcare, though it is still not replaced as in person consultation and treatment will always be an important parameter of healthcare. Despite this positive and promising nature of mHealth, there are also various challenges faced by mHealth. In this section, we will be focusing on the promises and the challenges faced by mHealth [23].

One of the major reasons behind mHealth's success is the promises it offers. Since mHealth works on the availability of the Internet, it makes sure that the data could be transferred to the clinicians and the practitioners in time, as seen in Figure 8.8. The in time monitoring and check of daily symptoms promise to track symptoms related to drug intake or even certain personalized allergies or medical conditions. Prediction of risk assessment is achievable with the combined data of the user with the help of Artificial Intelligence and other technologies. The passive data collection service provided by mHealth sets a benchmark for the positive development of technological growth [24].

Integration of Artificial Intelligence and Machine Learning in mHealth apps along with advancements in sensor technology has led to immense potential of mHealth technology. Several other factors contributed in this regard: acceptance of mHealth apps and generated data by medical practitioners and doctors, high level of digitalization in hospital and healthcare systems (such as telemedicine, teleconsultation, etc.), increased market size for smart devices, access to developers, political support and increase in available government funds to support the digital healthcare, increase in external collaborative support, and willingness of patients to pay for smart healthcare due to increased living standards, and awareness regarding healthcare, as shown in Figure 8.13a–c.

Analysis of voices, sleep-wake cycle, and active hours on social media helps in reading the behavioral pattern of the individual, which remarkably enables the assessment of the significant shift resulting in the precautionary alert to the user. With the advancement of technology and reduction in the cost of smart gadgets and biosensors, there is at our disposal a way to penetrate deep into the population beyond the socio-economic barriers. A careful analysis of real-time sensory data from both smartphones and sensory devices could prove to be just the tool needed to cope with these ever-increasing mental health issues.

During this ongoing pandemic, the world has shifted to digital platforms. The high rate of pathogenicity of virus has affected the medical system and led to shift of non-emergency cases to teleconsultation and remote consultation which created a boom in mHealth app downloads in different countries, as seen in Figure 8.13d. According to WHO, one out of four individuals is suffering from a mental or a physical ailment. mHealth provides us the opportunity to respect the rules regarding social distancing and making the individual self-aware by promoting patient empowerment. Apart from this, mHealth also makes the communication channel between the user and the clinician more transparent, which is both elaborative and

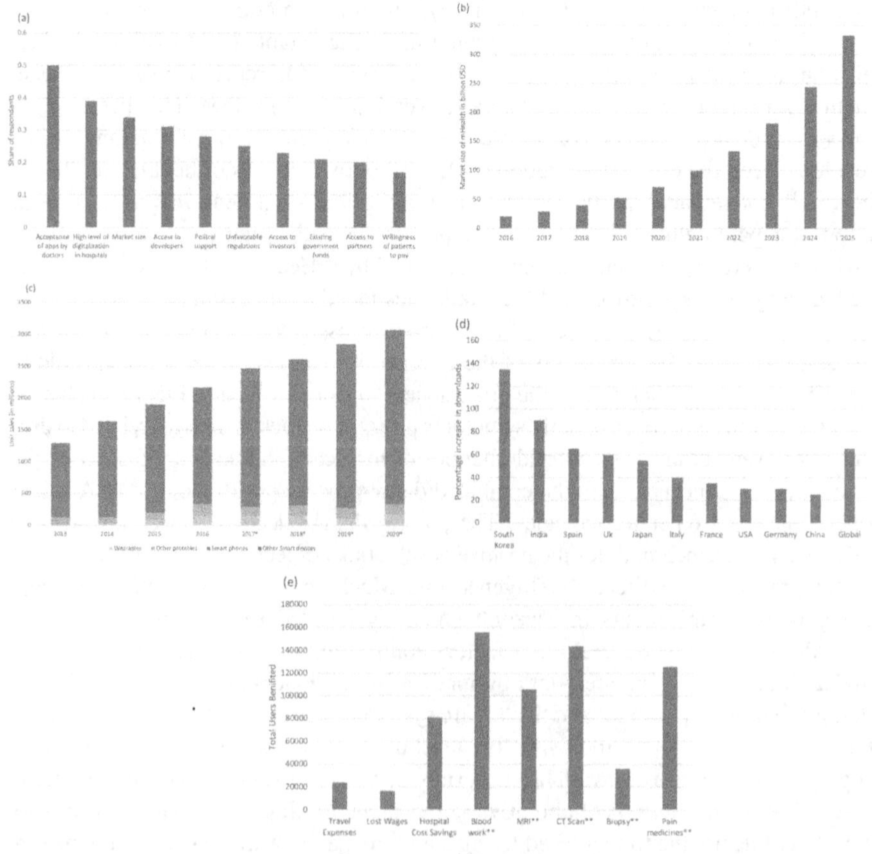

FIGURE 8.13 Factors behind acceptance of mHealth.

easily understood by the clinicians or medical practitioners and the users themselves. It provides user flexibility toward health with their schedule, while also being cost-effective (Figure 8.13e).

On the flip side, mHealth also faces multiple challenges. mHealth innovations require a massive amount of research to reduce the chances of incompetent validation and poor efficacy [25]. Since mHealth is still a new technology comparative to the one that already exists (evidence-based medicine), the medical practitioners and the general public are still coming to terms with accepting this and incorporating it as a part of their daily lives.

The mHealth industry is also concerned with ethical issues, security issues, as well as privacy issues for data sharing. It still has limited systematic integration and there is a huge gap between patient and the platform. Since it has not fully acquired as healthcare status, mHealth platforms are not covered under state or private insurances and are non-reimbursed. Moreover, these are a few controversial issues that have to be kept in mind while dealing with new technologies. The data consent is a sensitive topic and the handling of such data requires a lot of security and precautions. Since it is based on an individual's personal life and health statistics, any breach in the database can lead to severe repercussions. It is also important to take care of the flow of information between the user and the clinicians, so daily logging of information is mandatory (Figure 8.14).

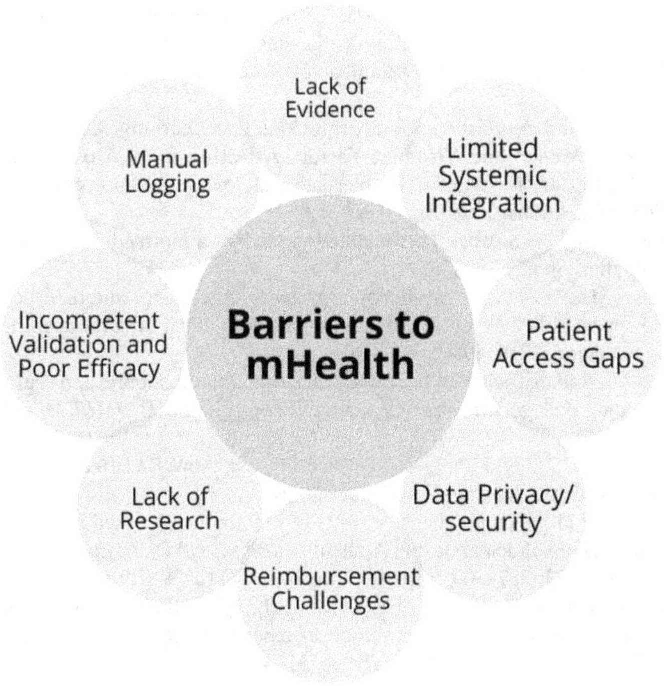

FIGURE 8.14 Barriers to mHealth services.

REFERENCES

1. Saxena, M., A. Deo, and A. Saxena. *mHealth for Mental Health. in* International Conference on Innovative Computing and Communications. 2020. Springer.
2. Saxena, M. and A. Saxena. Evolution of mHealth Eco-System: A Step Towards Personalized Medicine. in International Conference on Innovative Computing and Communications. 2020. Springer.
3. Who, D.-G., *Report of the Review Committee on the Functioning of the International Health Regulations (2005) in Relation to Pandemic (H1N1) 2009.* Sixty-fourth World Health Assembly: World Health Organization, 2011, pp. 49–50.
4. Nilsen, W., et al., Advancing the science of mHealth. *Journal of Health Communication*, 2012, **17**(supl): 5–10.
5. Saxena, M., M. Arora, and A. Saxena, Advancements in systems medicine using big data analytics. *International Journal of Information Systems & Management Science*, 2018, **1**(2), pp. 3.
6. Iyawa, G.E., et al., mHealth as tools for development in mental health, in *Impacts of Information Technology on Patient Care and Empowerment.* 2020, IGI Global. Pp. 58–80.
7. Cao, Z. Mobile phone GPS and sensor technology in college students' extracurricular exercises, in International Conference on Machine Learning and Big Data Analytics for IoT Security and Privacy. 2020. Springer.
8. Hermes, S., et al., The digital transformation of the healthcare industry: Exploring the rise of emerging platform ecosystems and their influence on the role of patients. *Business Research*, 2020, 13, pp. 1–37, doi.org/10.1007/s40685-020-00125-x.
9. Saxena, M., O. Singh, and A. Saxena, *Big Data and Personalized Medicine for Oncology*, in *2019* 6th International Conference on Computing for Sustainable Global Development (INDIACom). 2019. IEEE, pid 1352.
10. Agarwal, A. and A. Saxena. Analysis of machine learning algorithms and obtaining highest accuracy for prediction of diabetes in Women, in *2019* 6th International Conference on Computing for Sustainable Global Development (INDIACom). 2019. IEEE.
11. Agarwal, A. and A. Saxena. Comparing Machine Learning Algorithms to Predict Diabetes in Women and Visualize Factors Affecting It the Most—A Step Toward Better Health Care for Women, in International Conference on Innovative Computing and Communications. 2020. Springer.
12. Saxena, M. and A. Saxena, Personalized medicine: a bio-medicine derived from big data analytics. *Space*. **22**: 23.
13. Muntaner-Mas, A., et al., A systematic review of fitness apps and their potential clinical and sports utility for objective and remote assessment of cardiorespiratory fitness. Sports Medicine, 2019, **49**(4): 587–600.
14. Huberty, J., et al., Efficacy of the mindfulness meditation mobile app "calm" to reduce stress among college students: Randomized controlled trial. *JMIR Mhealth Uhealth*, 2019, **7**(6): e14273.
15. Longyear, R.L. and K. Kushlev, Can Mental Health Apps Be Effective for Depression, Anxiety, and Stress During a Pandemic? 2020.
16. Yousaf, K., et al., A comprehensive study of mobile-health based assistive technology for the healthcare of dementia and Alzheimer's disease (AD). *Health Care Management Science*, 2020, 23: 287–309. https://doi.org/10.1007/s10729-019-09486-0.
17. Murthy, P. and M. Naji, Role of digital health, mHealth, and low-cost technologies in advancing universal health coverage in emerging economies, in *Technology and Global Public Health*. 2020, Springer. pp. 31–46.

18. Karasneh, R.A., et al., Smartphone applications for period tracking: Rating and behavioral change among women users. *Obstetrics and Gynecology International*, 2020, 2, 1–9.
19. Franco, R.Z., et al., Popular nutrition-related mobile apps: a feature assessment. *JMIR mHealth and uHealth*, 2016, **4**(3): e85.
20. Granja, C., W. Janssen, and M.A. Johansen, Factors determining the success and failure of eHealth interventions: systematic review of the literature. *Journal of Medical Internet Research*, 2018, **20**(5): e10235.
21. Muchagata, J. and A. Ferreira. Translating GDPR into the mHealth practice, in *2018 International Carnahan Conference on Security Technology (ICCST)*. 2018. IEEE.
22. da Silva, P.E.F., et al., Development of a software for mobile devices designed to help with the management of individuals with neglected tropical diseases. *Research on Biomedical Engineering*, 2020, 36: 1–11, doi.org/10.1007/s42600-020-00090-8.
23. Baldauf, M., P. Fröehlich, and R. Endl. Trust me, I'ma doctor–user perceptions of AI-Driven apps for mobile health diagnosis, in 19th International Conference on Mobile and Ubiquitous Multimedia. 2020.
24. Goodman, R., L. Tip, and K. Cavanagh, There's an app for that: Context, assumptions, possibilities and potential pitfalls in the use of digital technologies to address refugee mental health. *Journal of Refugee Studies*, 2020, doi.org/10.1093/jrs/feaa082.
25. Brault, N., Saxena, M. For a critical appraisal of artificial intelligence in healthcare: The problem of bias in mHealth. *J Eval Clin Pract.* 2020 Dec 23. doi: 10.1111/jep.13528. Epub ahead of print. PMID: 33369050.
26. Available at: www.statistica.com.

9 Artificial Intelligence and Deep Learning for Medical Diagnosis and Treatment

Jai Mehta

CONTENTS

9.1 INTRODUCTION

Machines have been surrounding our lives since past century. Since the development of light bulb and electricity in 1878 by Edison, the whole system has been controlled by machines. So, whether it is multiple power generators supplying to the grid to bulbs operated by motion sensors, the machines are getting smarter and smarter. However, all these activities required a level of human interference as most of the machine's decisions were purely based on logic fed into it and not on its ability to think independently. Therefore, the capabilities of these machines were restricted by the capacity of the developers. As times changed, the big idea of making machines intelligent just like humans capable of making decisions resulted in lots of sci-fi movies and less of real applications. But as times further changed, we faced tougher problems, which led to the quest for intelligent machines. This quest resulted in the discovery of Artificial Intelligence, and it was formally introduced as an academic discipline in 1955 (Crevier 1993).

A large number of algorithms come under the umbrella of Artificial Intelligence and boast of making smart decisions; however, in essence they are limited by the training data. While mathematicians and statisticians were developing powerful models to predict outcomes using mathematical modeling, experts in computer science got interested in how the human brain learns and in building machines that can simulate the same learning processes. This led to some of the breakthrough algorithms, and leading among them is deep learning.

9.2 DEEP LEARNING

Deep learning is inspired by how the human brain learns from examples and stores information in the series of interconnected neurons. Let us first try to understand the human brain. Our whole body is interconnected with neurons, which collect signals and transfer to the interconnecting neurons through synapses. The information is finally processed in the brain. For most time it is learning through the incoming signals and when needed, it makes its decision; for example, when we touch hot thing, we remove our hand. Figure 9.1a symbolizes how neurons collect instructions from the environment and transmit it to the next neuron. Figure 9.1b depicts the role of neurotransmitters in transferring information.

This idea was initially incorporated in a perceptron model, which is a single-layer neural network, followed by backpropagation, and recently adapted as deep learning. The fast adaptation to deep learning has been primarily driven by high computational resources and availability of open-source platforms such as TensorFlow, PyTorch, and CNTK.

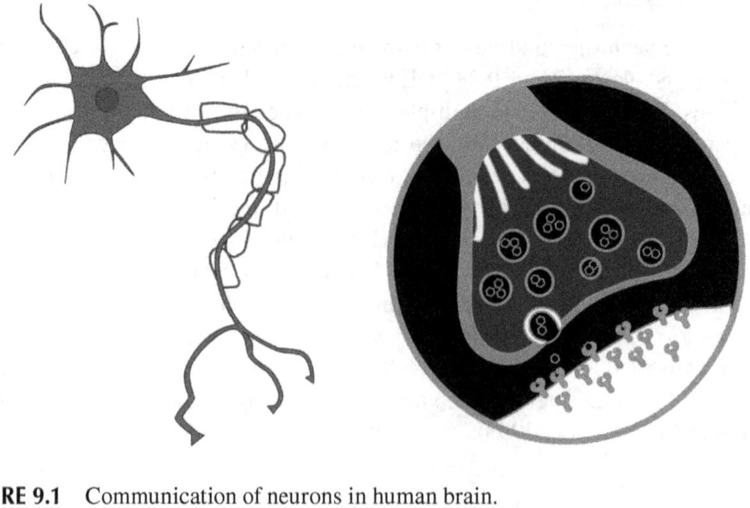

FIGURE 9.1 Communication of neurons in human brain.

9.3 DEEP LEARNING ARCHITECTURE

Deep learning architecture primarily consists of interconnected neurons. The number of input neurons and output neurons is decided on the type of problem we are trying to solve. In between the input and output neurons are the hidden neurons; the number of layers and the number of neurons in each layer vary based on the complexity of data. Each interconnection holds a weight, which at the start of training is assigned a random weight but the weight keep changing till the desired outcome is obtained.

9.4 TYPES OF DEEP LEARNING ALGORITHMS

Deep learning models are typical neurons connected in an architecture, by which predictions can be made. Different architecture and training methodologies have been developed to suit a wide range of applications. Here we discuss two of the common deep learning models:

1) **Feedforward Neural Networks (FNN):** One of the oldest training methodologies, FFN consists of fully interconnected neurons at each layer (Figure 9.2). The abstraction is captured in the interconnection between the hidden neurons. The model is trained with known outcomes and the error generated is backpropagated to modify the interconnecting weights using a stochastic gradient descent algorithm. The process of training is continued till the error sum of squares reaches the desired level. Multiple parameters need to be adjusted to achieve the desired learning and generalization levels.
2) **Convolutional Neural Networks (CNN):** Convolution neural networks are specialized type of deep learning networks and have a convolution layer along with other hidden layers (Figure 9.3). The convolution network is highly efficient in pattern recognition and therefore has been immensely

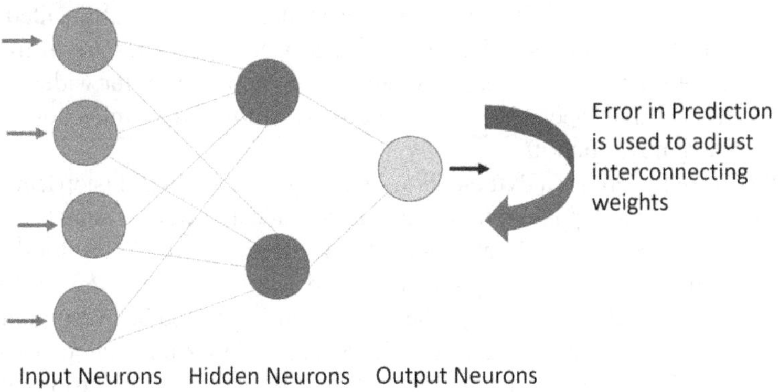

FIGURE 9.2 This diagram represents the errors in prediction is used to adjust interconnecting weights.

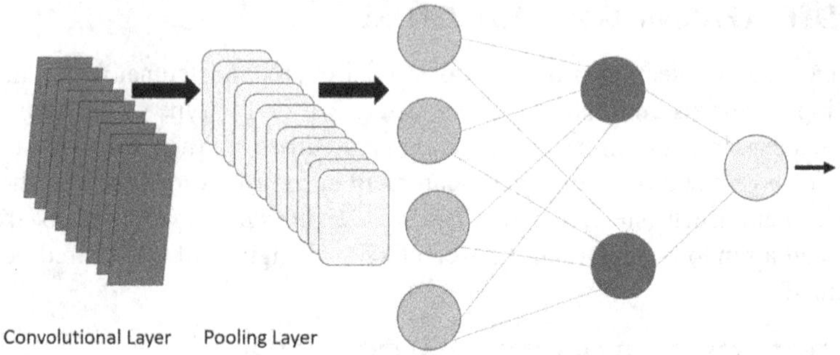

FIGURE 9.3 Illustration of convolutional layer.

popular in making predictions from the image. This has led to huge popularity in medical diagnostics and has potential to be used for automated scanning of X-rays, CT scans, biopsy, mammograms, and other areas of clinical diagnostics.

9.5 DEEP LEARNING LIBRARIES

1) **TensorFlow:** TensorFlow developed by Google is the most widely used library for commercial application of deep learning algorithms. TensorFlow runs on Python environment and provides all the tools and techniques for fast development and deployment of deep learning models. There is a library for web and mobile development applications. For more details, visit https://www.tensorflow.org/. COLAB is a web-based environment for new learners and includes all the needed libraries for quick learning and development of deep learning models. For getting started, visit https://colab.research.google.com
2) **Microsoft Cognitive Toolkit (CNTK):** CNTK, developed by Microsoft, incorporates most of the deep learning models. It is specially suited for developers working on .NET environment. CNTK libraries are available in C#, C++, and Python and therefore provide opportunity for wider range of software developers. For more details, visit https://docs.microsoft.com/en-us/cognitive-toolkit/
3) **PyTorch:** PyTorch is a Python library for easy development of deep learning models. It is more popular in research environment, given its quick learning cycle and flexibility in development of models. It is ideally suited for developers already working on Python. For more details, visit https://pytorch.org
4) **MXNET:** MXNET from Apache foundation is yet another very popular deep learning library for quick development and deployment of deep learning models. The advantage of using MXNET is in its APIs for various other languages, making it a perfect solution for integrated development and deployment. For more details, visit https://mxnet.apache.org/

5) **Keras:** Keras is a wrapper for various deep learning libraries. Keras is extremely easy to learn and a new user can get started in minutes. It runs on top of TensorFlow and other deep learning libraries. The syntax is very simple and easy to learn and implement. Keras library is developed in Python, so some knowledge of Python is necessary. More details are available at https://keras.io.

9.6 APPLICATION TO MEDICAL DIAGNOSIS AND TREATMENT

Times are changing fast and a large array of diagnostics are being used for life-threatening and chronic conditions. For many conditions, the indicators may not be so subtle, and doctors may miss out the chance for early diagnosis. In genomics, the data might be too large to make a sense of it without use of complex algorithms. Deep learning provides an opportunity to complement the traditional diagnostic methods by providing early and accurate detection, which may often be missed by the doctors. Deep learning can find its way in most of the life-threatening conditions in hospitals and has been successfully implemented in direct to consumer diagnostics. Some of the areas with high adoptability of deep learning is discussed below.

9.6.1 Imaging

X-ray, CT scans, MRI, and similar technologies have become a routine part of everyday diagnostics. A radiologist examines the images and inference is used to made diagnosis. Most hospitals struggle to have sufficient radiologists to examine the huge number of images. This leads to delayed diagnosis and treatment. Besides, sometimes the human brain can miss on early diagnosis of cancer or other life-threatening conditions, where early intervention can save lives. Deep learning models can work along the radiologist, acting as a second opinion, and reduce misdiagnosis. Most hospitals also face backlogs, sometimes up to months, especially if the diagnosis by the doctors is not flagged as urgent. Deep learning can examine the images as it is generated and can prioritize cases where it is seen something of concern (Selvikvåg Lundervold and Lundervold, 2019).

Developed countries have resorted to routine mammography for early detection of breast cancer. Such initiatives have been very effective in catching the disease before it has spread. However, it adds huge burden on the radiologist. The likelihood of radiologist to miss on early symptoms is much higher than when the patients come with symptoms. Machines if well trained can outperform radiologist in detecting breast cancer on routine mammography. Besides, it can even risk access the potential of development of breast cancer in future and those patients can go for more frequent mammography (Abdelhafiz et al., 2019).

One in five people in the Western world gets cancer at some point in their life. Early detection is often missed, and time is also lost in going through the GP and oncologist. Often in the busy schedule, people tend to ignore visiting doctors until it is too late. Skin Vision is a company from Amsterdam that has used deep learning and has developed a mobile app which can tell if a skin condition is a cancer, thereby helping people reach out to oncologist earlier than normal. Skin Vision has a sensitivity of 95% in detecting most common types of skin cancer. It also provides opportunity to track skin spots over time if a spot shows indication of being precancerous. Skin Vision is certified medical service and provide low cost home diagnostic solutions (de Carvalho et al., 2019).

Deep learning has the potential for routine screening of tuberculosis where the disease load is very high. It is particularly important in underdeveloped and developing countries, where qualified radiologists are at shortage. Deep learning trained on known tuberculosis X-ray can identify tuberculosis at an early stage. Early stage identification is critical for controlling damage to the lungs. Pasa et al. (2019) used convolution neural network to accurately diagnose tuberculosis; this neural network has a potential of large-scale screening of tuberculosis patients.

9.6.2 Genomics

Genomics is a potential area where deep learning can benefit in making intelligent decisions. The data have a very high dimension, making it a perfect problem to be solved using deep learning. However, deep learning models rely on thousands or maybe millions of data points, there are issues in getting such huge amount of data. With the huge genomic datasets come the problem of computing infrastructure. Deep learning is being under study by various groups, and with many research papers and data analysis library have been developed, it must find its applications in hospitals or diagnostic settings. Some of the developments of deep learning in genomics are discussed below.

Sakellaropoulo et al. (2019) used the drug resistance profile from 1000 cell lines to develop a deep learning algorithm to predict chemotherapeutic drug resistance in clinical samples. The study involved multiple mathematical models to develop prediction models and the deep learning models outperformed other models. Since the data was limited and originally developed from a cell line, there is a long way for it to be of clinical importance. However, the study demonstrated that deep learning has the capability to be explored in clinical settings.

Deepchrome (www. deepchrome.org) is a suite of deep learning tools for myriad applications of deep learning networks toward functional genomics. It consists of EpiGenome-DeepDiff, Genome-DeepMotif, Genome-gkmStringKernal, Protein-metaDeep, Protein-MustCNN, and BioText-SemiDeep, each with extensive application of deep learning toward functional prediction from genomics datasets.

DeepVariant (Poplin et al., 2018) is a variant caller for NGS data and it uses convolutional network to accurately identify genomic variation. Accurate SNP calling is often tricky, especially where the overlapping reads are less or the reads are of low quality. DeepVariant uses convolutional network and has ability to learn from one model and implement on another.

9.7 TUTORIAL

Before we start developing deep learning models, we need to set up the environment. This case study uses the Keras Python package, which runs on TensorFlow.

```
jpmehta@jai-ubuntu: ~
#The first 3 lines imports all the needed library
from keras.models import Sequential
from keras.layers import Dense
import numpy

# This line uploads the dataset. Place the csv file in the same folder where your code is, or p
rovide the complete path.
dataset = numpy.loadtxt("pima-indians-diabetes.csv", delimiter=",")

# Next 2 lines split input (X) and output (Y)
X = dataset[:,0:8]
Y = dataset[:,8]

# Next 4 lines constructs the model. It has 1 hidden layer and uses a mix of relu and sigmoid a
s activation function. The architecture can be changed by simple tweaks. Additionally, more hid
den layers can be added.
model = Sequential()
model.add(Dense(12, input_dim=8, activation='relu'))
model.add(Dense(8, activation='relu'))
model.add(Dense(1, activation='sigmoid'))

# Now is the time to Compile the model. It requires a loss function and an optimizer. There are
 multiple options available
model.compile(loss='binary_crossentropy', optimizer='adam', metrics=['accuracy'])

# Next we Fit the model
model.fit(X, Y, epochs=150, batch_size=10)

# Its time to evaluate the accuracy of model
scores = model.evaluate(X, Y)
print("\n%s: %.2f%%" % (model.metrics_names[1], scores[1]*100))
                                                                    27,64          All
```

FIGURE 9.4 Example code for development of deep learning network.

After installing Python 3.6, install PIP and use PIP to install TensorFlow, Keras, and Numpy package, e.g., pip install numpy, tensorflow, and keras. The dataset used is from https://www.kaggle.com/kumargh/pimaindiansdiabetescsv

The first eight columns correspond to pregnancies, glucose, blood pressure, skin thickness, insulin, BMI, diabetes pedigree function, and age and the last column is the outcome, i.e., diabetes versus no-diabetes. The eight parameters are supposed to predict if the person is likely to get diabetes in his lifetime. Once the model is trained, it can be used for making predictions for other patients and early intervention can be made to reduce chances of diabetes development.

Figure 9.4 shows the code which you can run on your computer or use COLAB. Once you execute the code, the model is developed, training performed, and the accuracy is reported. In our test drive, we obtained an accuracy of 76.56%. Try playing with parameters to obtain better prediction accuracy.

REFERENCES

Abdelhafiz, D., Yang, C., and Ammar, R. (2019) Deep convolutional neural networks for mammography: advances, challenges and applications. *BMC Bioinformatics* **20**, 281. doi: 10.1186/s12859-019-2823-4.

Crevier, D (1993), *AI: The Tumultuous Search for Artificial Intelligence*, New York, NY: BasicBooks.

de Carvalho, T.M., Noels, E., Wakkee, M., Udrea, A., and Nijsten, T. (2019) Development of smartphone apps for skin cancer risk assessment: Progress and promise. *JMIR Dermatology* **2** (1), e13376. doi: 10.2196/13376.

Pasa, F., Golkov, V., and Pfeiffer, F. (2019) Efficient deep network architectures for fast chest X-ray tuberculosis screening and visualization. *Scientific Reports* **9**, 6268. doi: 10.1038/s41598-019-42557-4

Poplin, R., Chang, P.C., Alexander, D., Schwartz, S., Colthurst, T., Ku, A., Newburger, D., Dijamco, J., Nguyen, N., Afshar, P. T., Gross, S. S., Dorfman, L., McLean, C. Y., and DePristo, M. A. (2018) A universal SNP and small-indel variant caller using deep neural networks. *Nature Biotechnology* **36**, 983–987. doi: 10.1038/nbt.4235.

Sakellaropoulos, T., Vougas, K., Narang, S., Koinis, F., Kotsinas, A., Polyzos, A., Moss, T.J., Piha-Paul, S., Zhou, H., Kardala, E., Damianidou, E., Alexopoulos, L.G., Aifantis, I., Townsend, P.A., Panayiotidis, M.I., Sfikakis, P., Bartek, J., Fitzgerald, R,C, Thanos, D., Mills Shaw, K.R., Petty, R., Tsirigos, A., Gorgoulis, V.G. (2019) A deep learning framework for predicting response to therapy in cancer. *Cell Reports* **29** (11), 3367–3373.e4. doi: 10.1016/j.celrep.2019.11.017.

Selvikvåg Lundervold, A. and Lundervold, A. (2019) An overview of deep learning in medical imaging focusing on MRI. doi: 10.1016/j.zemedi.2018.11.002.

Part III

Ethics

10 Ethical Issues and Challenges with Artificial Intelligence in Healthcare

Nicolas Brault and Benoît Duchemann

CONTENTS

10.1 MEDICAL ETHICS

10.1.1 A History of Medical Ethics: From the Hippocratic Oath to the Nuremberg Code and Beyond

10.1.1.1 Definitions

Before we deal with the history of medical ethics, it is important to define some important notions concerning this discipline, as it constitutes the major theme of this chapter. Our reader, who is not necessarily familiar with this field of research, must indeed have some kind of basic knowledge about what we are going to talk about.

First of all, the word "ethics" (ἠθικός or *ethikos* in Greek, *mores* in Latin), which can be used as a synonym of "morality," refers to both a descriptive and a normative aspect:

- The descriptive sense refers to the way people live in a specific group or a specific society, more precisely to a certain code of conduct, or to a certain set of values according to which an individual or a group lives, which specifies, more or less explicitly, the things or conducts that are permitted, valued, or forbidden.
- The normative sense is not about the way people live but rather about the way they should live. The idea is not to describe, for example, what is right or wrong in a given society, but to justify, for example, why a behavior must be considered as right or wrong, or good or bad. In other words, "ethics" in this sense is about the value of values. Some philosophers call it "normative ethics," to be more explicit about its subject.

The concept of "medical ethics" refers more to the field of "applied ethics," and constitutes a framework for the relations between medical doctors and their patients, but also concerning biomedical research. This notion is to be distinguished from the "medical deontology," which is the study of medical doctors' duties toward their patients. In most of the countries around the world, there are, for example, some kind of ethical codes which can concern journalists, lawyers, architects, and of course physicians and health professionals in general. Limits between "medical ethics" and "medical deontology" are quite vague, but we can consider that "medical ethics" refers to the philosophical reflection about what can or should be done in medicine, and the "medical deontology" refers to the legal aspects of the practice of medicine, that is to say what physicians are allowed or forbidden to do in their daily practice, and the disciplinary measures they can face if they are breaking the rules.

The last word to be defined is the word "bioethics": the term was coined by the American biochemist Van Rensselaer Potter (1911–2001) in his book *Bioethics: Bridge to the Future* (1971). According to Potter, bioethics applies to all the living world and Potter wanted to create a new philosophy that would integrate biology, ecology, medicine, and human values. Then, in the United States, bioethics became synonymous with the ethics of biomedical research. That's why Potter, in 1988, chose to use the term "global bioethics" to show more explicitly that his conception of bioethics encompasses both the humanity, present and future, and the environment.

The scope of this chapter is clearly about the normative sense of ethics, in the applied context of medicine, which includes both the physician-patient relationship, biomedical research and the healthcare system. We won't talk about animal ethics or environmental ethics: if we use the word "bioethics," it will be to designate the ethics of biomedical research.

10.1.1.2 The Hippocratic Oath and Its Values

Medical ethics has a long history, which dates back to Hippocrates (460–370 BC) and his famous Hippocratic Oath (which has probably not been written by Hippocrates himself). The new physicians, who were members of the Hippocratic School, were supposed to swear to uphold specific ethical standards. As the text of the Hippocratic Oath can be easily found on the Internet,[1] it is not necessary to reproduce it here *in extenso*. The most important aspect for us is that we can distinguish four ethical ideas or principles at stake in this oath:

1) First of all, medical doctors must respect a certain probity or integrity. This includes collegiality, i.e., respect for the other physicians and their family, especially the teachers. Physicians have to help them, morally and financially, in case they need it. Physicians should also respect the profession of physician in itself, and keep away from corruption.
2) The second idea refers to the importance of not doing harm to the patient: "I will abstain from all intentional wrong-doing and harm." This principle is often written in the Latin phrase *Primum non nocere*, which means "First, do not harm." In others words, it refers to the modern principle of non-maleficence. According to the Hippocratic Oath, this principle of not doing harm to the patient prohibits euthanasia, abortion, and even surgery, which must be left to specialists ("craftsmen").
3) The third idea is the corollary of the second: the physician must not do harm to his patient, but he must also do him good. This refers nowadays to the principle of beneficence. Of course, the Hippocratic Oath does not state explicitly this obligation, even if he says that the physician must "help the sick."
4) Finally, the Oath insists on the importance of medical secrecy and confidentiality: "And whatsoever I shall see or hear in the course of my profession, as well as outside my profession in my intercourse with men, if it be what should not be published abroad, I will never divulge, holding such things to be holy secrets." This appears as a cardinal virtue, which is still very important today, insofar as it is an essential component of a trustworthy relationship between the physician and the patient.

The values Hippocratic physicians promote are clearly centered on the physician-patient relationship, which is quite logical, given the fact that there was no biomedical research or healthcare system at that time. This is also due to the fact that Hippocrates is considered as the founder of clinical medicine (from the Ancient Greek κλίνειν *klinein* meaning to slope, lean or recline): the *klinikos* is thus the physician who visits his patients in their beds. This means that Hippocratic medicine is clearly centered on the patient, his individuality and his relationship with the environment. To put in other words, for Hippocrates, there was no such thing as diseases but only sick individuals. That's probably why his ethics is patient-centered.

10.1.1.3 From the Nuremberg Code to the Oviedo Convention

However, the birth of experimental medicine during the 19th century, due to Claude Bernard, changed the way medicine was conceived. Then, during the 20th century, several experiments were made upon people, most of the time without even their consent and sometimes without even informing them. We can make a short list of the most striking unethical experiments that took place all over the world during this period. First of all, in 1902, a German medical doctor, Albert Moll, dressed a list of more than 600 experiments where medical doctors inoculate pathogenic agents to patients without informing them. Then, in 1929, the French Army vaccinated population in Senegal without their ascent. In 1930, in Lubeck's hospital (Germany), 76 children died because they were vaccinated against tuberculosis. In 1932 began the longest experiment in history: the "Tuskegee Study," whose goal was to study the development of syphilis. This study included 600 poor Afro-American farmers: 399 with syphilis, 201 who did not have the disease. They were left uninformed (researchers told them they were being treated for "bad blood") and the authorities did not ask for their consent. Of course, they were not treated of their diseases, even after penicillin became the drug of choice for syphilis in 1947. The experiment was stopped in 1972 (40 years later), when the *New York Times* revealed the affair. In 1932, Units 731 and 100 were created by the Japan Army in China to make experiments on prisoners. The paroxysm of horror was reached by the Nazis, who made a series of medical experiments on a large number of prisoners, including children. It includes experiments on twins, freezing, malaria, jaundice, mustard gas, sea water, sterilization, poison, incendiary bomb, or high altitude.

Subsequently to the discovery of the horrors and war crimes committed by the Nazis during World War II were held the Nuremberg Trials from 1946 to 1949. One of these trials was dedicated to the physicians who made these experiments and was called the "Doctor's trial." This gave birth to the Nuremberg Code (1947), which states 10 ethical principles in medical research. The most important is the first one which states that "the voluntary consent of the human subject is absolutely essential." The code insists then on the risk-benefit balance of the experiment, and the fact that the experiment must be done for "the good of society" (second principle)

To be clear, the Nuremberg Code has never had any legal value in any country, nor it has been taken as official ethics guidelines by any association. The first international declaration, adopted by the World Medical Association, is the "Declaration of Helsinki" in 1964, which states "ethical principles for medical research involving human subjects, including research on identifiable human material and data," are largely inspired from the Nuremberg Code. Its basic principles are the respect for the individual and his autonomy (Article 8), their right to self-determination, and the right to make informed decisions (Articles 20, 21, and 22) regarding participation in research, both initially and during the course of the research: this is the notion of informed consent. Another important point is that "the subject's welfare must always take precedence over the interests of science and society" (Article 5), and that "ethical considerations must always take precedence over laws and regulations" (Article 9). It also recognizes the importance of not doing research on vulnerable individuals or groups. Its operational principles are that research should be based on a thorough knowledge of the scientific background (Article 11), on a careful assessment of risks and benefits (Articles 16, 17), but also have a reasonable likelihood of benefit to the population studied (Article 19), and be conducted by suitably trained investigators (Article 15), using approved protocols. Research must also be subject to independent ethical review oversight by a properly convened committee (Article 13). Of course, as the Declaration of Helsinki is a product of the World Medical Association, it has no real legal value, but it is considered as a set of ethical principles that every physician around the world should respect.

In fact, the only international legally binding instrument is the Oviedo Convention, or "The Convention for the Protection of Human Rights and Dignity of the Human Being with Regard to the Application of Biology and Medicine." It was created by the Council of Europe and entered into force on December 1, 1999. It has been ratified by 29 countries, although the Council of Europe has 47 members. Countries like the United States, the United Kingdom, the Russian Federation, the Popular Republic of China, the Republic of India, or Germany did not ratify it: this means that the vast majority of the world population did not ratify it. However, this convention is interesting for us, as it is not only about biomedical research, but also about biomedicine in general. It addresses issues such as "Consent," "Private life and right to information," "Human genome," "Scientific research," "Organ transplantation," or even "Public debate."

The Preamble to the Oviedo Convention thus states that "developments in biomedicine must benefit future generations and all of humanity." Its general principles are the primacy of the human being, an equitable access to healthcare, and professional standards. The issue of consent is of course pivotal to the Convention because of the relationship it has with individual autonomy. Medical intervention carried out without consent is a general prohibition within Article 5. Furthermore, consent must be free and fully informed. The Oviedo Convention also focus on the human genome: for example, genetic testing as a tool for discrimination is prohibited under Article 11. Article 12 allows genetic testing only for health or for scientific research linked to health purposes, and is reserved for health-related purposes only. In the same way, modification of the human genome, for reasons other than health-related, is generally prohibited under Article 13. Besides, a specific text about the human genome exists, which was issued by UNESCO in 1997: the "Universal Declaration on the Human Genome and Human Rights," where the human genome is considered as the "heritage of humanity" and forbids reproductive cloning.

To ensure that these ethical principles are being respected all over the word, several ethical committees were created at the end of the twentieth century: there are, for example, National Medical Councils in many countries, and experiments are supposed to be validated *ex ante* by an ethical committee. As already stated, some national and international ethical committees exist. The first committee on bioethical issues was created in France in 1983: it is called the "Comité consultatif national d'éthique" (*National Consultative Ethics Committee*) and was created in 1983. The Council of Europe has a *Committee on Bioethics DH-BIO*, created in 2012 (in replacement of the Steering Committee on Bioethics, created in 1992). And the United Nations has the *International Bioethics Committee* (IBC), which was created in 1993 and is composed of 36 independent experts.

10.1.2 The Philosophical Foundations of Medical Ethics: Deontology and Teleology

10.1.2.1 Ethical Dilemmas in Medical Ethics

After this brief overview on the legal and historical aspects of medical ethics, it is time to enter into its philosophical foundations. Most of the time, medical ethics is taught to students as a way to solve ethical dilemmas that they could face during their career as medical doctors: in this sense, medical ethics could furnish a kind of procedure to solve these dilemmas. Moreover, the recent progress in Artificial Intelligence may lead health professionals and some philosophers (for example, Nick Bostrom) to think that medical ethics (and ethics in general) could be implemented in some kind of Artificial Intelligence, and even a "superintelligence" according to Bostrom (Bostrom 2009). Of course, this implementation means that we could or should let Artificial Intelligence solve these ethical dilemmas, as Artificial Intelligence would be more objective or more powerful than the human brain to solve this kind of complex problems.

This is not the main point of this chapter: we focus here more on the multiple AI artifacts that are now used by physicians, patients, consumers, or the private and public sectors to analyze and improve medical practice, whether in a clinical or a public health context. Moreover, we consider that if some ethical principles are probably implementable, for example, utilitarianism and its calculus of pleasure and pain, it is however difficult, and maybe impossible, that an AI artifact could solve the ethical dilemmas in the medical context. We indeed consider medical ethics not as procedure that could automatically lead physicians to the solution to ethical dilemmas, but rather as a resource (just as AI artifacts) that physicians could use to think about all the moral implications of their decision (or non-decision) and explore the value of the values involved in various clinical or public-health-related issues.

However, it can be useful to state some of the ethical dilemmas physicians could face during their career: should a physician perform an abortion even if it were against his own beliefs? Should a physician tell to one half of a couple that the other half of the same couple is HIV positive, and thus break confidentiality? Should a physician prolong futile care for dying patient, to please, for example, members of his family? Conversely, should a physician stop life-sustaining therapies because of family demands? Should physician-assisted suicide be legalized? Should a physician refuse to take care of a patient because he has no health insurance and can't afford a treatment? Should it be legal to buy and sell organs for transplant?

As we can see, the list of dilemmas is almost infinite and can concern several issues such as confidentiality, professional integrity, medically assisted procreation, euthanasia, health insurance, but there are also some dilemmas concerning experimentations, reproductive technologies, or personalized medicine. The Covid-19 pandemic has also shed light, in a context of uncertainty, on critical choices physicians had to make as there was a shortage of vital equipment and supplies, for example, ventilators. In several countries, physicians had to make life-and-death decisions, according to criteria such as age or comorbidity, which were established in an emergency context.

Of course, most of the ethical dilemmas are in some way resolved by law or guidelines of states, institutions, or committees: for example, in France, the law on medical confidentiality strictly prohibits a physician from revealing HIV seropositivity to half of the couples who are not seropositive. And if the physician does it, he can be judged and put in jail for that. However, the laws and guidelines can vary a lot according to countries and times, and ethical dilemmas can be resolved in many ways according to the dominant culture of a country: abortion can thus be strictly prohibited in religious countries, for example. Another example is the possibility to sell and buy organs for transplant: in certain countries it is legal, in others it is forbidden. But sometimes laws and guidelines are just silent about what to do in certain circumstances, and the physician must be able to resolve a dilemma in order to act. That's why it is important to know and understand the two main positions in medical ethics: deontology and teleology.

10.1.2.2 Deontological Ethics

As we can see, the specificity of problems in medical ethics and bioethics in general is that it is not a choice between the good and the bad, or a problem concerning the weakness of the will (e.g., X did A rather than B, even though X was convinced that B was the better thing to do), but rather a choice between bad and bad: most of the time, you have to choose the lesser evil. Another way to state the problem in medical ethics is in terms of "values conflict": for example, euthanasia can be legal in a country, and a patient can ask you for euthanasia, and you can even be rather a pro-euthanasia person, but it can contradict the fundamental value of medical practice: "First, do not harm." This conflict between different personal, professional, and societal values is also a kind of ethical dilemma.

To simplify, we can say that there are two major ethical positions in medical ethics: deontology and teleology (also called consequentialism).

Deontological ethics is usually associated with the work of Immanuel Kant (1724–1804): according to his theory (Kant 1998), an action is considered as morally good if its intention is good, whatever the consequences of this action. In other words, the action is morally good if it conforms to a law or a principle, if it is made with respect to what he calls the "moral law." This is in relation to the fact that for Kant, the only virtue that can be unqualifiedly good is the "good will." No other virtue has this status because every other virtue can be used to achieve immoral ends (for example, the virtue of loyalty is not good if one is loyal to an evil person).

For him, there is a single obligation, which he calls the "Categorical Imperative," which is derived from the concept of duty. Categorical imperatives are principles that are intrinsically valid and good in themselves: this means that they must be obeyed, whatever the circumstances. Kant gives two different and successive formulations to his categorical imperative:

1) The first formulation of the categorical imperative is that of *universalizability*: "Act only according to that maxim by which you can at the same time will that it should become a universal law" (Kant, 1998, p. 31).
2) The second formulation of the categorical imperative is related to the fact that for Kant, only humans, considered as rational agents, are capable of morality and are to be considered as ends in themselves: "So act that you use humanity, whether in your own person or in the person of any other, always at the same time as an end, never merely as a means" (Kant, 1998, p. 38).

The two formulations are in fact two faces of the same coin. To understand his point, one has to remember that Kant makes a clear distinction between persons and things: persons (by which Kant means human beings) are ends in themselves and as such have a dignity; whereas things are means toward an end, and consequently have a price. This is summed up in Table 10.1.

Therefore, every human being has to defend his dignity and the dignity of any other human beings when he acts: for example, dwarf-tossing is more or less legal in some countries (for example, in Australia), if the person is of course consenting, but in some countries, it is considered as contrary to human dignity and thus prohibited. The rationale for this interdiction is that even if the person of short stature is consenting to this practice, and is thus autonomous, however, by consenting to being tossed, he infringes not only his own dignity but also the dignity of all the other human beings (according to the first formulation of the categorical imperative). In a medical context, it can be applied to euthanasia or medically assisted suicide: in a Kantian perspective, suicide is strictly prohibited because it cannot be universalized: "*First,* as regards the concept of necessary duty to oneself, someone who has suicide in mind will ask himself whether his action can be consistent with the idea of humanity *as an end in itself.* If he destroys himself in order to escape from a trying condition he makes use of a person *merely as a means* to maintain a tolerable condition up to the end of life. A human being, however, is not a thing and hence not something that can be used *merely* as a means, but must in all his actions always be regarded as

TABLE 10.1
Persons and Things

Persons	Things
Ends	Means
Dignity	Price

an end in itself. I cannot, therefore, dispose of a human being in my own person by maiming, damaging or killing him" (Kant, 1998, p. 38).

It is not better if it is medically assisted because, in this situation, it is the physician (or a member of the medical staff) who commits a murder, and murder is also prohibited, even if there are some exceptions. In the same way, one cannot sell his organs (for example, a kidney) because he is a person and as such he cannot use his body as a means to an end, which has a price, and not a dignity.

Finally, Kant distinguishes between three kinds of actions in relation to moral duty (or moral law):

1) *An action that is contrary to duty:* This action is necessarily immoral or bad because it is contradictory to categorical imperative and thus infringes the human dignity. Killing, or lying, or committing suicide are clearly actions contrary to duty.
2) *An action that is in conformity to duty:* This action is morally neutral. For example, a physician who keeps secret the information revealed by his patient because he doesn't want to lose his job acts in conformity to duty but not from duty. He's acting this way because of an interest or by fear and this is more an hypothetical imperative than a categorical one.
3) *An action from duty:* This is the only action that must be considered as good according to Kant. An action from duty is, for example, keeping the medical secret because it is the physician's duty, whatever the consequences. This is the only way to be in conformity with the moral law, and then with reason. It is about doing one's duty for duty sake.

As we can see, the main weakness of Kantian moral is its rigidity: It is quite difficult to apply it to the multiple situations met by health professionals in critical medical contexts, especially in multicultural societies. The other main weakness lies in its formalism: by focusing on principles and rules, Kantian ethics is doomed to be empty and powerless in real life, as principles always underdetermine actions. This critic was already tackled by Kant in a controversy with Benjamin Constant (the problem of lying to the murderer at the door), in his book *On a Supposed Right to Lie Because of Philanthropic Concerns* (1797). Conversely, the main advantage of Kantian moral is that it is quite easy to translate it into laws or norms, whose main function is to authorize or forbid conducts and actions. A second advantage is its appeal to autonomy and the idea, taken from Jean-Jacques Rousseau, that one is free when he obeys a law he prescribed for oneself. Autonomy is indeed a cardinal virtue in the field of medical ethics.

10.1.2.3 Teleological ethics (or consequentialism)

In opposition with the deontological view, the teleological position in medical ethics pays a special attention not to the intention (the good will) of the action, but to its results or its consequences: if the action has produced some good, or more good than harm, or even minimized harm, then this action must be considered as morally good. The most famous consequentialist theory is without a doubt utilitarianism, which was founded by Jeremy Bentham (1748–1832) and developed in his book *An Introduction to the Principles of Morals and Legislation* (Bentham 1789), first published in 1789. The main concept of utilitarianism is logically "utility" and Bentham's work opens with a statement of the principle of utility:

> Nature has placed mankind under the governance of two sovereign masters, pain and pleasure. It is for them alone to point out what we ought to do, as well as to determine what we shall do.
>
> **(Bentham 1789, Introduction, Chapter 1, p. 1)**

This sentence is interesting because Bentham adopts a heteronomous perspective: by "heteronomy," we mean that the ends are assigned by someone or something else than the individual himself—it could be Nature, as in Bentham's case, but it can also be God. Religions are typically heteronomous ethics, because God is supposed to have told humans what he ought and ought not to do (for example, the Ten Commandments). In an autonomous perspective, like in Kant's moral philosophy, any rational agent gives to himself the ends he wants to pursue: for Kant, as we saw, the end is duty, that is respect of the moral law and of the categorical imperative. For Bentham, it is "Nature" who gives us our ends: avoid pain and seek for pleasure, as pain and pleasure are our "sovereign masters who tell us what we ought to do."

By "principle of utility," Bentham means:

> that principle which approves or disapproves of every action whatsoever. According to the tendency it appears to have to augment or diminish the happiness of the party whose interest is in question: or, what is the same thing in other words to promote or to oppose that happiness.
>
> **(Bentham 1789, Introduction, Chapter 1, p. ii)**

And by "utility," Bentham means:

> that property in any object, whereby it tends to produce benefit, advantage, pleasure, good, or happiness (all this in the present case comes to the same thing) or (what comes again to the same thing) to prevent the happening of mischief, pain, evil, or unhappiness to the party whose interest is considered.
>
> **(Bentham 1789, Chapter 1, p. 2)**

As we can see, for Bentham, the concept of utility is synonymous with the concepts of "benefit, advantage, pleasure, good, or happiness" and the goal of every human being and of every society is to augment the happiness or the pleasure, and to diminish the unhappiness or pain. Bentham even creates some kind of "hedonistic calculus" or "felicific calculus" to calculate the amount of pleasure or pain that a specific action is likely to cause. He distinguishes between seven factors, which Bentham calls "circumstances," such as "intensity, duration, certainty or uncertainty" (see Bentham 1789, Chapter 4, p. 27).

Bentham thus proposes a kind of algorithm to calculate the amount of pleasure or pain caused by an action. This constitutes a major outbreak in moral philosophy because, for the first time, it is or it looks possible to quantify what is considered as purely a qualitative phenomenon, i.e., pleasure or pain. And this calculus includes not only the individual who acts but also all other persons who could be affected by this action.

In medical ethics, this idea of a calculus is particularly used in medical experimentation: one of the major criteria to authorize an experimentation on human beings is indeed the risk-benefit balance, which must be positive. The same kind of quantification is used in quality of life scales (QOLS), or also in quality-adjusted life years (QALY), which is a generic measure of disease burden, including both the quality and the quantity of life lived, used in economic evaluation to assess the value of medical interventions. Finally, several ethical dilemmas can be resolved with a teleological or consequentialist approach: selling one's organ can be, for example, morally justified because it saves someone's life, without causing too much harm to the person who gives his organ.

The main strength of teleological approach is that it is practical: its appeal to quantification makes it easy to implement it in public health policies, but also in data-driven approach. The second advantage is the idea that we can define or calculate objectively the good but also the bad: this leads to better take into account the pain and the suffering of the patient, but also his quality of life.

The main weakness of the teleological approach, and especially the utilitarian approach, is that it is not so easy and sometimes not possible to calculate what is a pleasure or what is happiness, and *a fortiori* a certain amount of pleasure or happiness: in multicultural societies, it is difficult to take for granted that every human being has the same conception of what are pleasure and pain. More precisely, there is always a risk of sacrifice: the maximum of happiness for the maximum of people is not the maximum of happiness for the totality of people. In a utilitarian perspective, it is not morally wrong to sacrifice one child to save ten children. Ultimately, utilitarianism can be summed up by the sentence: "The end justifies the means." Besides representing some kind of moral laziness, this moral principle can lead to serious misconducts in a medical context, and even to atrocities, as this was the case with the Nazis doctors, who were probably convinced that their horrible experiments on prisoners would greatly improve science.

10.1.3 From "Principlism" to Virtue Ethics:

10.1.3.1 The "Principlism" of Beauchamp and Childress

In 1979, a book was published that is still highly influential in the field of medical ethics: *Principles of Biomedical Ethics* (Beauchamp and Childress 2013), written by philosophers Tom Beauchamp and James Childress. This is an important book because its main idea is to provide a tool for health professionals and patients, both to identify moral problems and to make decisions about what to do. This practical approach for ethical decision-making is thus new, not because it would propose new ethical principles, or a new ethical theory, but because it proposes a set of four principles that are supposed to furnish "an analytical framework of general norms derived from the common morality that form a suitable starting point for biomedical ethics" and thus "general guidelines for the formulation of more specific rules" (Beauchamp and Childress, p. 13). These four principles are as follows:

(1) *Respect for autonomy* (a norm of respecting and supporting autonomous decisions),
(2) *Nonmaleficence* (a norm of avoiding the causation of harm),

(3) *Beneficence* (a group of norms pertaining to relieving, lessening, or preventing harm and providing benefits and balancing benefits against risks and costs), and
(4) *Justice* (a group of norms for fairly distributing benefits, risks, and costs). (Beauchamp and Childress, p. 13)

Nonmaleficence and beneficence are old principles, dating back to Hippocrates, as we saw before. They are also clearly teleological principles, as they are oriented toward the goal or the consequences of the action, i.e., patient's good. Conversely, autonomy and justice, which are more modern principles, are deontological principles: autonomy refers again to the patient and his capacity to an informed consent, whereas justice refers more to the socioeconomic aspect of medicine and healthcare.

By "common morality," Beauchamp and Childress mean "the set of universal norms shared by all persons committed to morality" (Beauchamp and Childress, p. 3), such as the prohibition of murder and of causing pain to others, the obligation of telling the truth, etc. In this sense, this common morality is "applicable to all persons in all places, and we rightly judge all human conduct by its standards." Hence, as the four principles are derived from this "common morality," they are supposed to be also universal. Therefore, the main advantage of principlism is that these four principles can be accepted as a basis for discussion, be it religion, or the moral principles, or the culture in general of all the participants to this discussion. This is crucial in modern multicultural societies. By stating the four principles, it allows the participants to the discussion (patient, patient's family, physician, medical staff, etc.) to be more explicit about the values they cherish the most and make their decision according to their most valuable value.

The main weakness of this theory can be that it is too narrow: maybe four principles are not enough and maybe some people can consider that they do not share neither of these four principles nor the principles of that "common morality" that every human being is supposed to share. For example, in a heteronomous perspective (whether the one fixing the rules is God or Nature, or anything else), these four principles may appear as totally irrelevant. The second weakness is that the conflict between principles may stay unresolved, because there are no unified moral theory from which they are all derived[2]: in other words, not only is there a conflict between teleology and deontology, but there is also a conflict inside teleology and inside deontology between the two principles of each side. For example, the principle of justice can be in contradiction with the principle of beneficence: during the Covid-19 pandemic, physicians had to made difficult choices between their patients, as the resources (for example, ventilators) were rare, according to the criteria that were not necessary fair (age, gender, social insurance, low or high socioeconomic status, etc.). In the same way, the distinction between non-maleficence and beneficence is not always clear: in the case of a terminally ill patient, doing good (beneficence) could lead to help the patient to die, which contradicts the principle of non-maleficence. Conversely, the physician could practice some kind of therapeutic obstinacy or aggressive treatment and thus not respect the principle of maleficence, in order to save a patient in conformity with the principle of beneficence. The formal aspect of principlism cannot furnish a solution to this kind of problems.

10.1.3.2 Virtue Ethics

It is impossible to present in a few pages all ethical theories that have been proposed more or less recently. We can cite *right theories*, which is a variant of contractualism, and focus on the concepts of contract, mutual agreement, and consent; *narrative ethics*, term coined by Adam Newton in his eponymous book (Newton 1997), an approach to ethical problems and practice that involves listening to and interpreting people's stories rather than applying principles or rules to particular situations; and *care ethics*, defended especially by Carol Gilligan from a feminist perspective in her book (Gilligan 1993), which holds that moral action centers on interpersonal relationships: the aim of care ethics is thus in particular to maintain relationships by contextualizing and promoting the well-being of caregivers and care-receivers in a network of social relations.

However, it seems important to mention virtue ethics for two main reasons: first, this is without doubt the oldest ethical theory, dating back to Aristotle and his *Nicomachean Ethics* (Aristotle 2009); second, since the article of E. Anscombe in 1958 (Anscombe 1958), virtue ethics has made a significant comeback in the philosophical discussions about medical ethics and bioethics (and ethics in general), precisely because of the absence, in deontological as well as teleological ethics, of the traditional themes of ethics in history: virtues and vices, moral character, moral wisdom, the problem of happiness, and the fundamental question: what is a good life? In medical ethics, virtue ethics insists not on the principles or the consequences of the action, but on the agent: the goal of ethics is not to know "what virtue is" but "to become good" (Aristotle 2009, p.24).

Virtue is for Aristotle a disposition, or a habit, or a "state of character," and acting virtuously is avoiding excess and deficiency, which are vices:

> Virtue, then, is a state of character concerned with choice, lying in a mean, i.e. the mean relative to us, this being determined by reason, and by that reason by which the man of practical wisdom would determine it
>
> **(Aristotle 2009, p. 31)**

For example, in a dangerous situation, a man must be courageous, which means neither rash, nor coward. But how does one know if he is courageous (i.e., virtuous) or rash or coward (i.e., vicious)?

The criterion here is a real person: the "man of practical wisdom" (the *phronimos*) embodies the virtue of practical wisdom (*phronesis*), which is derived from experience. But there is another criterion to recognize a virtuous action: pleasure. For Aristotle, when we act virtuously, we can feel the emotion of pleasure, and this emotion functions as a sign that we are doing something good. But pleasure is not an end, as it is for utilitarianism: it is rather a means towards a greater end, which is happiness, defined as an "activity in accordance with virtue" (Aristotle 2009, p.194).

The last important point about Aristotelian ethics in the context of medical ethics is the importance given to the specificity of a situation: if virtue is a state of character, this state of character must be in practice to be real, and this practice always refers to specific situations or cases:

> For instance, both fear and confidence and appetite and anger and pity and in general pleasure and pain may be felt both too much and too little, and in both cases not well; but to feel them at the right times, with reference to the right objects, towards the right people, with the right motive, and in the right way, is what is both intermediate and best, and this is characteristic of virtue.
>
> **(Aristotle 2009, p. 30)**

For physicians and healthcare professionals, the main advantage of virtue ethics is that it insists on their moral character (and physicians, for example, are supposed to have values and act virtuously, as their main goal is to cure patients and take care of them), their practical wisdom (acquired through experience), and also on the specificity of each patient and of each situation: the physician knows what to do, taking into account both general principles and the particular circumstances of a case.

The main weakness of virtue ethics is that it depends too much on the moral character of the agent and is too prone to individual definitions. It is thus extremely difficult to systematize or generalize and cannot furnish clear or explicit guidelines or healthcare professionals.

10.1.3.3 Synthetic Tables of Ethical Theories (Table 10.2)

TABLE 10.2
The Three Main Ethical Theories

Name	Deontology	Teleology	Virtue
Origin of moral principles	Autonomy	Heteronomy	Heteronomy
Motive of the action	Duty	Pleasure	Virtue
End of the action	Justice	Good	Happiness
Criterion of morality	Principles	Consequences	Mean between excess and deficiency
Weaknesses	*Rigidity:* difficulty to apply it to real situations, especially in the medical context *Formalism:* lacks empirical content	Sacrificial effects Difficulty to define what is good and bad	Depends too much on the moral character of the agent: too individual. Difficulty of systematization: cannot furnish explicit guidelines for action
Strengths	Easy to translate into laws and codes Appeal to freedom and consent	Objectivity of the good through quantification Easy to put in practice	Insists on the moral character and the practical wisdom of healthcare professionals. Attention paid to the specificity of each case
Main representative author	Kant	Bentham	Aristotle

10.2 ETHICS OF ARTIFICIAL INTELLIGENCE

10.2.1 Ethics of Technology and Ethics of AI

Technology has been perceived as a vehicle for economic, human, as well as social progress since 18th century. By showing the solar system through his telescope and by demonstrating a heliocentric theory of the universe, Galileo Galilei has highlighted our human senses fallibility and has freed us from it. Somehow the industrial revolution machinism freed us from ungrateful physical tasks and enhanced our individual and collective capabilities to perform tasks requiring more and more energy, force, and dexterity.

Nevertheless, this progressive dimension has been recurrently questioned. Lewis Mumford (Smith 1994)[3] has argued that technological innovations might threaten social and spiritual progress; similar conceptions, highlighting technicist issues, have also been put forth by other thinkers such as Langdon Winner, Jacques Ellul, or Ivan Illich.[4]

As Johnson and Powers (2005) dismiss the idea that technical innovation might be axiologically neutral, Langdon Winner's quote in Smith (1994) completes their statements:

> Technological systems, with their inherent political qualities, are not value neutral (...), societies, if they are to be equitable and effective, must understand precisely what sorts of implications new technologies may carry with them before they are introduced.
>
> **(Smith 1994)**

Hence, if a new technological system is not neutral, the value system it carries must be dependent on the societal environment in which it is to be implemented. The ethical responsibility for the development and implementation of such a system should refer to the political will for social justice. In order to remain ethically valuable, technological innovations should thus comply with regulations supporting the society's value system. In so doing, those regulations are society-driven and external to the technology itself, and should be the means to submit technology to some higher moral principles. Condorcet already mentioned this need for an "improved legislation" almost two centuries ago:

> In short, does not the well-being, the prosperity, resulting from the progress that will be made by the useful arts, in consequence of their being founded upon a sound theory, resulting, also, from an improved legislation, built upon the truths of the political sciences, naturally dispose men to humanity, to benevolence, and to justice?
>
> **(Condorcet 1791)**

Technical progress should then be coconstructed *de facto* by the Aristotelian necessary causes,[5] which lead the technical production as well as an outer ethical order that should be enforced by governments.

As any technology, AI should be subject to outer rationalized ethical policies. Moreover, as a disruptive technology which will potentially—and already does—change drastically working and leisure environments, there is a fundamental need for a normative framework guaranteeing the ethical production and usage of AI.

10.2.2 From the Myths of Artificial Intelligence to Neo-Luddism: A Plea for Regulation of AI

Further to our senses limitations as shown by Galileo Galilei, Herbert Simon (Simon 1955) has brought to light and modelized our limited rationality, "the psychological limits of the organism."[6] His theory was later echoed and developed by scientists of decision such as Tversky (1969), Kahneman and Tversky (1979), and Evans (1990), highlighting how human cognition is imperfect and subject to irrationality and biases.

The initial AI project[7]—in which H. Simon participated—was to deliver a clear understanding of our cognition and to create *in silico* a "common sense" at least equal to ours, and possibly better or at least more regular. AI then seems to be an innovative object aiming at extending our capabilities by freeing us from our cognitive limitations. It is the latest promise for technical progress, a systemic agent of our present and future modernity. This project is part of the present AI storytelling, the constructed myth of an enhancing technology meant for human good.

In the early 19th century, Luddites destroyed textile machines which were accused of replacing human labor and know-how; this idea has been regularly echoed by Marxist thinkers and in particular by Anders (2018a; 2018b), hence speaking of the alienation of human workers. Quite differently, Arendt (2018) considers that technology alienates our relationship with the world, and Kitcher (2001) considers that a more contemporary Luddite "lament" to science and technology is to see them as dehumanizing. On the other hand, instead of considering humans as being submitted to an anonymous system led by a technical rationality, Jonas' approach (Jonas 1985) considers a consequentialist "ethic of the future" where human responsibility is necessary to balance the potential consequences of our technique-driven actions.

While our societies are faced with these historical warnings against possible technical misdeeds of particular technical innovations, amplified by a form of technophobia that irrigates certain sectors, some new dangers and risks are emerging with the rise of AI technology. Some voices today[8] fear that AI will help replace humans in most industries not yet concerned by sole machinism. They fear that no human activity—even the cognitive ones—will actually be free from being performed by alternative machinic or AI processes. Some voices, conveyed by Bostrom (2014), warn against AI and the emergence of a new order that would sound the death knell for human sovereignty or at least for human autonomy. Some others still highlight the fear of job destruction[9]; it is then no longer only a matter of a "Luddite" fear of human labor replacement by the means of mechanization, but more broadly of the transformation of the very concept and the very value of labor. Finally, some are concerned with the transparency of AI solutions, the respect of privacy and confidentiality of information, and the manipulation of people.

Both ethical and legislative frameworks still remain deficient while facing such historical and emerging fears for machinism and AI. As a matter of fact, legislations from most countries have trouble keeping pace with the fast changes brought on by AI and the development of new applications. It is what Floridi (1999) calls a "policy vacuum," which is also noticed by Johnson and Powers (2005), Müller (2016), and Morley et al. (2020). In such circumstances, all actors are therefore calling for the foundation of a specific ethics that will enable AI to face these challenges. The industrial and institutional actors are trying to fill the gap but without any real coordination. Furthermore, besides the marketing promise of responsible innovations, the actual ethical purpose does not always appear clearly established.

Some private companies[10] and professional organizations[11] have so far managed to develop ethical principles in order to frame the AI innovations. Some governments together with professional organizations have also succeeded in legislating on certain AI-related innovations or so-called intelligent systems[12]; however, this remains limited to specific industries and oriented only toward an efficient while ethical use of technology. On top of this, many workshops and roundtables have been held in various countries, collecting the general public's perception of AI-related issues and relaying it in a bottom-up mode[13] to governments. Morley et al. (2020) identified nearly 70 AI ethics programs from major AI players,[14] institutional programs at a national or an international level, and the "AI for Good" program launched by the United Nations in collaboration with the ITU.[15]

However, this search for an AI ethics goes along with its myth. AI is considered mostly as an ethical object as it is presently designed. But it is assigned some capabilities that go far beyond its actual achievements and some voices want to rule AI as a possible futuristic—and much fantasized—autonomous subject.

10.2.3 AI for Social Good: A New Principlism?

10.2.3.1 What Ethics for AI ?

> Is not a mistaken interest the most frequent cause of actions contrary to the general welfare?
>
> **(Condorcet 1791)**

Hence, establishing an AI ethic and further implementing an AI applied ethic should consist in "hearing" the interest so that the action of an AI artifact remains in conformity with the general welfare.

It would involve answering questions: how do we define welfare we want to aim at; and consequently, how can we model an AI that complies with such a welfare or such a social good?

Answering such questions requires first to choose an ethical theory. A consequentialist version—as in Jonas (1985)—should involve a moral responsibility toward the future consequences of technology-driven actions. A contractualist would include some sort of a social contract built upon democratic deliberation in order to establish what general good is. A utilitarian one would necessitate a consensual value system in order to evaluate and balance the positive and negative impacts of technology. A virtue ethics would be based on character virtues of the individual and collective actors involved in the AI development and implementation. Finally, a principlist version is built upon clear ethical principles and their efficient usage.[16] The latter functions itself as a technical scheme, with a cybernetic feedback loop regulating the potential differences between practical misdeeds and the ethical axiomatic.

Broadly, knowledge engaged in the definition of general good principles is on the order of moral axiomatic. It can be considered in a transcendental way as resulting from a higher value system, for example, religious, or immanent, for example, conditional to a given sociocultural context. Whatever ethical theory is involved,[17] it is originated consensually from a public. We may note at this point the difference between the idealistic contractualism[18] based on Rousseau's social contract and the Hobbesian contractarianism[19] based on a self-interested deal. But there remains an ambiguity in the word "public" that needs to be clarified: besides the obvious group of all members from a society, there may be several publics as much as there may be several interest groups such as the industry, governmental institutions, activists, scientists, consumers etc. Thus, general good is based on a system of value within a given society and a given public. We may note a possible tension here as different publics within a common society may have different sets of values, this tension could be reinforced when considering different publics from different societies.

10.2.3.2 Principles and Factors

Further to Google's and IEEE's initiatives already mentioned, let us mention as well the Asilomar AI Principles[20] following the Conference for Beneficial AI, or else the Partnership on AI eight "tenets"[21] delivering a general creed for ethical AI developments.

Aiming at a synthesis of 47 AI ethical principles identified in four major international reports, Floridi et al. (2018) grouped them into five major categories: *beneficence*, *non-maleficience*, *justice*, *autonomy*, and *explicability*. The first four principles are precisely those edicted by Beauchamp and Childress (2013) in their foundational work for a biomedical ethics, with Floridi et al. adding the explicability as a principle specific to AI.

In doing so, Floridi et al. (2018) as well as Taddeo and Floridi (2018) propose a structural basis to standardize ethical behaviors in the chain of production and usage of AI. Then they categorize the action prescriptions into four groups: *to assess*, *to develop*, *to incentivize*, and *to support*; upstream evaluation of the capacity to manage risk, evaluation of the capacity to repair, evaluation of tasks that should never be delegated to the AI, evaluation of existing legislation and their capacity to deal with ethics; development of mechanisms that are still deficient or missing, whether technical (explicability), industrial (dynamic evaluation of misdeeds, unsuspected bias, etc.), institutional (reparation, financial responsibility), or academic (metric of trust in AI); emulate research; and finally support the "development of self-regulatory codes of conduct for data and AI-related professions, with specific ethical duties" or support training. It is therefore an important work of foundation of an ethical framework in order to support the development of an AI for good.

Cowls et al. (2019) resume the research initiated by Floridi et al. (2018), no longer on the theme of AI4People but similarly on that of AI4SG ("for Social Good").

Based on the study of 27 research projects dealing with examples of AI4SG, Cowls et al. (2019) propose a series of seven essential and presumed robust factors "that should characterise the design of AI4SG projects":(1) falsifiability and incremental deployment; (2) safeguards against the manipulation of predictors; (3) receiver-contextualized intervention; (4) receiver-contextualized explanation and transparent purposes; (5) privacy protection and data subject consent; (6) situational fairness; and (7) human-friendly semanticisation. The analysis of these factors is provided with "recommended best practices," the first of which, very Popperian in its formulation, is addressed to designers (efficient cause) to set up methods for testing their development (formal cause) in order to ensure users' trust (trustworthiness) in their object. To varying degrees, all other instructions are addressed to designers; even when it comes to considering the object appropriation by the user (receiver), it is a question of devising ergonomic strategies so that the solution, its expected beneficence, and its supposed non-maleficence are optimized according to the specifications.

10.2.3.3 Implementation

Following Floridi et al. (2018), Taddeo and Floridi (2018), and Cowls et al. (2019), we have established five general categories of ethical principles and four categories of action prescriptions and determined seven deontological factors aiming at a responsible AI design. Their proximity to biomedical principles will obviously serve our purpose of establishing an ethics of AI in a healthcare context.

In order to become applicable, they further require a detailed view of what concepts those ethical categories—beneficence, non-maleficence, or even justice—actually refer to. In a given context, they should refer to a social contract or agreement made between publics, institutional, and industrial actors. The 2018 *Montréal Declaration for a Responsible Development of Artificial Intelligence*[22] is an example of such an agreement proposal. It was born through the cooperation of "citizens, experts, public officials, industry stakeholders, civil organizations and professional associations" in order to guide AI toward a responsible industry. Such a concertation includes ten principles: well-being, respect for autonomy, protection of privacy and intimacy, solidarity, democratic participation, equity, diversity inclusion, caution, responsibility, and sustainable development. The well-being principle, which belongs to the category beneficence, is itself developed with five do's and don'ts guidelines such as "AIs must help individuals improve their living conditions, their health, and their working conditions,"[23] thus being focused on how AI can affect our societies in a utilitarian way. Hence, there is a need for a bridge between Floridi et al.'s principlistic deontology for an efficient ethical AI production and the Montréal contractualistic declaration for a responsible AI. Furthermore, the deontology factors framing technically an ethical AI production should refer specifically to the social agreement which is a result of a democratic concertation in a given industry and a given context, i.e., British healthcare system, human resources in Germany, IOT in France, etc.

This democratic control as specified in the "Democratic Participation" principle requires in particular that "the decisions made by AIs affecting a person's life, quality of life, or reputation should always be justifiable in a language that is understood by the people who use them or who are subjected to the consequences of their use."

This brings us to explicability as a principle category. It emphasizes a necessary commitment of AI designers to knowledge accessibility, hence calling for a bridge between ethics and epistemology. It requires also that the meaning of symbols conveyed by a given language from an artifactual emitter should be understood by the message receiver. It is then crucial that there exists a language common to AI developers as well as to AI artifacts and AI users, should the latter particularly be physicians. This is not only about ergonomics but also about creating the conditions of a meaningful access to the artifactual output so that the calculated result is justifiable.

10.2.3.4 Tensions

We have just seen how the AI deontology should be submitted to the democratically edicted ethical framework. Here is a point of friction between the economic and technical constraints related to the development processes and the ethical requirements initiated by the publics. It is as well a point of tension between sets of values that are possibly different or even divergent. The issue here is to resolve at least locally the tension emerging when putting agreed-upon principles into practice.

Whittlestone et al. (n.d.) has further identified four main tensions in the process of ethical principles implementation:

- Accuracy versus fair and equal treatment
- Personalization versus solidarity and citizenship
- Quality and efficiency of services versus privacy and informational autonomy
- Convenience versus self-actualization and dignity

In particular, can we solve these dilemmas involving conflicting values? For each of these dilemmas, is there a way to maximize both values or else is it possible to draw a clear ethical line maximizing the overall benefits while minimizing the costs? This would mean defining a metrics allowing us to quantify the ethical compliance with different sets of values.

For example, research on some CNN[24] artifacts dedicated to melanoma detection using digital dermoscopy images show overall some very accurate sensitivities and specificities.[25] However, the learning process is based on labeled image datasets from existing recorded cases. Wolff (2009) reports that the lifetime risk of dying from a melanoma is about 10 times higher for light skin individuals compared to dark skin ones. As a consequence, there are far less labeled images of dark skin melanomas available for the neural networks learning process and the diagnosis accuracy of such CNNs cannot be equivalent for all skin colors. In this case, overall accuracy is comparable to most dermatologists, but there is a lack of fairness in the accuracy expectations for a dark skin patient. Is this acceptable? What kind of trade-off would optimize the accuracy benefits without compromising the fairness principle?

10.2.3.5 Limitations

Based on Cowls et al. (2019), organizing the results of numerous studies published on arXiv and Scopus, among others, and of more than 70 "Ethical Codes of Practice" identified by Morley et al. (2020) in institutions and industry, we can observe that these applied research methodologies are only targeting the designer and the ethical modalities for developing an algorithm with the technical ambition of fitting the ethical principles. It may be objected that arXiv is dedicated to developers and scientists, but this is not the case with Scopus. Subsequent research on the Internet and in technology ethics journals has not given any more results in this direction. Hence, the current AI applied ethical factors present a first limitation in their scope: they are located only at the technical development level. On the one hand, it seems like an effective management strategy of the functional realization of explicitly pre-established principles; on the other hand, it denies both the user and the systemic environment the possibility to have an autonomy in their interaction with the AI artifact. The user is not considered an autonomous agent who can legitimately appropriate the AI object in an unplanned way. He/she is not considered a moral agent addressed by the ethical framework. The applied ethical system is intended for the "designer" as the only possible observer, as if the ethical approach is focused only at his/her position of action. And, in fact, all the recommendations are addressed exclusively to designers. Besides its projected technical efficiency, this applied technical ethics is unable to consider the implicit behaviors that might emerge apart from the intentional function the artifact has been programmed to fulfil.

Further to this limitation in the scope of AI, another limitation is directly related to the ethical theory choice. So far, the ethical frameworks were based on democratic social contracts, or else on principlistic deontology or contractarianism. Based on Beauchamp and Childress foundational work, this methodology aimed at establishing a technical framework ensuring compliance with ethical principles. We might then recall that Beauchamp and Childress' *The Principles of Biomedical Ethics* is presently in its 8th edition and has been extended in particular since its 4th edition in 1994. A new chapter was then arguing for the addition of five virtues—*trustworthiness*, *compassion*, *discernment*, *conscientousness*, and *integrity*,[26] thus advocating for the extension of principlistic ethics to virtue ethics. In doing so for AI ethics, it would be no longer only a question of constituting an ethical model for the AI development, but also of dealing with the responsibility that results from the action of every agent in the chain of production and use of AI, and therefore of refusing the modern substitution of *acting* by *doing*.[27] By adding those virtues, it is then a matter of acting responsibly and not only of doing ethics or even managing an ethical system.

The construction of an ethical system for AI should therefore be dual, principlistic as the only evaluable modality with demonstrable effectiveness, and reflective in the way responsible ethical behavior must be conducted, which is perhaps what Floridi et al. (2018, p. 692) referred to when mentioning the objective of "Enhancing Human Agency, Without Removing Human Responsibility."

10.3 PRINCIPLISM, VIRTUE ETHICS, AND AI IN MEDICINE

10.3.1 A New Principlism for AI in Medicine

Whether it concerns medicine or AI, it seems quite obvious that these two fields and industries raise many ethical problems, and thus generate a long list of declarations, conventions, codes, principles, guidelines, etc. For the different stakeholders working in the field of AI in healthcare, this great amount of texts probably makes their task more complex than it should be, though most of them may feel the necessity for an ethical regulation. That's why in this last part a framework for an ethical discussion is proposed, using as a basis what has been previously done in medical ethics and AI ethics. This framework is intended primarily for developers or engineers working in the field of AI related to healthcare, but also to users, i.e., both physicians (or healthcare professionals in general) and patients. More generally, it also encompasses, as medicine depends largely on a healthcare system in modern societies, the relationships between AI and healthcare in society. Our main goal is clearly not to supply the reader with some kind of recipe or method to solve ethical problems, a method or recipe that could be itself implemented in an Artificial Intelligence, but rather to make more explicit what is at stake in this nascent field of AI in healthcare and to point what should be considered as the major ethical principles which could or should be mobilized in any ethical discussion inside this field.

As a matter of fact, the most suitable tool or device is principlism, first proposed by Beauchamp and Childress (2013) and then completed by Floridi et al. (2018). Its main advantage is to put words on sometimes vague ideas and to allow people (computer and data scientists, engineers, physicians, patients, etc.) to state, discuss, and choose between different and sometimes contradictory values. As we saw, the four initial principles of principlism are beneficence, non-maleficence, autonomy, and justice. To these four principles, Floridi et al. (2018) added the principle of explicability, which is specific to AI and refers to both "the epistemological sense of *intelligibility* (as an answer to the question 'how does it work?') and in the ethical sense of *accountability* (as an answer to the question: 'who is responsible for the way it works?')" (Floridi and Cowls 2019). These five principles appear necessary to deal with the ethical issues raised by AI, but insufficient to tackle the specific issues raised by AI in healthcare.

More precisely, we may criticize the fact that the principle of explicability is too demanding or too stringent, not from an ethical point of view, but from an epistemic point of view. In other words, the "epistemological sense of intelligibility" is a good ethical principle but is very difficult or even impossible to realize in practice: most of the time, it is indeed not possible for the AI artifact's designer(s) and developer(s) to explain how it works in practice. As it is explained in the chapter on the epistemological issues of AI in healthcare, there is a gap between statistical correlations on which AI reasonings are based and a true causal relationship. And it appears that this gap is almost unsurmountable from an epistemic point of view. Therefore, it seems better and more efficient to adopt a semiological interpretability rather than a causal explicability: we thus propose to replace the principle of explicability by the principle of explainability. Explainable AI (XAI) has generated quite a huge literature in the last few years,[28] and many definitions of XAI can be found. For example, Barredo Arrieta et al. (2020) defined explainability as follows: "Given an audience, an **explainable** Artificial Intelligence is one that produces details or reasons to make its functioning clear or easy to understand.[29]" Wikipedia defines XAI as "methods and techniques in the application of artificial intelligence technology (AI) such that the results of the solution can be understood by humans."[30] We won't discuss that definition: the main idea is that XAI is opposed to the concept of "black box" where even the designers cannot explain the outcomes of AI reasoning, and thus is opposed to the principle of explicability. We thus consider that the principle of explainability is less stringent from an epistemic point of view than the principle of explicability, but as demanding as it is from an ethical point of view.

Furthermore, we consider that a sixth principle must be added, in order to restore an equilibrium: the principle of predictibility. By "predictibility," we do not refer to the "predictability" of AI, defined by the European High Level Expert Group guidelines, as the fact that for a system, "the outcome of the planning process must be consistent with the input," and which is considered "as a key mechanism to ensure that AI systems have not been compromised by external actors" (Fjeld et al. 2020). On the contrary, by "predictibility" we mean the capacity of AI to predict a result or an outcome, for example, in the medical context, of a disease, of a treatment, etc. This criterion of predictibility is originally a technical one: for example, in Machine Learning, prediction refers to the output of an algorithm after it has been trained on a historical dataset and applied to new data when forecasting the likelihood of a particular outcome. It the predicted outcome happens, it is a proof that the software is working properly. From an epistemological point of view, it refers to the criteria of verification or confirmation: if a scientific theory predicts correctly some events, then this theory must be considered as correct. From an ethical point of view, it is a way to morally judge AI not on the basis of its algorithm, or the way it works (and judge who is responsible for that) but to judge it on its results or on its consequences, without having to open the black box, i.e., account for the way it works. This appears particularly important in a medical context: in this context, medical predictions and medical decisions, whether they are or not produced or aided by AI, are a matter of life and death.

It has been noticed before that among the four principles of principlism defined by Beauchamp and Childress, two of them were deontological, namely, autonomy and justice, and two of them were teleological, namely, nonmaleficence and beneficence. This categorization can also be applied to the principles of explainability and of predictibility: explainability can be considered as a deontological principle and predictiblity as a teleological principle. Explainability indeed refers to the idea of responsibility: Barredo Arrieta et al. (2020) put, for example, this principle in relation to those of fairness and accountability. In other words, explainability appears as a matter of principle and not of consequences. Conversely, the principle of predictibility focuses on the results or the consequences of AI, and thus pertains to teleological ethics: the problem is not to know how it works or why it works that way, but to be sure that it produces good, or more good than harm.

10.3.2 The New Principlism in a Clinical and Public Health Context

To test the operationality of these six ethical principles, it is important to apply them first to the clinical or medical context, where the three actors are the physician, the patient, and an Artificial Intelligence; and then to the context of public health in a broad sense, where the private companies and the state are involved through

AI technologies (for example, the Big Tech), health insurance (private or public), and through several instances of regulation such as associations (of physicians or of patients) or diverse health agencies (for example, in the United States, the Food and Drug Administration and the Center for Disease Control and Prevention). The issues regarding the physician-patient relationship are individual, whereas the issues regarding public health are collective and societal. It appears that the six principles stipulated here constitute a simple and efficient solution to tackle the ethical issues at both the individual and the collective level.

For example, if we focus on the physician-patient relationship, the principle of autonomy commands that all the information (or almost all) given by the patient to his physician stay confidential, due to medical secrecy. This rule of confidentiality applies equally to the data provided by users of, for example, mobile health applications, even if there are clearly more actors involved here and if the ownership of the data is a tricky issue. The principle of autonomy can be linked to the principle of explainability: the idea here is that the functioning of an AI artifact can be understood, and can be understood differently according to the "audience," i.e., a patient or a physician. A last issue related to the principle of autonomy is the notion of informed consent: to be informed, the person consenting to something must know and understand what he consents to; the principle of explainability can serve as a way to inform the person on how an AI artifact is functioning and thus permit the consent to be valid. A similar reasoning can be made about the deontological principle of justice: the function of the principle of explainability is to ensure that every user is treated fairly and is not subject to several bias produced by an AI artifact. From a public health and populational perspective, the conciliation of the principles of justice and explainability is supposed to guarantee that the allocation of resources is fair, or, in other words, that the resources go to those who need it more. Ultimately, beyond the ethical issue, there is a social and political issue: in case there is a breach in the confidentiality, or bias that would lead to medical errors, or inequalities in the treatment of patients or in the allocation of resources, someone (an individual or a company) has to pay for it, that is has to be responsible for it. Blaming the algorithm cannot be a way to escape one's responsibility.

From a teleological perspective, the principles of beneficence and non-maleficence constitute an essential feature of the physician-patient relationship. Though it is merely science fiction, we can think about the first law of the Three Laws of Robotics created by Isaac Asimov which states that "A robot may not injure a human being or, through inaction, allow a human being to come to harm"(Asimov 1950). This could be applied to any AI artifact, especially in a medical context: though it is not sure if it can be implemented, these two principles must be considered if AI is to be considered as responsible. The principle of predictibility intervenes at this point to evaluate ex post if an AI artifact has done good, or has not done harm, or has done more good than harm. This can be applied to both a medical (drugs, surgery, etc.) or a public health action (vaccination, public health insurance) intervention, and both to a preventive or a curative action. Every action must indeed be evaluated or assessed on both its principles and its consequences on the global health of an individual patient or of a population.

10.3.3 The New Principlism and Virtue Ethics: For a Responsible AI in Healthcare

If the six principles stipulated here are necessary to address ethical issues regarding the use of AI in healthcare, they are however not sufficient. As seen before in Section 10.1.3.1, many conflicts between principles exist, for example, between teleological and deontological principles (such as beneficence and justice), or even between deontological principles or teleological principles themselves (for example, beneficence and non-maleficence). The two principles proposed here, explainability and predictibility, can of course be in conflict in certain medical situations: it is probable that, for example, the ability to predict an outcome can be achieved at the expense of the explainability of the outcome. According to us, this is why deontological and teleological ethics must be supplemented or balanced with virtue ethics.

As we saw in Section 10.1.3.2, virtue ethics, by referring to the "practical wisdom" of the actors involved in response to a specific action (or set of actions) in a specific situation, seems particularly adapted to clinical or public health situations or interventions. The main argument here is that insofar as a physician or a patient or other stakeholder has to choose between different ethical principles in a situation when there is no good solution, the only way to justify an ethical choice between principles in a specific situation is to appeal to the practical wisdom of the participants to this situation (physician, patient, etc.), i.e., to virtue ethics. In other words, principlism (the 6 principles) permit to name the values and to discuss about the value of these values for the participants, but the tensions that may arise between conflicting values, which determines the action to be done, can be ultimately resolved based on such practical wisdom. Thus, if the principle of beneficence or non-maleficence is chosen after a discussion, the patient must trust the virtue of the physician. Conversely, if the principle of autonomy is chosen, it is the physician who must trust the practical wisdom of the patient. The same argument applies to a public health context where the government would have to choose between, for example, beneficence and justice: in this case however, virtue ethics must be balanced by some kind of democratic procedure. The last point is that in relation to AI, it could also be a choice of the physician or of the patient (or of the government and the citizens) to choose between predictibility and explainability: the main point here is that AI artifacts should not decide by themselves and should propose different options, leaving the choice to its human operators.

Virtue ethics is probably the least implementable ethics, precisely because it refers to something that is specifically human: life experience, a kind of wisdom, an attention given to specific situations, and, finally, a sense of mankind. In a medical context as well, there are specific virtues which "derive primarily from experience with health care relationships": Beauchamp and Childress (2013) mention "five focal virtues: compassion, discernment, trustworthiness, integrity, and conscientiousness, all of which support and promote caring and caregiving." These virtues are surely a fundamental part of the practice of any healthcare professionals. That's why virtue ethics can constitute an invaluable help to put the six principles into practice, in order to create a responsible AI in healthcare. Of course, this won't solve automatically all

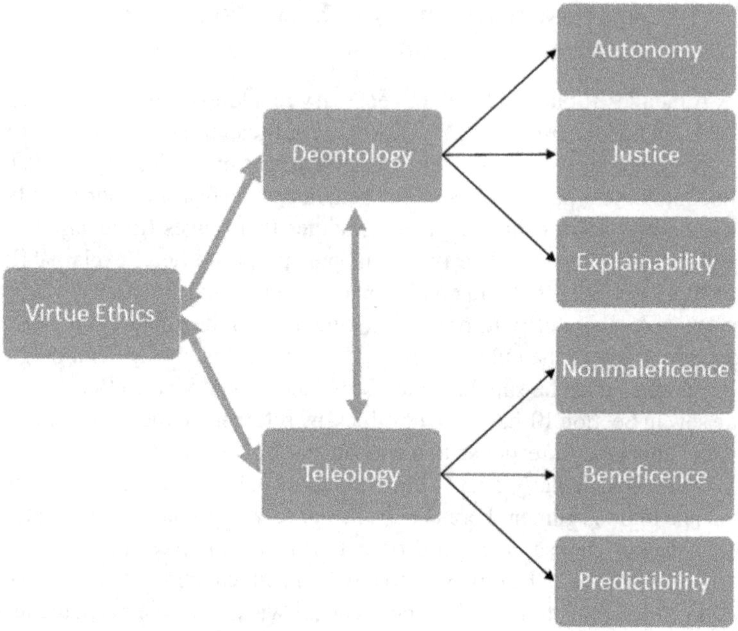

FIGURE 10.1 A proposal for an ethical AI in medicine.

the ethical dilemmas that exist in daily medical practice. But as it is about ethics, it is always about how things ought to be rather than how things are.

Figure 10.1 shows the proposal for an ethical AI in medicine.

NOTES

1. For example, https://en.wikipedia.org/wiki/Hippocratic_Oath.
2. For such a critic, see Clouser and Gert (1990).
3. See p. 28.
4. For further representative readings regarding the critical stance of Technic, see Ellul 1964; Illich 1973; Adorno and Horkheimer 1994; Marcuse 1991; Winner 2020; and Habermas 1987.
5. Formal, material, efficient and final causes which tell us the how, with what, who, and why of the physical emergence of an artifact. For more details, see Aristotle (2008).
6. Simon (1955, p. 101): "Because of the psychological limits of the organism (...), actual human rationality-striving can at best be extremely crude and simplified approximation to the kind of global rationality that is implied, for example, by game theoretical models."
7. As stated at the Dartmouth AI Conference, August 31, 1955, by J. McCarthy et al.
8. See, for instance, Arnaud Montebourg's candidacy to the French socialist party nomination for the 2017 Presidential election.
9. See Anders (2018a).
10. See Google's AI ethics principles: https://ai.google/principles/.
11. See IEEE's "Global Initiative on Ethics of Autonomous and Intelligent Systems": https://standards.ieee.org/develop/indconn/ec/autonomous_systems.html.

12. See regulatory framework for "Sofware as Medical Devices," initiated by the IMDRF (International Medical Device Regulators Forum), approved in 2018 by the American FDA and the UE.
13. See in particular the *Déclaration de Montréal IA Responsable*, retrieved on 24/ 09/2019 at: https://www.declarationmontreal-iaresponsable.com/rapport-de-la-declaration.
14. Such as the GAFAM: Google, Apple, Facebook, Amazon, Microsoft.
15. *International Telecommunication Union.*
16. A deontological ethics is thus principlistic.
17. Except for religious morality.
18. Ashford and Mulgan (2018): "According to contractualism, morality consists in what would result if we were to make binding agreements from a point of view that respects our equal moral importance as rational autonomous agents."
19. Ashford and Mulgan (2018): "Under contractarianism, I seek to maximise my own interests in a bargain with others."
20. See https://futureoflife.org/ai-principles/.
21. See www.partnershiponai.org/tenets/.
22. Retrieved on 24/09/2019 from https://www.montrealdeclaration-responsibleai.com/the-declaration.s
23. Ibid. p. 8
24. Convolutional Neural Networks.
25. See Haenssle et al. (2018); Esteva et al. (2017).
26. See Garchar and Kaag (2013).
27. See Arendt (2018).
28. For an overview of the literature on XAI, see Barredo Arrieta et al. (2020).
29. Italics in the original text.
30. https://en.wikipedia.org/wiki/Explainable_artificial_intelligence#cite_note-guardian-1 (retrieved on 09/01/2020).

REFERENCES

Adorno, Theodor W, and Max Horkheimer. 1994. *Dialectic of Enlightenment.* New York: Continuum.

Anders, Günther. 2018a. *Die Antiquiertheit des Mensche. Band 2: Über die Zerstörung des Lebens im Zeitalter der dritten industriellen Revolution.* 4., durchgesehene Auflage. München: C.H.Beck.

Anders, Günther. 2018b. *Die Antiquiertheit des Menschen. Band 1: Über die Seele im Zeitalter der zweiten industriellen Revolution.* 4., durchgesehene Auflage. München: C.H.Beck.

Anscombe, G E M. 1958. "Modern Moral Philosophy." *Philosophy* 33 (124): 19.

Arendt, Hannah. 2018. *The Human Condition.* 2nd edition. Chicago and London: The University of Chicago Press.

Aristotle. 2008. *Physics.* Translated by Robin Waterfield and David Bostock. Oxford World's Classics. Oxford and New York: Oxford University Press.

Aristotle. 2009. *The Nicomachean Ethics.* Translated by W. D. Ross and Lesley Brown. Oxford and New York: Oxford University Press.

Ashford, Elizabeth, and Tim Mulgan. 2018. "Contractualism." In *The Stanford Encyclopedia of Philosophy*, edited by Edward N. Zalta, Summer 2018. Metaphysics Research Lab, Stanford University. https://plato.stanford.edu/archives/sum2018/entries/contractualism/.

Asimov, Isaac. 1950. *I, Robot.* Garden City, NY: Doubleday.

Barredo Arrieta, Alejandro, Natalia Díaz-Rodríguez, Javier Del Ser, Adrien Bennetot, Siham Tabik, Alberto Barbado, Salvador Garcia, et al. 2020. "Explainable Artificial Intelligence (XAI): Concepts, Taxonomies, Opportunities and Challenges toward Responsible AI." *Information Fusion* 58 (June): 82–115. doi: 10.1016/j.inffus.2019.12.012.

Beauchamp, Tom L., and James F. Childress. 2013. *Principles of Biomedical Ethics.* 7th ed. New York: Oxford University Press.

Bentham, Jeremy. 1789. *An Introduction to the Principles of Morals and Legislation.* 1st ed. London: T. Payne.

Bostrom, Nick. 2009. "Ethical Issues in Advanced Artificial Intelligence." In *Science Fiction and Philosophy: From Time Travel to Superintelligence*, edited by Susan Schneider, 277–84. Hoboken, NJ: Wiley-Blackwell.

Bostrom, Nick. 2014. *Superintelligence: Paths, Dangers, Strategies.* 1st edition. Oxford: Oxford University Press.

Clouser, K. D., and B. Gert. 1990. "A Critique of Principlism." *Journal of Medicine and Philosophy* 15 (2): 219–36. doi: 10.1093/jmp/15.2.219.

Condorcet, Marie-Jean-Antoine-Nicolas Caritat, Marquis de. 1791. *Outlines of an Historical View of the Progress of the Human Mind.* The Online Library Of Liberty. http://oll-resources.s3.amazonaws.com/titles/1669/Condorcet_0878_EBk_v6.0.pdf.

Cowls, Josh, Thomas King, Mariarosaria Taddeo, and Luciano Floridi. 2019. "Designing AI for Social Good: Seven Essential Factors." *SSRN Electronic Journal.* doi: 10.2139/ssrn.3388669.

Ellul, Jacques. 1964. *The Technological Society.* Translated by John Wilkinson. Knopf. A Vintage Book. New York, NY: Vintage books.

Esteva, Andre, Brett Kuprel, Roberto A. Novoa, Justin Ko, Susan M. Swetter, Helen M. Blau, and Sebastian Thrun. 2017. "Dermatologist-Level Classification of Skin Cancer with Deep Neural Networks." *Nature* 542 (7639): 115–18. doi: 10.1038/nature21056.

Evans, Jonathan St B. T. 1990. *Bias in Human Reasoning: Causes and Consequences.* Essays in Cognitive Psychology. Hove and London, LEA.

Fjeld, Jessica, Nele Achten, Hannah Hilligoss, Adam Nagy, and Madhulika Srikumar. 2020. "Principled Artificial Intelligence: Mapping Consensus in Ethical and Rights-based Approaches to Principles for AI." *Berkman Klein Center for Internet & Society.* http://nrs.harvard.edu/urn-3:HUL.InstRepos:42160420

Floridi, Luciano. 1999. "Information Ethics: On the Philosophical Foundation of Computer Ethics." *Ethics and Information Technology* 1 (1): 33–52. doi: 10.1023/A:1010018611096.

Floridi, Luciano, and Josh Cowls.2019. "A Unified Framework of Five Principles for AI in Society." *Harvard Data Science Review*, 1(1). https://doi.org/10.1162/99608f92.8cd550d1

Floridi, Luciano, Josh Cowls, Monica Beltrametti, Raja Chatila, Patrice Chazerand, Virginia Dignum, Christoph Luetge, et al. 2018. "AI4People—An Ethical Framework for a Good AI Society: Opportunities, Risks, Principles, and Recommendations." *Minds and Machines* 28 (4): 689–707. doi: 10.1007/s11023-018-9482-5.

Floridi, Luciano, Josh Cowls, Thomas King, Mariarosaria Taddeo. 2020. "How to Design AI for Social Good: Seven Essential Factors." *Science and Engineering Ethics* 26 (3): 1771–1796. doi: 10.1007/s11948-020-00213-5. Epub 2020 Apr 3. PMID: 32246245; PMCID: PMC7286860.

Garchar, and Kaag. 2013. "Classical American Philosophy and Modern Medical Ethics: The Case of Richard Cabot." *Transactions of the Charles S. Peirce Society* 49 (4): 553. doi: 10.2979/trancharpeirsoc.49.4.553.

Gilligan, Carol. 1993. *In a Different Voice: Psychological Theory and Women's Development.* Cambridge, MA: Harvard University Press.

Habermas, Jürgen. 1987. *Knowledge and Human Interests.* Cambridge: Polity Press.

Haenssle, H A, C Fink, R Schneiderbauer, F Toberer, T Buhl, A Blum, A Kalloo, et al. 2018. "Man against Machine: Diagnostic Performance of a Deep Learning Convolutional Neural Network for Dermoscopic Melanoma Recognition in Comparison to 58 Dermatologists." *Annals of Oncology* 29 (8): 1836–42. doi: 10.1093/annonc/mdy166.

Illich, Ivan. 1973. *Tools for Conviviality*. London and New York: Marion Boyars.

Johnson, Deborah G., and Thomas M. Powers. 2005. "Ethics and Technology: A Program for Future Research." In *Encyclopedia of Science, Technology, and Ethics*, edited by Carl Mitcham. Detroit, MI: Macmillan Reference USA.

Jonas, Hans. 1985. *The Imperative of Responsibility: In Search of an Ethics for the Technological Age*. Chicago: University of Chicago Press.

Kahneman, Daniel, and Amos Tversky. 1979. "Prospect Theory: An Analysis of Decision under Risk." *Econometrica* 47 (2): 263. doi: 10.2307/1914185.

Kant, Immanuel. 1998. *Groundwork of the Metaphysics of Morals*. Translated by Mary J. Gregor. Cambridge Texts in the History of Philosophy. Cambridge, UK and New York: Cambridge University Press.

Kitcher, Philip. 2001. *Science, Truth, and Democracy*. Oxford Studies in Philosophy of Science. Oxford and New York: Oxford University Press.

Marcuse, Herbert. 1991. *One-Dimensional Man*. Boston: Beacon Press.

Morley, Jessica, Luciano Floridi, Libby Kinsey, and Anat Elhalal. 2020. "From What to How: An Initial Review of Publicly Available AI Ethics Tools, Methods and Research to Translate Principles into Practices." *Science and Engineering Ethics* 26 (4): 2141–68. doi: 10.1007/s11948-019-00165-5.

Müller, Vincent C., ed. 2016. *Fundamental Issues of Artificial Intelligence*. Synthese Library, Studies in Epistemology, Logic, Methodology, and Philosophy of Science, vol. 376. Cham: Springer.

Newton, Adam Zachary. 1997. *Narrative Ethics*. 1. Harvard Univ. Press paperback ed. Cambridge, MA: Harvard Univ. Press.

Simon, Herbert A. 1955. "A Behavioral Model of Rational Choice." *The Quarterly Journal of Economics* 69 (1): 99. doi: 10.2307/1884852.

Smith, Merritt Roe. 1994. "Technological Determinism in American Culture." In *Does Technology Drive History? The Dilemma of Technological Determinism*, edited by Merritt Roe Smith and Leo Marx, 1–35. Cambridge, MA: MIT Press.

Taddeo, Mariarosaria, and Luciano Floridi. 2018. "How AI Can Be a Force for Good." *Science* 361 (6404): 751–52. doi: 10.1126/science.aat5991.

Tversky, Amos. 1969. "Intransitivity of Preferences." *Psychological Review* 76 (1): 31–48. doi: 10.1037/h0026750.

Whittlestone, Jess, Rune Nyrup, Anna Alexandrova, Kanta Dihal, and Stephen Cave. n.d. "Ethical and Societal Implications of Algorithms, Data, and Artificial Intelligence: A Roadmap for Research," 59.

Winner, Langdon. 2020. *The Whale and the Reactor: A Search for Limits in an Age of High Technology*. 2nd ed. Chicago: University of Chicago Press.

Wolff, Tracy. 2009. "Screening for Skin Cancer: An Update of the Evidence for the U.S. Preventive Services Task Force." *Annals of Internal Medicine* 150 (3): 194. doi: 10.7326/0003-4819-150-3-200902030-00009.

11 Epistemological Issues and Challenges with Artificial Intelligence in Healthcare

Nicolas Brault, Benoît Duchemann, and Mohit Saxena

CONTENTS

11.1 KEY ISSUES IN PHILOSOPHY OF ARTIFICIAL INTELLIGENCE (AI)

11.1.1 A Short History of AI: From 17th Century's Calculators to the Dartmouth Artificial Intelligence Conference (2005)

11.1.1.1 From Pascal to Turing: A Prehistory of AI

Some set the computer science birth (without the actual naming) in the early 19th century and Charles Babbage's Analytical Engine,[1] the first mechanical programmable calculator using punch cards. We could go further in the past with Pascal's Pascaline[2] or Leibniz's Arithmetic Machine[3] as technical artifacts aimed at computing calculations. Those inventions were already simulating basic computations normally performed by human minds.

Much later, the turning point of computer science is more likely to be attributed to Alan Turing. With his 1936 abstract "a-machine,"[4] he is considered as the "mythological" father of computer science. He is the initiator of computer science as a theoretical and scientific discipline. With his abstract machine, he could prove the uncomputability of the *Entscheidungsproblem* ("decision problem")[5] and further the fundamental limitations in the power of performing mechanical computations. It was the first time a symbolic language combined with a complex logic system was conceived specifically for an automatic machine in order to represent and symbolize problems and the whole computation procedure leading to their solutions.

As for Artificial Intelligence, his contribution was more of a predictive and philosophical one.

In his 1950 publication, *Computing Machinery and Intelligence* (Turing 1950), he detailed his famous Imitation Game, or Turing Test dedicated to challenge future computers in their ability to ape human beings in their speech proficiency. Hence, he offered a first—although reductionist—definition of intelligence and implicitly a first definition of Artificial Intelligence.

In his test, a first human is considered as the blind evaluator. Facing him are a computer and another human. The computer succeeds if the evaluator cannot distinguish its communication with the other human's. John Searle later challenged the Turing Test validity with his Chinese Room model (Searle 1980). According to him there is no necessary correlation between mechanically answering the questions of the evaluator and understanding the questions and the answer delivered, even if right, hence putting the emphasis on the meaning rather than on the procedure.

11.1.1.2 From Turing to Dartmouth: A First Definition of AI

The period of time from Turing to Dartmouth is marked by the emergence of the first electronic[6] computers, such as the EDSAC created in 1949 by Maurice Wilkes' team at the University of Cambridge Mathematical Laboratory (the first computer with an internally stored program) or the EDVAC (*E*lectronic *D*iscrete *V*ariable *A*utomatic *C*omputer) at the Ballistics Research Laboratory with the collaboration of the University of Pennsylvania and based upon Von Neumann's theoretical project. ENIAC (Electronic Numerical Integrator And Computer) is considered the very first fully electronic computer, which was developed in 1945 at the Moore School of Electrical Engineering from UPenn, but it had to be recabled in order for every other program to be executed.

The aim of a computer is to process calculations that are normally processed by human minds. The very concept of computer is thus developed as a human mind imitation.

To that extent, this period is marked by the tension between two theories of the mind, between connexionists and cognitivists, and between a neurological and a symbolic conception of the mind.

Connexionists were willing to modelize it as a "black box" gifted with feedback or retraction mechanisms. The main success of this research is the mathematical modelization[7] of basic constituents of the brain: formal neurons (Figure 11.1).

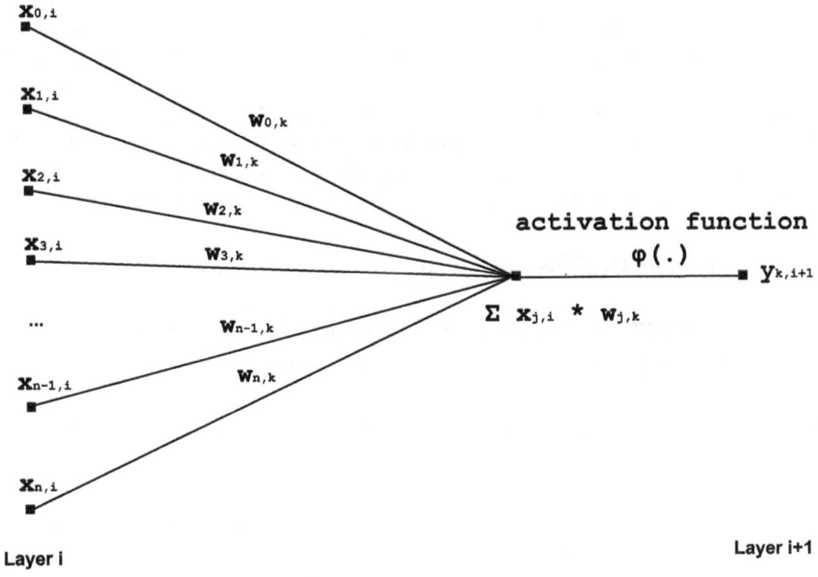

FIGURE 11.1 Mathematical modelization of a formal neural network.

McCulloch and Pitts proposed to simulate the brain behavior through a model using billions of basic neurons. Further to their research, the neuropsychologist Donald Hebb invented in 1949 the Hebb rule that enabled the neurons to learn:

> When an axon of cell A is near enough to excite B and repeatedly or persistently takes part in firing it, some growth process or metabolic change takes place in one or both cells such that A's efficiency, as one of the cells firing B, is increased.
>
> **(Hebb 1949)**

Using the Hebb rule, Franck Rosenblatt invented in 1957 the Perceptron: the first neural network with one layer and capable of learning.

On the other hand, cognitivists considered that thought can be described at an abstract level as a manipulation of symbols, whatever the materiality of the manipulation medium (brain or electronic machine). This approach supposes *a priori* a relationship between thought and language that can be formalized as a system of symbols.

One cognitivist (or symbolic) scheme consists in having machines manipulate language through symbols.

In 1956, four scientists, John McCarthy (Dartmouth College), Marvin Lee Minsky (Harvard University), Nathaniel Rochester (from IBM Corporation), and Claude Shannon (Bell Labs and theorist of Information Theory), invited some of their colleagues to a summer seminar at the Dartmouth College (New Hampshire, USA) to work on a new computation modality that is named for the first time : Artificial Intelligence. This is considered as the birth date of the AI field.

The seminar conclusions contain a formal definition for AI, thus including as a prerequisite a general definition for intelligence:

> "Artificial intelligence comprises methods, tools, and systems for solving problems that normally require the intelligence of humans. The term intelligence is always defined as the ability to learn effectively, to react adaptively, to make proper decisions, to communicate in language or images in a sophisticated way, and to understand."[8] Hence the field program was defined as follows: "The study is to proceed on the basis of the conjecture that every aspect of learning or any other feature of intelligence can in principle be so precisely described that a machine can be made to simulate it."

Thus, the newly created AI is based on the following conjecture:

(1) Human intelligence characteristics can be accurately described.
(2) That a machine can simulate these characteristics.

The AI appears at a key moment when two parallel fields are emerging almost simultaneously:

(1) A theoretical and scientific field dedicated to study the nature of intelligence and human mind from a materialistic perspective.
(2) A practical and engineering field aiming at the invention of machines able to process information and to calculate.

At that moment, Newell and Simon are fully convinced that real AI is within reach: "There are now in the world machines that think, that learn and that create" (Simon and Newell 1958).

11.1.1.3 Neural Networks versus Expert Systems

The short history of AI has been highlighted by the tension between connexionist and cognitivist theories. Is has thus been marked by the tension between those willing to simulate the brain behavior through its atomistic neural components and those willing to emulate the symbolic knowledge and reasoning.

On the one hand, the connexionist theory has known major impediments in the 1970s through the logical XOR crisis and a lack of practical achievements.

On the other hand, symbolic reasoning systems gave birth to expert systems. Restricting those programs to limited domains and with a small level of reasoning ambiguities managed to set limits to the combinatory explosion of rule production systems. An expert system encapsulates knowledge structured as rules and facts and can reason on that knowledge base by using some inference mechanisms as follows: if fact F is asserted, then action A. Its aim was then to emulate the human expert cognition within a limited domain.

For instance, DENDRAL (*Dendritic Algorithm*)[9] contained all the expert chemist knowledge and used it to solve problems of chemical components identification based on physical measurements. MYCIN[10] was dedicated to blood infectious diseases diagnosis (later to meningitis) and their associated medical prescription. For the first time, the inference engine is clearly separated from the knowledge and the expert system is able to explain its reasoning. In 1978, a clinical trial was conducted where MYCIN was challenged by nine physicians in the diagnosis of 80 patients suffering from meningitis. The results then evaluated by eight meningitis specialists were in favor of the algorithm. Many more examples of expert system achievements are available: PROSPECTOR in 1976 in Stanford, TAXMAN in 1977, or DELTA (Diesel Electric Locomotive Troubleshooting Aid) by General Electric in the beginning of the 1980s for assisting locomotive failure diagnosis.

Those systems were efficient for specific tasks where no algorithmic procedure was known in a specific narrow and technical knowledge domain.

11.1.1.4 Emergence and Development: Neural Networks and Machine Learning (ML)

In 1982, John Hopfield's research got neural networks research back on track. As a solution to neural network limitations, Hopfield proposed a fully connected (but non-reflexive) multilayer neural network. To make his point, he made an analogy with energy states of atoms in statistical physics and made it clear that physics was a field for a direct application of neural networks.

For every layer, neuron nods still work the same way as for the Perceptron, but some hidden layers are added and connected one to another.

The fundamental research that followed this moment, the emergence of personal computers, and the Internet bringing more and more computer power and foremost more and more data related to human behaviors created the conditions of development of modern AI, based on neural networks, and modern computers for the mathematical and technical part and so-called Big Data as the necessary fuel to Machine Learning, to the machine imitating human cognitive behaviors. As of today, we can classify AI learning in three main categories:

- *Unsupervised learning:* Can use examples without labels, or can generate its own examples. Needs the rules (of the game), in order to be able to play and evaluate an example, i.e. AlphaGo Zero learnt by playing against itself.
- *Supervised learning:* The system learns a labeled dataset (pairs input + expected output), it builds up the matrix of neural weights that will optimize a function *f* relating the input to its ideal output.
- *Reinforcement learning:* Optimization of cumulative reward.

11.1.2 The Modern Concepts of Artificial Intelligence and Big Data

The main AI industrial applications are nowadays based on supervised learning. The aim is to predict an expected output y for an input x or rather to compute an approximated output y_ε, which should be a good approximation of the ideal y with a maximum acceptable error ε, and a minimum acceptable probability p_ε: $p(y_\varepsilon - y < \varepsilon) < p_\varepsilon$. In order to achieve this end, during the learning stage, the program must calculate the matrix of neural weights at all neural nods.

To do so, a training dataset is input. This is a set of pairs of inputs and their expected outputs. In the case of a melanoma detection program, the dataset is a set of pairs (x_i, y_i), where x_i is an image of a cutaneous lesion and y_i is its known related diagnosis.

Neural weights are initiated stochastically. Initial outputs with initial weights are computed. So it is the initial error ε_0 to the expected output for every input. Using most often the retro-propagation of gradient, with output layer being layer number n, weights of layer $n - 1$ are tuned to reduce the initial error (cost function); according to layer $n - 1$, weights of layer $n - 2$ are tuned as well; and so on. When the full weight matrix has been recalculated, a new output is once again calculated with a new cost function ε_1, and so on, step by step, until the statistical error on the whole dataset is within range.

The main issue of those computations is obviously the dimensionality.

The dimensionality problem is correlated with the input data: a 2D image is worth approximately 10^6 pixels, an audio file 10^6 bits per mn, as for a text, a mole of matter is worth 10^{24} bits.

If the input data is to be represented using vectors,[11] it will first be represented atomistically in the input space. For instance, an image will be represented in a n-dimension space where n is the number of atoms of data present in the input. A black and white image of 10^6 pixels will be initially represented in a 10^6-dimension space where its coordinates will be the black color ratio for a given pixel.

Obviously, the dimensionality needs to be reduced in order to perform computations efficiently. There is a necessity to find regularities that will enable the system to represent parsimoniously the data, by compressing it in a reasonably big dimensional latent space without losing relevant data.

Hence, the learning stage is about the simultaneous mechanized construction

- of the parsimonious statistical representation of a given dataset in the latent space and
- of the neural weights matrix that enables to represent any given input not already present in the dataset.

This dual representation processing gives rise to a model, as defined by Minsky[12]. The probable prediction the AI program is aiming at concerning the input x is actually the output of a computation based on its representation or its model x^* in the latent space. This model can also be seen as a multidimensional measurement of its original input. For a given model, a chosen prediction[13] program should compute the probable end result.

11.1.3 AI: From Data to Knowledge

11.1.3.1 Truth and Proof

The epistemological issue related to software computations concerns the insurance that the end computed result is as expected; hence, it is true or a good enough reflection of the truth that shall be ascertained by proof.

A first way to consider the proof concept is the *tekhnê*'s "right rule"[14] that shall be used to produce a technical artifact. Software Verification and validation as defined by Mackall, Nelson, and Schumman 2002) is "the process of ensuring that software being developed or changed will satisfy functional and other requirements (verification) and each step in the process of building the software yields the right products (validation). In other words:

- Verification—Build the Product Right
- Validation—Build the Right Product"

A second version of the proof concept may be considered as in Tarski (1969, p. 70) as "a procedure of ascertaining the truth of sentences which is employed primarily in deductive science." In this case, the proofs show how the end result can be deducted logically from axiomatic premises.

Tymoczko claims:

> If we view proofs as abstract patterns, it seems obvious that the mere existence of a proof of a theorem guarantees the truth of the theorem (modulo axioms, etc.). There aren't any "gaps" in the (real) proof; it is rigorous, indeed the standard of "rigor." In the case of formal proofs, the idea of rigor can be explained in terms of logical validity.
>
> **(Tymoczko 1980)**

Would the difference in proof value be then only a matter of "rigor" ?

We find the difference to be more conceptual. While V&V proposes procedures managing the software development organization and testing the code for bugs or failures until their absence is reached, the deductive process aims at proving positively that the end result is logically true. Thus, there is an epistemic tension about the way of ascertaining truth between a technical approach based on pragmatic verification and validation and a scientific approach based on formal logic. The former's semantics is validity and evidence, while the latter's is truth and proof. The former is based on synthetic statements grounded on real phenomena, while the latter is based on analytic statements grounded on axioms and meanings. The former is aiming at decision and action, while the latter is aiming at certainty.

This is not a new tension in computer science as the past decades have shown numerous pessimistic arguments regarding the lack of proof of computer programs and the significant number of potential accidents related to unproven software. (Wiener 1985) mentions the original argument for proving limitations in a program development[15]; Dijkstra (1972) mentions the logical bias of program testing[16] not able to prove the absence of a faulty code; Thom (1971) mentions the human "impossibility of verifying all its steps."[17]

The tension rose dramatically in the late 1970s with the computer-assisted resolution of the 4-color problem.[18] It made even more pronounced the formal proof issue. This event is about the resolution of a mathematical problem with the help of mechanized computations. The question that arises is whether the proof should comply with mathematical proving norms or whether other scientific or technological norms could be used as a proving scheme. Tymoczko (1980) claims that "what has been checked is not rigorous" and that "what is rigorous hasn't been checked" and furthermore cannot be humanly checked. Thus, the computer-assisted proof does not comply with the standards of an acceptable mathematical demonstration proof. The noted lack of rigor draws a line between the possibility error, although small, and certainty.

We may consider as well the main proofs characteristics as in Tymoczko (1979) and in particular that they should be "convincing," "formalizable," and "surveyable," in particular that "a proof is a construction that can be looked over, reviewed, verified, by a rational agent." To that respect, the four-color demonstration proof is not formalizable and particularly not humanly surveyable.

By presenting this way the four-color problem resolution, our aim was not to criticize its demonstration[19] but to show that the way to manage proof in computer science was and is not self-evident.

In the end, we may regard this issue as related to our view of the computer science nature. Is computer science purely applied mathematics, does it relate to natural sciences with an empirical content, or is it merely an engineering discipline aiming at reliability and quality ? And should it be proven accordingly?

11.1.3.2 Machine Learning: Logic, Reliability, and Knowledge

This tension is slightly more complex where Machine Learning is concerned. Hoare (1996) noted that:

> the most dramatic advances in the timely delivery of dependable software are directly attributed to a wider recognition of the fact that the process of program development

can be predicted, planned, managed and controlled in the same way as in any other branch of engineering.

However, development of an ML software involves at least two objects. The first object is about the learning program which is the result of specific software engineering grounded on management rules and norms. The second object is the trained software. For neural networks with supervised learning, it is inherently a process grounded on a dataset which is itself a reduction of a limited series of experiments. It is also a process that is not directly programmed by human engineers but the result of step-by step complex computations.

The first programmed object (object P) is subject to engineering development standards such as verification and validation IEEE[20] Standard 1012TM[21] and testing IEEE Standard 829TM.[22] As a programmed software, the epistemic tension here is released by the application of engineering development management schemes. The program is planned, managed, controlled, and evaluated and then given evidence for the validity of its function, architecture, and interface.

As for the second object (object T), it is the result of an experimental training of object P using a chosen dataset as an empirical grounding. Object T must be evaluated in order to prove that the acquired but unformalized knowledge leads to proper results, that its outputs are as the existing human knowledge would predict them. If we consider object T as an engineering artifact, it should be V&Ved following previously mentioned standards. If we consider it to be the result of a natural science experiment, it should be proven as per the epistemic standards of the considered object, i.e., an AI software dedicated to detecting a melanoma in a dermoscopy image should be validated according to the clinical trials standards. Finally, if we consider it to be an artifact dedicated to formally modelizing knowledge by using applied mathematics, it should be proven using logic.

For example, similar experiments considering the AI software as a technical device or as a medical device will propose different ways of proving its reliability and truthfulness.[23]

On the other hand, if we were to have a logical approach to the Machine Learning processes, the question should arise as to what kind of logic could be used to validate formally the program resulting from the training stage, i.e., that the program produces true results. Truth is an assertion that needs a proof. And proofs can be given in different manners: first of all, by showing the reality of the assertion in all its occurrences, or through a formal causal argument using Aristotelian syllogistic, modal logic, or any other valid formal inference theory.

ML training using supervised learning is based on a dataset, i.e., on a set of individual experimental results in order to infer a general ability to compute any result from any input not present yet in the dataset. It is thus about inferring general propositions from particular ones, thus induction. Let us remind Mill's (1882, p. 208) definition for induction: "Induction may be defined the operation of discovering and proving general propositions."

By "proving," Mill meant inferring in accordance to his *System of Logic*. Hence, qualifying Machine Learning processes as inductive because they go from particular propositions to general processes goes without saying but qualifying the actual logic being used as induction seems a bit excessive without the formal proof that should go along with it.

However, there exists several theorems proving formally some of the behaviors of Machine Learning programs.

Those theorems supply a logical framework to the computations taking place during the training stage. However, they prove formally neither the validity of the dataset representation in the chosen space nor the validity of the predictions output from the unlearnt data, although there are proofs that under certain conditions an infinite size knowledge domain is learnable,[24] that the learning process can converge toward a final model, and that its predictions can be "probably approximately correct" (Shalev-Shwartz and Ben-David 2014). They do not prove, for example, that a domain is learnable within a reasonable machine-time cost, that the point of convergence is optimal, or that the learnt knowledge is bias-free.

Finally, the ambiguous Machine Learning epistemic position is well summarized by Stéphane Mallat (2019) in his lesson: "Machine Learning gives stunning results but we do not know why".[25] This situation is analogous to the steam engines of late 18th and early 19th centuries when steam power was efficiently used, although before the birth of the thermodynamics theory.

11.1.3.3 From Proof to Trustworthiness

Proof can be considered as a relevant decidability criterion for the truth proposition. Then what is it meant for? To communicate the guaranteed validity of the assertion, have a scientific community trust the result, be able to build more research, results, and theory upon those results. Proof means guaranteed truth or verified validity, which means trustworthiness.

But the question remains as to what community shall be targeted by the proof? Whose trust shall be looked for? The target is related to the way the proof itself has been built. Depending on the proof construction, the AI community or the community of practice related to the final usage of the AI artifact[26] may be aimed by the published research articles. Regardless of its construction, the proof may be forwarded using non-scientific or non-professional media in order to establish AI trustworthiness within the general public.

Furthermore, trustworthiness seems to be built as well upon performance taken in all its meanings: past performance as validating a general behavior, but also acting as stage performance where the results are exhibited in an implicit challenge with human performance given as the reference value. To that extent, it is now based on subjective arguments, socially and artificially constructed.

11.1.3.4 Explicability and Dependability

Proof, V&V, or statistic performance may not be enough. An AI artifact does not have a technical function by itself and for itself, it is not enough that its efficiency be validated in a white room. Such an artifact is meant to be in relationship with the world, interrelated with its working environment and its users. Decisions taken according to AI findings might engage human lives, i.e., in a deliberative physician-patient relationship, the detection of a breast cancer should be explained to the patient, this might be the case in high-reliability organizations such as nuclear and chemical industry, or in decisions with significant ethics content such as recidivism risk assessment in trials. Hence, an AI artifact should be able to communicate the results of its reasonings in a comprehensible manner including a "why" or at least a "how" to the computed outcome instead of being a "black box" delivering a *Pythian* prediction.

AI "reasonings" are a form of an artificial *mimésis* of cognitive activities normally performed by humans and already ruled by explicit and implicit knowledge, norms, cultures, etc. Hence, there is a tension between a new artificially conceptualized activity and its counterpart in the real world. Either the results communication is supported only by its assumed trustworthiness or else this communication comes with an explicit explanation. The former creates a situation of human dependence toward the machine authority. The latter supposes the possibility of a causal explanation and the possible commensurability of both artificial and human models. To that extent, if the AI "explicability" is considered as an ethical concept, its possibility is an epistemic issue based on causal inferences.

Let us recall that those AI "reasonings" are based on the computation of statistical correlations between empirical samples present in the dataset which are applied onto any new sample for a prediction. However, correlations between two events A and B do not disclose any directionality or directional temporality between A and B. Thus, causality cannot be inferred solely from correlations: "one cannot substantiate causal claims[27] from associations alone".[28] However, Fisher (1935) had assumed the possibility to draw valid statistical inferences from particular observations of their causes. Following Suppes (1970), Rothman (1976), Spirtes, Glymour, and Scheines (2000), or Pearl (1995; 1998; 2000; 2009), Halpern (2005a; 2005b), Pearl (2009), and later Pearl and Mackenzie (2018) have attempted to give a mathematical grounding to causal inferences in statistics based on the structural causal model (SCM), differentiating the "necessary cause"[29] from the "actual cause."[30]

In parallel, attempts from Hempel and Oppenheim (1948), Salmon (2006), Halpern (2005b), Pearl and Mackenzie (2018), and Pearl (2018) have also been made to supply causal explanations in statistic models.

In Hempel and Oppenheim (1948), the explanatory power is the possibility to deduce logically an *explanandum*[31] from an *explanans*,[32] the constitutive sentences of which must be true. Further to Hempel's *deductive-nomological* model (Hempel 1965) or Salmon's (Salmon 2006) *statistical relevance* model, Halpern and Pearl (2001b) developed their explanation scheme based again on the SCM. Although it is not fully clear from tensions, their model enables the display of clear graphical networks with directional relations disclosing the statistically "proven" causal path(s) between a cause X and its consequence Y.

However, the question remains as to what AI proposition needs to be explained and how. For example, let us consider an AI software capable of detecting melanomas in dermoscopy images of cutaneous lesions. Ideally, the user—dermatologist or physician—should be explained an individual categorization[33] using a "standard" medical interpretative theory.[34] However, the AI has built its own computed model using only selected images with their labels as learning material and such a "standard" theory has not been programmed as such. Thus, the AI software is unable to deliver an explanation comparable to the one a dermatologist would deliver to his/her patient. Further to this point, let us remind that the very notion of causal explanation as defined by Halpern and Pearl (2001b) cannot account for the correlation between the image of lesion and diagnosis as the symptom is not the disease cause just as the ABCDE theory is semiotic and not causal. All the detection AI software can account for is the way correlations are computed between representations of the learning dataset and a new image to be interpreted. The explainable interpretation does not account for the real phenomenon itself using existing theories but on a distant model, hence needing the construction of a distant semiology theory.

In our view, this necessity for a renewed semiology is acceptable. As any medical imaging device does not present the reality but a model to be queried using distant interpretation schemes, the computed AI digital representation is a model to be queried and requires the structuration of new semiotic rules in order to humanly infer the outcome thus to explain it. Here the explanation is a matter of semiology rather than a matter of epistemic causality and if the explained diagnosis refers to a real disease, its explanation and the semiotic rules shall refer to its computed virtual representation. The explanation syntax shall be directly related to the computations, while the meaning involved remains to be theorized.

11.1.3.5 Biases and Errors

We have just seen that performance and efficiency were the keys to trustworthiness. But this very performance may be biased.

As in Weisberg (2010), by bias we mean "the extent to which a particular measure of a causal effect has been systematically distorted." Thus, the concept of bias assumes a systematic error in a process evaluating a statistical cause. In Fisher's view (Fisher 1935; 1965), a "faulty" experiment is either due to an error in the statistics interpretation or an error in the experiment design or execution. The latter statistical error is directly related to what Fisher calls "Bias of Systematic Arrangements" (Fisher 1935), thus located in what he calls the *design of experiment.*

The AI training being based on mechanized statistical correlations, we may wonder what differentiates AI statistical biases from epidemiology's or social sciences'. AI as a general methodology can be considered as a class of *design of experiment.* A specific AI experiment would then be subject to errors in the process of statistical evaluation or in its own design process, or else in its execution—development and implementation. The statistical errors may reside in the initial data[35] or their label assignment, in the assumptions made to represent the data, or in the inability to identify confounding variables.

In our AI case, errors might first be located in the AI technique itself and then in the development methodology, the algorithm design, in wrong technical choices of software bricks or parameters during the development process. Those errors and biases can be related to human fallibility in a technical activity which is still at the research or at best at the innovation stage, still aiming at better solutions and better performance, hence not fully codified even when considering IEEE Standard 1012™. If they remain implicit and undetected, they might cause inaccurate data representation. Biases may also be located in the training itself. They may be related to wrong assumptions on hyperparameters value settings during the training stage. The training dataset itself may be biased. Its labeling structure may bear untested correlation hypothesis. It may involve information bias with inaccurate or even culturally biased labels. It may also be statistically too small, or integrating too small a number of certain minorities, of female versus male labels, of certain diseases. The bias may as well be located in the testing scheme, e.g., in the testing dataset, supplying wrong V&V results.[36] Those dataset biases are all too well-known in statistics as selection bias.

AI involving somehow some mechanized statistics technics, AI-related biases are consequently similar to biases in statistics but may be made implicit within veiled development choices and parameters, within hidden data representation and classification.

11.1.4 AI and Big Data: From the Myth to a New Paradigm?

We have seen how the original AI project had been built around the hypothesis that human thoughts or mental states were complex but mere calculations[37] and that computer models could eventually simulate such complex calculations and even explain them, thanks to memory and computation power continuous improvements.

Nowadays we live in an era saturated with data. Data are being produced firsthand by our individual Internet and mobile activities. Facebook reported warehousing 300 petabytes of data in 2014.[38] Data are also generated by social, professional, and scientific activities: commercial sales, electricity consumption, stock markets, medical data, scientific experiments, sociological data, etc. Together with the belief that knowledge is encapsulated within the data, the *Zeitgeist* or spirit of our time is that any knowledge is accessible through Big Data by the means of Machine Learning and furthermore that human intelligence can be outreached by AI agency.

Some say this myth is about to become a new paradigm. The question arises as to what paradigm and in what scientific field. It is probable that as a technology it will alter profoundly many sectors of activity that shall adopt it and even change the worldview. However, to that extent, it remains difficult to use the Kuhnian concept of paradigm. A profound environment alteration is not necessarily the crisis that should precede the scientific revolution. Furthermore, the knowledge representations involved in AI software shall be different one from another as they have been developed and trained with different processes, parameters, and datasets. In a given domain and for a given theory, what AI representations and scientific concepts should supersede the others and should an AI representation supersede the human theory given the AI representation do not deliver an explainable theory.

More generally, as a methodology, it could be some sort of a modern version of the 18th century empiricism, with the use of mechanized inductive processes simulating human reason. If we consider Galileo to have encrypted Nature regularities in a mathematical language, the AI project would be to further enable the artificial encoding of any human, social, or natural phenomenon. If so, the new AI paradigm would be about a new scientific methodology aiming at the mechanized encryption of general phenomena.

To this claim, we might object the absence of a formal proof, although it is the very proof that makes a proposition or a theory either surely true or surely false. AI is technically verified and validated, but that does not mean that its technical processes are proven formally using deductive or inductive logic. In that case, we may address this objection by using Peirce's pragmatic conception of an object as subsumed under its effects in the world: "Consider what effects ... we conceive the object of our conception to have. Then, our conception of these effects is the whole of our conception of the object" (Peirce 1978).

In this case, the effects being the whole of the artifact conception, a verification and validation based on the equivalence between what an AI artifact is and what its effects are in the world should be relevant considering Peirce's commitment to the truth or even to Dewey's instrumental commitment to "warranted assertibility."[39] The possible emergence of an AI paradigm as a scientific methodology would then result in the resurgence of scientific instrumentalism.

Given that AI has a claim for truth—or warranted assertibility—we might consider now the claim of AI as a neurobiological paradigm if AI happened to simulate entirely human thoughts. As Putnam (2001) puts it, "truth is not just a notion of folk psychology; it is the central notion of logic." But human intelligence is about psychology, i.e., not only logic but also heuristics and rationally limited cognitive processes.[40] Putnam adds that "intentionality is only a feature of folk psychology" and that according to Brentano's thesis, "intentionality won't be reduced and won't go away," where "intentionality is a primitive phenomenon that relates thought and thing, minds and the external world" (Putnam 2001). Thus, there is an essential contradiction here in aiming at simulating human reasoning while having a claim for truth.

Those non-exhaustive objections might be considered as what Hughes (1993, pp. 79–80) calls "reverse salient," i.e., impediments or components of a system which endangers the technical endeavor. However, in the history of a technical system, "reverse salients" can and must be resolved in order to develop, stabilize, and gain "momentum." Present AI is at the crossroads with many well-documented successes properly communicated in order to convince potential customers about its trustworthiness, with a technology that is still producing inventions and enhancements while already commercialized. But it still needs to solve its "reverse salients" in order to become a paradigm as such or at least a successful technological system that will change the "worldview."[41]

11.2 KEY ISSUES IN PHILOSOPHY OF MEDICINE: MEDICINE, HEALTH, AND DISEASE

11.2.1 The Hippocratic Conception of Medicine, Health, and Disease

11.2.1.1 Hippocrates and the Birth of Clinical Medicine

The first scientific revolution in medicine is due to Hippocrates of Kos (460–370 BC). Hippocrates is famous for being the founder of rational medicine, or more emphatically as the "Father of Medicine." At a time when medicine was strictly intertwined with religion and magic, he was the first to regard disease as a natural, rather than a supernatural, phenomenon. He thus encouraged the physicians to look for the physical causes of the disease and to use both clinical observation and inductive/deductive reasoning. By doing this, Hippocrates applied to medicine the method of the philosophers of his time, namely, Democritus (460–370 BC) and the sophist Gorgias (483–375 BC), whom he knew personally; but also, of course, Socrates (470–399 BC). This method consists in the replacement of a mythical explanation of phenomena by a logical or natural explanation; in the transition from "mythos" (the stories of gods, goddesses, and heroes, such as in Homer's *Iliad* and *Odyssey*) to "logos" (the development of rational philosophy and logic, such as pre-Socratic philosophers or, later, Plato and Aristotle's works).

More specifically, Hippocrates is considered as the father of clinical medicine: the word "clinical" refers to the patient in his bed (from Ancient Greek *klinikós*: "pertaining to a bed," from *klínein*: "to lean, incline"), and clinical medicine is defined as medicine at the bedside. By founding clinical medicine, Hippocrates insists on the necessity for physicians to use their five senses when examining their patient, as stated at *Surgery* 1.1: "It's the business of the physician to know … [things] which are to be seen, touched, and heard; which are to be perceived in the sight, and the touch, and the hearing, and the nose, and the tongue, and the understanding" (Thumiger 2018). Hippocrates distinguishes three steps in the examination of the ill:

(1) First, the "sensorial appraisal of the patient's physical state (body temperature, wetness and dryness; sweating or tremors; sensitivity of individual parts) and of the quality of his or her discharges (urine, faeces, and other bodily fluids) to be observed, touched, smelled, and even tasted by the physician" (Thumiger 2018).
(2) Second, a clinical interrogation or interview with both the patient and his family and friends. A passage at *Epidemics* 1.23 states the "things to be observed" according to Hippocrates: "the following were the circumstances attending the disease, from which I framed my judgements, learning from the common nature of all and the particular nature of the individual, from the disease, the patient, the regimen prescribed and the prescriber – for based on these things may become more favourable or less so; … from the custom, mode of life, practices and ages of each patient; from talk, manners, silence, thoughts, sleep or absence of sleep, the nature and times of dreams, plucking, scratching, tears" (Thumiger 2018). As we can see, the interview is about both what the patient is saying (the content of the interview) and the way he is saying it (the form of the interview), the latter being a rich source of information about the physical and mental state of the patient. This also includes what the patient is not saying, and could be said by his family or friends, or guessed by the physician.
(3) Third, taking the patient's history: this refers to of course the patient's previous illnesses but also to his "regimen," to his habits, his occupations, his familial situation, or in Hippocrates' words, "the custom, mode of life, practices and ages of each patient."

11.2.1.2 Hippocrates and the Theory of Four Humors

Hippocrates' conception of health and disease is based on the theory of four humors (blood, phlegm, yellow bile, black bile), which constitute the basis of the physiology of man, or, in other words, its nature. Health and disease are directly related to these humors: health is defined as an equilibrium or a balance of humors within the body (which Hippocrates calls "eucrasia"), whereas disease is due to a disequilibrium or a disbalance in the humoral composition of the body (which Hippocrates calls "dyscrasia"), which means that a humor is either in excess or in default, as Hippocrates states it at *Nature of Man* 4:

> "The human body has within itself blood and phlegm and yellow and black bile, and these are the nature of the body, and because of them it suffers and is healthy. So it is particularly healthy when these things maintain a balance of their power and their quantity in relation to one another, and when they are thoroughly mixed together. It suffers when one of them becomes either too small or too great, or is separated in the body and is not mixed with all the others."
>
> **(Hankinson 2018)**

These four humors are put in relation with the theory of the four elements (earth, water, air, fire), which was proposed by Empedocles (494–434 BC). The novelty of Hippocrates is to establish a correspondence between the four elements in nature with the four humors or fluids in the human body. Hippocrates goes even further by relating these elements and humors with the four ages of life, the four seasons, and also the four couple of qualities. This allows Hippocrates to distinguish between internal factors of disease (humors, for example) and external factors (season, for example). We can draw a table to see the correspondence between these different items (Table 11.1).

So, for example, if the physician has a patient who is a child, and if we are in the spring season (which is hot and wet), there is a high risk of the humor "blood" to be in excess: the physician can thus prescribe preventively a dietary habit such as the prohibition of eating red meat, or he can prescribe bloodletting as a preventive or curative treatment. This table of correspondence allows the physician to adapt the regimen of the patient to his individual characteristics but also to his environment. The occurrence of specific disease can also be prognosed, according to criteria such as season and thus avoided by prevention: the fact that the first printed medical book,

TABLE 11.1
Hippocrates and the Theory of Four Humors

Element	Humor	Couple of Qualities	Season	Age of Life
Air	Blood	Hot and moist	Spring	Infancy
Fire	Yellow bile	Hot and dry	Summer	Youth
Earth	Black bile	Cold and dry	Autumn	Maturity
Water	Phlegm	Cold and moist	Winter	Old age

by Gutenberg in 1457, is the *Laxiercalender*, a calendar of the bloodletting and purgation. That's also why regimen is the central concept of Hippocratic medicine, considering that regimen includes not only dietary habit but also habits of life, physical exercise, and even the art of sleeping and dreaming.

11.2.1.3 Hippocrates' Conception of Health and Disease

The last important point about Hippocratic medicine is that, ultimately, the real physician is Nature. We just showed that for Hippocrates, health and disease are directly related to the four humors and to the good balance of these humors within the body: the patient and the physician must thus find a way to maintain that balance, either through preventive or curative measures. But there is a serious limit to that, and especially to the power of the physician. Hippocrates is supposed to have said that "Nature is the true physician of diseases," which has been translated in Latin under the expression "*Vis medicatrix naturae.*" The exact citation is: "The body's nature is the physician in disease. Nature finds the way for herself, not from thought. ... Well trained, readily and without instruction, nature does what is needed" (*Epidemics* VI, section 5, chapter I[42]). This means that the role of the physician is not to go against nature but to help the patient and his body to restore his equilibrium, for example, by regimen or by bloodletting. This also shows that for Hippocratic physicians, each patient has to be considered both as an individual or particular patient and also as a whole organism in relation with his environment, with, for example, *Airs, Waters and Places* (Hippocrates and Jones 2010), to cite one of the books of the Hippocratic Corpus dedicated to that kind of environmental issues. This is also why the physician-patient relationship is so important in the Hippocratic tradition. The first aphorism of his famous book named *Aphorisms* is a good summary of the difficult art of medicine: "Life is short, and Art long; the crisis fleeting; experience perilous, and decision difficult. The physician must not only be prepared to do what is right himself, but also to make the patient, the attendants, and externals cooperate" (Hippocrates and Jones 2005).

11.2.2 The Modern Conception of Medicine, Health, and Disease: From Anatomo-Clinical to Experimental Medicine

11.2.2.1 Bichat and the Foundations of Anatomo-Clinical Medicine

The second scientific revolution in medicine takes place more than 2000 years after the clinical revolution initiated by Hippocrates, at the end of the 18th century. This revolution is the product of many evolutions that cannot be described in this chapter. Two of them can nonetheless be emphasized: the first one is the development of anatomy in the 16th century, thanks to Andreas Vesalius (1514–1564) and his famous book *De Humani Corporis Fabrica* (*On the Fabric of the Human Body*), published in 1543. At a time when the anatomy of Galen is still the medical orthodoxy, even if Galen only dissected animals and not humans, Vesalius establishes anatomy as a scientific discipline by insisting on direct observation as the only reliable source of anatomical knowledge, and no longer the authority of Galen or Hippocrates. The second evolution is more due to political and social reasons and takes place after the

French Revolution of 1789: according to Michel Foucault (2003), between the end of the 18th century and the beginning of the 19th century, hospitals in France ceased be a place for charity toward the poor, the homeless, or the orphans, to become a genuine medicalized place. The advantage of this evolution is that physicians can observe a vast number of patients but also dissect them when they die. These two evolutions largely explain the advent of anatomo-clinical medicine.

Anatomo-clinical medicine is defined as the systematic correlation between the clinical data and the autopsy data, or, in other words, between the medicine at the bedside and anatomo-pathology. The founder of modern anatomical pathology is Giovanni Battista Morgagni (1682–1771), who has been for 56 years Professor of Anatomy at the University of Padua (as Vesalius before him), one of the most prestigious faculties of medicine in the world at this time. His main thesis is that most diseases are not vaguely dispersed throughout the body, but originate locally, in specific organs and tissues. However, it is the French anatomist Xavier Bichat (1771–1802) who is considered as the true founder of the anatomo-clinical method: as Morgagni, Bichat dissected hundreds of corpses and was able to find the lesions which were the causes of the disease. More precisely, Bichat, who founded histology and histopathology, was convinced that diseases were due to some specific lesions in the various tissues of the human body. The works of Bichat modified the vision that physicians had of the body: the human body became more transparent to them, as they were able to identify the lesion inside the body through clinical examination, at least for some diseases.

The last important point about Bichat is that he was a vitalist. Vitalism is traditionally opposed to mechanism: the mechanistic doctrine was defended, for example, by René Descartes (1596–1650) who considered that all living beings, except humans, are just machines. This theory of beast-machine states that only human beings have a soul, but also that all biological phenomena (even if the word "biology" appears only during the 18th century and become common during the 19th century) are reducible to physical laws or physico-chemicals laws. On the contrary, vitalism considers that living phenomena are subject to specific laws or that vital properties could not be explained through physics or chemistry. The difference is that some kind of "vital principle" (or "vital force" or "élan vital" in French) exists and distinguishes living beings from all other beings. We can distinguish three main thesis in vitalism:

(1) Vital phenomena are not reducible to physicochemical phenomena.
(2) Vital phenomena can only be observed and cannot be experimented: any experimentation on vital phenomena just distort them.
(3) Vital phenomena must be conceived in their totality: each organism is an organized totality, with hierarchized functions.

That's why Bichat, in his *Physiological Researches upon Life and Death* (Bichat 1809), defines life as "the totality of those set of functions which resist death": each living being has from his birth a certain quantity of vital energy, which decreases throughout life and through the struggle with everything that is dead.

11.2.2.2 C. Bernard and the Foundations of Experimental Medicine

One of the greatest revolutions in the history of medicine is clearly operated by Claude Bernard (1813–1878), in his book *An Introduction to the Study of Experimental Medicine*, published originally in 1865 (Bernard 1927). This revolution can be divided into three aspects: first, a revolution in the method; second, a revolution in physiology, through the discoveries Bernard made; and finally, a revolution in the conception of health and disease.

Bernard's main goal is to establish the use of scientific method, i.e., experimental method inherited from Isaac Newton and Descartes, in medicine through the knowledge of physiology. The purpose of physiology is no longer to understand how the human body is organized through organs or tissues, but to understand how the human body functions or works, and the various organs and tissues work together, or, in other words, to understand their determinism. For Bernard indeed, and contrary to Bichat's thesis, vital phenomena are as much determined as non-vital phenomena. He considers that this determinism is an "experimental axiom" that could give physiology and medicine the status of a scientific discipline:

> We must acknowledge as an experimental axiom that in living beings as well as in inorganic bodies the necessary conditions of every phenomenon are absolutely determined. That is to say, in other terms, that when once the conditions of a phenomenon are known and fulfilled, the phenomenon must always and necessarily be reproduced at the will of the experimenter. Negation of this proposition would be nothing less than negation of science itself.
>
> **(Bernard 1927)**

Moreover, for Bernard, the vitalistic concept of a "vital force" is not an explanation of the phenomenon of life: "what we call vital force is a first cause analogous to all other first causes, in this sense, that it is utterly unknown" (Bernard 1927). However, Bernard agrees with Bichat on the specificity of vital phenomena. He considers that physical and chemical sciences provide the foundation for physiology, although physiology is not reducible to them. But the specificity of the object (vital phenomena) does not correspond to a specificity of the scientific method:

> So, if the sciences of life must differ from all others in explanation and in special laws, they are not set apart by scientific method. Biology must borrow the experimental method of physico-chemical sciences, but keep its special phenomena and its own laws.
>
> **(Bernard 1927)**

This unity of scientific method is in strict correlation with the way Bernard considers what a good scientific method is: it is only through experiments and through the hypothetico-deductive method, that science can make progress. Bernard thus distinguishes different steps of any experimentation: first, the experimenter makes empirical observations, then he proposes hypotheses to explain these observations (a cause-effect relationship), then he tests his hypotheses through an experiment, and it is only the experiment that can tell if the initial hypotheses are confirmed and infirmed. When a hypothesis is confirmed, then we have a theory. But the theory is always subject to future revisions: "Theories are only hypotheses, verified by more or less numerous facts. Those verified by the most facts are the best, but even then they are never final, never to be absolutely believed" (Bernard 1927).

This method justifies for Bernard the passage from dissection to vivisection in order to study physiological determinism: dissection only gives information about dead structures, but not about how an organ properly performs its function. It is through the practice of vivisection that Bernard discovered, for example, the glycogenic function of the liver. This led him to create the concept of "internal secretion" and then to the concept of "milieu intérieur" or "internal environment":

> The living body, though it has need of the surrounding environment, is nevertheless relatively independent of it. This independence which the organism has of its external environment, derives from the fact that in the living being, the tissues are in fact withdrawn from direct external influences and are protected by a veritable internal environment which is constituted, in particular, by the fluids circulating in the body.
>
> **(Bernard 1974)**

It is important to note at this point that Bernard's experimental medicine did not have a real impact on medicine as it was daily practiced in the second half of the 19th century. If physiology is today legitimately considered as a science, the scientific status of medicine is still debated.[43] The main progress was the fact that the laboratory was at that time introduced at the hospital. Physicians thus got used to going back and forth from the bedside to the laboratory. The laboratory played also a major role in the development of microbiology and bacteriology with the works of Louis Pasteur (1822–1895), who discovered the principle of vaccination (against rabies), microbial fermentation, and pasteurization; or Robert Koch (1843–1910) who identified the specific causative agents of anthrax (*Bacillus anthracis*), tuberculosis (*Mycobacterium tuberculosis*), and cholera (*Vibrio cholerae*) and theorized what is known as the "Koch's four postulates":

(1) The organism must always be present, in every case of the disease.
(2) The organism must be isolated from a host containing the disease and grown in pure culture.
(3) Samples of the organism taken from pure culture must cause the same disease when inoculated into a healthy, susceptible animal in the laboratory.
(4) The organism must be isolated from the inoculated animal and must be identified as the same original organism first isolated from the originally diseased host.

This exemplifies the statement of Bernard, for whom a good physician is first a good scientist and a good experimenter. However, contrary to Bernard's work, bacteriology had a huge impact on clinical medicine and "Pasteur, a chemist without medical training, inaugurated a new era in medicine" (Canguilhem 2000).

11.2.2.3 The Modern Conception of Health and Disease

Talking about a modern conception of health and disease should not mislead the reader: by "modern," we refer to the conceptions that evolved from the end of the 18th century to the beginning of the 20th century. It started with the anatomo-clinical medicine that identifies disease with the lesion of an organ, lesion that prevents the organ to perform fully or normally its function. It continued with the conception of the physiology of the human body defended by Bernard. According to him, the only difference between physiology and pathology is a quantitative one. Disease is not a result of disequilibrium or a disbalance in the humoral composition of the body as in the Hippocratic tradition (though the idea of internal secretion and internal environment are quite similar to the fluidic conception of health and disease defended by Hippocrates), or the result of a lesion, as in anatomo-clinical medicine, but the result of the deregulation of a normal function, or a dysfunction of an organ. In other words, the normal and the pathological are identical if we except quantitative variations: there is only a difference of degree between health and disease, and not a difference of nature. These two conceptions of disease (lesion of an organ and quantitative variation of a physiological variable) have in common that the individual patient is erased behind his disease. In other words, the patient is reduced to his organs and its functions, or to his physiological variables such as blood pressure, heart rate, blood sugar levels, etc. This conception was clearly reinforced during all the 20th century with the invention of a huge quantity of monitoring devices (starting with the electrocardiogram) and of paraclinical exams which reduced the patient to a set of numerical values and intervals of normality. Health and disease have thus become a quantitative notion, and not anymore, as in the Hippocratic conception, a qualitative one. As Canguilhem says:

> Contemporary medicine is founded, with an efficacy we cannot but appreciate, on the progressive dissociation of disease and the sick person, seeking to characterize the sick person by the disease, rather than identify a disease on the basis of the bundle of symptoms spontaneously presented by the patient.
>
> **(Canguilhem 2012)**

Finally, the bacteriology of Pasteur and Koch "led to a profound epistemological revolution in medicine" (Canguilhem 2000), and on the way health and disease are conceived. Canguilhem says that, after bacteriology, "the object of medicine was no longer so much disease as health" (Canguilhem 2000). The reference to this passage from a "medicine of disease" to a "medicine of health," described by Canguilhem and Foucault, is crucial to understand contemporary conception of medicine, health, and disease.

11.2.3 The Contemporary Conception of Medicine, Health, and Disease

There were so much of discoveries and progress in all areas of medicine and science in general during the 20th century that it is almost impossible to list them. However, we can distinguish two major—and contradictory—trends in the evolution of medicine throughout the 20th century: the molecularization of medicine and the advent of modern epidemiology, understood here as a mix of new statistical methods and study design applied to medicine and a new conception or a new approach of epidemiology often characterized as "risk factor epidemiology" (Giroux 2011).

11.2.3.1 The Molecularization of Medicine in the 20th Century

First, the molecularization of medicine is a by-product of the molecularization of biology and of life in general, in relation to the progress of genetics made during the 20th century, often epitomized by the discovery of DNA Double Helix by J. Watson, F. Crick, and R. Franklin in 1953. This molecularization culminated in the human genome sequencing achieved in 2003 through the Human Genome Project. As N. Rose explains:

> This new genetics was bound up with a mutation in the very image that we have of life. The body that 20th-century medicine inherited from the 19th century was visualized via a clinical gaze, as it appeared in the hospital, on the dissection table and was inscribed in the anatomical atlas. The body was a vital living system, or a system of systems. ... In the 1930s, biology came to visualize life phenomena at the submicroscopic region—between 10^{-6} and 10^{-7} cm .... Life, that is to say, was molecularized.
>
> **(Rose 2001)**[44]

This molecularization can be considered as the logical continuation of the reduction of disease to lesions or quantitative variations of physiological variables. Now, the disease is located at a molecular level: it could concern the cell or, at a lower level of reality, the gene. For example, Linus Pauling published a paper in *Science* titled: "Sickle cell anemia, a molecular disease" (Pauling et al. 1949), where he shows that "hemoglobin from patients with sickle cell anemia (Hemoglobin S or HbS) differs from hemoglobin of normal patients" (Strasser and Fantini 2020), due to a "difference in the physicochemical properties of the protein, namely the different numbers of electric charges of the macromolecule" (Strasser and Fantini 2020). In 1959, J. Lejeune, M. Gautier, and R. Turpin published the first study which identifies a genetic disease: trisomy 21 (each cell in the body has three separate copies of chromosome 21 instead of the usual two copies) showed that a numerical chromosome abnormality could be responsible for the disease. This study constitutes a landmark in the beginnings of medical genetics. In other words, the progress made by molecular biology during the 20th century gave birth to a new medicine: biomedicine. This concept of "biomedicine" is not just a kind of merging of biology and medicine but embraces a whole worldview. S. Valles shows, in his article "Philosophy of Biomedicine," three key features of biomedicine:

(1) "First, specific to biomedicine: the domain of disease and its causes is restricted to solely biological, chemical, and physical phenomena;
(2) Second, shared with many natural sciences: an emphasis on laboratory research and technology and, as translated to health research, a discounting of research questions that cannot be studied by randomized clinical trials (or their analogs, e.g., 'natural experiments'); and

(3) Third, an embrace of 'reductionism,' a philosophical and methodological stance … that holds that phenomena are best explained by the properties of their parts" (Valles 2020).

Biomedicine thus appears as the reductionist medicine: patient is once again reduced to the physical, chemical, and biological constituents—there is no place for his individuality and his relation to environment. Moreover, the experimental methodology, inherited from Bernard, is completed by the introduction of new statistical methodologies just after World War II, which profoundly modified the conception of the etiology of diseases but also the way drugs are evaluated.

11.2.3.2 The Quantification of Medicine[45] and the Birth of Evidence-Based Medicine (EBM)

Just after World War II, a new way to understand the causes of disease appears: in 1950, one of the most famous articles in the history of epidemiology was published: it was written by R. Doll and A.B. Hill (1950) which demonstrated a correlation between smoking and lung cancer and paved a new way to understand the etiology of a disease by using statistical method. It provides a new methodology for observational studies: the "case-control study," which is retrospective. In 1954, Doll and Hill published a new article (Doll and Hill 1954) about the correlation between smoking and carcinoma of the lung. Due to several critics addressed by prominent statisticians such as J. Berkson[46] or R. A. Fisher[47], to the methodology of case-control study and the risk of bias it introduces, Doll and Hill decided to adopt "some entirely new approach … characterized by looking forward into the future" (Doll and Hill 1954), or, in other words, a prospective study, also known later as a cohort study. A few years before, A.B. Hill has conducted, with his colleagues of the Medical Research Council, what is considered as the first randomized clinical trial in history (Hill 1990), which evaluated the potential of streptomycin to treat tuberculosis. The double-blind randomized clinical trial (random allocation of subjects to the two groups, treatment versus placebo, neither the researchers nor the subjects know who receives the treatment and who receives the placebo) soon became the gold standard in medical experiments (Jones and Podolsky 2015). The introduction of these new methodologies, both to assess the etiology of disease and to evaluate the safety and benefit of new drugs (Marks 2000), modified both the conception of the etiology of several diseases and the way medicine was practiced. This gave rise to a new epidemiology, called "risk factor epidemiology" (Giroux 2011).

The problem is that it generated an enormous amount of medical literature, from observational to experimental studies: for example, if in 1950 there were around 86,000 articles indexed in PubMed, in 2018, there are more than 1.3 million[48]: how does the clinician is supposed to find his way through all these results? Besides this problem of quantity, there is a problem of quality: how is the clinician supposed to assess the scientificity of an observational or an experimental study? How is he supposed to choose between the results of a cohort study and the results of randomized clinical trial? How is he supposed to be sure that such behavior, or such substance (tobacco for example, or alcohol), cause a disease, but only in a probabilistic manner?

It was to answer these questions that EBM appeared at the beginning of the 1980s. The term "Evidence-Based Medicine" was coined by Gordon Guyatt in 1992, and it was first considered as a new "approach to teaching the practice of medicine" (Guyatt 1992). However, it soon became a new to practice medicine and its definition changed:

> Evidence based medicine is the conscientious, explicit, and judicious use of current best evidence in making decisions about the care of individual patients. The practice of evidence based medicine means integrating individual clinical expertise with the best available external clinical evidence from systematic research.
>
> **(Sackett et al. 1996)**

This EBM is historically a product of two main evolutions in medicine, in relation to the development of observational and experimental studies after World War II: the first one is the development of what is called "clinical epidemiology," defined by Sackett as "the application, by a physician who provides direct patient care, of epidemiologic and biometric methods to the study of diagnostic and therapeutic process in order to effect an improvement in health" (Sackett 1969), and which A. Feinstein prefers to call "clinimetrics," whose domain is "concerned with quantitative methods in the collection and analysis of comparative clinical data, and particularly with improved 'measurement' of the distinctively clinical and personal phenomena of patient care" (Feinstein 1983). In other words, clinical epidemiology or clinimetrics is an attempt to quantify clinical medicine and to make it more scientific.[49]

The second main evolution is the notion of "critical appraisal" of the medical and clinical literature, praised by E.A. Murphy (Murphy 1976) and D. Sackett essentially to avoid bias. Sackett considers that critical appraisal constitutes the origin of EBM: "By the early 1990s we began to extend the Critical Appraisal concepts to include clinical decision making for and with individual patients. This was labelled Evidence-Based Medicine by our former graduate student, Gordon Guyatt" (Haynes and Goodman 2015). This double evolution led to the hierarchization of the levels of evidence, starting from the opinion expert to the observational studies (case-control study, cohort study), and to the experimental studies (non-randomized and randomized clinical trials) to finish by the category of critical appraisal which includes systematic reviews and meta-analysis. This pyramid of evidence is thus a way to assess the quality of evidence, and a tool for the physician to make better decisions and provide the best treatment to his patient. However, EBM appears as a pure product of biomedicine and tends to adopt a reductionist approach to the patient. Once again, the patient is forgotten.

11.2.3.3 From the Medicine of Disease to the Medicine of Health

G. Canguilhem is probably the most prominent critics of both the reduction of medicine to a science and the reduction of health and disease to a quantitative or objective definition. These two theses are strictly intertwined, and are due to the definition of health and disease (or normal and pathological) given by Canguilhem. He opposes to

Bernard's thesis "that in biology the normal and the pathological are, but for minor quantitative differences, identical" (Canguilhem 2000). For Canguilhem, "there is no objective pathology. Structures or behaviors can be objectively described but they cannot be called 'pathological' on the strength of some purely objective criterion" (Canguilhem 1989). Health is indeed not identical to normality:

> Health is more than normality; in simple terms, it is normativity. Behind all apparent normality one must look to see if it is capable of tolerating infractions of the norm, of overcoming contradictions, of dealing with conflicts. Any normality open to possible future correction is authentic normativity, or health.
>
> **(Canguilhem 2000)**

In other words, "life is this polarized activity of debate with the environment, which feels normal or not depending on whether it feels that it is in a normative position or not"(Canguilhem 1989). Thus, health cannot be defined statistically or mechanistically, but is rather the ability to adapt to one's environment. In this sense, every patient is unique and must be treated as such, and the main goal of medicine and therapeutics is to establish or restore the normal, by which he means "the subjective satisfaction that a norm is established." Health is therefore something eminently subjective, and the patient knows better than the physician if he is healthy or not. And the difference between the normal and the pathological is one of nature and not of degree. The difference between these two states is clear-cut for the patient, because it is a "new way of life for the organism" (Canguilhem 1989): for example, diabetes is not just a biochemical problem of high blood sugar level, or a set of symptoms such as frequent urination or increased thirst: in reality diabetes modifies completely the way of living of the patient and has a global impact on his daily life. In other words, there are no diseases, only sick individuals.

Therefore, medicine is not an objective science, but "a technique or art at the crossroads of several sciences" (Canguilhem 1989). For him, clinical medicine, or medicine at the bedside, comes first, long before any pathological science:

> In pathology the first word historically speaking and the last word logically speaking comes back to clinical practice. Clinical practice is not and will never be a science even when it uses means whose effectiveness is increasingly guaranteed scientifically. Clinical practice is not separated from therapeutics, and therapeutics is a technique for establishing or restoring the normal whose end, that is, the subjective satisfaction that a norm is established, escapes the jurisdiction of objective knowledge. One does not scientifically dictate norms to life. ... The physician has sided with life. Science serves him in fulfilling the duties arising from that choice. The doctor is called by the patient. It is the echo of this pathetic call which qualifies as pathological all the sciences which medical technology uses to aid life. Thus, it is that there is a pathological anatomy, a pathological physiology, a pathological histology, a pathological embryology. But their pathological quality is an import of technical and thereby subjective origin.
>
> **(Canguilhem 1989)**

In other words, it is because health and disease are subjective that pathological sciences exist: pathological refers etymologically to the suffering (the pathos) of someone, and the very existence of medicine is to relive this suffering, to care much more than to cure.

One of the main points of Canguilhem's conception of health and disease is the importance given to the environment. For him, the environment—and not the body—comes first and that it is the relation with the environment that determines the normal or the pathological:

> Thus, in order to discern what is normal or pathological for the body itself, one must look beyond the body. With a disability like astigmatism or myopia, one would be normal in an agricultural or a pastoral society but abnormal for sailing or flying. Hence we cannot clearly understand how the same man with the same organs feels normal or abnormal at different times in environments suited to man unless we understand how organic vitality flourishes in man in the form of technical plasticity and the desire to dominate the environment.
>
> **(Canguilhem 1989)**

The distinctive feature of man is that his environment is not only and not essentially biological but social: this means that social norms (technological, economic, juridical, political, or moral norms) are more important than vital norms. Yet, one of the most prominent traits of modern societies is the medicalization of society, criticized by both Canguilhem and M. Foucault, that every aspect of life is now susceptible to receive a medical treatment. Foucault says, for example, that "the medicine of the last decades, already acting beyond its traditional boundaries defined by the patient and by the diseases, begins to no longer have any domain outside it."[50] Canguilhem describes how this process of medicalization modifies both the medical act itself and medicine in general. Medicine is no more the response to a pathetic appeal from a patient, but is now a response to a demand.

> This gave new impetus to a medical discipline that had enjoyed prominence in England and France since the end of the eighteenth century—public health or hygiene. ... The political pressures stemming from public health concerns gradually resulted in changes in medicine's objectives and practices. The accent was shifted from health to prevention to protection. The semantic shift points to a change in the medical act itself. Where medicine had once responded to an appeal, it was now obedient to a demand. Health is the capacity to resist disease; yet those who enjoy good health arc nevertheless conscious of the possibility of illness. Protection is the negation of disease, an insistence on never having to think about it. In response to political pressures, medicine has had to take on the appearance of a biological technology. Here, for a third time, the individual patient, who seeks the attention of clinician, has been set aside.
>
> **(Canguilhem 2000)**

In other words, the traditional medicine of diseases has become nowadays a medicine of health. This means that now medicine is relying essentially on prevention and prediction. This is partly due to what is called "epidemiological transition" (Omran 1971), whose most prominent manifestation is the replacement of infectious diseases by chronic diseases. Contemporary medicine is founded on a new individualization of the patient: the patient is now identified according to his risk factors (blood pressure, body mass index, genes of predisposition to some diseases, etc.). The object of contemporary medicine is no longer the sick individual or the diseases, but the risk of disease: every individual is now a potential sick individual. Consequently, all the behaviors of all the individuals are now the target of public health policies and advertisements: every citizen is supposed to do sport or physical activity, to eat fruit and vegetables, to avoid smoking or any risky behaviors, etc. The problem is that these policies of health promotion[51] or of empowerment tend to make the individual responsible of his state of health or of disease, without considering his familial, social, economic, or ecological background. In other words, it can lead to a form of guilt for getting sick. Lastly, the main objective of this medicine of health is to produce a normalization of the behaviors by exerting a pression on the individuals in order for him to adapt to the existing social norms and to be physically and psychically performant in a competitive world. The concept of biopower and biopolitics, theorized by M. Foucault, and defined as the practice of modern nation states and their regulation of their subjects through "an explosion of numerous and diverse techniques for achieving the subjugations of bodies and the control of populations" (Foucault 1978), has never been so relevant, when the Covid-19 pandemic imposes unprecedent measures of restriction on civil liberties for the sake of public health.

11.3 CONCLUSION: PERSONALIZED MEDICINE OR THE INTRODUCTION OF AI AND BIG DATA IN MEDICINE

The sequencing of human genome achieved in 2003, whose main goal was to identify and map all the genes of the human genome from both a physical and a functional standpoint, opened a new era in biology and medicine called the "post-genomics era." It gave birth to "omics" sciences: genomics, transcriptomics, metabolomics, interactomics, epigenomics, proteomics, pharmacogenomics, etc. The main progress of "omics" sciences is that, instead of analyzing a single gene, protein, or metabolite, it analyzes the entirety of a genome, a proteome, or a metabolome. According to the US National Academy of Sciences, there are two main reasons to conduct omics research:

> One common reason is to obtain a comprehensive understanding of the biological system under study. For instance, one might perform a proteomics study on normal human kidney tissues to better understand protein activity, functional pathways, and protein interactions in the kidney. Another common goal of omics studies is to associate the omics-based molecular measurements with a clinical outcome of interest, such as prostate cancer survival time, risk of breast cancer recurrence, or response to therapy.
>
> **(Committee on the Review of Omics-Based Tests for Predicting Patient Outcomes in Clinical Trials et al. 2012)**

In other words, the general idea is the individualization of the diagnosis, prognosis, and therapeutics according to the genetic profile of a patient. Many authors consider that these omics sciences opened a new era in medicine and constitute a scientific revolution. Some authors called this new medicine "personalized medicine"[52]

(Langreth and Waldholz 1999); its aim was to "target drug for each unique genetic profile." Ten years later, for the anniversary of the article, the tone was less optimistic: "we know that it was a new era that started, and we have already seen the first important results, even though the promise of 'targeting drugs for each unique genetic profile' is far from being fulfilled yet" (Jørgensen 2009). However, the main characteristics of personalized medicine is that it first continues the molecularization of medicine which started in the 20th century, and then it inaugurates the computerization of medicine (Lemoine 2017) through the use of Artificial Intelligence and Big Data. In 2008, L. Hood proposed to call this new medicine "P4 medicine," defined as "a result of two convergences: systems medicine and the digital revolution" (Hood 2013). But to what correspond these four P's?

1. *The first P stand for "predictive":* "Within the next 10 years, we should be able to sequence entire genomes in less than an hour's time at the cost of a few hundred dollars. ... In 10 years, we may have a little hand-held device that will prick your finger, make 2,500 blood measurements, and will longitudinally follow the organ-specific proteins for 50 different organs. This will allow us to detect many diseases at the earliest detectable phase, weeks, months, and maybe years before symptoms appear" (Hood 2013).
2. *The second P corresponds to "personalized":* "In the future, diseases will be stratified according to the genetic make-up of the individual, and, in turn, treatments will be individually optimized" (Hood 2013).
3. *The third P is for "preventive":* "Instead of medicine focusing on disease as it does today, the focus in the future will be on wellness" (Hood 2013).
4. *The last P stands for "participatory":* "Patient-driven networks are going to be the driving force of this revolution in medicine" (Hood 2013).

In other words, the main idea behind P-medicine is that all medical decisions, practices, interventions, or products would be tailored to the individual patient. For some authors, P-medicine will radically transform the healthcare sector and society: with the emergence of mHealth through the multiplication of wearable devices (smart watches, for example, which integrate more and more sensors), which makes possible "mathematically sophisticated 'big data' analyses of billions of data points generated for each individual in the population" (Flores et al. 2013) and thus a continuous self-monitoring of each individual which could be cross-checked with his genetic data, the possibilities are great. In this sense, it could surely "make disease care radically more cost effective by personalizing care to each person's unique biology and by treating the causes rather than the symptoms of disease" or "provide the basis for concrete action by consumers to improve their health as they observe the impact of lifestyle decisions"(Flores et al. 2013).

But the risks are as much great as the possibilities: for the moment, nothing guarantees that the analysis and reasonings of Artificial Intelligence are not prone to random and systematic errors. Nothing guarantees neither that these new technologies, in a sector entirely controlled by the Big Tech companies, could not be used in another way, not only to make profit, but to exert some kind of huge biopower on the population and increase social and health inequalities between the individuals. In other words, what we need, from an epistemological point of view, is a real critical appraisal of Big Data and Artificial Intelligence in healthcare (Brault and Saxena 2020) to assess the validity of the Big Data and the way Artificial Intelligence thinks or reasons. What is needed is not only to open the black box of Artificial Intelligence, but to make it explicable, explicability referring here to both "the epistemological sense of *intelligibility* (as an answer to the question 'how does it work?') and in the ethical sense of *accountability* (as an answer to the question: 'who is responsible for the way it works?')" (Floridi and Cowls 2019). At least, as we explained in the previous chapter, we can make AI "explainable," by which we mean the semiological interpretability of Artificial Intelligence technologies. This explainability appears to us as the only way to make AI understandable by the public, and to make possible for the public and the citizens to exert a democratic control on it. As health is defined by the World Health Organization as "a state of complete physical, mental and social well-being and not merely the absence of disease or infirmity," physicians and patients, and not just algorithms, should be the main actors of this well-being, in all its dimensions.

NOTES

1. Menabrea Luigi Federico (1843).
2. Pascal (1645).
3. Leibniz (1710).
4. Namely a Turing Machine.
5. In mathematics and computer science, the *Entscheidungsproblem* ("decision problem") is a challenge posed by David Hilbert in 1928. The problem requests an algorithm to be able to decide whether a given statement is provable from the axioms using the rules of logic.
6. That is, not electromechnical.
7. By Warren McCulloch and Walter Pitts. See McCulloch and Pitts (1943).
8. For the full text, see: www-formal.stanford.edu/jmc/history/dartmouth/dartmouth.html.
9. Developed by Edward Feigenbaum, Bruce Buchanan, Joshua Lederberg, and Carl Djerassi.
10. Developed (starting) in 1972 by Edward H. Shortliffe, mentored by Bruce Buchanan.
11. Which is rather common but the representation can be made using tensors as well.
12. Marvin Minsky, *Matter, Mind and Models*, 1963: *"To an observer B, an object A* is a model of an object A to the extent that B can use A* to answer questions that interest him about A"*, in (Minsky 1968).
13. Depending on the request, for instance: categorization, probability computation, etc.
14. The Aristotelian *orthos logos.*
15. "A proof represents a logical process which has come to a definitive conclusion in a finite number of stages. However, a logical machine following definite rules need never come to a conclusion."
16. But program testing can be a very effective way to show the presence of bugs, but is hopelessly inadequate for showing their absence.
17. René Thom (1971) as quoted in (Tymoczko 1981): "Let us suppose that we have been able to construct for a formal theory S an electronic machine M capable of carrying out at a terrifying speed all the elementary steps in S. We wish to verify the correctness of one formula F of the theory. After a process totaling 1030 elementary operations,

completed in a few seconds, the machine M gives us a positive reply. Now what mathematician would accept without hesitation the validity of such a 'proof,' given the impossibility of verifying all its steps?"

18. See (Appel and Haken 1977).
19. It is not considered a problem anymore but a theorem.
20. Institute of Electrical and Electronics Engineers, see also ISO standards.
21. Standard for System, Software, and Hardware Verification and Validation, last version in 2016.
22. Standard for Software and System Test Documentation, last version in 2008.
23. As examples we might consider Li et al. (2016) and Haenssle et al. (2018).
24. See Shalev-Shwartz and Ben-David (2014).
25. Translation by the author.
26. That is, dermatologists in the case of a melanoma detection software, oncologists in the case of breast cancer detection, etc.
27. Such as explicability.
28. See Pearl (2009, p. 99).
29. X is a necessary cause of Y if Y would not have occurred provided X had not occurred.
30. X is an actual cause of Y if X is at the origin of a logical sequence of events ending in the occurrence of Y.
31. Empirical phenomenon.
32. Mainly general laws derived from general regularities.
33. To make it simple: melanoma or non-melanoma.
34. For example, the ABCDE semiology model.
35. Sampling bias.
36. Often, the whole dataset is split: two-third of the dataset is used for training, while the last third is used for testing. In that case, bias in the training dataset is probably present in the testing dataset as well.
37. See Hobbes, Putnam.
38. See https://engineering.fb.com/core-data/scaling-the-facebook-data-warehouse-to-300-pb/ (retrieved August 28, 2020).
39. See Dewey (1941).
40. See Simon (1955).
41. See Kuhn (1970).
42. Hippocrates and Smith 1994.
43. See, for example, Canguilhem (1989).
44. On the molecularization of biology and medicine, see also Chadarevian (2003).
45. For a history of quantification in medicine, see Matthews 1995) and Jorland, Opinel, and Weisz (2005).
46. See, for example, Berkson (2014 [1947]; 1955; 1958; 1963). For a short history of Berkson's bias, see Brault (2020).
47. See, for example, Fisher (1959). On the controversy around the association of smoking with cancer of the lung, see, for example, Parascandola (2004); White (1991); and Vandenbroucke (2009). For a general history of epidemiology, see Morabia 2004); Leplège, Bizouarn, and Coste 2011); and Brault (2017).
48. Alexandru Dan Corlan. Medline trend: automated yearly statistics of PubMed results for any query, 2004. Web resource at http://dan.corlan.net/medline-trend.html (accessed November 29, 2020).
49. For an overview of link between public health epidemiology and clinical epidemiology, see Giroux (2012) and Brault (2017).
50. "Crise de la médecine ou anti-médecine ?", in Foucault (2000).

51. See, for example, "The Ottawa Charter for Health Promotion," published in 1986, accessible at: https://www.who.int/teams/health-promotion/enhanced-wellbeing/first-global-conference.
52. For an overview of the philosophy of personalized medicine, see Lemoine (2017); Darrason (2017); Giroux (2017); Chadwick (2017); and Guchet (2017).

REFERENCES

Appel, Kenneth, and Wolfgang Haken. 1977. "The Solution of the Four-Color-Map Problem." *Scientific American* 237 (4): 108–21. doi: 10.1038/scientificamerican1077-108.

Berkson, J. 1955. "The Statistical Study of Association between Smoking and Lung Cancer." *Proceedings of the Staff Meetings. Mayo Clinic* 30 (15): 319–48.

Berkson, Joseph. 1958. "Smoking and Lung Cancer: Some Observations on Two Recent Reports." *Journal of the American Statistical Association* 53 (281): 28. doi: 10.2307/2282563.

Berkson, Joseph. 1963. "Smoking and Lung Cancer." *The American Statistician* 17 (4): 15–22.

Berkson, Joseph. 2014. "Limitations of the Application of Fourfold Table Analysis to Hospital Data.*,†." *International Journal of Epidemiology* 43 (2): 511–15. doi: 10.1093/ije/dyu022.

Bernard, Claude. 1927. *An Introduction to the Study of Experimental Medicine*. Translated by Henry Copley Greene. MacMillan & Co.

Bernard, Claude. 1974. *Lectures on the Phenomena of Life Common to Animals and Plants*. American Lecture Series, Publication No. 900. A Monograph in the Bannerstone Division of American Lecture Series in the History of Medicine and Science. Springfield, Ill: Thomas.

Bichat, Xavier F.M. 1809. *Physiological Researches Upon Life and Death*. Translated by Tobias Watkins. Philadelphia: Smith and Maxwell.

Brault, Nicolas. 2017. "Le Concept de Biais En Épidémiologie." Paris VII.

Brault, Nicolas. 2020. "Le biais de Berkson, ou l'histoire d'un quiproquo épistémologique." *Bulletin d'histoire et d'épistémologie des sciences de la vie* Volume 27 (1): 31–49. doi: 10.3917/bhesv.271.0031.

Brault, N., Saxena, M. "For a critical appraisal of artificial intelligence in healthcare: The problem of bias in mHealth." *J Eval Clin Pract*. 2020 December 23. doi: 10.1111/jep.13528. Epub ahead of print. PMID: 33369050.

Canguilhem, Georges. 1989. *The Normal and the Pathological*. New York: Zone Books.

Canguilhem, Georges. 2000. *A Vital Rationalist: Selected Writings from Georges Canguilhem*. Edited by François Delaporte. 1st pbk. ed. New York: Zone Books.

Canguilhem, Georges. 2012. *Writings on Medicine*. New York: Fordham University Press.

Chadarevian, Soraya de. 1998. *Molecularizing Biology and Medicine: New Practices and Alliances, 1920s to 1970s*. 1st ed. London: Taylor & Francis. doi: 10.4324/9780203304235.

Chadwick, Ruth. 2017. "What's in a Name: Conceptions of Personalized Medicine and Their Ethical Implications." *Lato Sensu: Revue de La Société de Philosophie Des Sciences* 4 (2): 5–11. doi: 10.20416/lsrsps.v4i2.893.

Committee on the Review of Omics-Based Tests for Predicting Patient Outcomes in Clinical Trials, Board on Health Care Services, Board on Health Sciences Policy, and Institute of Medicine. 2012. *Evolution of Translational Omics: Lessons Learned and the Path Forward*. Edited by Christine M. Micheel, Sharly J. Nass, and Gilbert S. Omenn. Washington, D.C.: National Academies Press. doi: 10.17226/13297.

Darrason, Marie. 2017. "Médecine de précision et médecine des systèmes: La médecine personnalisée se trompet-elle de cible ?" *Lato Sensu: Revue de la Société de philosophie des sciences* 4 (2): 66–82. doi: 10.20416/lsrsps.v4i2.983.

Dewey, John. 1941. "Propositions, Warranted Assertibility, and Truth." *The Journal of Philosophy* 38 (7): 169. doi: 10.2307/2017978.

Dijkstra, Edsger W. 1972. "The Humble Programmer." *Communications of the ACM* 15 (10): 859–66. doi: 10.1145/355604.361591.

Doll, R., and A. B. Hill. 1950. "Smoking and Carcinoma of the Lung: Preliminary Report." *British Medical Journal* 2 (4682): 739–48. doi: 10.1136/bmj.2.4682.739.

Doll, R., and A. B. Hill. 1954. "The Mortality of Doctors in Relation to Their Smoking Habits: A Preliminary Report." *British Medical Journal* 1 (4877): 1451–55. doi: 10.1136/bmj.1.4877.1451.

Feinstein, Alvan R. 1983. "An Additional Basic Science for Clinical Medicine: IV. The Development of Clinimetrics." *Annals of Internal Medicine* 99 (6): 843. doi: 10.7326/0003-4819-99-6-843.

Fisher, Ronald A. 1935. *The Design of Experiments.* London: Oliver & Boyd.

Fisher, Ronald A. 1959. *Smoking. The Cancer Controversy: Some Attempts to Assess the Evidence.* Edinburgh, Scotland: Oliver and Boyd.

Fisher, Ronald A. 1965. "The Place of the Design of Experiments in the Logic of Scientific Inference." *Sankhyā: The Indian Journal of Statistics, Series A (1961-2002)* 27 (1): 33–38.

Flores, Mauricio, Gustavo Glusman, Kristin Brogaard, Nathan D Price, and Leroy Hood. 2013. "P4 Medicine: How Systems Medicine Will Transform the Healthcare Sector and Society." *Personalized Medicine* 10 (6): 565–76. doi: 10.2217/pme.13.57.

Floridi, Luciano, and Josh Cowls. 2019. "A Unified Framework of Five Principles for AI in Society." Harvard Data Science Review, June. doi: 10.1162/99608f92.8cd550d1.

Foucault, Michel. 1978. *The History of Sexuality. Volume 1: An Introduction/The Will to Knowledge.* 1st American ed. New York: Pantheon Books.

Foucault, Michel. 2000. *Dits et écrits: 1954 - 1988. 3*: 1976 –1979. Nachdr. Bibliothèque des sciences humaines. Paris: Gallimard.

Foucault, Michel. 2003. *The Birth of the Clinic: An Archaeology of Medical Perception.* London: Routledge. http://site.ebrary.com/id/10639215.

Giroux, Élodie. 2011. "A Contribution to the History of Risk Factor Epidemiology." *Revue d'histoire des sciences* 64 (2): 219–24. doi: 10.3917/rhs.642.0219.

Giroux, Élodie. 2012. "De l'épidémiologie de santé publique à l'épidémiologie clinique. Quelques réflexions sur la relation entre épidémiologie et clinique (1920–1980)." *Bulletin d'histoire et d'épistémologie des sciences de la vie* 19 (1): 21. doi: 10.3917/bhesv.191.0021.

Giroux, Élodie. 2017. "Médecine de précision et Evidence-Based Medicine : quelle articulation ?" *Lato Sensu: Revue de la Société de philosophie des sciences* 4 (2): 49–65. doi: 10.20416/lsrsps.v4i2.683.

Guchet, Xavier. 2017. "Médecine personnalisée versus médecine de la personne : une fausse alternative." *Lato Sensu: Revue de la Société de philosophie des sciences* 4 (2): 36–48. doi: 10.20416/lsrsps.v4i2.813.

Guyatt, Gordon. 1992. "Evidence-Based Medicine: A New Approach to Teaching the Practice of Medicine." *JAMA* 268 (17): 2420. doi: 10.1001/jama.1992.03490170092032.

Haenssle, H. A., C. Fink, R. Schneiderbauer, F. Toberer, T. Buhl, A. Blum, A. Kalloo, et al. 2018. "Man against Machine: Diagnostic Performance of a Deep Learning Convolutional Neural Network for Dermoscopic Melanoma Recognition in Comparison to 58 Dermatologists." *Annals of Oncology* 29 (8): 1836–42. doi: 10.1093/annonc/mdy166.

Halpern, J. Y. 2005a. "Causes and Explanations: A Structural-Model Approach. Part I: Causes." *The British Journal for the Philosophy of Science* 56 (4): 843–87. doi: 10.1093/bjps/axi147.

Halpern, J. Y. 2005b. "Causes and Explanations: A Structural-Model Approach. Part II: Explanations." *The British Journal for the Philosophy of Science* 56 (4): 889–911. doi: 10.1093/bjps/axi148.

Hankinson, Jim. 2018. "Aetiology." In *The Cambridge Companion to Hippocrates*, edited by Peter E. Pormann, 1st ed., 89–118. Cambridge: Cambridge University Press. doi: 10.1017/9781107705784.006.

Haynes, R. Brian, and Steven N. Goodman. 2015. "An Interview with David Sackett, 2014–2015." *Clinical Trials: Journal of the Society for Clinical Trials* 12 (5): 540–51. doi: 10.1177/1740774515597895.

Hebb, D. O. 1949. *The Organization of Behavior: A Neuropsychological Theory.* New York: John Wiley & Sons, Inc.

Hempel, Carl G. 1965. *Aspects of Scientific Explanation and Other Essays in the Philosophy of Science.* New York: MacMillan & Co.

Hempel, Carl G., and Paul Oppenheim. 1948. "Studies in the Logic of Explanation." *Philosophy of Science* 15 (2): 135–75. doi: 10.1086/286983.

Hill, Sir Austin Bradford. 1990. "Memories of the British Streptomycin Trial in Tuberculosis." *Controlled Clinical Trials* 11 (2): 77–79. doi: 10.1016/0197-2456(90)90001-I.

Hippocrates, and William H. S. Jones. 2005. *Hippocrates. Volume IV.* Reprinted. Loeb classical library 150. Cambridge, MA: Harvard Univ. Press.

Hippocrates, and William H. S. Jones. 2010. *Hippocrates. Volume I.* Nachdr. Loeb Classical Library 147. Cambridge, MA: Harvard University Press.

Hippocrates, and Wesley D. Smith. 1994. *Hippocrates. Volume VII.* Loeb Classical Library LCL477. Cambridge, MA: Harvard University.

Hoare, C. A. R. 1996. "How Did Software Get so Reliable without Proof?" In *FME'96: Industrial Benefit and Advances in Formal Methods*, edited by Marie-Claude Gaudel and James Woodcock, 1051: 1–17. Berlin, Heidelberg: Springer Berlin Heidelberg. doi: 10.1007/3-540-60973-3_77.

Hood, Leroy. 2013. "Systems Biology and P4 Medicine: Past, Present, and Future." *Rambam Maimonides Medical Journal* 4 (2): e0012. doi: 10.5041/RMMJ.10112.

Hughes, Thomas Parke. 1993. *Networks of Power: Electrification in Western Society, 1880 - 1930.* Softshell Books ed. Softshell Books History of Technology. Baltimore, MD: John Hopkins Univ. Press.

Jones, David S., and Scott H. Podolsky. 2015. "The History and Fate of the Gold Standard." *The Lancet* 385 (9977): 1502–3. doi: 10.1016/S0140-6736(15)60742-5.

Jørgensen, Jan Trøst. 2009. "New Era of Personalized Medicine: A 10-Year Anniversary." *The Oncologist* 14 (5): 557–8. doi: 10.1634/theoncologist.2009-0047.

Jorland, Gérard, Annick Opinel, and George Weisz, eds. 2005. *Body Counts: Medical Quantification in Historical and Sociological Perspective / La Quantification Medicale, Perspectives Historiques et Sociologiques.* Montréal ; Ithaca: McGill-Queen's University Press.

Kuhn, Thomas S. 1970. *The Structure of Scientific Revolutions.* [2d ed., Enl. International Encyclopedia of Unified Science. Foundations of the Unity of Science, v. 2, No. 2]. Chicago: University of Chicago Press.

Langreth, null, and null Waldholz. 1999. "New Era of Personalized Medicine: Targeting Drugs for Each Unique Genetic Profile." *The Oncologist* 4 (5): 426–7.

Leibniz, Gottfried. 1710. "Brevis description Machinæ Arithmeticæ, cum figura", in *Miscellanea Berolinensia ad incrementum scientiarum*, Berlin (Germany): Berlin-Brandenburgischen Akademie der Wissenschaften, 317–19.

Lemoine, Maël. 2017. "Neither from Words, nor from Visions: Understanding p-Medicine from Innovative Treatments." *Lato Sensu: Revue de La Société de Philosophie Des Sciences* 4 (2): 12–23. doi: 10.20416/lsrsps.v4i2.793.

Leplège, Alain, Philippe Bizouarn, and Joël Coste. 2011. *De Galton à Rothman: les grands textes de l'épidémiologie au XXe siècle*. Paris: Hermann.

Li, Yunzhu, Andre Esteva, Brett Kuprel, Rob Novoa, Justin Ko, and Sebastian Thrun. 2016. "Skin Cancer Detection and Tracking Using Data Synthesis and Deep Learning." *ArXiv:1612.01074 [Cs]*, December. http://arxiv.org/abs/1612.01074.

Mackall, Dale, Stacy Nelson, and Johann Schumman. 2002. "Verification & Validation Of Neural Networks For Aerospace Systems." Dryden Flight Research Center and NASA Ames Research Center.

Mallat, Stéphane. Lesson at the Collège de France, January 23rd 2019.

Marks, Harry M. 2000. *The Progress of Experiment: Science and Therapeutic Reform in the United States, 1900–1990*. Cambridge History of Medicine. Cambridge: Cambridge Univ. Press.

Matthews, J. Rosser. 1995. *Quantification and the Quest for Medical Certainty*. Princeton, NJ: Princeton University Press.

McCulloch, Warren S., and Walter Pitts. 1943. "A Logical Calculus of the Ideas Immanent in Nervous Activity." *The Bulletin of Mathematical Biophysics* 4 (5): 115–33.

Menabrea Luigi Federico, Lovelace Ada. 1843. "Sketch of the Analytical Engine invented by Charles Babbage... with notes by the translator." Translated by Ada Lovelace. In Richard Taylor (ed.), *Scientific Memoirs*, London: Richard and John E. Taylor, 666–731.

Mill, John Stuart. 1882. *A System of Logic*. New York: Harper and Brothers.

Minsky, Marvin Lee. 1968. *Semantic Information Processing*. Cambridge, MA: MIT Press.

Morabia, Alfredo, ed. 2004. *A History of Epidemiologic Methods and Concepts*. Basel and Boston: Birkhauser Verlag.

Murphy, Edmond A. 1976. *The Logic of Medicine*. Baltimore, MD: Johns Hopkins University Press.

Omran, A. R. 1971. "The Epidemiologic Transition. A Theory of the Epidemiology of Population Change." *The Milbank Memorial Fund Quarterly* 49 (4): 509–38.

Parascandola, Mark. 2004. "Skepticism, Statistical Methods, and the Cigarette: A Historical Analysis of a Methodological Debate." *Perspectives in Biology and Medicine* 47 (2): 244–61. doi: 10.1353/pbm.2004.0032.

Pascal, Blaise. 1645. *La Machine d'arithmétique. Lettre dédicatoire à Monseigneur le Chancelier.*

Pauling, L., H. A. Itano, S. J. Singer, and I. C. Wells. 1949. "Sickle Cell Anemia, a Molecular Disease." *Science* 110 (2865): 543–8. doi: 10.1126/science.110.2865.543.

Pearl, Judea. 1995. "Causal Diagrams for Empirical Research." *Biometrika* 82 (4): 669–88. doi: 10.1093/biomet/82.4.669.

Pearl, Judea. 1998. "Graphs, Causality, and Structural Equation Models." *Sociological Methods & Research* 27 (2): 226–84. doi: 10.1177/0049124198027002004.

Pearl, Judea. 2000. *Causality: Models, Reasoning, and Inference*. Cambridge, U.K. ; New York: Cambridge University Press.

Pearl, Judea. 2009. "Causal Inference in Statistics: An Overview." *Statistics Surveys* 3: 96–146. doi: 10.1214/09-SS057.

Pearl, Judea, and Dana Mackenzie. 2018. *The Book of Why: The New Science of Cause and Effect*. New York: Basic Books.

Peirce, Charles S. 1978. *Collected Papers of Charles Sanders Peirce. Volume 5: Pragmatism and Pragmaticism*. 4. print. ed. by Charles Hartshorne ...; Vol. 6. Cambridge, Mass: Belknap Press of Harvard Univ. Press.

Putnam, Hilary. 2001. *Representation and Reality*. Reprinted. Representation and Mind. Cambridge, MA: MIT Press.

Rose, Nikolas. 2001. "The Politics of Life Itself." *Theory, Culture & Society* 18 (6): 1–30. doi: 10.1177/02632760122052020.

Rothman, Kenneth J. 1976. "Causes." *American Journal of Epidemiology* 104 (6): 587–92. doi: 10.1093/oxfordjournals.aje.a112335.

Sackett, David L. 1969. "Clinical Epidemiology." *American Journal of Epidemiology* 89 (2): 125–28.

Sackett, David L., William M. C. Rosenberg, J. A. Muir Gray, R. Brian Haynes, and W. Scott Richardson. 1996. "Evidence Based Medicine: What It Is And What It Isn't: It's About Integrating Individual Clinical Expertise And The Best External Evidence." *BMJ: British Medical Journal* 312 (7023): 71–2.

Salmon Wesley. 1970. "Statistical Explanation", in Robert Colodny (ed.). *The Nature and Function of Scientific* Theories, Pittsburgh: University of Pittsburgh Press, 173–232.

Salmon, Wesley C. 2006. *Four Decades of Scientific Explanation.* 1. Univ. of Pittsburgh Press paperback ed. Pittsburgh, PA: Univ. of Pittsburgh Press.

Searle, John R. 1980. "Minds, Brains, and Programs." *Behavioral and Brain Sciences* 3 (3): 417–24. doi: 10.1017/S0140525X00005756.

Shalev-Shwartz, Shai, and Shai Ben-David. 2014. *Understanding Machine Learning: From Theory to Algorithms.* New York: Cambridge University Press.

Simon, Herbert A. 1955. "A Behavioral Model of Rational Choice." *The Quarterly Journal of Economics* 69 (1): 99. doi: 10.2307/1884852.

Simon, Herbert A., and Allen Newell. 1958. "Heuristic Problem Solving: The Next Advance in Operations Research." *Operations Research* 6 (1): 1–10. doi: 10.1287/opre.6.1.1.

Software and Systems Engineering Standards Committee. 2016. *IEEE Std 1012™-2016*, IEEE Computer Society.

Spirtes, Peter, Clark N. Glymour, and Richard Scheines. 2000. *Causation, Prediction, and Search.* 2nd ed. Adaptive Computation and Machine Learning. Cambridge, MA and London: The MIT Press.

Strasser, Bruno J, and Bernardino Fantini. 2020. "Molecular Diseases and Diseased Molecules: Ontological and Epistemological Dimensions," 27.

"Streptomycin Treatment of Pulmonary Tuberculosis. A Medical Research Council Investigation." 1948. *British Medical Journal* 2 (4582): 769–82.

Suppes, Patrick. 1970. *A Probabilistic Theory of Causality.* Acta Philosophica Fennica, Fasc. 24. Amsterdam: North-Holland Pub. Co.

Tarski, Alfred. 1969. "Truth and Proof". *Scientific American* 220: 63–7.

Thom, René. 1971. "'Modern' Mathematics: An Educational and Philosophic Error?" *American Scientist* 59 (6): 695–99.

Thumiger, Chiara. 2018. "Doctors and Patients." In *The Cambridge Companion to Hippocrates*, edited by Peter E. Pormann, 1st ed., 263–91. Cambridge: Cambridge University Press. doi: 10.1017/9781107705784.013.

Turing, Alan M. 1950. "Computing Machinery and Intelligence." *Mind* 59 (236), 433–60.

Tymoczko, Thomas. 1979. "The Four-Color Problem and Its Philosophical Significance." *The Journal of Philosophy* 76 (2): 57. doi: 10.2307/2025976.

Tymoczko, Thomas. 1980. "Computers, Proofs and Mathematicians: A Philosophical Investigation of the Four-Color Proof." *Mathematics Magazine* 53 (3): 131–38.

Tymoczko, Thomas. 1981. "Computer Use to Computer Proof: A Rational Reconstruction." *The Two-Year College Mathematics Journal* 12 (2): 120. doi: 10.2307/3027374.

Valles, Sean. 2020. "Philosophy of Biomedicine." In *The Stanford Encyclopedia of Philosophy (Summer 2020 Edition)*, edited by Edward N. Zalta, Summer 2020. Stanford: Metaphysics Research Lab, Stanford University. https://plato.stanford.edu/archives/sum2020/entries/biomedicine.

Vandenbroucke, J. P. 2009. "Commentary: 'Smoking and Lung Cancer'–the Embryogenesis of Modern Epidemiology." *International Journal of Epidemiology* 38 (5): 1193–96. doi: 10.1093/ije/dyp292.

Weisberg, Herbert I. 2010. *Bias and Causation*. Hoboken, NJ, USA: John Wiley & Sons, Inc.
White, Colin. 1991. "Research on Smoking and Lung Cancer: A Landmark in the History of Chronic Disease Epidemiology." *Lung Cancer* 7 (3): 180. doi: 10.1016/0169-5002(91)90089-O.
Wiener, Norbert. 1985. *Cybernetics or Control and Communication in the Animal and the Machine*. 2d ed., 4. print. Cambridge, MA: MIT Press.

Index

CPSIA information can be obtained
at www.ICGtesting.com
Printed in the USA
BVHW092107240621
610373BV00002B/233

PASSING ENGLISH

PASSING ENGLISH
OF THE VICTORIAN ERA

A DICTIONARY OF HETERODOX ENGLISH, SLANG, AND PHRASE

BY

J. REDDING WARE

As forests shed their foliage by degrees,
So fade expressions which in season please.—BYRON.

LONDON
GEORGE ROUTLEDGE & SONS, LIMITED
NEW YORK: E. P. DUTTON & CO.

This Work forms a Companion Volume to

FARMER AND HENLEY'S
'DICTIONARY OF SLANG AND COLLOQUIAL ENGLISH'

IN THE SAME SERIES.

PREFACE

HERE is a numerically weak collection of instances of 'Passing English' It may be hoped that there are errors on every page, and also that no entry is 'quite too dull'. Thousands of words and phrases in existence in 1870 have drifted away, or changed their forms, or been absorbed, while as many have been added or are being added. 'Passing English' ripples from countless sources, forming a river of new language which has its tide and its ebb, while its current brings down new ideas and carries away those that have dribbled out of fashion. Not only is 'Passing English' general; it is local, often very seasonably local Careless etymologists might hold that there are only four divisions of fugitive language in London—west, east, north and south But the variations are countless. Holborn knows little of Petty Italia behind Hatton Garden, and both these ignore Clerkenwell, which is equally foreign to Islington proper, in the South, Lambeth generally ignores the New Cut, and both look upon Southwark as linguistically out of bounds, while in Central London, Clare Market (disappearing with the nineteenth century) had, if it no longer has, a distinct fashion in words from its great and partially surviving rival through the centuries—the world of Seven Dials, which is in St Giles's—St James's being practically in the next parish. In the East the confusion of languages is a world of 'variants'—there must be half-a-dozen of Anglo-Yiddish alone—all, however, outgrown from the Hebrew stem 'Passing English' belongs to all the classes, from the peerage class who have always adopted an imperfection in speech or frequency of phrase associated with the court, to the court of the lowest costermonger, who gives the fashion to his immediate *entourage* Much passing English becomes obscure almost immediately upon its appearance—such as 'Whoa, Emma!' or 'How's your poor feet?' the first from an inquest in a back street, the second from a question by Lord Palmerston addressed to the then Prince of Wales upon the return of the latter from India. 'Everything is nice in my garden' came from Osborne. 'O.K.' for 'orl kerrect' (All Correct) was started by Vance, a comic singer, while in the East district, 'to Wainwright' a woman (*i.e.* to kill her) comes from the name of a murderer of that name. So boys in these later days have substituted 'He's a reglar Charlie' for 'He's a reglar Jack' meaning Jack Sheppard, while Charley is a loving diminutive of Charles Peace, a champion scoundrel of our generation. The Police Courts yield daily phrases to 'Passing English', while the life of the day sets its mark upon every hour. Between the autumn of 1899, and the middle of 1900, a Chadband became a Kruger, while a plucky, cheerful man was described as a 'B.P.' (Baden Powell). Li Hung Chang remained in London not a week, but he was called 'Lion Chang' before he had gone twice to bed in the Metropolis. Indeed, proper names are a great source of trouble in analysing Passing English. 'Dead as a door nail' is probably—as O'Donnel. The phrase comes from Ireland, where another fragment—'I'll smash you into Smithereens'—means into Smither's ruins—though no one seems to know who Smithers was. Again, a famous etymologist has assumed 'Right as a trivet' to refer to a kitchen-stove, whereas the 'trivet' is the last century pronunciation of Truefit, the supreme Bond Street wig-maker, whose wigs were perfect—hence the phrase. Proper names are truly pitfalls in the study of colloquial language. What is a 'Bath Oliver,' a biscuit invented by a Dr Oliver of Bath; again there is the bun named after Sally Lunn, while the Scarborough Simnel is a cake accidentally discovered by baking two varying superposed cakes in one tin. In Scarborough, some natives now say the cake comes down from the pretender Simnel, who became cook or scullion to Henry VII. Turning in another direction, it may be suggested that most exclamations are survivals of Catholicism in England, such as 'Ad's Bud'—'God's Bud' (Christ); 'Cot's So'—'God's oath'; 'S'elp me greens'—meaning groans; more blue (still heard in Devonshire)—*morbleu* (probably from Bath and the Court of Charles II.)—the 'blue death' or the 'blue-blood death'—the crucifixion. 'Please the pigs' is evidently pyx; while the dramatic 'sdeath is clearly 'His Death'; even the still common 'Bloody Hell' is 'By our lady, hail', the lady being the Virgin. There are hundreds of these exclamations, many wholly local.

Amongst authors perhaps no writer has given so many words to the language as Dickens — from his first work, 'Pickwick', to almost his last, when he popularised Dr Bowdler; anglicization is, however, the chief agent in obscuring meanings, as, for instance, gooseberry fool is just gooseberry fouille, moved about—of course through the sieve. Antithesis again has much to answer for. 'Dude' having noted itself, 'fade' was discovered as its opposite; 'Mascotte' a luck-bringer having been brought to England, the clever ones very soon found an antithesis in Jonah, who, it will be recalled, was considered an unlucky neighbour. Be it repeated—not an hour passes without the discovery of a new word or phrase—as the hours have always been—as the hours will always be. Nor is it too ambitious to suggest that passing language has something to do with the daily history of the nation. Be this all as it may be—here is a phrase book offered to, it may be hoped, many readers, the chief hope of the author, in relation with this work, being that he may be found amusing, if neither erudite nor useful. *Plaudite.*

J. R. W.

ABBREVIATIONS USED

ab.	about
abbrev.	abbreviation
Amer.	American
art.	artistic
Austral.	Australia
Bk.	Book
Ca.	Canto
c. Eng.	common English
cent.	century
cf.	compare
ch.	chapter
C. L.	common life
com., comm.	common
commerc.	commercial
corr.	corruption
crit.	criticism
D. C.	*Daily Chronicle*
D. cls.	Dangerous Classes
D. M.	*Daily Mail*
D. N.	*Daily News*
D. T.	*Daily Telegraph*
E.	East
e.g.	for example
E. N.	*Evening News*
Eng., Engl.	England, English
Hist.	historical
i.e.	that is
I. L. N.	*Illustrated London News*
Ind.	Indian
L.	Low Class
L. C. and D.	London, Chatham Dover
L. C.	Lower Class
Lit.	literary
Lond., Lon.	London
M. Class	Middle Class
Metrop.	Metropolitan
Mid.	Middle
Milit.	Military
M. P.	*Morning Post*
Mus. Hall	Music Hall
N.	North
Newsp. Cutting	Newspaper cutting
N. Y.	New York
O. Eng.	Old English
on	onwards, as 1890 on= 1890 and years following
O. S.	old style
P. House	Public House
Peo.	*The People*
Peop.	Peoples'
polit.	political
Pub. Sch.	Public School
q. v.	which see
qq.v.	which (plural) see
R.	Railway, Royal
Ref.	*Referee*
S.	South
Sat. Rev.	*Saturday Review*
Soc.	Society
Span., Sp.	Spanish
st.	stanza
St.	*Standard*
S. Exch.	Stock Exchange
Theat., Theatr.	Theatrical
Tr.	Trade
Univ.	University
U.S.A.	United States of America
v.	against
W.	West

PASSING ENGLISH

A. D. (*Ball-room programme*). A Drink, disguised, thus:

PROGRAMME OF DANCES.

1. Polka..................	Polly J.
2. Valse..................	A. D.
3. Valse..................	Miss F.
4. Lancers..............	Polly J.
5. Valse..................	A. D.
6. Valse..................	Miss M. A. T.
7. Quadrille............	Polly J.
8. Valse..................	A. D.
Etc., etc.	

The ingeniousness of this arrangement is that young ladies see 'A. D.', and assume the youth engaged.

Abernethy (*Peoples'*). A biscuit, so named after its inventor, Dr Abernethy (*see* Bath Oliver).

Abisselfa (*Suffolk*). Alone. From 'A by itself, A'; an old English way of stating the alphabet.

Abney Park (*East London*). About 1860. An abbreviation of Abney Park cemetery, a burial ground for a large proportion of those who die in the East End of London. Cemetery is a difficult word which the ignorant always avoid. Now used figuratively, *e.g.*, 'Poor bloke, he's gone to Abney Park'—meaning that he is dead.

We had a friendly lead in our court t'other night. Billy Johnson's kid snuffed it, and so all the coves about got up a 'friendly' to pay for the funeral to plant it decent in Abney.—*Cutting.*

About and About (*Soc.*, 1890 on). Mere chatter, the conversation of fools who talk for sheer talking's sake, *e.g.*, 'A more about and about man never suggested or prompted sudden murder.'

In an age of windy and pretentious gabble—when the number of persons who can, and will, chatter 'about and about the various arts is in quite unprecedented disproportion to the number of those who are content to study these various arts in patience, and, above all, in silence—there was something eminently salutary in Millais' bluff contempt for the more presumptuous theories of the amateurs. —*D. T.*, 14th August 1896.

Above-board (*Peoples'*). Frank, open. From sailors' lingo. Not between decks or in the hold, but above all the boards in the ship.

Abraham's Willing (*Rhyming*). Shilling. Generally reduced to willing, *e.g.*, 'Lend us a willing.'

He don't care an Abraham's willing for anybody.—*Newsp. Cutting.*

Absolutely True (*Soc.*, ab. 1880). Absolutely false, from the title of a book, the statements in which, of a ghostly character, were difficult of acceptation.

Abyssinian Medal (*Military*). A button gone astray from its button-hole, one in the region of the abdomen. Introduced after the Abyssinian War. (*See* Star in the East.)

Academy (*London*). A billiard-room. Imported from Paris, 1885.

An edict has been promulgated (Paris) forbidding the playing of games of chance on public thoroughfares or in cafés for money, and it is chiefly directed against the billiard rooms, or academies as they are called here.—*D. T.*, 26th July 1894.

Academy Headache. When art became fashionable to a severe degree this malady appeared; now applied generically to headaches acquired at any art galleries.

Art critics complain of 'Academy headache' and of the fatigue produced by leagues of coloured canvases.—*D. N.*, 15th April 1885.

There has yet to arise the philosopher who can explain to us the precise cause of the 'Academy headache'. . . . It is an experience familiar to many who 'do' the great collection at Burlington House. Most persons who go to the Academy know the malady well.—*D. N.*, 4th June 1885.

Academic Nudity (*Oxford*). Appearance in public without cap or gown.

After a tranquil pipe in a friend's room we set out again. Shall we take cap and gown, or shall we venture forth in a state of 'Academic nudity'? Perish the slavish thought! We go without them.—*Cutting*.

Accident. A child born out of wedlock.

Accidented (*Lit.*, 1884). Liable to surprise.

An operatic season thus accidented can hardly prove prosperous, but may be pregnant of good if it teach intending managers of Italian opera to rely on general excellence of *ensemble*, rather than on stars that may at any moment be eclipsed.—*Globe*, 1st July 1885.

According to Cocker (*Peoples'*). Quite correct, according to rule. Cocker flourished in 1694, when the first edition of his *Arithmetic* appeared at the sign of the Black Boy on London Bridge. In the beginning there was no sense of the preposterous in declaring a thing was 'according to Cocker'. Probably the quaintness of the name brought down the dignity of the phrase.

According to Gunter (*Peoples'*). Used precisely as 'according to Cocker'. Gunter was a distinguished arithmetician, and the inventor of a chain and scale for measuring. 'Gunter's chain' is dragged over the land to this day. 'Give me the Gunter' is as common a phrase amongst surveyors as 'Give me the chain'.

Acknowledge the Corn (*Amer. English*). Adroit confession of minor offence to intensify the denial of the major offence: *e.g.*, 'Sir, I believe you are after my wife—and you certainly pocketed my meerschaum last Sunday evening at 10.30.' To which the answer might be: 'Well, I acknowledge the corn—I took the pipe by incident, so to speak; but as to Mrs H., I'm as innocent as the skipping lamb.' Said to arise from an ordinary horse-lifting case in the West of U.S.A. The victim was accused of stealing four horses from one point and four feeds of corn from another for the said four horses. 'I acknowledge the corn,' said the sufferer — but legend says he was lynched in spite of the admission.

Acting Ladies (*Theatrical*, 1883). Indifferent *artistes*. Mrs Langtry, moving in society, having (1882) appeared as an actress in London, and in the same year gone to America, where she made vast sums of money, many ladies of more education than dramatic ability turned their attention to the stage. Eleven out of a dozen totally failed, and few 'twelfths' kept before the public: hence an 'acting lady' soon came, amongst theatrical people, to represent an incapable actress: *e.g.*, 'She isn't a comedian, you know, she's an acting lady.'

Acting ladies, in my opinion, should be severely left alone. There is no pleasing them or their friends.—*Entr'acte*, February 1883.

Actor's Bible (*Theatrical*). *The Era.* This phrase was one of the first directed against sacred matters, about the time when *Essays and Reviews* was much discussed (1860-70).

Mr Sydney Grundy, whose sensitiveness sometimes outruns his discretion, issued a challenge to Mr Clement Scott in 'the Actor's Bible'.—*Ref.* 1883.

There was a motion in the Court of Chancery on Friday, before Mr Justice Chitty, to commit the proprietor of the 'Actor's Bible' for contempt of Court for allowing certain remarks about 'unprincipled imitators' of Miss Geneviève Ward to appear in print.—*Cutting*.

Adam and Eve's togs (*Peoples'*). Nakedness. (*See* Birth-day suit.)

Adam's Ale (*Peoples'*). Water—probably from the time of the Stuart Puritans. If so, it forms a good example of national history in a word or phrase.

Ad's my Life (*Peoples'*; 18 *cent.*). An 18 cent. form of 'God's my life'. (*See* Odd's life.)

Ad's Bud (18 *cent.*). God's Bud, *i.e.*, Christ. Common in H. Fielding.

Advertisement Conveyancers (*Soc.*, 1883). Street Advertisement Board Carriers. (*See* Sandwich Men.) Brought in by W. E. Gladstone (2nd May 1883), during his speech at the inauguration dinner of the National Liberal Club in these words:

These fellow-citizens of ours have it for their lot that the manly and interesting proportions of the human form are in their case disguised both before and after by certain oblong formations which appear to have no higher purpose than what is called conveying an advertisement.—*Newsp. Cutting.*

Society accepted the phrase and the Premier's enemies shot many a shaft anent it.

Ægis (*Latin*). A shield, hence protection, patronage, from Minerva's habit of putting her invisible shield in front of her favourites when in battle.

Madam Adelina Patti appeared yesterday afternoon under the ægis of Messrs Harrison, and once more gathered a great audience round her.—*D. T.*, 4th June 1897.

Æstheticism (*Soc.*, 1865 - 1890). Ideal social ethics, represented outwardly by emblems, chiefly floral, the more significant flowers being the white lily and the sunflower.

The women wore their dresses chiefly in neutral tints, and especially in three series, viz.:—greens, dead leaf (the yellows, or yellowish, of the series); olive (the middle path of colour); and sage (the blues of the series). In each of these series there were scores of tints. The pomegranate was also a fetish. (*See* Grego.)

The joke of æstheticism and sunflowers had been smiled at and had died once or twice between 1865 and 1878 before it was familiar enough to the public for dramatic purposes.—*D. N.*, 27th January 1887.

Affigraphy (*Coster*). To a T, exactly. A corruption of autograph—the vulgar regarding a signature as of world-wide importance and gravity. (*See* Sivvy.)

Afters (*Devon*). Sweets—pies and puddings. 'Bring in the afters' is a common satirical remark in poor Devonshire houses, especially when there are no 'afters' to follow. Also used in Scotland, *e.g.*, 'Hey mon, a dinner, an' nae afters!'

Afternoon Calls (*Soc.*, 19 *cent.*). Referring to exclusive society, who have never accepted the afternoon 'drums' and five o'clock teas, but adhered to the more formal 15-minute afternoon visit.

You had not observed that sort of thing before marriage? Never. What I saw of her was at afternoon calls.—Lord Gerard's evidence in Lord Durham's Nullity of Marriage suit, March 1885.

Afternoonified (*Soc.*). Smart.

What may prove a popular new adjective made its first appearance last week. A lady entered a fashionable drapery store. The lady found nothing to please her. The shopwalker then was called. This individual, with a plausible tale or compliment, will invariably effect a sale after all other means have failed. In reply to his question whether the goods were not suitable, the fastidious customer answered: 'No, thank you; they are not "afternoonified" enough for me.' In the case of a lady armed with an argument of such calibre what was the shopwalker to say or do? Like a wise man, he expressed his regret and beat a dignified retreat. The lady did the same, but the adjective remained.—*D. T.*, July 1897.

'After you with the push' (*Peoples'*). Said, with satirical mock politeness, in the streets to any one who has roughly made his way past the speaker, and 'smudged' him.

Aggeravators, Hagrerwaiters (*Costermongers*). Side-curls still worn by a few conservative costermongers. Of two kinds—the ring, or ringlet (the more ancient), and the twist, dubbed, doubtless in the first place by satirists, 'Newgate Knockers'. Indeed the model of this embellishment might have been the knocker of the door of the house of the governor of that gaol. The aggravation may mean that these adornments excite envy in those who cannot grow these splendours, or that they aggravate or increase the admiration of the fair sex. The younger costers wear rival forehead tufts—such as the Quiff, the Guiver, or the Flop. There is, however, one golden rule for these fashions—the hair must stop short of the eyelids.

Agony in Red (*Soc.*). Vermilion costume. When the æsthetic craze was desperately 'on' (1879-81), terms used in music were applied to painting, as a 'nocturne in silver-grey,' a 'symphony in amber,' a 'fugue in purple,' an 'andante in shaded violet'. Hence it was an easy transition to apply terms of human emotions to costumes.

There are many terrible tints even now to be found among the repertory of the leaders of fashion—agonies in red, livid horrors in green, ghastly lilacs, and monstrous mauves.—*Newsp. Cutting.*

Agreeable Rattle (*Soc.*, ab. 1840). A chattering young man. The genus has long since disappeared. The A. R. went out with the great Exhibition of 1857.

Roderick Doo appeared to be what the ladies call an agreeable rattle.—Albert Smith, *Mr Ledbury* (1842).

Ah, dear me! (*Soc.*, 18 *and* 19 *cents.*). An ejaculation of sorrow, perhaps from 'Ah, Dieu mais!' which in its turn came from *Ay de mi* (*q.v.*). Probably introduced by Catherine of Braganza or one of her French contemporaries at Whitehall ('Ah, dear me, but it's a wicked world').

Ah, que je can be bete! (*Half-Soc.*, 1899). A new macaronic saying—French and English. Amongst the lower classes another ran 'Twiggy-vous the chose?'

'Aipenny Bumper (*London Streets*). A two-farthing omnibus ride, descriptive of the vehicles in question which were not generally great works in carriage-building, until the London County Council started (1899) a line of ½d. 'busses between Waterloo Station and Westminster along the Strand. The L.C.C. 'busses were as good as any others, and better than most.

Air-hole (*Soc.*, 1885-95). A small public garden, generally a dismally converted graveyard, with the ancient gravestones set up at 'attention' against the boundary walls.

For some years past the churchyard has been disused, and the Metropolitan Public Gardens Association, with a keen eye for what it not inaptly terms 'air-holes,' has been making strenuous efforts to secure it as an ornamental space.—*D. T.*, 1st June 1895.

Air-man-chair (*Music-hall* transposition). Chairman — effected by taking the 'ch' from the beginning and adding it, with 'air', to the termination. Very confusing and once equally popular, *e.g.*, 'The air-man-chair is got up no end to-night,' *i.e.*, is well dressed. The chairman has now been abolished in music-halls. He was supposed to keep order and lead choruses. The modern public now do these things for themselves.

Albany Beef (*Amer.*). Unattractive viands.

The *New York Herald* concludes by observing that 'ioukkà', which it calls 'really the national soup of Russia', to 'one of simple tastes, must resemble Hudson River sturgeon, otherwise known as Albany beef, struck by Jersey lightning'.—G. A. Sala, in *D. T.*, 30th June 1883.

Albertine (*Soc.*, 1860-80). An adroit, calculating, business-like mistress; from the character of that name in *Le Père Prodigue* (A. Dumas *fils*). She is in his play an economical housewife, but looks to her own ledger with remorseless accuracy. The word is used and understood in England only by persons of high rank. In France it is used by all classes as a term of reproach, addressed even to a wife for any display of niggardliness. (*See* Nana, *Cheri.*)

Alderman hung in Chains (*City*). A fat turkey decked with garlands of sausages. From the appearance of the City fathers, generally portly—becoming more so when carrying their chains of office over their powerful busts.

Alderman (*Peoples'*). Half a dollar = half a crown, which by the way is fivepence more than the American 'half'. Its origin beyond the reach of discovery; it is probably derived from some remote alderman who when on the bench habitually ladled out this coin to applicants for relief.

Alexandra Limp (*Soc.*, ab. 1872). An affected manner of walking seen for several years amongst women. Said to have been imitated from the temporary mode in which the then Princess of Wales walked after some trouble with a knee. (*See* Buxton Limp, Grecian Bend, Roman Fall.)

Alhambra War Whoop (*Theatrico-political*, 1870). The 'historical' defiance cast at each other by the Germans and French in London during the Franco-German war. Speaking of the destruction of the theatre by fire (Dec. 1882) G. A. Sala wrote at the time in *The Illus. London News*:

Do you remember the 'War Whoop at the Alhambra'? That was during the Franco-German war in 1870—in the late Mr Sawyer's time, and just after the refusal of the dancing licence to the place. The enterprising lessee, not to be baffled by the unkind action of the Areopagus of Clerkenwell Green, determined to 'take it out' in international noise; so every evening towards the close of the performance he organised one band which played the 'Marseillaise', the strains of which were immediately followed by the enlivening notes of the German 'Wacht am Rhein'. Then ensued the Alhambresque 'War Whoop'. The Frenchmen in the house cheered their own melody to the echo, and groaned, whistled, and yelled at the Teutonic air The Germans, on their side, received the 'Wacht am Rhein' with clamorous exultation, and hooted and bellowed at the 'Marseillaise' The English portion of the audience impartially screamed and howled The appalling *charivari* nightly drew crowds to the Alhambra; but the excitement did not last long

All (*L Peoples'*). Perfect, extreme, complete, absolute—the sum of street gentlemen's admiration, *e g*, 'She's all there,' 'All a lark,' 'All on,' 'All a neat bit'

'It's all bosh' All is a big word Does he refer to the meeting, the Royal Exchange, the speeches, the speakers, or the existence of unemployed thousands? His favourite word comes in again in the supplementary remark. 'It's all a game' My friend says he is a French polisher, and he smells like one He further informs me that he belongs to some mysterious commonwealth, that he is a teetotaler, a vegetarian, a non-smoker When I hint to him—emphasizing his own term—that he is all too good for me, he cheerily comforts me with 'Not a bit of it, it's all right' This is as it should be—all bosh, all a game, all right.—*D. N*, 5th February 1885 (*See* Neat)

All his buttons on (*C L*, 1880 on). Sharp, alive, active, not to be deceived

He is eighty-three years of age, but as we say hereabouts, has all his buttons on (laughter), and he says, 'I never heard of greater nonsense in all my life Here I am, W G of the "Blue Boar", who, if the Duke of So-and-So gives me notice in September to quit next Lady Day, have to leave my licence behind me without any compensation'—Sir W. Harcourt, *Speech in Bermondsey*, 20th May 1890.

All a-cock (*Peoples'*) Overthrown, vanquished. It may be a version of knocked into a cocked hat, (*q.v*), or, more probably it is derived from cock-fighting, *e g*, 'He's all a kick,' meaning a dying bird, from the motion of the legs during the agony of death This would pass into 'cock' readily, seeing that the conquering bird was always called 'a game' one, or 'he just only tripped me, an' I was all a-cock in a one-two'.

All a treat (*Street*). Perfection of enjoyment, sometimes used satirically to depict mild catastrophe.

All-fired (*Amer*). A euphemism for hell-fired, used as a general intensive, *e g*, 'I was in an all-fired rage'

All it is worth (*Amer*) To the fullest extent, as fully as possible

Scalchi, to use a side-walk phrase, played Siebel for all the character was worth, and was evidently the favourite. —*N Y Mercury*, 1883

All my eye and Betty Martin (*Peoples'*) An expression of disbelief, evasive declaration that the person addressed is a liar Perhaps the finest example extant of colloquial exclamations reaching to-day from pre-Reformation times St Martin was, and is, the patron saint of beggars The prayer to St Martin opens, 'O, mihi, beate Martine'

This phrase was used by English mendicants (and is still used by South-Italian beggars) when asking for alms When indiscriminate charity 'went out' in England at the date of the Reformation, this phrase fell into bad repute as representing a lazy and lying class. It is still used by the commoner classes as an expression of doubt, though it has been very widely superseded by 'humbug' (*q v*)

All my own (*London Apprentices, 19 cent*). Freedom, mastership Its use is disappearing with the tendency to abolish apprenticeship

I'm quite in the world alone
And I'll marry you
If you'll be true,
The day I'm all my own —(1896).

All my eye and my elbow (*London*, 1882). Fictional. appears to be a flight of genius starting from 'all my eye and Betty Martin', got into form, not because Betty Martin had become vulgar, but possibly because her vague identity led to conventional divergencies There is a smart aspect about this term, for, while eye and elbow offered a weak alliteration, there is some sort of association and agreement in the action of these personal belongings, for one can wink with the eye and nudge with the elbow at once

All of a piece (*Peoples'*) Awkward, without proper distribution or relation of parts, *e g.*, 'He lounged in—all of a piece.' 'Have you seen his new Venus? Awful—all of a piece.'

All over grumble (*Peoples'*). Obvious.

In some of the things that have been seen here it has been a case of *all over grumble*, but Thursday's show was all over approval.—*Ref.*, 28th March 1886.

All over red (*Railway, to public*, 1840 on). Dangerous, to be avoided. From red being the colour signal of danger throughout the railway world. The phrase has been accepted by the public at large. (*See* Be Green, White Light, Paint the Town Red.)

All poppy cock (*Amer.*). Mere brag, nonsense. Perhaps a figure of speech drawn from the natural history of the field-poppy, which looks very braw, military, cockish, and flaunting, but which tumbles to pieces if touched, or droops and faints almost directly it is gathered.

All right up to now (*Street*). Smiling, serene. Derived from *enceinte* women making the remark as to their condition. Used by Herbert Campbell as a catch-phrase in Covent Garden Theatre Pantomime, 1878.

All-round muddle (*Stock Exchange*, 1870). Complete entanglement.

Her 'bondage' is not of lengthened duration, inasmuch as the husband, finding himself in an all-round muddle, shoots himself dead.—*Cutting*.

When reporters get hold of a new phrase they are liable to work it to death. At present they are grinding away at 'all-round'. They tell about the all-round fighter, the all-round baseball player, the all-round reporter, the all-round thief, and the all-round actor. One reporter said the other day that whisky was the best all-round mischief-maker there was in the world, and he probably hasn't been all-round either.—*Cutting*, 1888.

All very fine and large (*Lond.*, 1886). Satirical applause; from the refrain of a song sung by Mr Herbert Campbell.

How many people passed the turnstiles at the Alexandra Palace I am not in a position to say, but that the attendance was all very fine and large is beyond dispute.—*Ref.*, 7th August 1887.

Alley (*Peoples'*). A go-between. Evidently from 'aller', to go.

Mrs Cox was an alley for her.—Bravo Coroner's Inquest.

Allee samee (*Pidgeon English*). All the same. Used by Chinese cheap abourers when detected in trying to cheat. 'Washy money allee samee,' applied by Anglo-Asiatics in a satirical spirit where things are not quite satisfactory. 'It appeared that they were not quite married, but that they lived together allee samee.'—*N. Y. Mercury*, February 1883.

Alligators (*Amer.*). People of Florida, so named from the alligators there; used also because the Floridans are supposed to be as greedy as these reptiles. Of course, an invention of some other State or States.

'Will you kindly tell me which way the wind blows?' asked a Northern invalid of the landlord of a Florida hotel. 'Certainly, sir,' replied the landlord, stepping to the door; 'the wind now blows due north, sir.' 'Thank you.' A little later the landlord said to the bookkeeper: 'Have you made out Mr Smith's bill yet?' 'No, sir.' 'Well, just charge one dollar to his account for information about the direction of the wind.'

Alls (*Public-House*). Waste pot at public-houses. On all public-house pewter counters may be seen holes, down which go spillings of everything. Popular mistrust runs to the belief that these collections are used up —hence the comment upon bad beer. 'This must be alls.' As a fact, the brewer allows a barrel of good beer for every barrel of alls forwarded to the brewery. What does the brewer do with it? This is indeed wanting to know, at the end of the book, what became of the executioner? Probability is in favour of the sewer-grating.

Allsopp (*Peoples'*). Short for Allsopp's Pale Ale.

Ally Luja lass (*Lond. Street*, 1886 on). Hallelujah lass was the name given to the girl contingent of the Salvation Army, when the movement rose into importance in London, and General Booth made an effort to purchase all the theatres, succeeding, however, only in one case, that of the Grecian Theatre, City Road.

She sed thay wur Ally Luja's lasses. 'Ally Luja's asses,' I sed; 'thay wants kikkin.'—*Comic Report of a Salvation Meeting* (1870).

Ally Sloper (*Street*, 1870 on). A dissipated-looking old man with a red and swollen nose. Invented by Mr Charles Ross, who ran him in print for a score of years.

Almighty dollar (*Amer*). This expression, a derisive synonym for money or Mammon, originated with Washington Irving It is found in his *Creole Village*, and reads thus

'The Almighty Dollar, that great object of universal devotion throughout our land, seems to have no genuine devotees in these peculiar villages'

Alphonse (*Soc*, 1870 on). A man of position who accepts money from a married woman or women richer, and probably older, than himself, as recompense for remaining her or their lover. Quite understood in Paris—not known out of society in London From the play *Monsieur Alphonse* (Alexandre Dumas, *fils*).

There was yesterday evening and up to the small hours of the morning a serious riot in the Latin Quarter, caused by the students who continue from time to time to make violent demonstrations against those professional allies of certain women—men who bear the name of 'Alphonse'—a sobriquet invented by Alexandre Dumas, one which has passed into the language —*Newsp Cutting*

Altogether (*Soc*, 1894) The nude in art. From Du Maurier's *Trilby*, who is an artist's model 'I sit for the altogether.'

The *New York Mercury*, 27th September 1895, has this heading: Will the next fad be photographs of modern woman taken in the 'altogether'? Society women now have their busts done in marble, their hands and arms in bronze, and their legs photographed

In *The Demagogue and Lady Phayre*, the labour leader appears as a figure of rude nobility The proportions are not heroic, they are simply life-size In the altogether they make up an individuality rich, massive, and imposing —*Weekly Sun*, 29th December 1895

They wore little underclothing—scarcely
anything—or no—thing—
And their dress of Coan silk was quite
transparent in design—
Well, in fact, in summer weather, something like the 'altogether',
And it's there I rather fancy, I shall
have to draw the line!
—Mr W S Gilbert's 'The Grand Duke', March 1896

There was no earthly necessity why the *Hôtel du Libre Echange* should be an improper play, except that the modern French audience revels in impropriety They like it, they wallow in it, and they destroy their native ingenuity in construction and invention with what we may call 'the cult of the altogether' —*D T*, 30th April 1896

Altogethery (*Soc.*). Drunk—from the tendency of a drunken man to lounge himself. Byron uses the term in a letter of 1816.

Amen Corner (*Californian*). A church

Sunday found them, judge and lawyers, seated in the 'amen corner' —*All the Year Round*, 31st October 1868

A'mighty (*Amer*). One of the first evasions of an oath-like word It is, of course, a corruption of 'almighty'.

As you know, young fellur, them goats is a'mighty kewrous anymal—as kewrous as weemen is

Ammedown Shop (*Poor*) Corruption of Hand-me-down Shop A good example of a phrase getting bastardized into one meaningless word 'George, my dear, ammedown my gal's Turkey-red frock'

Amok *See* Run a-muck.

Anatomy (*Peoples'*, formerly *Literary*). A thin needy boy, or old withered soul In common English, it has been reduced to natermy, *e g*, 'He were a perfick 'nattermy'

A boy of twelve stood leaning against a fence on Duffield Street, hat pulled down, feet crossed, and his right hand going up occasionally to wipe his nose, when along came another anatomy about his size —*Detroit Free Press*

Ancient Mariners (*Cambridge Univ*) Graduates still associated with the University who continue to row

At Cambridge Fawcett rowed stroke (the necessary position of a blind man) in the crew of 'Ancient Mariners', as the older members of the University who still ply the oar are called —*D N*, 7th November 1884

Androgynaikal (*Art*) Appertaining to the nude figure, and to the anatomy of both sexes

Simeon Solomon's notion of the classic ideal in his picture called 'Sacramentum amoris', a small figure, as nude as may be, girt with a skin of a panther and a light blue sash, and background of yellow drapery, but of that peculiar type of form to which the term 'androgunaikal' is applied in art, and holding a long thyrsus.—*Newsp Cutting*.

Angel (*N London Street*) A woman of the town fringing the Angel at Islington, *e.g*, 'What are you doing here? *you* ain't a Angel—you're only a Sluker' (*i.e.*, St Luker, from the Parish of St Luke, in the City Road, which is considered at the Angel as socially below Islington, as it is comparatively depressed in its physical want of elevation in comparison with the Angel, which is quite at the top of the hill).

Angel-makers (*Peop.*, 1889 on). Baby-farmers; because so many of the farmed babies die. Probably from the French 'Faiseuses des anges'.

'ANGEL-MAKING'.—Another case of baby-farming, or 'angel-making', as it is called in Austria, has just been discovered by the Lemberg police, who have arrested three women on the charge of systematically starving to death infants committed to their care.—*Newsp. Cutting*, December 1892.

They are not only under a cloud owing to the deaths of Miss Thompson and Mademoiselle Madet, but every day a fresh charge is laid at their doors, and some people have even gone so far as to describe them as members of a band of what Parisians call 'angel-makers'.—*D. T.*, 7th December 1896.

Angels on Horseback (*Virginia*). Fricasseed oysters—meaning exquisite. Origin not known.

Anglican Inch (*Church*, 1870 on). Description given by the ritualistic clergy of the short square whisker which is so much affected by the Broad Church party. The Rits (*q.v.*) call themselves the 'Church of England', the generally accepted Broad Church, or Taits as they were called in Archbishop Tait's time, are 'Anglicans'—hence the 'inch'. (*See* St Alban's Clean Sweep.)

Anguagela (*Transposed*) Language. A good example of the confusion produced by transposing and repeating a syllable or letter; *e.g.*,

How the Lord Chamberlain's people pass this stuff goodness only knows. Perhaps they don't understand the French anguagela.

Animal (*L. C. and D. Railway Passengers*, 1860). Synonym for the 'Elephant and Castle' station. 'Third-class Animal' is, or was, quite understood by the railway booking-clerks of the district.

Animal (*Tavern*). A disguised, or flippant, reference amongst boon companions to the tavern, used in common when the sign is zoological, such as the Bull, Bear, Lion, Dragon—but more especially referring to the Elephant and Castle (S. London); until (1882) this place was exceptionally dubbed 'Jumbo' (*q.v.*).

Anno Domini, B.C. (*Soc.*, 1890 on). Relating to unknown longevity.

'He must be very anno domini, mustn't he?' 'A.D.? my dear fellow, say B.C.'

Anonyma (*Soc.*, 1862). A name given to women of gallantry in an article in the *Times* commenting on a well-known Phryne of that day. The word lasted many years and came to be synonymous with a gay woman.

She could kick higher in the can-can than any anonyma there.—*N. Y. Mercury*, 1882.

Anti-queer-uns (*Soc.*, 18 *cent.*). A perversion of 'antiquarians', due to Foote.

So many interesting associations cluster around the remains of the old nunnery at Godstow, a mile or two out of Oxford, that it is rather surprising so little attention has been bestowed on the ruin. Perhaps it may be difficult even for 'Anti-queer-uns', as Foote calls them, to get up much enthusiasm over nameless graves.—*D. N.*, 3rd February 1885.

Anti-Tox (*Amer.*, reaching England 1885). A drug to sober a drunken person. Tox is, of course, the abbreviation of intoxication.

A reporter noticed the singular fact that nearly every one who went into a leading saloon was under the influence of some powerful stimulant, and nearly every one who came out was painfully sober. Then he determined to go in and see about it. 'Have a dose of Anti-Tox?' asked the barkeeper, recognising the reporter. 'It's the greatest thing on earth; you come to me rocking from one side of the saloon to the other and reeking with the fumes of the vilest whisky, and I will make a new man of you while you are getting out a twenty-cent piece.'—*Minneapolis Gaz.*, 1885.

'Apenny-lot day (*Costers'*). A bad time for business—really, when everything has to be sold cheap.

Apostle of culture (*Soc.*, 1880). An individual who sets up as a perfect judge of taste. Probably started by Sir Francis Burnand in *Punch*.

Our self-elected apostle of culture has told us that it is as ridiculous to say that such and such a colour is the fashion as it would be to assert that B flat was the fashionable key.—*D. N.*, 13th January 1885.

Apostles of murder (*Polit*, 1867 on) A name given generally to political agitators who included assassination in their programme.

To say nothing of dynamite, and of that horrible compound found at Liverpool which presents the innocent appearance of sawdust but of which every grain is an explosive agency, the apostles of murder are reported to have employed methods of offence even more diabolical. —*D. N*, 6th April 1883

Apple-jack (*Amer.*) Spirit distilled from cider or from the pulp of apples already pressed for cider (*See* Sweet Waters) 'Jack' is a common term for spirits in U S A In Normandy this liquor is calvados.

'A grindstun can,' remarked a weazened farmer, who had just called for some apple-jack —*Newsp Cutting*, 1883.

Apples (*Corruption of Rhyming Slang*). Stairs, as thus 'Apples and pears—stairs' 'Bill an' Jack's gone up apples'

'Apples and pears in no birdlime —time.'—(*Rhyming Street*, 1882)

An obscure mode of describing sudden ejection from a house, *e g.*,

The flunkeys had me down stairs (apples and pears) in no time (birdlime).

'Appy dosser (*Low Life*, 19 *cent*) A satirical description of a homeless creature, so wretched as not to have the few halfpence necessary to pay for a 'doss', or bed in a common lodging-house

Elizabeth, poor storm-tossed bit of one of the myriad wrecks that strew the ocean of life, homeless and starving, dying of an agonizing ailment, was, having neither money nor friends, what is professionally known as a ''appy dosser'. That is to say, she would crawl at night into the open passages of a low lodging-house, and fall down where she could—in the yard or the passage—and sleep —*Ref*, February 1882

Archer up (*London*, 1881) Safe to win Formerly a popular phrase of congratulation. A man was seen running for and catching a 'bus · 'Archer up,' shouted the on-lookers. A man appeared in new clothes 'Archer up!' Another threatened to knock another down 'Archer up!' here used probably satirically. The phrase took its rise from a celebrated jockey who suddenly sprang to the front in 1881, and carried everything before him It is short for 'Archer is up in the saddle'. He rode with an absolute recklessness which may account for his end, for he shot himself At once the phrase passed away utterly, and was heard no more.

Arctics (*Amer*) Winter clothing, which in the earlier settled States is decidedly built on a vast scale

I hate a hotel where you have to get up at 4 15 A M, dress in a cold room, and walk down to the station because the 'bus doesn't go to that train, and about half-way down you discover that you left your arctics in the office —*Newsp. Cutting*

Ardent (*Soc*, 1870) A shortened form of 'ardent spirits' From the Mexican *aqua ardente*, through America

After this we all felt in such good humour that the bottle passed freely, and I fear that more than one of our number swallowed a little too much of the ardent —*Newsp Cutting*, 1878

Arer (*Peoples'*) More so. From 'are', emphatically used 'We *are*, and what's more, we can't be any arer'

'Arf-a-mo' (*Peoples'*, 1890 on) Abbreviation of 'half a moment', *cf.*, 'half a sec.' and 'half a tick' (of a watch).

I'll bet you never noticed all the things that you can do
In half a mo'—half a mo',
So cock your ears and listen and I'll mention one or two,
In half a mo'—half a mo'.
Tho' you're as sane as Satan you can go clean off your dot,
And then start backing gee-gees on a system very hot,
Have five-and-twenty thousand quids and lose the blessed lot
In half a mo'—half a mo'
Chorus In half a mo'—half a mo'
Your pluck and perseverance you can show,
You can go with other people
Down a sewer, climb a steeple,
Fall an' break your blooming neck in half a mo'.
—1896

Arf-an-arf (*London Public-house*, 19 *cent*) Half-and-half A mixture half of black beer (porter) and half ale (*See* Cooper)

Arf'arf'an'arf (*Peoples'*) A figure of speech, meaning 'drunk', the substitution of cause for effect, the intoxication being the latter, 'arfarf-anarf' the former. It may be thus explained, arf' = half pint of; arfanarf = half and half = half ale and half beer = half and half. This liquor is fourpence the quart, therefore, the mystic refreshment is called for as 'arf o' four d arfanarf', the 'd' being used to express pence = *denarii*. Is used to describe drunken men, *e.g.*, ''E's very arfarfanarf'—really meaning that he has had many 'arfs'.

Argol-bargol. To have a row. May be argue turned into argol, from the old term 'argil' (*see* the Grave-digger in *Hamlet*), corrupted from 'ergo'. The 'bargol' is a rhymed invention following a common habit. The whole term, however, is pervaded apparently by depreciation:—'Well—well—d'yer want ter argol-bargol?'

Aristocratic veins (*Theatrical*). Blue lines of colour usually frescoed on the temples, and sometimes on the backs of the hands and wrists. Supposed to be a mark of high and noble birth. Sometimes adopted by women in society. 'Pass me the smalt, girl—I want to put in my veins.' (*See* Mind the Paint.)

Arkansas tooth-pick (*Amer.*). A bowie-knife. Arkansas is notorious for sudden blood-letting.

And he jabbed an eighteen Arkansas tooth-pick into—whoever it happened to be.—*Mark Twain.*

He had a seductive way of drawing his 18-inch Arkansas tooth-pick, and examining it critically with a sinister smile, while humbly requesting the temporary loan of five dollars.—*Texas Siftings.*

'Arrydom (*Soc.*, 1885). The kingdom and rule of 'Arry, the typical London cad.

It seems a pity that the *Whitehall Review* did not confine itself to saying, in the speech of 'Arrydom, 'You're another,' instead of appealing to a special jury.—*Sat. Rev.*, 26th March 1885.

'Arry's Worrier (*Peoples'*, 1885 on). The deadly and bronchitical concertina common to 'Arry's hand, and as deadly as his fist or his 'Hinglish'.

If our readers are inclined to be curious, they may, on further investigation, discover the player of ''Arry's' favourite 'worrier' in the form of a patient-looking little lady, who sits on the stonework of the railings which guard the select piece of grass and trees.—*People*, 19th February 1897.

'Arrico Veins (*Common people*, 19 *cent.*). Varicose veins.

'Bless yer, 'arrico veins don't kill. I know an old lady o' ninety-one, an' she's 'ad 'em these forty years. Ill-conwenient, but they ain't dangerous—on'y a leak.'

Artful Fox (*Music-hall*, 1882). A nonsense rhyme for 'box'.

You capture the first liker at him in a snug artful *fox* at some chantin ken where there's a bona varderin serio comic, and Isle of Francer engaged.—From *Biography of the Staff Bundle Courier*, the gentleman who accompanies 'serio-comics' from music-hall to music-hall when 'doing turns'.

Artistic Merit (*Society*, 1882). A satirical criticism of a flattering portrait. A celebrated sculptors' case (Belt *v.* Lawes, 1882) brought this term into a general use. Belt complained that Lawes had said of him that he (Belt) had no 'artistic merit,' and that all his many busts were artistically finished by competent men, commonly called 'studio ghosts'. Belt and his friends maintained that he possessed not only good modelling power, which was also denied, but finishing power also. For Lawes, the then President of the Royal Academy (Sir F. Leighton) and many other eminent art followers gave evidence that Belt had no artistic merit. Gradually, during a long trial of over forty days, the public grew to comprehend that in sculpture 'artistic merit' might mean the use of flattering refinement in finish. Hence arose the use of the phrase as an euphemism for flattery.

Sincerity may raise a costume ball from the mere pastime of an evening to an undertaking involving culture, patience, and self-denial, and bring about a result not perhaps without 'artistic merit'.—*Newsp. Cutting*, February 1885.

Fancy asking a policeman to decide upon the morality or immorality of a ballet! You might as well ask a policeman to pass judgment on the decency of a statue of Venus, and at the same time to criticise its 'artistic merits'.—*Ref.*, 11th February 1883.

Ashkenazic. German and Polish Jews.

Ash-plant (*Military*, 1870). Light, unvarnished, unpeeled, rough-cut ash swish, for carrying in the hand. Subalterns at Dover first carried these swishes, value about 1d., the head formed by a knot got at a branching. They became very fashionable, and soon, owing to their valuelessness, very common. Therefore, after a time, they were mounted in gold or silver, the swish remaining unpeeled, and in no way polished or varnished.

Bringing his ash-plant down on the counter with ten Slade force, he said, 'If that's the sort of man you are, I'm off to take tea with Miss Murnford.' And he offed.—*Bird o' Freedom*, 7th March 1883.

Ask another (*Street*, 1896 on). A protest against a reiterated or worn-out joke, an expression of boredom; directed at a 'chestnut', *e.g.*, 'I say, Joe, when's a door not a door?' to which Joe disgustedly replies, 'Oh, ask another.'

Aspect (*Lond.*, *chiefly Hatton Garden district*). A look of eager love. Used chiefly in the Italian quarter, but spreading. Where there is a foreign colony in London, as French in Soho, Italian in Clerkenwell Road, German in Clerkenwell, the English amongst them, to some extent fraternizing, adopt any forcible word or phrase used by them, as, for instance, in the Whitechapel district the Jewish 'selah' (God be with you, or good-bye) has become 'so long', a phrase which has spread all over England. Amongst Italians 'aspetto' is a very common word. Used alone no doubt it may be translated, 'Hold on a bit!' but it retains its meaning 'look', 'aspect', and it is this translation which has been accepted by the observant English lower-middle-class in the Italian district. A fiery youth looking too fiercely into the eyes of a gutter donzella, she observes, 'aspetto —aspetto!' Her English sister has accepted the word, and under similar circumstances cries, 'Not too much aspect, Tom!' Applied also in other ways, *e.g.*, 'Well, Jack, not too much aspect, or you might run agin one o' my fists!'

Aspinall (*Peoples'*). Enamel. Also as a verb. From Aspinall, the inventor and manufacturer of an oxidized enamel paint.

Astarrakan (*Street*, 1890). A jocular mispronunciation of the astrachan fur. Used satirically, after Mr Gus Elen's (1898) song, the first line of the chorus running:

Astarrakan at the bottom of my coat.

Atavism (*Society*, *c.* 1890-5). The antithesis of decadent. The difference between these newly meaninged words is very marked. The decadent may show ability, genius even, but his life demonstrates that he is in a general way mentally, morally, and physically inferior to his forebears; and, as a rule, he dies childless, or his children have no families. The atavist, on the other hand, is a human being who is relegated by some hidden natural force to a condition assimilating to an early form of mankind. He is therefore, as a rule, a physical improvement upon his immediate or modern forebears, and even possibly a mental superior—but morality from the modern standpoint has little or no existence for him. He tends to the animal life—he takes what he wants; society calls him a kleptomaniac; plain people dub him a thief, while as a dipsomaniac he again imitates the mammal, which, once indulged in liquor, becomes a hopeless drunkard. An atavist may become a decadent; a decadent never becomes an atavist.

Athletic Drolls (*Music-hall*, 1860 on). Comic performers whose songs were interspersed with gymnastic feats. (*See* Knockabout Drolls, Singing Drolls.)

Atlantic Greyhounds (*Soc.*). Quick Atlantic steamers.

The booking of passengers desirous of securing berths on board one or other of the 'Atlantic greyhounds' now plying between the Old and New Worlds far exceeds the accommodation available for their reception.—*D. T.*, 20th May 1895.

Attorney-General's Devil (*Legal*).

He was chosen by Sir John Holker, whose practical shrewdness was seldom at fault, to succeed the present Lord Justice Bowen as junior counsel to the Treasury, commonly called 'Attorney-General's Devil'.—*Newsp. Cutting*, 1883.

The working barrister who does the heavy work of a K.C. or other legal big-wig is generally called a 'devil'. But the term is dying out owing to increased legal amenities.

Auctioneer (*Peoples'*). The fist—because it 'knocks down'.

Milo, the boxer, was an accomplished man. He did not, however, use the sculptor's hammer, but rather the 'auctioneer' of the late Mr Thomas Sayers.—*D. N.*

Auditorium (*Press*, 1870). The portion of a theatre occupied by the audience—called the theatre until Dion Boucicault took 'Astley's', spoilt the ceiling by cutting ventilating holes in it, and then wrote a long letter to the *Times* in which he spoke of the improvements he had made in 'the auditorium'. The word was at once accepted with much laughter. Now used seriously.

Some time before the curtain rose large crowds of seat-seekers might have been observed surging down the tunnels that lead to the auditorium of this house (Opera Comique, now swept away).—*Ref.*, 14th June 1885.

Aunt Sally (*Low London*). A black-faced doll. Early in the century the sign of a rag-shop; afterwards adopted as an entrancing cock-shy, a pipe either forming the nose or being placed between the teeth. From Black Sall and Dusty Bob, characters in the elder Pierce Egan's *Life in London*, and probably adopted owing to the popularity of that work, precisely as in a later generation many of Dickens's characters were associated with trade advertisements. Aunt Sally is vanishing, even at race-courses. Soon, but for a portrait, she will be only a memory. Very significant of Pierce Egan's popularity, which from 1820 to 1840 was as great as that of Dickens, whose fame threw Egan into obscurity.

Aunt's sisters (*London Middle-class*). A foolish perversion of 'ancestors'.

Corrie Roy was once more restored to the home of his aunt's sisters.—*Comic Romance.*

Away (*London Thieves' Etiquette*). A man is never spoken of as 'in prison', though he is there for many a 'stretch'. It would evince great want of etiquette to mention the detaining locality, *e.g.*, 'Mine's away, bless 'is 'art,' the grass-widow of lower life will say, as indicative that her husband is in jail. The answer should be, 'A 'appy return 'ome to 'im, mum.'

'Awkins (*Lower Classes*, 1880 on). A severe man, one not to be trifled with. Name-word from the Judge, then Sir Frederic Hawkins, who about this time impressed the lower and criminal classes as a 'hanging' judge, *e.g.*, 'Joe, don't you play around Tom Barr—'e's a 'Awkins, and no mistake.'

'Awkins (*Mid-London*, 1905). A princely costermonger. From a music-hall song sung by Albert Chevalier, with the catch line, 'And 'Enery 'Awkins is a first-class name'.

And, indeed, if not in Walworth, where should Mr Hawkins be supreme? It is the epical home, so to speak, of his race—a district traversed by that Old Kent-road in which their lyric hero 'knocked' the passers-by with the unexpected splendours of his attire and turn-out. Disestablishment is not understood to trouble his repose, and the downfall of the Welsh Church would probably leave him as unmoved as the just man in Horace, so long as the 'Harp' of the same nationality continues to open its hospitable doors to himself and Mrs Hawkins on their 'Sundays out'.—*D. T.*, 14th May 1895.

Axe to grind (*Amer.-Engl.*). *I.e.*, a personal end to serve, originally a favour to ask; from men in backwoods pretending to want to grind their axes when in reality they required a drink. Mr Ebbs, an American etymologist, says that the origin of this phrase has been attributed to Benjamin Franklin. It is true, many of his sayings in *Poor Richard* bear a striking similarity to the saying; still, not one of them can be tortured into the above phrase.

Every one seems to have had what the Americans call 'an axe to grind'.—Yates, *Recollections* (1884).

Finally, Mr Irving stepped forward, and in a voice trembling with emotion, bade farewell to his American friends. He said among other things: 'Now that I can speak without fear or favour, and without the suspicion that I have an axe to grind, I can say for the first time how deeply grateful we are for the innumerable acts of kindness received from the American people.'—*Newsp. Cutting*, April 1885.

Conservatives with axes to grind will soon make the word Beaconsfield as wearisome by mere iteration as the word Jubilee.—*D. N.*, 7th April 1887.

Axe-grinders (*American*). Men who grumble, especially politically.

Willard's Hotel was closed, and, even if it had not been, with its *clientèle* of bar-loafers, swaggerers, drunkards, and axe-grinders (a class of politicians peculiar to Washington hotels), it would not have been the place for Mr Dickens in his state of health.—Dolby, *Dickens as I knew him.*

Ay de mi, sometimes **Ay de my** (*Hist.*). It pervades all Western European literature. It is found in

Tom Cringle's Log, also in *Gil Blas*, bk. xi. 5.

Ay de my ! un anno felice
Parece un soplo ligero ;
Perô fin dicha un instante
Es un siglo de tormento.

Smollett translates the phrase 'alas'. It was Carlyle's favourite protest, and is found frequently in Froude's biography of him :

The dinners, routs, callers, confusions inevitable to a certain length. *Ay de mi* —I wish I was far from it.

It was probably brought to England by Catherine of Braganza. (*See* 'Oh dear me !')

B

B's. (*Fenian*, 1883). Patriotic Brotherhood. In questionable taste. The members of the Patriotic Brotherhood, or Irish Invincibles, thus styled themselves. It may have had some absurd association with the 'busy bee'.

Patrick Duffy was sworn, and deposed —Finnegan and Devlin were at a meeting of the society held in the spring of 1881. I knew James Hauratty and Patrick Geogeghan, who were both 'B's'. —*Report of the Patriotic Brotherhood Conspiracy* (Trial at Belfast, 26th March 1883).

B.C. play (*Theatrical*, 1885). Classical drama ; *Before Christ*. Invented *apropos* to Claudian (Princess's Theatre).

The authors are wise to eschew low comedy. There wasn't much of it in the time of Pericles. George cannot come in and talk about milking his hay and mowing his cows as he did in 'Claudian'. One of our best low comedians, he is not at home in a B.C. period.—*Ref.*, 28th March 1886.

B.H. (*Peoples'*, 1880). Bank holiday.

B.K.'s (*Military*). Barracks. Used by officers, non-coms., and privates, down to the drummer-boy. (*See* H. Q.)

B.P. (*Theatrical*). British Public. (*See* Pub.)

'Have you read Leader's manifesto on taking possession of Her Majesty's Theatre ?' 'We have, and feel sure there's a good time coming for the B.P.'—*Bird o' Freedom*, 1883.

Harvey writes and arranges, not to please me, who don't pay, but the great B.P., who do.—*Ref.*, 9th August 1885.

'My dear Wilfred,—They tell me you are in a wax about the exceptions I took to your article. I am extremely sorry to touch any line of yours, but B.P. must be considered, you know !'—Ouida, *An Altruist*, 1896.

B. and P. (*Lond.*). Initials of two young men whose public proceedings resulted, about 1870, in a long police-court inquiry and trial. (*See* Beanpea.)

B Flat (*Peoples'*). Proof of advance of education, being a sort of pun lying between *si bémol* or B flat, and an intimate insect (now rapidly being evicted by a survival of the fittest), which has been too fatally associated with the family of Norfolk Howard (*q.v.*).

Baby (*Tavern*, 1875). The conviction amongst men given to creature-comforts that the cheapest soda and spirits refresher rose to sixpence at least, led the ærated water manufacturers to invent the half-bottle (2d.), which from its small size was dubbed 'baby' by all men. 'Give me a baby lemonade' was understood by all barmaids, who never blushed. The term has lapsed.

Baby and Nurse (*Tavern*, 1876). A small bottle of soda-water and two-penny-worth of spirit in it. This is the nurse. Accepted terms even by queens of the taps and handles. Where more than 'two' of spirits is required numerals come by their own again. The phrase has lapsed.

Baby's public-house (*Peoples'*). Nature's fount.

Among them is a six-year-old baby that is suckled at the breast when it asks for baby's public-house, and that fills up the intervals between refreshment by smoking cigarettes. Fact !—*Ref.*, 5th October 1884.

Bab'sky (*Liverpool*). Corruption of Bay o' Biscay.

The place where the arch was erected is about the most exposed part of the town when the wind is high, and in consequence is generally styled the 'Bab'sky'.—*Newsp. Cutting*, May 1886.

Back answers (*C. Eng.*, 19 *cent.*). Sharp retorts, quick-tongued replies, dorsal eructations, without any concession to the laws of etiquette.

He went to the station and gave no 'cheek' or 'back-answers' to any one.—*Cutting*.

Back down (*American*). To yield.

If we may—we indicate an apologetic foreign policy by remarking that the Government 'backs down'.

That is to say, 'makes a back', as boys at leap-frog, to enable the other players to get over.

Back-hairing (*Street*). Feminine fighting, in which the occipital locks suffer severely.

His Honour said no doubt there had been a great deal of provocation, but the rule was when a woman had her back hair pulled down and her face scratched, she back-haired and scratched in return. *Newsp. Cutting.*

Back-hair parts (*Theatrical*). Rôles in which the agony of the performance at one point in the drama admits of the feminine tresses in question floating over the shoulders.

Like the famous lady who never would undertake any but 'back-hair' parts, the Parisian *comédienne* could only with difficulty be prevailed upon to become a stage heroine whose garments have to express the depths of an unpicturesque poverty.—*D. N.*, November 1884.

Back o' the green (*Theatre and Music-hall*). This is a sort of *rebus*, the 'green' being an imperfect rhyme for 'scenes', also referring to that historical 'green' curtain which has now almost passed away. It represents 'behind the scenes'.

Back row hopper (*Theatrical*). Chiefly used in taverns affected by the commoner members of 'the profession'. 'He's a back row hopper' is said of an impecunious man who enters one of these houses on the pretence of looking for somebody, and the certain hope of finding somebody ready and willing to pay for a drink.

Back slang it (*Thieves'*). To go out the back way.

Back-scene (*Devonshire*). Literal. The second word direct from the French '*seant*', and an interesting example of evasive French-English—found only in Devon.

Backs, The (*Cambridge*). Literally the backs of several of the greater colleges, notably Trinity and John's—seen from the opposite side of the Cam.

St Andrews boasts her links, Oban is proud of her bay, Cambridge has her 'backs', and whoever visited Liverpool without hearing of her docks?—*D. N.*

Backsheesh (*Anglo-Arabic*). Bribe. The origin of this word is historical. When Mohamed Ali endeavoured, after his lights, to bring Egypt within the pale of civilization, he sought to abate the endless begging exercised by most of his subjects. To this end he assured his people that if they did not beg, foreigners would always make them a *backsheesh*, or 'present'. The natives accepted the theory, but only to apply it to their old practice. They begged, as they beg to this day, as much as ever; but they made their entreaties elegant by asking for a backsheesh—the one word of Arabic that every Englishman in Egypt learns, even if he acquire no other.

The people who talk of bribery and 'backsheesh' in such circumstances are imperfectly informed as to desert customs and slang. To give a Sheikh who gets for you a hundred camels, say £60, is not an act of bribery. It is merely paying him a commission.—*D. N.*, 16th March 1883.

Bad cess to ye! (*Irish*). Cess—board and lodging. An amiable Celtic benediction. An Act of Parliament was passed during Strafford's viceroyalty 'for the better regulating of Ireland', wherein we find these words: 'Whereas there are many young gentlemen of this kingdom (Ireland), that have little or nothing to live on of their own, and will not apply themselves to labour, but live coshering on the country, cessing themselves and their followers, their horses and their greyhounds, upon the poorer inhabitants,' etc., etc. This phrase is in common use in England—where the two words are supposed to mean ill-luck, as indeed they do, *e.g.*, 'Bad cess to you, Joe—wherever you go!'

Bad crowd (*Californian*). A man of indifferent character.

She then went out to tell the feminine convention on the back stoop what a bad crowd Jabez used to be when he kept a chicken-ranch on the Stanislaus in '51.—*San Francisco Mail.*

Bad egg (*Peoples'*). A person hopelessly beyond cure, perfectly disreputable. Originally American, though no longer used in the U.S. Colloquial in England.

A man out West, by the name of Thomas Egg, having committed some crime, his neighbours gave him the appellation of a 'bad Egg', which, in its application to vice, with man, woman, or child, they are invariably called bad eggs. It is also used to denote a good man, by calling him a good egg. And this is used either to denote his moral or pecuniary standing.—*American Paper*.

Bad form (*Soc.*, 1860 on). The opposite of Correct Fashion. Derived from the racing stable.

The very low bodices of some seasons ago are now considered 'bad form' (a quite untranslatable phrase).—*D. N.*, 'Dresses for dances', 15th December 1885.

This ingenious piece of tactics in taking cover was looked upon as 'bad form', even by the other hill men, who appreciated the scruples of British humanity.—*Newsp. Cutting*.

(*See* No class).

Bad hat (*Middle-class*, 19 *cent.*). A queer chum, dissatisfactory mess-mate, disreputable person. Probably Irish, from the worst Hiberian characters always wearing bad high hats (caps are not recognised in kingly Ireland).

What a shocking bad hat! is the next cry, with something of an historical flavour about it, that I can recollect. The observation is not yet wholly extinct, I should say, although its meaning has entirely vanished from the public ken; but, according to Sir William Fraser, in his *Words on Wellington*, the origin of this derisive criticism on a gentleman's head-gear was as follows: 'When the first Reform Parliament met, the Duke went into the Peers' Gallery of the House of Commons—Sir William Fraser says that it was the Bar, but this part of his statement is due, I should say, to a slip of the pen—to survey the members. Expecting, of course to be questioned, and knowing that his words would be repeated, the Duke, prompt as usual, was ready for the inquisition; and when asked, on walking back to the House of Lords, what he thought of the new Parliament, he evaded responsibility by saying, "I never saw so many shocking bad hats in my life." The catchword soon lost its political associations, and after a few years, was merged in the purely imbecile query, "Who's your hatter?'"—G. A. Sala, in *D. T.*, 28th July 1894.

Bad Shilling (*Common*). The last, *e.g.*, 'That's a bad shillin', that is, for there ain't another beyinde it, you know.'

Bad young man (*L. Peoples'*, 1881). Antithesis to Good Young Man (*q.v.*).

That the fatted calf, who had never been a prodigal, should suffer death in honour of the bad young man has never seemed to me strict dramatic justice.—*Ref.*, 18th January 1885.

Badger, to (*Peoples'*). To worry. From worrying a badger in his hole until he comes out to show fight. (*See* Draw.) It forms a remarkable example of complete inversion of the original meaning, for it was the badger which was worried—he was never the worrier. Nowadays he is the aggressor.

Immediately after the explosion at the House of Commons on Saturday I went to see 'the scene'. Thanks to the courtesy of the officials in charge—sorely badgered by M.P.'s, peers, and public persons, who had come out of idle curiosity—I was able to make a thorough inspection both of the House and of Westminster Hall.—*Ref.*, 1st February 1885. (*See* also G.O.M.)

Badges and Bulls' eyes (*Army*, 1899). In the Boer Revolt (October 1899), the officers' medals and badges offered fatal bulls' eyes for the Bore rifles.

The question has been much discussed whether, in view of the terrible gaps made in the roll of officers, they were not even yet too much marked out as Boer targets by what General Gatacre called badges and bulls' eyes.—*D. T.*, 21st December 1899.

Bag o' Beer. (*Lowest people's*). Bacchanalian brevity—for it means, and nothing else than a quart—half of fourpenny porter and half of fourpenny ale. This once stood 'pot o' four 'arf an' 'arf', reduced to 'four 'arf', and thence to 'bag o' beer'.

Bags o' Mystery. (*Peoples'*). A satirical term for sausages, because no man but the maker knows what is in them.

'If they're going to keep running-in polony fencers for putting rotten geegee into the bags of mystery, I hope they won't leave fried-fish-pushers alone.'

This term took its rise about 1850, long before the present system of market-inspection was organised. But this term remained long after sausages were fairly wholesome. The 'bag' refers to the gut which contained the chopped meat.

Bag and Baggage. Thoroughly, completely. It once more became popular from a phrase in a speech by Gladstone in reference to the Turk in

Europe, whom he recommended should be turned out of Europe 'bag and baggage'.

The truth of the matter is that all the petty States which won over the sympathies of sentimental politicians by their eternal whinings against that 'big bully, the Turk', have proved themselves past masters in the art of oppressing minorities, now that the tables have turned. They would like to carry into effect the 'bag and baggage' theory, and make a clean sweep of foreigners, to whatever race or religion these latter may belong.—*D. T.*, 13th August 1885.

Bagger, Bag-thief. (*Thieves'*). A stealer of rings by seizing the hand. Possibly from the French 'bague', a ring.

Baiard (*Peoples'*). A good fellow. Still now and again heard in the provinces; of course from Bayard, the chevalier '*sans peur et sans reproche*'.

'Thou'rt a real baiard—thou art. How now, mates, what baiards have we here?'—Garrick, *Abel Drugger*.

Bailiff of Marsham (*Fens*, 17 *cent.*). Ague.

There was so much water constantly lying about Ely, that in olden times the Bishop of Ely was accustomed to go in his boat to Cambridge. When the outfalls of the Ouse became choked, the surrounding districts were subject to severe inundations; and after a heavy fall of rain, or after a thaw in winter, when the river swelled suddenly, the alarm spread abroad—'The Bailiff of Bedford is coming'—the Ouse passing through that town. But there was even a more terrible bailiff than he of Bedford, for when a man was stricken down by the ague, it was said of him, he is arrested by the Bailiff of Marsham, this disease extensively prevailing all over the district when the poisoned air of the marshes began to work.—Smiles, *Lives of the Engineers.*

A fine example of passing English being helped by old phrases, for when the draining of the fens had been practically accomplished, ague ceased as an endemic disease. The term, however, is still heard now and again at any point between Boston in the north and Chelmsford in the south. It is metaphorically used to suggest approaching death.

Baked dinner (*Jocose, Prison*, 19 *cent.*). Bread—which is baked. The phrase was habitually used at Bridewell, this prison having been utilized until quite recently as a place of detention rather than as a prison for the punishment of troublesome city apprentices bound to freed men of the City of London. They were taken before the City Chamberlain, who in extreme cases sent the youngsters to Bridewell, in Bridge Street, Blackfriars, where a painting or two of Hogarth's are still to be found. Here the offenders were kept in honourable durance for a fortnight or more without labour, their only punishment being the absence of liberty. It was upon these neophytes that the trick was played of telling them that they were to have 'Baked Dinner'. Their disappointment, and the explanation of the term afforded huge merriment, reiterated on every possible occasion.

Baker's Dozen. Thirteen—grimly used for a family of twelve and another.

The 'baker's dozen', meaning thirteen, dates back to the time of Edward I., when very rigid laws were enacted regarding the sale of bread by bakers. The punishment for falling short in the sale of loaves by the dozen was so severe that, in order to run no risk, the bakers were accustomed to give thirteen or fourteen loaves to the dozen, and thus arose this peculiar expression.—*Newsp. Cutting.*

Balaclava (1856-60). A full beard, first seen upon the faces of the English army upon their return to England from Crimea. The new departure was instantly dubbed with the name of the most popular of the three great battles (Alma, Balaclava, Inkermann), the name probably being chosen by reason of the brilliancy of the charge of the Light Brigade. French writers who had visited the Great Exhibition of 1851, and who had been struck by the absolute absence of the moustache (except in the case of some military men), and the utter absence of the beard, without exception, were astonished upon return visits half-a-dozen years afterwards, to find Englishmen were bearded like the pard. Britons upon the principle of reaction always going the whole hog, grew all the hair they could, and the mere moustache of Frenchmen was nowhere in the fight. Interestingly enough, exactly as the wild, unkempt beard of 'The Terror' dwindled into the moustache for the young, and the côtelette (mutton-chop) for the elderly, so the Balaclava (which abated the razor, as a daily protesting sacrifice to anti-gallicanism) toned down by '70, into the various beards of to-day—the Peaked, the Spade, the Square, and other varieties of Tudor beards. These remained until the Flange, or Dundreary (*see* 1872-73), came in and cleared the chin, to be followed by the Scraper. To-day the 'York' prevails—the short, pointed beard still worn by the Prince of Wales.

Bald-head (*American*). An old man.

The house-fly flies an average of three miles per day. He can't be biting babies and bald heads all the time, you know.—*Texas Siftings*.

Byron used this term contemptuously in *The Two Foscari*, Act iii., sc. 1. MARINA.—'Held in the bondage of ten bald heads,'—referring to the Council of Ten.

Bald-headed Butter (*Com. London*). Butter free from hairs. First publicly heard in a police-court case, where the satire had led an indignant cheesemonger to take law in his own hands.

'Waiter, I'll take a bit of bald-headed butter, if you please.'

Balley, To (*Com. Lond.*). To be off, *e.g.*, 'I thought it was time to be off, so I balleyed.' (*See* Skip, Valse, Polka.)

Balloon (*Tailors'*). A week's enforced idleness from want of work. French, *bilan*, officially a balance-sheet book, figuratively a sentence, condemnation.

Balloon-juice (*Public-house*, 1883). Soda-water; presumably suggested by its gassy nature.

It's as good as a bottle of balloon-juice after a night's hard boozing.—*Newsp. Cutting*.

Balloon-juice Lowerer. A total abstainer, the 'lowerer' from the use of 'to lower' for 'to swallow'.

To be a booze fencer now, is to be a mark for every balloon-juice lowerer who can't take a drop of beer or spirits without making a beast of himself.—*Newsp. Cutting*.

Bally (*Sporting*, 1884 on). Excessive, great. Perhaps an evasion of 'bloody'.

'Too bad, too bad! after getting fourteen days or forty bob, the bally rag don't even mention it. I shall turn teetotal'. . . . 'Has that bally Ptolemy won, d'ye know? What price did he start at?' . . . 'If you had been born an elephant instead of a bally jackass, you would have had your trunk on the end of your nose, when you could have seen to it yourself.'—*Sporting Times*, 11th April 1885.

Balmedest Balm (*Low London*). Balm in the extreme.

'It is just a little the balmedest balm you ever plastered on your love-stricken heart. Try it, Annetta; and don't be afraid of it; spread it on thick.'—*Newsp. Cutting*.

Balsam (*Sporting*). Money. From both medicaments being of such an agreeable character. Originally confined to dispensing chemists.

Ban (*Com. Irish*, 18 *cent.* on). Lord-Lieutenant. There is a supposed association between 'ban', curse or edict, and 'banshee', the precursor of sorrow. Still in use, *e.g.*, 'Bedad, one ban or anoder, 'tis the same man.'

Banbury (*London*, 1894). One of the more recent shapes of 'jam', 'biscuit', 'cake', 'confectionery', 'tart' (*qq.v.*)—a loose woman.

Witness took several names and addresses, and some of the females described themselves as 'Banburys', and said they got their living as best they could.—Raid on the Gardenia Club, *The People*, 4th February 1894.

Baned (*Prov.*). Poisoned, *e.g.*, 'I'll have 'ee baned like a rat.' Abbreviation of henbane.

What if my house is troubled with a rat,
And I be pleased to give ten thousand ducats
To have it baned?
—*Merchant of Venice*, Act iv.

Banded (*Low London*). Hungry. May be Romany, or literal, hunger pressing like a band on the stomach, *e.g.*, 'I've been fair banded all the blooming week.'

Bang (*S. Exchange*). To loudly and plentifully offer a certain stock with the intention of lowering its price.

When any adventurers—call them bears or bulls, or any other animals—start to bang the shares, do not lend yourself to the game they are playing; sit close on your shares.—*D. T.*, 2nd June 1898.

Bang (To) (*Fashion*, 1870-95). Mode of dressing the hair in a line of fixed curls over the forehead. Chiefly used by women in England. Introduced by the then Princess of Wales. Commonly called to 'fringe' the hair.

An American lady has written: 'If for

a few brief hours of triumphant bang you are willing to undergo a long night of anguish, roll three rows of these wooden fire-crackers in your perfumed tresses.'—*D. N.*, 21st October 1886.

The man who bangs his hair hasn't enough sense to blow out his brains, even if he possessed any.—*N. Y. Commerc. Advertiser.*

This fashion at last gave way (1895) to 'undulated bands' covering the forehead, and, more fashionably, also the ears.

Bang Mary (*Kitchen*). The English cook's translation of 'bain Marie', the small saucepans within another saucepan of boiling water, an apparatus devised by a French cook named Marie. This obvious simplification of French is a good example of the vulgar habit of fitting foreign words to well-known English ones of something like similar sound ('folk-etymology').

Bang through the Elephant (*Low London*). A finished course of dissipation, as thus: drunk rhymed into elephant's trunk, abbrev. to elephant.

'You're no fool, don't you know, you're up to slum; been right bang through the elephant.'

Bang Up (*Low London*). First-class, superior. 'Bang' probably from the commanding cry of a cannon or gun, while 'up' is always an aspiring adverb, or even verb. However, 'bang' may be a vivid translation of 'bien', an exclamation certainly used at the court of Charles II.

Bang up to the Elephant (*London*, 1882). Perfect, complete, unapproachable. The 'Elephant' ('Elephant and Castle Tavern,' South London), had for years been the centre of South London tavern-life when (1882) Jumbo, an exceptionally large elephant at the Zoological Gardens, became popular through certain articles in the *D. T.* The public were pleased to think Jumbo refused to leave England and the gardens for America. He, however, did ultimately, with no emotion, leave behind him this bit of passing English.

'The fly flat thinks himself so blooming sharp, so right bang up to the elephant, that he's got an idea that no sharper would ever try to take him on.'

Banian Day. *See* Banyan Day.

Banjoeys (*Soc.*, 90's). Banjoists. A happy application of the comic joey—comic since the time of Grimaldi. An evasion of the 'ist' and invention of a friendly term at the same time. Said to be a trouvaille by the Prince of Wales, who brought banjo orchestras into fashion, being a banjoey himself.

Bank Up, To (*N. Country coal districts*). To complete, to more than complete—referring to building up a huge fire, *e.g.*, 'Us sooped yell till niight, an' then us poot away room! Then we banked up with a jolly dance—and the tykes did go it.'

The Helston Flora Day—or 'Furry Day'—was a go-as-you-please sort of festivity, where people danced in the streets, waltzed in and out each other's doors, and hilariously 'banked up' these entertainments by holding a bird show and running foot races.—*D. T.*, 20th August 1896.

Banker Chapel Ho (*E. London*). Whitechapel, and, in another shape, vulgar language. The word got in this way. In the first place, it is a ludicrous Italian translation—*Bianca*, white; *cappella*, chapel = White Chapel. Then Anglicization entering in, the first word got into 'Banker' and the second back into Chapel, with the addition of the rousing and cheery 'Oh!' 'Ah, Mrs Dicks, but you know the force of the sweet Italian quotation "Giotto Cimabue di Fra Angelico in Sistine"!' To which Mrs D——, originally from the district, might reply: 'Now, Ned, there's a good feller, none o' your Banker Chapel Ho!'

Bant, To (*Soc.*, 1860 on). To reduce stoutness. From the name 'Banting', that of a very fashionable funeral undertaker, who reduced himself many stones by the use of non-fat-producing food. He had a whale-bone frame made to fit his once large waistcoats and coats, and wore the whole over his reduced size—removing this armour to produce a full effect.

The Globe Dime under Meehan and Wilson has not been behind its neighbours in furnishing attractive novelties, leading off with John Craig, a champion of obesity, who has 'banted' down to a net weight of 758 pounds avoirdupois.—*N. Y. Mercury*, 13th January 1885.

Banyan Day (*Middle-class*). No meat; only 'bread and cheese and kisses' through twenty-four hours. Of course from India and the Army, the cooling banyan suggesting that all the rupees went yesterday.

If the actor has been taking the M.P. unawares on banyan day, when there wasn't enough cold meat to go round, I certainly think he owes him an apology. —*Ref.*, 25th February 1882.

In Devonshire the word is even applied to scrappy, tawdry dressing, *e.g.*, 'What a banyan sight to be sure!' (The word must be pronounced as a spondee).

Those were the halcyon days of British industries. The banyan days have been with the miners since then, and seem likely to stay.—*Ref.*, 2nd May 1886.

They told me that on Mondays, Wednesdays, and Fridays, the ship's company had no allowance for meat, and that these meagre days were called banyan days, the reason of which they did not know; but I have since learned they take their denomination from a sect of devotees in some parts of the East Indies, who never taste flesh.—Smollett, *Roderick Random*, ch. xxv.

'Banyan' is sometimes used for the skin.

The first hour found him beastly drunk; the second, robbed and stripped to his banyan. — *Rattlin the Reefer*, ch. xliii.

Barbecue (*Old English*). Any animal, bird, or large fish cooked whole, without cutting, from beard (*barbe*) to tail (*queue*).

The triumphal procession of a band of music, to welcome Mrs Langtry, was a comparatively ancient device smacking somewhat of both the circus and the institution known in America as a '*barbecue*' (a festival where a bullock or sheep is roasted entire, set to music).—*Newsp. Cutting.*

In the United States the word now represents a noisy political meeting.

I see they announce a big, old-fashioned barbecue to be given next week by the Brooklyn Democrats, at which Cleveland and Hendricks, Presidential candidates, are to participate. This barbecue holdin' used to be a very popular form of political excitement in the olden time.—*Newsp. Cutting.*

The barbecue was announced as a 'Monster Democratic Rally', and 'A Grand Political Carnival and Ox-Roast'. —*Newsp. Cutting.*

Barber's Cat (*Peoples'*). A skinny man. Perhaps a corruption of 'bare brisket', also used for a thin fellow—the brisket being the thinnest part of beef.

Barclay Perkins (*Peoples'*). Stout From the brewing firm Barclay, Perkins & Co.

Barges (*Peoples'*, *c.* 1884). Imitation breasts, which arrived from France, and prevailed for about four years. Named probably from their likeness to the wide prow of canal-barges.

Bark up a wrong Tree (*American*, *e.g.*, 19 *cent.*). Mr Rees, an American etymologist, says:

This is a very common expression at the West. It originated, as many of these vulgarisms do, from very simple causes. In hunting, a dog drives a racoon, as he imagines, up a certain tree, at the foot of which he keeps up a constant barking, by which he attracts the attention of his master, who vainly looks on the tree indicated. While endeavouring to find the animal he discovers it on another tree, from which it escapes and gets beyond his reach. Hence the phrase 'To bark up the wrong tree'. It has become general in its application, denoting that a person has mistaken his object, or pursuing the wrong cause to obtain it, etc.

Barkis is Willin' (*Peoples'*, 1850). Form of proposal of marriage, still very popular in lower-middle classes. From Dickens' *David Copperfield*, ch. v.

'Ah,' he said, slowly turning his eyes towards me. 'Well, if you was writin' to her p'raps you'd recollect to say that Barkis was willin': would you?'

Characters hardly less distinguishable for truth as well as oddity are the kind old nurse and her husband, the carrier, whose vicissitudes alike of love and mortality are condensed into three words since become part of universal speech, *Barkis is willin'*. Foster, *Life of Dickens*, vol. iii., p. 18.

In cross-examination she said that the drinking fits usually occurred when Mr Dunn was from home. She did not think that the Walls were fit company for Mrs Dunn. Mr Wall did not pay the witness any attention. Mrs Wall wanted to force her son on the witness, but she resented it. — Sir C. Russell: 'Was "Barkis willing"?'—The witness: 'No.' (Laughter.)—*Dunn* v. *Dunn & Wall*, 30th January 1888.

Barmy (*Peoples'*). Generally 'a bit barmy', rather mad, 'cracked'. From St Bartholomew, the patron saint of mad people. The pronunciation of the saint's name was Barthelemy—passing into Bartlemy (*cf.* Bartlemy Fair), and Barmy became the final form, *e.g.*, 'The family has always been a bit barmy in the crumpet.' (Why crumpet should stand for head is, so far, beyond discovery.)

Barn. A public ball-room; probably because one of the last of the London garden ball-rooms was Highbury Barn, North London. (*See* Barner.)

Barn-stormers (*Theatrical*, 18 *cent.* on). Inferior actors who play in barns. Used, of course, in scorn by those comedians who have reached permanent footlights. The term has now almost passed away in consequence of the enormous increase in the number of theatres which now exist, even in the smallest towns. The 'barnstormers' hire a barn near a village, and there give their performance—frequently of Shakespeare.

Miss Helen Bancroft, who recently played in this city, was announced as with a barn-storming company. *N. Y. Mercury*, 1883.

Barner (*North London*, 1860-80). A 'roaring' blade, a fast man of North London; from Highbury Barn, one of those rustic London gardens which became common casinos. The term remained until the Barn was swept away for building purposes.

Barneries (*Strand*, 1887). Last outcome of S. Kensington exhibitions ending in '-ries'.

Considerable commotion ensued at the Adelphi Stores, Strand, on account of the new proprietress, Miss Barnes, being presented with a testimonial. Miss B. has already won favour in her new venture, and it is thought the 'Barneries' will be much affected by *the* profession. —*Ref.*, 20th February 1887.

Barney (*L. Eng.*). A quarrel, row, generally of an innocuous character.

Then Selby runs out, and goes into the lodging-house to get another knife, but I stops him, and the barney was all over, but as we was agoing along to the hospital up comes a copper. — *People*, 6th January 1895.

Baron George (*S. London*, 1882). A portly man. This term was derived from the Christian name of a Mr George Parkes, a portly theatrical lessee in S. London, who came to be called Baron George; *e.g.*, 'He's quite the Baron George!'

Barrel of Salt, To take with a (*American*). To accept under reserve, with incredulity. From the Latin phrase *cum grano salis*.

He is therefore to be taken with a barrel of salt.—*Newsp. Cutting*.

Barrel of Treacle (*Low London*). The condition of love, suggested by the sweetness of this cloying synonym.

'Pon our sivey, we don't want to poke fun at chaps who've fallen into that barrel of treacle called love, and make up to their little lumps of soap in the operpro sort of way, and no blooming kid.—*Newsp. Cutting*, 1883.

Barrered (*Low Life*). A corruption of barrowed, from to barrow or put in a barrow, not that of the gardener but of the coster. Distinct from 'shettered' (*q.v.*), intimating that the drunken gentleman was removed by his friends and not by the police; *e.g.*, 'Which mum, we 'ad to barrer 'im 'ome. He were too that 'eavy to carry.' In St Giles the highest shapes of involuntary locomotion is 'wheeled' (in a cab)—then follows barrered—then the declension is reached in 'shettered' (shuttered). This term is passing away with the shutters themselves.

Barrikin (*Com. London*). Barking, chatter.

Let 'em say what they like, and howl themselves dotty. Their barrikin only makes 'em thirsty, and when they've got hot coppers through chucking the barrikin out too blooming strong they go in for a little quiet booze themselves, make no error.—*Newsp. Cutting*.

Barrister's (*Thieves'*). A thieves' coffee-house, derived from a celebrated host of this name.

The witness remarked that he could not waste his time; and Richards said he could not make out where he was, and he would go to the 'barrister's' and look for him. (The witness explained, amid a roar of laughter, that a 'barrister's' was a slang term for a coffee-house frequented by thieves.)—*Cutting*.

Baseball (*American*, 1880 on). Small, insignificant. Sometimes heard in Liverpool. Suggested by the small size of the ball in question.

Yesterday a *Mercury* reporter saw Heer within the prison walls. As he stepped into the corridor from his cell he evinced some nervousness, and stroked a 'baseball' moustache faintly perceptible on his upper lip, with his cigarette-stained fingers.—*N. Y. Mercury*, 1880.

Bash (*Thieves'*, 1870). To beat heavily with the fist only. Probably the most modern onomatope — the word doubtless being an attempt to vocalize the sound made by a fist striking full in the face

This real lady said, 'I ain't any the wuss for being able to take my own part, and I should think myself very small beer, and no kid, if I couldn't bash any dona in our court.'—*Newsp Cutting*

Women of susceptible and nervous temperaments are asked to come to theatres and see for themselves how they hocuss and 'bash' people at low riverside houses.—*Cutting*

Mr Chaplin. 'Bless me, yes! Didn't you know that he had offered Greenwood, of *The Telegraph*, a Civil List pension if he would get Lord Randolph "bashed" and dropped into the Thames?'—*Ref.*, 1882.

Basher (*Mod Low Lond.*). A name applied to low fighting rowdies paid to bruise and damage

The villain of the piece and the 'bashers', or hireling assassins, are supposed to carry on their trade unchecked in Ratcliffe Highway and Wapping

Basket of Oranges (*Australian, passing to England*) Pretty woman. A metaphor founded on another metaphor—the basket of oranges being a phrase for a discovery of nuggets of gold in the gold fields. One of the few flashes of new language from Australasia, *e g.*, 'She's a basket of oranges fit for any man's table'

Bastile (*Street*, 18 *cent.* on) Any place of detention, but generally a prison or a workhouse More commonly 'Steel'. The horror of the Bastile felt by all Frenchmen in the 18th century spread to England, and the name was associated with oppression. The word was particularly applied to 'Cold Bath Fields prison, Clerkenwell, which was called 'The Steel' until its final fall about 1890. The last new application of this word was (1870) to the Peabody Buildings for working men, erected in the Black Friars Road, London. It was the first of these buildings, which have long since been accepted and even battled for by working people. But at first the prejudice was very marked. The term has not been applied since 1880.

Bath Oliver (*W. Eng*, 18 *cent* on) A biscuit with a historical character

'Bobs' fights on 'Bath Olivers'. Shortly before leaving for the Cape he paid a visit to his sister, Mrs Sherston, of Bath, and took away with him to the front a bountiful supply of Bath Olivers. He sent home for a further supply, which Lady Roberts took with her when she went to join him It is not every one who has heard of the Oliver. It is a biscuit, and owes its name to the celebrated Dr Oliver, a Bath physician, and the friend of Pope, Warburton, and other eighteenth century notabilities When on his death-bed, the doctor called for his coachman, and gave him the recipe for the biscuits, ten sacks of flour, and a hundred sovereigns The lucky fellow started making and selling the biscuits in a small shop in Green Street, Bath And there they are made and sold to this day.—*M A. P*, 19th May 1900

Batter through (*Peoples'*). To struggle, beat thro', from French *battre*, to beat, probably used in the time of Charles II, *e g*, 'He battered through the part somehow!'

Batty-fang (*Low London*) To thrash thoroughly Evidently *battre à fin.* But how it passed into English, or whence it came, unless from the heated court of Charles II., it would be difficult to say

Baub (*Cockney*, 19 *cent.*). One of the commonest modes of evasively referring to the Deity—modes in which some idea of the original word, either in length, syllable, or letters, or even rhyme, is to be traced; *e.g.*, 'S'elp me Baub, I didn't go for to do it' However, the word really comes from Catholic England, and is 'babe'—meaning the infant Saviour.

Baudinguet (*Parisian*). A nickname given to Prince Napoleon in 1848, from the name of the mason who aided the Prince to escape from Ham, where he was imprisoned It stuck to Napoleon III. even to 1870, when a war correspondent at Sarbruck (July 1870) asked a soldier if he knew whether the emperor had arrived The reply was 'Oui, Baudinguet est arrivé.'

Bayreuth Hush (*Soc.*, 1890) Intense silence. From the noiselessness of the opera house at Bayreuth (Bavaria) when a Wagner festival is about to commence

If it cannot be said that the peculiar order of stillness known as the 'Bayreuth hush' made itself felt in the Covent Garden opera house last evening, yet there is no denying the spirit of expectation and attention in which a full audience brought itself to the opening performance of the long-expected *Ring* cycle.—*D T*, 7th June 1898.

Bazaar Rumour (*Army*, 1882 on). Doubtful news. Equivalent to 'Hamburg'. The result of the Egyptian occupation, referring to native news spread through the bazaars of Cairo.

I am able to contradict on official authority the statement published in London that there was a bazaar rumour that the Mahdi and his followers were marching on Dongola.—*D. N.*, 10th November 1884.

Bazaar'd (*Soc.*, 1882). Robbed. From the extortion exercised by remorseless, smiling English ladies at bazaars. Applied everywhere. Replaced, 'rooked' in society; *e.g.*, 'I was awfully bazaar'd at Sandown.'

A gentleman coming home from a bazaar met a highwayman, who accosted him with the professional formula of 'Your money or your life.' 'My dear sir,' said the gentleman, 'I should be most happy to give you my money if I had any, but I have just been to a bazaar.' The highwayman at once acknowledged the force of this argument, and further was so touched by the circumstances that he offered the victim a small contribution.—*Newsp. Cutting.*

Beach-comber (*Nautical*). A pirate, a beach-loafer, or a yachting tourist. In its earlier shape it referred to the pirate who made a landing and swept up all he could—that is, he 'combed the beach'. The pirate being quite dead in the Western Seas, this sense of the term is now only applied in the East, and generally to the Chinese *marin d'industrie.* The use of the word in its earlier meaning is sometimes figurative, especially on the American coast, *e.g.*, 'I was beachcombed out of every red cent.' In its later sense the word means a globe-trotter, or rather a beach-trotter, who travels only on land within easy distance of his wandering yacht.

It would be better to enter the army from the ranks, or to go gold-mining in Chiapas, or try ivory and Central Africa, or even to be a beach-comber in some insular paradise of the Southern Seas, which, as Mr Stevenson is showing, is the best kind of lotus-eating life left to mankind.—*D. N.*, 11th February 1891.

Probably Mr Stevenson would not be displeased at the title of a literary beach-comber.—*D. N.*, 27th December 1890.

Beadles (*American*). People of Virginia; probably from their high, old-fashioned behaviour, which the Northerner associates with that expiring church functionary.

Beak (*Low London*, 18 and 19 *cent.*). A magistrate. Probably from lawyers, as Thackeray has somewhere remarked, being celebrated for a vast expanse of aquiline nose. Mr G. A. Sala (*D. T.*, 28th July 1896), urges a different origin:

A contributor to *Notes and Queries* states that Hookey Walker was a magistrate of much-dreaded acuteness and incredulity, whose Roman nose gave the title of 'beak' to all his successors. The term is derived from the Anglo-Saxon 'beag', a necklace or collar worn as an emblem of authority. Sir John Fielding, half-brother of the novelist, was known as the 'blind beak', and he died in 1780, sixty years before the cry of 'Hookey Walker' became popular.

Beak-hunter (*Thieves'*). Annexer of poultry.

Bean-eater (*New York*). A term of scorn for a citizen of Boston, referring to the former Sunday custom observed by some Bostonians of accepting for dinner on that day cold belly of pork, and colder beans. (*See* Stars and Stripes.)

Circus tricks! circus tricks! you bean-eaters! Can't you tell when a feller's a-dying:—*Cutting.*

Beanfeast (*Peoples'*). A treat. Used generally in reference to enjoyments, and derived from the yearly feast of employees in factories and shops, of which much of the expense is borne by the employer. Originally the treat consisted of broad beans and boiled bacon, which must have been a great delight when few green vegetables were obtainable throughout winter.

Oh, it was quite a beanfeast—only one mouse [=black-eye].—*Cutting.*

Sometimes it is used satirically to denote a riot, *e.g.*, 'What a beanfeast!' parallel with the American 'picnic'.

Beano (*Peoples'*). Great rejoicing. From bean-feast, reduced to bean, with the ever rejoicing *o* added. (*See* Boyno.) It may be a connected coalition with 'bueno'—common in London Docks—being Lingua Franca.

One day last week I said 'Good-bye!'
To my kids, my wife, and home,
I met some pals, and away we went
For a 'beano' by the foam.
—*Cutting*, 1897.

Beaner (*Peoples'*). Chastisement. 'To give beans' is to inflict punishment, a phrase derived from boys beating each other with a collection of horse-beans in the foot of a sock The word 'beaner' is sometimes used ironically, calling something agreeable which is quite otherwise, *e g*, 'That's a beaner—that is!'

Beanpea (*London Streets*) A coalescing of B and P (*q v.*) into one word, the *d* being dropped. Doubtless the outcome of time, and the droll idea of combining the two vegetables which come in almost at the same time Still hastily, too hastily, applied to effeminate youths The case was thrown out of Court when it came before Lord Chief-Justice Cockburn

Beans Sovereigns Possibly a corruption of *bien* (a sovereign being certainly a 'bien'). But it may be a market-gardeners' trade phrase But if so, why beans? Why not strawberries, or asparagus, or some other of the more valuable products?

Be-argered (*Peoples'*). Drunk The 'argered' is 'argumentative', a drunken man being commonly full, not only of beer, but also of argument.

Beast (*Youths'*, 1870). A bicycle—the first endearing metaphor bestowed upon this locomotive Used in no way derogatively, but as though a horse—a hunter. (*See* Bone-shaker, Craft, Crock) But, as time went on and the 'byke' became a power, it ceased to be associated with a mere animal, by 1897 no term could be too distinguished by which to designate the all-conquering machine

Beat-up (*Soc.*, 19 *cent.*). To call upon unceremoniously, from beating-up game, which is certainly not treated with politeness when wanted, *e g*, 'I'll beat you up on Monday, or when I can' (*See* Stir up, Have out)

Beau (*Peoples'*). A man of fashion —early 18 century, of course direct from the French, and evidently from 'est il beau?' for before 'homme' it changes its formation 'un bel homme!' Johnson says, 'A man whose great care is to deck his person.' Still used in country places. 'What a beau ye be, Tummis!' Earliest classic use by Dryden, 'What will not beaux attempt to please the fair?' Swift says, 'You will become the delight of nine ladies in ten, and the envy of ninety-nine beaux in a hundred' Never now heard in towns (*See* Spark)

Beau-catcher (*Peoples'*, 1854-60). A flat hook-shaped curl, after the Spanish manner, gummed on each temple, and made of the short temple hair, spelt sometimes *bow catcher*. It is synonymous with 'Kiss curl' Now obsolete on this side of the Pyrenees.

Beaver-tail (*Mid -class*, 1860) A feminine mode of wearing the back-hair, turned up loose in a fine thread net (called 'invisible') which fell well on to the shoulders When the net is now worn, generally by lazy girls of the people, it is fixed above the neck Obviously from the shape of the netted hair to a beaver's flat and comparatively shapeless tail The well-marked fashion in hair for the people's women folk which followed was the 'Piccadilly Fringe' (*q v*)

Bedder (*Oxford-'er'*). Bedroom.

Bedford Go (*Tavern*, 1835-60) A peculiar oily chuckle usually accompanied by the words, 'I b'lieve yer my bu-o-oy.' From the style of Paul Bedford, an actor for many years with Wright, at the old Adelphi Bedford always was famous for his chuckle, but he raised it to fame in connection with the above credo, uttered in the celebrated melodrama, *The Green Bushes* (*See* Joey, O. Smith.)

Bee (*American*) An industrious meeting—as quilting, or apple-gathering

One day the boys over in the Bend had a hanging bee and invited us to come down and see a chap swing for his crimes —*Detroit Free Press*, January 1883

Beef (*Theatrical*, 1880) A bawl or yell Probably the career of this word is—'bull—bellow—beef,' the last word elegantly suggesting the declaration of a noisy bull.

At the back was the musical box, and an obliging hammer-whollopper beefed the names of the different squallers and bawlers as they slung on the boards. —*Cutting*

Beef (*Clare Market*—extinct). Cat's meat, *e g*, 'Give me my mouser's one d. of beef'

Beef a Bravo (*Music-hall*). To bellow, bravo like a bull, in order to lead the applause for a friend who has just left the stage.

Beef-à-la-Mode (*Com. London*) Stewed beef called *à-la-mode* on the *lucus a non lucendo* principle—for it is not a fashionable dish It came from Paris, where, in the days of sign-boards, a restaurant where this dish was sold showed the sign of a bullock seated in clothes of fashion.

You can swill yourselves out with *beef-à-la-mode*, as toffs call it, for two d., or you can indulge in the aristocratic sausage and mashed and half-a-pint of pongelow all for four d.—*Cutting.*

Beef-heads or Cow-boys (*American*). People of Texas and the West of U.S.A.—from the general employment of the inhabitants being the harrying of cattle.

Beef-headed. Stupid. Cattle being heavy, stolid, and torpid.

Beef-tugging (*City*). Eating cook-shop meat, not too tender, at lunch-time. Dinner is not clerkly known in the E.C. district as occurring between 1 and 2 P.M.

Been and gone and done it (*Peoples'*). Very general mode of saying that the speaker has got married, *N.B.*—gone is in this relation generally pronounced 'gorne'.

Marius and Florence St John have 'been and gorne and done it' at last. The registrar of hatches, matches, and dispatches has tied what for them is the 'dissoluble' knot.—*Newsp. Cutting.*

Been there (*Amer.-Eng.*, 1870). Had experience; *e.g.*, 'Thank 'ee—no betting; I've been there.'

Some reasons why I left off drinking whiskey, by one who has been there.—Paper in *Philadelphia, Sat. Ev. Post*, 1877.

He wants a man who understands his case, who sympathises with him, who has been there himself, and who will give him a vent for his emotions at a reasonable rate per line.—*N. York Puck*, 14th September 1883.

Beer and Skittles (*Peoples'*). A synonym for pleasure; *e.g.*, 'Ah, Joe, if a bloke's life was all beer and skittles *we* shouldn't be doing time.'

But life on a yacht is not all beer and skittles, nor is it always afternoon. There is the dreadful morning time, when the crew begin to stir on deck, and earthquake and chaos seem to have come.—*D. N.*, 22nd August 1885.

Beerage (*Soc.*, 19 *cent.*). A satirical rendering of peerage, referring to the brewery lords, chiefly of the great houses of Allsopp and of Guinness.

Dr Edwards as a temperance worker had some very strong things to say a few months ago on the subject of the ennoblement of rich brewers. Of course he opposed it on moral grounds, but some of the old nobility would be inclined to agree with his denunciation of the 'beerage' for other reasons—*Newsp. Cutting.*

Beer-bottle (*Street*). A stout, red-faced man.

Beer-eaters (19 *cent.*). A great consumer of beer, one who more than drinks it—who lives on it.

The Norwaygians are a fine and a sturdy race, but not at all like I had imagined them, after all I had read about Sigurd and Sintram and Sea-egg-fried, and the Beerseekers, who must not be confounded with a race peculiar to London, found mainly upon licensed premises, and distinguished among their kind as the Beer-eaters.—*Ref.*, 21st August 1887.

Beer-juggers (*Amer. Miner's*). Bar-women.

The only busy people in the place were the wife of the pianist, who sat by him industriously sewing, and the women who sold drink. These latter are called beer-juggers, and fill a large place in the evening life of the miner. *Journey Round the World*: 'of LEADVILLE.'—*D. N.*, October 1883.

Beer O! (*Trades*). The cry when an artisan does a something, or omits to do a something, the result of which in either case being a fine to be paid in pongelow. The exclamation is taken up by the whole shop, or rather was, as the custom is now obsolete.

Beetroot Mug (*Street*). A red face—passed for many years into Ally Sloper, a character in comic fiction since 1870, invented by Charles Ross, a humorist of the more popular kind.

Before the War (*Soc.*, 1880). From America. A new shape of 'the good old times'. Whenever a ganache in the U.S.A. wants to condemn the present he compares it with the time 'before the War (1860-65)'.

'How beautiful the moon is to-night!' remarked an American belle to her lover, as they spooned in the open. 'Yes,' was the reply; 'but you should have seen it before the war!'—*Newsp. Cutting.*

Begorra, also **By Jabers** (*Irish*). Solemn Irish oaths. Both words have been adopted by common English folk.

Spoken—Yes, by jabers; he's the best boy that ever was. Sure he's shown such powers of discernment ever since the first day he was born, that begorra he knows more now than ever I've forgotten.—*Newsp. Cutting.*

Behind Yourself (*Peoples'*, 1896 on). Too far behind, quite in the rear, far from absolutely up to date. Antithesis of Too previous, *e g*, 'What—you thought to-day was Thursday? Why, it's Saturday afternoon You're behind yourself, man, and a deal at that'

Behindativeness (*Soc.*, 1888). Referring to the dress pannier—one of the shapes with which fashion is for ever varying the natural outline of the feminine frame, *e g*, 'That lady has got a deal of behindativeness.'

Belcher (*Sporting*, 19 *cent*). A handkerchief pattern, round spots, light or dark upon a dark or light ground From a prize-fighter, Jim Belcher, who always carried into the ring a wiping handkerchief of this kind After Belcher's time, the 'belcher' split up into colours, every prize-fighter having his own tints. Belcher's original was white spots on dark blue ground Until quite recent years, a spotted neck-tie was called a Belcher: now called a 'moon-tie'.

At one time 'belchers' were made of that pattern which is affected in that spotty coat which Mr H B Conway sports in *The Widow Hunt* —*Entr'acte*, June 1885

Belittle, To. To make little of. An old word not found in most dictionaries, but brought into fresh use in 1898 by Mr Joseph Chamberlain, who about this time frequently used it.

Our whole policy has been belittled and ridiculed by the men who, when they were in office, kept our Colonies at arms' length —*Mr J. Chamberlain*, 8th December 1898.

The hard-won victories he gained in the old times are belittled and made nothing of —*Sun*, 6th December 1899.

Bell the Cat (*Peoples'*). To risk the lead Still used without any real knowledge of its origin, but with thorough comprehension of its application, *e g.*, 'Yes, but who'll tell him she's no good—who'll bell the cat? Some of us know he's got a bunch of fives.'

The proverb is of Scottish origin, and was thus occasioned: The Scottish nobility entered into a combination against a person of the name of Spence, the favourite of King James III It was proposed to go in a body to Stirling to seize Spence and hang him, then to offer their services to the king, as his natural counsellors, upon which the Lord Gray observed, 'It is well said, but who will bell the cat?' alluding to the fable of the mice, who proposed to put a bell round the cat's neck, that they might be apprized of her coming. The Earl of Angus replied that he would bell the cat. which he accordingly did, and was ever after called Archibald Bell-Cat

Belle à croquer (*Soc.*, 1860) Beautiful enough to command desire Dating second French Empire, it lasted into 1883, in English Society, becoming in lower circles 'beller-croaker'.

It possesses the further advantage of being blue enough to make a blonde *belle à croquer*, and yet not too blue to make her darker sister look as delightful as Nature meant her —*Newsp. Cutting*, 1883

Bellering Cake (*School*) Cake in which the plums are so far apart that they have to beller (bellow) when they wish to converse.

Belly-washer (*Amer. Saloon*). Lemonade or aerated water (*See* Rattle-belly-pop)

Bellywengins (*E Anglian, chiefly Suffolk*) A violent corruption of 'belly-vengeance', a cruel comment upon the sour village beer of those regions

Belt (*Anglo-American*). To assault. From the army, where the belt was often used for aggressive purposes.

Mrs Tice, who saw her approaching, said 'There comes that old maid, belt her'—*Newsp Cutting*

Belt Case, The (*Soc*) A symbol for years of wearisome tardiness From a celebrated libel case, Belt *v.* Lawes (1882), which lasted on and off for weeks

It is more interminable than the Belt case —*D. N.*, 25th October 1883

Ben (*Theatrical*, 19 *cent*). Short for 'benefit'—'benefit' never being used under any consideration by any self respecting actor when speaking in the profession 'Benefit' succeeded 'bespeak', which was in use when Dickens wrote *Nicholas Nickleby*

Ben (*Soc.*, 1880). A fib, a tarradiddle. The history of this word is fortunately preserved A well-known Italian proverb was converted into *Se non e vero—e Benjamin trovato.* The 'Ben' was too evident to be resisted. Hence a fib was described as a Benjamin Trovato, passing into Ben Trovato, then Ben Tro, and finally Ben, whence it has got fatally confounded with 'ben', the abbrev. of 'benefit'

The papers were rampant as to the

Czar's forty thousand dollar diamonds, and Modjeska's jewellery was one of the attractions of the season. Perhaps this story isn't true. Anyway, it will do to go into the Benjamin Trovato series.—*Ref.*, 29th March 1885.

Here is a little story which, if not true, ought to be, for it is at least of the Benjamin order.—*Newsp. Cutting.*

Ben-cull (*Thieves'*). A friend. Ben is from the Hatton Garden Italian *bene.*

Bench Winner (*Soc.*). A dog which has won many prizes at dog-shows—from the exhibits being placed upon benches.

The result is a series of paintings very aptly termed 'A dog show on canvas and paper', for not only are all the Royal favourites represented, but there is scarcely a bench winner of note not included.—*D. T.*, 11th February 1897.

The hounds are the property of Mr Edwin Brough, who has devoted himself to bloodhound breeding. It has been Mr Brough's practice not only to breed for bench points, but to train his animals to exercise those peculiar faculties with which they have been endowed by nature.—*D. N.*, 10th October 1888.

Bench Points (*London*). Ascertained and classified physical advantages. From show animals, especially dogs, being exhibited on benches. Applied also to women, *e.g.*, 'Her bench points were perfect, but I shouldn't like a wife of her build.'

Bend o' the Filbert (*Low*, 18 *cent.*). A bow or nod, filbert being elegantly substituted for the 'nob' or 'nut', both signifying head.

She gives him a bend o' the filbert as much as to crack 'ight-ri, its oper-pro for your nibs, you can take on'.—*Cutting.*

The above describes a serio-comic lady accepting by a nod, while acting or singing, the attentions of an admirer.

Bender (*London*). A sixpenny piece; so called from the rapidity with which this coin wears thin, and thereupon easily bends. This was especially the case thirty years since.

Bender (*Anglo-Amer.*). *E.g.*, 'Three sailors on a bender,' *i.e.*, 'on a drunken spree.' Possibly a conception of a 'Bon Dieu' used exclamatorily='My eye!' or 'Good heavens!' or it may be from some Spanish word adopted by Texas cow-boys after that State was wrested from Mexico (1845), creeping up north. It is common to sailors 'over the ditch'.

There was a distant rumbling and groaning, as if old Vesuvius was on a bender.—*Newsp. Cutting.*

In England the Bender is the elbow. (*See* Over the Bender.)

Bengal Blanket (*Anglo-Ind.*, 19 *cent.*). Used by soldiers who have been in India to describe the sun; *e.g.*, 'Yere's a London May—fifteen days, and I ain't seen a corner o' Bengal Blanket—what a climate!' (*See* Blue Blanket.)

Benjamin (*Maritime*, 19 *cent.*). A sailor's blue jacket, larger than the 'monkey' jacket which barely passes the hip-bones. It was the merciful invention of a Hebrew sailors'-tailor on Portsmouth Hard. The grateful tars appear to have given the name of this watcher of their winter comforts to the garment he invented. The word is now in general use for a jacket of dark-blue or black cloth made long and fitting to the figure. Generally called an 'Upper Benjamin'. Sailors also call the rare nautical waistcoat a 'Benjy'. Probably this was another invention, used in the diminutive form of the beneficent Benjamin.

Benjo (*Sailors'*, 19 *cent.*). A riotous holiday, a noisy day in the streets, probably from 'ben', or *buen giorno*; *e.g.*, 'Jim's out on a benjo.'

Beong (*Thieves'*). A shilling—probably a form of the French 'bien'; for indeed a shilling is very well when coppers only are, as a rule, ours.

Bermondsey Banger (*London*). A society-leader among the South London tanneries. He must frequent 'The Star', be prepared to hold his own, and fight at all times for his social belt.

Bespeak (*Theatrical*, 1830-50). A performance for the benefit of an actor or actress. The name took its rise from the patrons called upon by the beneficiare at the country theatre, giving a comparative consensus of opinion as to the piece in which the applicant should appear. It was superseded by 'benefit', which yielded to 'ben'. A good deal concerning bespeaks may be found in Dickens' *Nicholas Nickleby.*

Best Eye Peeled (*Amer.*). A figure of speech for extreme alacrity.

I tell you a driver on one of those vans has got to keep his best eye peeled every minute.—*Newsp. Cutting.*

Bet yer sweet life (*Amer.-Engl.*). Perfect assurance, complete conviction.

'Oh, no, certainly not,' said Mr Jones, smiling blandly. 'There are ups and downs in theatrical life, can't always make money—unless you have the right kind of a show. We've got a daisy, haven't we, Lunk?' 'Bechersweetlife,' said Mr Lunk emphatically.—1884.

Bet you a million to a bit of dirt (*Sporting*, 19 *cent.*). The thing is so sure that there can be no uncertainty. The betting man's Ultima Thule of confidence.

Bet your boots (*W. Amer.*). Absolutely safe betting—the boots being the most serious item of expense in the Wild West uniform.

'You bet', or 'you bet yer life', or 'you bet yer bones', while to 'bet yer boots' is confirmation strong as holy writ—in the mines, at least.—*All the Year Round*, October 1868.

Betty Martin. *v.* All my eye and Betty Martin.

Between the Devil and the Deep Blue Sea. Scylla on the one side, Charybdis on the other—between two equal menaces. The phrase has no meaning as it reads—the devil and the deep blue sea have no relation. May this not be one of the frequent perversions of proper names to words well understood of the people? For instance, may it not refer to a couple of French admirals or generals 'Deville' and 'Duplessy'—'Between Deville and Duplessy'—inferring disaster for the middle party. The phrase is quite historical.

'I had to pay up—there was Hook on one side, and Crook on the other—I was between the Devil and the Deep Blue Sea.'

He may indeed be said to be between the devil and the deep sea—victims alike of Kurd and Turk.—*Joseph Hatton*, 6th February 1898.

Bever (*E. Anglian*). A four o'clock halt on the road for a drink. An interesting word, evidently from the Norman conjugation of *boire*. (*See* Levenses.)

Bexandebs (*E. London*, 18 *cent.* on). A young easy-go Jewess in the Wentworth Street district. A combination of Becks (Rebeccas) and Debs (Deborahs), used satirically, *e.g.*, 'The bexandebs are in full feather—it's Pentecost Shobboth!'

Beyond, The (*Amer.* 1878). Heaven.

To this, one venerable old gentleman in the circle responded that he could now see around him daily his friends who had gone to the beyond, and that if he is riding in a street car and it is not crowded, they enter and sit beside and opposite him.—*N. Y. Mercury*, April 1885.

Beweep (1898). A new form of 'weep' brought in by the Tzar of Russia (20th May 1898) in a telegram referring to the death of W. E. Gladstone. It took the fashion at once.

The whole of the civilised world will beweep the loss of the great statesman whose political views were so widely humane and peaceful.—(Signed) Nicholas.

Bianca Capellas (*E. London*). An elegant evasion in describing White Chapellers—cigars understood, a very bad brand.

There was adjoining this a smoking-room or *salle d'attente*, in which were some stale English papers and the odour of equally stale cigars, also English—veritable Bianca Capellas—but of the sort of thing that we wanted there was no sign whatever.—*Ref.*, 6th June 1886.

Bible Mill (*Com. London*, 19 *cent.*). A public-house. An attack upon Bible classes. Said of noisy talking in a tavern.

Bible Class, Been to a (*Printers' Satire*). A gentleman with two black eyes, got in a fight.

Bi-cameral (*Polit.*, 1885). Two chambers, Lords and Commons. First heard in 1885—used satirically by the opponents of a second chamber.

Mr Labouchere complained that of the sixteen members of the Cabinet—thirteen are peers, or the near kinsmen of peers. This fact is an evil resulting from several causes. The first is the bi-cameral system, to adopt the convenient pedantry of Continental writers.—*D. N.*, 9th September 1885.

Bi-cennoctury (*Theatrical*, 1870). The two hundredth night of a run, with which explanation we leave this marvellous bit of etymology to the mercy of a critical world.

Big Beck (*Kent*). A local oath, *e.g.*, 'By the big beck'—heard only in remote places. Probably refers to Thos. à Becket, and has come down from his canonized bones. Sometimes (still in Kent) 'By the Blessed Beck'. (*See* More blue.)

Big Bird (*Theatrical*). A hissing figurative reference to the goose (*q.v.*)—a figure in itself for hissing; *e.g.*, 'Tom had the big bird last night, and he is in bed this morning.' However, this phrase sometimes has another meaning. At the Britannia Theatre the audiences began (about 1860) to compliment the accomplished villainy of the stage-villain by politely hissing him at the end of one act, to prove how well he had played the scoundrel. This thoroughly indigenous E. London fashion came West about 1878 where it was heard, perhaps at the Princess' for the first time. It has since spread, notoriously to the Adelphi (when still a dramatic house) and Drury Lane; but it has never become a W. London institution. In the E., if the villain did not get the 'big bird', he would consider that he was not on a par with Titus, and that he had lost his day, or rather evening, and he might fear for the renewal of his engagement.

Big end of a month (*Anglo-American*).

'The "big end of a month" is three weeks. I heard a market man speak of the "big end of a dozen" chickens.'

Big Heap (*Amer.*—old mining districts). A large sum of money—now current also in England.

Sam Adams had a ben. at the Pav. on Thursday night, and I hope he's made a big heap out of it.—*Newsp. Cutting.*

Big Numbers (*Anglo-French; old*). Bagnios. From the huge size of the number on the swinging door, never shut, never more than two or three inches open. The English grooms, stable-men, and their like in France often use this phrase: 'Joe's fond o' the big numbers.' 'Tom Four can't run over to the old home for Christmas—he's left too many of Nap's likenesses in the big numbers.' So extensively known throughout Europe was the association of big numbers and shady houses that, when about 1880, people began to place the numbers of their houses on their fanlights, for night observation, their neighbours were often quite unhappy (for a time); while even now many people shrink from the convenient custom.

Big Pot (*Music-hall*, 1878-82). A leader, supreme personage, the 'don'. This phrase is probably one of the few that filter down in the world from Oxford, where, in the 50's it was the abbreviation of potentate. It referred to a college don, or a social magnate. It has remained permanently a peoples' phrase—the pot being associated with the noblest pewter in a public-house.

'Some of the failures you meet at the "York" will try to impress you with the fact that the comic singers in receipt of big salaries have made their reputation by means of "smut", and that if they (the unsuccessful ones) were to resort to a similar method of gaining the applause of audiences, the "big pots would not be in it".'—*Newsp. Cutting.*

The 'York' is an hotel in the Waterloo Road, S. London, where music-hall people still meet.

Billy born drunk (*L. London*). A drunkard beyond the memory of his neighbours.

He did not have 30 or 40 pots of beer that day. He could do a good many, but he was not going by the name of 'Billy born drunk'.—*People*, 6th January 1895.

Billy-cock (*Provincial*). A brimmed low, felt hat; a modern amelioration of bully-cock, a term now having little or no meaning, *e.g.*, 'Do you cock your hat at me, sir?' was the reply to this challenge—the cocking of the hat. Other authorities hold the word to refer to William III., and his mode of wearing the hat.

Billygoat in Stays (*Navy*, 1870-85). A term of contempt: probably the outcome of the astonishing use, by young naval officers, of waist-stays, during or about these years. Introduced by a young naval officer of the highest, who afterwards, on shore, came to be called 'cuffs'.

Billy-ho (*Peoples'*, *Hist.*). In excelsis; suggests extreme vigour. May be from a proper name, 'Hough' for instance, confounded with the big 'O' so commonly used as a suffix to words of congratulation—as 'What cheer ho!' 'What ho!' etc.

The Marquis of Salisbury and Mr Biggar were having a cigar together. Said the Marquis: 'Weather keeps very dry; we want rain badly. I think Canterbury ought to issue a prayer for it.' 'Arrah! be asy wid yer Canterbury,' exclaimed Mr Biggar; 'it's just a new hat I'll be afther buying, and it's my umbrella I'll be lavin' at home, and shure it'll rain like billy-ho!'—*Ref.*, 9th August 1885.

Billy Turniptop (1890 *sqq*). An agricultural labourer. Probably an outgrowth of Tommy Atkins.

'Billy Turniptop' does not seem a very respectful description of the agricultural labourer, especially during election times, and the Unionist candidate for Doncaster has been sharply pulled up for using that cognomen. His explanation was that he was only quoting the speech of a representative of the opposite party.—*D. T.*, 10th July 1895.

Bin (*Harrogate*). A mineral spring. Satire based upon the wine-cellar.

It is considered high treason at Harrogate to drink from the Old Sulphur, or any other 'bin', as a Scottish robust invalid calls it, without first consulting medical authority.—*D. N.* (Harrogate), 31st August 1883.

Binder (*Lower Class*). An egg. Pint o' wash, two steps, an' a binder'—'a pint of tea, two slices of bread-and-butter, and an egg.' Alludes to its constipating action.

Bindery (*Amer.-Eng.*, 1879). A bookbinder's workshop.

The word 'bindery', a new-comer in England, though in common use in Canada and the United States, has recently been welcomed with something like a bonneting by correspondents of *Notes and Queries*.—*Newsp. Cutting*, 1879.

Binned (*Lond.*, 1883). Hanged; a ghastly word, referring to Bartholomew Binns, a hangman appointed in 1883.

Bird (*Theatrical*). Hissing—the bird being the goose (*q.v.*), whose general statements are of a depreciatory character.

Professor Grant, Q.C., had both 'the bird' and 'the needle' at the Royal on Monday.—*Age*, January 1884.

Pantomimes and Blackmailers. Threats of 'the bird'. Already three or four of the most prominent artistes engaged at one house have been molested after leaving the theatre at night, and threatened with 'the bird'—that is, hissing—unless their tormentors are well paid to remain quiet.—*People*, 6th January 1895.

Bird (*Theatrical*, 1840). A figurative name of The Eagle, which was the title of the tavern and pleasure-grounds out of which grew the Grecian Theatre, an elegant name never accepted by its patrons, except a few who called it the Greek. 'Bird' it remained until General Booth of the Salvation Army bought it up (1882). To this day an effigy of the 'bird' surmounts the main building. (*See* Brit., Vic., Eff., Delphy, Lane.)

Birdlime (*Low Class*, 19 *cent.*). Nonsense-rhyme for 'time'.

We have been awfully stoney in our birdlime, and didn't know where to turn for a yannep, so we've had to fill up our insides on something less than two quid a week.

Birdofreedomsaurin (*Amer.*). Bird-of-freedom soaring. A jocular mode of describing the altitude of the American eagle. Used mildly in England to deprecate any chance American extreme expression of patriotism.

I think that Prince Louis Napoleon was over-dressed. I know that in his green or purple stock (I forget which) he wore an immense breastpin representing an eagle in diamonds—not the eagle with displayed wings, that is, the American 'birdofreedomsaurin'—but an aquiline presentment with the wings closed—the eagle of Imperial sway.—G. A. Sala, in *D. T.*, 16th June 1894.

Birds may roost in my bonnet, Any (*Devonshire*). Self-praise. Speaker so little given to slander that the most Aristophanic birds could carry no disparagement of hers between heaven and earth; *e.g.*, 'Don't 'ee b'lieve it, Mrs Mog—any bird may a-roost in *my* bonnet.' 'A little bird told me' is in close relation with this phrase. The origin is to be found in Ecclesiastes, x. 20. 'For a bird of the air shall carry thee voice, and that which hath wings shall tell the matter.' The belief that birds carry messages between earth and heaven is common to all countries and times. In Europe the dove and the robin are the birds most associated with this charming superstition.

Birmingham School (*Soc.*). A polite evasion of radical; *e.g.*, 'We do not like his politics at the Duke's—he belongs too thoroughly to the Birmingham School'—about 1885. Since then Birmingham has climbed down or up; and the centre of radicalism is supposed to be Newcastle. 'The Newcastle Programme should be backed by the Marquis de Carabas!' (*See* Newcastle Programme.)

Biscuit and Beer Bet (*Street*, 19 *cent.*). A swindle—because the biscuit backer invariably loses, it being intended that he should lose—to the extent of glasses round, for instance. The bet is as follows: that one youth (the victim) shall not eat a penny biscuit before his antagonist has swallowed a glass of beer by the aid of a teaspoon without spilling any of the beer. The biscuit is so dry, and the anxious bettor so fills his mouth in the desire to win that he generally loses; *e.g.*, 'Yere's a mug—let's biscuit an' beer 'un.'

Bismarck (*Political; South German and French*, 1866). A term of contempt.

A good story is told of a Bavarian who, quarrelling the other day with one of his fellow-countrymen, abused him in the most violent language, and, after exhausting a very extensive vocabulary of invectives, at last called him 'Bismarck!' The phlegmatic German had borne all previous insults with praiseworthy patience; but, on hearing himself thus apostrophised, he flew into a tremendous passion, and cited his enemy before the courts. He was non-suited on the plea that 'Bismarck' is a name, and does not necessarily imply an insult—at least, no such interpretation was to be found in any of the Bavarian law precedents. This is not the first time that the name of a Prime Minister has thus been popularly applied as a term of contempt. Under the Restoration it was a common incident to hear a cabby apostrophising a sulky or restive horse, 'Va donc, hé, Polignac!' and during the early part of the reign of the Grand Monarque, 'Mazarin' was equivalent to the refined exclamation, 'You pig!' which an attentive listener may be edified by hearing exchanged by the *gamins* of Paris in the present year of grace.—*Morning Star*, 1867.

After 1870, Bismarck was 'accepted' by Bavaria.

Bit-faker (*Thieves'*). Counterfeit money-maker — from 'bit', money, and 'fake', to make, or rather cunningly to imitate.

Bit o' Beef (*Vulg.* 19 *cent.*). A quid of tobacco; less than a pipeful. A playful, or possibly a grim, reference to tobacco-chewing staying hunger. (*See* City sherry; Pound o' bacca.)

Bit o' blink (*Tavern*). Drink—rhyming slang.

Bit o' crumb (*C. L.*, 1882). A pretty plump girl—one of the series of words designating woman immediately following the introduction of 'jam' as the fashionable term (in unfashionable quarters) for lovely woman.

Then Joe fell in love with a dona—oh, what a bit of crumb.—*Newsp. Cutting.*

Bit of fat from the eye, Have a (*L. Class*). Suggestive of compliment—this phrase being seriously used at a spread, or dinner of sheep's head, the orbits of the eyes being lined with a fat supposed by the accustomed consumer to be exceptionally delicate.

Bit o' grease (*Anglo-Ind. Army*). A Hindoo stout woman of a smiling character, *e.g.*, '*She's* a nice bit o' grease—*she* is.'

Bit of haw-haw (*London Tavern*, 1860 on). A fop. Possibly suggested by the hesitating commencing syllable used by many well-bred men—more frequently from modesty or caution than from any sense of impressing the idea of superiority.

When these young bits of haw-haw borrow a swallow tail coat and a crook stick, and a bit of window to shove into their weak peepers, and then go into the Gaiety with an order, strike us purple if they're not at their best then. They know all the actresses of course, and the way they talk about some of 'em would make a red stinker turn blue.—*Newsp. Cutting.*

Bit o' jam (1879). A pretty girl—good or bad.

He kisses me, he hugs me, and calls me his bit o' jam, and then chucks me down stairs just to show me there's no ill feeling; yet I love him like anything.—*Newsp. Cutting.*

Everything you see you just feel you would like to buy and take it home to the bit of jam.—*Newsp. Cutting.*

Bit o' pooh (*Workmen's*). Flattery—generally said of courtship—obtained very oddly. The exclamation 'pooh' generally expressing nonsense, the phrase suggests flattering courtship or blarny.

Bit o' prairie (*Strand*, 1850 on). A momentary lull in the traffic at any point in the Strand, so that the traveller can cross the road. From the bareness of the road for a mere moment, *e.g.*, 'A bit o' prairie—go.'

Bit o' raspberry (*Street*, 1883). An attractive girl. When 'jam' came to be used to describe a girl, the original *double intendre* suggested by a comic song having become known—raspberry, as the most flavoursome of conserves, was used to describe a very pretty creature. Then the jam was dropped, and the 'bit o' affixed, and this phrase became classic.

'So,' said Bill, 'you're the bloke who's spliced my bit o' raspberry'.—*Cutting.*

Bit o' red (*Historical*, 18 *and* 19 *cent.*). A soldier, *e.g.*, 'A bit of red so lights up the landscape.'

Bit o' stuff (*Street*, 19 *cent.*). A lovely woman — not perhaps of a Penelope-like nature—rarely at home.

He waited for a bit of stuff near the stage door of the Comedy Theatre. He was an elderly cove and he had great patience.—*Cutting.*

Bit o' tripe (*L. Class*). One of the endearing names given to the wife —probably a weak rhyme.

This paper always comes useful, if it's only to wrap a Billingsgate pheasant in to take home to the bit of tripe. — *Cutting.*

Bit on, To have a (*Sporting*). To have a bet on—a 'bit' of money on—a race.

I hear that all the shining lights of the music hall who are accustomed to have a little 'bit on' were on the right side.—*Newsp. Cutting.*

Bit to go with (*Amer.-Eng.*). Generosity — as the result of self-satisfied superiority.

An American railway train can give most things in this world a bit to go with in the way of noise.—*Ref.*, 20th February 1887.

Bitch the pot (*University*, down to 1850). Amongst a tea-drinking party of men it was asked, 'Who'll bitch the pot?'—meaning who will pour out the tea.

Bitched (*Printers'*). Spoilt, ruined, in reference to type.

Bite the tooth. To (*Thieves'*). To be successful. Origin unknown.

Bite-etite, perhaps **Bitytite** (*Peoples'*, *E. London*). Grotesque substitution of bite for the first four letters of 'appetite'. (*See* Drinkitite.)

Bite off more than one can chew (*American-English*). Referring to plug tobacco, and meaning that the person spoken of has undertaken more than he can accomplish.

Bits of Grey (*Soc.*, 1880). Elderly victims of both sexes present at balls and marriages, especially the latter, to give an air of staid dignity to the chief performers. 'Don't tell me—we had a small and early, all young—most miserable, growling, towering failure I ever endured. No stir-up for me without my bits of grey. They give tone to the whole thing.'—*Society Novel*, 1883.

Bits o' soap (*Com. Lond.*, 1883). Charming girls—of a kind.

I can imagine General Booth jumping in his boots when he piped that article in his paper. I wonder what all the converted bits o' soap thought about it.—*Cutting*, 1883.

(Booth became the self-appointed general of the Salvation Army, 1882-83.)

Bitter oath (*Peoples'*, 19 *cent.*). Emphatic intensification of oath; *e.g.*, 'I'll take my bitter oath.' Oaths may be divided into two classes—those which appeal to heaven, as 'By God', and those which relate to an antithesis, as 'By hell', the former being the better oath. The masses, incapable of discriminating one kind from the other, simplified 'better oath' into 'bitter oath', as possessing more emphasis.

Bitties (*Thieves'*). Evasive term for skeleton-keys.

Bivvy (*London*). Beer; evidently from the French 'buvez' (Italian 'bevere') — the imperative mood of the verb being applied to the beer itself. The difficulty is to find the descent. It may have come from French prisoners very early in the nineteenth century, or from the French colonies in Soho, or (more likely) from the Italian organ-grinding regiment in the neighbourhood of Hatton Garden.

Black and white (*Thieves' rhyming*). Night. It would mean, when used, 'to-night'.

Black-bagging (1884). Dynamitarding—from the fact that where dynamite proceedings had failed at certain railway-terminuses the explosive charges were found in black bags.

Five thousand pounds reward for the discovery of the perpetrators of the outrage at London Bridge is too much. It is an encouragement to others to go black-bagging.—*Ref.*, 4th January 1885.

Black-ball (*Club*, 19 *cent.*). To reject by ballot. The word is now absolutely inappropriate, though still used by 'correct' clubmen. It had meaning when club elections were effected by each elector being given one white and one black ball, so that upon opening the ballot-box the colours decided, black naturally being a negative. So far as the declaration of the election was concerned, nothing could be better than this mode; but unfortunately every elector was troubled by the possession of the second ball, which he might drop and thereby betray his vote. This ball the voter certainly would have some inconvenience in depositing, apart from the watchfulness of neighbouring eyes. Hence the new mode of club-balloting with a box, having a hole in front large enough for the entrance of the hand, the bottom of the box being divided by a high partition, while the outside is marked 'Yes' (or 'Ay') and 'No'—referring to the two boxes formed by the partition. Only one ball is given to each voter, and thus he gets rid of his responsibility by depositing the ball either on one side or the other. Unfortunately nervous voters are frequently fogged the moment they lose sight of the right hand, while the ballot-box-carrier (where it is carried, instead of being placed on a table for the approach of the voter) has a frequent habit of tilting up the 'No' side of the box, so that if the ball is not firmly manipulated when inside the palladium, it may have a better chance of favouring the 'Ay'. Even this word itself is a difficulty, for its complication between 'ay' and 'ayes', together with its infrequency except as an interjection, helps to confuse timid voters. More recently the ballot boxes have been bearing the legends 'yes', 'no'—the affirmative always preceding the negative.

Black-bottle Scene (*Dublin*, 1822 on). Black beer-bottle throwing at obnoxious persons.

On the 14th of December 1822, on the occasion of the Marquis Wellesley, visiting the Theatre Royal, Dublin, an organized disturbance on the part of the Orangemen took place, in resentment of his Excellency's sympathy with Catholic Emancipation. The affray is always referred to as the 'black-bottle' riot; a black bottle having been flung at the Viceroy by an Orangeman in the top gallery.—*Newsp. Cutting.*

On any other occasion the incident might have passed unnoticed, but now the rumour of a 'black bottle' scene was in every one's mind.—*A. M. Sullivan*, 1877.

Black Eye (*American, political and social*). A reverse, especially political.

A black eye for Platt.—An Albany jury has decided that Governor Hill was right, and Quarantine Commissioner Platt wrong, and that the latter has all along been a resident of Owega, while holding office in New York.—*N. Y. Mercury*, 15th January 1888.

Often used to designate theatrical failure.

This inheritance proved a black eye to all concerned, because the new company lacked all the vocal and comedy requisites for a successful interpretation of this very popular work.

Black Ivory (*Slave-dealers*). A disguised way of referring to negro slaves.

Mr Steyn, a former Landdrost of Potchefstroom, in both letters and speeches, complained that 'loads of "black ivory" were being constantly hawked about the country'.—F. W. Chesson, in *D. N.*, 5th November 1883.

Black Jack (19 *cent.*). A black portmanteau of peculiar make.

William Wall deposed that he repaired the portmanteau produced, and recognised Burton as the man who brought it. Burton also brought another second-hand portmanteau called in the trade 'Black Jack'.—*Dynamite Case Report*, 4th March 1885.

Blackleg (*Labour*, 1889-90). A non-striker in industry. Blackleg had long been used for a swindler, but at this date it was first applied to non-Union men or non-strikers. Directly used in relation to the dock-strikes. Common to the labouring classes by June 1890.

It will be seen from the full report of the situation, which we print elsewhere, that the present stage of the conflict turns on the presence of the 'blackleg', to use the designation which the Dock labourers first popularised.—*Chaos in the Post Office*, in *D. N.*, 10th July 1890.

Black Maria (*Thieves'*, 19 *cent.*). The prison van, probably Anglicizing 'Black V.R.', this public conveyance being ink-coloured, and bearing V.R. on each side of it. To the ignorant V.R. would have no meaning; while Maria would; or it may be a rhyming effort. The New York prison van, though of course very different from the English carriage, bears the same name.

He 'protested' against entering the Black Maria, and on the way up 'would not admit' that he was going to the Workhouse, but by this time he probably feels at home up there.—*N. Y. Police Report*, 1883.

Upon the death of Queen Victoria, necessarily the initials on the prison van were changed to E.R.—the term for the vehicle, however, still remaining. A phrase was immediately found for E.R.—Energy Rewarded—a term accepted by even the nation, with applause. (*See* V.R., Virtue Rewarded, Vagabonds Removed, Sardine Box.)

Black-silk Barges (*Ball-room*). Stout women who ought to avoid dances. They dress in black silk to moderate in appearance their amplitude.

'It's time I sounded a retreat from dancing—I've had to dance with seventeen black-silk barges this blessed evening. Never again—never again.'

Black Strap (*Peoples'*, *Old English*). Port wine. A corruption of 'black stirrup' cup. Sherry or sack (the first a corruption of Xeres, the second, an abbreviation, was always white wine; clarets and burgundies red; port black). The stirrup cup was always potent. The passage from black stirrup to black strap is too evident when port came amongst the people—more accustomed to strap than the stirrup. To this day strap is used for port.

Blank please (*American*). A negative euphemism for the unending 'damned'—with a polite request added.

. . . that matter-of-fact business manager of ours says that, although we may put what we blank please in the editorial columns, he won't put a six-inch display in the advertising end of the paper for less than several hundred dollars cash, quarterly in advance.—*Texas Siftings.*

Blarney (*Irish*). Flattery. The *Blarney stone* is a protruding one, standing out from below a ruined window of ruined Blarney Castle (near Cork). Whoever kisses this stone, a very difficult feat, and one which requires help and strong holding hands while the aspirant leans over and down into space, is supposed to possess for ever after the gift of successful flattery.

The traditions respecting the kissing of the Blarney stone, to impart to the devotee a peculiar suavity of speech, is about three hundred years old.—*Newsp. Cutting.*

Blasé (*Fr.*, 1840). Wearied, bored. Brought to England with a farce called *L'Homme Blasé*, subsequently produced for Wright (Princess Theatre), in which version this actor was called Blasé. Succeeded by 'bored' about 1860.

Bleed (*Peoples'*). A perversion of the word 'blood', as 'She'll have his bleed'—usually said of a woman who is rating her husband.

Blenheim Cloud (*Polit.*). The influence of the Dukes of Marlborough over Woodstock, which lies in the shadow of Blenheim.

Against this the more sanguine point to the advantage of being free from what they call 'the Blenheim cloud', the Duke having formally declared that he takes no part in this election, and that all his people are free to vote as they choose.—*D. N.*, *1st July* 1885.

Blenheim Pippin, The (*Polit.*, 1883). An application of the name of a known variety of pippins, always a small apple, to describe Lord Randolph Churchill, a diminutive man, who, as a son of a Duke of Marlborough, was associated with Blenheim, the family seat in Oxfordshire.

. . . the Tories are, as a rule, followers of the strongest; and after the Blenheim Pippin's latest manifesto they will hardly know whether to throw in their lot with Tweedledum or Tweedledee.—*Entr'acte*, 7th April 1883.

Bless me soul (*Peoples'*). Bless me—Saul. Probably one of the few Puritanic exclamations—all of which were Biblical, 'Bless me, or my, soul' is nonsense, as it stands—for who blesses? Hence probably arose 'God bless my soul'. But this phrase is also meaningless, for the soul needs no blessing. 'God bless me' is reasonable. But here, 'soul' is the important word. In this conversation it should be remembered that Saul was held in high Puritanic esteem—as a patriarch of much power.

Blessing (*Irish*). Gratuity. Poetic way of putting it; will contrast with 'backsheesh' (*q.v.*) 'Sure, he's a man gives me a blessing every time he passes without pretending not to see me, he does.' In Devonshire a 'blessing' is a handful thrown in, *e.g.*, 'Plase to give' us a half-peck o' pays, and give us a blessing.'

Blew, To (*Com. Lond.*). To dissipate. This word is by no means to 'blow', but is suggested by 'blue'. 'I blewed' (or 'blew') means 'I spent', and probably is suggested by the dismal blue appearance of a man, penniless and recovering from a drunken fit. The word was turned to very droll account by a comic-singer, Herbert Campbell, in 1881. A medicinal pad to be worn over the liver was very much advertised; and a half life-size cut of a masculine and healthy patient with the 'liver pad' *in situ* created a great deal of comment. The singer put both together and came out with a ballad. 'Herbert Campbell's favourite song now is called "Clara blued her Liver Pad"', meaning that she had sold her specimen and spent the proceeds in drink—for you only 'blew' money when you do spend it in drink.

In about an hour he reached the Strand, and in less than another hour he had blewed his half-a-dollar, so he sat on a doorstep and wept as only boys who have run away from home and have got the stomach-ache can weep.—*Cutting.*

Blewed his red 'un (*Peoples'*). 'Red 'un' is an anglicization of 'redding' (a thieves') word for a watch, probably the name of a watch-receiver. The phrase therefore means 'Spent in drink the money raised on his watch.' Here brevity is indeed triumphant.

Blighter (*Theat.*, 1898). An actor of evil omen: it took the place of Jonah (*q.v.*).

'I never care about acting in a play which is likely to fail. Look at Jones. Splendid actor, but he has been connected with so many failures that he has got to be known as a blighter, and no one will engage him.'—*Cutting.*

Blind Hookey (*Peoples'*). A leap in the dark; *e.g.*, 'Oh, it's Blind Hookey to attempt it.' From a card game. The centre card is the banker's—the players put money against either of the four other cards. If the dealer's centre card is the highest of the five he takes all the bets. If his card is the lowest, he pays all four.

Blink. *See* Bit o' blink.

Blister, To (*Peoples'*, 1890 on). To punish with moderation: a modification of 'to pound'; *e.g.*, 'I'll blister 'im when I ketch 'im'—a promise of fisting. Used chiefly by cabmen in relation to magisterial fines, *e.g.*, 'I was blistered at Bow Street to-day for twenty hog.'

Blizzard Collar (*Soc.*, 1897). A high stand-up collar to women's jackets, coats. Suggestive of cold weather.

I must mention the very pretty Russian vests of fur that our élégantes have now adopted. They are tightly fitting, and fasten on the side; they have a short basque all round, a blizzard collar, and a fancy belting of jewelled enamelled plaques.—*D. T.*, 16th January 1897.

Bloater (*Peoples'*). An abbreviation of Yarmouth bloater: a fat person. From the fact that the first smoking process applied to the herring results in a remarkable swelling, which afterwards abates.

If intended for immediate eating, the herring is taken down after one firing, when it is swelled and puffed out like a roasted apple. It is then known to the true East Anglian as a blowen-herring—the word bloater is rejected by philologists as a foreign corruption—and here you probably have the true etymology of the familiar word. — *Yarmouth*, by W. Norman (Yarmouth, 1883).

Blob (*Cricket*, 1898). No runs. 'Blob' has taken the place of 'duck', or 'duck's egg'.

Block (*Scotch Thieves'*, 1868). A policeman in one syllable.

I think it would be a good idea for my mother to get the block privately and make an appeal to him; he would have a little feeling for her, I think.—Dundee garotter's letter, 1868.

Block (*Linen Drapers'*). A name applied curiously to the young lady of fine shape who in the mantle department tries on for the judgment of the lady customer.

Block a quiet pub. (*Peoples'*). To stop a long time in a tavern; *e.g.*, 'I don't care for theayters or sing-songs; but I like to block a quiet pub.', said the commercial; *i.e.*, to remain quietly drinking in an out-of-the-way public house. Generally said of a sot.

Bloke (*Lower Classes*, 19 *cent*). A friendly soul, inclined to be charitable.

This word has not the objectionable meaning it is often supposed to possess. On the contrary, it is mighty affectionate, *e g*, 'Got a bit o' bacca, bloke?' if asked you in the streets is by no means offensively said. It is less than 'gentleman', more than 'mate'. 'He's a proper bloke' is simply a pæan

Bloke is also a lover, or even an acquaintance

Master Edward Graham, aged eight, and Miss Sarah King, aged nine, appeared at Bow Street as inseparable and incorrigible beggars in the Strand 'Sally and her bloke' is said to be the unpoetical designation of the pair in the Strand —*D. N*, 1882

In universities, an outsider, a mere book-grubber, *e g.*, 'Balliol mere blokes. But they carry off everything' (*See* Old Put, Muff)

Blood (*Old*). By our Lord—one of the old Catholic exclamations

Blood—it is almost enough to make my daughter undervalue my sense. — Fielding, *Tom Jones*, bk vii, ch. 4

The extended form is 'bloody'—by our lady—an asseveration referring to the Virgin, which becomes an apostrophe in the shape 'What the bloody hell'—'By our lady, hail.' 'What' thus appears to be a Protestant addition. About 1875, when the London School Board had influenced the metropolis for some half dozen years—this word and phrase were superseded by 'blooming', a sheer evasion which has survived the nineteenth century, and has quite passed into the lower layers of the language. In 18th century literature may be found the form 'blady hell', which suggests the origin very forcibly

Some actors have been known to mutilate the speech in *Macbeth*, 'Be bloody, bold, and resolute', lest it should suggest the inconceivably wicked thought, 'Be bloody-bold, and resolute'. Now this extremely shocking word is nothing more nor less than a corruption of 'By'r lady'. How little do the dregs of our population, who, when they hurl out the word, imagine that it contains some frightful explosive, dream that they are appealing to the Virgin.—*D T*

Blood and 'ounds (*Irish*). Blood and *wounds* (Christ's)—an old pronunciation rhyming with 'pounds'; *e g*, 'Blood an' 'ounds — how the blood runs out uv 'un thin' This phrase is a good example of the anglicization of words whose original meanings are from various causes lost Probably most of the Catholic adjurations have been applied in the same such manner as this.

Blood Ball (*London Tr*). The butchers' annual hopser, a very lusty and fierce-eyed function. The female contingent never wear crimson—as being too trady. (*See* Bung Ball)

Blood Hole (*E London*, 1880). A theatre in Poplar.

The irreverent ones of the district, whenever they mentioned the place, called it 'The Blood Hole'—in allusion, I presume, to the style of drama presented.—*Newsp Cutting.*

Blood or Beer (*Street*). A challenge to fight or stand, *i e*, 'pay for' malt refreshment. A jocular phrase bordering on bullying. Real fighting is inducted by the phrase 'Take off your coat'! This is serious. 'Come on, ruffian It's blood or beer'—is simply friendly suggestion

Bloods (*Lowest Classes*) Wall-flowers, from a not too clear association of colours. A higher figure of speech than Bugs (*q.v.*), but still painfully disgusting in association with this fresh-breathed blossom. 'Bloods, bloods—penny a bunch, bloods.'

Bloods (*Navy*). Sailor boys' title for 'Penny Dreadfuls'.

They expect lots of blood, wonderful adventures, gruesome illustrations and a good deal of cheap sentiment', and they get it. As they get older, their tastes change. — Rev. G. Goodenough, Navy Chaplain.

Blood-worms (*London*, 19 *cent*). Sausages in general, but a black-pudding of boiled hog's blood in particular. 'S'elp me sivvy, I've come down to blood-worms' (*See* Sharp's Alley)

Bloody carpet rags (*Amer.*, imported to Liverpool) A mutilated man.

All of a sudden the burly coloured man drew a razor from his pocket and started for the light-weight with the remark that he'd make bloody carpet rags of him —*Newsp Cutting.*

It should be added that the razor is the American negro's favourite weapon, carried as a rule in a high boot — something after the manner of a Scotch dirk in a Scotch sark.

Blooming Emag (*Street*, 1870). Back spelling: 'Emag' is 'game'. Selfishness in its perfect degree.

There nothing like cheek, yobs, whatever you're blooming emag may be. But be honest, even if you have to go out nailing to be honest.—*Cutting.*

Bloomeration (*London*, 1891). Illumination. First heard 9th November at Prince of Wales' illuminations.

Blooming little holiday (*Lowest Peoples'*). Saturnalia — liberty to be free, to be perfectly tyrannical.

An English defeat and panic, on English soil, would seem to the English rough the very beginning of the millennium, or, in his own language, 'a blooming little holiday.'—*Newsp. Cutting*, 1879.

Blouser (*obscure*). To cover up, to hide, to render nugatory, *e.g.*, 'Joe—you won't blouser me!" From the French, evidently. Probably used in an anti-Gallican spirit, when the blouse first appeared to cover over an honest Englishman's waistcoat; or it may be from the court of Charles II.

The Army is warned that the clergy will try to 'blouser' or mislead them, and to persuade people to refuse the use of halls, while all the time professing interest in the Army's holy labours.—*Newsp. Cutting* (about 1881).

Blow (*Peoples'*). To boast—from the noise made when a whale blows water through and up from the nostrils, with much noise. Introduced by sailors in the whale trade, common to England and America, and still surviving amongst the lower classes. A good example of a word arising from a new industry and passing away with it.

About the veracity of big game shooters, one is sometimes obliged to feel now and then a lingering doubt. They might remind an Australian reader of 'him who tried to blow', in a well-known line of a modern poet. 'Blow', it may be necessary to explain, is the Australian equivalent for 'brag' or 'boast'. Thus Othello 'blew' in the account of his adventures with which he obliged Desdemona.—*D. N.*, 25th February 1885.

'Blow' and 'blow upon' are sometimes still used in their old form, in the sense of to expose or betray.

All he asks is to pass him along his plate with whatever happens to be handy round the pantry, and he won't go away and blow how poor the steak is. He just eats whatever is set before him, and asks no questions.—*Cutting.*

Blow me tight (*Peoples'*). Below me with a firm hand—that is, sent to Hades. Used generally as a protest on the part of the speaker, and an assurance of truth. Generally followed by 'if', and sometimes 'but'. He means that he is willing to be damned if he lies.

It was reckoned out we'd get to Brighton at six o'clock last Saturday, blow me tight.—*Cutting.*

Blow-out (*Peoples'*). Dissipation—literally stretching the digestive apparatus.

At the end of a month a miner finds himself in possession of from £25 to £30, and, as a corollary, has what he calls 'a blow-out'.—*Newsp. Cutting*, 1883.

Blowing (*Thieves'*). 'A pick-pocket's trull', quotes Byron in a note to the line 'Who on a lark with black-eyed Sal (his blowing)' (*Don Juan*, ca. xi. st. 19). Sometimes 'blowen'.

Blowsa-bella (*Theat.* 18 *cent.*). A vulgar, self-assertative woman, generally stout. Blowsa is probably from the French 'blouser', a verb got from 'blouse', meaning to attract by gutter arguments. Bella is of course an abbreviation of Isabella, and the whole phrase probably would mean a vulgar woman of the people giving herself false airs of grandeur. *The Daily News* (22nd Feb. 1883) throws perhaps some light on the word in reference to the Salvation Army.

Bluchers (*Mid. Class*; 1815 on). Plural of blucher, referring to the commonest of boots. From General von Blücher, the Prussian general-in-chief at the battle of Waterloo. When some clever *bootmaker* invented the now extinct Wellington boots, a humble imitator followed with the handy Blucher, and made quite a large fortune out of this idea—and the boots—the most frequent name for workmen's boots known to Britons, who have found this manufacture a handy weapon. (*See* Wellingtons.)

Blue (*Old English*). Dismal—evidently from the appearance of the countenance when showing anxiety or mistrust—as distinct from red anger. In this sense it is used in U.S.A. to this day, *e.g.*, 'This news will make our return to Yonkers rather blue', *i e*, melancholy. It will be found temp George III in a ballad, published in Dublin by Trojanus Laocoon, called *The All-devouring Monster*; *or New Five per C—t*, a satirical work which attacked a project, dating from England, of course, to put a duty of 5 per cent upon all imports. Here is a triplet from the ballad in question

The effects of the Tax will soon make us look Blue,
Its nature, its drift being known but to few,
Reverse of the Glass Act—this all men saw through.

In England, 19th century, 'blue' has been abandoned as describing melancholy, owing to its new meaning—one of vulgar, coarse, *double entendre*; *e g.*, 'Have you got any new blue?' may be asked by one who is athirst for erotic entertainment. Perhaps comes in some obscure way from the French, where a bluette certainly means a short song, which skirts the wind of impropriety The earlier meaning of blue is however still sometimes applied.

And yet, though things are all so blue, it's funny,
My missus never lets me *blue* the money.
—*Elephant and Castle pantomime*, 1882.

Blue Blanket (*Peoples'*, 19 *cent*) The sky. 'I slept under the blue blanket last night. (*See* Bengal Blanket)

Blue Caps (*Indian Mutiny*, 1857). Dublin Fusiliers

The Dublin Fusiliers are 'The Blue Caps' A despatch of Nana Sahib was intercepted, in which he referred to 'those blue-capped English soldiers who fight like devils'. The name stuck At the Siege of Lucknow the bridge of Char Bagh was raked by four guns and defended on the flanks by four others. 'Who is to carry it?' asked Outram. 'My Blue Caps', replied Havelock, and they did —Rev. E J Hardy.

Blue Damn Evasive swearing Celestial curse—the blue referring to the sacred purple blood of the Crucified.

Blue Funk (*Pub Sch.*). Absolute panic—from the leaden colour of the skin when the owner is beyond question afraid.

Of Mr Weedon Grossmith's assumption it may be further said that it is calculated to develop his most approved strain of humour, which in schoolboy parlance is known as blue funk —*People*, 28th February 1897.

He will, no doubt, tell people at home that he left the Soudan because he was invalided. That is not the case He left us because he was in a blue funk —*D. T*, 6th July 1897.

Blue Grass (*Amer.*) People of Kentucky—from the peculiar tint of the grass.

The Kentucky correspondent of the *Cincinnati News-Journal* is evidently hard hit This is what he writes: When the Bona Dea, out of her bounteousness, makes a Bluegrass woman, she takes care never to spoil the job A soft, white, warm body, translucent with divine light, and curving to lines of beauty as naturally as the tendrils of a vine, is the groundwork upon which nature limits the human angel . . The brow of Juno and the bust of Hebe, the sea-nymph's pearly ear, the wood-nymph's springy step—these are a few of the charms nature gives the maiden of the Bluegrass —*Newsp Cutting*

Even accepted as the title of a paper.

Blasphemous Libel.—Louisville (Ky), 21st April —Mr C E. Moore, Editor of a newspaper, published here, known as *The Blue Grass Blade*, and who has been in prison for the last fortnight —*Newsp. Cutting*

Blue Grass Belle. A Kentuckian beauty

While down in Kentucky last Fall, buying horses, he tipped a wink at a blue grass belle —*Newsp Cutting*

Blue-handled Rake The railing and steps leading to the platform of a fair-booth stage

Blue Hen's Chick (*Devonshire*). A clever soul, *e.g*, 'You're a blue hen's chick hatched behind the door'—said satirically

Blue Jack (*Nautical*) Cholera morbus—from the colour of the skin in this disease. (*See* Yellow Jack)

Blue-jacket (*Peoples'*, 19 *cent*) A sailor—given from the colour of jacket (*See* Lobster, Robin Redbreast)

Blue Moon (*General, in all classes*). Absolutely lost in mystery, but probably an Anglicism of a word or words with which neither 'blue' nor 'moon' has anything to do It imports indefinite futurity. Possibly meaning 'never', because a blue moon is never seen.

'I ain't a going to make a speech', said he, in a voice husky with emotion, 'because if I was to jaw till a blue moon I couldn't tell you more about her we've been and buried than you know already.' —'Cadgers in Mourning', *D. T.*, 8th February 1883.

Blue Noses (*American*). Canadians —obviously from the force of sharp weather on the Canadian nose. Probably contemptuous.

In Nova Scotia, has died a centenarian who had fought under Nelson and under Wellington. Did a grateful people follow the hero to the grave with proud tears? Not much. John Aberton was buried in a rough box on the day he died. There were no prayers, no funeral procession, no formalities, but the old patriot received the burial of a dog. This ought to make recruiting brisk in Canada and incite the blue noses to volunteer in a mass to defend Queen Victoria's codfish.—*N. Y. Mercury*, 1st January 1895.

Blue o'clock in the morning (*Street*). Pre-dawn, when black sky gives way to purple. Rhyming fancy, suggested by two o'clock in the morn. Suggestive of rollicking late hours.

The birdcatcher has often to be up 'at blue o'clock in the morning'. The rime is on the grass when he lays his nets. It is bitterly cold standing about in the fields.—*D. N.*, 12th October 1886.

Blue Pencil (To) (*Theat.*, 1885 on). Cutting down literature—first applied to dramatic pieces. From the colour of the pencil used. 'More blue pencil', said Mr Tree—it is the only way of writing a successful piece.

The actor will have a better chance after the blue pencil has eliminated the unnecessary verbiage in the dialogue.—*D. N.*, 17th February 1899.

Blue Pig (*Maine*, U.S.A.). Whisky. Maine is a temperance state, therefore liquor has to be asked for under various strange names, which have generally been satirically distinguished by a strange contradiction in their component parts, as in this instance. The phrase common in Liverpool.

There have been remarkable animals discovered in Maine before now—to wit, striped and blue pigs and Japanese dogs of scarlet hue. These creatures, however, have usually been found to be of the genus stalking-horse — that is, they merely served as screens for the sale of prohibited intoxicating fluids.—*D. N.*

Blue Ribbonite (*M. Class*, 1880). A sort of pun between 'nite' and 'knight', and one which gave the phrase rapid popularity. Outcome of the custom of wearing a blue ribbon on left breast of coat to demonstrate that the wearer was an abstainer.

With respect to the inconsistencies in the man who married Miss Dash drinking champagne and port, it should be remembered that he had not taken the pledge, and that he was concealing his identity. Besides, he said before the wedding breakfast that he was almost a blue-ribbonite—Brighton Bigamy Case, 20th and 24th October 1885.

Blue Ribbon Fakers (*London*, 1882). The progress of abstinence principles, practically started by Father Mathews (1815-71), is very interesting. The original abstainers made no daily public parade of their principles, and were not forbidden to associate with men who drank fermented liquors, or to have 'drinks' in the house, or to pay for drinks. Then followed the Good Templars (1860), who prohibited their followers from paying for others' alcoholic drinks, from having liquor in the house, or entering a tavern, even to buy a biscuit, but they showed no visible signs of their temperance. Then came the Blue Ribbon Army who (1882) instituted the daily assertion of their principles by wearing a scrap of bright blue ribbon in the left breast buttonhole of the coat. Street satirists dubbed them Blue Ribbon fakers.

The Blue Ribbon fakers may say what they fair like, but there are times when good brandy is new life—ask the squirts. About 1896 these blue ribbons became in some degree unpopular with abstainers, and were discarded. But so far no abstinence supporters had tabooed tobacco. It remained for the Salvation Army to add to all the abstinence principles hitherto adopted that of the rejection of tobacco in all its forms. As they operated chiefly amongst youths, their success as anti-tobacconalians was considerable. So far moderation or abstinence in relation to animal food has not yet been advanced—but it must follow in due course.

Blue Roses (*Literary*). Unattainable — sometimes blue dahlias, or tortoise-shell Tom cat, equal to squaring the circle Blue roses is the most poetical of these phrases.

The blue cloud of a fame beyond Doré's reach floated ever before him; he was eternally allured by the blue roses of an impossible success.—*D. N.*, 25th June 1885.

Blue 'un (*Sporting*) A journal named *Winning Post*—so named from its tint, no doubt given to enter the ranks with the 'Pink 'un' and 'Brown 'un' (*see*)—all three fine examples of language produced by the habitually obvious, and of the tendency to shorten frequent phrases Technically, blue 'un is a learned woman.

The application of the term to women, originated with Miss Hannah Moore's admirable description of a 'Blue Stocking Club' in her 'Bas Bleu'—*Mill*

Bluchers (*London*). Outsider cabs, not allowed, except upon emergency, to enter railway termini—probably in contradistinction to Wellingtons, just as the Wellington boot was the aristocratic foot-covering—the Blucher that of the general. The Blucher boot survives, the Wellington is a fossil.

It appears that when there is a deficiency of cabs at any station, outside or non-registered vehicles are called in on payment of a penny for the right of taking stand in the yard With a nice regard for history, the drivers of these 'understudy' cabs are, in the vernacular of the fraternity, dubbed 'Bluchers'—*D T*, 'Cab Strike', 23rd May 1894

Bluff (*Californian*, 1849 on) To humbug, hector, bully, from an American card-game wherein the player sheerly seeks to domineer over his opponent, and gain by sheer audacity, without absolute reference to the cards he (the bluffer) holds. Probably from 'bluff', Californian for cliff, the word suggesting tall boasting

'I bluffed 'im for a hour, but 'e wouldn't 'ave it at not no price Mr Newton, the magistrate at Marlborough Street observed. This is a case of bluff—Sir George Lewis If you have made up your mind, I will retire from the case—Mr Newton Can you contradict the constables?—*People*, 3rd October 1895

Tom Gossage afforded in his own character and habits an amusing example of how a man could get imbued with the peculiar vice of the time—and that was the game of brag—brag and the hard old vices of its kindred—bluff and poker—*Newsp. Cutting*

Bluffer (*Californian*, 1849 on) The noun followed the verb very rapidly.

The stranger went away and returned with the bluffer.—*Newsp Cutting*

Bobby (*Scottish*) A faithful person—abbreviation of Greyfriars Bobby, who has become a household word in the Canongate, Edinburgh. He was a devoted little terrier who kept watch and ward for a dozen years over the grave of his unknown master, buried in the strangers' corner of Greyfriars Cemetery, Edinburgh. Lady, then Miss Burdett Coutts, was so touched by this fidelity that she erected a little monument to his memory 'Hey, mon, nae mair thanks, or maybe ye'll be getting the name o' Bobbie'.

Bobby Atkins *See* Tommy Atkins.

Bobby's Labourers (*Volunteers*, 1868) Name given to special constables, chiefly volunteers, during this year—one of Fenian alarm—upon the principle that the s.c's did the work of the policemen—that is 'bobby'.

Bob, Harry and Dick (*Rhyming*, 1868) Sick—disguised way of admitting a crushed condition, the morn following a heavy drink (*See* Micky)

Bobolink (*American*) A talkative person, from being like a bird of this name. Abbreviation of Bob o' Lincoln

This is the way somebody translates the bobolink's libretto: 'Chink a link, chink a link, tink tink, tinkle tootle, Tom Denny, Tom Denny, come pay me, with your chink a link, tinkle linkle, toodle loodle, popsidoodle, see, see, see!' making not the slightest pause from beginning to end

Bobs (*Soc*, *passing to People*, 1900). Plural of Bob, exactly as Roberts is the plural of Robert—hence the genesis of the familiar name for General Roberts Bobs was much applied in this year, especially to smart Irish terriers B.P (passing to Bups), was also in great vogue—of course the initials of General Baden Powell. This pluralising of nicknames had been growing for years

Mr Ernest Wells, one of the founders and managers of the Pelican Club, and familiarly known in sporting, dramatic, and literary circles by his journalistic pseudonym of 'Swears', has, etc.—*D. T.*, 25th July 1900

Tales, old Chestnuts, Hairs, Pots,

Pumps, were some of the plural nicknames in use about this period.

If a limber's slipped a trace,
'Ook on Bobs;
If a marker's lost 'is place,
Dress by Bobs;
For 'e's eyes all up 'is coat,
An' a bugle in 'is throat,
An' you will not play the goat,
Under Bobs.
—*Rudyard Kipling.*

Bobtail (*Peoples'*). Name given early in the 19th century to the dandies who wore the pointed tail-coats which followed the wide skirts of the 18th century, tails which must have been very striking. Name still given to a waiter by common classes. (*See* Claw-hammer.)

Bobtail (*Irish*). Appealing to the masses, to the passing penny. Irish, and probably dating from the introduction of the swallow-tail coat from England—doubtless despised at first, but still retained by the peasantry.

Boucicault said 'I introduced *The Poor of Liverpool*—a bobtail piece—with local scenery and Mr Cowper in the principal part (Badger). I share after £30 a night, and I am making £100 a week on the damned thing. I localise it for each town, and hit the public between the eyes; so they see nothing but fire. I can spin out these rough-and-tumble dramas as easily as a hen lays eggs. It's a degrading occupation, but more money has been made out of guano than out of poetry.'

Body Lining (*Drapers'*). Bread—very opposite, lining in this trade being what goes inside the bodice (or body) of a dress. 'Pass me half a yard of body-lining.' Body-lining itself is a strong twill.

Body Snatcher (*Street, London*, 1840-1860). A cabman—from the habit, before higher civilization amongst cabmen prevailed, of snatching their victim-patrons. Suggested by that other body-snatcher—the resurrection-man, who was but a memory in 1840.

Bohemian Bungery (*Strand District*). Public-house patronized by struggling authors. Bohemian having been introduced by Murger for a fighting author, artist, or musician, and the tea-pot brigade having dubbed a licensed victualler a bung, from that adjunct to the beer barrel—this phrase became one of the results of time. The Nell Gwynne was once a Bohemian Bungery.

Bohemian down to his boots (*Art and Lit.*). Bohemian in excelsis. 'He is a . . .—such as they are'—that is 'the boots'.

At that time a young man, Nelson Kneass, a scion of an old and proud family, was horrifying 'society' by going round blacking his face as a negro minstrel. He was a brother of District Attorney Kneass, of this city, was highly educated, but was a 'Bohemian down to his boots'.—*N. Y. Mercury*, 15th January 1888.

Boiled Owl (*People's*). Drunk—as a boiled owl. Here there is no common sense whatever, nor fun, wit, nor anything but absurdity. Probably another instance of a proper name being changed to a common or even uncommon word. May be drunk as Abel Doyle—which would suggest an Irish origin like many incomprehensible proverbs too completely Anglicised.

It is a well-known fact in natural history that a parrot is the only bird which can sing after partaking of wines, spirits, or beer; for it is now universally agreed by all scientific men who have investigated the subject that the expression, 'Drunk as a boiled owl' is a gross libel upon a highly respectable teetotal bird which, even in its unboiled state, drinks nothing stronger than rain-water. —*D. T.*, 12th December 1892.

Also whitish, washed-out countenance, with staring sleepy eyes.

Both were admirably made up, and Twiss had just the boiled-owlish appearance that is gained by working all night in a printing-office.—*Ref.*, 31st May 1885.

(*See* Dead as O'Donnel, Smithereens.)

Boiled Shirt (*Middle Class*). Clean, white—from the fact that if the shirt is not boiled it remains dull grey. W. America, but common in England.

'Waal now, say, you with the boiled shirt. What did Miss Maslam reply when you put the question?'—*Newsp. Cutting*, 1897.

Boko (*Common*). A huge nose. Corruption of 'beaucoup', the 'o' being national and preferred to the French 'ou'. Said to be descended from the time of Grimaldi, who would observe while 'joey-ing' (*q.v.*) 'C'est beaucoup', and tapping his nose. The phrase still remains, Anglicised, for a rough observing to another rough of a third gentleman's nose, will make the statement, 'I say—boko!' When one Espinosa, a French dancer, came to London (1858), the size of his wonderful nose drew so much gallery observation of 'boko' that Mr J. Oxenford, in the *Times*, especially referred to the organ and assumed it was art. Thereupon, Espinosa wrote explaining that the nose in question was *un don de la nature*.

He was as thin and pale as a coffee palace bit of roast beef, and his boko was as high and red as the sun on a foggy morning.

If he thought he had a black spot on his boko he'd go into convulsions.

Boko-smasher (*Street*) For elucidation of this elegant occupation *see* Boko.

Bolt-upright (*Peoples'*) A good example of graphic application From the rigidity of a bolt, *e.g.*, 'he was bolt-upright, mum—and were so all the time, as 'is dear father was a-thrashin' of him.'

Bolted to the Bran (*Polit*) Thoroughly sifted—one of the few puns or jocular phrases of which Gladstone could ever be accused.

Now the great questions are initiated, discussed, sifted, 'bolted to the bran', to use an expression more than once adopted by Mr Gladstone, before they come formally under the notice of the House of Commons —*D N.*, 12th August 1885

Bombast (*Hist.*). Windy words—from Bumbast—the word, with a *double entendre* used for the material for stuffing out trunk hose, 16th and 17th centuries.

When I came to unrip and unbumbast this Gargantuan bag-pudding, I found nothing in it but dog's tripes —*Gabriel Harvey*.

I. Disraeli says '*Bombast* was the tailors' term in the Elizabethan era for the stuffing of horse-hair or wool used for the large breeches then in fashion—hence the term was applied to high-sounding phrases "all sound and fury, signifying nothing".'

Bone (*London*, 1882). A thin man Hence—'The bone has made a remark.' (Surrey Pantomime, London, 1882)

Bone-clother (*Medical*). Port wine—which is popularly supposed to induce muscle

Bone Idle (*Scottish*) Could not be more so Probably the one atom of slang, if this can be called slang, which Carlyle exercised; may be found in a letter to his mother (15th Feb 1847) 'I have gone *bone idle* these four weeks and more, and have been well done to every way.'

Bone-shaker (*Youths*, 1870 on) The earliest bicycle—which tried to break bones incessantly.

Bone-shop (*Lower Classes*). Workhouse—another of the more figurative and satirical names for this establishment Here it refers presumably and untruly to the nature of the nourishment as producing nothing visible over the pauper bones.

'Two of 'em lives in the blooming bone-shop and the other little devil is in the small-pox hospital'

Boner Nochy (*Clerkenwell*, Italian quarter) Good-night—imitated by the Clerkenwellians, from the *bona notte* of the Italians in Eyre Street Hill, Little Bath Street, and Hatton Garden; or it may be from the Spanish 'noche'—through the U S A

'In any case', said Don Miguel, rising and preparing to retire for the night, 'in any case, can you wonder that I hate the Argentine, and everything connected with it? Buenas noches, senor!'—*Ev. News*, 9th December 1898

Bonner (*Oxford 'er'*). Bonfire. This specimen of 'er' shows a spice of satirical wit, for it is suggestive of Bishop Bonner, who certainly lit up many bonfires—Smithfield way.

Bonnet (*Lower Class*). To smash another's hat over the eyes. From French (*bonnet-a-cap*), and time Charles II Bonnet passed into hat, but 'to bonnet' went sliding down until now it is in the gutter (*See* Cloak, In his sleeve, Shawl)

Bonny Robby (*Provincial*). Pretty but frail girl, probably from 'buona roba'—common in the time and court of Charles II.

DRUG. There visits me a rich young widow? FACE. A bona roba?—Garrick's *Abel Drugger*.

Bono Johnny (*Pigeon Chinese*). A good fellow. A Chinese invention; used by English sailors as warrant of good intentions

Bonse (*School*). Head. 'Look out, or I'll fetch you a whack across the bonse'.

Boo; Boo-ers (*Theatrical*, 1900). First-night gallery critics who replaced the goose (hissing) by 'booing'—probably because it was easier and more secretive.

Who would have thought, when an ill-mannered gallery 'booed' Mr Kerker's sparkling entertainment more than twelve months ago that it would achieve an unparalleled success at the Shaftesbury?—*D. T.*, 9th May 1899.

(*See* Wreckers.)

Boobies' Hutch (*Military*, 19 *cent.*). A drinking point in barracks, which, under certain circumstances, is open after canteen is closed. Satire probably upon the fools who have never had enough.

Boodle (*Liverpool*). One of the New York terms for money. Probably from the Dutch.

Hangman ain't such a bad fellow. He always treats the boys after he receives 'the boodle' from the Sheriff for sending an unfortunate to the other side; although some folks are really afraid to go near him, and wouldn't even pass his house, I'd just as leave drink with him as I would with you.—*N. Y. Mercury*, 3rd May 1885.

In vain did one of the American comic journals some time ago depict, with becoming scorn, a hoard of needy European nobles struggling for the possession of a demure American beauty who bears a bag of what is locally known as 'boodle', and in polite society as lucre, in her shapely arms. — *D. N.*, 15th September 1890.

Book-maker (*Racing*, 19 *cent.*). A professional betting man who makes a betting book upon every race, or about every race in a season. He lays against all horses. A bookmaker of position must make immense profits, under the two conditions of betting with men who can pay and with men who will accept all the conditions offered by the bookmaker. In fact, under these 'circs', he rarely loses, while the money he may make is almost limitless. Sometimes, however, when a favourite wins, the 'ring' (that is the mass of betting men), is hit heavily.

Bookie (*Sporting*, 1881). The endearing 'ie', common in Johnnie and chappie, adapted to bookmaker. The 'maker' dropped — the suffix added.

Booking (*Public School*). Anything but—for it is casting volumes from you as missiles at the enemy for the time being, *e.g.*, 'Jannery split—book him together!'

It would be a pity to deprive them of the chance of such 'glorious fun' as the 'mobbing' and 'booking' (that is pelting with books) of the model school tyrant. —*Newsp. Cutting.*

Boomerang (*American*, 1882). A vain folly, the consequence of which returns upon the perpetrator. This phrase is of course based upon the peculiar trajectory of the Australian boomerang, which, properly thrown, returns to the feet of the missile-thrower. In 1883 a play was produced by Mr Daly in New York, with the title '728—or Casting the Boomerang'. A New York dramatic critic in the course of an article upon this play, wrote:—'the various follies or boomerangs of the principal characters return in the course of the play to plague them'.

Boomlet (*City*, 1896). A small 'boom'. Satirical invention used to attack the prosperous enemy.

Without troubling you with details, I may mention that during the recent West Australian boom—or, as some of my Stock Exchange friends prefer to call it, 'boomlet'—we succeeded in realising, etc.—Mr H. Bottomley, 10th December 1897.

Boomster (*City*, 1898). One who booms.

Boost (*Liverpool - American*). A hoist, toss, elevation—from the mode of raising one in the world hurriedly, exercised by an angry bull or even cow.

The cowcumber kin be made an ornament, will stand in any climate, and the placques and chromos will encourage art and give a fresh boost to decoration.

Boot (*Tailors' and Bootmakers'*, 19 *cent.*). Money — one of the trade applications to describe money — just exactly as the grocer calls coin 'sugar' or the milkman 'cream'. 'We've had the boot for that job.' Probably an abbreviation of 'beautiful', this being an obviously likely, vulgar, poetical name for money. (*See*

Needful) Sometimes only a shilling 'Can I have the boot?'—asked for at the end of a day's work Indeed 'boot' in its most ordinary form is an advance on the weekly wages—but one never under a shilling. The lower advance, sixpence, is called a slipper. Also used in the tailoring trade A worker will say at closing time, 'Please, sir, could you oblige me with the boot', while a more retiring soul would ask—'Could I have a slipper, sir?'

Booth Star (*Minor Stage*) Leading actor or actress in a 'booth'. 'Let me tell you a booth star is a good thing You often get four parts a night It is great experience—and it is the first step to Drury Lane.'

Booze (*Low London*). Intoxicants of all kinds, but particularly beer. May be from a name, but probably is an onomatope of quite modern date, from the boozing noise made by drunkards when falling off to sleep Booze is drink in general—boozy, the result of drinking slowly and tandem, also to sleep.

At the hearing of the Southampton election petition, witness describing a procession of costermongers said. 'I heard some men shout that they wanted some more booze' Mr Justice Wright. 'What?' Mr Willis: 'Booze, my lord, drink'. Mr Justice Wright: 'Ah!'

Booze plausibly claims a sort of corrupt descent from the genuine, if low, English word to 'bouse,' which occurs in our literature as early as 1567.—*D T.*, 2nd December 1895.

Mr O'Donovan, the Eastern traveller, said to a press-interviewer (*World*, 31st January 1885), 'this word is Persian for "beer"' Was he indulging in one of his ordinary jokes? If not, then the coalescing of these words and meanings is a very remarkable etymological fact

Boozer (*Street*, 19 *cent*) The public-house, as well as the public-house frequenter

Big Tim goes with him, while I pops around the boozer —*People*, 6th January 1895

Booze-fencers (*Com Lon.*, 1880) Licensed victuallers — from 'booze' drink, and fencers sellers — probably a wilful corruption of 'dispensers'

You may run down booze fencers as much as you like, but you take my tip that there are more real gentlemen among them than among any other class, upper ten included —*Newsp. Cutting*

Booze-pushers (*Low London*, 19 *cent*) Variant of booze-fencer.

When a bloke is flatch kennurd the booze pushers will give him any rot in the house, and that's very hard lines —*Newsp. Cutting*.

Booze-shunters (*P. House*, 1870). Beer-drinkers

They have never robbed a man of a hard day's work, and are the best booze shunters in the world without ever getting slewed.

To 'shunt' in railway life is to move from place to place. The booze-shunter moves the beer, or 'booze,' from the pot into his visceral arrangements The term was started by the S W.R porters and guards, who use the larger public-houses in the neighbourhood of the terminus in the Waterloo Road (London).

Bo-peep (*Nursery*). Exclamation of fun. Johnson does not comprehensively elucidate this word when he gravely says it is from 'bo' and 'peep'. 'The art', he says, 'of looking out, and drawing back, as if frighted, or with the purpose to fright one another.' SHAKESPEARE, who has everything, has this phrase once—

'Then they for sudden joy did weep
And I for sorrow sung,
That such a king should play bo-peep
And go the fools among.'

DRYDEN has: 'There devil plays at bo-peep, puts out his horns, etc.'

Bor (*E Anglian*) May be a shortening of neighbour, but is probably a corruption of boy—politely applied even to the oldest male inhabitant.

Bore (*Soc*, 19 *cent*) Weary. From tunnelling operations — steady, deadly, incisive 'jaw'. One of the trade metaphors which has passed into society and still stops there Never has come down in the social scale. 'Lord Tom bores one to death with Tel-el-Kebir'

To bore in the hills, is it? Well—don't bore me about it. — MISS M. EDGEWORTH, *The Absentee* (1809)

Born Days (*Peoples'*). Intensifier. Days that are born in an individual life 'In all my born days I was never so insulted' Other authorities maintain it should be 'borne,' or burdened, days — while still more recondite etymologists maintain it is 'bourn' — from our progress daily to that bourn whence no traveller returns. Fine example of three different words with the same sound offering as many meanings. Almost as good or as bad as 'mala'.

Born a bit tired (*Soc.*, 1870 on). Sarcastic excuse for a chronically lazy man. 'You can't reasonably expect him to work a couple of hours per day—he was born a bit tired'.

According to Mr Alderman Taylor, of the London County Council, there exists the man who is 'born a bit tired'.—*D. T.*, 13th February 1897.

Born with a sneer (*Literary*, 1850 on). Said of an implacable critic, attributed to Douglas Jerrold, who was good at sneering himself.

'Lord X would laugh at the Holy Sepulchre—he was, etc.'.

Light opera has familiarised the public with the man who was 'born with a sneer'.—*D. T.*, 13th February 1897.

Bosh (*Lower Official English*). A term applied by market inspectors to butterine, oleomargarine and other preparations practically too long-windedly named to please the official mind. Now extended to all adulterants or adulterated food. Mr O'Donovan declared this word to be Persian, and that it means 'empty'. Certainly the word used as an exclamation is replete with the idea of emptiness. (See *World*, 31st January 1883.)

Boss Time (*Anglo-Amer.*). Great pleasure, a supreme holiday; *e.g.*, 'Eve had a boss time last winter hunting deer up in Michigan.'

Now used in England.

Botany Beer Party (*Soc.*, 1882). A meeting where no intoxicants are drunk. In this year temperance, which had been growing in society for years, became drunk on affectation.

Botany Beer, it has recently been decided on judicial authority, is not beer at all.—G. A. Sala, in *Ill. Lond. News*, 10th March 1883.

Botherums (*Agricultural*). Yellow marigolds.

Among the turnips the yellow marigolds flourish mightily, so mightily that they are called locally 'botherums' by the farmers, for they are most difficult to get rid of.—*Newsp. Cutting.*

Bottle Nose (*Amer. Boys*). Scornful designation of the aged nose—an organ which so frequently derogates from the promise of youth. Applied without mercy to those no longer young. Heard in Liverpool. (*See* Bald-head, Scare-crow.)

Bottle up (*People's*). To refrain, restrain oneself; in another sense, to hem in the enemy, literally or figuratively.

The old story of Spanish lack of preparation was repeated; vessels were foul from long absence from dock, coal was deficient, ammunition ran short, and instead of commanding a fleet 'in being', Admiral Cervara was glad to bottle himself up in the harbour of Santiago.—*D. T.*, 17th June 1898.

Bottled (*People's*, 1898). Arrested, stopped, glued in one place—re-introduced during the American-Spanish war, immediately after the U.S.A. squadron had bottled the Spanish fleet in Santiago by closing the narrow opening to the harbour of that city; *e.g.*, 'My wife's come to town—I'm bottled. Next week, Jane.'

Bottle o' Spruce (*Peoples'*, 18 *cent.*). Zero, nothing, abbreviation of Bottle of Spruce Beer, which was cheap, commonplace, almost valueless; *e.g.*, 'Of course, you say I don't care a bottle of spruce.'

It also implies twopence; this sum, early in the 19th century being the price of a bottle of spruce beer. A man now seeking twopence asks for the price of a pint. His grandfather would have asked for a bottle of spruce.

Boughten or Bought (*Provincial*). Adjective of disparagement. Bought as distinct from superior home-made goods. No longer heard. Very pleasant, as illustrating a time when every country-house, large and small, had its spinsters, weavers, stocking-knitters, and straw-plaiters. This word is the more interesting from a modern instance in Ireland, where vanned bread that is carted from the baker's is a term of disparagement as compared with home-made bread.

Bouguereau quality (*Art*, 1884). Riskily effeminate. From the name of the great French painter, whose style is almost unwholesomely refined. The word has become cruelly perverted by its translation into common-place art chat. Now very extensively used The Bouguereau quality is not only applied to figure painting and to sculpture, but reaches landscape and portrait painting, decoration, and even literature The Bouguereau quality in letters is now very marked, and refers to work by both sexes. It is also applied to manners, speech, and even dress—remarkable example of rapid growth of a word.

The exhibition includes several notable works by famous painters M Bouguereau's group called 'Spring' is alone worth seeing, being a very refined example of his exquisite painting of the nude —*D N*, 19th July 1886.

Boulevard-journalist (*Fr.*, 1856). Immediately after Louis Napoleon seized upon the throne of France, a number of contentious little journals appeared, mostly of a personal and scandalous character, for politics had been practically slain The serious journals styled these new issues 'journaux des boulevards', their writers 'Les journalistes boulevardiers'. These literary gnats especially attacked England, as a rule, hence the English press willingly Anglicised the term to describe an unscrupulous writer until 'Society journalist' was discovered and accepted

Boulevardier (*Franco-Eng.*, 1854-70). Paris man about town of third-rate position, accepted in England, *e g.*, 'He is only a boulevardier'

Bounced (*Amer.*, 1880). Ignominiously ejected. Derivation speaks fatally for itself.

While he did not feel greatly injured by being bounced from a club which numbered only seven lame old men and two dogs, he wanted to feel that justice was on his side, and he therefore appealed to the Lime-Kiln Club for its decision.—*Newsp Cutting*

Quite accepted in England.

Bounced muchly (*Amer. Tavern*). To be expelled with exceeding vigour Bounced is a modern discovery, but the adverb 'muchly' is due to the wild philology of the mirth-provoking Artemus Ward

Bouncer (*P House*, '80's) Expeller of noisy or even mildly drunken customers (*See* 'Chucker out'.)

The 'bouncer' of the House of Commons, going into the gallery, tried to find the guilty individual.—*Newsp. Cutting.*

Every one who mixes much in society in Whitechapel will understand the functions of the bouncer When tavern liberty verges on licence, and gaiety on wanton delirium, the bouncer selects the gayest of the gay and—bounces him. To 'bounce' is simply to prevail on persons whose mirth interferes with the general enjoyment to withdraw from society which they embarrass rather than adorn. The bouncer almost invariably uses gentle means and moral persuasion. He bounces the erring 'as if he loved them'. His reputation for strength and science are so great that no one cares to resist the bouncer, and the boldest hold their breath and let themselves be bounced without a murmur. (*See* 'Chucker out'.) —*D N*, 26th July 1883.

Bouncing (*Peoples'*). Big, rotund —probably from bonse—a huge round marble.

Moreover, he has females in his employ who have been with him ten years, and many of them are the healthy mothers of bouncing boys and girls. I'm not quite sure under what circumstances children bounce, but I believe the expression is applied to strapping infants, though, again, I do not know under what circumstances children strap —G. R. Sims, *Ref*, 28th December 1884.

Bound to Shine (*Amer*) Praise The antithesis of 'clouded over' (*q v*)

Bournemouth (*Theatr.*, 1882-83). The deported Gaiety Theatre (London) —said satirically The house was very icy that winter, and produced colds, while Bournemouth is the sanatorium for weak-chested invalids.

We don't care about Bournemouth—our pleasant name for the Gaiety, as everybody there is dying of coughs and colds.—*Sporting Times*, 3rd February 1883

Bowl for Timber (*Cricketers'*) To send the ball at the martyr-player's legs—the timber. Discountenanced in later years—rather as waste of time than with any view of repression of personal injury 'Try for timber—he's quivery'—that is to say, nervous

Bowl (*Thieves'*, 19 *cent.*) Discovery —from 'bowl out'—a cricketing term. Good as illustrating how a national pastime always provides new language.

Grizard went with them, and said he wanted them to look sharp and get to Covent Garden before the market was open, in case it came to a 'bowl' This was at four in the morning. The Alderman. What is a 'bowl'? Witness. I understand it to be a find-out.

Bowler (*Middle Class*). Hard, dome-shaped, man's felt hat. This hat ('80) took the place of the deer-stalker, which was the first modern felt hat produced in London. The bowler was a make of a smaller kind altogether. Origin not known—but probably from the name of the manufacturer. Has quite passed into the language.

All the description that the railway officials can give of the man is that he appeared well dressed, and wore a dark overcoat, closely buttoned, and a bowler hat.—*D. T.*, 15th February 1897.

Bow-wow-mutton (*Naval*). So bad that it might be dog-flesh.

Boxing out (*Austral. from Amer.*). Boxing outing—or bout.

Boy (*Bolton*). Man. There are no men in Bolton—all are boys, even at ninety. This quality they share alone, throughout England, with post-boys—who never grow up.

Boy Jones, The (about 1840). Secret informant. A chimney boy-sweep of this name tumbled out of a chimney at Buckingham Palace, or was found there under a bed, and was supposed to have heard State secrets as between the Queen and the then Prince Albert. Event supposed to have accelerated chimney-sweeping by machinery. For years 'the boy Jones' was suggestive of secrecy. 'The person who told me, my son, was the boy Jones.' (*See* 'Jinks the Barber', 'Postman's Sister'.)

Boyno! (*Nautical*—from Lingua Franca, or S. American). Friendly valediction; sometimes been used at meeting as 'Hullo!' 'Boyno—how is it?'

At parting, 'Well—so long! Boyno!' From the Spanish 'bueno', equivalent of 'God speed you.'

'Bueno, senoretta!' said the dwarf, and walked away with the superintendent.

Brace up (*Thieves'*). Pawn stolen property. Corruption perhaps from Fr. 'Braser', to fabricate—at length; 'braser des faffes'—to fabricate false papers. May have been introduced by French criminals.

Bracelets (*Thieves'*). Humorous title for hand-cuffs; in itself a satirical description.

Brads (*North Country*). One of the trade names for money—in this case halfpence. The word comes from the boot-making trade, and is still in use in the north. Brads are small nails.

'Hey, lass, thee shalt hev' thy tay-tray when t' brads coom along.'

Bradshaw (*Middle Class*). Precise person, great at figures. From 'Bradshaw's Railway Guide'; *e.g.*, 'Quite a Bradshaw—my dear.'

Brag (*Soc.*, 1800-30). A game of cards in which the players tried to give the idea that they held better cards than they did. Hence the phrase, 'Don't brag by the card.'

Speculation does not greatly surprise me, I believe, because I feel the same myself; but it mortifies me deeply because speculation was under my patronage; and, after all, what is there so delightful in a pair royal of Braggers? It is but three nines or three knaves, or a mixture of them.—Jane Austen's *Letters*, 1809.

Bran New (*Peoples'*). A corruption of brand new, that which is branded with the name of the maker. Probably from Sheffield.

Brandy and Fashoda (*Soc.*, October 1898). Brandy and soda, of course. Good example of droll pleonasm. From the discovery of the French captain, Marchand, at Fashoda, almost immediately after the conquest of the dervishes at Omdurman (1898). (*See* S. and B.)

Brandy-shunter (*L. Class*). He that swalloweth frequent eau-de-vie.

Thomas Spencer Carlton, the eminent brandy-shunter, was born about thirty-five years ago of wealthy yet honest parents.—*Newsp. Cutting.*

Brass (*Metallic England*). Money. The commonest term for cash all over England, and almost the only one used in the copper and iron industries.

The prisoner and another man stopped the prosecutor, and explained that it was 'money to buy beer' that they wanted. 'Haven't any' said he. 'Yes, you have' shouted Quain; 'and we've got to have some of it. Now, then, brass up, or we'll shove you through it.'—*Newsp. Cutting.*

Brass-knocker (*Cadgers'*). Broken victuals. This may be a corruption from the Romany, but it is now suggestive of a house whose superior respectability warrants the absence of complete economy and the presence of pieces.

Brayvo Hicks (*Theat.*, 1830). A peculiar form of applause only used in approbation of muscular demonstration on the lower stage — especially broadsword exercise. Derived from Hicks, a celebrated favourite actor for many years, more especially 'upon the Surrey side' After he passed away the applausive phrase first applied to him was inherited for many years by his natural successors. It may still be heard in out-of-the-way little theatres Applied in S London widely, *e g*, 'Brayvo Hicks—into 'er again Mary — give 'er the gravil rash.'

Brayvo Rouse (*E. London*). Applause—approval. From the name of an enterprising proprietor of 'The Eagle', afterwards 'The Royal Grecian', a theatre situated in the City Road, now the Central London headquarters of the Salvation Army. This clever man was one of the first managers to give a long series of well-presented French light operas in English All the best of Auber's work was dressed in English by Rouse — who, it is to be feared, annexed without 'authorial' complications. Whenever he appeared it was always 'Brayvo Rouse'. Old players still show his house in the City Road 'Buck up — to it again — brayvo Rouse!'

Bread and Meat Man (*Military*). An officer of the Army Service Corps.

Bread-basket (*London Trade, 19 cent.*) Obvious invention of genius for stomach. Hence never extended to Ireland, where the equivalent is tater-sack, the mouth being tatur-trap.

Miss Selina Slops was invited before his Worship, on the charge of smearing the face of B O 44 with a flatiron, while hot, and also with jumping upon his bread-basket, while in the execution of his duty —*Cutting*.

Break (*L Class*) Ruin, overcome, expose, injure — justly or unjustly. Expression of victory—'I broke 'im —I broke 'im through and through!' In middle classes 'to break a man' is an abbreviation of break away from him—to cease to know him—to cut him. This word obtains ever-increasing significations.

Breakdown (*Negro-plantation*) A particular kind of dance, for one generally, where the steps are varied, but the performer does not move far from his place, coming from the old French settlements of America, probably a corruption of 'Rigodon' — Anglicised or rather Americanised

I have heard of burlesque actors dancing a 'breakdown', but the other day the *Echo*, on its broadsheet, announced, 'breakdown of an excursion train!'—*Entr'acte*, January 1883.

Breakers Ahead (*Nautical*). Necessarily, warning of coming danger.

'Melita' enjoyed a very short and inglorious career It started with 'breakers ahead' and ended with brokers on the spot, I believe —*Ref*, 14th January 1883.

Breaking Camp (*American backwoods*) To change one's camping place; figuratively, to leave it by way of death.

I could have braced up under it if my poor Mary had got sick and died at home with me holdin' of her hand and consolin' her as she was breakin' camp for the other world —*Newsp. Cutting*.

Breast the Tape (*Sporting*). Conquer, lead, overcome—from touching the tape with breast in running matches.

Leeds at the best of times does not rejoice in a very clear atmosphere; but when she wraps herself in a fog, she can give London a good start in the race for objectionableness and breast the tape an easy winner at the finish —*Ref*, 27th November 1887

Breath strong enough to carry coal (*Anglo-Amer*) Drunk

. comes home at three o'clock in the morning with a breath strong enough to carry the coal —*Newsp Cutting*

Brekker (*Oxford 'er'*) Breakfast —a great find in the 'er' dialect, but probably in origin dating from the nursery.

Bremerhaven Miscreant (*Amer polit*, 1883). At this place were made the clock-work dynamite torpedoes which ('80 - '83) alarmed European society

'Bremerhaven miscreant' These toys, in which a charge of dynamite is exploded by clockwork, are manufactured, it is commonly believed, by Mr Crowe, of Peoria. In a free country, of course, where there is a large Irish vote, a clever mechanic may make what he pleases, and we are far from expressing the futile hope that the Government of the United States will interfere with the industry of Mr Crowe and his followers But our nation, though averse to a policy of

Protection, might not unreasonably lay a heavy prohibitive duty on 'infernal machines'.—*D. N.*, March 1883.

Briar (*Peoples'*, 1870). A briar-root pipe. A modern invention, supposed to be of god-like comfort. 'Briar-root is sometimes used to describe a corrugated, badly-shaped nose.'

Brickfielder (*Australian*). Hot north wind, bringing with it a red impalpable dust from the interior. It penetrates even locks, and stains fabrics in drawers of a dull brick red—hence the graphic name. Generally comes after great heat in January, and portends a grateful change in the weather. 'What a brickfielder you are!'—meaning nuisance.

Bricky (*Peoples'*). Brave, fearless, adroit—after the manner of a brick; said even of the other sex, 'What a bricky girl she is.' (*See* 'Plucky', 'Cheeky'.)

Bridges-bridges (*Printers'*). A cry to arrest a long-winded story. Probably corruption of 'abregeons-abregeons'—in a deal Anglicized. (*See* 'Grasses', 'Chestnuts'.)

Bridges and no Grasses (*Printers'*). Secret. A bridge is an absentee without leave, who has not sent a substitute, or grass. When a combination is made to prevent a master from getting out his paper by the printers absenting themselves, this would be called Breaking the Bridge. The whole system belongs to a system of rattening, a system which is being swept away by the strides of education.

Bridgeting (*Amer.-Eng.*, 1866 on). Obtaining money under false pretences, or even by criminal process, from servant girls. This word has taken astounding journeys. It dates from Ireland, where so many female children are named after Saint Bridget that the name became as typical of the Irish serving-girl in New York as Pat (from St Patrick) is typical of the Irish working-man. From the fifties onward Bridget became synonymous in New York with domestic servant. In the sixties the Fenian leaders in New York discovered a new way of getting money by issuing notes of the Bank of the Republic of Ireland at 50 per cent. discount. Large sums were obtained through many years, and money is obtained even now from sentimental Irish servant women in New York—much of which has, it has been declared, aided the Irish Nationalist movement in the House of Commons. Term now applied in many directions.

Brief (*Peoples'*). Letter, or piece of paper with writing. Probably ancient. May be from the use by the First or Second George of this term for letter.

Brief (19 *cent.*). False reference. The system of false references has so increased that many masters do not ask for references, but accept the servant or clerk, discovering him to be honest or dishonest, as the peculiar disposition of the employer lies.

Brenner said, 'I've given the Jew boy another brief. I hope he'll pay me this time.' Alleged conspiracy to defraud Licensed Victuallers.—*Morning Advertiser*, 25th February 1892.

Brief (*Lawyers' Clerks'*). Pawnbroker's ticket, suggested perhaps by the shape. The synonyms for this signal of woe are countless, and the list is always growing.

'Ah, Sam, how are yer? 'ere, will you buy the brief of a good red 'un, in for a fifth its value?'—*Newsp. Cutting.*

This mystic enquiry refers to the duplicate (this paste-board being a simulacrum of a card firmly pinned to the pledge) of a pawned watch—a red 'un, a term which is probably the corruption of a proper name—say Redding. (*See* Tombstone.)

Brighton Bitter (*Public House*). Mild and bitter beer mixed—satirical reference to some Brighton ale-house keepers, who, knowing Sunday and Monday excursionists are only chance customers, never give these customers bitter beer, though they pay its price.

Brim (*Thieves'*). A fearless woman of the town. Origin evidently foreign—probably the French army, where a 'brimade' is equal to English military 'making hay', and introduced to London by way of Soho.

Bristols (*Soc.*, 1830 on). Visiting cards, from the date when these articles were printed upon Bristol—*i.e.*, cardboard; a superior Bristol make.

Inside Madame Bernhardt's house there is a register open for the signatures of callers, and the card basket shows a large collection of 'Bristols'.—*D. T.*, 17th February 1898.

Brit (*Theatr.*). An endearing diminutive conferred by its denizens on the Britannia Theatre; as, 'How do you get to the Brit?' 'Take a train east—one station this side of Jericho' (*See* Bird, Vic, Eff, 'Delphi, and Lane)

British Roarer (*Peoples'*) Our heraldic and symbolical lion

The tribunes are dressed in red cloth, and are guarded by four comic Byzantine lions, which act as symbols of our British roarer.—*D. N.*, May 1883.

Broad Faker (*Thieves'*) Card-player, probably not wholly dissociated from cheating Broad may simply refer to the width of the card, but it probably refers to the name of an early maker of cards—probably marked for cheating

Broad-gauge Lady (*Railway Officials', passing to Peoples'*). One who makes rather a tight fit for five on a side 'I know I'm a broad-gauge lady—but I can't help it, can I?' Herbert Campbell's 'gag', Drury Lane Panto. 1884-85. Passed away with the broad-gauge in the '90's

Brogue (*Irish*). Local lingual accent—from the name of the foot-covering worn by the peasants 'From the brogue to the boot' (gentleman) 'all speak the same of him, and can say no other' Maria Edgeworth, *The Absentee*, ch. 9.

Broken Brigade (*Soc*, 1880 on). Poor, younger sons living on their wits. 'Broken'—another form of 'stone-broke'

The younger son has been brought up in almost precisely the same fashion as his elder brother . . When, therefore, he finds himself without the legitimate means to live and enjoy life, as he has been trained to do, he must either find illegitimate means or else join that party which has earned for itself the unenviable name of the broken brigade. —*D N*, 26th September 1887

Brokered (*L. C*, 1897). A specimen of the daily making of language—here upon the pre-historic basis of the noun creating the verb How much more concise than 'got the brokers in', and so much nearer the literal, for one broker who brokers, as a rule, suffices

Defendant complained that she had been 'brokered' by mistake, and that she had to go out to wash to help pay this debt for another man, as her husband was only surety —*D T*, 20th November 1897.

Brolly (*Public School*, 1875 on) Umbrella This is evidently a corruption of umbrella. How did it come about? It descends from good society. Let us suppose the then Prince of Wales hears one of his children when very young make an effort to say umbrella, with 'brolly' for result, that he therefore applies the word very naturally to his umbrella; that he is heard at the Marlborough, where the word is adopted, and so passed on to the sons of the members of the club, who carry it down into their schools—whence it spreads. In King's College the word is quite naturalised (*See* 'Gamp,' 'Gingham,' 'Sangster')

Brompton Boilers (*Art*, 1870 on) A three-roofed iron-built museum at S Kensington. It got this name from the aspect of the building, and retained it nearly fifty years They were only demolished in 1898

As little is there room or reason for carting them (the pictures left to the nation by Sir Richard Wallace), off to South Kensington, especially so long as the administrative powers leave the 'Brompton boilers' in their present absolutely disgraceful condition.—*D. T.*, 2nd April 1899

Brooks of Sheffield (*M. Cl.*, 1853 on). *Nemo*—warning to be careful as to names. 'Who was he?' oh—Brooks of Sheffield From the first three numbers of David Copperfield—where David is referred to by Mr Murdstone in this name. Now passing away—but still used in the '80's On all fours with Binks the Barber.

Never mind, I hear that Smith, the champion pugilist of the universe and all England, is going to find out who that there Brooks of Sheffield is who boasts that he knocked Smith out in a private glove fight.—*Ref*, 31st July 1887.

Broom (*Soc*, 1860 on). A would-be swell—a total pretence. Corruption of Brum, with the 'u' long, it being an abbreviation of Brummagem, which is a contemptuous pronunciation of Birmingham—for many years, until the '80s, a synonym for pinchbeck manufactures Good example of substituting a known word for another less known — on this occasion the process taking place in Society itself

Broomstick (*Canadian*). A gun or rifle. No word could more perfectly outline the peaceful character of the Canadian as distinct from his American brother, when it is borne in mind that the latter calls his gun, shooting iron. The domesticity of 'broomstick' yields history in itself.

Brother Bung (*London Tavern*). A fellow-publican; as, 'Oh, they're brother bungs', said contemptuously. However, after the usual smart English manner of taking even Mr John Bull by the horns, the less dignified publicans have accepted the situation amongst themselves, and will frequently say when meeting, 'How goes it, brother bung?'

Brougham (*Soc.*, 1820 [?]). A small, close carriage, named after Lord Brougham—it is even said invented by him. The name has lasted to this day as 'broom' amongst high-class people — though less well-informed souls will give the two syllables. Recently a smaller brougham with rounded front has come to be called, by leading people, 'cask', and even 'tub'.

Brown (*Mooney's, Strand*). Two pennyworth of whisky. Evasive, delicate mode of getting a 2d. drink, the usual whisky-gargle being half sixpence. Good example of a singularly local passing word. Mooney's is the Irish whisky-house of the whole Strand.

Brown George (*Oxford fin*, 1890 on). Large jug holding bath-water, from its colour, and the name of the earthenwarer.

Brown Polish (*Anglo-Amer.*). A mulatto. Outcome of the use of tan-coloured boots. Grotesquely graphic — on the lines of Day and Martin (1840) describing a negro, because D. & M.'s blacking was *so* black.

Brown Stone Fronts (*Amer. political*). Aristocrats.

The dream of the rich New Yorker, realised in the case of Mr Vanderbilt, is to live in a brown stone house.

In New York politics, efforts are sometimes made to bring about what are called the primary elections in July, because in that month, as it is said, 'the brown stone fronts are out of town'.—*D. N.*, 10th October 1883.

The height of respectability is to live in a brown stone-fronted house—that is to say, to show a bold veneer of brown stone to the world that passes along the main street, putting off your neighbours at the back with ordinary brick.—*Newsp. Cutting.*

Brown Study (*Soc.*) Deep study. But why brown? Blue, or black and white would be more appropriate. Possibly from a celebrated 'varsity man given to being lost in thought.

Brown to (*Com. Classes*). To understand. Origin very obscure—probably from a keen man of this name. 'He didn't brown to what she was saying—not a little bit.' Possibly from meat proving its goodness by handsomely browning while on the roast.

Brown 'un, The (*Sporting*, 1870). *The Sporting Times*—from the then tone of its paper. (*See* Pink 'un.)

Brownies (*Lower London*, 1896). Common cigarettes—three for one halfpenny. From proper name, Brown. Outcome of cigarette-smoking.

To meet humbler feminine wants there are now halfpenny packets of cigarettes containing three, known as 'Brownies.'—*D. T.*, 3rd March 1898.

Bruffam (*Soc.*, 1860 on). A droll variation of Brougham, the small carriage known by that name—Brough itself being pronounced **Bruff**. Another illustration of the 'gh' eccentricities.

A story runs that Brougham, on being rallied by the Iron Duke as a man whose name would go down to posterity as a great lawyer, statesman, etc., but who would be best known by the name of the carriage which had been christened after him, retorted that the Duke's name would no doubt go down to posterity as that of a great general and the hero of a hundred fights, but that he would be best remembered by having a particular kind of boot named after him.—*Newsp. Cutting.*

Brulée (chiefly Naval, 1863). A very obscure word. Term is used at Vingt et un, and consists of the dealer helping himself to two cards, one from the top of the pack, the other from the bottom. This is permissible before the new dealer commences his deal. He has the option of making the brulée or not. If the two cards are not a natural (one ace and one court card or ten), he pays the unit to each player of the money played for—if it is a natural, he takes from each player from four to six times the stake, according to agreement. Sheer gambling. Not good form. 'N.B. Nap' (Napoleon) has completely swept away Vingt et un—and 'brulée avec' — as the French golden youth might say. Probably from the name of the inventor.

Brums (*R. S. Exchange*). N.W. Railway stock. All railway stocks have names of convenient brevity.

The nicknames of stocks at the Exchange are, on the whole, disrespectful. Thus, the ordinary stock of the London and North-Western Railway is known as 'Brums', although 'Brummagem' is anything but a proper description of so solid a property. 'Mids' will readily be recognized as Midland Railway stock; and an equal facility of identification may be claimed for 'Chats' (Chatham and Dover), 'Mets' (Metropolitan), 'Districts' (Metropolitan District), and some others. 'Dovers', however, would scarcely sugggest at first sight the South-Eastern Railway, nor 'Souths' the London and South-Western; while the North Staffordshire shares are irreverently spoken of as 'Pots,' after the Potteries.

The pet names are in every way preferable. Who would not cheerfully lose money on 'Berthas' (Brighton Ordinary), on 'Doras' (South-Eastern Deferred), on 'Noras' (Great Northern Deferred), on 'Saras' (Manchester, Sheffield, and Lincoln Deferred), or even on 'Dinahs' (Edinburgh and Glasgow Ordinary)? On the other hand, there is an added exasperation in the thought of having rashly 'put one's pile' on 'Caleys' (Caledonian Ordinary) or 'Haddocks' (Great Northern of Scotland Ordinary.)—*Newsp. Cutting.*

Brush (*Public House*). Odd name for a small glass, which is an inverted cone fixed on a thick stem of glass; used for dram-drinking in London—and thus fancifully named from its outline to a house-painter's brush.

That little bloke, with no more flesh on him than on a one and ninepenny fowl, put away six pots of four-half, three kervoortens of cold satin in a two-out brush, a 'arf kervoorten of rum, and a bottle of whisky.—*Newsp. Cutting.*

Brush Power (*Artists'*, 1882). Simply—painting, *e.g.* 'Never was Mr Millais' brush power so manly and assured.'—*Crit. of R. Academy*, 1883, John Forbes-Robertson.

Bryant & May's 'Chuckaways' (*E. London*, 1876). Girls employed in B. & M.'s lucifer match factory. Here one reading is droll, the other perhaps very cruel—a combination too frequent in peoples' wit. Chuckaways is one of the graphic names given to lucifer matches, simply because after striking and using, the remainder of the lucifer is thrown or 'chucked' away. Here, in effect, the lucifer is applied to the cause, the maker. The rhyming too should be remarked. This same cruel meaning of chuckaway may be left to the imagination. Of course girl lucifer match-makers, following a miserable and unhealthy industry, are not the equals of Belgravian match-making mothers.

Bub (*Old Eng.*—now American). In *The Country Girl* the author often calls her husband 'bub.' In the States it is a friendly term addressed to a boy.

'Your husband ought to be arrested for working on Sunday!' 'Working on Sunday—come here, bub! Now, bub, if you'll prove that my husband ever worked on Sunday, or any other day in the week, I'll give you a dollar! I've lived with him for twenty years, and have always had to buy even his whiskey and tobacco, and now if he's gone to work I want to know it!' The boy backed off without another word.—1882.

Bubble (*Soc.*, 17 *cent.*). To cheat. 'To bubble you out of a sum of money.' Decker's *Horn-book*, 1609.

The well-meaning ladies of England, when they subscribed for that monument, had not the faintest notion of what they were doing. They were indeed 'bubbled', to use a phrase of Queen Anne's time.—*D. N.*, 1882.

POLLY. I'm bubbled.
LUCY. I'm bubbled.
POLLY. Oh, how I'm troubled.
—*Beggars' Opera.*

Still used by the lowest. 'I bubbled 'im to rights.' Equal to 'bilk'—a more modern word.

Bubble around (*Amer.-Eng.*). Rather a strong verbal attack, generally by way of the press. 'I will back a first-class British subject for bubbling around against all humanity.'—Besant & Rice, *The Golden Butterfly*, ch. 18.

Buck (*Soc.*, 18 *cent.*). Young man of fashion, derived not from the male deer, but a diminutive of 'buckram', a stiffening fabric used in setting out the full-skirted coats of the eighteenth century. The word lasted fashionably to about 1820. It is now only used by thoroughly vulgar people. Its fashionable equivalent in the middle of the nineteenth century was 'swell', which is rapidly being vulgarized. 'Toff' is an invention of the envious enemy. Buck obtained another meaning during the '70's—a sham cab fare. During the evening the Strand being gorged with crawler cabs, it was determined to keep empty cabs out of that thoroughfare from 10 to 11 P.M. Cabmen desirous of getting through on the chance of obtaining a fare from a Strand theatre or restaurant would ask passing young men—fairly dressed, if poor, to pretend to be a fare in order to get past the line of police. This fraudulent passenger came to be called by cabmen, and afterwards by the police, 'a buck', used no doubt satirically.

When a cabman wants to drive past the police to get access to theatre exits out of his own turn he puts a man into his cab and drives rapidly on, as if taking a fare away. This sham fare in street parlance, we learn, is 'only a buck'.—*D. N.*, 26th September 1887.

Mr Bridge said in this case it had not been shown that the man was 'a buck' in the ordinary acceptance of the term. Defendant had evidently allowed his friend to ride on the spring. This was an offence against the regulations, in addition to entailing extra labour on the horse. He hoped it would be understood that in future in such cases, and where 'bucks' were employed, the full penalty would be imposed. — *Newsp. Cutting*, October 1887.

Buck against (*Anglo-Amer.*). To oppose violently. From the stubborn bucking habit of stag and goat.

Buck up and take a chilly (*Navy*). Advice to a man to pull himself together after a hard drink. The 'chilly' may be literal, since cayenne is supposed to be a signal help in restoring the collapsed patient to sense and sobriety.

Buck or a doe (*Anglo-Amer.*). A man or woman, obviously from the habit and mode of thinking by backwoods' men.

The startled girl gave him a glance, but no other demonstration of recognition. 'It's kinder rough to rattle 'em along like freight in this way (coffined, dead), but where you ain't got no plantin' facilities of yer own it's got to be done. Was the lamented a buck or a doe?'—1883.

Buck Parties (*Soc.*). Bachelor meets. From Australia.

The one drawback to our pleasure has been the delicate state of Mrs Pen's health. This sent me out to what are called here 'buck parties', *i.e.*, parties of men only, when otherwise I should have gone with her to (what she calls) more civilised gatherings.—*Ref.*, 19th September 1888.

Bucket-shop (*City*, 1870 on). Stockjobber's, or outside broker's office. From U.S.A.

RUINED BY BUCKET SHOPS — A once prosperous merchant's defalcation and suicide. Montreal. Samuel Johnson . . . absconded. . . . Two detectives started with him for this city. . . . This morning he jumped from the train at the Tanneries, and was found dead with two bullets through his brain. Johnson is another victim of bucket-shop speculation. It is known that he has lost thousands of dollars in these places. The community is indignant at the manner in which so many citizens are being ruined by bucket shops, and steps will certainly be taken to close them.—*N. Y. Mercury*, 2nd October 1887.

Bucking match (*Negro*). Fight with heads. Fine example of throwback to savage life. Sheer atavism.

Stacey appeared to be the more belligerent of the two, insisted on having the quarrel out, and challenged Kline to fight him without fists or weapons. This is the usual manner among Philadelphia negroes to denominate a 'bucking match', which is not an infrequent method of settling disputes. — *Newsp. Cutting.*

Bucking the Tiger (*Anglo-Amer.*). Gambling heavily.

Entering by a green baize door, the visitors found themselves in a large and well-lighted room—the lair of the tiger. Gamblers usually speak of faro playing as 'bucking the tiger', but if any one imagines that the animal is other than a fat, sleek, attractive-looking feline they make a great mistake. Only the furry coat is exposed; one must join in the play in order to get a glimpse of the fangs and claws.—*Newsp. Cutting.*

An oil region correspondent of a Philadelphia journal, who evidently 'has been there'—at both places—says that 'boring for oil is like "bucking the tiger"', or eating mushrooms; if you live it is a mushroom; if you die it is a toadstool. If you strike oil you have bored in the right place, if you don't you haven't.—*Newsp. Cutting*

In the United States the operation of staking all one's money in a gaming hell is called 'bucking the tiger'.—G. A. SALA

Bud (*Amer.-Eng.*). A young girl. Real original American discovery.

The American novelist is in rather a tight place. When he is in a tight place—or, indeed, whether he is or not—he usually takes the world into his confidence. His grievance at present is the censorship of the 'bud', or young girl, of his native land.—*D. N.*, 31st May 1889.

Buff to the Stuff (*Thieves'*, 19 *cent.*). Accomplices who swear to stolen property as theirs.

They might as well have the twenty quid as not, for they were sure to get out of it, as they were going to send some people to 'buff to the stuff', a slang term for claiming the property supposed to have been stolen, and stating that they had sold it.—*Newsp. Cutting*.

Buffalo Boys (*Music Hall*). Comic negroes, affecting stupidity, probably from one of the earliest nigger melodies.

Buffer (*Peoples'*). A catspaw, intermediator, illustrator of the couplet

'Those who in quarrels interpose
Often get a bloody nose.'

Comes in one line from the railway buffer, which breaks the impingement of railway carriages, and in another line from buffo, who in comic Italian opera is always ill-used. 'Poor old buffer,' said by Robson to the ghost of Lablache, the buffo, in *The Camp at the Olympic*, by J. R. Planché.

Buffer (*Navy*). A boatswain's mate—probably because he is the buffer state, so to speak, between boatswain and able seaman.

Buffer State (*Political*). A small territory dividing the countries or colonies of two greater states—as Belgium, which is a buffer state between France and Germany. Holland is another buffer state. So also is 'Andorre'. So also were Monaco and Mentone the 'buffer' once between France and Italy.

Buffs, Buffaloes (*Secret Society*). A jovial, so-called, secret society—'Ancient Order of Buffaloes.' Probably in the commencement from 'beau fellows'—as Hullo! my beau fellows!—beau being a word much used in the last century. The process of being made a buffalo fifty years ago was very simple, the victim being sworn on the sacred ibis. Before him and everyone of the elect a cork was placed, when the president told the acolyte that upon a given word every man was to seize his cork, the last to touch his cork having to pay 2s. 6d. The word was given, the victim seized his cork, and as no one budged or moved a hand, evidently he was the last to touch his cork. So he paid his half-crown. The Buffaloes (A. S. O. B.) have been for a long time a well-ordered society—possibly too jovial, but certainly in some degree charitable. They have proper officers, give annual jewels of gold, not perhaps of a very high carat, to their officers, and have ceremonials, in some degree choral, as the astonished outsider may learn for himself as, on passing a lodge, he hears the brethren proclaiming their intention to 'Chase the Buffalo', though where they would find the buffalo it would be difficult to say. Sisters, *i.e.*, brethren's wives, come without to hear these things, and go home trembling and minatory. The Buffs are strictly non-political.

Buffy (*Com. Lond.*). Drunk—probably Anglicized from bevvy. 'He always goes to bed buffy.' Or it may be swelled with drink, from French *bouffi—temp.* Charles II.

He, the driver, must get up earlier and go to bed without getting buffy, which he hadn't done for a week of Sundays, before he found that little game would draw in the dibs.—*Newsp. Cutting*.

Bug (*Amer.*). Abbreviation of bugbear—a nuisance.

The phraseology of Edison, to judge from his day-book records, is synthetic, strongly descriptive, and quaint. . . A 'bug' is a difficulty which appears insurmountable to the staff. To the master it is 'an ugly insect that lives on the lazy, and can and must be killed.'—*Newsp. Cutting*.

Bugaboo (*Amer.*). A panic—of an absurd and unreasoning character. 'The recent Fenian bugaboo.'—1867.

Bug-eaters (*Amer.*). People of Nebraska. This word must be read 'beetle' in English. Refers to the enormous amount of insect life in this territory.

Bug-shooter (*Schools and Univs.*). A volunteer—volunteers not being popular with gown—the system being left to town.

If you join the Volunteers you are discourteously spoken of as a 'bug-shooter'. —*D. T.*, 14th August 1899.

Bugs (*Lowest Classes*). Wall-flowers. From their colour, signal example of lower class tendency to horribly vulgar association of ideas, even in relation to such pleasant visitors as these blooms—the first of the year—frequently seen in penny bunches in poorest neighbourhoods early in February. Who'll 'av a pennorth o' bugs? (*See* Bloods.)

Build up (*Thieves'*). To array in good clothes, for trade purposes.

Jennings agreed to 'build up' Archer with clothes, and at another meeting brought him a coat in order that he might appear respectable when he visited his old fellow-servants at the Lodge.—*Newsp. Cutting.*

Bulge, To get the (*Anglo-Amer.*). To gain an advantage; from the approaching conqueror in wrestling or fighting overcoming the opponent, so that the conqueror's chest-muscles are forward, or bulging.

Mr Dodsley has, to use the new phrase of American slang, 'the bulge' on Messrs Longmans.—*D. N.*, 19th June 1891.

'You wanted to get the bulge on it, didn't you?' 'Wanted to do what?' 'Wanted to get the bulge on it.' 'What do you mean by bulge?'—*N. Y. Mercury*, 1892.

Bull (*Common Lodging-House*). A second brew of tea.

The lodgers divide their food frequently, and a man seeing a neighbour without anything will hand him his teapot, and say, 'Here you are, mate; here's a bull for you.' A 'bull' is a teapot with the leaves left in for a second brew.—G. R. Sims, *Horrible London.*

Bull and Cow (*Rhyming*). A row.

Bull-doze, To bull-doze (*Amer.-Eng.*, 19 *cent.*). Political bullying. The origin of this phrase is absolutely lost, always supposing that it was ever found. Mr Rees, an American authority on obscure words, says (1887):

'A bull-doze is a term used in inflicting punishment upon an unruly animal; the weapon a strap made out of the hide of a bull. During the existence of slavery the term "bull-doze" was used when a negro was to be whipped; the overseer was instructed to give him as many lashes as was applied to an animal, hence the term 'bull-doze'." Maybe 'doze' has reference to dozen.

This word is also used in private life to describe pestering conduct:

Serves you just right for bull-dozing me a whole month to make this infernal excursion.—*Newsp. Cutting.*

The following quotation will show that even in the U.S.A. themselves this term is not fully understood:

'What do they mean by bull-dozing?' asked an inquisitive wife the other evening. 'I suppose they mean a bull that is half asleep.' And the injured one kept on with her sewing, but said nothing.

Bulley (*Westminster School*). The lappet of a King's scholar's gown—probably rather meant to describe the wearer than the gown.

Bullfinches (*Hunting*). High hedges—probably from the name of some owner or farmer opposed to hunting.

To the stag, we imagine, it is a matter of small concern whether his enemies are counter-jumpers or leapers of bullfinches. —*Newsp. Cutting*, March 1883.

A bullfinch in Ireland is a stone hedge. —*Athenæum*, 17th Feb. 1887, p. 221.

Bullock's horn (*Artizans' rhyming*). Pawn.

Put your kicksies in the bullock's horn.—*Cutting.*

Bully (*O. Eng.*). From bullocking and bull-tossing.

Yes, you villain, you have defiled my own bed, you have, and then you have charged me with bullocking you into owning the truth. It is very likely, an't please your worship, that I should bullock him.—Fielding, *Tom Jones*, bk. ii. ch. 6. (*See* Bully-rag.)

Bully (*Amer.*). Capital, good, excellent — perhaps from French Colonial times in the south, and from 'bouilli'—the stewed beef which equals in Gallic popularity and stability the 'roast' of England and the States.

'What's the matter with you?' 'My leg's smashed,' says he. 'Can't yer walk?' 'No.' 'Can yer see?' 'Yes.' 'Well,' says I, 'you're a —— Rebel, but will you do me a little favour?' 'I will,' says he, 'ef I ken.' Then I says, 'Well, ole butternut, I can't see nothin'. My eyes is knocked out, but I ken walk. Come over yere. Let's git out o' this. You pint the way, an' I'll tote yer off the field on my back.' 'Bully for you,' says he. And so we managed to git together. We shook hands on it.—1863.

Mr Rees (N. York) says 'Bully' is used as indicating satisfaction amongst lower English classes—as 'Never mind, as they say in the waxey crowd, he's a bully boy.'

Captain Townshend saw an omnibus pole strike a gentleman's horse in the flank, knocking over both steed and rider, and the man, calling out 'Bully for you,' drove away laughing

Bully about the muzzle (*Dog-fanciers'*). Too thick and large in the mouth.

'Angelina [a terrier] is bully about the muzzle,' said Maulevrier; we shall have to give her away.'—Miss Braddon, *Phantom Fortune.*

Bully-fake (*London*, 1882). A compound of 'bully'—here meaning advantageous and 'fake' action, or result. Fake is said to come from *facto.*

It's a bully fake for a dona when she has the fair good luck to snap hold a husband who will cut up to rights—*Newsp. Cutting.*

Bully-rag (*Peoples'*, 19 *cent.*). To scold at length, said of a woman Probably suggested by the irritation caused to the bull in the ring, or perhaps pit, by being driven frantic with a perpetual red flag—the rag 'Don't bully-rag *me*, woman!'

Bum-boozer (*Theatr*). A desperate drinker It is to be feared that the following line has been seen in the advertisements for artistes in the commoner theatrical papers.

'Bum-boozers—save your stamps.'

Bumble puppy (*Provincial*). A tossing game used to cheat simpletons—hence bumble-puppy means idiot and idiocy Origin unknown.

By the-bye now that we are to be legalized into such goody-goodies that little or no sport is to be allowed except battledore and shuttlecock, egg-hat, push-pin, etc, I am about to offer a prize for the championship of Bumble puppy, *i e.*, if the police authorities will allow it to take place.—*Newsp. Cutting.*

Bummaree (*Billingsgate*) A middleman at the fish auctions. Corruption of bonne marée French seaside term for high tide or flood, and also for salt-water fish.

The 'bummarees' or middlemen whip up all the plaice, and carry them off to turn a penny on them by breaking them up into smaller lots—*Newsp Cutting.*

Bummarees (*Cooks'*) Corruption of Bain marie, a cooking utensil consisting of a number of little pots in a bath, or 'bain', of water contained in a large pot The French phrase is as difficult to comprehend as the corruption—for Marie is beyond analysis—unless it is the name of the inventor. English books of a later school making an effort to avoid the first syllable and be truly Parisian, call the contrivance a 'bang Mary'—a very alarming rectification

Bummer (*Anglo-Amer.*, 1880). Originally a commercial traveller, from one who 'booms'. (Now—a noisy cad.)

'You are nothing but a third-class society bummer, fit only to associate with your own class of New York scum'—*N Y Mercury*, 8th October 1883

Bun Feast (*Boys'*). A woeful description of a very poor and meagre feast, where buns need not necessarily serve to swell up the juvenile stomach

Bunce (*Drapers'*) Goods—probably from a proper name.

Bunch of Fives (*L. Class*) The fist simply—ingenious mode of proving the speaker can count up to five.

One of the associates of the eccentric Marquis of Waterford formed a collection of door-knockers, brass plates, bell pulls, little dustpans, golden canisters, and glovers' 'bunches of fives', of which, in the course of a roystering career, he had despoiled private houses and tradesmen's shop-fronts—G A Sala, *Illust Lond. News*, 27th January 1883.

Buncombe or Bunkum (*Amer-Eng.*, 19 *cent*) Politically, or possibly any publicly, spoken flattery. This word is an admirable instance of a name at once passing into a language and even yielding to phonetic spelling. The press, both in the U S A and in England, accepted immediately the name as a synonym for humbug. From a celebrated orator of honied phrases named Buncombe Vulgarised rapidly into Bunkum; but the Americans, permanently accepting the word, have restored the original spelling This name-word has as absolutely passed into the English language as 'burke', or 'boycot' Mr Rees (New York) says of this word:—

The origin of this expression was in the lower house of Congress. A member from North Carolina, and from the county of Buncombe, was speaking when some of the members showed disapprobation, manifested in the usual manner by coughing and sneezing. The member was not long in making the discovery that he was making himself very obnoxious, nor willing to yield an iota of his time to any one, and fully determined to have his 'talk', addressed the disaffected members thus:—'Go, gentlemen, if you like; clear out, evaporate, for I would have you to know that I am not addressing the house but—Bunkum!'

Bundling (*Welsh*). Courting—in a reclining position.

That peculiar Welsh institution, 'bundling' has almost disappeared, a son of the Cymry tells me, from the Principality. It was a sort of union by which a man and woman agreed to take one another on trial for twelve months. If at the end of that time harmonious relations still subsisted between them, they usually took one another, for better for worse, in the orthodox manner. But, if they separated, no sort of disgrace or stigma attached to either; they went their ways, and the world thought none the worse of them for having lived in open adultery.—*People*, 17th January 1897.

Bung (*Peoples'*, 1850 on). A landlord—sometimes endearing when used by dearest friends, but generally and increasingly suggestive of contempt and superiority on the part of the speaker. Used by a client towards a publican whilst he is holding his court in his own particular gin palace; might lead to an immediate call upon the chucker-out to eject the traitor. Only a complete 'pal' could afford, with an elegant but risky sense of fun, to say, 'Dear Bung, I'll take another bitter'—beer being understood.

Bung (*Public Schools*). A lie—probably from some notorious liar's name, known in some leading school, whence it has drifted to most schools.

Bung Ball (*London Tr.*). A great annual Terpsychorean meet of the bungs, or publicans. Celebrated for the grandeur of the diamonds—or what are said to be diamonds—and other precious stones. At this function artificial hops and grapes are never worn, they being too suggestive of the bar. (*See* Blood Ball.)

Bungaries (*Peoples'*, 1870 on). Public-houses. As taverning came to be looked down upon, the landlord, once mine host, honest John Barleycorn, etc., became a 'bung'—whence, as general contempt for pubs. increased, bungary for his house came to be good English. 'Bungs and bungaries must pass away.'

Buniony (*Art*, 1880). Term to express lumpiness of outline, from a a bunion breaking up the 'drawing' of a foot. 'He has still go, but he's getting very buniony.'

Bunk (*Peoples'*). To retreat judiciously. 'I shall bunk', very common in public schools.

Bunker (*L. Class*). Beer—Anglicizing of 'bona-aqua'—an idea of some light-hearted Italian organ-grinder in the Italian quarter behind Hatton Garden.

Bunko (*Amer.-Eng.*). Doubtful, shifty. From S. America. Heard in Liverpool.

At Mackinac they took him for a lord, and at Cleveland he was taken for a bunko man, and had to identify himself by telegraph.

Bunter (*Thieves'*). A woman thief of the lowest possible kind. The very gutterling of crime to whom no 'perfect lady' would condescend to fling a ''ow d'ye doo?'

Bunting-tosser (*Navy*) Signalman. The signals are small flags made of bunting, and they are run up at or near the mast-head.

Bupper (*Peoples'*, 19 *cent.*). Universal infantile reduction of bread and butter used, as a rule, until the specimen gets his first paternal spanking over his first pair of breeches, when the word passes into 'toke' for the whole term of his natural boy's life, *e.g.*, 'Bit o' bupper, p'ease'—too often heard in the watches of the night. Said to be of royal descent. 'Upon my word', said the old general, 'I think I prefer bup to anything.'

Burgle (*Soc.*, 1880). To commit burglary. Introduced (at all events to London) by Mr W. S. Gilbert in *The Pirates of Penzance*.

Burick (*L. Class*, 19 *cent.*). A wife—said to be Romany. To administer manual correction to her is 'to slosh the burick'.

When your burick gets boozed, smashes the crockery, and then calls in her blooming old ma to protect her from your cruelty, that's the time to do a guy.—*Cutting*, 1883.

Burke (*Polit.*, 19 *cent.*). To stifle, quash, abate—from one Burke, who with another, Hare, for some years early in the nineteenth century, systematically murdered persons of all ages, in Edinburgh, for the purpose of selling their bodies to medical men for hospital purposes. Their mode was by stifling with pitch-plasters, which prevented outcry. Their victims were first generally made drunk, except in the case of women. Hence the appositeness of the word for silencing First used in Parliament by way of attack, afterwards accepted as a good verb full of meaning

Burst (*Policemen's*, 1879). Outpour of theatrical audiences about eleven (of course P.M), into the Strand 'The burst gets thicker every month,' said the sergeant 'All the world goes to the play now' The sudden popularity of the play-house began about 1879, and went on increasing in the most marvellous manner

Burst her stay-lace (*London*). A sudden bust-heaving feminine indignation, which might even literally, and certainly does figuratively, bring about this catastrophe.

Burst your crust (*Prize ring*, 1800, etc.). Breaking the skin. Went to America

It is not good manners to do so, and you might slip and burst your crust by so doing —*American Comic Etiquette for Children*

Bury (*Low Life*) To desert.

Buryen' face (*Amer.*) Solemn, serious countenance—burying face.

Soon's I could git my buryen' face on, I takes Spider in ter whar the fuss wuz goin' on.—*Tobe Hodge*

Bus (*Soc*, 1881). Dowdy dress Applied only to women; when a badly-dressed victim enters a drawing-room this fatal word may be used—meaning not so much that the lady has come by bus as that her style of dress is not fitted to any sort of vehicle higher in character than the once popular one named

Bus-bellied Ben (*Street*, E C, 1840 on). An ordinary name for an alderman, who used to be frequently corpulent. The wave of abstinence, however, has swept even over the corporations of the City of London The satire was completed by a couplet—

Bus-bellied Ben;
Eats enough for ten.

Bush-ranger (*Austral*) Highway man. Interesting as a comparative term; for while the word is fairly equivalent to our highwayman, it is significant to compare both with the American evasive 'road agent'.

Bushy Park (*Rhyming*, 1882). A synonym for 'lark'.

Oh, it is a bushy park to see the Salvation souls toddling about arm-in-arm —*Cutting*.

Business end of a tin tack (*Amer*). The point.

The joke about the pin in the chair, and the suggestion that the business end of a tin tack would be preferable, are essentially American —*D N*, 1882.

Persons unaware of the existence of such agents as buckram or crinoline muslin might be forgiven for supposing that such flounces were maintained in order on the principle of an air cushion, and that the introduction of the business end of a pin would produce sudden collapse —*D. N.*, 27th March 1883.

Busker. He who goes busking 'Now, gentlemen, don't break out the bottom o' the plate with the weight o' silver you 'and this old busker. I'd send round my 'at as more civil, but yer liberality 'ud knock the bottom out.'

Busking (*Street-singers'*). Going from pub to pub singing and reciting, generally in tow with a banjo.

'Hang it, I hope I shall never come down to regular busking; yes, now and again when bis is bad, but for ever—Lord forbid'

'That pub's no good—don't you see the notice—no buskers after 7. They've got their evenin' reglers'—*Cutting*

Busnacking (*Navy*) Equals Paul Prying—unduly interfering

I wish old Nobby wouldn't come 'busnacking' about, worrying a chap out of his life I wasn't doing any harm! To 'busnack' is to be unnecessarily fussy and busy.—*Rev G. Goodenough, R.N.*

Buss me—bub (*London*, 18 *cent.*). Baise-moi—evidently. (*See Country Girl.*)

Bust (*Street*, 1875) Burst, or explode with rage, and so join the majority. As a noun it means a heavy drink.

A vulgar critic asserts that Poe must have been on a bust, and raven mad when he wrote his famous poem.

A sculptor can be on a bust without losing cast.—*Newsp. Cutting.*

Busted (*Amer.*, 19 *cent.*). Bankrupt.

'We're busted miners, missus,' began Black Dan, with a wink to his comrades, 'completely busted, an' can't pay. What you give us to eat must be fer charity.'—*Newsp. Cutting.*

Buster (*London*, 1844 on). A penny loaf. This word has rather a pathetic origin. When the abolition of the corn laws reduced the price of bread, it increased the size of the penny loaf, which at once obtained this eulogistic title—a corruption of burster, a loaf large enough to rend the enclosing stomach. This term remains, but not in its appositeness, for whereas the baker in those early free trade days took a pleasure in showing how much bread he could give for a couple of halfpence, the more recent baker has practically abolished the object. Even his penny roll is not overpowering as to size.

Buster (*Music Hall*, 1882). A special giantess, called Maid Marian. For some time after she left London the word was applied to big women, and for some years the boys in the Leicester Square district would shout at a big woman, 'My high—yere's a Maid Marian for yer!' Marian was a Bavarian giantess brought to London in this year. She appeared at the Alhambra in the autumn so successfully that the dividends paid to shareholders were doubled. She was sixteen only, more than 8 feet high, and was 'still growing'. The use of the word 'Maid' before Marian grew out of the suggestion the two words formed—that of the sweetheart of Robin Hood. Doubtless this title accelerated the popularity of the giantess, who died before she was twenty.

Bust yer (*Street*, 1880 on). A recommendation to ruin; *e.g.*, 'Bust yer, what do I care about that?'

Busy Sack (*Travellers'*). A carpet bag. Good word, and capital equivalent to the American 'hand-grip', given to the small hand-bag.

Butcher (*Public House*). One of the synonyms for 'stout'—obtained probably from general observation that few butchers are thin and narrow.

Butter, To (*Cricket*, 1898). To miss, fail to catch—from butter-fingers, or rather buttered, so that they have no hold. In cricket generally applied to the miss of an easy catch.

Butter-churn (*Music Hall Artistes'*). Rhyming for 'turn'—the short appearance of the performer on the stage, which he or she occupies about a quarter of an hour.

When the dona's finished her butter churn, he fakes his way to her, and if there's no other omee mouchin for the music why he takes her to her next flippity flop.—*Biography of a Toff Bundle Carrier.*

Butter-fingers (*Household*). A servant careless in all her ways—especially as to crockery. As though the fingers are so greased that no grip can be made.

Butter upon Bacon (*Household English*). Extravagance—resulting out of the condemnation of eating bread and butter with bacon, instead of the plain loaf. 'What—are you going to put lace over the feather—isn't that rather butter upon bacon?'

Buttock and File (*Thieves'*, 18 *cent.*). Shop-lifter, evidently French; *filer*—meaning 'to escape quickly'.

Button-maker (*London*). A nickname of George III.

The King was familiarly called the 'Button Maker' by one generation of his faithful subjects, and 'Farmer George' by another. His son is still sarcastically referred to as the 'First Gentleman in Europe'.—*Newsp. Cutting.*

Buxton Limp (*Buxton*). Reference to the hobbling walk of invalids taking the waters. Borrowed from the Alexandra Limp (*q.v.*, also Grecian Bend, Roman Fall).

If walking is too severe exaction just at first and the 'Buxton limp' is too decided, the patient secures a seat in the omnibus.—*D. N.* (Harrogate), 31st August 1883.

Buy your Thirst (*Amer.*, passing English 1894). To pay for drink.

Buz (*Oxford Common Room*). Turn of the don or visitor to whom this word is addressed to fill his glass—the liquor, as a rule, being priceless port. 'It's your buz!' Very ancient—

supposed to be a corruption of 'bouse', or booze, common London for 'a drink', and to drink.

'In bousing about 'twas his gift to excel,
And from all jolly topers he bore off the bell'

Buz-faker, Buz-faking (*L. London*). One of the applications of 'booze'—a buz-faker being an individual, generally a woman, or rather one that was a woman, who makes the victim drunk before the robbery is effected

Buzzards (*Amer.*) People of Georgia — probably from the wild turkeys which once abounded there. Singular return to Red Indian customs, the Red Indian being always designated by the name of something in natural history associated with his surroundings. Nearly every state has its inhabitants named after this system (*See* Blue Grass.)

Buzzer (*Peoples'*, 1898 on). A road-motor of any kind, from the noise made during progress.

Byblow (*Lower Peoples'*). An illegitimate child. Suggested by an aside breath May be from Carolian times, and a corruption of 'bibelot'—(a valuable small art object)—a term which any one of the famous French 'beauties of the Court' might apply to her nursling—and one that may have been translated satirically into byblow. The *bas peuple* of France to this day style an illegitimate—'un accident'

By the Holy Grail (*Hist*) The blood of Christ A solemn invocation to this day in thoroughly Catholic countries, and heard in provincial France now and again—'Par le sang real' It is heard in England, in the west only, and there very naturally reformationised into 'By the Holy Grill'—for Grail has no meaning, while 'grill' has a deal Probably here the grill refers to St Lawrence, who was completed by being grilled. In Paris this invocation is represented by 'Sacré', and 'Sacré Dieu'—'Sang Réal de Dieu.' The English phrase has much exercised English etymologists Many have assumed that the 'grail' was a round dish in which the Redeemer broke the bread Nay, there has been published a drawing of this very dish. The phrase is derived from 'sang real' in this way The 'g' of 'sang' thrown upon the following 'r'—we have greal, then the remaining 'san' has been taken for 'saint'—holy, and then some blundering early printer has taken the verbal phrase 'san greal'—and translated it 'Holy Grail'—and thus it remains to this day a phrase utterly without meaning (*See* More Blue).

By th' good Katty (*Lancashire and North generally*) An ancient Catholic oath, evidently—By the good Catherine—St Catherine of Alexandria, whose popularity in England is probably proved by the number of wheel-windows in Gothic architecture. 'By th' good Katty, aw feel like as if aw should ne'er ha' done'

C

C B. U (*Commercial*, 1897) Legal initials of Court of Bankruptcy, Undischarged Arose from the process of one H H who obtained goods while an undischarged bankrupt by letter headed with these initials which he held, freed him from a charge of fraud

The superintendent of police stated that there were hundreds of cases against the accused, who pleaded that the letters 'C B U' which appeared on his notepaper informed his creditors that he was an undischarged bankrupt, the exact interpretation of the letters being 'Court of Bankruptcy, undischarged'.—*D T.*, 23rd March 1897.

C H (*Popular* from Nov. 1882-83) Conquering Hero. The term took its rise consequent upon the incessant reception of the soldiers engaged in the Egyptian War (1882), by the playing of 'See the Conquering Hero Comes.'

It will soon be a military distinction not to be a C H.—*Ref.*, 19th November 1882.

C. O (*Military*). Soldiers' Greek for 'the Colonel'

C S (*American Civil War*). Abbreviation of Confederate soldiers.

U S. and C. S. slept together on blankets —*Newsp Cutting*

Cabbage, The (1883) A familiar name given to the Savoy Theatre, opened in 1881, and named after the old 'Savoy' liberties, within which it was built.

When I saw the Cabbage Theatre full I thought to myself, etc.—(1883).

Cabbage Garden Patriots (*Polit.*, 1848 on). Cowards.

The phrase 'cabbage garden patriots' refers to the way in which Smith O'Brien, the uncrowned king of forty years ago or so, was discovered hiding in a bed of cabbages after his followers had fled in all directions, when they were informed as to the coming of the horrid Saxon's minions.—*Ref.*, 20th October 1889.

Cackle (*Theatrical*). To cackle is neither to gag, nor to pong—it is both, with cackle added. A ceaseless unpunctuated flow of words and phrases more or less unconnected and meaningless.

'Cackle' is a convertible substantive or verb which carries a meaning for which it would be most difficult to substitute any other word nearly so effective, and there is a world of satire in its application to a human goose.—*Stage*, 21st August 1885.

Cackle-tub (*Thieves'*). A pulpit. The dangerous classes evolved this term in prison, where they probably see a pulpit for the first time.

Cackling Cove (*Cadgers'*). An actor—the cadger seeing no difference between observing Shakespeare, and whining floridly for pence.

Cadaver (*Anglo-Amer.*). A financially 'dead 'un.'

Three fresh Cadavers. Last week the Crawford Mutual Relief Association, of Ohio, notified the Insurance Commissioner of that State that it was in the throes of dissolution. The day following the Northern Ohio Mutual Relief Association and the Eureka Life surrendered their hungry ghosts.—*Newsp. Cutting.*

See Dead 'un.

Cad-mad (*Oxford*, 1880). The vain glory and superciliousness which overcome, and permanently, the better sense of *nouveaux riches*, *parvenues*, mushroomers (*see*), 'Poor devil—forgive him — he's a cad-mad emancipated haberdasher.'

Cads on Castors (1880). Bicylists.

It will come as a severe blow to fastidious people, who, adopting and freely using the rather stupid phrase that stigmatised all bicyclists as 'cads on castors', fondly thought that they could kill by ridicule a pastime to which they took exception. — *D. N.*, 10th September 1885.

Cady or Kadi (*Whitechapel*). A hat—probably from the Hebrew. It has the distinction of offering one of the rare rhymes to lady. In 1886 a song-chorus began—

Met a lady!
Raised my cady!

The lady probably being of insufficient virtue — the context borne in mind.

Caesaration (*American*). A remarkable shape of evasive swearing—really damnation.

'Ow! ow! Caesaration! I'll kick the head off you!' he roared, catching hold of a fence and glaring at the boy.—*Newsp. Cutting.*

Cake (*London*, 1882). A foolish stupid fellow. Used in good society, Borrowed by Mr Emanual Duperré for a comedy of English manners called *Rotten Row*, produced at the Odeon (Paris, 1882).

Cake-walk (*Music Hall*, 19 *cent.*). Negro step-dancing.

The science of 'cake-walking' does not appear to be a particularly abstruse one. Indeed, it may be said to have been anticipated by the English minuet. Cake-walking is, in fact, a graceful motion, conducted upon the toes and ball of the foot. Yet there must be an unsuspected amount of merit in it, for we are informed that the Farrells won first prize at the Madison Square Gardens in New York before 10,000 interested spectators. . . . As the reward to the dancers generally consists of an elaborate cake we are at once enlightened as to the genesis of a colloquialism, which has become quite acclimatised in our own land.—*D. T.*, 14th March 1898.

Calf Round (*Amer. Agricultural*, 1870). To dawdle about, asking for some kind of help — suggested by a calf worrying its mother.

'No, sir; I'll die first. Integrity in business transactions is the rule of my life. When I set a time to pay you, calf 'round.' — *Kentucky State Journal*, 1882.

Calico Hop (*Amer.-Eng.*). A free and easy calico ball. This function was invented to evade expenditure by providing that all the dresses, ordinary or fancy, should be strictly of cotton. However cunning people held cotton velvet to be within the bounds of a calico ball, and so contrived to make rare displays of themselves.

The Pleasure League gave a calico hop to their numerous friends on Wednesday evening, at Gerstner's Hall, which was largely attended —*N Y Mercury*, April 1883

Calicot (*French*). Originally a trade phrase for a linen-draperman both in France and England—used to describe a 'snob' or cad 'What a calicot he is!' E Zola in *Au Bonheur des Dames* (1883) uses the word in its original acceptation —'Hein—des calicots qui vendent des fourrures!' Derived from linen-drapers' young men dressing expensively, but not purchasing good manners

Call it 8 Bells (*Nautical*). Early drink It is not etiquette in good nautical circles to have a drink before high noon; 8 Bells So the apology for alcoholics before that hour takes this form · 'Come along — I fancy the bar is this way Call it 8 Bells.' And they do

Call-money (*Police*) Money paid to policemen for calling artisans early in the morning at a given hour.

Attention to 'call-money' appeared to receive more favourable consideration, and sixpences per week for rousing sleepy shopkeepers were matters not to be lightly estimated, even though it is written in the rules, we believe, that no fees are to be received from the citizen who requires to be roused —*Papers on Metrop Police.*

Calloh (*Hebrew-Yiddish*). A bride. Proper spelling of the ordinary term, kollah (*q.v.*)

Camberwell Death-trap (*Camberwell, 19 cent*). Surrey Canal

Mr Powell, whose little nephew was recently drowned in the Surrey Canal, has called attention in a contemporary to the dangerous condition of that waterway. He regards it as a pitfall for little boys who walk on or play about its banks, and he tells us that it is locally known as 'the Camberwell Death trap'. —*D N*, 27th September 1883

Cambric (*Soc*, 18 *cent*). A shirt of fine linen; later a handkerchief of cambric Derived from name of place of manufacture of fine linen. 'Cambray' or Cambrick, after the fashion of calico. (*See* Lully.)

Cambridge lot (*Oxford Univ.*). General term of scorn for men of the more eastern of the two universities

The distinction of this 'Cambridge lot' is of a kind which is not merely official but individual, and of an individuality specially suitable for recognition by a University.—*Newsp. Cutting*, 1883.

Camera Obscura (*Amer - Eng*). *Le queu.*

The Arkansan walked behind the stooping darkey, swung his right boot into the air three or four times, and then sent the sole whizzing against the darkey's camera-obscura —*Newsp Cutting.*

Came up (*Street*, 1890) Come up. Amongst the masses it is a common shape of small wit to replace the present by the past tense 'Came' for 'come' is very common and used by most drivers—who invariably say 'Came up'.

Camp (*Street*) Actions and gestures of exaggerated emphasis Probably from the French. Used chiefly by persons of exceptional want of character 'How very camp he is'

Can (*Navy*) A. B 's familiar abbreviation of Canopus. Why classic when you can be colloquial, and 'can' is still very colloquial in the Navy

Can I help you with that? (*Peoples'*, 1895 on). Said generally to a man with money, or eating, or more especially drinking. Drolly begging, in fact—mean invention. When said to the fairer sex the import is different.

Can you say uncle to that? (*Dustmen's*) To which the usual answer appears to be (in a dust-yard) 'Yes—I can' Uncle in this relationship appears to equal 'reply'.

Can you smash a thick 'un? (*Peoples'*). Can you change a sovereign. A grim sign of woe—suggesting the common experience that the moment a sovereign is changed, it is 'smashed' or gone

Canader (*Oxford* 'er') A Canadian canoe—this word being canoer. Accent on the second in Canader.

Canaries (*London*, 1882) Charity subscription papers. This term took its rise from the use of the word by Booth, the General of the Salvation Army. The colours of the Army were red and yellow, probably in close imitation of the scarlet and gold of the officers of the Guards. The idea of using yellow paper for subscription lists probably arose from the combined facts that yellow paper is cheap and that yellow was one of the Army colours. On the other hand, red paper is very expensive. General Booth, who had a marked tendency to very simple forms of humour, named these papers 'Canaries'. The word 'took' at once.

Canary (*Music Hall*, 1870). Chorus-singer amongst the public—generally in gallery. Invented by Leybourne, a comic singer, probably to give him rest between his verses, he being pulmonary. 'Go it, canaries', he flatteringly would say, meaning that they sang like canaries.

Chorus-singing by the canaries has long been a South London Institution.—*Ref.*, March 1886.

Canary (*Costermonger*, 1876). An ideal hip adornment.

Upper Benjamin built on a downy plan, velveteen taoc, kerseymere kicksies, built very slap up, with the artful dodge, a canary, very hanky panky, with a double fakement down the side.—*Cutting.*

Very difficult of explanation, and in true descent from the cod-piece, though not so glaring in its declaration. It has also some association with 'Il Ruossignuolo', as spoken of in the sprightly pages of Boccacio.

Canary Bird (*Peoples'*). A sovereign. Canary, as something charming, is often associated with pleasant things that are yellow. 'Yes, it's a canary bird, but it will soon fly away to my landlord. He gets them all!'

Candid Friend (*Soc.*, 1860). Equivalent of the damned kind friend of Sir Peter Teazle's. One who says what a mere acquaintance would studiously avoid. Man who urges what he should only admit with reluctance.

Mr Foster has for a long while taken upon himself the unpleasant rôle of 'candid friend' with regard to the Government, and every now and again considers it his bounden duty to chide the members of it when even those who are in open Opposition would remain silent.—*Ref.*, 8th March 1885.

Candle, To (*Peoples'*, 18 *cent.*). To investigate or examine minutely. Figure of speech derived from the use of candles to test eggs, and to ascertain if a second sheet or other enclosure was included in a letter. In the last century the candle was practically the only mode of illumination—a common object. Now, except in the 'wax' division of society, a candle is frequently not seen from year's beginning to end.

It requires a stretch of fancy to picture forth an old-fashioned post-office, with clerks 'candling' the letters as if they were doubtful eggs. The conditions of a single letter were that it should be written 'on one sheet.' The letters were held up to the light to show whether they required a surcharge for an enclosure.—*D. N.*, 1st August 1883.

Candle-shop (*Broad Church*). A Roman Catholic chapel, or Ritualistic church—from the plenitude of lights.

Canister (*Street*). A preacher. Evidently a corruption of a street preacher whose name was something like, for instance, 'Kynaster', and popularly Anglicised. (*See* Sky Pilot.)

Cant. Sneaking, mean, lying, faced with assertion of religion. Probably first used opprobriously after the Reformation, when Canterbury fell out of grace for the time being, as the metropolis of the English Church. Long after the destruction of the monasteries Kent was the headquarters of English beggars. It is so perhaps to this day. Dickens, who died in 1870, was always accompanied in his walks from Gad's Hill House by several mastiffs, which he declared were for his protection from beggars. The author certainly cleared the roads about Gad's Hill from beggars—and the lieges as well for that matter, for the dogs were as fierce as Bismarck's. The abbey-loupers always begged with canticles in their noses and mouths, especially with the prayer to S. Martin, patron saint of beggars. Cant may be from Kent, Canterbury, or canticle, or all three, but it certainly means, as it meant, whining imposture on a basis of religion, as 'He doesn't preach—he cants.' 'Don't cant, Bert, or I won't pay a doit of your debts.' All the great writers of the eighteenth century use this word—Swift, Addison, Dryden, and many others. Dr Johnson, of course, gives the word a Latin origin—'Cantus'—but does not say how the journey was made. In Scotland they believe the word came from two Andrew Cants, father and son, time of Charles II., and both very violent

Presbyterian preachers. But the word went north to them, the Cants did not send it south, 'I write not always in the proper terms of navigation, land service, or in the cant of any profession '—*Dryden* 'A few general rules, with a certain cant of words, has sometimes set up an illiterate heavy writer for a most judicious critic.' The word in Ireland is still used for selling by bids. 'Numbers of these tenants or their descendants are now offering to sell their leases by cant '—*Swift*

Terra del Fuégo is, as the cant phrase goes, beyond the sphere of British influence for either ambition or greed, but it has not been forgotten by the British missionary societies.—*D N.*, 14th May 1889

Cant of togs (*Beggars'*). A gift of clothes Here the mode of begging for clothes affords a word to describe the present or benefit gained by canting Good example of low satire satirising itself.

Can't see a hole in a forty-foot ladder (*Colloquial*) Drunk in the extreme degree, for such a ladder offers quite forty opportunities.

Every night does my husband come home blue, blind, stiff, stark, staring drunk, till he can't see a hole in a forty foot ladder, sure —*Comic Song*, 1882

Can't see it (*Peoples'*) Reply in the way of objection, such as 'Do lend me five pounds!' 'Can't see it'

Can't show yourself to (*Peoples'*, 1880) Not equal to; as thus · 'You can't show yourself to Jack Spicer'—or of a play—'It can't show itself to *The Golden Prince.*'

Can't you feel the shrimps? (*Cockney*, 1877) *I e*, Smell the sea. Heard on a Thames steamboat when approaching Gravesend, the metropolis of shrimps (*See* Speak the Brown To-morrow, Taste the Sun, See the Breeze.)

Cantillory Realism (*Soc.*, 1897). Onomatope applied to singing. The linguistic 'find' of 1897 Means singing in which the sounds suggest the words sung. Very open to ridicule, but intended quite gravely. At once burlesqued — where 'kiss' was used the lips were smacked If 'thunder' came in the words, the singer used all his bass voice, etc., etc.

Owing to his powers as a vocalist, Mr Louis James, of Walthamstow, may be on the high road to fortune, but unless he promptly ceases to follow what the new-fashioned jargon calls cantillatory realism his rosy prospects may become overshadowed — *D T*, 1st February 1898.

Cap (*Eng -Amer.*). Equivalent to 'Sir' — but really abbreviation of 'Captain'. Common in America—gaining ground in England.

'Fact, Cap,' asserted a bystander

Cape Smoke (*Cape Town, S A*) Indigenous whiskey of the colony, which is very cloudy in tone.

Mr Cecil Ashley strongly insists on the terrible effects of the 'Cape Smoke' At present this evil vapour may be bought at sevenpence a bottle, and traders wander about the country with waggon lòads of it, which they almost force on the natives —*Newsp. Cutting*, 1878.

Captain Bates (Been to see)? (*Thieves' and Street*). A satirical enquiry of the 'How d'ye do?' character — applied to a gentleman once more restored to ungrateful society after a term in jail Captain Bates was a well-known metropolitan prison-governor.

Captain Macfluffer (*Theatr*) Sudden loss of memory on the stage, *e.g*, 'He took Captain Macfluffer awfully bad' Its origin is beyond the hope of discovery Cut down to Fluff and fluffy

The prompter's voice is dumb in America. Actors and actresses there are alert and ready for their work, they don't 'fluff' —Clement Scott, October 1900.

Captain Swosser (*Peoples'*). Naval cousin of the military Captain Jinks, both blustering specimens of the services. Derived from a character of Marryat's.

The inducements of Captain Swosser, of the Royal Navy, to have his portrait taken are far less than they were.—(1882)

Carachtevankterous (*Amer.*) Desperately wanting in self-possession Perhaps an intensification of cantankerous, which in its turn is a term beyond investigation Both probably wild onomatopes.

I have seen folks upon this river—quiet-looking chaps, too, as ever you see—who were so teetotally carachtevankterous that they'd shoot the doctor who'd tell them they couldn't live when ailing, and make a die of it, jist out spite, when told they *must* get well.—*Newsp. Cutting.*

Carambo, Caramba (*Span.-Amer.*, going north, and passing to Eng.). Hearty good wishes—but more honoured in the breach than the observance. In fact honestly translated, and loudly expressed to a departing friend—might lead to the interference of any policeman with salvationary or even merely denominational tendencies. Meaning elegantly evaded in Spanish-English dictionaries. Much used in the extreme south-west of France—especially at Tarbes. Implacable etymologists may apply at any Spanish embassy—perhaps the Spanish door-keeper, if there be one, is the safest professor of Spanish to trust to, during this lingual search after useful knowledge.

Carara (*European* passing, 1898). A murderer who cremates his victim.

As she was conveyed to prison the Mantes people shouted 'A mort la Carara,' giving her the name of the Italian mushroom merchant now awaiting trial in Paris for the murder of the bank messenger at Bicêtre.—*D. T.*, 4th April 1898.

Carding (*Irish-Fenian*, 1867-82). A local torture.

Cardings have very likely been rare in county Wicklow. A carding is a highly-spirited operation. About twenty persons, more or less well armed and disguised, break into a cottage, and subject persons who have basely paid rent to a more or less severe form of torture. According to the old Parliamentary reports, carders 'tool' with a board stuck full of nails, but perhaps modern science has provided, or modern spirit suggested, some less severe instrument of correction.—*D. N.*, 1881.

Carlylese (*Liter.*, 19 *cent.*). Benevolent despotism, Tory democracy (1880-85).

To him' (Bismarck) says Mr Lowe in the middle-class Carlylese which he affects, 'to him the ballot-box was only a dice-box.'—*D. N.*, December 1885.

Carnival (*Amer.*, 1882). A fashion or sudden practice.

It not unfrequently happens that such prominent events are followed by an epidemic or 'carnival'—to use a much-abused word—of suicides and murder. (1882).

Caroon (*Peoples'*). A five-shilling or crown piece. From *Corona*, and nearer the mark than the modern word. (*See* Cart-wheel.)

Carpenter Scene (*Theatr.*). Cloth or flats, well down the stage, to allow of some comic dialogue while the next scene is setting.

The old, feeble device of 'forward', or, as they were sometimes derisively called, 'carpenter' scenes—because notoriously written only to give time for the building of more elaborate sets behind them—have now almost entirely disappeared from the stage.—*Newsp. Cutting*, 6th April 1885.

Carpet-bagger (*Amer.—coming to England*). A general term for a poor person who arrives with a carpet-bag, and becomes prosperous by audacity or unfair trading. Originated by the Confederates, as against the Federals, when after the civil war hungry and place-seeking political adventurers from the north were appointed to places in the conquered south, and, arriving in a poverty-stricken condition, soon showed signs of wealth and general prosperity.

Carpet Dance (*Soc.*, 1877). A familiar dance for a few unfortunates in a drawing-room, as distinct from a large dance to which everybody is invited. It was voted bad taste to offer champagne at a carpet dance—or indeed to drink any wine whatever, except claret. White soup was often served, and became as fashionable as rational, *e.g.*, 'Do come and christen our new carpet with a valse or two.'

Carried (*Rhyming*). Married; *e.g.*, 'He was carried yesterday, poor bloke'—very ominous, and searchingly graphic. The word is obtained merely by supplanting the 'm' by a 'c'—but what a suggestion there is of harrying and rallying on the part of the bride!

Carriwitchet (*Peoples'*). A puzzling question. Probably an invented word, in itself suggestive of bewilderment. Or it may be from the name of a woman notorious for asking difficult questions—say Carrie Witchet!

Carrots (*L. Class*). Red hair. This is an interesting instance of aggressive Anglicization. It has not in origin anything to do with 'carrots', the colour of which has never yet been seen in association with human, or perhaps any other hair, except, possibly, that of one of the 'lemurs'.

It is a corruption from Catholic times in England when a red man or woman was called 'Iscariot', the 'betrayer' in the Roman Church, and especially in Rome where red hair amongst the people has always been a rarity—because Judas Iscariot was historically supposed to have had red hair. The Protestant religion in England more or less parting with Iscariot, the historical name became associated with the vegetable, which, by the way, may have gained its name, seeing its colour, from the same source as did red hair.

'Hello—carrots—what cheer now, my lad!'

'Deceptive—what can you expect of her? Isn't she carroty?' Indeed to this day there is a firm belief that red-haired women are faithless and deceptive—probably from their frankness, possible rudeness, yet general desire to please. In Scotland 'carrots' has degenerated into 'sandy', invariably applied to red-haired men, but never to women. Supposed by correctly thinking people to be a nickname for Alexander; but really a substitute for Iscariot, and a good one, for there is plenty of 'sand', or 'grit', or 'go' in most men or women with hair more or less auburn.

Carry me out (*Peoples'*, 18 *cent.*). A satirical expression, pretending defeat, humiliation, and pardon. Sometimes 'carry me out and bury me decent.' The latter portion is possibly an Irish addition. Derived from the prize ring, when the senseless, defeated hero was, when quite vanquished, as scrappers once were, ignominiously carried out. Or it may be from cock-fighting, or both. The dead birds were certainly carried out.

Carry on proper (*Common Lond.*, 19 *cent.*). To behave well.

Carsey (*L. London*). A house; corruption of casa—from the Italian organ-grinders in Saffron Hill district.

If you're a bank director and broken up a thousand carsers of poor honest people, that's the time to do a guy.—*Newsp. Cutting.*

Cart (*Peoples'*, 18 *cent.*). A metaphor for the gallows—to which terminal its victims were jolted in a cart. Still heard in provincial places—'You be on'y fit for the cart'—doubtless now used without the least idea of its original meaning. In London the cart travelled, only too often, several miles from Newgate to Tyburn Tree, whose site was that of the Marble Arch in Hyde Park. Used by all the dramatists in the last century.

'I care not—welcome pillory or cart.'—Garrick, *Abel Drugger.*

Now would I sooner take a cart in company with the hangman than a week with that woman.—Farquhar, *The Inconstant.*

Cartocracy (*Soc.*, 19 *cent.*). People distinguished enough to keep carts—especially dog-carts. (*See* Gigmanity.)

Carts (*L. London*). A pair of boots—generally those of noble size. Onomatopoetic—reference to the noise a young navvy can make with his understandings as equal to that of the passing waggon.

Cartwheel (*Peoples'*). A five-shilling piece. From its noble weight and thickness. (*See* Crown.)

Carve up (*Amer.*). To annihilate completely.

That dear grave holds a disappointed chap who cum out here from Reno to carve me up.—*Newsp. Cutting.*

Case (*Fast Life*, 1850 on). Abbreviated form of Casino, and referring to the rowdy cafés for which the Haymarket was once celebrated. The word has survived the abolition of late houses and the closing of public-houses at 12.30. The word is applied to any common public-house or confectioner's where the business carried on is not wholly one of stomachic refreshments. 'He kept a case for years in Panton Street'—may be from Casa. 'Case' is also thieves' English for a counterfeit five-shilling piece.

Though Neal kept what is vulgarly known as a case, and was assisted in his unholy work by Mrs Neal, and though both of them at different times were concerned in the management or direction of other cases, he seems to have considered it his wife's duty to remain,' etc.—*Ref.*, 16th March 1890.

Casket (*Amer.*). Evasion of 'coffin'. First mentioned in Webster, in edition of 1879. Coming to England slowly.

When he got to the house the child was laid out in a handsome white casket that must have cost at least twenty dollars.—*N. Y. Mercury*, 1884.

Cast-iron and double-bolted (*Amer.*, 1880). Samsonly strong.

Striking outcome of the spread of engineering work.

'Stranger, onless yer made of cast-iron and double-bolted, ye hadn't better go in till the row is over!'—1883.

Cast an Optic (*Sporting*). A paraphrase of 'look'.

Cast skin, To (*Soc.*). To rejuvenate—from the serpent throwing off its skin annually, and coming forth radiant. Still used.

'Why, sir, you've cast your skin.'—Farquhar, *The Inconstant*.

Castor (*Street*). A hat. Of course from the first hats being made of the fur of the castor, or beaver; passed down to the streets, where any hat is called a castor. Superseded by Gossamer.

Casuals (*Hotel*). One-day stayers in luxurious hotels at marine and mineral water stations. From the casual, or night pauper, as distinct from the superior settled unionist.

Another day the 'casuals' at the hotel were mystified exceedingly by a carefully printed programme announcing that a performance of wax-work would be given in the drawing-room. — *Newsp. Cutting*.

Casualty (*Peoples'*). A black eye. From the first Soudan war, when slight injuries were cabled under this head.

In one of these contests, in the affair of the Cross Causeway, indeed, Scott became what is now called a 'casualty'. He suffered a contusion.—*D. N.*, 21st March 1885.

Cat (*Thieves'*). Woman in general, and a bad one in particular. Suggested probably by her smoothness, the uncertainty of her temper, and the certainty of her claws.

Cat and Fiddle (*Hist.*). A very common sign for a tavern until words supplanted rebuses, which were for the ignorant. The country arrival who could neither pronounce 'The Bacchanals', nor understand these three dancing graces, could nevertheless know he 'was there' when he saw as a painted sign the 'Bag o' Nails'. The use of the house-sign was its power to paint the sound of a word or words by objects which had a relation of sound only to the actual meaning of the sign. Hence a goat and a pair of compasses, one of the Cromwellian signs after the Restoration, represented 'God encompasses us.' Probably all the old Catholic signs, especially those on the road to Canterbury, are still in existence. For instance, the rendezvous for the Blackfriars as distinct from the Southwark pilgrims was 'The Hand and Flower,' which lent itself readily to the painter's art. It refers to the Virgin and her emblem, the lily. This house was at the corner of Gravel Lane and Union Street, about half a mile from the Tabard, and it only lost this sign some thirty years since. The Cat and Fiddle is the 'Catherine fidèle', probably brought over with the Conqueror, for 'à la Catherine fidèle' is still a common sign in Normandy. Obviously the Anglo-Saxon knew nothing of the great saint of Alexandria—but a painted Cat and Fiddle was quite within his means. Necessarily these signs were in the old parts of London, which in time became all the low parts of London. For a hundred years or more 'Cat and Fiddle' has meant a doubtful house, where thieves and loose women abound.

He's come down in the world, has Jim. He keeps a Cat and Fiddle.

Cat and Mutton Lancers (*E. London*, 1870). Name given to the militia in the district of Dalston when drilling in Cat and Mutton Fields. When time, elegance, and the wave of progress have swept these 'fields' far away from their present elysium the term will remain an enigma. Probably from a chapel or chantrey (11th to 15th century) dedicated to Catherine Martyr (of Alexandria). It is a good instance of human stupidity in accepting sheer ignorance as gospel truth that within the precincts of these fields a publican had for sign a cat running away with a leg of mutton; his rebus perpetuated the absurdity.

Cat-lap (*L. Soc.*). Tea and coffee; terms used scornfully by drinkers of beer and strong waters. Cat-lap in club-life is one of the more ignominious names given to champagne by men who prefer stronger liquors.

Bell rings, and enter Emperor and Empress; and then there takes place the general presentation. A vast crowd, but not much animation; plenty of card tables, but few players; no supper, but plenty of soup; also 'catlap' in abundance. Empress retires very soon; Kaiser stays.—*Newsp. Cutting*.

Cat-meat pusher (*Street*). A merchant of cooked horse-flesh, the final term being derived from his truck—albeit pusher means generally a maker or doer of something Linendrapers' young men are calico-pushers, while the trimmers up of old clothes are called faker-pushers.

Cat o' Mountain (*Peoples'*) A shrew. A very common example of confused origin, for whether this term comes from catamaran, a wild, over-sailed S American craft, or from catamount (a panther) it would be difficult to say. Very common still in London street feminine statements. Yer catter mountin', go 'ome an' wash yer pore childring an' don't dare ter haddress *me*, mum!

Cat on testy dodge (*Soc.* 1870 on) A ladylike beggar worrying ladies at their houses for money—if only a sixpence (tester), and bringing testimonials in favour of some charitable institution. These 'cats', generally strong-minded ones, take commission on the sums they get.

Catafalque (*Fashion,* 1897). The high plumed hat—especially black feathered, which rose to its greatest height in 1897, towards the end of which year they were sometimes removed to laps by their wearers when in theatres and a good temper

The ladies with the huge hats have capitulated, and George Alexander has added another to his many conquests. At the last Saturday matinée there was not a catafalque to be seen on any head, but towers of plumes in many laps —*D. T.*, 25th November 1897

Cataract (*Soc*, '40's) Voluminous and many folded falling cravat, which swarmed over the length and breadth of the fashionable masculine chest

Cat-sneaking (*Thieves'*). Stealing public-house pots Probably an easy disguise for 'pot' Creatures of a felonious turn so fallen as to take to this trade would have little invention

Catch Cocks, To (*Low Military*) To obtain money by false pretences Catch cocks are contrived by characterless soldiers who address gentlemen, invent tales of distress, and often thereby obtain money. 'Joe, let's go cock-catching.'

In the Kensington Gardens a soldier told a gentleman that he lost his railway ticket, which was to take him to Windsor to join his battalion, and he would be punished if not at his quarters at a certain time The gentleman gave him the money for his fare, but saw the man go in a contrary direction to that of the railway station. He followed him, but he ran into a public-house and got out by the back-door, and the gentleman saw no more of him He ascertained that he was a Grenadier Guardsman, and that his battalion could not be at Windsor, as the Fusilier Guards were there There is not a day but soldiers are guilty of such disgraceful acts of 'loafing', and they glory in it They call it, in the Guards, 'catching cocks' and 'throwing the hammer' These terms may have a far more cogent or obscure meaning —*Newsp Cutting*

Catch on, To (*Amer.* probably from New Eng) To make a hit; to succeed beyond question

'Come down to The Bric-a-brac and I'll show you some of the gentlemen thieves, the fellows who have discovered a way by which they can commit highway robbery by daylight and in the presence of witnesses, and not to be amenable to the law', said Old Sport to the reporter 'I don't catch on,' replied the reporter.

'I don't catch on worth a cent', sadly murmured the managing editor, 'but as you have worked on the great dailies, I suppose it's all right'—*Newsp Cutting*

I hear that Miss Helen Dauvray is coming to the Prince's to play 'One of Our Girls', the comedy which Bronson Howard wrote expressly for her The piece seems to have caught on in the States.—*Newsp Cutting*

Catch-penny (*Street*). Gutter Ballads

The origin of the phrase 'catch-penny' is that after the execution in London of Thurtell for the murder of Weare (1824), a publisher named Catchpin printed a penny ballad entitled *We are Alive Again.* When cried on the streets it sold to the extent of 2,500,000 copies, the persons buying supposing from the sound that the ballad had reference to Weare It came, therefore, to be spoken of as a 'Catch penny affair'

Catechism (*Bankruptcy Court*). Interrogatories

Caterpillar (*Soc*, 1848 on) A ladies' school. (*See* Crocodile)

Caterwauling (*Peoples'*). Cat-music Johnson gives up the attempt to derive this word 'What a caterwauling do you keep here.'—Shakespeare (*Twelfth Night*). Used now only by the vulgar.

'So I cannot stay here to be entertained with your caterwauling.'—Gay, *Beggars' Opera*.

Cats' Party (*Sporting*). Chiefly women. Probably from the high tone of women's voices.

Upon one occasion she was at a party given at 88 Adelaide Road. It was termed a 'cats' party', owing to the number of ladies who were present. (Laughter.)—Mr Justice Butt: Descriptive of the music, I suppose. (Laughter.)—Divorce Court, *Dunn* v. *Dunn & Wall*, 1st February 1888.

Caucus (*Amer.-Eng.*). Vehmgericht, or council of many tens, who secretly combine on a given line of action. The word came from U.S.A. about 1870. Primarily 'caucus' like 'gueux' in Flanders (16th century), and 'frondeur' in France (17th century) was a term of reproach, which was adopted by the party attacked with this word; and used by themselves to distinguish themselves. Very wide in its application. Mr Joseph Chamberlain has done much to popularise this very important word — not yet admitted into dictionaries.

Gordon, in his history of the American Revolutions, says, 'About the year 1738, the father of Samuel Adams, and twenty others who lived in the north or shipping part of Boston, used to meet to make a caucus and lay their plan for introducing certain persons into places of trust. Each distributed the ballots in his own circle, and they generally carried the election. As this practice originated in the shipping part of Boston, caucus may have probably been a corruption of caulker's meeting.'—(1830).

'The House of Lords', says Mr Chamberlain very truly, 'has become, so far as its majority are concerned, a mere branch of the Tory caucus—a mere instrument of the Tory organisation.'—*D.N.*, 9th October 1884.

'Then the noble lord says I am the Birmingham caucus. This description is flattering as to my influence and ability, but it is a total mistake.'—Mr J. Chamberlain, House of Commons, 30th October 1884.

Caucus-monger (*Political*, 1883). A political agitator. Introduced by Lord Randolph Churchill (1883), and accepted by the Conservative party as representing the average radical.

They now knew beyond all manner of doubt, that on the 4th of May last the Government of Ireland was handed over to Mr Chamberlain, the caucus-monger of Birmingham—and to Mr Sheridan, the outrage-monger of Tubbercurry — Lord Randolph Churchill. Dinner at Woodstock, 27th February 1883.

Caulk, Calk (*Naval*). Go to bed and to sleep, probably from tucking in the clothes under you in the hammock or bunk, and so suggesting the action of caulking a seam in the vessel's side; also used for a short sleep—forty winks:—'I'll caulk it out.'

From this word grows out 'caulker'. Four of Irish hot; *i.e.*, four pennyworth of Irish whiskey. Quite naval, and equal to the mere landsmen's 'nightcap'—caulk meaning to make all tight and weather safe.

Cave (Cave of Adullam) (*Polit.*, 1866-97 on). A secret political combination — distinct from illegal conspiracy.

You recollect a new institution brought into the House of Commons at that time (1886). It is called the 'Cave'. Into the 'Cave' entered, as was historically correct, all the discontented—those who did not like the Bill on the opposite side of the House, and some on our side who did not like it; and the result was that the Bill was destroyed, and the destruction of the Government followed it. We supposed the 'Cave' would come into office. They came into office, not all the 'Cave', but some of them.—J. Bright: Bright Celebrations, Birmingham, June 1883.

Many of you will no doubt remember that a strenuous effort was made by the Opposition in which they were joined by some 'Cave' men from our side to frustrate the Government Bill, which was rejected, and the Government itself overthrown. — John Bright, Leeds, 18th October 1883.

Cave Dwellers (*Soc.*, 1890 on). Atavists—people whose habits are on a par with those of the pre-historic races.

A certain mining camp of cave-dwellers was wont to beguile its Sabbaths by tying up in the same bag a cat, a terrier, a monkey, and a parrot, and speculating on the issue.—*Newsp. Cutting*.

Caved out (*Amer.-Eng.*, 19 *cent.*). Come to an end—finished. From the metal ceasing in a tunnel. The end of the vein.

Cawfin (*Marine*). A badly found ship. Corruption of 'coffin'—name given as suggestive of a sailor being as bad as dead who sailed in her. Became popular when Mr Plimsoll forced his Bill.

Celestials (*Theatrical*) Gallery occupants, a synonym of 'gods'—from their superior position to pit and even boxes

One of the 'celestials' visiting Toole's Theatre (pulled down in 1897) recently complains that, although he was elevated, his seat wasn't sufficiently high to enable him, with Tam o' Shanters and Gainsboroughs on the heads of the ladies in the upper boxes, to see more than the top of the scenery —*Ref*, 5th October 1884

Cellars (*Street*) Boots Probably because these apartments are the lowest necessities in connection with ordinary sumptuary arrangements (*See* Garret)

Centipedes, The (*Military*). 100th Foot From the insect of that name. One of the punning regimental cognomens. (*See* $\frac{2}{\text{D.G}}$ and XL's)

Cess. *See* Bad cess to ye !

Chain lightning (*L Class, Lond.*) Potato spirit, imported from Germany. Filthy mess—poisonous to a degree. Smuggled chiefly

On telling him the charge he exclaimed, 'It's all nonsense, I only gave her some chain-lightning,' which he understood to be some foreign spirit.—*D. N.*, 22nd December 1885

Chair Days (*Soc.*) Old age.

Why should a cruel and humiliating malady torture the kindly, upright, conscientious spirit, and rack the strong, temperate bodily force spent in the service of his age, deserving, if any ever did, easy 'chair days' and the supreme blessing of the natural euthanasia of old age?—Sir E. Arnold, writing of Gladstone's death, June 1898

Chair Warmer (*Theatrical Anglo-Amer*). A beautiful or pretty woman who does nothing on the stage beyond helping to fill it

'Richard Whalen fired a pistol shot at Carrie Howard, a 'chair-warmer' at Esher's Alhambra, St Louis, at the close of the performance on Friday night. A 'chair-warmer' is a lady whose talent is comprised in her physical charms, and who can neither sing, dance, nor act. —*Newsp Cutting*

Chairmarking (*L. Industrial*, 19 *cent.*) Secret markings of licences and employés' characters by masters, foremen, and others. Probably marking by the chairman or master On 4th August 1894 (*see D. T.*) a complainant, whose name did not transpire, by a solicitor, summoned a cab-proprietor for (through his foreman) marking a licence with secret signs.

What two witnesses for the complainant regarded as 'chairmarking' was some additional writing in the date column

Mr Hopkins (the magistrate at Westminster) said it is possible that the licence is marked in a manner to be understood in the trade, but if cabmen are able to combine to make their terms —they have a powerful union of their own—why should not the proprietors also combine and by marking a licence in a particular way, let it be understood that the holder of it is not a desirable person to be employed ? They are entitled to do it —*D T*, 4th August 1891

Chalk against (*Peoples'*). Resentment or desire for explanation In the last century when very few of the smaller shopkeepers could write, a score was kept in chalk on a square of wood (*See* Hogarth's *Distressed Poet*) It is most figuratively used to designate an unsettled misunderstanding or grudge. (*See* Score.)

Chalk marquis (*Peoples'*) A false marquis. Never applied to any other title than this Probably the result of some forgotten pun or play upon a name.

Chalk out (*Peoples'*) Distinct directions Nothing so vivid as this in any well-known modern language 'If you miss it now — you *are* a juggins I've clean chalked it out.'

Challik it oop (*Theatrical*) A grotesque request to obtain credit—the primitive way of marking up a credit in public-houses before education was extended.

Chamber of Horrors (*Soc*) The name of the corridor or repository in which Messrs Christie (King Street, St James's) locate the valueless pictures that are sent to them from all parts of the world as supposed genuine old masters; sent, as a rule, with directions to sell at certain prices most preposterously fixed very high Phrase borrowed from Madame Tussaud's wax-work, where this chamber is coloured black, and filled with the effigies of murderers

Chamber of Horrors (*City*) Room at Lloyd's (Royal Exchange) where are 'walled' notices of shipwrecks and casualties at sea.

Champagner (*Mus. Hall*, 1880). Lorette. Within the last twenty years the marvellous increase in the consumption of champagne—or what seems like it to the unlearned in wines—has been most marked. Directly the tap-stopper was invented and 'fizzing' wine came to be sold by the glass, the ladies who chiefly frequent the better parts of music-halls at once showed their elegance by deserting gin, rum, and other horrors for this less damaging, however adulterated, drink. Hence the poor souls who could not command the 'sparkling' and its adjuncts, either from want of good looks, good breeding, or good clothes, assimilated the new popular drink and its female consumers.

'Oh, bless you, she won't speak now—she's quite the champagner.' (*See* Tip-topper.)

Champagne Shoulders (*Soc.*, 1860). Sloping shoulders. From the likeness to the drooping shoulder of the champagne bottle as distinct from the squarish ditto of the sherry or port bottle.

Champagne Weather (*Soc.*, 1860 on). Bad weather—said satirically.

Champion Slump of 1897 (*London*, 1897). Motor car. On and after Lord Mayor's Day of 1896 the motor car claimed English highways for their own. On the 10th there was a procession from Westminster to Brighton, with such a lamentable result that the 'slump' or catastrophe prefaced 1897—for some time.

Has the great motor car demonstration, which was to revolutionize British humanity, fizzled off into this?—*D. T.*, 15th February 1897.

As this year wore on a dozen or so of pale yellow motor-cabs, which came to be satirically styled 'The Butter-coloured Beauties,' made their appearance. But they had not plied for hire three months before one of them killed a hanger-on boy with its back wheel gear, while in November a driver went drunk and amok with his motor-cab; the two in combination doing considerable damage.

By the end of November they were called the 'Margarine Messes', which grew out of their first satiric name—'The Butter Beauties'—from their colour.

Towards Christmas the motor once more took to its initial behaviour—and ran away.

The Champion Slump of 1897 was not appreciably modified by the natural history of the motor car in 1898.

Chancellor's Eggs (*Legal*). Day-old barristers.

Every term a new batch of what were once humorously called 'Chancellor's eggs' is incubated..—*D. T.*

Change breath (*Amer. tavern*). Take a 'go' of whiskey—this certainly does change the smell of the breath.

The other day as three or four of the old boys were sitting around the stove in Schneider's sample room stirring in the grated nutmeg, Bill Matson came in to change his breath.—1882.

Chant (*Sporting*, 1886 on). To swear—the last satirical popular verb to describe 'language'.

Chanting-ken (*L. London*). A music-hall.

Chapel (*Printers'*). Secret meeting and decision. The congregation of unionists in a 'shop', to confer upon any given matter of trade, or even personal importance. Little notes are sent about, a chapel never being called at a moment's notice. They generally take place at tea-time, when the assembly sit in some quiet corner, drink their tea quietly, and as quietly discuss the question. Probably from 'chapter'—especially as printing in England dates from the chapter-house, Westminster Abbey. (*See* Garret.)

Chapper (*L. London*). Mouth—from associations with chaps, chops, and cheeks.

Chapper, To (*L. London*). To drink.

Chappie (*Soc.*, about 1880). Replaced chum, which had become vulgar. There was quite a friendly meaning in the word; it was by no means contemptuous, and thereby varied from the meaning put upon 'Johnny', which appeared about this same time. Dropped rapidly in the world, and vanished from society in the '90's.

The hue of vine and mulberry just now is delicious, and makes us regret somewhat that the Mulberry Gardens liked by Pepys when the 'chappies' and 'Johnnies' of his day did not carry him off to 'Fox Hall,' have made way for the peculiar ugliness of Buckingham Palace. —*D. N.*, 1882.

Charity Bob The quick, jerky curtsey made by charity school-girls, now (1883) rapidly passing away.

A little mite about eighteen inches high on the O P side wins loud applause for her correct rendering of the charity bob —*Newsp. Cutting*

Charley (*Street*, 1662-1829) London street watchmen

In New Boswell Court might be seen until recently (1868) a relic of the light of other days in the shape of an ancient box (which used to be drawn up from the pavement during the day), fitted for the protection of those slow, antiquated, muffled-up guardians of the night, covered with their many-caped dark coats, called watchmen . At length the Charley found himself one fine morning superseded by that admirably constituted and well organized body, the new police, as modelled by Sir Robert Peel, who appeared in the London streets for the first time, 20th September 1829 —Diprose's *Clement Danes*, vol i. p. 101

Between the bellmen and the London watchmen there was always a close alliance, and in the reign of the Merry Monarch, from whom the Charlies took their name, their identities were more or less merged —*D T*, 17th January 1894.

This same word is used by 'the general' to describe women's breasts when well developed It is said this term also comes down from Charles II., and refers to his many mistresses, who certainly displayed their charms as never women did before. Wilder etymologists assume the word to come from Carolian French—'cher lis'—referring to the painted whiteness of the attribute in question

Charlie Freer (*Rhyming, Sporting*) Beer, *e g.*, 'He can put down Charlie Freer by the gallon, he can.'

Chateau Dif (*S. Exchange*). A grotesque play upon Chateau d'If. Here the exchange is the castle of diff, or diffs—*i e*, 'differences' on settling days.

Chatham and Dover (*London public-house rhyming*) 'Over' This phrase is generally used as a pacificating one —in a tavern quarrel, a friend will say, 'Come—Chatham and Dover it' —meaning give it over

Cheap beer (*Police*) Beer given by publicans at night-time to officers.

'There are innumerable publicans who make a practice of allowing this "cheap beer", and it is tacitly understood that all cases will be treated leniently in which those houses may choose to form the scene of future action The first enquiry of a constable whose beat is changed to his brother officer, who shows him "his new relief", is, which are the houses where "cheap beer" may be relied upon to be ready when punctually called for '—*Newsp Cutting*

Cheat (*Thieves'*, 18 *cent.*) Gallows Fielding's *Jonathan Wild*

Check up (*Gallery, Theatrical*). To 'check up' is to obtain entry to the gallery, not by the ordinary mode of payment, but by waiting at the bottom of the gallery stairs and asking passers out, 'Have yer done with yer check, sir?'—the pass-out check, by production of which the holder obtains re-admission to the theatre. When the applicant gets the check, he 'ups' at once—the gallery stairs Theatrical managers hold that these transfers are not legal, but magistrates, certainly in London, will not convict checkers up if brought before them upon charges of fraud 'I've checked up three times this blessed week!' said the youth 'I checked it up—I wasn't goin' to pay no bloomin' shillin'.'

Cheek-ache (*Artisans'*) Blushing or turning red in the face rather for the meanness of another than your own. 'I got the cheek-ache over him '

Cheeky (*Peoples'*). Adjective form of cheek—smart sauciness.

Cheese and Crust (*Low Classes*). Exclamation — perversion of Jesus Christ Frightful at first sight, this phrase suggests a slight sense of respect by its veiling of the oath. Also a little touching as being a phrase associated with comfort to those amongst whom comfort is little known (*See* Corkscrew)

Cheri (*Soc*, 1840-55 and on) A charming woman Derived from Madame Montigny, of the Gymnase, Paris Her stage name remained Rose Cheri She was a singularly pure woman, and an angelic actress. Word used by upper class men in society, in the 'forties', to describe the nature of their mistresses Word now forgotten

Cheshire, The (*Peoples'* 19 *cent.*). Perfection Figure of speech, a metaphor wherein the perfection of Cheshire cheese is made to stand for perfection itself. Good example of homely coining of words, *e.g.*, 'She's the Cheshire —I can tell you.' A variant is—'That's the Stilton.' Charles Steyne was very funny as the ratcatcher, who calls everything 'the Cheshire'.

Cheshire Cats (*Provincial*). Amiable result of adjacent county criticism, —that of Lancashire. Chiefly used in association with the comparison to 'grin like a Cheshire cat'. Cat may have been derived from kit—Christopher.

Chest Plaster (*Theatrical*, 1883). Satirical description of the young actor of the day by his much older and more 'legitimate' brother actor. From the heart-shaped shirt-front worn with a very open dress waistcoat, and starched almost into a cuirass. 'Bah—he is but a chest plaster humbug.' (*See* Shape and Shirt.)

Chesterfield (*Soc.*). A long, white coat—originally made with capes—now applied to white coats generally, but sometimes to blue (1840-50). Good example of qualifying name being used for the object qualified.

Chestnut (*Amer.-Eng.*). An old joke offered as new. Brought to England officially in 1886 by A. Daly's Company at the Strand Theatre in 'A Night Off', where the heroine tells the hero the play was found in an 'old chest'—to which he replies, 'Very old —chestnut!'

Chevalier Atkins. *See* Tommy Atkins.

Chevaux de frise (*Lit.*). Friesland Horse, or cavalry—a tangle of spikes set at right angles as a rule. The Dutch had no cavalry in the 17th century. Invention of the Frieslanders; named by the French (17th century) in scorn of Dutch enemies. Good example of a phrase by its construction suggesting an apparently more obvious meaning, for the frise suggesting 'friser', the temptation to write Cheveux-de-frise, as describing the tangle, has in many instances been fatal.

Chevy-chase (*Rhyming*). Face—in common use.

After listening for a while her chevy-chase gets serious looks.—*Newsp. Cutting.*

Chew into dish-cloths (*Amer.*, 1882). To annihilate.

The wolf came down with his ears working with delight, and had only reached the earth when the goose sprang upon him and chewed him into dish-cloths.—*New American Fables.*

Chic (*Franco-English*, 1865 on)—Dash, smartness.

'Chic' in its original acceptation meant simply 'trick' or 'knack', and was applied to dexterity of performance before it acquired its application to elegance of result. A painter, for instance, was said to have 'du chic'—that is, the knack or dodge of using his brush with effect. It was only later that a 'stylish' toilette was described as displaying the same quality. The phrase came in, if we remember rightly, in the early sixties, and with the vogue of Offenbachian opera-bouffe.—G. A. Sala.

Chicago Reform Lawyer (*Amer.-Eng.*, 1890 on). A lawyer of lawyers—from the fact that Chicago is supposed to be the most alert spot on the mere earth. 'No—he's not an American advocate—he's a Chicago reform lawyer.'

She devotes herself to finance, looks after railway interests and her bonds, assisted therein by her son and daughter, who lives with her, and she defies even a 'Chicago reform lawyer' to get the better of her.—*D. T.*, 10th February 1897.

Chickaleary-cove (*Costermongers'*, 1860). A perfect personage. Introduced into society above the gutter by Vance, a comic singer, who used the word in a song-chorus. 'I'm the chickaleary cove, with my one, two, three'—the numbers probably referring to the mere trinity of blows required to floor the enemy.

The barrowman's one aim and ambition is to be chickaleary.—*D. T.*, 6th April 1893.

Enterprising clothiers at the East End make the construction of 'chickaleary' attire a leading feature of their business. —*Newsp. Cutting.*

Chi-ike (*Anglo-Amer.* 19 *cent.*). A distance call used by American trappers, and borrowed by them from the Red Indians. 'Hullo—don't chi-ike me like that over there—you'll wake Westminster Abbey.'

Mr G. A. Sala (*D. T.*, 28th August 1894) says of this phrase. 'Chi-ike!' I have not the remotest idea when this slang cry was first heard or what it means. Emitted, however, from a powerful pair of lungs, 'Chi-ike' could be made almost as far-reaching as the Australian cry, 'Coo-ee' Often sent in unfriendly salute by street arabs along the street 'Whoa-chi ike' addressed to a 'toff'

And then a crowd got round and began to chi-ike the couple —*Cutting.*

Chinwag (*Hist*) Talk

I have not been out of my pyjamas all day and no further from the tent than to the next one for a 'chinwag' —*People* August 1898, Letter from near Klondyke.

Chin-music (*Costers' defiant talk*).

One of the toughest fights Geoghegan had ever was with Jim M'Govern The two had indulged in a lot of 'chin music' on various occasions, and finally met in a saloon on the Bowery and Hester street one winter's night, when it was snowin' hard —*Newsp Cutting.*

Chin-chin (*Naval—passed into club society*) 'Hail!' 'Good health!' 'Here's to you!' 'Chin-chin, old chap.' The answer is 'Pa-pa' Origin obscure, probably—'Same to you!' Dates from the Chinese of Singapore 'We went into the temples, and our pockets were not rifled; we went into the prisons, and we were not brained by manacled villains, we mixed in crowds and were never hustled; and the only cries we heard were 'Chin, chin!' or 'Pa, Pa!'—which means welcome or good fellows —Clement Scott, *D. T.*, 1st August 1893

Chip in (*Anglo-Amer*) To join in discussion, to subscribe money.

'Gentlemen, let's chip in enough more to buy her a new dress I'm a poor man, but here's a quarter for the old lady'—*Newsp. Cutting*

Chirrup, To (*Music-hall*, 1886 on) Applaud, cheer. The word was made classical on 5th March 1888, when a man was 'sent' for a month as the result of levying blackmail upon music-hall artists as they entered at the stage door to pay for applause, with the alternative of being hissed if they did not 'stump up'. This case killed the process

Pike, the stage-doorkeeper at the Canterbury, proved seeing the prisoner for some time carrying on the system of obtaining money for what in the slang of the gang is called 'chirruping' He had seen the prisoner receive money, and had cautioned him —*Police Court Report*, 6th March 1888.

Chiv(e) (*Historical*). A knife Said to be Romany, but it may be a curtailment of Shevvle, as the metropolis of knife manufacture, Sheffield, is called to this day If so, on all fours with 'jocteleg'—Jacques de Liège — who manufactured in the 14th century a splendid knife, long before Sheffield rose to glory

Chiv is used on the stage 'I've had to be chivved' Mr H. Marston (1870)—meaning stabbed in the course of the piece

Presently Selby pulls out a chivy (knife), and gives Big Tim a dig or two —one on his arm and one at his face, and another at his leg Big Tim says to me,' 'Costy, I've got it a bit thick, suppose I give him a bit of chivy, and see how he likes it' Then we all laughed, and Big Tim pulls out the chivy, and makes a dig or two at him.—*People*, 6th January 1898.

Chiv(e)-fencer (*Criminal*). One who harbours, fences, wards off from arrest—murderers

'He's a chive fencer, the director of a railway, or a swell'—*Newsp Cutting*

A chive-fencer is also a purveyor in the streets of cheap razors and knives.

Chivy (*Criminal*) Relating to the use of the knife

Chivy Duel (*Thieves'*) A fight with knives

A 'Chivy' Duel—Described by a 'Costy'—At Southwark evidence was given in the charge of 'intentionally and maliciously wounding and inflicting grievous bodily harm on each other by stabbing each other', preferred against two men, etc —*People*, 6th January 1895.

Chivy, To (*Hist*). To hunt down, worry A corruption of Cheviot (Hills), whence this kind of attention was much practised by the early English of the north when swinging into the Cheviots after the cattle stolen, or to use the more northern term—'lifted'—by the Scotch more or less all along the border

'Which a pore cove were never chivied as I'm chivied by the cops.'

Choice Riot (*Street*, 1870) A horrid noise, such as the festive marrow bones and cleavers Mildly satirical. 'That there baby's making a choice riot'

Choke off, To (*Peoples'*, 18 *cent* on). To get rid of. From the necessity of twisting a towel or other fabric about the neck of a bull-dog to make this tenacious hanger-on let go his biting hold. Used against persons of pertinacious application.

'Choke off' in the U.S.A. means to reduce a pleading man to silence.

Choker (*Peoples'*). A lie, in its most direct form. 'What a choker!'—such a bare-faced lie that the hearer is nearly choked. Also applied to very large neckties and for similar reasons—the huge adornment appearing to choke the wearer. The masculine choker was at its greatest in England in the time of George IV., and the fashionable lead of Beau Brummel, when it was over a yard in length. Now and again a choker breaks out about the masculine neck, but in the '80's and '90's it was steadily replaced by the 'ties'. The feminine choker is always with us, and assumes a new shape once a month.

Chokey (*Sailors'*). Imprisonment—derived from the narrow confines of the ship's lock-up and the absence of ventilation—chokey generally being fixed as near the keel as conveniently it can be managed. However, some authorities maintain that this word is an Anglicising of the Hong-Kong Chinese 'Chow Key'—a prison.

Been run in? Been locked up? Been in chokey? What!—what do you take me for? Who are you blooming well getting at? Who're you kidding?—*Cutting.*

In a very short time the whole of them were safely in the chowkey. The parties implicated have been brought up at the Fort Police Court, and committed for trial.—*Bombay Times.*

Chonkey (*Lond. Street*). A meat pie—derivation beyond the bounds of mere discovery. Probably from the name of a once historic pieman, whose fame remains a name alone.

Chop up (*L. Class; last cry of the* 19th century). To annihilate; a variant of cut up.

Chopping (*Nursery*). Big, lusty, handsome. Johnson says:

'A child which would bring money in the market'—suggested by chopping and changing. 'Perhaps,' he says, after admitting all the etymologies to be doubtful—'a greedy, hungry child, likely to live.'

'Both Jack Freeman and Ned Wild
Would own the fair and chopping child.' —*Fenton.*

Chortle, To (*Peoples'*). To sing. Probably an onomatope. Chortled like the nightingale, and smiled like anything.

Many present on Boxing Night fully expected that when he appeared he would chortle a chansonnette or two.—*Ref.*, 29th December 1889.

Mr Wilford Morgan has been engaged to chortle the famous song, 'Here's to the maiden of bashful fifteen!'—*Ref.*, 18th August 1886.

Chortle also means to praise excessively. 'Joe chortles about his kid pretty loudly—it's 'is fust!'

It seems a curious time for an American critic to chortle over the recent success of Miss Minnie Maddern Fiske.—*D. T.*, 31st March 1897.

Chouse (*Peoples'*, 17 *cent.*). A cheat, to cheat. Henshaw derives it from the Turkish word chiaus, an interpreter, and referring to an interpreter at the Turkish embassy in London in 1609. He robbed the embassy right and left. In 1610 Ben Johnson in *The Alchymist* made the word classic.

'What do you think of me—
That I am a chiaus?'

Johnson has this word, but his modern fine brethren have rejected it, though Johnson gives Swift and Dryden as his authorities. 'Freedom and zeal have choused you o'er and o'er' (*Dryden*). 'From London they came, silly people, to chouse' (*Swift*). Butler also uses it in *Hudibras.*

Chow-chow (*Anglo-Ind.*). A hash, or resurrection pie, from Hindustanee word for mixed confectionery.

Christ-killers (*Peoples'*, 19 *cent.*). Jews. Passing away—chiefly used by old army men. 'What can you expect?—he's a Christ-killer. Pay up your sixty per cent., and try and look pleasant!'

Christen a jack (*Thieves'*). A grim use of baptismal ceremony—to replace the name on a stolen watch by another, to defeat detection. (*See* Church a Jack.)

Christmas (Oh) (*M. Class*). Evasive swearing. Used by Rudyard Kipling in *The Day's Work.* Of course it is 'Christ's Mass'.

Chronic (*M. Class*, 1896). Ceaseless, persistent. 'Oh! Joe's chronic.' 'Charley's Aunt's chronic'—said of a piece that ran perpetually.

Chronic Rot (*Peoples'*). Despairingly bad. Rot may or may not be from erotic, it is more likely an application of the original meaning of the word, but it is now quite understood Chronic is used in its original application, but more widely as—'Oh, that theatre's chronic'—means that never is a good piece seen there These two words intensify each other 'Jack's swears to swear off' (drink) 'is chronic rot.'

Chuck (*Naval*) A biscuit—hard tack (*see*) Probably an onomatope from the noise made in chewing, or perhaps from the hand-broken biscuit (for to snap it with the teeth were out of the question), being thrown or chucked carelessly into the mouth, which is the tar's mode of coaling up

Chuck, To (*Old Eng.*). To fling Johnson gives half a dozen meanings to this word, but not fling, which is its most forcible meaning Everything is chucked amongst the common folk, from a farthing or a chunk of bread, to a wife or a mistress. Now applied to the process of divorce

She had three children by him and two by some other fellow, which is the habit of some great ladies, so Sir John chucked her.—*Newsp Cutting*

Jones and Dimsdale were arrested in court, as they were heard to say, referring to the evidence against the prisoner Foster, 'He's sure to get chucked'—a slang expression for discharged.—*Police Report*, November 1890

So I takes the knives away and chucks them over a bridge Selby then picks up an iron bar, and makes a drive at Big Tim, but I catches hold of it, and stops him —*Chivey Duel, People*, 6th January 1895

They would blush a maidenly pink if certain words were uttered in their presence, and then shake off with relentless severity and austerity any erring sister who has, in modern parlance, 'chucked everything' —*D. T*, John Strange Winter, 5th August 1899

Chuck a Chest (*Street*) Generally said of a soldier who has a full bust. To throw forward the chest, as though prepared to meet the world

Chuck a Dummy (*Tailors'*). To faint Very interesting as illustrating the influence familiar objects have in framing new ideas—from the similarity of a falling fainting man to an overthrown or chucked tailor's dummy—a figure upon which coats are fitted to show them off for sale. 'I chucked a dummy this mornin', an' 'ad to be brought to with o-der-wee!'

'Chuck it out, Creswick'—then manager of Surrey

'Yes, and chuck it out quick, cully,' observed Sir John Adamant.—*Cutting*

Chuck a Shoulder (*Costers'*) To turn away—said chiefly by the male coster of the female, *e g*, 'Which she chucked me a shoulder, an' not the one I want—an' 'av been on hice ever the mortal since'

Chuck a yannep (*Back Slang*) To throw a penny

'The Lord loveth a cheerful giver', but there's no use chucking a yannep into the collection plate loud enough to make the people in the back seats think the Communion service has tumbled off the altar—*Cutting*

Chuck his weight about, To (*Milit*) To demonstrate his physical magnificence—generally said of any soldier who is showing off, but more particularly one of the household brigades 'So 'e turned up, and chucked 'is weight about all over the blooming place—he did'

Chuck out ink (*Press Reporters'*) To write articles

Suddenly it came across my mind that the boss might be waiting about for me somewhere with a big boot and genteel language, and that it might be better for my health if I chucked out ink—*Cutting*

Chuck over the lug (*Peoples'*) To thwack over the ear—lug being high Scotch for the auricular (*See* Poultice over the peeper, One over the gash)

Chuck up, To (*L. London*). To abandon.

Did she mean, we says, to chuck us up? Of course she did, says she, flaring up like a mill on fire—*Cutting*

'But after all, cullies, being mashed on a dona is nothing, it's when the bit of jam chucks you up—that is the stinger'—*Cutting*

Chuck up the bunch of fives (*Pugilistic*) To die The one poetic figure of speech engendered by the prize ring. The fives are the two sets of four fingers and a thumb—the fists—the 'bunches'—flaccid in death 'Pore Ben—'e's been an' gorne an' chucked up 'is bunches o' fives'

Chuck up the sponge (*Prize Ring*) To admit defeat—by way of a pugilist's attendant, at his chief's failure, throwing up the sponge with which he has been refreshing his principal. This custom was, and is, applied to death. All trades yield these figurative modes of referring to birth, marriage, death, and money.

'Bill chucked up the sponge this morning.'

Chuck your money about (*Street*, 1894 on). A satirical but good-tempered reproach cast at meanness, or insufficient reward. 'Jack—you've done me a real good turn—yere's the price of a pint.' To which Jack may reply, 'Well—you do just chuck your money about—you do!'

Chuck-barge (*Naval*). Cask in which the biscuit of a mess is kept. Also equivalent to bread-basket. (*See* Bread-barge.)

Chuck-bread (*Beggars'*). Waste-bread, that which would be thrown away but for mendicants. 'No chuck-bread for me.'

Chuck-out (*L. Theatrical*, 1880 on). This verb has the force of 'vigorous'. 'Can't he chuck it out?' would mean that a singer or actor has a powerful delivery. Therefore the recommendation 'Chuck it out' is equal to 'Louder—if you please' of the public dinner.

Chuckaboo (*Peoples'*). A name given familiarly to a favourite chum. No meaning; but probably the 'chuck' is a conversion of 'duck'.

Chuckaways (*London*). Lucifer matches—graphic description of the act of rejection after the match is done with. Bill—'I want a light—got any chuckaways?' (*See* Bryant and May.)

Chucked all of a heap (*Street*). Fascinated, ravishingly overcome, mashed, enthralled.

When he gazed upon her soft and gentle beauty, and heard the gurgling sound which smote his ear like the rushing of many waters he was chucked all of a heap.—*Cutting*.

Chucker-in-Chief (*Public-house*). A prince amongst mere chuckers-out.

The magnificent figure of the gentleman, who was late literary adviser to Gussy (Sir A. Harris, of Drury Lane Theatre) and chucker-in-chief, is now to be seen nightly at the Princess's, where its owner finds his services appreciated.

Chucker-out (*Public-house*, 1880). The name given to a barman who turns out noisy tavern customers. Chuckers-out are simple and compound. The first argues the case, he being generally not a giant of strength. The 'compound', who gets his name probably from his size—large enough for a 'compound' of men—'bounces' without a word—which he seldom has.

Chuckers-out are of two blooming sorts generally—simple and compound. The simple chucker-out is sometimes a bit barmy in the crumpet, and is only kept for the sake of show, and to prevent the sweet tarts behind the bar hollering out. . . . He's a warm 'un, is the compound chucker-out. You generally find him at music-halls and about the bars of pubs. which blokes use that aren't afraid of a couple of black peepers.—*Cutting*.

Chucking-out Time (*Lond. Public-house*). Half-past twelve, the closing hour for metropolitan taverns, when those who do not go willingly are 'chucked out'.

Chuffy (*Peoples'; rare*). Surly; *e.g.*, 'Don't be chuffy'—probably from the behaviour of one 'Chuffs'—who may have once been powerful in the cadger world.

Chum (*Universal*). A familiar friend. This term is probably the only one that has steadily remained patronised by all classes. Dr Johnson, who always sought the unexpected, says this word is 'Armorick'. He adds, 'a chamber fellow'; a term used in the universities.

'The princes were quite chums.'

'I had a chum, etc.'—Fielding, *Tom Jones*, book viii., ch. 2.

'The two actors were very, very friendly indeed. We dressed in the same dressing room, and were very friendly. In fact, Mr Crozier bought some colours from Mr Franks on Saturday, I believe.' The Coroner: 'They were what is called in vulgar parlance "chums".' Witness: 'Yes. I never knew them to have any quarrel or speak any angry words to each other.'—Evidence of Mr C. Lillford at an inquest upon Crozier, an actor accidentally killed at the Novelty Theatre, London (10th August 1896).—*D. T.*, 14th August 1896.

Chump (*Peoples'*). The head. Chump initially is a fine onomatope, being the sound made by horses in grinding oats. Hence the use of the word to represent head, of which the dentition is only part. Then extended to the human head. (*See* 'Orf Chump', 'Orf his Chump'.)

Spain had her flirtations, and Marie Antoinette was frivolous and fond of pleasure until she lost her chump —*Cutting*

Take off yer blooming 'at, take off yer blooming chump as well.—Said in a theatre

Chump (*Ang -Amer* , 1895). Equivalent to Juggins. A youth (as a rule) who is in any way cheated of his money — especially by the so-called gentler sex.

What's a chump? 'Say, pa, what's a chump?' asked young Tommy as his father was taking him out walking 'See that young man in there?' (they were just passing an ice cream saloon) said the father, pointing in 'Yes, I see him, the one with the girl in the red dress?' 'Yes; well, he's buying ice cream for his girl with money he ought to save to buy his lunch with till next pay day He's a chump '—*Cutting*

Chumps Elizas (*London*, Five Pounder Tourists', 1854 on). A grotesque pronunciation of Champs Elysés—still in Paris.

Church a Jack, To (*Thieves'*) To remove the works of a watch from its case, and put them in another, of course with the view of destroying the identity of the article. (*See* Christen a Jack.)

Church-bell (*Rural*). A talkative woman 'Ah ca'as ma wife choorch bell, cas 'er's yeard arl over t' village '

Church parade (*Soc.*, 1885 on) The display of dress after morning church Quite the thing to carry prayer books Began in Hyde Park; imitated now all over the country

Mr Dutton asked, with respect to some wearing apparel which prosecutrix paid £4 for on delivery for Mrs Gardiner, whether she did not part with the money to enable 'the countess' on the following Sunday to accompany her to the Church parade in the Park. Prosecutrix: 'Church parade was never mentioned.' —*D. T*, 17th March 1893

Church-piece (*Soc.*). A threepenny piece—the smallest silver the genteel mean can put in the absurdly-named offertory

Churched (*Com Lond.*) Married —amongst the common, attendance at prayers after childbirth amongst higher-class women The commonest possible term amongst lower classes for marriage, and singularly expressive as marking the distinction between ordinary come-together marriage, and the real ceremony.

He did grand before we was churched, and used to blarney and call me good-looking, and squeeze my blooming waist. —*Cutting*

Churchyard Cough (*Peoples'*). A fatal cold — sometimes in these later times synonymised by 'cemetery catarrh'.

Churchyard Luck (*Peoples'*) The 'good fortune' which the mother of a large family experiences by the death of one or more of her children *e g*, 'Yes, mum, I hev brought 'em all up —ten boys, and no churchyard luck with it.'—Said by a Liverpool woman to a district-visitor

Cigaretticide (*Soc.*, 1883) A word invented to meet the theory that the cigarette is the most dangerous form of smoking More common in America than in Great Britain.

That young man's grit is indeed remarkable in this age of dudism and cigaretticide —*Cutting*

Cinder (*Peoples'*, 19 *cent*) Hot—especially alcoholic heat, *e g*, 'That's a cinder for him '

He had been a teetotaller himself for seven years, and really left his last lodgings because the landlady was too fond of putting 'a cinder in her tea', that is to say, flavouring her Mazawattee with a plentiful supply of rum —*D T.*, 12th May 1896.

Cinder-knotter (*Navy*). A stoker — very descriptive, and necessarily modern, phrase, for he does knot the living coals into heaps

Cinder-sifter (*Fashion*, 1878). A hat with open-work brim, the edge of which was turned up perpendicularly On all fours with the poke bonnet, called 'coal-scuttle', or the high collars introduced by George III, and styled gills

Cinderella (*Society*, 1880). A dance which ends at twelve — the name fancifully suggested, it is not known by whom, in reference to that successful young professional beauty who, at midnight, was by force majoi compelled to give up dancing Adopted in France—1880.

N'ayez pas peur, ma chère, ce n'est qu'une Cendrillon, à minuit — finis et silence

The hours at which balls begin grow later and later The stroke which sends the last guest hurrying away from the Cinderella dance scarcely ushers the first arrival to a season ball —*D. N.*, 27th March 1884.

Circlers (*Theatr.*). Occupants of dress-circle. Applied with envious derision by the pit.

Circs (*City*, 1860). Abbreviation of 'circumstances'.

The Duke and Duchess of Teck patronized the performance of *Iolanthe* at the Savoy Theatre on Monday last. Under the circs I am disposed to exclaim, 'What extravagance!'—*Cutting*, August 1883.

The royal couple at this date were about economising by leaving England and going to Rumpenheim.

Circuit Rider (*Amer., provincial*). A peripatetic preacher.

There was no 'circuit rider' or other evangelical authority to be relied upon. —*Cutting*.

Circumbendibus (*Peoples'*). Evasion—adopted probably from some author playing with Latin formation—based upon circumlocution. 'He allowed the accusation by a circumbendibus.'

Circus (*Amer.*) Excitement, adventure—from the pother created when a wandering circus heaves in sight. A circus is the most favourite form of American provincial amusement.

Lafayette got the check cashed and spent the money, and then Coghill found out that he had paid Lafayette just three times too much for the Louisiana lands. Then there was a circus.—*N. Y. Mercury*, 23rd May 1885.

The next day old Hays and young Hays started out in search of Reed's companion—Stephens. The pair found Stephens in his room. He made a desperate fight, but there was no 'circus' this time, the two Hays bein' too many for the one Stephens.—*Cutting*.

City Road Africans (*Street*, 1882). —Hetairæ of that quarter. Origin not known.

City sherry (*Peoples'*, E. London, 1880). Four ale, which in colour may be said to resemble the worst description of sherry or the highest quality of rectified varnish. The East London people have a modified mistrust of those living amongst them, who get their living in the city, especially of the great body of exclusive clerks, whose general poverty they satirise in many ways, of which this is one. 'City sherry' used to be the basis of a great perennial practical joke at the 'European,' once a prosperous tavern in the Poultry (E.C.), where this liquid was set out in imperial half pints and royal array on the counter awaiting the 'ready' pennies of the passing public. The humble little joke took its rise from this opportunity of helping oneself to these drinks without calling for a barman, and then planking the money down.

Country cousins were told that tumblers of city sherry were given away at this particular house all day long. The victim was taken in, was handed a glass of fourpenny from the counter, while the operator gave a well-known wink to the attendant barman who instantly comprehended this joke. When the wondering eye of the country cousin was off the counter the town relative paid for the drinks.

This 'sherry house,' the European, fell before the improver at the end of 1884, and the jocular 'halves' ceased to be drawn for ever. However, city sherry, *in* the City, is still cloaked satire for a pretended 'free drink'.

Clackbox (*Hist.*). Male or masculine of chatterbox—generally applied to a woman, and especially a girl. This word rarely comes to town.

Claim (*Ang.-Amer.*). To recognise in travelling. In a railway carriage one may frequently hear the enquiry—'Surely I claim you—we met at Suez?'

Clamp (*N. Eng.*). A kick, from the name given to the heavy boots clamped or tipped with iron. Very formidable weapons.

Clap-trap (*Theatrical*). Commonplace. Trap to catch a clap from the audience, as:—

'The man who lays his hands upon a woman, except in the way of kindness, ought to be yard-armed.'

Clare Market Cleavers (*Strand*). They were the butchers in this once densely populated place—now a sixty yard street. The rival community was Seven Dials—half a mile away—with which country there were frequent wars. The glory of Clare Market began to pitch in '70, rocked in the early '90's, and was practically gone in '98. The Cleavers were great fighters, Princes in Clare, and heavy blackmailers of newly-married couples of that ilk—who were always obliged with a concert of marrow-bones and cleavers. These cleaver serenades had to be paid for. 'Oh—he's a cleaver bloke—I can tell you.' As it has been said, the glories of Clare Market and her cleavers began to fade in '70. Her commercial and butcherly bravery, beginning in the west at Drury Lane, and swinging south east down to Temple Bar, with a dash over into Strand Lane (*see* Diprose's St Clement Danes), fell before the demands of the new Law Courts Two-thirds of the parish were swept away, and with the old crowded houses the Clare Market customers. The butchers shared in the fall—but they still remained a combined power in the old slaughter-houses, until in the '80's their 'cleavin' propensities ended in a steel fight, which finished one of the later cleavers Resulting precaution, and two School Board schools slowly suppressed the cleavers, who vanished, while the market faded into a mere street

Clare Market Duck (19 *cent*). Baked bullock's heart stuffed with sage and onions—which gave a faint resemblance to the bird The term is one of those satirical associations of cheap food with luxurious dishes, of which there are several specimens (*See* 'Billingsgate Pheasant,' 'Two-Eyed Steak,' etc.)

Clarkenco (*Polit*). A new political party. When the Gladstone Government went out (June, 1885) and that of Lord Salisbury came in, Mr Ed Clarke, Q C, who was expected to get office was left out in the cold He was supposed to lead a new party which took the place of that led previously by Lord R Churchill

'Mr Edward Clarke and Co', as the new Fourth Party is called in the House, will let the Churchill lot 'have it' at every convenient, and at several inconvenient, opportunities—*Ref*, 19th July 1885.

Claw-hammer (*Amer-Eng*) Tail-coat, accepted in England about 1880. Description of the divided tail, like in shape and lines to the claw of a hammer. (*See* Bobtail)

Clean Time (*Amer*) A figurative expression for honesty, derived from the old phrase, 'clean hands' 'He never would do the clean thing'

Clean tuckered out (*New Eng*) Utterly exhausted—probably from the name 'Tucker'.

He was clean tuckered out all but his eyes (and he could just barely turn them in his head) and his bill.—*Newsp Cutting*

Cleavin (*Clare Market*). Boastful—from the Clare Market Cleavers (1750-1860)—the king-butchers of that once popular market who were the equal pride and terror of that place,—terror because of their readiness to fight, pride, because of the warfare, continual and unflagging, they carried on over the border amongst the Pict-pockets and mauraudmg Scots of the adjacent Drury Lane They made much coin by marriage in the neighbourhood, and far around by their rough marrow-bone and cleaver orchestras

Clicker (*Printers'*) The sub-foreman in printing office Gives out copy and conveys orders from foreman to men Probably contemptuous, and from the French—Claqueur. The clicker also puts the type into pages Most obscure phrases or words in printing come from France

Climb in on, To (*U S*) To overcome easily, to get the better of another by cunning

'I climbed in on him proper'

Dr Hall says it is very unhealthy to live on the ground floor of a house. Doctor's right A fellow's creditors can climb in on him with so little trouble.—*Newsp Cutting*

To lower pride

Climb the Golden Staircase, To (*Amer.*) One of the U S A equivalents to the Latin 'join the majority'.

Edward's Folly Dramatic Company is reported as having climbed the golden stairs The cash assets are alleged to have been carefully secured in a pill box—(1883)

D'Arcy and his company, with Josie Batchelder as star, climbed the golden staircase last Monday They are said to have been kindly assisted on their tour homeward by sympathizing citizens—*Cutting*

Climb the Mountain of Piety, To To pawn, from the first governmental pawnshop being situated on a height in Rome called Monte di Pietà, so named, of course, from a group of the dead Christ and the Virgin called in art a Pietà

Mr Candy On one occasion, I think, you had to resort to what is called 'climbing the mountain of piety'?—Evelyn *v.* Hulbert, *D N*, 15th April 1896

Clinger (*Ball-room*) A lady who holds on in waltzing, *e g.*, 'She's a bad 'un to go, but she's a real clinger.'

Clobber (*Jewish, E. London*). Superior, or rather startling clothing. In Hebrew 'KLBR'.

'My high—look at Beck.'

Clobbered (*N. Eng. Prov.*). Well nourished and dressed. Common in Yorkshire.

'Eh, he looks well clobbered.'

Clock (*London*). A dynamite bomb, when carried in a small square Gladstone bag. Took its rise in the '80's, during the dynamite scare, when a dynamiter, being stopped by a policeman and asked what he had in his bag, replied—'A clock'.

Clock stopped (*London, Peoples'*). No credit. 'No *tick*'—hence the clock has stopped. 'No tick' means 'no ticket'—given by master or other to obtain credit.

Cloddy (*Dog Market*). Aristocratic in appearance. Applied to human beings by some divisions of the lower classes.

''E's a cloddy bloke—don't yer make no mistake about it!'

A bull-dog should be low to the ground, short in the back, and thickset. An animal that possesses these qualifications is known as one of the 'cloddy', the correct expression among dog-fanciers. —*D. T.*, 13th November 1895.

Close out, To (*Amer.*, 1883). To finish. Quite local until recently. Now sometimes heard in England.

Do not close out the last of your soup by taking the plate in your mouth and pouring the liquid down.—*Cutting.*

Clou (*Theatr.*). From the French. Equal to 'heart' or central idea of a tale or drama. Of course, literally 'nail'—upon which the piece or book hangs.

Whatever may be the decision arrived at, the case will be memorable as fairly placing before the world entirely opposite views as to the degree of copyright in the central idea, or '*clou*', as it is called in France, of a drama or romance.—*D. N.*, 4th August 1883.

'The field of the French writer is almost unlimited. He writes for men and married women. His first thought when hammering out the *clou* or mainspring of his play is "What shall I do with my adulteress?"'—G. W. Gilbert, *D. N.*, 21st January 1885.

Clouded over (*American*). Overwhelmed by misfortune. (*See* Bound to shine.)

Clove-hunters (*Amer.-Eng.*) Frequent nip-drinkers, especially between the acts of a play, when the nibbled clove vainly sought to hide the higher perfume of the alcohol. Came to be used (1884) for the refreshment itself.

Pleasing example of modern metaphor.

A belief prevails among Union Square Theatre patrons that the trick chairs which adorn the auditorium were designed to trap and hold in place between the acts clove-hunters.—*N. Y. Mercury*, December 1884.

Coal-oil Johnny (*Amer. coal-oil fields*). The derivation of this word is interesting. Many of the uneducated and more wasteful men who struck oil squandered their money, while Johnny in American is the equivalent of English Sammy, Sappy, or Softy—hence a coal-oil Johnny was at first a suddenly enriched coal-oil miner, who wasted his easily-gained wealth. The term soon spread, and stood for a description of a stupid, extravagant, vulgar person.

He played a 'coal-oil Johnny' career; treated to champagne by the basket, had the handsomest carriage and pair in the city, and paid cabmen five dollars to drive him a few blocks.—*Newsp. Cutting.*

Coal Sack (*Peoples'*). Cul de sac—one of the most egregious Anglicisations in the language.

'Which we bolted up a blind alley, and found ourselves in a coal sack.'

Coal up, To (*Trade. Stokers'*). To feed. 'Let's coal up on bread and cheese—nothing better, sonny.'

Cock (*Printers'*, 1874). In throwing types to decide who shall pay for drinks or other matters, by the number of nicks which turn up, the types used sometimes catch together, and do not fall flat on the imposing stone, the general arena for these adventures. 'That's a cock' is said—abbreviation of 'cock and hen'. The question is once more tried.

Cock and Bull Story (*Peoples'*). Every etymologist has had an attack of analysis of this phrase, which Sterne uses as his abrupt and unintended termination of 'The Sentimental Journey'. No one has solved this difficulty. Possibly a phrase on all fours with 'By hook or by crook,' 'A miss is as good as a mile,' etc., and meaning 'A. Cock, and D. Bull, story'—and may refer to two witnesses of these names in some once notorious case.

Dr Brewer of course goes off at score upon this phrase. He says. 'A corruption of "a *concocted and bully story*". The catch-pennies hawked about the streets are still called *cocks, i e*, concocted things Bully is the Danish *bullen* (exaggerated), our bull-rush (an exaggerated rush), *bull-frog*, etc, etc' All this is confused, contradictory, wanting in relation of parts. Probably corruption of perchance Cockaigne Bill—a forgotten teller of inconsequent tales — like the more modern Mrs Partington

Sir Francis Jeune said the petitioner had shown a great deal of carelessness His wife told him a cock-and-bull story about having been married before, and he took no steps to verify it until some years afterwards —*Sir F. Jeune, Div. Court*, 29th October 1896

Cock and Hen Club (*Soc*, 1880) One of mixed sexes—then spoken of contemptuously probably because they had not at that date quite succeeded

He takes advantage of his wife's absence from home to 'make a night of it', and take supper with a strange young lady at a club which, I believe, would be called of the cock-and-hen order —*Carados.*

What are described as working men's clubs (often enough falsely described thus), very early breakfast clubs, cock-and-hen clubs, with one or two other clubs whose names and descriptions will to the initiated suggest themselves, are all flagrant and distinct violations of the Licensing Acts —*Ref.*, 19th May 1889

Cock of the Walk (*London, Sporting*, 18 *cent*). Leader—derived from cock-fighting, or from farmyard, where one cock alone holds the central ground

Directly you get up one or two steps in the ladder, you want to be cock of the walk—*Cutting.*

Cock one's chest (*Navy*) To throw the chest out, after the manner of vain creatures Generally used with the addition—'like a half-pay Admiral'—not a full-pay, mark you.

Cockatoo (*Austral*, 1880). A small farmer. The name is given by the squatters or sheep breeders to the agriculturists, from the cockatoos following the movements of the farmer over his land, especially at sowing time The word is offensively used, for there is, or perhaps it is better to say was, bitter war between the settled farmer and the unsettled squatter, whose sheep often ruinously injured the unenclosed agricultural stretches, while too frequently, it is to be feared, the squatter made a path for his sheep, even where an enclosure had been made. The squatter still knows the cockatoo has the sympathy of the legislature, and he 'hates him accordingly'.

Cocked Hat, To knock into a (18 *cent*). To conquer, tumble about in all directions. Perhaps no phrase is more obscure than this. It is probably one of the expressions which result out of a change in dress, especially where the change is associated with political movement The hat which preceded the cocked was the cavalier, which possessed a flat flopping brim, above which showed the white feather, which swung round and trailed between the shoulders Hence arose the Puritan term for cowardice—showing the white feather—this dancing adornment displaying itself very ineffectively when the cavaliers took to flight, which they did upon occasion The cocked hat might figuratively be described as a cavalier hat, whose brim had been knocked up and in by three spaced blows round the circumference Now as the cocked hat came in with the Guelphs and the Whigs, it can readily be understood that the Jacobites accepted the new cocked hat as a head-gear that had been assaulted by cavaliers—hence probably a Jacobite term, 'I'll knock the Whig into one of his own cocked hats'—an idea so practical that it was accepted by the people. It has lasted to this day, when the three-cornered cocked, or up-turned hat has absolutely vanished in England except amongst mayors and aldermen, and by way of the black cap worn by judges while uttering the death sentence. The tricorne is still worn in Germany, and even in France and Italy

I thought that was the worst play I had ever seen, but *Nadine* knocked it into several cocked-hats —*Newsp. Cutting*, 8th March 1885

Wilson Barrett licks everything else into a cocked hat —*Newsp Cutting.*

Cock-linnet (*East London*) A dapper boy, a tiny buck from the East End of London, where bird fairs are held every Sunday morning It is also rhyming slang for 'minute'.

'Hold on for a cock linnet—now barney.'—*Newsp. Cutting.*

Cocks (*Dispensing chemist*). Concoctions.

Cock-sure (*Sporting*, 18 *cent.*). Absolutely certain. In the good old days of cock-fighting the vanquishing bird always crowed—but never until he was quite sure, by various modes of proof, that his enemy was either dead or insensible. Then he gave gullet.

Used disparagingly in these later days.

In the identification of prisoners police constables sometimes blunder, and rarely, if ever, hesitate. They are very 'cock sure' in their evidence.—*D.N.*, 8th December 1884.

Cocker up, To (*Chaunters'*). To make a horse look young for sale. Evidently from the French 'coquet'; the more likely that Chaunter is certainly from Chanteur—an unscrupulous and daring cheat.

Cockowax (*Peoples'*, 18 *cent.*). Obscure—used satirically. 'Hullo my cock'owax.' Probably corruption of cock of wax, which may have been said in cock-fighting days of a bird which had no mettle in him—a poor soft, waxy, creature, opposite of cock of the walk.

Cock-pit (*Political*). A convenient place for settling a sanguinary quarrel. From the pit or enclosure in which the cocks fought, and which would become much blood-stained—hence the name was given to that portion of a warship to which the wounded were taken for treatment.

England cannot consent to make Egypt the cock-pit in which the diplomatic intrigues of Europe are to find a new arena.—*D. N.*, 21st January 1885.

Cocoa (*Nautical*). Comic shape of Toko—(*see*). Schoolboy expression, probably from Negronia. When a word has become time-weary, it is often newly editioned by being exchanged for a well-known word which rhymes with it.

Charlie Wyndham and W. H. Vernon must mind their eye, or Onesimus will give 'em 'cocoa' before long.—*Newsp. Cutting.*

Cocotte; Cocodette (*Franco-English* 1860-70). Non-virtuous French, or other young woman of large income. The second is to the first as a first officer is to the captain.

In the circle of cocottes, and cocodettes, by which the French Court has during the last fifteen years managed to surround itself, fast American women have furnished no inconsiderable contribution.—(1867.)

Cod (*Printers'*). A fool; *e.g.*, 'the fellow's a cod.'

Cod (*Peoples'*). Humbug, swindle, more generally coddem, cod em, cod them.

Cod, To (*Thieves'*, 18 *cent.*). To cod is to cheat meanly by way of familiarity in relation to eccentric erotics. To comprehend this term an intimate acquaintance with Balzac's *Vautrin* is required.

Cod, To (*Theatr.*). To flatter; *e.g.*, 'Don't try to cod me'—from Coddem—a game of deception.

Cod (*Trade. Tailors'*). A drunkard. The word is suggested by the fallen cheeks and lips' corners which are some of the facial evidences of a drunkard, and which certainly suggest the countenance of a cod, which fish, furthermore from its size, is typical of huge drinking. 'He's a bigger cod every day.'

Cod, Coddem (*Mid. Class*). To ridicule by appealing to the sanity of one codded.

'Cod' is peculiar as a word signifying ironical chaff, and perhaps it has not much to recommend itself beyond its brevity.—*Stage*, 21st August 1885.

I don't know all the perfessionals. Irving don't play coddem in our taproom.—*Cutting.*

I hear that at the end of Adelphi Terrace there is a theatrical club where coddem is now the favourite pastime.—(1882.)

Shoreditch isn't what it was; but there's some fun in the old village still. You can show off your Sunday togs in the Aquarium. You can play coddem.—(1883.)

Cod-bangers (*Great Grimsby and Billingsgate*). Gorgeously arrayed sailors. Good example of an obscure phrase or word having a solid foundation. The cod are brought in alive from the North Sea to Great Grimsby, and are knocked or banged on the head as wanted for market. The fishermen in this trade make, and waste, considerable money. They keep to the blue worsted jersey, but it is complicated with rich silk squares hauled round the neck, and by frequent rings. This gorgeousness has begotten the half-contemptuous, half-envious name It has spread to Billingsgate and beyond the cod-trade 'Whoa — yere comes a cod-banger' The word may also have another meaning, easily sought and found

Coddem (*L Class*) A tavern game—for from two to say ten, and the equivalent of the American bluff or brag. All the shapes of this word come from Coddem, which is played by the operators dividing into two sets—each set seated opposite the other—a table between them One side have a bean, or other small object—the hands belonging to this side are lowered under the table, the bean is placed in one of the hands, and all the fists are brought up in a row on the table The other side now have to guess where the bean is He must not touch the fists, but he points to one, and says either 'tip it' or 'take it away'. If he says 'tip it', the hand pointed at is opened, and if it is empty, the other side has lost one, and the holders of the bean score one. Then they begin again, and again bring up their fists Now as to the other term 'take it away', upon this direction, the owner of the hand pointed at takes it off the table—if it is empty On the contrary shows the bean if it is in his hand—then the other side loses another point This hand being lowered, the guesser begins again with the remaining hands, until he either guesses right, or again loses a point—all of which may appear to the reader very simple On the contrary, it is one of the most psychological games ever invented It calls for immense intelligence, and there is not probably a village in England without its champion codder—a man who invariably wins at this game When a guess is right, the bean passes to the other side that has guessed rightly Money is won or lost at this game—but the process is too complicated for clear explanation

Codger (*Peoples'*). Roystering, ageing, boon companion The earlier dictionaries will have nothing to say to this word, which does not appear to have come from the Persian or other equally next-door language. A modern dictionary describes him as a stingy, clownish fellow, whereas he is rarely stingy, and never clownish There was, until perhaps 1880, a Codger's Hall for political discussion and drinks, under the shadow of S. Bride's, Blackfriars. Word probably invented itself, in the gutter, or near about Byron first gave it houseroom in an occasional address to 'Thomas Moore', 'Oh you who are all, etc.' Learned etymologists assume this word to come from cogito, but do not suggest the itinerary. Nor indeed do codgers ever think They have no time for cogitation

Codocity (*Printers'*, 1874). Stupidity—capacity for being codded.

Coffee-and-B (*Night Tavern*, 1880) Coffee and brandy

On being served the barmaid asked him to treat her. He inquired what she would have, and she said coffee and 'b' He asked what she meant by 'b', and she said brandy, or as they called it 'coffee and cold water'.—*Newsp Cutting*

Coffee-sisters (*Germany*, 19 *cent*). Malignant gossipers From the women drinking in coffee and scandal at the same eager moment Much after the use of the word tea-talker in England 'What is she — a mere coffee-sister'

A well-known society lady in Germany is credited with the statement that coffee not only keeps those who indulge in it wakeful and gay, but is likewise endowed with the mysterious 'virtue' of bringing to light all the vices of a not too-populous city. And it is well understood that herein lies the attraction it has for the critical sisterhood of mature German ladies known as 'coffee-sisters', or, as we should say, gossips —*D. T*, 26th September 1895

Coigne (*Printers'*). A clever trade term for money. A play upon coin and coigne, or coin, or quoin, a wedge, generally named thus in printing offices. Pun suggested by the force of coin as a wedge, and a wedge as a coign

Gascoigne, I am willing to believe, has little 'gas' about him, and not more coigne than he knows what to do with — *Newsp Cutting*

Coker-nuts (*Low London*) Well-developed feminine breasts. (*See* Prize Faggot)

Cold (*London Tavern*). The antithesis of 'warm with' and 'hot with' (sugar) Cold is short for cold water Hence, the usual order in times of heat is 'Three of cold'—say gin

Cold Coffee (*Artisans' Secret*, 1874) Beer In some offices, especially in some printing houses, beer is only allowed at certain hours, while coffee is admissible at all times. Coffee-house mugs are therefore kept, and the errand boys go for 'cold coffee'. The coffee-house keeper has the beer ready, and to such an extent was the effort at deception carried that in some cases milk was mixed with the beer to complete the deception — many young printers being very moderate drinkers.

Cold Cook (*London*). An undertaker—for dead humanity being by the lower classes called 'dead meat', clearly the undertaker who looks after the dead is a cold cook.

Cold-creams (*Military*). Linesman's name for the 'Coldstreams', to designate their assumption of superior manners and distinction. 'Look out, mate—yere comes a cold cream.' (*See* Porridge Pots, Grinning Dears, Muck, Gee-gees.)

Cold Day (*U.S.*). Bad luck—good instance of climatic influence in producing phrases.

'It's a cold day when I get left anywhere that I can't find my way back. Well, good-bye, old potatoes.'—*Newsp. Cutting.*

This essentially American phrase (now common in England) intimates that he is very clever, adroit, and rarely bested. A cold day in America is indeed cold, the phrase therefore means—only a very dreadful state of weather would result in his discomfiture.

'It's a cold day when the trotting-horse reporter gets left,' said the law reporter to the managing editor.—*Newsp. Cutting.*

Cold Deck of Cards (*Californian*, 1849-80). Cards marked for the purpose of cheating.

During the early days of California, a witness giving evidence in court referred to the operation technically known as 'ringing in a cold deck' at poker. For the information of the judge, the witness explained that, at the game of poker, it was not uncommon to introduce a pack, or as the American phrase goes, 'deck' of cards, which was said by professional cardsharpers to be 'cold' when duly marked and arranged for the purpose of fraud. The judge asked if any person was present who could give an explanation of the *modus operandi.* To his amazement the audience rose like one man.—*Newsp. Cutting.*

He denied the alleged 'cold deck' business *in toto*, and made some vigorous remarks about the moral weakness of a man who puts up all he can raise on four aces, with a view to scooping in the parties of the other part, and then turns round and 'squeals' when another fellow takes the pot with a straight flush.—*Newsp. Cutting.*

Cold Four (*Public-house*). One of the more opprobrious terms for the cheapest description of beer. The cold does not refer to the low temperature of four-ale, or four 'arf-an-'arf, but to its fatal want of warmthful generosity.

Cold Meat (*L. London*). Dead humanity.

The wicked Scorcher says a dead wife is the best bit of cold meat in the house. —*Cutting.*

Cold Shake (of the hand) (*Amer.*). A new form of cold shoulder, or dismissal. 'Leave you,' he cried—'do you give me the cold shake?' 'No, no,' she said, 'only for a minute.' He watched—it was her false back hair. She fixed it and returned radiant.

Matsada S. Ingomar, a Japanese athlete, who had married a rich Quakeress—one Miss Lodge of Philadelphia—for a month or so forsook the arena, and gave his former companions the 'cold shake'.

Cold Shoulder (*English, coming from the Italian of Dante's time*). To turn the shoulder upon an applicant. It is interesting, as illustrating how personal wit will deflect a meaning, or add to it, that Douglas Jerrold totally changed the aspect of this phrase. He made it refer to cold shoulder of mutton, and 'cold shoulder' became synonymous with inhospitality, as it remains to this day. The climax was reached by the comicality (attributed also to Douglas Jerrold) of Paterfamilias (at dinner table). 'For what we are about to receive may we be truly thankful—cold shoulder again!'

Shakespeare used the phrase as turning the human shoulder from a suppliant.

If you are too clever, people are sure to find you out, and call you red-hot treats, and will give you the shoulder of mutton for ever.—*Cutting.*

Cold Snap (*Amer.-Eng.*). The first premonitory frost—figuratively a quick, markedly cool reception.

When the first 'cold snap', as the Americans call it, arrives, then many of us must wish to be hibernating animals —*D N.*, 20th November 1884

Young Blunt had his overcoat in pawn during the cold snap and wanted to get it out, so he called on Mr Moses to see about it —*Newsp Cutting*

Cold Tub (*Soc.*, 19 *cent*) A cold morning bath Good example of homely metaphor. Here the water gets dubbed by its containant

The speech of the Chancellor of the Exchequer, so far from encouraging illusions in the mind of clever youth, was as bracing as cold tub —*D. T*, 11th November 1899

Colder'n a wedge (*Western Amer*) Dead—colder than a wedge, the iron quoin used for splitting timber, and which in American winters is cold enough to take the skin off upon touch.

Colinderies (*Soc*, 1886) The Colonial and Indian Exhibition, South Kensington. The last of the droll names given to the series of four industrial exhibitions at South Kensington (1883-86)

The Colinderies was patronized by no fewer than 81,516 people, making a total since the opening of 2,240,536.—*Ref.*, 8th August 1886

Even the authorities accepted this droll titling, which began with Fisheries, followed by Healtheries, continued with Inventories, and ended with Colinderies Even the attendants bore upon their caps the legend 'Colindia'

The epilogue was called 'Colindia', and was a very pleasant entertainment It was a sort of ten minutes' pantomime —*Ref*, 8th August 1886

At a Royal Commission of Inquiry into the Metropolitan Board of Works (7th August 1888) Mr Emil Loibl, a witness, added the last invention in 'ries'.

A song mentioned was *Ten to One on the Lodger*, and the songs were said to have put to the blush two Chinese mandarins. Witness replied: That was another trick of the briberies —*Public Press*, 8th August 1888

Collah Carriage (*Street Negro Minstrels*) A railway carriage filled with women — Collah being Yiddish for young girls. 'Git into a collah carriage.' Said while waiting on a railway platform by one negro minstrel to another, both with their musical instruments of torture, their banjos, ready

Until stopped by the police, these tiresome persons found it pay to take shilling third-class return tickets some way down a line, and change their carriage at every station—making a collection before every change The victims fixed, and many of them nervous, it was a poor collection that did not produce threepence. Granted twenty stations there and back, five shillings was the result—a profit of three shillings—while they had their ride to some fair or festive occasion and back for nothing Probably derived from Hebrew negro minstrels in the first place — practically all Jews singing from birth, while most acquire some aptitude on some musical instrument

Collar (*London*) In work. Said of a horse when he gets into swing, or perhaps when he begins to get wet with work Applied to human beings when in work, and therefore making money

'Joe's in collar'

College (*Poor Peoples'*) The workhouse Term by no means satirical, and used to avoid the true expression.

'The old gent is gorne inter the college at last.'

'Mother ain't 'ome now—she's at the college' (*See* 'Lump', 'In there')

Colleggers (*Oxford* '*er*') Academical collections

A ceremony at which the whole host of Dons, sitting in solemn boredom, frankly say what they think of you—are 'colloggers'—*D T*, 14th August 1899.

Collie shangles (*Soc*, 1884) Quarrels Brought in by Queen Victoria, in *More Leaves* (1884).

'At five minutes to eleven rode off with Beatrice, good Sharp going with us, and having occasional collie shangles (a Scotch word for quarrels or rows, but taken from fights between dogs) with collies when we came near cottages'

Colloquials (*Soc*, 1890 on) Familiar conversation—good example of adjective passing into abstract noun

Well—well—let us give up the higher culture now the teapot's here, and have some colloquials

Colour (*Amer Soc*, 1860 on) Applied to negroes in American as more delicate than black or even negro This euphemism commenced with the popularity of 'Uncle Tom's Cabin'

Why there should be an objection to the word 'negro' is strange It defines a person of a certain African origin and complexion, and it is gratifying to know that sensible black men are beginning to see it, and despise the studied over-politeness of some white people who talk and write of 'color' without knowing what it really means.—*N. Y. Mercury*, 1883.

'Color' at a Discount. — Attorney-General Brewster has bounced all the Africans in the Department of Justice. He found that the 'color' of money was a little too much for the 'man and brother.'—*N. Y. Mercury*, 1883.

Colour Ball (*Amer.-Eng.*, 1880 on). In England a vulgar black Sal and Dusty Bob kick-up. In U.S.A. a negro or 'dignity' dance.

Colour the meerschaum, To. Drinking to the extent of reddening the nose. 'Aint 'e colourin' 'is meerschaum?' The phrase arises from an association of ideas—those in the first place of darkening the colour of a meerschaum pipe by steady smoking, and in the second, intensifying the hue of the nose by steady drinking. The colour harmony between the pipe and the nose above it is very droll, the hintful phrase itself a singularly good example of the keenness of the common people masking itself in a mock politeness which is worse than the plain truth.

Coloured grave (*Amer. Puritanism*, 1882). That of a negro — striking instance of class prejudice creating phrases of its own.

Presently the undertaker came up, and I asked him. He said he didn't know; that he had told them to dig a coloured grave.—*Newsp. Cutting.*

Colt (*Anglo-Amer.*). A revolver. Good example of the name of the manufacturer being given to the manufacture. Colonel Colt was the inventor of the commercial as distinct from the historical revolver. 'I put down five pounds for my 'colt.' 'This is the colt that is bound to win.' Supplanted by one 'Derringer', a small pocket revolver, sometimes called a 'saloon' from its possible conveyance by way of the waistcoat pocket into polite society.

Colt Party (*Anglo-Amer.*). A soirée of all young people—no elders. Much more in vogue in United States than in England.

'I'll never give another all young party again,' said her grace—'it was too, too stupid.' 'Dear duchess,' replied Lord Claud, 'the colt party is impossible. The charm of maturity, to say nothing of age, dares everything.'

Com (*Business*). A commercial traveller.

I loved the good old 'com.' I have spent many a pleasant evening in commercial rooms with the shrewd men of the world who used to be bagmen, and who had strange tales of the road to tell. —G. R. Sims, *Ref.*, 28th December 1884.

Comb and Brush (*Rhyming*). Lush. At one time this word signified 'drink', and drink only. 'Won't yer lush us?' meant Will you not pay for some drink for us? Now the word has been extended in its meaning, and includes all shapes of liberality. 'Jack lushed us all three to the Surrey Theayter.'

Comb-cut (*Sporting*). Trimmed, manipulated; applied to a man who has been completely vanquished. From the comb of fighting cocks being removed to prevent the opponent from seizing it; may be suggested by the vanquished bird having had his comb torn across by the victor.

Come and have one (*Peoples'*, 1880). Drink is understood. A jocular application of the phrase 'One of those'.

Come and have a pickle (*Soc.*, 1878). An invitation to a quick unceremonious meal.

Come and wash your neck (*Navy*, 1860). Take a drink—from the liquor flushing the throat.

Come-day, go-day (*Military*). An extravagance, *e.g.*, 'It's come-day, go-day with him'—meaning that he receives on 'come'-day money or pay that is spent or goes the same day.

Come-down (*Common Life*). Disaster, ruin, degradation, humiliation, *e.g.*, 'What, no bonnet! What a come-down; an' I knoo 'er mum when she 'ad six of everything.'

Come down (*Theat.*). The act of moving towards the audience from up the stage.

Come off, To (*Amer.-Eng.*, 1892). To cease, refrain, desist, etc. Very graphic—probably from the American call to fighting dogs, or men.

'How much does yez ax for this book?' 'Six dollars,' replied the smiling clerk.

'Six dollars! Oh, come off!'—*N Y Mercury*, February 1892.

Come in, To (*Society*, 1880). To become fashionable, *e g*, 'You mark my words, the horrid old Victorian furniture, especially from 1840 to 1851, will come in. Already spindley Chippendale is a pill'—(1883)

Come on (*Theat*) No invitation to fight, but a direction to appear upon or 'come on', the stage. (*See* 'Go off' and 'Go up'.)

Come over on a Welk (or Wilk) Stall (*Coster satire*) *E g.*, 'Where did yer dad come from? Come over on a whilk-stall?' This may be a folk-satire upon 'Coming over with the Conqueror,' or the 'whelk' may have that broad reference which was applicable to 'He's got 'em on'—when first this satirically eulogistic phrase came out

Come out, To (*Soc*, 19 *cent.*) To appear in society—applied to young women in society The crown which finishes the work of coming out is presentation at Court.

Mr Francis Knowles called, and examined by Mr Clarke, said: I have known Lady Durham ever since she 'came out'.

General Reilly, examined by Mr Clarke, said I have known Lady Durham ever since she came out in society.—*Evidence in Lord Durham's Nullity Suit*, March 1885

Come the old soldier over, To (*Peoples'*) Cajolery, pretended poverty, specious lying statement 'Don't come the old soldier over *me*'—from fraudulent uniformed beggars after Waterloo

A great amount of imposture was practised by means of the 'old soldier' dodge upon the Duke of Wellington during the latter part of his life To 'come the old soldier' is in some quarters still a familiar expression signifying the practice of an artful trick, and the 'old soldiers' after Waterloo were so numerous and so pestered the Duke of Wellington that he was fain to hand over all applications for alms to the Old Mendicity Society.—*D N.*, 3rd March 1885.

Come to grief, To (*Sporting*, 1880). A riding man's term for a smash or spill; gradually accepted on all sides to depict failure.

'He tried Hamlet, but to the surprise of his family, though not of his friends, he came to distinct grief.'

Come to stay (*Amer.-Eng*). Come to remain

What he had to say about the origin and development of that remarkable institution, which, as the Americans put it, 'has come to stay', was very interesting —*D. T.*, 20th May 1899.

Come up with (*Amer -Eng*) To be on equality, *e g*, 'I came up with him instanter and he took a back seat'

Come up to the rack, or jump the fence (*Amer*) To decide to do a thing or take departure. Rack is short for 'racket', this word representing noise Racket gives a capital idea of the bustle of American life, while 'jump the fence' is singularly suggestive of new settlements, and enclosed homesteads

'Well, I want to bring this young man to time. Fact is, he's either got to come up to the rack—or jump the fence'—*Newsp Cutting*.

Comfy (*Soc*, 1880 on) An endearing diminutive of comfortable. Probable origin—a royal nursery.

Felice is lonely, homesick These dear girls are very nice and kind, but the simple tastes and simple conversation of the truly rural is apt to pall on your *blasé* old Diogenes She feels as if half only of her were here, and the sensation is not 'comfy'—*D N*, 4th July 1895 (Craigie *v* Craigie).

Comic-song faker (*Music Hall*, 1880) Music-hall way of describing music-hall song-writers

Mr Joseph Tarbar tells me he is the boss author of this or any other country—as far as comic song-faking is concerned.—*Cutting*

Coming bye-and-bye (*Amer -Eng*, 1876 on.) Eternity The evangelical nature of the ballads, and other musical compositions for the voice, became very marked after 1870, and even preachers thought it elegant to refer to the second personage of the Trinity as 'our mutual friend J. C.'—evidently without any thought of offence; indeed with true sincerity. A ballad entitled 'In the coming bye-and-bye', very namby-pamby, and referring of course to the after life brought (about 1880), this style of composition into sudden contempt—more especially when Mr W. S. Gilbert imported it into a ballad for the Lady Jane (*Patience*), wherein, lamenting the lapse of her charms, she fears that in the coming bye-and-bye —meaning a few years—her charms will be gone.

It seems to me that there will be plenty of calls on that 'Actors' Benevolent Fund' in the coming by-and-by. —(1883).

Commandeer, To (*Transvaal War*, 1899). Required—in Dutch; but in England held to be robbery. To commandeer was to press unwilling men into the Dutch army, or 'take' whatever the Dutch came across, and with no concurrent effort to pay for the property annexed.

Some of the recruits from the inland districts were wild and uncouth beings, arrayed in rags and patches, and without boots or shoes. With these attractions were combined the external polish of uncombed bushy hair and beard, and skins rarely washed. Mausers and ammunition were all they possessed in many cases. One of them commandeered —otherwise stole—a native's horse, borrowing a saddle from one Britisher and stirrup leathers from another.—*D. T.*, 24th October 1899.

Mr Labouchere suggested that Sir Michael Hicks-Beach should make a commando among the melodramatic millionaires of Park Lane.—*D. T.*, 24th October 1899.

The 'last cry' of this term, and practically closing it and the war, was in the *D. T.* for 2nd March 1900—the day of the relief of Ladysmith.

Scores of them had commandeered the contents bills of the morning and evening papers announcing the 'Relief of Ladysmith', and, sticking them on their chests, they marched on, blowing trumpets and waving flags.

President Kruger, before leaving the capital, commandeered a quantity of gold.—*D. T.*, 7th June 1890.

Commander of the Swiss Fleet (*Polit.*, 19 *cent.*). An impossible title; satirical attack upon titles and positions which exist only for the money they produce. This is the best of them, Switzerland being not only in the centre of Europe, but generally two miles above the sea-level.

It sounds quaint enough to talk of an Admiral 'winning his spurs', articles not generally associated with seamanship, except in the case of the legendary Commander of the Swiss Fleet.—*D. N.*, 6th July 1883.

Commando (*Transvaal War*, 1899). A regiment. Name found by Dutch. In a few days it was in London differentiated from commandeering—which was found to be sheer pressing of men, and annexation of property.

I believe that the first attack will be made on the large Free State commando. —*D. M.*, 25th October 1899.

Commercial Drama (*Theat.*, Nov. 1900). Drama that pays—without relation to literature, art, wit, poetry, or any other comfortable quality. Generally depends upon surprise scenery and machinery, or the reproduction of well-known places, or common objects of street life. Used satirically, but started quite seriously in a lecture, with this title; given before the O. P. club, a society of patrons of the drama. The lecturer warmly applauded the commercial drama, of which he declared himself a successful producer (at Drury Lane), while he intensified his position by an attack upon Shakespeare, of whose plays he declared that some were so pervaded by horrors that they were thereby objectionable, while he maintained that some half dozen could not be produced on the modern stage.

'Oh, yes, quite a commercial drama —thousands of pounds in it, and not one sentence worth hearing.'

Commercial legs (*Recruiting sergeants*'). Bad ones—unfitted to drill.

A slender, awkward, shambling youth, with the 'confounded commercial legs', which show that he has never taken the Queen's shilling, etc.—*Newsp. Cutting.*

Common-roomed (*Varsity*). Had up before the head of the college—the common room being the principal's chamber of state. Good example of substitution of place for person.

The descendants of Mr Dickenson may not mind a story as to how he climbed the college gates, and was being 'common roomed', when cries were heard of 'Dickenson for ever!' from the Quad, and it was found that he had won the Latin verse prize.—*D. N.*, 7th October 1886.

Commonsensible (*Soc.*, 1890 on). The condition of common sense.

English jurisprudence has had a blunt and downright way of presuming a man's motives from the results of his conduct— a somewhat rough and ready method no doubt, but still eminently 'commonsensible'.—*D. T.*, 21st January 1898.

Compos, Non (19 *cent*). Abbreviation of non compos mentis—and a very lame one too.

The churchwardens proved that he raised the disturbance before the collection had commenced It was stated that this was not the prisoner's first appearance on a similar charge, and a doctor had certified that he was not altogether compos —*D T*, 23rd February 1897

Comstockism (*Amer.-Eng*, 1885 on) Opposition to the nude in art. Comstock was quite a public man in America He for some years had a formidable following in his attacks upon 'naked art'

Comstock on Nudity —He admits that it is not necessarily obscene — the proprieties observed. Anthony Comstock (in heated bath-room) 'Hello! Hello! I say, porter! Bring me a match I can't see to fix my necktie.' Servant (hastening to the door) 'Did the gas go out, sah?' 'No, I put it out I've been taking a bath'—(1889) (*See* Horsleyism)

Con (*Polit.*, 1883). An abbreviation of Constitutionals, a designation fugitively borne by the Conservatives in this year. This rather contemptuous word was bestowed by the Radicals in return for the discovery of Rad (*q v*)

Mr Wilson Croker in *The Quarterly Review* more than forty years ago recommended the Tory party to abandon that designation and call themselves instead the Conservative party *The Quarterly Review* of the present day seems disposed to think that the title of Conservative should be quietly dropped, and that of 'Constitutional' adopted instead.—*D N*, 20th October 1883.

Con (*Thieves'*) Simply disguised convict.

Concertize (*Musical*). From America—to assist musically in concerts

M Ovide Musin, the great Belgian violinist, has returned to this city to concertize under Mr L M. Rubens' management.—*Newsp. Cutting*, November 1885

Concrete Impression (*Art.*, 1890 on) Conviction. One of the most absurd of the art critical 'finds' of the '90's

Thus, Mr Peppercorn's 'Bosham, Early Morning', is all breeze and grey light, but not much else; the study is not distinctive enough to call up a definite and concrete impression —*D. T*, 4th January 1896

Condemned; Condemnation (*Sporting*, 1870). Damned, a damn A sort of jocular avoidance of even mild swearing.

David out-gagged even himself, and caused great laughter Nobody else was worth a condemnation.—*Ref*, 11th December 1884

'Ducks!' I says, 'you condemned lunatic, them ain't ducks, them's mud hens!'—*Cutting*

Confidence-queen (*Ang.-Amer*, 1883). A female detective—outcome of American state of society.

The confidence queen of Miss Caroline Hill revealed that lady's stage qualities to great advantage, especially in the scene of the third act.—*N Y Mercury*, June 1884.

Confidence man (*Thieves'*) —He is a specious gentleman who asks his way of one who appears to be a promising victim, and whom he never meets, but overtakes, after allowing him to pass, and so take stock of him. He then enters into conversation, asks the victim to have a drink—as they approach the tavern where the confederate awaits results If the victim accepts, the confederate, who appears to be a stranger, begins showing what appears to be gold, and making foolishly weak bets The confidence man then whispers confidentially to victim that they may as well have the fool's money as another. If the victim is as much rogue as fool, he consents, and by some one of twenty dodges (*see* 365 Straightforward Ways of Cheating), he is robbed If he is honest, however, his honesty saves his pocket

Congo patois (*Amer*, 1884). Slang Term heard at Liverpool.

The professor had, probably, been reading those shockingly poor books, the Grandissimes, Dr Sevier and the Creoles, in which Congo patois, as it is called, is ascribed to educated white people.—*Newsp. Cutting*

Considerable amount of united action (*Parliamentary*, 1883). Conspiracy. Early in this year Mr Herbert Gladstone charged the Conservative opposition with 'malicious conspiracy' to oppose the government Called to account, he modified the statement into this phrase, which henceforth remained a satirical euphemism amongst the younger Conservatives for 'conspiracy' in general.

Mr Herbert Gladstone, however, is mildly of opinion that his words were 'stronger than the occasion justified', and that he would more accurately have expressed whatever amount of meaning was present in his mind by substituting for 'malicious conspiracy' the phrase 'a considerable amount of united action'.—*Globe*, 16th March 1883.

Conspiracy of silence (*Soc.*, 1885). Evasion of comment. Created by the silence of general press in relation to certain terrible articles in *The Pall Mall Gazette.*—(1885.)

Some of the clergy and some of the judges have at last been aroused to the danger of the situation, and many journals are now breaking through the 'conspiracy of silence', and boldly denouncing the shameless creatures, etc. —*Ref.*, 31st August 1885.

Constant-screamer (*Peoples'*, 1860 on). Concertina — A satirical onomatope of the musical instrument in question—which is a machine played by an upward pull, and a downward pressure of the construction, which has much the appearance of a tubular Japanese lantern.

Tommy of the Artillery and Army Service is brimful of music hall talent, and nightly upon the foredeck to the melody of a 'Constant-Screamer' he warbles, solo or chorus, 'Off to Ashantee'. —*D. T.*, 20th December 1895.

Constructive Assault (*Sporting*, 1880). Attendance at a prize-fight.

Some time ago the whole of the common law Judges met to decide the question, what is an assault? The point arose out of a decision of a Chairman at Quarter Sessions, who had ruled that any one 'assisting' at a prize-fight was guilty of a 'constructive assault'. The Lord Chief Justice of England agreed with the Chairman, and carried a majority of the Court with him.—*D. N.*, 14th October 1884.

Consume salt (*Theat.*). English equivalent of *cum grano salis.*

A recent Modjeska poisoning item in the country papers suggests that some stars must consume a great deal of salt if they read about their reported doings. —(1883.)

Contango (*Stock Exchange*). Practically, suspense or renewal of a transaction. (*See* Bull, Bear, and especially Backwardation.) These entries read and furthermore understood—contango may possibly be comprehended. No gain being made on a transaction, and the backwardation being paid, the contract is renewed, in the same terms, upon the price at the commencement of the transaction, and without reference to the price of the day when the contango is arranged. This process is more generally indulged in when there has been no, or very little, variation in the price of a given security between purchase-day and settling-day.

Context, To (*Printers' and Typewriters'*). To try to ascertain, or to discover a badly written word in 'copy', by its context, by studying the words on both sides of it; *e.g.*, 'Oh, context it, and do the best you can.'

Continent (*Amer.*, 1880). The latest shape of oath in the States; *e.g.*, 'What the continent do you mean by it?' It refers of course to the continent of America. Origin obscure. Not in any way the transmutation of a word like it.

Not one of them even looked up. Not one of them seemed to care a continental whether his old ore assayed 15 or 95 per cent. They had all 'been there'.—*Wall Street News* (1883).

Conversation, A little. Violent swearing.

Coo-ey (1860 on). Shout of good-fellowship. This cry, with a long accent on the 'ey' is an imitation of the Australian aborigines' friendly call to another from long distances in the bush. It is therefore naturally a friendly call here in the home country, and is never used in an inimical spirit. It is generally used to find a friend lost in a crowd, or far ahead by night in the street. Probably introduced by sailors, the starters of so much hearty, vigorous, popular passing English—probably miners who have tried their luck at the gold fields, and found it only trying. The gold diggers were the first to adopt the 'coo-ey'—which, properly pitched, appears to travel with exceptional vigour. The e-e-e-y is always half a tone below the 'coo', which is generally pitched as high as the individual voice will allow. The Australian starts upon the 'C' in alt, or that *ut de poitrine* which is the ambition of every operatic tenor in the world.

Cooking Day (*Navy*). Twenty-four hours devoted to Bacchus.

Cool (*Back-phrase*) Means look, 'c' being used in place of 'k', probably because being a true word it is more misleading

Cool her on Sunday in a black velvet costoom, with boots, gloves, and gamp to match —*Cutting*.

Cooper (*Nautical*). One who sells liquors on the sly, also one who buys illicit spirits. Applied (1884) to the vessels, generally Dutch, which follow English fishing smacks into the North Sea Also applied to the cooper's vessel

Another matter in which he took deep interest was the suppression of those floating grog-shops in the North Sea which have done so much injury, and no inconsiderable step was taken in that direction when he made arrangements by which duty-free tobacco is now supplied from the mission smacks in the North Sea to the fishermen, who have not now the inducement to board the 'Coopers' which before existed —*Prince of Wales, Birkbeck Testimonial Fishmongers' Hall*, 31st October 1885

There is a queer craft always hanging about. She is called a 'cooper', and no man cares whence she comes She flies sometimes an English, sometimes a foreign flag, and is in fact defined by the Duke of Edinburgh as a floating grog-shop of the worst kind.—*D. N.*, 20th June 1883.

Cooper (*Peoples'*) The name of a beer-mixture of common beer (3d per quart) and stout (6d. to 8d per quart). Named from the coopers who invented the mixture

Cooper up, To (*Boer War*, 1899-1900) To surround, fix, render immovable—from the fixing of the staves of a tub by its hoops.

The pursuit of De Wet failed, and the swoop in a semi-circle from Pretoria to Pinnaar's Poort, miscarried in so far as 'coopering up' De la Rey, Theron, or any of the lesser Boer leaders and raiders was concerned —*D T.*, 20th October 1900.

Cop (*Thieves'*) Complex rhyming Taken, seized, thrashed, struck, caught by disease, well-scolded, discovered in cheating—a universal verb suggesting defeat or damage of some kind. There has been more discussion over this widely applied word than any other in the kingdom of phrase. It is a very obscure, complicated, abbreviated, back-phrasing example. It is to 'pocket' (in the shape of receiving)—the tek being elided—when poc being spelt backwards 'cop' appears When the police cop a man he is practically 'pocketed' So with all the many applications of this word—with a little indulgence—its vigour will be seen Its common use is 'cop the yenneps', penny backworded, with an 'e' added for the sake of euphony, the plural being made in the ordinary way 'I've copped the yenneps, and I'm off to the carse and the burick'—that is, home and wife Cop has another meaning—to take too much to drink. In universal use

Cop a mouse (*Artisans'*). Get a black eye. Cop in this sense is to catch or suffer, while the colour of the obligation at its worst suggests the colour and size of the innocent animal named.

Cop on the cross, To (*Thieves'*). To discover guilt, by cunning

A good way of copping her on the cross is to pretend to go off into the country for a day or two, and come down on her in the middle of the night. —*Cutting*

Cop the brewery, To (*L. Class*, 19 *cent*) To get drunk

Cop the curtain (*Music Hall, passing into the theatres*, 1880) To gain so much applause that the curtain is raised for the performer to appear and bow. 'The Basher copped the curtain twice, and was a great go'

Copper (*Street*, 1868 on) A policeman. The term superseded Peeler, Robert, Bob, Bobby. From the common street verb 'cop' 'There's a copper round the corner will (1884) scurry a covey of toddlers wrangling in the gutter more rapidly than a four-horse waggon.' Copper is perhaps the first word the infantile street arab thoroughly comprehends

This word is also used as an exclamation amongst work-people when any one of their number is blustering. It means giving himself the airs of police authority.

'Copper! copper! we shall soon be a sergeant!'

The incident of the trial which will probably pass on and become history when the rest is forgotten was the enquiry of Mr Justice Hawkins as to the meaning of the word 'copper'. The witness kindly explained to the innocent judge that a copper is a policeman—one who 'cops'.—*Ref.*, 15th August 1888.

'A Lady' writes to a fashionable rag that the low-necked dress is an abomination, 'into which it is the duty of the press to look.' Look! No, old gal. If any of 'em come near me I shall cry 'copper!'

'I cry copper' was the refrain of a popular song (1882) in which the policemen 'got it'.

Copper Captain (*Queen's Bench Prison*, Southwark). A captain found in neither Army nor Navy List. An officer of self-promotion.

'The Affable Hawks and other varieties of copper captains have taken flight from the Borough Road. Flash songs are no longer heard behind the high walls, on the inner side of which the racquet courts are still marked out, and a ghastly stillness has fallen upon the once thickly peopled spot.'—Article upon Queen's Bench Prison (1881), then about to be pulled down. 'But the modern practitioner has shown a notable advance in method from the copper captains, table knights, and Dandos of yore.'—*D. N.*, February 1882.

'The company contains many copper captains, brazen adventurers, and women whose character is advertised in their countenances.'—*D. N.*, 26th August 1883.

Copper-clawing (*Street.*) A fight between women. Probably a corruption of 'cap-a-clawing'—a pulling of caps—a phrase which ceased to be applicable when lower-class women ceased to wear caps.—(1820.)

Copper-rattle (*Navy*). Irish, generally Irish, or other stew—from the hubble-bubble of this boiling delicacy —called in London city restaurants, 'French Pie'.

Copper's Nark (*Thieves'*). A policeman's civilian spy.

Upon this the prisoner, who was standing by, accused witness of being a 'copper's nark' (*i.e.*, a police spy), and dealt him several severe blows.—*D. T.*, 18th October 1897.

Copper's Shanty (*C. L.*). A police station. Shanty is from the backwoods of America—a small, cosy house.

'Do you think I've arrived at my time of life without seeing the inside of a copper's shanty?'—*Cutting.*

Copper-slosher. An individual with the mania of 'going for' policemen.

Miss Selina Gripp, the well-known copper-slosher, returned to the buzzim of her family on Tuesday from Tothill, where she had been staying for some months.—*Mock Fashionable Intelligence*, 1882.

Copy (*Printers'*). The matter to be set up in type, and which must be one of two kinds, the ever legitimate MS. or manuscript, and the frequently stolen reprint.

The copy's bad, as though with skewer the author wrote, and watery ink. 'What word is this?' quoth one. 'Elephant, elegant, or telephone?' 'Oh, I don't know, at this time of night; put it what you like, and let the reader find it out.'—*Cutting.*

Coqcigrues (*European*). Utopias, impossibilities. The word evidently refers to something that will never happen. It is on all fours with the French folksaying: 'That will happen in the week of the four Thursdays.' May it be Coqs aux Grues—cock fowls that are half storks or cranes—more especially referring to the differences between the gallinaceous claw and the long leg and web-foot of the stork. The anticipation of arrival is also consistent with the migratory habits of storks, and also of the coqs de Bruyère. 'Coqcigrues' may have originally been booth clowns—professional jesters; applied afterwards generally to foolish people. They were dressed as cocks, with feathers and cocks' heads, and danced upon stilts, hence the reference to storks—'grues'; or cocks on storks' legs.

If reform can only come from within, the teaching of history warns us that we cannot expect reform till the coming of the Coqcigrues.—*D. N.*, June 1885.

The king sent John de Shoreditch to ask the Dean and Chapter for a loan of the hundred marks left by Bishop William de Marcia, and kept at Wells *usque ad generale passagium ad Terram Sanctum* —'till the general passage to the Holy Land;' that is to say, till the coming of the Coqcigrues, or *usque ad adventum Coqcigruorum.*—*Newsp. Cutting.*

Corfee-'ouse cut (*Cheesemongers'*). The back of bacon, without bones, and exceptionally used by coffee-house keepers.

Cork (*Workshop*). The cork (probably from the American caucas) is the complainant who brings a charge before the shop constable and the garret. He may bring a complaint against a fellow-workman of a technical character, or of some social nature or even crime. The restraint upon the cork takes the shape of the rule which compels him to pay five shillings if he lose the case, while the defendant, when losing, is mulcted in but half-a-crown. Of these fines half is generally spent in drink in the shop, the other forwarded to the secretary of the Union, who applies it to the General Purposes Fund

Corkscrew (*L Lond.*) An evasive pronunciation of God's Truth—used satirically (*See* Cheese and Crust)

Corn-crackers (*Amer*) The people of Kentucky, probably from the immensities of corn grown there.

Corner Boys (*Dublin*) Loafers, who generally affect street corners, as presenting more scope (1) for seeing, and (2) for bolting.

Kilmainham was reached a few minutes before five o'clock There were only a few corner boys present in the neighbourhood of the prison, and there was no demonstration of any kind — Report of Arrest of Mr Dillon, M.P, 1881.

The term comes from America

Cornichon (*Soc*, 1880) A muff Direct from French—gherkin

Yet are not all French sportsmen good shots, indeed, for every decent gun you must reckon twenty highly developed *cornichons*—French for muffs —*Newsp Cutting*

Cornstalks (*Austral.*) The people of New South Wales, from this province growing quantities of corn. Given by the people of Victoria

Being usually of good height, but wanting in depth and breadth, they have gained for themselves the epithet of cornstalks, which is saying a great deal for the value of their heads.—Baden Powell, *New Homes for the Old Country* (*See* Gum-suckers)

Cornucopia (*Amer*) A rich individual

We who dine at noon, live in one-story cottages with mortgages on them, and have wet blankets thrown over us as we slowly elbow our way through life, sometimes envy the old cornucopias as we see them go down to the bank to draw their dividends —*Cutting*

Correctitude (*Soc*, 1900) Correctness. Latinised word first seen and heard in England in 1900 Probably from U.S A

M Delcassé, it is true, has all along been a pattern of 'correctitude', but the Waldeck-Rousseau Cabinet had a difficult people to deal with —*D T*, 29th December 1900

Corroboree (*Nautical*) A drunken spree, in which there is much yelling Supposed to be derived from a term used by some unknown South Sea Islanders to describe a wordy and excited interview Every sailor knows the word, sometimes used disparagingly as 'It just *was* a corroboree'

Gould (*Handbook of the Birds of Australia*) says it is the Australian native word for a discussion, or pow-wow 'The males' (of an Australian bird) 'congregate and form corroboree places.'

Corpse (*Theat.*). To balk a fellow-actor on the stage while he is acting, by some by-play or facial action which attracts attention. Very emphatic. 'Look here, Joe, if you corpse me again to night in the second act, while you are up, I'll pull your long nose!'

Corpse-worship (*Club*, 1880 on) The extreme use of flowers at funerals This custom, set by the Queen at the mausoleum (Frogmore) immediately after the death of the Prince Consort, grew rapidly, until the custom had extended to quite the lower classes, amongst whom neighbours vied in forwarding expensive floral tributes Finally, in the '90's, many death notices in the press were followed by the legend, 'No flowers'

Corsey (*Sporting*). Stiff betting or play—not from race course, as it might well be supposed, but from French *corse*.

Baccarat may be played for any sums, from the *petit baccarat de santé*, the family baccarat, up to the sport which is usually described as *corsé*, or in stronger language, reckless —*D. N*, 18th January 1884

Cosey (*Slums*) A small, hilarious public-house, where singing, dancing, drinking, etc, goes on at all hours

Cosh (*Amer*) One of the veiled ways of naming the Deity

The word 'Oshkosh' is the name of a town, and not a form of profanity in use by the Scandinavians, from whom the

Americans have obtained it in the modified form of 'Cosh! Good-morning'—said satirically, of course, as to Scandinavia.

Coss (*Hatters'*). A blow. Origin obscure—probably the name of a pugilist.

Coster (*Low Life*). Short for costermonger, a great being in low life, generally a sort of prince, and often a king o' the costers. To be really royal he must make money, but save nothing, dress beautifully (*see* Pearlies), be handsome in a rough way, be always flush of cash and liberal with it, possess a handsome girl or wife (generally the latter), and above all, fight well, and always be ready to fight. Reign generally extends to five years (nineteen to twenty-four), when he either takes a shop and does well, takes to drink and does worse, or growing ancient, grizzly, or broken with disease, loses a fight, abdicates, and sinks into the ranks. Said to be derived from 'Quatre saisons'—the 'Marchand des quatre saisons'—that is fruit and vegetables of spring, summer, autumn, and winter.

Costermonger Joe (*Com. London*). Common title for a favourite coster.

Costermongering (*Musical*, 1850). Altering orchestral or choral music, especially that of great composers. From the habit Sir Michael Costa sometimes showed of modifying the score of Handel. Happy hit, as contrasting the guerilla business of the coster with the proper professional and established tradesman.

But the costermongering was worse than ever this time, and, in mingled sorrow and anger, amateurs cried, 'Et tu, Brute!' Better things were expected of Mr Manns, but it was found that Cæsar and Pompey are very much alike—specially Pompey.—*Ref.*, 28th June 1885.

Costume Play (*Theat.*). A drama in which the dresses are any before those of the 19th century, but not before say the tenth; *e.g.*, 'Thank God,' she observed, 'I've got a costume play at last. I shall klobber in crimson and gold for the first act, blue and amber for the second, and pure white and silver for my death in the third. I shall make a great success. Redfern will make.'

A new play by Robert Buchanan is, however, being rehearsed at the Vaudeville. Like *Sophia*, it is a 'costume' piece.—*Ref.*, 5th February 1888.

Costume plays are, to the thinking of some folk, handicapped because they are costume plays. It is sneeringly said that the modern young actor cannot be at ease unless he can dive his hands into his pockets.—*D. T.*, 18th July 1899.

Cot so (18 *cent.*). An evasion of God's oath—the Redemption. Common in Richardson.

Cottages (*Fast youths'*). Vespasians; retiring points for half a minute. Said to be derived from the published particulars of an eccentrically worded will in which the testator left a large fortune to be laid out in building 'cottages of convenience'. Passing away in favour of the underground palaces dedicated to Cloacina—palaces generally termed 'Fountain Temples' or 'Palaces'.

Cough Drop (*Peoples'*, 1860 on). Poison, or even anything disagreeable. 'Lor', what a cough drop she are!' From the ominous motto used many years since with a cough lozenge—'Cough no more'. The gruesome *double entendre* here was first seen by W. Brough, who incorporated it in a burlesque—for when you are dead you *cough no more!*

'Honest John Burns,' who has been returned for Battersea by the skin of his teeth, and who would have benefited considerably had his constituents given him a holiday, objects to being called 'a cough drop'.—*Ref.*, 27th July 1895.

'Oh, he's awful leary—a very cough drop—a genuine red hot treat, make no blooming error.' 'Oh, she's a cough drop, a red hot treat, and no mistake.'—*Cutting.*

Couldn't speak a threepenny bit (*Street*, 1890 on). Utter temporary incapacity for speech. 'I couldn't speak a threepenny bit, but I made myself a luvverley cup o' tea, an' I were soon better.' The lady had probably been drinking—indeed the phrase may be an elegant evasion of the admission of, at least, partial intoxication.

Counting-house (*Street*, 1870). A stupid perversion of countenance—supposed to be comic. 'Just take a squint at his counting-house.'

We get into the shop and see a really fine-looking dona smiling all over her counting-house.—*Cutting.*

Country Cousin (*Rhyming*) A dozen, *e.g.*, 'They put away about three country cousins o' Bass'

County-crop (1856) A closely-cropped head of hair, such as is imposed upon prisoners sent to the county jails In 1856 when the Crimean soldiers returned with long heavy beards, which for many years remained a national fashion, it was found that longish hair, such as had been worn all the century, gave with the heavy beard too top-heavy an appearance. The hair was therefore cut down, and the result was dubbed a county crop, while the beard was called a door-mat, shortened to mat 'He's got a crop and mat' quite described the swell of 1856 1857 The door-mat has vanished—the 'crop' (1897) remains

Couple of Flats (*Theat.*). Double meaning. In the old time, before the advent of elaborate set scenery, two scene screens run on from opposite sides and joining in the centre were called a 'couple of flats' Applied to two bad actors (*See* 'Camp at Olympia', by Planché)

Course-keeper (*Winchester School*) A bully's bully The Wykehamist strong enough to compel fagging officered the 'course-keeper'—a medium between the oldest and youngest of the scholars He deputed his work to one of the smallest boys

The offices which the Eton fag performs are amongst the lightest of the duties of the Winchester fag Besides these he had to clean dirty boots, clean frying-pans, cook breakfasts, and fetch water The infliction of some of the most offensive of these duties, as *e.g.*, cleaning frying pans, was often deputed to a middle boy, or 'course-keeper' as he was called, who gratified any personal grudge he might have against any particular small boy by selecting him for the odious task.—Letter to *Daily News*

The term remains, but fagging at Winchester is a thing of the wretched past.

Couscousou (*Algerian French*, 1840) The native rendering of qu'est-ce que c'est, the enquiry a French soldier always puts upon every possible occasion, and which the Algerian has supposed to be the name of a stew. Hence in imitating this dish they apply the enquiry it would elicit from a French onlooker—equivalent to our 'kickshaw'. Used to be used in London eating-houses — derived undoubtedly from the same French origin

Cover to Cover, From (*Soc.*, 18 *cent* on) Through and through Good example of the spread of education and reading yielding new phrases, for of course this figure of speech is obtained from reading a book from first page to last

I can vouch that Sir William White, who knew him 'from cover to cover', never entertained this view of his character.—*D T*, 12th June 1897.

Covered Brougham (*Peoples'*, 1870). A waggon with tarpaulin over the top Given to the vehicles which once plied from the Bank to the East of London, taking up customers too late for even the last 'bus They were in especial force on Saturday night, and were generally very convivial The increase in the number of 'buses swept away the covered brougham (*See* Virgins' 'Bus)

Cow-boy (*Local Amer.*) A Texas farmer, from his cattle-raising — boy being a common term for men of all ages 'The graziers of Colorado have come to the title of 'cow-boys'

Cow with the iron tail (*Peoples'*) Pump. A way of attacking milkmen who until about 1865 sold extensively watered milk This phrase was very familiar until certain municipal acts were passed which by penalties put down the watering of milk (*See* 'Simpson', 'Hard Simpson', 'Liquor', 'Dill').

Cow-juice (*Amer*) Milk — used by Buckstone, the actor, in *Our American Cousin*.

Cowlick (*Peoples'*) A wisp of growing hair, of different colour from the general tone 'Lick' is evidently a corruption of 'lock', and cow has nothing whatever to do with kine Good example how the Anglicizing of one word modifies another in association with it. The first word having been turned into 'cow', and lock having no meaning in connection with 'cow', it became lick, and the double error suggested a cow-lick which had turned the colour of the wisp of hair. Probably in the first place from a lock common to the head of a clan, the

Gow or Gough, Irish or Scotch. This wisp of hair in all probability frequently became a birth-mark, and was probably often imitated by art when nature arrested the inheritance. A very powerful French drama, in which Fechter was famous in Paris was built up on a cow-lick (*Les Fils de la Nuit*). A superstition of luck or ill-luck attaches to the cow-lick. 'Ha! he always had a lucky cow-lick.' The 'widow's lick' or 'lock' is a tuft of unmanageable hair which grows lower than the rest of the forehead hair, and is always at or near the centre of the top of the forehead. The belief that a woman possessed of this lock, generally of a greyish tone, must lose her husband has, in past generations, prevented many a good woman from getting even a worse husband. Johnson has nothing to say to this word.

Coxey (*Ang.-Amer.*, 1894). A wild political leader. From an American politician of this name who pioneered a number of out-of-work mechanics, who seized trains and invaded Washington.

The march of the 'tramps' in America is a very live thing. The 'Coxeyites' are having a tremendous amount of fun, and the eyes of the world are upon them. —*Ref.*, 29th April 1894.

Coxies (*Low Class*). Corruption of cock's eyes. A term at dominoes for double I. A good example of rebus phrasing. Probably a translation from the French *œil de coq*—especially as a single one is called 'udder cock'—*œil de coq*, although rarely. 'Cock's eye' is the general term. The other names for dominoes are evidently French—2, tray; 3, duce; 4, quarters; 5, sinks. The whites are called 'blanks', while the sixes have become quite English. Interesting to mark that 'tray' and 'duce' are used still by old-fashioned people for 2 and 3 at cards, while even the French 'valet' is still 'varlet'.

Coy-gutted (*Devonshire*). Difficult in the matter of eating. Generally used with an addition more emphatic than elegant.

Crabby (*W. Eng.*). A carpenter—said despitefully. Origin vague.

Crack (*Jovial*, 18 *cent.*). A roystering meeting, derived from 'cracking' and finishing a bottle of wine.

'My poor old mother', he wrote, 'comes in with her sincere, anxious old face. "Send my love to Jane, and tell her" (this with a woeish face) "I would like right weel to have a crack" (conversation) "wi' her once more." '—FROUDE, *Carlyle's Life in London*, vol. ii., p. 96.

Crack (*London*). A narrow passage of houses; *e.g.*, ''Ave yer seen the grand duchess of our crack this blessed mornin'—gorne to the Cristial Pallis in 'lectric blue—she 'av.'

Crack a case (*Thieves'*). To break into a house. 'Case' from *casa* (Italian) anglicized.

Crack a wheeze (*Theatrical*). To utter the last thing out—'wheeze' probably from the alcholic guffaw which follows the tale, especially if it is erotic.

'Cracking a wheeze' is a phrase which has always struck us as extraordinary, especially as it has not the recommendation of brevity. It is synonymous with the sailor-slang phrase, 'spinning a yarn'.

Crack the bell (*Peoples'*). To produce failure by speech; or even act, to reveal a secret unintentionally; to muddle—the phrase in fact has many meanings. Derived from the necessity of being silent while casting a bell, the belief, coming down from monastic times, that a mere word spoken during casting may produce a flaw in the bell; *e.g.*, 'What! told Tom—Jack's going to marry Jill? Then you *have* cracked the bell.' 'She dropped in the mud with all her new togs on, and cracked the bell in a jiffy.' (*See* Let the Cat out of the Bag.)

Crack the monica (*Music-halls*). The chairman, who once ruled in these places—he vanished in the '80's—had before him a table-bell, which he sounded after certain ways, one of which informed the audience applauding a singer who had retired that he or she would appear again. 'He cracked the monica, an' on she came smilin' like "jam" '—the monica is the bell.

Cracker (*American*). A biscuit. The English word, evidently meaning 'twice cooked', or baked, is a misnomer, while the States'-wide synonym is at least a good specimen of onomatope.

I, a lone bachelor, a lone fisherman, with infinite pains and great pleasure, first dipped these ink-pots in the freshest of eggs beaten up; after that into the finest and crisped cracker dust.—*Newsp Cutting*

This ink-pot is cuttle-fish, named after a protective secretion it throws out when pursued. Its more fish-mongerly title is squid. It abounds in New York waters. They are capital eating when 'dusted' and fried.

Cracker (*S Carolina*). Native—origin unknown.

Imagine a tall, gaunt, loose-jointed man, with long grizzled hair, deep-set eyes that glow like coals of living fire, high, square shoulders, a stooping, slouching gait, skin wrinkled and dirty beyond pen description, hands and feet immense, the former grimy and with protruding knuckles, the latter incased in cowhide boots with soles an inch thick and of astonishing width; clothes beside which Joseph's coat would sink into insignificance, so covered are they with patches of divers colours—this is a South Carolina 'cracker'.—*Newsp. Cutting*, 1883.

Crackpot (*Stock Exchange*, 1880). A doubtful company promoter, a man who has the appearance of prosperity and who is but an impostor. This word may come from New York. 'A crackpot in the city' is a term so familiar that it was taken for the chorus in a comic song. It appears even in France where a commercial crash of a swindling nature or a political breakdown is called a 'krach' (pronounced crack), which may represent either crack or 'crash'—more probably the latter—bearing in mind French spelling of most English words. 'Crackpot' replaced the phrase 'Lame Duck'.

They take the honours, and they should do some of the work. Besides, they might improve their minds by listening occasionally to 'The Crackpot in the City' and 'Tiddy-fol-lol'.—*Ref*, 28th January 1883.

'We do a tremendous business in our bank,' said one crackpot to another. 'Why, through buying ink at a new place we save £200 a year. Fancy the amount of writing we do.'—*Cutting*.

Cracksman (*Thieves'*, 18 *cent*). A man who cracks buildings—a burglar, as distinct from a high toby man or a low toby fellow. (*See* High Toby.)

Craft (*Youths'*, 1870). A bicycle, from liking the machine to a ship. (*See* Beast, Bone-Shaker, Craft, Crock.)

Crambo Song (*Peoples'*). Still heard in the remoter parts of England. Roystering ballad, of a cavalier, wine, and women swing. From the eternal Spanish carambo or caramba, shortened by the omission of the first vowel. Probably brought over by Philip of Spain, or a countess in the suite of Catherine of Braganza, or Charles II may be answerable. This cry would be a beloved one in the mouth of a man who did not object to be called 'Old Rowley'—Charles II indeed was rather proud of the distinction. Rowley himself was an étalon in the royal stables.

'The secret flew out of the right pocket of his coat in a whole swarm of your carambo songs, short-footed odes, and long-legged pindarics.'—Farquhar, *The Inconstant*.

Cranky gawk (*Chicago*). Equal to Scotch 'dazed gowk'—said of a stupid, awkward lad.

Crazy quilt (*Amer Mid Cl*). A quilt of patchwork, made at random.

The old woman's dress looked like a crazy quilt, and two of the boys had only one trousers-leg apiece.—*Texas Siftings*, 1883.

Craythur, Craytur, or Craychur (*Irish*). Whiskey; *e g.*, 'Oh, for the love o' God giv me now a taste o' the craythur.' The origin of the word may be of singular significance in considering the history of Ireland and the Irish if it is really 'creator' and not 'creature', as it is generally supposed. In the latter case 'creature' means Satan. This is certain, that for years after the middle of the 18th century whiskey was not known in Ireland, while during the period of Home Rule (1782-1800) Grattan himself in the Dublin House of Commons declared every seventh house in Ireland was a whiskey shop.

Cream Ice Jacks (*London Streets*). Street-sellers of ½d ices. Jacks—probably from Giacomo and Giacopo. 'They've a bad time of it, 'ave the cream ice Jacks, for whenever a kid gits ill the mother goes for the jack an' 'as it out with 'im.'

Creams (*London Street*). Abbreviation of cold-creams, in its turn a droll mode of describing the Coldstream Guards. Intimates that they are dandies, and know how to get themselves up. 'Now then, my creams—gods of the essences,' he observed. 'Then there was a shindy!'

Credit Draper (*Peoples'*). A smooth-spoken seeming cheat—from the tallyman system, whose practitioners have bestowed upon themselves this evasive and hypocritically benignant name. 'Don't believe a word 'e 'ave to say—'e's on'y a credit draper.'

Cremorne (*Society*, 1884). An open-air place of amusement frequented by doubtful women. From public London gardens of that name, long since built over. Applied in 1884 to the 'Inventories' (*see*) when that entertainment was so frequented by 'tarts' that it became in the evening scarcely a place to which a girl could take her mother. Now applied generally.

But as it is certain that no porter with a flaming sword can possibly stand at the gate to decline the shillings of persons not immaculately virtuous, so it is probable that some day a cry will be raised about a 'Cremorne'. When once that ominous word is whispered people begin to be shy of their natural pastime of letting the evening pass in the open air.—*D. N.*, 10th November 1886.

Creoles (*Amer.*). People of Louisiana—probably a satire by the north upon the illegitimate mingling of slave-owners' and slaves' blood previous to 1862.

Crib (*Street*, 1800-40). To conquer with the fists fairly. From Tom Crib, a celebrated pugilist early in the 19th century. To crib, meaning to thrash, is still heard in the slums of London and other great cities. In the nautical novel, 'Rattlin the Reefer' (chap. lxii.), is this paragraph:

Apt quotation!—you are cabined—you are cribbed—you are confined—*cribbed*—look at your countenance—as I said before, 'tis the hand of Providence. —*Cutting*.

Crime (*Army*). Small fault. Often intentional. 'Squinting on parade' is a crime. 'What will a sergeant not go for to say—ain't you got a crime?'—that is to say, confinement to barracks or extra drill scored against a soldier.

Crimea (1856). The full-beard—given to the first long beards worn in England from the time of Elizabeth to that of Victoria. The fashion of shaving, which passed from France (Louis XIII.) to England, prevailed here long after Frenchmen had begun to grow hair. The severity of the winter 1854-55 (in the Crimea) caused the issue of an order to wear beards, and these were retained. Upon the return of the few survivors, their strange and fierce beards were thus dubbed, and amongst the people the term has remained. 'My eye, what a Crimeer Bill have got along o' the doctor for 'is bronkikkis (bronchitis).'

Before the invasion of the Crimea no man, 'unless an officer in Her Majesty's cavalry, ever ventured to wear a beard or moustache'.—Sir A. West, *Memoirs*, 1897.

Criss-cross (*Peoples'*). A corruption of Christ's Cross—one of the few religious exclamations which have not become vulgarized since the Reformation. Generally refers to right angles in textile fabrics, wood, and metal work. Sometimes used exclamatively. 'S'help me criss-cross' (or crass), 'I didn't!'

Not many who use this word appear to have any idea of its meaning, yet it is one of the few old Catholic oaths which have retained much of the original sound.

Croak (*Society*, 19 *cent.*). To be hypocritical, suggested by the lamentable declaration of a frog when he tunes up.

John Hollingshead for some time past has been telling his patrons how they croaked in 1807.—*Newsp. Cutting*, March 1883.

Crock (*Youths'*, 1870). A bicycle. One of the more obscure names for this apparatus. Perhaps from part of the name of a builder. (*See* Beast, Boneshaker, Craft.)

Crocks (*Art jargon*, 1880). Ornamental china. This term came in when, from 1870 to 1880, the porcelain mania raged, and huge sums were given for even poor specimens of china. This word of meek unobtrusiveness is an abbreviation of crockery-ware. (*See* Rags and Timbers.)

Crocodile (*Society*, 1850). A lady's school out walking. A ballad in the forties went:

'I'd rather meet a crocodile
Than meet a lady's school.'

Crocodiles' Tears (*Peoples'*, 19 *cent.*). Imitation sorrow.

Many visitors have probably passed by the alligator in the somewhat out-of-the-way corner where he at present sojourns; but others know him well, and love to stir him up until he swells out with anger, and emits from the corners of his eyes the queer little bubbles which pass for crocodiles' tears. —*D. N.*, 21st March 1883.

Crocus (*Thieves'*). A mock doctor—a cheap-jack gentleman with a wonderful cure. Simple derivation 'croak', to kill, or cause to croak, and 'us'.

Crony (*Peoples'*). A friend, or rather trusted and loved companion Johnson says of this word: 'An old acquaintance, a companion of long standing' Generally used with the qualifying adjective 'old'. Swift has this word.

'Strange an astrologer should die
Without one warder in the sky!
Not one of all his crony stars
To pay their duty at his herse!'

Pepys (30th May 1665) says·
'Died Jack Cole, who was a great crony of mine.'

Probably one of the few words came from one of the universities If so, it is possibly derived from Chronos.

Crooked 'un (*Peoples'*) Crook. The reverse of a straight 'un. Generally said of a husband who turns out bad. 'He was about as crooked as they make 'em.' (*See* By Hook or by Crook.)

Crop up (*Society*, 1850) To suddenly appear, or introduced. 'Then Jack cropped up'—from geological term referring to a sudden stratum. Accepted when geology became modish.

Croppie (*Scottish*). Equivalent of Roundhead, and used precisely in the same way Strangely enough, in the 1798 Irish rebellion, the rebel Irish were called croppies, equally from the shortness of their hair. A Hanoverian song was popular, called 'Croppies, lie down,' which suggestion of treating them as dogs made the rebels very wild In one historical instance a servant of thirty years' standing shot at the family after hearing one of them singing this song.

Cross-bench mind (*Society*, 19 *cent.*) Undecided, hesitating, from the cross benches in both Houses of Parliament, upon which those peers or members seat themselves who have not made up their minds to which party they belong 'Poor man, with his mother to the right of him, and his wife to the left of him, he has but a cross-bench mind.'

Lord Glenaveril is brought up partly in Germany, is born to great estates, and takes his seat on the cross-benches of the House of Lords But poor Lord Glenaveril with his title, and his land, and his patronising disposition, and his 'cross-bench mind', is merely a puppet through whom, about whom, and starting from whom, Lord Lytton may expound his social and political philosophy.—*D. N.*, 30th March 1885

Crosses (*Peoples'*) Woes, miseries, sorrows. This may be derived from 'across', or more probably from Catholic times, and a reference to carrying the cross.

Cross-grained (*Peoples'*) Ill-tempered, hard to manage. A trade metaphor, from the carpenter's shop, where cross grained wood is hard to deal with.

Cross-life men (*Thieves'*, 1878) Men who get their living by felony Used amongst themselves — rather plaintively it would seem, and in remarkable contrast with the 18th century term, 'gentlemen of the road', 'high toby men', and others

Sir H James—What do you mean by men of your class? Witness—Men of the world—(laughter)—men like myself. I did not tell him that I had seen gentlemen's servants there—I am certain of that I did not use the term that the room was the resort of cross-life men (thieves) —*Bignell* v. *Horsley*, 1880.

Cross the Ruby (*Fast World, early* 19 *cent*) A grotesque abbreviation of 'cross the Rubicon', with the same meaning. Ruby was then the name for port wine

Crocheteer (*Society*, 1880) A patron of crotchets.

Within later years the ladies and gentlemen who feel so strongly on the subjects of vivisection, compulsory vaccination, teetotalism, Sunday closing, and other cognate topics, have been called crotcheteers.—G A Sala, *I L N.*, 12th May 1883

Crotchetty (*Society*, 19 *cent*). Eccentric, unexpected. Trade metaphor, from music. Probably from the time when solemn, slow church music was enlivened by the comparatively quick crotchet; or it may be from a man named Crotchet

Crowbar Brigade (*Irish*, 1848) The Irish Constabulary. From the crowbar used in throwing down cottages to complete eviction of tenants.

After a while the whole *posse*—sheriff, sub-sheriff, agent, bailiffs, and attendant policemen—came to be designated the 'Crowbar Brigade'.—A M Sullivan, 1878

Still used to deride policemen in Ireland.

Crowbar Landlord (*Ireland*, 19 *cent.*). Outcome of Crowbar Brigade.

I recommend my countrymen to shoot the crowbar landlord as we shoot robbers or rats, at night, or in the day, on the roadside or in the market-place!—T. Mooney, California, 1865.

Crowd (*Theatrical*, 1870 on). Simply the audience; *e.g.*, 'What sort of a crowd is it to-night?' Also a theatrical company; *e.g.*, 'Who's in the crowd?' 'Lal Brough and Arthur Roberts.' 'Oh, then, there will be at least half-a-dozen laughs.' Also said of the mass of supers, whose numbers increase yearly; *e.g.*, '*I*? What do *I* do? Oh, I go on with the crowd.'

Crows' feet (*Soc.*). Diverging Delta wrinkles at the outer angles of the eyelids.

Crow's nest (*Soc.*, 1850 on). Small bedroom for bachelors high up in country houses, and on a level with the tree tops; *e.g.*, 'Give me a crow's nest, and pray save me from the state bed-chamber.'

Cruel classes (*Soc.*, 1893). Used by the Duke of York, 6th February 1893, on the occasion of his first public speech, as chairman of a dinner in aid of the Society for Prevention of Cruelty to Children. At once took, as distinguishing the savages of the lowest classes from the lowest classes generally.

Until this Society came into existence the lives of young children belonging to the cruel classes of the community could not be considered secure. Their very helplessness made them an easy prey.

Crumb. *See* Bit o' Crumb.

Crumpet. *See* Barmy.

Crush the stur (*Thieves'*). To break from prison—stur being abbreviation of sturaban.

A short time after I ascertained from the jailor who payed me a visit, that my two 'fly' friends had 'crushed the stir', and were at large, ready to prey on the community again.

Crushed (*Soc.*, 1895). Spoony, in love with.

Quite new is the slang 'crushed'. It is used in place of the expression, 'mashed', 'struck', etc., and is quite *au fait* with the summer resort girls. One hears everywhere murmurs of Charlie Binks being utterly 'crushed' on Mabel Banks, and so on with regard to various things. Dora tells Flora that she is 'crushed' on Jim's new sailor, when she really isn't damaging his headgear at all, and so it goes. The English language is getting awfully queer!—*American Paper.*

Crusher (*Peoples'*). A policeman—evidently a word suggesting respect for the force. Mr W. S. Gilbert used this word in the *Bab Ballads*.

'One day that crusher lost his way,
In Poland Street, Soho!'

Crushers (*Navy*). Ships' corporals, who are the rank and file of the master-at-arms. Descriptive term, borrowed from ashore, where this term is still applied satirically to policemen.

Crusoe (*Iron Trade*). A good example of anglicising; name given by English ironmasters and workmen to the great French ironworks at Creuzot—a reminiscence of Robinson Crusoe.

Cry! (*Peoples'*). Shape of Carai—probably introduced by English gipsies passing from Spain. One of the libidinous good-wishes at nightfall, similar to Carambo. Both words more or less known to the oi polloi. Now applied indiscriminately to express surprise of a satiric character.

Cry haro (*Jersey*). A synonym of justice. Word used by people calling upon their lords for interference. One of the first railway engines run out of St Helier's was named 'Haro'. Now used as a 'jollying'.

It is characteristic of the satirists of the hour that they make their victims' very sobriety a reproach. If he is perfectly well dressed, an excellent thing in youth, is exceptionally quiet and well bred, and goes frequently to the theatre, they dub him a 'masher', and 'cry haro' upon him.—*Newsp. Cutting*, 1883.

Cuff-shooter (*Street*, 1875 on). A clerk. Name invented after the introduction of shirt-cuffs wide enough to come down well over the hands; a movement of the arm to throw forward the cuffs was called cuff-shooting; said scornfully or enviously of young clerks popularly supposed to consider themselves leading gentlemen; *e.g.*, 'Well, what if I am a coster? I earns a dollar (5s.), where a blooming cuff-shooter don't make a 'og' (1s.).

This wide cuff was introduced by the late Duke of Clarence. He also invented the high collar. Indeed the prince's designation was familiarly 'cuffs and collars'—finally 'cuffs'.

Culver-head (*Lower Classes*). A fool; practically calf-head. Probably from Dutch fishermen (chiefly with eels) frequenting Billingsgate, once the matrix of so many vigorous phrases. If from Holland of course the word is a corruption of Kalver, which gives a name to one of the chief streets of Amsterdam

When the culver-headed yeknods are down in the dumps, strike us pink if they're not as humble as a blackberry swagger.—*Cutting*

Cum grano (*Anglo-Amer*). Abbreviation of 'cum grano salis'—with the same meaning To listen—with allowances

Managers as a rule agree with Talleyrand that words were made to conceal thoughts, hence theatrical announcements are always received cum grano by the public.—*Newsp Cutting*, 1883.

Cummifo (*Peoples'*). Cockney for *comme il faut.*

Were it not that she is a lady, and possesses the cachet of foreign and not home production, there are folk who might begin to have a dawning suspicion that she is within a couple of miles or so of being not quite as cummifo as she might be.—*Ref.*, 28th April 1889

Cup o' tea (*Colloquial*, 1870). Consolation—probably suggested by a cup of tea being 'so very refreshing' to persons who do not drink any shape of alcohol. Used satirically of a troublesome person.

'Oh, don't yer though You are a nice strong cup o' tea.'—*Cutting*

Cupboard (*Lower Classes*) Hungry. Hunger suggested by mentioning a food receptacle

A pleasant hour or so was spent here, and then we turned our faces back towards Valletta, full ready for the lunch on which in my mind's eye, Horatio, I had been feasting for some while before my internal economy set up its cry of 'Cupboard'!—*Ref*, 6th June 1886

Cupboardy (*Com Lond*) Close and stuffy

I ain't one of them fellers as thinks that you can't keep healthy without yer drinks rose water and eats cream cheese, but, surely me, if the air of the alley ain't a-gettin' raythor too cupboardy for my stomach —*D T* (Greenwood).

Curled Darlings (*Soc.*, 1856) A name given to military officers immediately after the Crimean War, which once more brought soldiers into fashion. Referred to the waving of the long beard and sweeping moustache.

But it is needless to cite instances to be found by the score in warlike annals, from the 'Gentlemen of the French Guard fire first' at Fontenoy to the well-fought field at Inkerman, when the 'curled darlings' approved themselves metal of the right temper —*Newsp. Cutting*, May 1883.

Curmudgeon (*Anglicized French*, 17 *cent*) Cœur méchant. Probably from court of Charles II. The phrase is colloquial in France.

But he would be a curmudgeon, indeed, who grudged the warmest praise for an entertainment light, lively, and melodious, appealing to the eye and grateful to the ear —*D T*, 9th May 1899 (*See* Quandary)

Cœur méchant is much objected to as the origin of this word. It is fully accepted here on the principle that the more obvious derivation is preferred to the more erudite, on the ground that corrupters of phrases are generally uneducated.

Curse o' Cromwell (*Irish*). One of the more vigorous civilities exercised by the lower Irish to their equals. No one seems to know what the 'curse' was—probably his presence in his life-time—possibly tertian fever after the death of the Protector

Curtain (*Theatrical*, 1860 on). A tableau at finish of act or play, to obtain applause

It matters little for the purpose of romance whether or not Nelson saw Miss Emma Hart in Romney's studio before he met her a married woman at Naples These things have to be done for stage-craft, for theatrical tricks, for what are vulgarly called 'curtains'.—*D. T*, 12th February 1897.

It is singular, considering how excellently French dramatists write, that they so frequently fail in getting a good 'curtain' —*Ref*, 15th March 1885

Also a 'call before the curtain' at the end of an act or a piece.

Edward Russell plays well as Peggotty. His acting, if a little too hurried, was full of power, and he revealed considerable pathos He was rewarded with several 'curtains'.

(*See* Take a curtain—Quick curtain)

Curtain-taker (*Theatrical*, 1882) An actor more eager even than his brethren to appear before the curtain after its fall. (*See* Take a Curtain, Lightning Curtain-taker, Fake a curtain.)

Curtains (*Regimental.*) A name given to one of the first modes of wearing the hair low on the military forehead (*1870*) The locks were divided in the centre, and the front hair was brought down in two loops, each rounding away towards the temple. The hair was glossed and flattened.—*Guiver.* (*See* Sixes, To put on the, Scoop, etc.).

Cut a finger (*Lower Classes*). To cause a disagreeable odour; *e.g.*, 'My hi! some cove's cut 'is finger.'

Cut and run (*Peoples'*). Make off rapidly, retire without permission. Trade metaphor. From sailoring, and act of cutting a vessel in the night-time from her moorings and then running before the wind. Very general; probably accepted from T. P. Cook in *Black-Eyed Susan.*

Cut one's stick (*Old Eng.*) To travel for work—the stick being cut or obtained for helpful and probably defensive purposes.

Cut the line (*Printers'*). To knock off work—for a time; origin obscure, but may refer to the line of type.

Cut the record (*Peoples' sporting*). Victory. Here cut is used as surpassing.

People are saying that the Inventions Exhibition is not so much talked of as previous displays at South Kensington have been; but I think that as soon as we get hot weather, the admission returns will cut all previous records.—*Entr'acte*, 30th May 1885.

Cut-throat (*W. Amer.*). Destructive, reckless—applied to card-playing.

It is not uncommon, therefore, to see merchants (especially American) having a social game of 'cut-throat monte', 'eucre', or 'poker', with piles of gold before them.—*All the Year Round*, 31st October 1868.

Cycling fringes (*Cycling*, 1897). Especially prepared forehead-hair to be worn by such women bikers as had not abjured all feminine vanities.

It may be, of course, both libellous and ungallant to suggest that there could be any possible connection with those wonderful 'cycling fringes, warranted never to come out of curl,' at present filling the barbers' windows.—10th March 1897.

Cyclophobist (*Literary*, 1880). An invented word to describe haters of tradesmen's circulars.

The word 'cyclophobist' is still comparatively new to the English language, and perhaps it is not a very scholarly compound to express 'a man who hates and dreads tradesmen's circulars'.—*D. N.*. 6th January 1882.

Naturally came to be applied to the opponent of the bicycle, as this vehicle became ubiquitous.

The chairman, on whose suggestion the communication was laid on the table in the first instance, explained that he was not a 'cyclophobist', but he did most emphatically object to scorchers, and racers, and pacemakers, and also to careless riders, of whom he and many other people went in daily terror.—*D. T.*, 9th December 1897.

Cyrano (*Soc.*, 1900). A huge nose. Due to the popularity of Rostand's play, *Cyrano de Bergerac*, whose hero had a phenomenal nose, imitated in pasteboard by French and English actors who played the part. Pronounced Sée-ra-no, with the accent on the first. A dactyl.

Miss Annie Hughes was as unlike Sam Weller as it is possible to conceive. The immortal 'man' was not a dandy 'tiger' with a Whitechapel accent and a Cyrano nose.—*D. T.*, 16th April 1900.

(*See* Boko, Duke.)

D

D. B. (*Theatrical*). A masked mode of condemnation.

Although Miss Deby was d. b.—which being interpreted means deucedly bad—some of those about her were deucedly good.—*Newsp. Cutting.*

D. D. (*Naval*). Discharged—dead.

The usual way on board a man-of-war of writing a man's epitaph; as: 'Bill? Oh! he's D. D.—this year agone.'—Captain Chamier, 1820.

D. T. Centres (*Lit.*, 1880 on). Minor Bohemian, literary, artistic, and musical clubs—from the jollity, or supposed jollity, of a Bacchic character which continually proceeds within their walls. D. T. is a reduction to the absurd of delirium tremens—or 'tremenses,' as some comic folk style that self-imposed disease.

D. V. (*Atheistic*). A satiric and not very adroit application of the initials of 'Deo Volente', to 'Doubtful—very'.

Fred Hughes says that the letters 'D. V.' in his advertisement referring to his appearance at the Jumbo Theatre, mean 'doubtful—very'. I thought so.

D. V. (*Soc.*). Divorce. Another shape of satire upon Deo Volente—Heaven, of course, having certainly nothing to do with the performance, if papal authority is of any value

Daddles (*Pugilistic*) Hands.

All was in readiness, and the men having shaken daddles, the seconds retired to their corners, and at 12 56 commenced the fight.—*Newsp Cutting*, 1862

Daisy (*Amer , passing to England* 1870). A charming, fresh, delightful person or thing

An enthusiastic admirer of 'The Silver King' lately, in the upper circle of the Grand Opera House audibly proclaimed Wilfrid Denver to be 'a daisy' —*Newsp. Cutting*, October 1883

This morning a young man walked into the office with a huge watermelon in his arms Placing his burden on the counter he addressed the agent. 'Now, isn't that melon a daisy?'—*Newsp. Cutting*

Specially used (and abused) as a sentimental basis, hence 'Daisy' came to be synonymous with humbug.

He took me by the ear and said I couldn't come no 'daisy' business on him.—*Detroit Free Press*, 1883.

Also a satirical term for a drunken man.

Detective Lanthier had hardly approached the platform where the 'Female Dudes' were on exhibition when a piping voice exclaimed familiarly · 'Vote for me, mister, I am a daisy!'—*N Y Mercury*, 8th October 1883

Daisy Crown of Cricket (*Sporting*, 1883 on). Poets have their imaginary bays, warriors their imagined laurels—the field daisy, therefore, is the appropriate floral emblem given to the champion bowler, batter, fielder, *et hoc*

Oxford, so far, is retaining her maritime supremacy, though the daisy crown of cricket is decorating other brows —*D. N.*, 6th July 1883

Daisy-five-o'clocker (*Amer.-Eng*) A charming five o'clock tea An extreme application of daisy, as a term of approbation.

Dam (*University*) Abbreviation of 'damage' in relation to payment for entertainment or entry to place of amusement; *e g.*, 'What's the dam?' 'A sov per fellow'

Damager (*Theatrical*, 1880) A nonsense name for manager. Perhaps some covert reference to his autocratic power of sweeping out a comedian.

The green room became so crowded that at last the damager was compelled to put up a notice.—*Newsp Cutting*

Then a damager took him in hand and engaged him to come on first.—*Newsp Cutting*

Dame (*Eton*). A master who confines his attention to mathematics To some extent a supercilious term.

'Badger' Hale went to this school as a mathematical teacher, and though for the last twenty years he took the classes in natural science, he remained, to use the Eton term, a 'dame'—that is to say, a house-master who did not teach the classics, and whose boys consequently always had a 'tutor' as well outside —*D T*, 26th July 1894

Damfino (*Anglo-Amer*) The last instance of abbreviation and obscure swearing 'I am damned if I know' is its origin.

A vicious college student being asked what he intended doing after graduating, replied. 'Damfino, preach, I s'pose'

Damfoolishness (*Amer*, *passing to Eng*) Intensification of foolishness, and abbreviation of damned foolishness

'Now, Hennery, I am going to break you of this damfoolishness, or I will break your neck'—*Newsp Cutting*.

Damned (*Theatrical*, 18 and 19 *cent*) Condemned utterly, *e g*, 'The piece was damned from the gods to the groundlings.'

Damned good swine up (*Peoples'*, 1880) A loud quarrel Suspected to be of American origin In the States the 'swine' are more demonstrative than at home Here even the common pig is quarrelsome; *e g.*, 'Tell Cecil to tone himself down a bit, or we shall have a damned good swine up'

Damirish (*Amer* , 1883) A disguised euphemism for 'damned Irish'

When I read the story in the papers about the explosion in the British Parliament pa was hot He said the damirish was ruining the whole world.—*A Bad Boy's Diary*, 1883

Damp bourbon poultice (*Amer. Saloon*) A 'go' of whiskey

'Postage stamps', replied the country merchant, as he slammed the door and went out to soothe his feelings with a damp bourbon poultice.—*Newsp Cutting*

Dampen (*Amer* , *Theatrical*). A euphemism for 'to damn'.

Most interesting, but the 'heroine' dying so soon, rather dampens the piece in her opinion —*Newsp Cutting*.

Damper (*Soc* , 1886 on) A dinner-bill—a document which has steadily increased in importance through many years Term recognised in the lines attributed to Theodore Hook.

Men laugh and talk until the feast is o'er,
Then comes the reckoning, and they laugh no more!

Curiously enough the French found a correlative title to Damper, viz., La Douloureuse.

La Douloureuse! Few know that in modern French slang it means the bill that is offered to a generous host after the dinner is over and the reckoning is at hand.—*D. T.*, 29th June 1897.

Dance (*Fashion*, 1890). A ball—this latter word being only used for solemn state and aristocratic functions.

The Duke and Duchess of Devonshire gave a large dinner party last evening at Devonshire House, followed by a dance reaching the dimensions of a ball, only that the word has fallen out of favour save for public functions.—*D. T.*, 6th July 1899.

Dance upon nothing (*Peoples'*, 18 *cent.*). To be hanged—the convulsive motions of the legs in the air suggesting the phrase. Probably took the place of 'Mount the cart' (*q.v.*), when the place of hanging was in the prison, or its shadow, and a cart was no longer in vogue. Passing away in appositeness, now that the hangman uses a long rope, so that the neck is broken, and the victim does not struggle. (*See* Hemp is grown for you.)

Dancing dogs (*circa*, 1880). A satirical title applied to 'dancing men' when dancing began to go out.

Then drop in those supercilious masters of the situation, the dancing young men, the 'dancing dogs', as they have been called.—*D. N. Leader*, 27th March 1884.

Dander riz (*Amer.*). Classic in *Sam Slick*. 'Dander' is indignation; 'riz', a diminutive of 'raised'. Dander is probably from the old Dutch of the early American settlers — the source of so much American droll phraseology.

I don't for a moment say that she would; but, quoting from one of the Claimant's own letters, 'Anna Maria has got a timper of her own', and there is no knowing what she might say if her 'dander were riz'.—*Entr'acte*, 1st November 1884.

Darbey (*Thieves'*). A haul (of course of stolen goods).

'Ben—You ought to be in London on the 10th of this month. The Prince of Wales will be married, every place will be .luminated, and all the "lads" expect to make a good "darbey" (good haul, or robbery). Old Bill Clark expects about 24 reddings (gold watches), and old Tom and Joe expect twice as many.'—*Thief's Intercepted Letter*, March 1863.

In the plural this word represents the common name for handcuffs. It were curious to trace the first of these bracelets to Derby, which 'on the spot' is, or at all events was, pronounced 'Darby.'

Dark as a pocket (*Merchant Seamens'*). Very expressive.

Darkies (*Lower Lond. Soc.*, 1860 on). A synonym for the coal-hole, the shades, and the cider cellar—places of midnight entertainment in or near the Strand, all famous in the mid-nineteenth century.

The days of The Cider Cellars, and The Shades, called in slang terms 'The Darkies' and 'The Coal Holes', and the low music-halls with their abominable songs, and the Haymarket orgies and the dancing saloons disappeared.—*D. T.*, 20th November 1896.

Darn (*Eng.-Amer.*). A United States evasion of damn, and very suggestive of household occupation and equally innocent swearing. (*See* Dern.)

When Sacramento was being destroyed by fire some of the merchants managed to save some champagne, and, going outside the town, drank 'Better luck next time. This is a great country.' Next day a tavern-keeper had a space cleared among the ruins, and over a little board shanty hastily run up was this inscription: 'Lafayette House. Drinks two bits. Who cares a darn for a fire!' —*All the Year Round*, 31st October 1868.

Some writers maintain that this term went to U.S.A. from England, upon the argument of the phrase, 'Darn my old wig,' which cannot be American. Here a kind of pun was intended, for wigs were economically darned. Wigs have passed away, as a fashion, over a hundred years, yet this phrase is still heard at and about Plymouth, which suggests that the word may have crossed the ditch in due course, sailing long after the *Mayflower*.

Vance thinks that the management of Her Majesty's Theatre are a darned sight too particular.—*Newsp. Cutting*, March 1883. (V. was a very clever comic singer, and most comic in petticoats).

Dash my wig (*Peoples'*). Another version of 'darn' in the time of wigs. Still heard, though wigs are seldom referred to, if worn; rarely worn amongst men. Some wild etymologists hold this to be a perversion of 'Dish the Whigs', but they do not give the clue. Dishing the Whigs, by the way, may mean 'douching' them, though, on the other hand, there is a common expression, 'Well, I'm dished!' but this is supposed to be a corruption of dashed, in its previous turn a corruption of d—dash—d, the printer's moral evasion of 'damn' when the printing of this word was in bad taste, and was bad in law'

Daverdy (*Devon*). Careless. Probably from an individual notoriously untidy—possibly David Day

Day-bugs (*Essex schools*) Day scholars, *e g*, 'Don't row with that fellow, he's only a day-bug'—said by a night-flea or boarder This phrase is interesting as showing that the U S A habit of using 'bug' for beetle went from England.

Dead as a door-nail (*Peoples'; from Ireland*) Dead as O'Donnel, on all fours with 'I'll smash you into smithereens'—that is to say, Smithers' Ruins—S having had his house pulled about his ears. O'Donnel being dead and Smithers no longer alive, the two folk-phrases become, the one anglicized into 'door-nail', the other into a powerful word representing complete destruction, one which is heard to this day amongst the Irish lower classes wherever found. Probably many phrases, such as 'The Twinkling of a Bed-post', etc., are built upon proper names which have faded from memory, while the phrases relating to them remain Dickens begins his *Christmas Carol* with this phrase: 'Morley was dead as a door-nail—to begin with!'

Falstaff What! is the old king dead?
Pistol. As *nail in door*. the things I speak are just. *Shakspeare.*

Dead-beat (*Amer.-Eng.*). A pauper—lost his last copper.

'Hang *me* ef I savvy! He didn't pungle, he ain't got no kit, and nobody don't know him' Now it's my opinion he's a dead beat—that's how I put *him* up!'—*Newsp. Cutting.*

Dead broke (*Amer -Eng*). Another reading of dead beat.

'Cheap enough—dog cheap for the fun I had, but I'm dead broke Had 60 dollars yesterday morning, but she's gone—all gone—not a red left.'—*Newsp Cutting*

Dead give away (*Amer.*) A swindle, deception.

He would seem to argue with her that a brood of chickens would be a dead give away on them both —*Newsp Cutting*

Dead-eye (*Sailors'*, 19 *cent.*) Generally 'A bit o' dead-eye' Figurative reference to esoteric effort. In ordinary nautical language 'dead-eyes' are the small clean-cut holes worked in rigging blocks, and in ships' woodwork generally They certainly have an appearance of shadowed sight, which is very startling at times. Mr W. S. Gilbert gave this term to his hero, Dick Dead-eye, in the opera-bouffe *H M S Pinafore*—(1878).

Deadhead (*Theatrical, from Amer.*). One who does not pay his or her entrance fee Critics are professional deadheads. Hebrews are the great sinners in this connection, they getting their free passes, they themselves only knowing where All 'theatrical people' are deadheads, for they never pay to enter a theatre. 'The female deadhead was in a red opera cloak—she always is.' This vermilion stain, however, has now vanished

I have not paid a cent for a seat at the theatre in twenty years I boast of this sometimes Why is this? I am supposed to have 'influence'. I am one of the old 'men about town'. Really I am without influence But no matter. Let me live out the remainder of my theatrical days in peace I shall be a real deadhead soon —*Soliloquy by 'Old Deadhead'*

Mr E V Page has written a good song for Miss Tilley on the 'deadhead' lay After this, how can I expect him to pass me into the Cambridge stalls?—*Entr'acte*, 30th May 1885. (*See* Order deadhead)

He wished also to add that there were quite 'Deadheads' enough visiting theatres Mr Chance asked what that meant. Mr Parkes said it meant a class of persons who under various excuses obtained or attempted to obtain admission to theatres and places of public entertainment without paying —*Newsp. Cutting*, 1882.

The experienced eye can always divide the deadheads from the 'plank-downers' in a theatre The deadheads are always dressed badly, and give themselves airs when looking at the inferior parts of the house The plank-downers never give themselves airs, mean business, and only look at the stage. Deadheads are very emphatically thus described by a theatrical official 'Here come two more deadheads; look at their boots.'

Dead-lock (*Street*, 1887 on). A Lock Hospital. Very significant; *e g*, 'Don't muck about—always go to the dead-lock' Applied from the habit of stags clinching their horns, and fighting thus to the death.

Dead number (*Com. Lond.*). The last number in a row or street; perhaps the *end* of the street.

Dead 'un (*City*). A bankrupt company; *e.g.*, 'The All Round Blessing Assurance is a dead 'un.' (*See* Cadaver.)

Dead wood (*Amer. forest*). Advantage. Origin very obscure. In clearing trees a skilful axeman so acts as to take every advantage from the hang of the tree that it may heel over and save him as much cutting as possible. The gain is 'dead wood'.

She extracted a twenty dollar bill, and remarked: 'I reckon I've got the dead wood on that new bonnet I've been sufferin' for.'—*Texas Siftings.*

Deal of weather about (*Nautical*). Bad meteorological times. For sailors fine weather is no weather at all. On the sea the word always means discomfort and struggle, as may be seen in its use, 'weather the storm'.

Deaner, The (*Oxford 'er*). The Dean.

The dean of a college is the 'deaner' or the 'dagger', while even this is reduced by some to 'the dag'.—*D. T.*, 14th August 1899.

Dear me (*Soc., passed to people*). Exclamation used by the best people; may be a corruption of Dio mio. Possibly introduced by Maria Beatrice of Modena, second wife of James II.

As a matter of fact, women do appeal a good deal, and often when they do not know it. What is the meaning of 'Dear me'? As English it is absolutely meaningless. It is a mere phase, an expletive, until we understand it as a corruption of 'Dio mio'.

Or it may be 'Dieu mais', an exclamation which came into use immediately after the Restoration—introduced by one of the French Court beauties.

Death on (*Amer.*). Determined, even at the risk of life.

Birmingham, to use the Yankee vernacular, which is well understood in that locality, is 'death on' Woman Suffrage.—*Newsp. Cutting.*

Death - promoter (*Amer.*, about 1880). An ominous synonym for alcoholic drink. This phrase is a very fine instance of the etymological landmarks sometimes — perhaps often— afforded by passing English. Here is seen subterfugal conviction of the danger of alcoholic indulgence, even taking possession of the intelligence of the very patron of whiskey himself. Throughout history there is no period before the end of the 19th century where alcohol is associated with death —if we except *L'assommoir*, a cudgel, and used in France to describe a drinking-bar. (*See* 'Pisen'.)

Decadent (*Soc.*, 1885 - 90). A synonym for degenerate (noun and adjective), and the antithesis of atavism, atavistic (*q.v.*).

The most extravagant guesses were made as to its authorship—the writer having for obvious reasons cloaked himself with anonymity—and it was even whispered that the book came from the hand of a famous decadent, who 'dropped out' some time back.—*Sun*, 7th November 1899.

Decencies (*Theatrical*). Pads used by actors, as distinct from actresses, to ameliorate outline.

Deck (*Gaming*). A pack of cards.

John Kernell tells of an actor who spouted his trunk for his board, claiming that it contained fifty-three pieces. When the landlady opened it she found a paper collar and a deck of cards.—*Newsp. Cutting.*

Deck (*Costers'; local*). The Seven Dials (W. London). 'He's a decker' means he lives in the classic dials. (*See* Seven Dials' Raker.)

Degenerate (*Soc.*, 1899). A libertine (male), a woman of gallantry (female). Its antithesis was regenerate, which probably meant a return to a reasonable life, and church at least once on Sunday. A play styled *The Degenerates*, by Sydney Grundy, with Mrs Langtry for lead, was set before the public in the autumn.

To-night you receive—and receive most hospitably and graciously—a member of the theatrical profession. Whether your taste in this respect is better or worse than your father's, whether you are degenerates or regenerates I must ask others to decide.—*Charles Wyndham* (at Argonaut Club), 13th November 1899.

Degrugger (*Oxford 'er'*). A degree.

When you passed an examination you obtained a testamur or certificate, which was labelled a 'testugger', and thanks to it you could proceed to take a 'degrugger', which is Oxford for Degree.—*D. T.*, 14th August 1899.

Delo diam (*Back slang*). An old maid; in common use.

When a bloke's hard up it's the delo diam who is his friend When a poor girl goes wrong it is the delo diam who gives her shelter until the kid is born. Delo diams are angels on this muddy earth, and if there is a heaven delo diams will take a front seat there —*Newsp Cutting*, 1883

Delo nammow (*Back slang*) Old woman

'If he doesn't pay that delo nammow eighteenpence for washing there will be a bankruptcy at his door' — *Newsp. Cutting*

Delo nam o' the Barrack (*Thieves'*) 'Old man', which is back spelling, and 'Master of the house'—barrack, used for house, probably being obtained from soldiers on furlough

'Delphi (*Theatr*). Mass pronounciation of 'Adelphi', the great house, through the Victorian era of melodrama in the Strand. (*See* 'Lane)

Demijohn (*Peoples'*) Large measure, swingeing draught Probably from a measure of the time of King John; *e g.*, 'All gorne—well, that was a demijohn, that was.' Johnson has nothing to say about it.

Demons (*Austral*) Old hands at bushranging; derived from men who arrive from Van Dieman's Land (Tasmania), some of whom are popularly supposed to have inaugurated bushranging in Australia

Den (*Public-house*) A name generally given to a public-house frequented night after night by the same set, and bestowed by them half ruefully, half-satirically.

Dennis (*Sailors'*). Nothing except below contempt; *e g*, 'Hullo, Dennis!' 'Oh, I'm Dennis, am I?' Sailors always call the 'pig' Dennis This may have reference to a certain sister isle—and it may not. (*See* Mud)

Derby (*Sporting*) To pawn. At a time when men still were foolish enough to take their watches to races, and especially the crowded Derby, they were frequently 'rushed' (that is, 'pushed at', but passing language is always industriously inclined to be lazy enough to save a word) for their watches This became so common that men who pawned their watches would say they had been stolen on the Derby or other course Satirical friends saw the point, and hence a new verb for 'to pawn' was added to the countless stores of changing English

Dern (*Amer.*) Another of the evasive stages of 'damn'

'Never held such derned hands in my life. Beat the game, though.'—*Newsp Cutting*. (*See* Darn.)

The study of evaded swearing in English may be interestingly compared with the same process in French In the former the evasion is always a concession to religious thought, in the latter it is always an attack For instance, 'Sacré nom de Dieu' has fallen to 'Cré nom de Chou' Any one can mark the sound similarity of the final words—the pronounciation of 'chou' being something like the mode in which 'dieu' is uttered by Alsacians and Auvergnats. But how needless is the offence of calling the Almighty a cabbage.

Desert (*Soc.*, 1892 on). Ladies' Club—from the absence of members

Deuce Dusius—the erotic God of Nightmare, passing (15th century in England) into Robin Goodfellow. Also applied to the four two's of a pack of cards—here from the French 'deux', playing cards having arrived from Paris, precisely as the three is called 'tray' — from trois. There is no association between dusius and the deuce of clubs say, or any other card deuce.

'It's true, I admit, that women have babies, but who the dooce has to keep 'em!'

The most familiar shape of Deuce is Robin Goodfellow, whose pictorial representation has long since been turned out of good society If any curious reader is desirous of seeing him in his habit as he lived, he must be prepared to pay him five pounds for a copy of Mr Thomas Wright's remarkable little book upon Phallic worship Its study will enable him to comprehend Shakespeare's allusions to this alarming personage—probably Robin Goodfiller.

Deucid or **Deuced** (*Peoples'*) Either corruption of decided, or meaning devilish in the more daily use of that word, as in 'He's a devilish good fellow' In the latter case it is derived from deuce George Eliot, in 'Felix Holt,' ch. 17, makes it 'deuced'. 'He has inherited a deuced faculty for business.'

Deuce o' denas (*Thieves'*). From deux, two, and dena, shilling

If you ask them to lend you a deuce o'

denas, very likely you won't get it.—*Newsp Cutting.*

Deuce take you (*National*). Ejaculation desiring that Satan may fly away with you. Sometimes impersonal—'Deuce take it.' From Dusius—Dusii.

'They were in fact the fauns and satyrs of antiquity, haunting, as they did, the wild woods. As incubi they visited houses at night. They made their presence known as nightmare. They were known at an early period in Gaul by the name of dusii, from which, as the church taught that all these mythic personages were devils, we derive our modern word deuce used in such phrases as "Deuce take you!"'—R. Payne Knight, *Worship of Priapus.*

Devil doubt you, The (*Peoples'*). Very commonly used in this form, but in full, 'I don't' is added. Used to concede a violent assertion on the other side. 'I'm a scorcher, I am,' to which the reply would be, 'The devil doubt you—*I* don't;' probably from the time when compliments were still passed to Satan on the Persian plan. Means 'I am not clever enough to dispute your theory; it requires one as clever as Satan to question your assertion.' Probably the most familiar oath, if it is an oath, in the English language.

Devil's dinner hour (*Artisans'*). Midnight, the hour for all Satanic revels. Said in reference to working late.

Devil's luck and my own (*Peoples'*). No luck whatever. The demon having been lamed early in life, and frequently cheated of his prey, even of the Fausts of this world, his luck is not extensive; *e.g.*, 'Getting on? Bless me no; I've the devil's luck, and my own too. When I pay my way I fancy I'm somebody else.'

Devonshire compliment (*W. Country, except Devonshire*). Doubtful politeness; *e.g.*, 'Do 'ee 'ave this cup o' tea in the pot; 't'ull on'y be thrawed away!'

Dew o' Ben Nevis (*Lond. and Edin. Taverns*). A fortunate name discovered by a Scotch distiller to distinguish his whiskey. 'Dew' was poetic, and 'Ben Nevis' was already in the heart of the Scotch customer. The name is now used in place of the word whiskey, much like 'Guinness' for stout, 'Alsopp' and 'Burton' for ale, and 'Kinahan' for Irish whiskey. 'Twa o' bennévis' (the 'e' pronounced short) is a common request, always complied with in the hard-working land o' cakes.

Dick's hat-band (*Peoples', provincial*). A makeshift. The hat-band in general use, even in Mr Weller's time of widowhood, was a portentous sweep of crape, draped and bowed behind. It slipped into a band of cloth on the hat, and has now passed to the arm as a strip, in imitation of the mourning worn by the late Queen's servants for the Prince Consort. Who was Dick? 'Tis all that remains of him. 'What be that, gammer—that bean't a bonnet?' 'No, bless thee, 'tis a Dick's hat-band.'

Dicky, Dickey (*Peoples'*). Very doubtful; *e.g.*, 'It's Dickey, ain't it?' Origin obscure. May refer to Richard III. as conquered. A courtier of Henry VII. may have started the phrase as a flattery to the Conqueror.

The columbine was less fortunate in his opinion. 'She's werry dicky; ain't got what I call "move" about her.'—Greenwood's *Night in a Workhouse.*

Die in a horse's night-cap (*Thieves'*). To die in a halter. Supposed to be very brilliant satire.

Die Dunghill (*Sporting, 18 cent.*). Said of a cock that would not fight—and applied to human curs; *e.g.*, 'I never die dunghill—always game.' In our days the term has changed to 'die on a dunghill', meaning the person spoken of will have no home in which to die.

Diff (*Soc.*). Abbreviation of 'differences', *e.g.*, 'No—it is not I love her—she loves me.—That's the diff.'

Probably came from the Stock Exchange, the birthplace of so much passing English.

There is a great diff between a dona and a mush. You *can* shut up a mush (umbrella) sometimes.—*Newsp. Cutting.*

Diffs (*Theatr.*). A euphemistic abbreviation of 'difficulties', cruelly common with lessees until the prince, about 1870, completely brought the theatre into fashion.

Diffs (*Vulgar*). Abbreviation of 'difficulties'. 'For gentlemen in difficulties arrested in the county of Surrey there was a single spunging-house in a street somewhere off the Blackfriars

Road I remember visiting a friend there once, who told me that the apartments were extremely comfortable. The sheriff's officer was an accomplished whist player, and he had a musical daughter who used to play and sing to the gentleman in "diffs".'—G A Sala, *Fifa and Ca Sa, in T D.*, 15th August 1893.

Dig (*Mid. Class, Elegant*) Abbreviation of 'dignity', *e g*, 'So I stood upon my dig, and told him his room was nicer than his company.' Sometimes 'otium dig' (from 'otium cum dignitate', *e.g.*, 'Come and see me in my summer-house, there I am in my otium dig'

Dig me out (*Soc*, 1860). *I e.*, call for me, tear me from lazy loafing in the house

Digger (*Milit*) The guard-room. Short for 'Damned guard-room'.

Digs Short for 'diggings' Australian for lodgings, from the time when gold miners lived on their claims, or diggings. In common use by theatrical touring companies.

The strolling 'mummers' have alighted from a cheap excursion train, and are imbibing hot whisky and water before commencing their chilly exploration of the quiet little country town in search of 'digs'.—*D. T.*, 23rd March 1898.

Dill (*Chemists'*) A disguised title for water—no such simple liquor as mere water being named before the public. 'Dill' sounds more medicinal than dill water. The word is a liquidising of 'distilled water'.

Dilly-dally (*Peoples'*) Hesitative. An equivalent of shilly-shally, both generally used as an attack upon the spoonery of lovers. Probably rhymed from the latter.

Dimber-damber (*Street*) Smart, active, adroit One of the alliterative phrases with no absolute meaning—a false onomatope Namby-pamby and nimmeny-pimmeny are on similar lines.

He is a bit dimber-damber, and up to everything on the carpet —*Newsp Cutting*

Dime Museum (*Freak Show, applied to theatres*, 1884). A common show—poor piece. From New York, which has a passion for monstrosity displays, called Dime Museums—the dime being the eighth of a dollar.

Dimensions, To take (*Police*). To obtain information.

I said, 'Are you sure?' and he said, 'Yes, she's been murdered in a railway carriage.' At eleven that same night Sergeant Cox came to the house and took 'dimensions'.—*Newsp. Cutting.*

Dinah (*Com London*). A favourite woman, *e g*, 'Is Mary your Dinah?' Corruption of 'dona'.

Dipping (*Thieves'*). Picking pockets —literally dipping.

Mr Selfe What is meant by 'dipping'?
The policeman It's the last new word —it means picking pockets —*Newsp. Cutting*

Dirt Road (*Amer*). The highway, as distinct from the railroad, which is gravelled Probably railway official satire.

His Honour talked to him in a fatherly way, and told him to start for home by the dirt road, and David went out —*Newsp Cutting*

Dirty Half-Hundred (*Milit.—O.S.*). 50th Regiment.

The gallant 'Fiftieth,' otherwise known as the 'Dirty Half-Hundred,' a regiment with a splendid record, retains its title as 'The Queen's Own', with a local habitation in West Kent —*D N*, July 1881.

Disagreeable Bore (*Soc.*). The antithesis of Agreeable Rattle.

Discommons (*University*) To boycott, send to Coventry, exclude

A man is supposed, on leaving school and going to college, to be learning to take care of himself Except by 'discommonsing' dishonest tradesmen, a form of permitted Boycotting which might be more widely exerted, we fail to see how the Heads of Houses are to make extravagant young fellows careful.—*D. N*, 20th March 1885.

Disguised (*Soc*) One of the numerous evasive synonyms for 'drunk'

Most of Bob Prudhoe's customers are noblemen disguised—in liquor.—*Newsp. Cutting.*

Bob was a very handsome and dashing licensed victualler in the 'neck of the Strand', between St Mary's and St Clement Danes—long since demolished.

Disguised Public-House (*Polit.*, 1886) Workmen's political clubs. First used in the House of Commons, *e g*, 'Call it a club if you like—this is a free country—but it's an after 12 30 p.m. public, and nothing else.'

Dish (*Parliamentary*). To overcome, to distance—figuratively, to present the enemy trussed in a dish, displayed before the conquerors and the nation.

It is alleged that Liberals have stolen a march upon the Conservatives, that non-political candidates have turned out to be Radicals in disguise, and, in short, that the Tories have been dished.—*D. T.*

The Whigs had been dished, to use the historic phrase of the great Lord Derby.—*D. T.*, 20th May 1899. (*See* Dash my Wig.)

Dismember for Great Britain (*Soc.* 1886). The last political nickname given to Gladstone. About the time of the Home Rule Bill.

They used to call him the Member for Midlothian. Now they call him 'the Dismember for Great Britain.'—*Ref.*, 18th April 1886.

Distinct(ly) (*Society*, 1880). Thorough(ly). The use of this word in this sense in many cases became a mania. 'He is a distinct fool.' 'She is a distinct fraud.' 'They are distinctly in the wrong.'

Ditch, the (*Local Lond.*, 1850). Abbreviation of Shoreditch, one of the chief eastern thoroughfares of London.

The Ditch is the oldest village in London. A bloke named Shore hung out there once. His missus went wrong with a King. When the King snuffed it the dona had to walk through the streets in her nightgown. She died in a ditch did Jane. Hence the name Shoreditch. —*Cutting*, 1883.

A frequenter of the Ditch is a Ditcher.

Ditch (*Anglo-Amer.*). The Atlantic. A playful allusion to its immense width (*See* Herring Pond.)

Ditch and Chapel (*E. London, street*). An abbreviation of Shoreditch and of Whitechapel

You only know me, maties, in Ditch parlours and Chapel bagatelle rooms.—*Cutting*, 1883.

Ditched (*Anglo-Amer.*). Off the highway; halted. Accepted by the States from old coaching days.

A portion of Doris's Inter-oceanic circus was ditched on Friday on the Missouri Pacific Railroad, near Booneville, Mo.—*Newsp. Cutting.*

Now figuratively used; *e.g.*, 'I was ditched completely, and did not know what to say.'

Ditto, Brother Smut (*Peoples'*). Your tongue is as coarse as you say mine is. Probably from chimney-sweeps.

Dive (*Amer. Eng.*). An underground drinking bar. Reached England through Liverpool—from 'diving under to reach it'. Equivalent to the lost London word 'Shades'—from the underground darkness of these resorts. The last 'shades' were in Leicester Square. The first dive is scarcely more than a gun-shot away in Piccadilly.

In many places (U.S.A.), especially in the cities, the existence of the law makes no real difference; in some few, by fits and starts, it is rigidly enforced, and the consequence is that the drinking is driven underground, into what they variously call 'dives', 'speak easies', and 'kitchen bar room' in the North; and 'blind pigs' and 'blind tigers' in the South. The liquor sold deteriorates at the same time. Little but spirits is dealt in, and much of it is of the vilest quality. —G. A. Sala, *D. T.*, 25th October 1893.

A grand entrance takes the place of the tavern, which is relegated to 'down below,' and is called a 'dive'.—*Ref.*, 10th May 1885.

Diver (*Thieves'*). A pickpocket—obviously from diving the hand down into others' pockets.

Divine punishment (*Naval*). Divine service.

Jack has little faith, and does not know, perhaps cares little, what to believe; and as to worship, it has long been known in the forecastle as 'divine punishment'.—*Newsp. Cutting*, 1869.

Diviners, or Divvers (*Oxford Univ.*). Reduction in Oxford 'er' of the Divinity Examination, which replaced the Rudiments of Faith and Religion.

Dixie (*Polit. Amer.*). The pet name given to the South, or Dixie-land. A popular negro song went, 'I wish I was in Dixie', that is to say, 'In heaven'.

Dizzy Age (*Soc. of a kind*, 19 *cent.*). Elderly. Makes the spectator giddy to think of the victim's years—generally those of a maiden or other woman canvassed by other maiden ladies—or others, *e.g.*, 'Poor dear; but though she is really very well, especially at a distance, on a dull day, she must be, the dove, quite a dizzy age.'

Dizzy flat (*Chicago*). A fool whose foolery makes the hearer giddy.

Do (*Peoples'*). In one capacity, as a neuter verb, praiseful, as 'He'll do'. Convert it into an active verb, 'He'll do you', and it becomes the most emphatic possible warning against a cheat. Rare instance of one word serving two distinctly opposite purposes. To 'do', as meaning to fight and conquer, has quite passed into common English life. 'I got done in three rounds', simply means that the speaker cried *Væ victis* after he had been grounded for the third time. A serio-comic singer, Bessie Bellwood, turned this word to great account while singing a song as a girl who boasts of her prowess, saying—'Yoho, you come down our court If I can't do yer, me and my sister Jemima 'ull do yer proper,'—proper in this case meaning completely

Finally, this (the emphatic auxiliary verb of the eight auxiliary verbs) is used to describe murder.

Her ladyship replied· 'The two men have been trying to do for me '—Lady Florence Dixie, concerning an armed attack upon her, 1883

Quite classic in the criminal division of Irish society, and is even used to express—hanging by law.

'What sort of a *do* did Walsh get?' Asked by Patrick Joyce, the principal assassin in an agrarian outrage, when almost a whole family were swept away (Nov. 1882). He asked this question of a jailer immediately after he had been condemned to death. Walsh had some time previously been hanged at Galway

Arthur Chewster, of Boston, U S, was committed for trial from the West Ham Police Court on Saturday for severely wounding a labourer at Walthamstow with a bowie-knife. The prisoner informed the police that he was an Irish-American, and meant 'to do' for all Englishmen.—*Globe*, 5th October 1885

In Lancashire is used to express suffering, *e g.*, 'I've had a severe do this time—bronchitis, three weeks in bed '

Amongst thieves to 'do' is to serve a term of imprisonment

In middle-class life 'do' represents a joke, as, 'What a do!'

Chiefly applied to cheating, as—'I was done Brown'—that is, completely cooked.

Carlyle's favourite Cockney, who affirmed that every lottery had 'a do at the bottom of it', would find his rather cynical view of the gambling world strengthened by a case heard at the Guildhall Police Court.—*D. N.*, 25th May 1885.

Judge: Will you speak to what you know of the morality of Mr Doulton?—Well, I will only say that he has 'done' me out of my money (The word 'done' aroused the curiosity of the Court, and the witness said, emphatically, 'Well, then, robbed me of my money.'—*Newsp. Cutting*

Do again (*Navy*). Contemptuous reference to some one who never achieved much. Generally applied to marines, who, being neither enrolled sailors nor soldiers, are the 'buffers of both, and get pressed hard'.

'Pick him up and pipeclay him and he'll do again '—*Newsp Cutting*

Do a bunk (*Public School*) To retire with precaution

Do a bust (*Thieves'*). To burst a house open; burglary.

Redfern and his mate told him they were 'going to do a bust', meaning a robbery —*D T*, 14th December 1897.

Do a Dutch (*prob Amer Knickerbocker*). To remove one's furniture without the preliminary of paying the rent due.

The Spitkinses did a Dutch with all their stock just before quarter day —*Newsp. Cutting*

Do a moan (*Navy*) To growl. Moans are of frequent occurrence.

Do a smile (*Amer*, 1860 *on*). To take a drink Now rarely heard.

Do a stamp (*Amer*, *passing to England*) To go for a walk.

Do him a treat (*Pugilistic*) To give him a thrashing.

'He's a gee-gee of another colour. Whoa, my rorty pals, he's a hot 'un, though some of you can do him a treat when he gets a trifle cheeky.'—*Cutting*.

Do in (*Sport*, 1886 on). To adventure, bet, plank down, etc,

I am utterly unable to understand the unhealthy state of mind of a young fellow of one or two and twenty who in little more than a twelvemonth loses between three and four hundred thousand pounds, and who now rushes to 'do in' every spare fiver or tenner that comes into his possession.—*Ref.*, 19th May 1889.

Do one's bit (*Thieves'*) To carry out one's enforced contract as a felon with the Government.

It is not easy to persuade a wealthy employer who can buy what labour he requires in the cheapest and best market to take a man who has 'done his bit' in a correctional institution.—*Newsp Cutting*.

Do oneself well (*Colloquial*, 1881). To make an effort to succeed in life

He was heard to remark to the lady of the house, in confidence, that this was what he appreciated, that he adored domesticity and 46, and that he intended to do himself well.—*Newsp. Cutting*, 3rd February 1883.

Do over for (*Low London*). To extract money by flattery or threats.

When they comes back, Selby says to me, 'All I could do him over for was a couple of bob.'—*People*, 6th January 1895.

Do the aqua (*Public-house*). To put in the water, as 'Jo, do the aqua', and Joe pours the water into the held-out glass, observing 'Say when!' 'When', says the other—at the point he considers the dilution absolute.

Do the graceful (*Peoples'*). A paraphrase: to fascinate, to charm by elegance of attention or behaviour.

On Saturday last, on the occasion of the 300th performance of *Iolanthe*, D'Oyly Carte did the graceful by presenting every lady visitor with a choice bouquet. —*Newsp. Cutting.*

Do to rights (*Lower Classes*). To effect perfectly; achieve quite satisfactorily. Has shades of meaning. 'Did me to rights.' May be said eulogistically of a meal. 'I'll do you to rights' may be a promise of high delight, but it may mean, when addressed to a man, that the addressee will be thrashed awfully by the speaker.

Do ut Des (*Soc.*, 1883). Selfish people whose philosophy is 'I give' that thou 'mayest give'.

THE 'DO UT DES' AT HOME: Since the time of Bismarck's famous 'do ut des' policy, we have known that the statesmen of the Fatherland are not inclined to give favours for nothing.—*D. T.*, 29th December 1900. (*See* Doddies.)

Do yer feel like that? (*Lower Classes*). Addressed to a person generally lazy who is being industrious, or who is doing some unusual work. Used satirically.

Do you know? (*Peoples'*). The history of this initial phrase is very odd. It was first heard in the East of London, used by a popular preacher who often preached colloquially in the streets, and whose voice had very droll changes in it. The phrase spread (1883) over the East district, and reached the West towards the end of the year. It became public early in 1884 through its adoption by Mr Beerbohm Tree, in *The Private Secretary*. The piece was soon removed to the Globe when Mr Tree's part was taken by Mr Penley, who made the phrase more marked still throughout the year. It helped to make the piece popular. The oddity of the phrase was got out of its strange musical character..

The 'Do' was used short, as a grace note. Then followed the 'you' a third higher, and held about an ordinary crotchet's length. The 'know' was then taken a sixth below the 'you'. The whole had a most droll effect. Mr Penley began on the middle A, rose to C, and fell to E. The phrase was in common use in all stages of society. It went to America.

The Secretary has little more to say than 'Do you know', which is delivered in amazingly sepulchral tones, and which is likely to become a 'gag' expression on the street.—*N. Y. Mercury*, 1884.

Do you savey? (*Half-society*, 1840). Mongrel French—Savez-vous?

'All right—I shall savey in a minute.'

'I couldn't savey that in a month.'

Do you to Wain-rights (*Lower classes*, c. 1874). Intensification of 'Do you to rights,' by introduction of the name of a more than usually notorious murderer, one Wainwright. (*See* Wainwright you.) The phrase was used by men to women, meaning a threat of murder, sometimes used quite earnestly. Wainwright had killed a mistress who troubled him very much. Phrase still heard in East London, where the crime was committed.

Doc (*Amer.*). Short for doctor.

'Now, doc, I want you to tell me the worst. Is she dangerous?' The doc said it was not his nature unnecessarily to frighten any one, but he said doctors often had a duty to perform that they would prefer to transfer to other shoulders.—*Newsp. Cutting.*

Doctor Brighton (*Soc.*, 19 *cent.*). Brighton: said to be the invention of George IV.; one of his few small witticisms.

'Doctor Brighton' is the prince of fashionable physicians, and does not dose his patients with nasty physic. The 'Doctor' has a pleasant face and an agreeable manner at all times.—*D. T.*, 13th August 1885.

Dr Jim (*Peoples'*, 1896). A soft felt hat, with wide brim. When soft felt hats began (1895) to overcome the eternal hard black or brown 'un bowler, they obtained several names of little account, the quotation of which was more honoured in the breach than the observance.

Upon the arrival, late in 1896, of Dr Jameson from the Transvaal, the wide rim of his soft Africander felt was at once accepted. For some weeks these models were called Jemmysons, but the hero in question becoming more popular as Dr Jim, the wide soft felter became a Dr Jim—very soon reduced to Jimmunt, sometimes a Jimkwim—the outcome of a coalescing between the earlier and later titles.

Do without (*Yorkshire*). To dislike. A Yorkshire man is generally too cautious to say he hates a man. He circumambulates, and says, 'Eh, ah could do wi'out him.' (*See* Nice place to live out of.)

Dod rabbit it (*Amer.*). In Charles II.'s time it was God rebate (assuage) it. This passed finally in England into 'Od rabbit it'. Going over to America the phrase was there further changed.

Doddies (*Peoples'*) Corruption of *Do ut des*; reduction of Doddies-man; *e.g.*, 'E's a doddies—give a sprat to catch a herring any day in the week, and any hour.'

Dodo (*Amer.*, beginning to be known in England). A human fossil, a man who clings to the past, and condemns future days and present—a *ganache*, to use a French term.

Dodo (*Press*, 1885). Scotland Yard—figuratively to express that the metropolitan police were fossil in their organisations.

The old dodo at Scotland Yard, roused into a state of feverish activity by the comments of the press and the public on the failure of Monday, yesterday converted itself by a tremendous effort into a gigantic turkey-cock, or, to use the much more expressive Scotch word, a great bubbly-jock—which strutted and rattled and stamped and made its guttural gobble all over the metropolis yesterday, with the most alarming result.—*Pall Mall Gaz.*, 11th February 1886.

Dodrottedest (*Amer.*, 1883). An example of evasive swearing.

The Apaches war well mounted, and I recko'nized the leader as a feller they called Chief Billy, the dodrottedest thief and cut-throat that ever pestered a community.—*Newsp. Cutting.*

Doesn't give much away (*Peoples'*, 1880). Yields few or no advantages—seizes all chances. Very cogent, and full of folk-keenness.

Edgar, who doesn't give much away, arranges to have Rayne drugged with a wonderful potion, two drops of which will make a man silly for the time being.—*Newsp. Cutting.*

Dog (*Peoples'*). Clever, cheery, hearty fellow—age not considered. Derived from the active, cheerful nature of dogs in general.

An Irishman has always been 'a dog at a ballad', as a Shakespearian character (oddly anticipating modern slang) calls himself 'a dog at a catch'.—*D. N.*

Dog-cheap (*Peoples'*). Very cheap. Who or what was the dog? Certainly not canine, for the word would not be apposite—cat-cheap would be nearer the mark. Probably a pedlar, whose name might be Diggory, abbreviation to dig, and thence dog—'I bought it dog-cheap'. Johnson, who was cruelly puzzled by some of the compounds in 'dog', says, 'dog and cheap—cheap as dog's meat; cheap as the offal bought for dogs.' Dryden uses the word—'Good store of harlots, say you? and dog-cheap?'

Dog-gone (*Peoples'*). Devoted; from the pertinacious devotion of the doggie. In U.S.A. it is an evasion of 'God damn'.

Dog my cats (*Amer.*). An example of concealed swearing—God damn my eyes.

Dog my cats if she didn't make a nest of it and set three weeks on the buttons!—*Newsp. Cutting.*

Dog's legs (*Soldiers'*). The chevron, designating non-commissioned rank, worn on the arm, and not unlike in outline to the canine hindleg.

Doggie (*Milit.*, 1850). Officer's servant, especially cavalry. The increase of education amongst the men has swept the term away. Men were proud of it in times when officers and their servants were more familiar than at present.

Doggie (*London Youths'*). All-round upright collar. (*See* Sepulchres, Poultice, Shakespeare navels.)

Doing (*Peoples'*). A thrashing; *e.g.*, 'I'll give 'im a doin'—which 'e won't see out of 'is eyes for a fair week after I've done 'im over.'

'I've had a bad doing this week—lost thirty quid.'

Doing the bear (*Span.-Amer., passing over U.S.*). Courting which involves hugging.

Courtship is carried on in a most extraordinary manner in Mexico. The part a man plays in a courtship is called 'doing the bear', which is a translation of 'hacer el oso'. It is quite a common expression in Mexico to say: 'I am doing the bear to Miss So-and-so'; or for the girl to say: 'That young man is doing the bear to me.'—*Newsp. Cutting.*

Dol (*Peoples'*). Abbreviation of dollar.

Dollars to buttons (*Anglo-Amer.*). A sure bet.

'She has got to put those clothes on, and she feels that it is dollars to buttons that when she picks up an under-garment from the floor by the table leg, that she will be blown through the roof.'—*Newsp. Cutting.*

(*See* Million to a bit of dirt.)

Dolly mop (*Peoples'*). An over-dressed servant girl. Probably a form of Dollabella and Mopsa, both names used in 18th century for weak, over-dressed, slovenly women.

Dolly worship (*Nonconformist*). The Roman Catholic religion. From the use of statues, etc.

Dominoes (*Tavern*). The teeth, when bad and yellow. When white, they are ivories.

Don Cæsar spouting (*Soc.*, 1850 on). Haughty public elocution—especially after dinner. Probably a satirical combination of 'the Don'—a memory of Mary Tudor's husband, and Julius.

Dona Highland Flingers (*Rhyming—Music Hall Singers*). One of the names of the serio-comic—generally one who sings or flings high notes—hence the term. 'Many a dona Highland Flinger gets nailed when she thinks she marries a toff, and finds out that he's a bad egg.

Dona Jack (*Lower Classes*). Lowest description of Jack—man who lives on the dona, a man who preys upon men of all designations.

Done (*Texas*). Completely. Done is the commonest of adjectives; *e.g.*, 'We are done tired';

'The kitchen is done swept';
'The baby is done woke up.'

Done Fairly (*Sporting*, 1860). Completely cheated.

Fairlie has taken the Novelty Theatre. Let's hope that nobody will be able to say he's done Fairlie.—*Cutting.*

Donkey's breakfast (*London*, 1893 on). A man's straw hat. Satiric reference—a protest against the then new fashion, with suggestion as to the wearer. Died out as the century wore to an end. 'Which when a gent puts a donkey's breakfast a-top of his nut—he wants jollying.' It took several years for the streets to accept the straw hat. Even now it is far from universal.

Donnybrook (*Anglo-Irish*). Riot, disturbance, down to a shrew's squabble. Applied in a thousand ways. On 19th February 1900 the *Daily Telegraph* had a paragraph about a number of torpedo-boat destroyers, one of which broke away in harbour from her moorings, and did much mischief. This par was headed 'The Destroyers' Donnybrook'.

From the historical conviction that Donnybrook Fair (Ireland) is *all* noise.

Don't be a chump (*E. London*, 1889). Do not lose your temper. Derived probably from the act of fixing the teeth in passion as though chumping—that is, biting hard.

Don't care a Pall Mall (*Club*, 1885). A synonym for a damn. In July 1885 the *Pall Mall Gazette* gained wide notoriety by the publication of articles entitled 'The Maiden Tribute'. Hence the phrase, 'He may say what he likes; I don't care a Pall Mall.'

Don't dynamite (*Peoples'*, 1883). Avoid anger. Result of the Irish pranks in Great Britain with this explosive. Their chief result was to add a word to the army of phrases.

Don't know who's which from when's what! (*Street*, 1897). Total sentence of stupidity. Speaks for itself.

Don't lose your hair (*Peoples'*, 19 *cent.*). Don't lose your temper. Came in when wigs went out, and replaced 'dash my wig'. From the tendency to tear the hair in a rage, or, at all events, to seize it. (*See* Keep your hair on.)

Don't mention that (*Common London*, 1882). A catch word which prevailed for some time in consequence of Mr Baron Huddleston's frequent use of the phrase during the endless hearing (for over forty days) of a libel case between sculptors—Belt *v.* Lawes.

Don't seem (*Colloquial*). Equivalent to 'incapable of'; *e.g.*, 'I don't seem to see it, my dear fellow; where does the advantage come in?'

Don't sell me a dog (*Soc.*, 1860). Do not deceive me. Derived from the experience that the purchase of a dog, most fanciers being thieves, was ever a deception. Very popular until 1870.

Don't think, I (*Mid. Class*, 1880). Emphatically meaning *do* think; *e.g.*,

'So you've nailed my young woman—well that's a nice thin job, I don't think'—simply because he's quite sure of it.

Don't turn that side to London (*Peoples'*). Condemnation of any kind—of a patched coat or boots, the worst side of a joint of meat, some injury to the body, etc., etc. From the supposition that everything of the best is required in the metropolis. (*See* Turn the best side to London.)

Doogheno (*London, Back*, 19 *cent.*). This is a remarkably complicated specimen. It is composed of 'good' backwards, the letter 'h' to prevent the softening of the 'g' when brought next an 'e'. 'Eno' is of course 'one'.

It can't be denied that Booth has made a doogheno hit, and you ought to nark his bucket.—(1882.)

Edwin Booth was an American actor who (1881-82) obtained considerable success in London in Shakespearian characters.

If a chap happens to be a dab tros he gets on better than a doogheno who keeps himself quiet and never lets anybody Tommy Tripo know how clever he is.—*Cutting.*

Dook (*Peoples'*). A huge nose. Corruption of 'duke,' and referring to *the* 'Duke'—time of Wellington, who during the first half of the 19th century was, with intervals of unpopularity, styled 'the duke'. His Grace's high nose was hereditary. The title became shortened to this one word, and his nose being so exceptional, the title of the owner came by metaphor to represent a huge nose. To this day it is used. (*See* Boko.)

Dookin (*Thieves'*). Fortune-telling. Sixpenny horoscopes in by-ways and cast upon the lines of the palm of the hand, the left, that being nearest the heart. Hence the word—dook, dookes, being ancient slang for hand; generally used in plural. 'Put up yer dooks.' 'Dookin' has now become fashionable, and is called palmistry. Where all the hand is concerned (this in telling character), the term is chiromancy.

Door and hinge (*Lond., Peoples'*). Neck and breast of mutton, a joint which bends readily amongst the cervical vertebræ. Very graphic and humorsome. (*See* Stickings, Hyde Park Railings.)

Door-knocker (*Peoples'*, 1854). A ring-shaped beard formed by the cheeks and chin being shaved leaving a chain of hair under the chin, and upon each side of mouth—forming with moustache something like a door-knocker.

Charles Dickens had a moustache and a door-knocker beard.—E. Yates, *Recollections*, vol. i., p. 256.

Door-mat (*Colloquial*, 1856). The name given by the people to the heavy and unaccustomed beards which the Crimean heroes brought home from Russia in 1855-56, and which started the beard movement, much to the astonishment of French excursionists. By 1882 the term came to be applied to the moustache only, probably because about this time the tendency to shave the beard and wear only a very heavy moustache became prevalent.

While writing, a pal comes in and tells me that the City peelers are to be allowed to grow doormats.—*Cutting.*

The Corporation of London, always very conservative, only allowed the City police to wear moustaches in 1882.

He was a little joker with a red smeller and a small red doormat over his kisser.—*Cutting.*

Doormat (*Common Lond.*, 1880). Victory (*see* Grease-spot), meaning that the enemy was overcome, and so fallen that the victor wiped his feet upon the conquered—Væ Victis!

I guess that chucker-out won't hit me any more. I made a doormat of him.—*Cutting* (1883).

Doping (*Racing*, 1900). Hocussing rather than poisoning racehorses when about to run. In 1899-1900 large sums of money had been made by American betting-men at English race meetings. Gradually the conviction gained ground that runners were being tampered with in new and dangerous ways, resulting in more than temporary injury to the horses. Especially in the U.S.A. it was remarkable how frequently racers either died at or shortly after a race, or that they so went back that they were never raced again. In the U.S.A. the term used for the exercise of this nefarious usage of horses was called 'doping'—said to be derived from a proper name. The term came to be heard in England in the summer of 1900. In November of this year the Animals' Aid Society held a weakly organised meeting to devise means to meet these fraudulent practices. But it turned out that nobody present knew anything at all about the matter.

Dorothy (*Soc.*, 1888). Rustic love-making. From the mode of an opera-comique of this name (1887-88).

Those (letters) of the defendant were of the most amatory character, containing repeated promises, in Dorothy style, to be true to the plaintiff.—*D. N.*, 7th July 1888.

Dorsay (*Soc.*, 1830-45). Perfect. Count d'Orsay, of an old French family, led the fashion generally during these years; so much so that it was the highest praise to say he was a dorsay.

Dose of Locust (*N. York Policemen's*). A beating with fists.

Mullaley, smarting under the pain of the wound, gave Mr Supple a dose of locust, which induced him to accompany the officer to court.—*Newsp. Cutting.*

Dossy (*Street*). Elegant. Probably from Count d'Orsay (*q.v.*).

Dot and carry one (*Street*). Person with a wooden leg.

The 'dot' is the pegged impression made by all wooden legs before the invention of the modelled foot and calf. The 'one' is the widowed leg.

Dotted (*Tavern*, 19 *cent.*). Black-eyed. To 'dot' a gentleman is to punctuate him emphatically with a black-eye.

The chucker-out he dotted,
He got so blooming tight.
—*Cutting.*

Dotties Man (*Peoples'*). Greedy, grasping—giving a sprat to catch a herring.

Double-breasted water-butt smasher (*Street*). A man of fine bust—an athlete.

The Bobby said that Joey Fanatty (aged), described on the charge-sheet as the double-breasted water-butt smasher, was charged with a salt.—*Newsp. Cutting.*

Double intenders (*Peoples'*). Knock-down blows—labial or fistful.

Double-plated blow-hard (*Amer.*). A loud and contemptible boaster.

They went away believing I was an old liar and a double-plated blow-hard, and in a week no one would stop here.—*Newsp. Cutting.*

Double Scoop (*Military*, 1890). Hair parted in centre, and worn low—gave way to the quiff.

Dough-nut (*Amer. passing to England*). A baker, especially the German variety.

'Shut up, thou dough nut, or thy last moment may be thy next.'—*Cutting.*

Probably from the too frequent pale, flabby, doughy face of this sickly operative.

Dover Castle boarder (*Prison; Debtors'*). A circumscribed district around the Queen's Bench prison (Southwark Bridge Road), pulled down in 1881, was called the 'rules of the Bench'. Certain debtors, not imprisoned in the Bench itself, were compelled to sleep in this district, and they were thus called because the most prominent tavern in the neighbourhood was styled 'The Dover Castle'—much frequented by these poor debtors, who were therefore called 'boarders'. The house still exists. It was not a stone's-throw from the prison.

Down the banks (*Irish colloquial*). Failed; *e.g.*, 'I got down the banks for my pains'—meaning I failed only as a result. Probably the outcome of life amongst the bogs, which are scored with deep ditches, as the peat is cut perpendicularly. The water at the foot of the banks is frequently quite deep, often enough to go over a man's head.

Down the Lane and into the Mo (*Central London, Low*). Here the Lane is that called Drury; the 'Mo' is abbreviated 'Mogul Music Hall' (established 1850), and afterwards baptized The Middlesex. But the Lane clung to 'Mo'—probably a name given to the place generations since, when a public garden there was kept by some wonderful Indian.

What was the good, thought we, of saving your rhino, if you've got no girl to take for trots down the Lane or into the Mo.—*Cutting*, 1883.

Down the Road (*E. London Streets*). Showy, flashy. The road is the Mile End Road, which to frequent on a Sunday, in a good cart or 'shay', is the ambition of every costermonger and small trader in that district.

Down to the ground (*Peoples'*) Completely—from head to heels

The character suits Rignold 'down to the ground' —*Newsp. Cutting.*

Drag (*Theat*) Petticoat or skirt used by actors when playing female parts Derived from the drag of the dress, as distinct from the non-dragginess of the trouser.

Mrs Sheppard is now played by a man —Mr Charles Steyne, to wit I don't like to see low coms in drag parts, but must confess that Mr Steyne is really droll, without being at all vulgar —*Ref.*, 24th July 1887

Also given to feminine clothing by eccentric youths when dressing up in skirts.

Dragon (*Cornish*) Opprobrious distinction conferred on the men of Helston by their Cornish neighbours—especially the nearest.

A neighbourly legend of Helston—formerly Hellstone—in Cornwall, says that the borough was dropped from the clouds by the Evil One in the course of a provincial tour over the western county To this moment, I understand, it is a deadly affront to call a Helston man a 'dragon' —*D T*, 20th August 1896.

Drapery Miss (*Com. Class*) A girl of doubtful character, who dresses in a striking manner Libellous generally Degenerated from the time of Byron, who says in a note to st. 49 ca. xi. of *Don Juan* —

'Drapery Misses'· This term is probably anything now but a *mystery* It was, however, almost so to me, when I first returned from the East, in 1811-12 It means a pretty, a high-born, a fashionable young female, well instructed by her friends, and furnished by her milliner with a wardrobe upon credit, to be repaid, when *married*, by her *husband*.

Drasacking (*Devon*) Draw-sacking —idle, slow, dragging

'Drasacking' is a common and cheap pastime, consisting of an aimless, pointless, shambling sauntering The 'drasacking' householder, while an absolute tortoise himself, believes that a wise and just dispensation intended his servant-girl or hired man to be a hare —*D T.*, 19th October 1895

Draw iron (*Amer.*) To present a pistol.

If every person who fancied himself aggrieved by his cabman were to 'draw iron', the nature of the cabman's shelter would have to be altered and made to correspond with the iron huts familiar to Irish police.—*Newsp Cutting.*

Draw the Badger. (*See* Badger)

Draw the dibs (*Bootmakers'*) To take wages—dibs being a trade term for money. Dibs are small nails, hence coins.

Draw the line at tick (*Serio-comics'*) A euphemism for declaration of virtue on the part of a serio comic lady singer. 'I may sing a hot line or two, or take a present here or there, but I draw the line at tick,' the material in question being not a scheme of credit or 'tick', but a covered allusion to the textile fabric used for the covering of beds and mattresses.

Dree his weird (*Lancs.*). To bear trouble sadly.

Little do the unthinking youths who nowadays assemble at a wedding to 'guy' the 'best man' suspect that a generation ago a victim of this description would not have had to 'dree his weird' alone His weird would have been dreed conjointly with him by a second best', a third best, down sometimes in a descending scale of excellence to an eighth best man.—*D T.*, 3rd September 1895

Dress for the part (*Society—drawn from Theatre*, 1870) —To act hypocritically

The only two authors of real celebrity whom I can remember as having looked 'like themselves'—I mean their books—were Douglas Jerrold and Alexandre Dumas the Elder Sham celebrities, on the other hand, 'dress for the part', and contrive to look that which they are, really, not —G A Sala, in *Ill. Lond. News*, 16th December 1882

Dressed up to the nines (*Com. London*) A eulogistic or sarcastic expression of opinion as to another's dress—according as the accent and manner of the speaker go Corruption of 'Dressed to the eyen'. When 'eyen' (pl of 'eye') was departing English, an 's' was added to give 'eye' a modern plural—while the knowledge of 'eyen' remained. After a time 'eyen' lost its meaning, and the old plural was colloqualized into a comprehensive expression, and 'nines' followed Concurrently, the expression 'dressed to the nines' took form, and is still used

Drilling (*Workpeoples'*) Punishment by way of waiting, applied to needlewomen who make errors in their work

There is a common punishment in these sweating warehouses when work is wrongly done. It is termed 'drilling'.

The woman could not, it seems, be sufficiently 'drilled' by merely being sent home to undo the work and do it again. She must be taught to be more careful by punishment a little more drastic than that, and accordingly she was told her bundle would be sent down to her, and till it came she must wait. 'The woman stood there expecting the parcel every minute for three days.'—*D. N.*, 26th February 1885. (*See* Sweater.)

Drinkitite (*Peoples' : East London*). Thirst. The struggling populace, who chiefly joke (when they joke apart from abuse) over their struggles, having discovered 'bite-etite' as a jocose conversion of appetite—came naturally to give it a correlative in 'drinkitite'. There is also grim satire in the application of the last syllable, which is the common word for 'drunk', hence 'drinkitite' as a pendent to 'bite-etite' is positively perfect. An East London gentleman gently referring to his continued libations would evasively but emphatically observe: 'I've been on the drinkitite right through the week.'

Driving at (*Peoples'*). Energetic action. Good example of phrase coming out of general characteristic vigour of the race. 'He must be driving at something.' Even the word drive, without the progressive 'ing' or the emphatic 'at', is a perfect English word.

Drop (*Amer.-Eng.*). To cause to drop.

About two minutes after he had the revolver his body was swung a little on one side, when I pointed my revolver and fired where I thought I could drop him.—*D. N.*, 5th September 1884.

Self-defence of a burglar named Wright. Also, to understand.

'Ah?' sobbed the girl, 'you do not drop.'—*Newsp. Cutting.*

Drop (*Society and Sporting*, 1850). To lose (money). A racing man or society man who fails to win money on a race never loses it—he always drops it; *e.g.*, 'I dropped awfully on the Leger.'

Drop (*Thieves'*). The modern gallows. A very significant word to describe modern capital punishment. At Tyburn tree the man stood in the cart, which was drawn from under him. Afterwards, at Newgate, the sufferer was pulled up. But when some genius invented the falling flap, which dropped from under the feet of the victim, the significance of the word became evident.

Drop the cue (*Billiard-players'*). To die.

Drouthy (*Scotch*). Wavering person; one of no settled will.

Leading citizens were occupied the greater part of the night before the polling-day watching doubtfuls, known locally as 'drouthies'; every voter was pledged; not a few were 'nursed'; the halt, the blind, and the deaf were escorted to the polling-booth.—*D. N.*, 27th October 1884.

Drum (*Thieves'*, 1860). A house.

Close to the gardens the prisoner said 'What do you think of those "drums" there?' and witness said, 'I don't think much of them.'—*Felon's Queen's Evidence.*

Drum is not usually applied to a respectable quaker-like house, but to any one frequented by, say, soldiers. Fielding uses this word in *Tom Jones*, Bk. xvii., ch. 6.

Drum (*Thieves'*). A cell—precisely because a drum is an enclosure.

Drunk as a lord (*Streets*). Very intoxicated. Descent from 18th century middle-class—when drunkenness was honourable.

'Drunk as a lord' and 'Sober as a judge' have ceased to have any recognisable application to the nobility and the Judicial Bench. Judges, in these later days, are as sober as other folk, take them as a class, no more and no less, and the same applies to the Peerage.—*D. T.*, 27th May 1888.

Drunk as Floey (*Peoples'*). Who it appears was dead drunk—may be a corruption of Flora, but probably a confusion between that comparatively familiar name and 'Chloe'. If the latter, good instance of the power Swift had to popularize. In the dean's poems Chloe is always more or less under the influence of drink.

Drunk as a polony (*Lond.*). At first sight this expression might be accepted as very literal, seeing that a sausage cannot stand, and that a polony (corruption of Bologna—celebrated for its sausages) exists under the same conditions. But it is more probably one of frequent but obscure expressions derived from the French, who to this day say: 'Soul comme un Polonnais'—this probably took its origin in reference to Maurice Maréchal de Saxe, who, in his drinks, was more

Polish than French On the other hand, the Pole, for drinking companions, has long held in France the position maintained in England by the cobbler—'drunk as a cobbler'

Druriolanus (*Theat*, 1885). Drury Lane Theatre. Playful outcome of calling Mr Augustus Harris, afterwards Sir Augustus Harris, the Emperor Augustus. The word also suggests that other directorial personage, Coriolanus

The vast stage of Her Majesty's is not a whit less advantageous for the display of its spectacular effects than that of the house which gives to Mr Harris's telegraphic address of 'Druriolanus' its special fitness and significance —*D N*, 12th October 1886.

Augustus Druriolanus is their president, and they are going to bring off a four-oared race from Barnes to Hammersmith on October 31 —*Ref*, October 1886

Dry Bobs (*Eton*) A cricketer. (*See* Wet Bobs)

Dry canteen (*Milit*) (*See* Wet canteen.)

Dry guillotine (*Franco-English*) Severe imprisonment. From the penal French colony at Cayenne, a fearful place.

Cayenne is so malarious that transportation thither used to be styled the dry guillotine.—*Graphic*, 1st November 1884

Dry land (*Rhyming*). To understand.

Whenever you see a chap after your judy, the best thing to do is to go up to her and tell her that you don't mean to stand her blooming kid, that you dry land her emag —*Cutting*.

Dry up (*Anglo-Amer*). To cease because effete—from mining districts of W. America, where, when the mountain torrents dry up in summer, mining operations necessarily cease

Duca di Somevera (*Peoples'*). Liberal Italian translation of Duke of Somewhere On a par with the Earl le Bird, Sir Tinly Someone, and Swift's Lord Nozoo.

The unhappy purchaser of a supposed masterpiece must be prepared to hear that his picture is a replica of one in the Isle of Wight, or at Madrid, or in Lord Blank's gallery, or in the Palazzo of the Duca di Somevera—*D N*, 16th June 1883

Duchess (*Silk trade*) The shapely girl upon whom mantles and jackets are tried to enable ladies to judge of the effect

The Duchess—living lay figures receive that title, in addition to a whole pound a week —Besant & Rice, *The Golden Butterfly*, vol i, ch 11.

Duchess (*Peoples'*). Mother — invariable title given between familiar friends when the mother of either is being asked after. 'How's the Duchess, Bob?'

The wife, under similar conditions, would be asked after as 'The Old Clock' — a title whose derivation a sharp witted man may find in the first chapter of Sterne's *Tristram Shandy*

Duck-pond (*Navy*). The shallow bathing-place on the lower deck, effected by a rig-up of sail-cloth, made watertight, fixed to the deck, and in which the cadets wash and roll themselves, in batches, under the watchful eyes of a warrant officer

Ducks (*Soc*, 1840) White trousers of a peculiarly woven cotton fabric—mentioned here because it has been said to be a corruption of 'dux', the name given to the material by the Scotch manufacturer who discovered it. Dux was, if not is, used much by the Scotch (*See* Lindley Murray's *English Grammar*)

Duffer-fare (*Lond Cabmen's*). In the neighbourhood of the theatres, as closing time approaches, the police will not allow cabmen to drive empty cabs through the Strand highway In order to get past the police, and so obtain a chance of a fare when the theatres vomit their thousands, cabmen will ask a pedestrian to be 'chummy' enough to jump in, and be driven into the Strand Here arrived the 'duffing-fare', quits the cab, the driver is in the Strand—and keeps there till 11 P M, when the theatres disgorging, he gets a fare that is no duffer, and who pays more or less nobly

Duffing (*Soc. and Peoples'*, 1880 on). The outcoming adjective of 'duffer' and 'duff'. By 1897 this word became one of the most active qualitatives in the language. As a verb it had by this time come to be thoroughly conjugated; *e g*, 'He duffs everything he touches' 'He is the most duffing duffer that ever duffed' 'He has duffed, he does duff, and he will duff for ever.'

Duke (*Street*). Nose. (*See* Dook.)

Duke o' Seven Dials (*Low Class*, 1875). Satirical peerage bestowed upon any male party dressing or behaving above or beyond his immediate surroundings. There is no corresponding duchess. A young person of airs and graces is generally spoken of as about to marry the peer in question; *e.g.*, 'I'm going to be the duchess of the Dook o' Seven Dials.'—*Parody Song, Drury Lane Pantomime*, 1884.

Duke's (The) (*Lond.*, 19 *cent.*). A nickname of the Argyll Rooms in Windmill Street, Haymarket, W., now replaced by the Trocadero. In allusion to the Duke of Argyll.

Why should the Argyll be suppressed and the Pavilion be tolerated? Of the two 'the Pav.' is far worse than 'the Duke's'.—*Newsp. Cutting.*

Dukey (*Street, Boys'*). A penny gaff. The four-farthing theatre obtained this title from a Jewish proprietor of one of these temples of art. His nose was very prominent (1840-50). In these days such a feature begot its owner the title of duker, from the hero of Waterloo, emphatically 'the duke' from 1815 to 1850. The 'y' here is an instance of endearing addition.

Dumbed (*Amer. Puritanic*). Evasion of 'damned'.

The man who believes that the Jews are such a pack of dumbed fools, as to seriously entertain any such plan, should be shut up in an asylum for the feeble-minded.—*Newsp. Cutting.*

Dummy (*Thieves'*). Loaf—probably from the softness of the crumb.

Dumplin' on (*L. Classes*). *Enceinte.*

Dun (*Peoples'*). To worry for money. One of the forcible words gleaned from proper names. Of course lexicographers trace it to Early English, Anglo-Saxon, or some other remote source. Webster says it is taken from the Saxon *dynan*, to claim. But the Saxons did not dun—they recovered their debts by more forcible means.

Here is its true origin: It owes its birth to one John Dun, a famous bailiff of the town of Lincoln; so extremely active, and so dexterous was this man at the management of his rough business, that it became a proverb when a man refused to pay his debts, 'Why don't you dun him?' It originated in the reign of Henry VII.

Durn (*Amer.-Eng.*). Another evasion of 'damned'. (*See* Darn.)

Worms that rise early are caught—gobbled up by birds every time. The worm's a durn fool to get up so early.—*Newsp. Cutting.*

Dust (*American Teamsters*). A mere light touch of anything.

The visiting, the music, the marching, the cheering and the excitement of the reunion, with a little dust of liquor, had made him feel quite excited.—*Newsp. Cutting.*

Dust (*Amer.*, 1880). To walk quickly—suggested by the dust thrown up in the act. Indirect proof of the dry nature of American weather.

One grabbed a rope that was on the sidewalk where they was moving a building, and pa got up and dusted. You'd a died to see pa run.—*Newsp. Cutting.*

Dusting (*Boer War*, 1899-1900). Finishing the war—complement of 'Sweeping up'.

North of Pretoria there is still a good deal of dusting to be done.—*D. T.*, 2nd November 1900.

Dustman's bell (*Nursery*). Time for bed. Origin obscure. Is it Dowse man's bell—curfew bell—time to put out ('dowse') the lights? Has it any association with 'dowse the glim'? Johnson gives: 'To fall suddenly into the water'—which would certainly put out the light.

Dust out (*Amer.-Eng.*). To retreat quickly, 'levant'. Suggested by dust thrown up by rapid walking.

I quickly got inside, locked the door, and dusted out the back way.—*Newsp. Cutting.*

Dust up (*Milit.*, 19 *cent.*). An engagement—from the dust made by the movements.

A member of the Royal Army Medical Corps, who, in his own words, 'got through the Graspan dust-up nicely', was sent, etc.—*D. T., Boer War*, 16th January 1900.

Dusty (*Navy*). A ship's steward's assistant—probably because this hard-worked official looks it.

Dutch (*Peoples'*). Retreat—especially from a creditor, and still more especially when accompanied by furniture removed from a tenancy, the rent of which has not been handed over.

'We did a dutch with everything—even down to the coal-hammer.'

'Yere comes 'Anner's young bloke—I think I'll do a quick dutch.'

I make myself agreeable, and then say, 'I must do a Dutch'.—*Cutting*

Dutch cheese (*Low London*, 1882) A bald head; derived from the fact that Dutch cheeses are generally made globular.

Dutch daubs (*Amer.*, 1883) Common paintings of still-life, imported into America by the ten thousands. Introduced by the *New York Herald* (April 1883) in reference to a political measure which placed a 35 per cent *ad valorem* duty upon imported pictures. The term soon came to mean a bad picture of any kind

The term 'Dutch Daub' has fetched me a little I call to mind that in almost every refreshment buffet and miner hotel bar in the Southern and Western States you come across oil-paintings of still life —G A Sala, *Ill London News*, 28th April 1883

Dutch row (*Street*). A got-up unreal wrangle. Rarely heard On all fours—with 'une querelle d'Allemand'.

Dutchman (*Soc of a sort*, 1870 on). Name for champagne of Deutz and Gelderman. Here the first name is pronounced Dutch, and the last syllable of the second name is added

Duty (*Lower Class, Respectable*). Interest on pawnbrokers' pledges Evasive synonym for interest

Dying duck in a thunderstorm (*Peoples'*) Lackadaisical

'Whoa, call her good-looking? That dona with a mug like a dying duck in a thunderstorm, and smiling as if she'd had a dose of castor oil and didn't like it.'—*Cutting*

Dynamite (*Mid.-class*, 1888) Tea Early in February two men, Americans, were tried in connection with Irish-American attempts to do injury in this country with dynamite In the course of the trial (*D N*, 4th Feb 1888) it came out that dynamite was always called 'tea'—for the purposes of concealment The word took at once

Dynamite Racket (*Amer - Eng.*, 1885). Invented contemptuously to describe this sort of explosion.

New York loves a show, whether a parade, a big funeral, a blazing fire, or a dynamite racket.—*Newsp. Cutting*

Dynamiter (1882). A user of dynamite for illegal purposes It soon came to be a synonym for any violent man or woman, especially the latter; *e g*, 'My eye, ain't she jest a dynamiter?' When 'tart' came to be common passing English, it was applied to this word, *e g.*, 'Well, she may be tasty, but to my mind she's a dynamitart.' (*See* Petroleuse)

Dyspepsia (*Milit. Hospital*) Drink delirium. D T.s.

E

E C. Women (*Snob Soc*, 1881). Wives of city people, so named from the city forming the East Central postal district of the metropolis

E P. (*Theat*). Experienced Playgoer.

The experienced playgoer will readily guess that Branson compasses the (apparent) destruction of Gerald, and anon returns to Ballyvogan to personate the heir—and the e p will be right —*Newsp Cutting*

E R (*Oxford 'er'*). Suffix applied in every conceivable way to every sort of word Began early in the Queen's reign and has never lapsed. A new word in 'er' is generally started by some quite distinguished Oxonian —generally a boating man, sometimes a debater

There has been a furore at Oxford in recent years for word-coining of this character, and some surprising effects have been achieved A freshman became a 'fresher' in the earlier Victorian era, and promises to remain so for all time and existence —*D T.*, 14th August 1899

Ear-mark (*Parliam.*, 19 *cent.*) ?—Note of interrogation, or enquiry. Used by M P 's when reading Bills and other papers to draw their future attention. A sort of rebus, from this character being something like an 'ear'. Word often heard in Parliament.

Nervous reference is made to the assertion of the Chancellor of the Exchequer that certain items of Transvaal revenue would be ear-marked for the purpose of the war contribution —*Newsp. Cutting*

Early riser (*Anglo-Amer.*—returning emphasized to England). A sharp, business-like person. Probably from 'Early to bed and early to rise, Makes a man healthy, and wealthy, and wise,' or again ''Tis the early bird catches the worm' (who unfortunately is for himself, too early a riser). In U.S.A. this phrase takes several shapes—the best being 'You'd have to get up early to be before me!'

The general idea is that anybody who is going to over-reach Hetty Green (New York), or do her out of a fraction of those millions, will have to be a very early riser indeed. She gives no costume dances, and never will; she would be better liked if she did.—*D. T.*, 10th February 1897.

Early purl (*Street*, 19 *cent.*). A drink made of hot beer and gin, so named because taken early on a cold morning. A song ran—

'I'm damned if I think
There's another such drink
As good early purl.'

When princes and princesses are born there is a lavish distribution of 'caudle', a mysterious beverage of the nature whereof we confess ourselves as ignorant as of that of 'early purl'.

Early-turners (*Music-hall*). Scornful reference to an inferior artist who takes his 'turns' early in the evening, before the audience is thrang, or fashionable, or both. From 8.0 to 8.30. (*See* Enders.)

Earth-hunger (*Political*, 1880). Greed to possess land. Supposed to have come from Ireland, and in that relation to refer to the desires of peasants to obtain a bit of land. In England used to define the passion of landed proprietors to add to their land at any cost.

East of the Griffin (*W. London*). East London. Replaced 'East of Temple Bar'. Outcome of the city Griffin on his wonderful pedestal replacing Temple Bar.

At the Pavilion Theatre, you ought to know by this time, even if you never go east of the Griffin, they do things in a way that is not excelled at many West End theatres that I am acquainted with. —*Ref.*, 11th October 1885.

Eat strange meat (*Soc.*, 19 *cent.*). A delicate evasion of cannibalism.

We feel much less horror than in face of the naked fact of cannibalism practised by civilized men for the sake of dear life. Life is not worth the imputation of having 'eaten strange meat'.—*D. N.*, 14th August 1884.

Eat the leek. To apologize. From Shakespeare.

Eat vinegar with a fork (*Peoples'*). The extreme of acid sharpness—in conversation. The vinegar alone would set teeth on edge, the fork intensifies the condiment.

Eatings (*Peoples'*; old). An ancient word now represented by board; *e.g.*, 'The room 'ull be 'arf-a-crown a week, without eatin's'—for there are lodgers who would expect banquets thrown in with a sixpenny bed for the night.

Eautybeau (*Music-hall transposition*). Beauty.

Do I know him? Do I rumble the eautybeau? What do you think?—*Cutting.*

Ebenezar (*Puritanic*). An exclamation of rejoicing—from the Hebrew. George Eliot often uses this word in her diary.

Eccer (*Oxford 'er'*). Exercise—both c's hard.

Every man after lunch devotes himself to 'eccer', which is, in ordinary parlance, exercise. This may take the shape of 'footer', or a mild constitutional known as a 'constituter', while if any one lounges idly about he is, of course, a 'slacker'.—*D. T.*, 14th August 1899.

Edgarism (*Club*, 1882). This was the new satirical name given to agnosticism, or rather atheism upon the production of Tennyson's prose play *The Promise of May*. The villain-hero, Edgar, is an educated man of position, who bases his arguments for free love and free will upon a denial of the deity. This bit of historical passing English died with the play, which, while never successful, was most unfairly damned by critics and public. The former appear to have resented the poet's despotic associations of free thought with immorality —as a necessary outcome of atheism.

Edge (*Criminal*). To bolt, escape. Probably from 'dodge'—and retire.

One of the other two called out 'Edge' (a slang term to be off), and they ran away.—*D. N.*, November 1886.

Eekcher (*Peoples'*, 1882). Inversion of cheek—audacity.

Well, modesty is not marketable nowadays, and perhaps Tippy is right to pin his faith to the doctrine that there's nothing like 'eekcher'.—*Newsp. Cutting.*

Eel-skin (*Soc.*, 1881). A name given to the tight skirt worn at this date; *e.g.*, 'She wore an eel-skin of London smoke.' (*See* One leg.)

Eenque (*Streets*; *transposition*) Queen A very popular example of this queer mode of word making.

So shout, you beggars, shout, God save the Eenque.—*Cutting*.

Eetswe (*Transposition*). Sweet—a very common word in low life; *e g.*, 'Lord, I *am* eetswe on that udyju' (judy)

Eff, Effy (*Theatr.*) Abbreviation of Effingham, a small theatre once in E London.

Efficient effrontery (*Soc*, 1885). Clever audacity—brought in by J W. M'N Whistler in February by a lecture at Prince's Hall, called 'Ten o'clock', from the hour at which it began—P.M. It was an attack upon art-critics in general, and Ruskin in particular. The lecturer used this term, which at once became familiar in society in a hundred ways

Mr Whistler's lecture is distinctly a surprise He deprecates the tone in which such subjects are too frequently handled. The commonplace world endowed with 'efficient effrontery' no longer reverently approaches Art as a dainty goddess, but 'chucks her under the chin' —*D N*, 21st February 1885.

Eicespie (*Transposition*) Pieces An interesting example of the rough logic used in phrase-making 'Pieces' is a figure of speech for money, and there is the ordinary transposition But that is not all The *i* being left as the initial would destroy the ordinary vowel sound of 'piece'; therefore the *e* is placed before the *i*.

Does the artful, and he draws the eicespie —*Cutting*

Eighteen-carat lie (*Amer*, 1883). A good. sound lie, 18 carat gold being good, thorough metal

Eighty Club (*Soc*) A club formed in the year ''80', shortly before the general election, with the object of promoting political education, and stimulating Liberal organization by supplying Liberal meetings in London and the country with speakers and lecturers

Eiley Mavourneen (*Commercial*) A non paying debtor Refers to the line in Moore's song, 'It may be for months, and it may be for never.'

Elaborate the truth (*Soc*) To lie.

Elderly Jam (*Peoples'*, 1880 on). Aging woman Qualified jam; *e.g.*, 'Elderly jam is—elderly jam, and heaven preserve it, for man turns from it'

Electrate (1890 on) To describe locomotion by electricity.

They go by train to Bourne End, where they take to the river and 'electrate' to Medmenham Abbey and Henley Electrate is one of the recently-invented verbs to express the new mode of locomotion, to which the words sail and steam are inapplicable —*Newsp Cutting*

Applied more recently to violent and eccentric meetings, *e g*, 'They electrated from 8 to 11 15 P.M Everything was amended, and then they amended the amendments'

Electrocution (*Amer -Eng*, 1890) Execution by electricity Built upon execute

Elephant's Trunk (*Street, rhyming*). Drunk. The phrase became incomprehensible by the dropping of the rhyming. 'Oh, he's elephants' (*i e*, intoxicated) will, in time to come, exercise many an etymologist

(Daddy) And what am I to be? (Mother G) Get out—you're drunk. (P Char.) You shall be—let's see—Baron Elephant's Trunk.

A capital example of a common bit of slang phrase locally applied, for this line is found in an Elephant and Castle Theatre Pantomime. It should be added that 'daddy' was a satire upon the Blue Ribbon movement—he belonging to it, and yet always being 'elephant's trunk'

Elevator (*Soc*, 1882 on). The crinolette. For some years the dress below the back of the waist was almost flat, when in this year bows were seen there, and then followed the crinolette, which, throwing up the dress, obtained this satiric name amongst young men, and was afterwards accepted literally.

Elijah Two (*Amer -Eng*). A false prophet From one Dr Dowie, an American peripatetic preacher who first gained this title. His son was dubbed Elijah Three.

Ellersby (*Peoples'*, 1870 on). The initials of the London School Board No particular point beyond brevity—said to be the soul of wit

L S B Extravagance. The extraordinary extravagance of the London School Board is strikingly shown by the constant increase in the amount paid by the Strand Board of Works —*People*, 20th September 1896.

Ellessea (*L. Compositors*). The initials of London Society of Compositors.

Elongated kisser. A wide mouth.

'Yer looks like a lady,' I says; 'then why do yer wipe yer elongated kisser with a whopping great red stook?'—*Cutting.*

Empress Pidgeon (*Naval*, 1876 on). Pigeon is discussion, and Empress Pigeon was a palaver with Queen Victoria for a basis. Now Emperor Pidgeon.

Endacotted (*Socialist*, 1887). Illegally arrested. Attributed to Mrs Annie Besant. Derived evidently, by partial similarity in sound, from Boycott, and referring to a policeman of the name who was tried and acquitted (1887) upon an indictment for illegal arrest of a young dressmaker, whom he swore was a well-known woman of the town. After a time the term was reduced to 'cotted' following the common tendency to shorten phrases and even words.

Ender (*Music-hall*). A performer of inferior quality, even inferior to an 'early-turner,' (*q.v.*) who only 'goes on' after the great hours. Enders perform from 11 to 11.30—when most music-halls are emptying—except on 'bens'.

End-men (*Negro Minstrels*). The two comic black souls who enliven with small wit a negro entertainment, and sit at either end of the line of seated performers. Now passed to black comics who even sit in the midst.

On the stage there are sixty of these dark coloured minstrels, whose voices are interposed with striking effect in many of the choruses. The 'end men' are numerous, and amply endowed with a boisterous humour.—*Newsp. Cutting.*

Engineer (*Amer.-Eng.*, 1880). To manage, manipulate, direct. Outgrowth of railway and steam era generally.

Afterwards you may look out for Daly's Company from New York, engineered by Terriss.—*Ref.*, 8th June 1884.

English pluck (*Peoples'*). Money, figuratively; *e.g.*, 'Got any English pluck to-day?' (Have you any money with which to gamble by means of tossing?)

Enobs (*Back slang*). Bone, in ordinary plural. A very favourite specimen because by chance the inversion is a sort of rebus, bones showing affording a study of 'knobs'.

But he swallowed a box of matches one day which burnt away all the fat and left the mere enobs you see now.—*Cutting.*

Enthuse (*Amer.*). Abbreviation of 'create enthusiasm'. Not yet accepted in England.

An entirely new play, called *Uncle Tom's Cabin*, with muzzled bloodhounds in their stellar rôle, did not enthuse the manager nor his patrons of the past week.—*Newsp. Cutting.*

Enthuzimuzzy (*Soc.*, 19 cent.). Satirical reference to enthusiasm. Attributed to Braham the terror.

Entire Squat (*Amer.*, *reaching Eng.* 1883). A household, including wife, children, servants, and furniture.

Espysay (*Stable*, 1880 on). A word composed of the letters S.P.C.A.—initials of the Society for the Prevention of Cruelty to Animals. Secretive in its nature, being created by people about horses and cattle, many of whom go about in savage fear of this valuable society.

Essex calves (*Provincial*). A contemptuous designation of Essex-men, always looked down upon by more prosperous Suffolk.

Essex lion. Lion is a variant of calf. Not used in Essex, but against it; especially by superior Kent, over the way, on the south side of the Thames. Interesting as showing inter-county hostilities, now passing away. The men of Kent or Kentish men (between whom there would appear to be great differences) have always belonged to an advanced part of England, and have escaped satire by reason of their superiority. Probably they gave their county neighbours their well-known sobriquets—Hampshire Hogs, Sussex Sows, Surrey Swine. Middlesex they avoided, but Essex, separated from them by the Thames, and inferior, as a county, to Kent, as indeed it remains to this day, was specially honoured with a title.

Establish a funk (*Oxford*). To create a panic—invented by a great bowler, at cricket, who enlivened this distinction with some cannon-ball bowling which was equivalent amongst the enemy to going into action. Funk for panic, dismay, alarm—is superior to origin Probably from establish a suit in whist.

Euro ! (*Navy*) Seamen's name for the Europa—a happy example of the sailor's love of getting in a final *o*, as in 'what oh !', 'what cheer oh !', etc

Europe on the chest (*Army*). Home - sickness. Used chiefly by soldiers in India, who commit offences sometimes in order to be sent home.

Sir, they are not all bad at the bottom of them, but they have had at times the fever, and ague and their heart grows faint for England, and then they get what the driver terms Europe on the chest, and at the same time he is not particular what he does as long as he has a chance of coming to England —*Letter by Convict, D N.*, 3rd November 1885.

Even with, To get. A vigorous use of this word, to procure equality with one who has bested the speaker, *e g*, 'Never fear, I'll get even with him yet'

Evening wheezes (*Peoples'*). False news, spread in evening half-penny papers in order to sell them

Eventuate. To result. A direct importation from America, and not at all wanted

'It appeared as though we were committed to a conflict with the House of Lords of a nature so strenuous and so exciting that it might possibly have eventuated in something like a revolution'—*H Richard, M.P*, *Speech*, 1st January 1885

Everlasting knock (*Amer.-Eng*) The stroke of death

And so he closes his career He may be far happier as a man than he has ever been, but as a ruling prince he has taken the everlasting knock.—*Ref.*, 10th March 1889

Everything is nice in your garden (*Soc*, *passing to People*, 1896 on) A gentle protest against self-laudation; *e g*, 'I don't wish to praise myself, but I believe I'm the greatest living tenor, in this world at all events!' Reply · 'Yes, yes, everything is nice in your garden!' This is said to be derived from one of the young princesses (probably a daughter of the Princess Beatrice) who made this reply when something in her garden at Osborne was praised by Her Majesty If this is a true statement, it forms one of the very rare phrases that have come down from the precincts of the throne

Ewigkeit (*Soc*, 1880) This German word for 'eternity' came to be used not so much in adulation of Carlyle as in order to fall in with the bantering spirit of treating religious speculation, which began to grow rapidly in this year. It spread slowly, and by 1883 was found in popular journals

All these things have vanished temporarily into the 'ewigkeit', to yield the field to beer and spirits—the people's drink, the birthright of every free-born Briton —*Ref*, 17th May 1885.

Exceedings (*Oxford*) Expenditure beyond income A delicate evasion

Extra (*Theatrical*). An individual of the great brigades who 'go on', but do not speak, sing, or dance An extra does but fill the eye Generally a pretty girl, of no talent, perhaps with a passion for the stage—perhaps with ulterior intentions.

Extra pull (*Operatives'*). Advantage, or disadvantage, as the case may be. As an advantage, it is a figure of speech from the extra pull of the handle of the beer engine in public-houses (*See* Long Pull)—a pull which flushes a spirt of beer into 'their own jugs' after the proper measure, in the publican's pewter, has been shot in As a disadvantage—refers to the extremely troublesome tooth in the dentist's grip All depends on the context.

Extradition Court (*Polit*). The second justice-room at Bow Street (London) Name given jocularly by officials Good example of the mode in which passing English grows out of the history of the day

The case was taken in the second court, which is commonly called the Extradition Court, because nearly all the extradition cases are heard in it —*D. N.*, 10th April 1883.

Extreme Rockite (*Clerical*). One who believes in the Rock newspaper, and preaches on its basis.

In a recent issue of a contemporary, for instance, we find a 'liberal' rector asking for a fellow labourer, who among other qualifications must be 'an extreme Rockite' —*Newsp Cutting.*

Eye in a sling (*Peoples'*) Crushed, defeated. From the doleful appearance presented by a sufferer with a bandage over the suffering eye

Eye peeled (*W. Amer.*). Eyes well opened; peeled away from drooping lids; on the watch.

The Librarian was instructed to keep his eye peeled for a stray copy of a Chinese hymn book which might be bought cheap.—*Newsp. Cutting.*

F

F.C.'s (*Theat.*). False Calves (*i.e.* paddings used by actors in heroic parts to improve the shape of the legs).

F.F.V. (*Anglo-Amer. Soc.*). Distinguished. Initials of First Families (of) Virginia. Used quite seriously in the South of the U.S.A. and satirically in the North. The origin of the use of the letters may be traced to Massinger's *City Madam*, Act V., sc. 1 (acted in 1622).

Face the music. To fearlessly meet difficulties.

Before sailing Mr Cecil Rhodes gave a brief interview to some reporters. He stated that he would not resign his seat in the Cape Parliament. 'I shall meet my detractors. I will face the music.'—*D. T.*, 18th January 1896.

Face ticket (*British Museum*). A ticket is required for the Reading Room. It is never asked for when a constant reader passes the janitors. Nothing is said—the passer-by has a face ticket.

Fade (*Pure Amer.*). Antithesis of masher and dude. Either of these ornamental beings gone shabby.

A young lady employed at one of the Exposition displays rather took the shine off of a fade the other day. The fade, recently a dude, walked up to the place where she was stationed, etc.—*Newsp. Cutting.*

Fair cop (*Thieves'*). Undoubted arrest; 'fair' here means 'thorough', while 'cop' is from Early English for 'catch'.

Fair herd (*Oxf. Univer.*). Good attendance of strangers.

Foreigners are sometimes busy, or indifferent, or afraid of the Channel, and many promising schemes for a 'fair herd' on Commemoration Day have broken down owing to this cause.—*D. N.*, 13th June 1883.

Fair itch (*Street*). Utter imitation. Equally vulgar and vigorous.

Fair trod on (*Street*, 1887 on). Most ill-used.

'Oh, the yeroines o' them penny novelettes—yer good old penny ones—none o' yer 'apenny ones for me—o' them yeroines—arn't they fair trod on!'—Bessie Bellwood (serio-comic, Jan. 1891).

Fair warning (*Street*). Manly and frank intimation.

Faire Charlemagne (17 *cent.*, *Court*). To know when to leave off—especially at cards. A corruption of 'faire chut la main'—to make quiet the hand; that is, do not go on manipulating the cards, 'chut' being the equivalent of the English 'hush'. Said to be used by Louise de Querouilles, known as Mother Carwell, and afterward as the Duchess of Portsmouth—a very economic and long-headed Bretonne.

That feat which the French describe by the mysterious expression, 'faire Charlemagne'—the feat of leaving off a winner—is one of the most difficult in the world to perform.—*D. T.*, 22nd April 1896.

Fairy (*Lower Peoples'*). A debauched, hideous old woman, especially when drunk.

Fairy, To go a (*Theat.*). To toss for a penn'orth of gin, meaning that a fairy takes very little. In use amongst the minor literary men.

Fairy tales (*Mid. Class*, 1899 on). Untruths.

Mr Kruger, for the information of his sympathisers in America, has told a Chicago journalist one of his pretty little fairy tales, the only truth in which is that some burghers are again taking up arms.—*D. T.*, 4th July 1900.

Fake a curtain (*Theat.*, 1884). Reference to 'Take a curtain', 'Curtain-taker', and 'Lightning curtain-taker', will alone enable the student to comprehend this term. To fake a curtain is to agitate the act-drop after it has fallen, and so perhaps thereby induce a torpid audience to applaud a little, and justify the waiting actor to 'take a curtain'. The manager himself may direct this operation, but it is generally the stage-manager who manipulates the manœuvre.

Fake a picture (*Artistic*, 1860 on). To obtain an effect by some adroit, unorthodox means. In this sense it is difficult to say where swindling ends and genius begins. It is much used by inferior artists.

Fake a poke (*Thieves'*) To pick, or manipulate, a pocket. This phrase is a singular revival. Johnson has 'Fake—amongst seamen a pile of rope,' and as to poke—'a pocket or small bag' 'I will not buy a pig in a poke!'—Camden.

He denied that when entering the music hall he was accused by a lady of picking her pocket, and further said that when called out he did not say he had never 'faked a poke' in his life —*People*, 6th September 1896

Fake pie (*Straitened Soc.*, 1880) — A towards-the-end-of-the-week effort at pastry, into which go all the 'orts', 'overs', and 'ends' of the week. *See* Resurrection pie—a term which this has superseded.

Fakement Chorley (*Dangerous Classes*) A private mark, especially on the outside of houses and in thieves' kitchens

Fal (*Rhyming*, 1868) Represents 'gal' (girl)

Fall in the thick (*Street*) To become dead drunk Full of metaphor Black beer is called thick, so is mud, the phrase suggests equal misery whether the patient plunged in the mud, or rambled into drunkenness.

Fall-downs (*Street*, 19 *cent*) The fragments of cookshop puddings which fall down while rapidly slicing up the puddings for sale, fragments which are finally collected on a plate, and sold for a halfpenny A boy will rush in, and, with the air of a general at least, say· ''A'porth o' fall-downs' Conquered when the reply comes, 'Hall sold!'

Fancy oneself (*Mid Classes*). On good terms with oneself.

They had never known a Government which, if he might use the language of the street 'fancied itself' to the extent to which the present Government did —*D T*, 14th December 1897

Fanned with a slipper (*Amer-Eng*, 1880 on). Simply spanked, the vibratory action suggesting the fanning

Miss Lulu Valli made a hit at once as the demon child, Birdikins, who is threatened to be 'fanned with the slipper' of her devoted but erratic mother —*D T*, 2nd February 1897

Fanning the hammer (*W Amer*, 1886) Brilliantly unscrupulous Instantaneously active, equal to energetic in the highest. Example of application of one term to varying meanings Derived from West American gamblers wiring back the trigger of their revolvers, so that its stop-action is arrested The six barrels of the revolver are discharged by rapidly striking back the hammer with the outer edge of the right hand, while the revolver is held in the left This vibratory action of the right hand is the fanning No aim can be taken, and fanning is only successful in a crowd Six bullets will generally clear a crowd So rapid is word adaptation in the States that already the term 'fanner' is used to describe an unscrupulously brave man

Far away (*Lower Classes*, 1884) Pawned. From a song, a parody upon 'Far, far away'. One line ran, 'Where are my Sunday clothes?' To which the singer answered, 'Far, far away'. The 'far away' is mine uncle's Passed into a verb, *e g*, 'I far-awayed my tools this blessed day —I did!'

Far gone (*Theat.*, 1882) Exhausted, or worn out, figuratively.

Miss Gilchrist, who has now matured into a well-formed young woman, is what I should call a vocal defaulter, her singing being 'far gone'.—*Entr'acte*, April 1883

Farcidrama (*Theat.*, 1885) A failure comedy of a farcical character, tied with a thread of serious interest Discovered by Mr Ashley Sterry to describe a posthumous half-finished comedy by H J Byron, and named *The Shuttlecock*—one which Mr Sterry quite finished It failed, and this word at once came to be used to describe a failure of any light piece 'It was a farcidrama'—meaning a 'frost'

To begin with, the description of *The Shuttlecock* as a 'farcidrama in three acts and a song' may be set down to the living rather than to the dead dramatist. —*Ref*, 17th May 1885.

Farthing-faced chit (*Peoples'*) Small, mean-faced, as insignificant as a farthing Chit also means small and contemptible.

Farthing-taster (*Street Children's*, 1870 on) Lowest quantity of commonest ice-cream sold by London street itinerant ice-cream vendors

In other shops may be seen hundreds of the thick, small glasses in which the 'farthing-taster' will be dealt out to their juvenile consumers.—*Newsp. Cutting*, 27th June 1898.

Fastened (*Lancs.*). Pawned.

Fastidious cove (*London*, 1882). A droll phrase for a fashionable swindler, who pretends to be of the upper ten.

You can always tell the 'fastidious cove' by his sending twenty-seven cuffs and collars to the laundry accompanied by a single shirt.—*Cutting*.

Fat ale (*Peoples'*, *early* 19 *cent.*). Strong ale—as distinct from weak ale, which is 'thin'.

'I was stupefied as much as if I had committed a debauch upon fat ale.'—Marryatt, *Rattlin the Reefer*, ch. 58.

Fat will burn itself out of the fire (*Peoples'*). Antithesis of 'All the fat's in the fire'.

After a while, however, the fat burnt itself out of the fire, and the happy couple seemed to get on very comfortably.—*Cutting*.

Favourite vice (*Jovial*, 1880). General habitual strong drink.

'I have watched the Prince's progress,' says His Worship, 'and I am glad to say there has been progress; for at one time I did not entertain a particularly high opinion of him. I rather thought that the Prince cared more for his pleasures and, I may as well say, for his vices, than for the duties of his high position.' Of course, the word 'vices' is here used in a harmless sense: for example, when the bottles and the cigar-case are to the fore, even a bishop may enquire of you, with a jovial smile of boon companionship, What is your favourite vice?—*D. N.*, 6th October 1885.

Fearful frights (*Peoples'*). Kicks, in the most humiliating quarters.

I shouldn't like to be in James Carey's boots—his trousers either, if all I hear is true. He's had some fearful frights, you bet.—*Cutting*.

Fearful wild fowl (*Soc.*). From Shakespeare's line, any extraordinary creature not often seen; even applied to men making antic fools of themselves.

A full programme of the Show is a formidable study, but a patient plodding through it shows that the fearful wild fowl mentioned are really to take a part in the pageant.—*D. N.*, 10th November 1884.

Feather in her mouth (*Marine*). Capable of showing temper, but holding it in. Poetical description of the merest idea of foam at the point where a ship's cut-water touches the wave, and which shows there either has been, or will be, dirty weather.

So to Elba the *Foam* was now directing her course, dancing lightly along upon a sparkling and nearly smooth surface, with only just enough movement during the later portion of the day to keep a very small 'feather in her mouth'.—Sir E. Arnold, in *D. T.*, 31st March 1897.

Feather in the cap (*Hist.*). Probably from Scotland, where only he who had shot an eagle dared to wear a feather in his cap.

Features. Practically no features worth talking about. Satirical-like expression, *e.g.*, 'Hullo, Features!' 'Face' is used similarly.

Fed (*Amer.*, 1860-65). Abbreviation of federal, given to themselves by the Northerners, whereupon the Southerners cut themselves down to Confeds, and met the Northerners at that.

Fed up with (*Boer War*, 1899-1900). Overdone, oppressed, filled with.

'Oh, I'm about fed up with it' is the current slang of the camps when officers and men speak of the war.—*D. T.*, 20th October 1900.

Feeder (*Theat.*, 1880). Actor or actress whose part simply feeds that of a more important comedian. Took the place of the 'confidante' in opera.

Feeding birk (*Thieves'*). Cook-shop — 'birk' being possibly a corruption of 'barrack'.

You have to be a bit cheeky to go into a feeding birk to order pannum good enough for a prince without a D in your clye.—*Cutting*.

Feel cheap (*Peoples'*, 1890). Humiliated, *e.g.*, 'Every other girl was in white, and I felt quite cheap.'

Feel like (*Amer.-Eng.*, 1884). Inclined towards.

'Do you feel like brandy and water?' is certainly an incorrect question (even grammatically) in England. Across the sea we believe the observation means, 'Do you feel inclined to partake, at my charge, of the refreshment of cognac and water?'—*D. N.*, 16th April 1885.

Feel like accepting it (*Amer.*). To repent, be humble.

In his death we has lost a good man, but we has at de same time gained some waluable experience, in case we feel like accepting it.—*Lime-kiln Club*, 1883.

Feel one's oats (*Amer.-Eng.*). Certain to be active. Figure of speech from the work got out of a well oat-fed horse, *e.g.*, 'You needn't be afraid—he's a man that feels his oats.'

Feel the collar (*Stable*). To perspire in walking.

Feel very cheap (*Mid.-class Eng.*, 1885 on). Antithesis of self-sufficiency. Generally refers to condition when recovering from dissipation.

Does some brother officer adjacent 'feel very cheap' after some midnight revelry; or how comes it that my host is not in the way?—Clement Scott, in *D. T.*, 21st January 1893.

Female personator (*Music-hall*). Another misnomer (*see* Male impersonator), for the performer is a male who impersonates female appearance, singing, and dancing. A man who dresses and acts like a woman, while the male impersonator is a woman who dresses and acts like a man. These interchanges of sexual appearance are still much relished on the music-hall stage.

Fenian (*Peoples'*, 1882 on). Three cold Irish, *i.e.*, threepence worth of Irish whisky and cold water. Brevity is the soul of cruel as of brilliant wit. In this instance the wit is very cruel, for it refers to the hanging and therefore coldening of the three Fenians who were hanged for the murder of Lord Frederick Cavendish and Mr Burke, Under-Secretary for Ireland, in the Phœnix Park, Dublin, on 6th May 1882. Other authorities say that the three Irish, here referred to with such grim humour, were the Fenians Allen, Larkin and O'Brien, hanged at Manchester for the murder of Police Sergeant Brett. They are called by the Irish national party 'the Manchester martyrs'. In Manchester itself the '3 cold Irish' became at public-house bars—'Give me a Fenian'. The term spread all over England. (*See* Got a clock.)

Fewer of him (*Amer.-Eng.*, 1880). Expression of congratulation at absence of numbers in the given case.

An English judge is a much more conspicuous personage than a judge in any foreign country. His salary is higher, his social position is better, and there are, to use an expressive Americanism, 'fewer of him'.—*Newsp. Cutting.*

Fiddle-face (*Peoples'*). A doleful face, widening abnormally at the temples and jaws, and sinking at the cheek bones.

Put on a fiddle-face and jaw to him about his future, and it's most likely he and his mates will slosh your mug for you and sneak your yack.—*Cutting.*

Fiddler (*Racing*). *Fille de l'air*—a French horse. The Anglicization of the names of foreign horses is a positive study in itself. English racing men who speak French always accept the English baptism.

Another stud horse, Peut-Etre, always called in the English betting ring 'Potater' was, as well as a few other lots, bought in.—*Newsp. Cutting.*

In the case of Volodyovski (Derby winner, 1901) no Anglicization was possible, so the pencillers tried an assonance, and styled him Bottle o' Whisky, and it is interesting in this connection to observe that in all professions and trades uncommon proper names are always Anglicized—roughly, absurdly, no doubt; but this process clears away all doubt as to pronunciation. For instance, in the Navy sailors always simplify a hard-named ship. A person had a vessel named the *Spero*, which was corrupted into Sparrow. As for *Psyche*, what they called her can scarcely be mentioned in decent company. Another person bought a vessel called the *Dœdalus*, which was called the Dead-loss.

Field Lane duck (*Holborn, Lond.*). Baked bullock's heart. A good example of lower peoples' habit of satirising their own poverty. This bake is made savoury, and is the nearest approach to duck possible, exactly as baked liver with sage and onions is called 'poor man's goose'. Field Lane was a near neighbour of Saffron Hill, where Dickens's Fagin reigned; London improvements have nearly swept it away. Field Lane is great in the annals of charity as the locality where first a night refuge was opened.

Field-running (*Builders'*, 1860). Building rickety houses rapidly over suburban fields. Introduced when the district railways brought small sub-urban houses into fashion.

Fiery cross (*Liter.*, 19 *cent*). Warning of danger. Probably from Scott—who introduces this flaming mode of carrying news of clan-risings.

The Police send round the Fiery Cross:—'Idle Panic' was the headline by which we described in our later editions of yesterday the extraordinary alarm which seized upon the metropolis, and nothing which occurred during the evening calls for any modification of that description. — *P. M. G.*, 11th February 1886.

Fifteen puzzle (*Mid.-class Eng.*). Complete confusion. The fifteen puzzle was an arrangement of moveable cubes bearing numbers which were to be arranged in a square, so that every line counted fifteen. It was very difficult and became a rage (1879). It soon came to represent confusion, incomprehensibility.

The syrup cup was, for a while, a fifteen-puzzle for the bear.—*American Bear Story*, 1883.

Fight space with a hair-pin (*Oxford Univ.*, 1882). A figurative way of describing the impossible.

Fighting Fours (*Milit.*). The 44th Regiment.

The 44th East Essex loses nothing of its identity in being called 'The Essex Regiment' except, perhaps, that the signification of The Fighting Fours is hardly so clear as it was.—*D. N.*, July, 1881.

Fighting the tiger (*San Francisco*). Gaming, with all its consequences; some of which are desperate. Practically applied—desperate game.

He asked me if I had ever heard of Faro, and if I knew the meaning of 'fighting the tiger'. Soon afterwards I learned that I was conversing with the keeper of one of the most notable among the gaming hells of San Francisco.—*Cutting*.

Figure-head (*Nautical*). The head simple, and suggested of course by the prow-terminal of most English ships.

A cove can, too, if he likes, spend the half of his bob in pongelow and the other tanner in bread and cheese, but we think he's likely to stop out of collar longer than a cove who doesn't cloud his blooming figure-head with booze.

We have once or twice landed our blooming figure-head on the kerb.

Filbert (*Street*). Head—variety of 'nut' to describe the same. Probably applied to a long-shaped head. Derived from prize ring.

'Yere—come and look at the bloke standin' on his filbert,' said the boy.

Filibuster (*Amer.*). To obstruct, impede business.

The Senate had an all-night sitting, the Republicans filibustered from six P.M. till early morning. To 'filibuster' means in its Parliamentary sense to obstruct.—*Newsp. Cutting*, 1882.

Filing-lay (*Thieves'*, 18 *cent.*). Pocket-picking. Fielding's *Jonathan Wild*. Probably from the French 'fil'—thread—from threading the fingers in the pocket.

Fill the bill (*Amer.*) To suit.

I have a tree claim and homestead, am a good cook and not afraid to work, and willing to do my part. If any man with a like amount of land, and decent face and carcass, wants a good wife, I can fill the bill.—*Newsp. Cutting*.

Fill, To give a (*Thieves'*). To deceive, *e.g.*, 'I gave the blue belly a fill'—would mean that you sent the policeman on a wrong scent.

Fills a gentleman's eye (*Sporting*). Shapely—possessed of thoroughly good points.

What do we not suffer from other people's dogs? Our own, of course, is a treasure of love and loyalty, he has a splendid nose, is perfectly purely bred, and, in short, as doggy people say, 'he fills a gentleman's eye'.—*D. N.*, 1875.

Filly (*Ball-room*). A lady who goes racing pace in round dances, *e.g.*, 'She's the quickest filly in the barn.' Either from French 'fille', or in reference to the use of the word in stables. 'Colt' is often applied to an active boy.

Filly and foal (*Peoples'*). A young couple of lovers sauntering apart from the world.

Fin de siècle (*Soc.*, 1897 on). Extreme in literature, art, and music. From Paris—adopted here in a condemnatory spirit. Within a year in London was introduced the phrase 'New Century'—first applied in a public manner to the 'New Century Theatre Society'—whose plays were based upon the Ibsen theories of life. The authors appear to have thought these words typical of the 20th century, whereas Ibsen towards the close of the 19th century had been writing for more than fifty years, and had long been a classic in Scandinavia and, in a less degree, throughout Germania.

Find cold weather (*Public-house*) To be bounced, or expelled; *e g*, 'Yere you—if you ain't quiet you'll soon find cold weather *I* can tell yer'

Finger and thumb (*Rhyming*) Rum

Finger in the pie (*Peoples'*). Obvious—and based upon the philosophy of too many cooks spoiling the broth

Finish (*Soc.*, 1830) A house where the night (which was next morning about 4 A M) was finished by the exhaustion of the *debauché*

'We are writing of the days when the Elysium, Mother H 's, The Finish, Jessop's, etc, were in their zenith and glory'—Diprose's *Clement Danes*, vol i, p 98

'Let us go to a finish—say Jessop's' Jessop's finally expired about 1885 It was the building afterwards occupied by the *Echo* newspaper Opposite was the celebrated place of accommodation, 'The Fountain'—significant title, which had then been established hundreds of years

In 1896, King William Street, Strand, saw the opening of a brilliantly-appointed lounge entitled 'The Finale', assuredly good Italian for finish, a sign the proprietor had brought with him from South Africa

Fire (out) (*O Eng, now Amer.—reaching Eng.* 1896) To eject Probably from 14th century, the phrase being invented from the summary process of the first cannon. 'Let us fire him' is equivalent to 'bounce him'.

Then they thought his objection to the spending of £20 on a lecture—and its necessary or needful accompaniments—on the interesting and entertaining subject of 'Bacteriology' too much of a good thing, so they had him 'fired' from the meeting —*E N*, 10th Feb. 1899

The Americanism 'to fire out' is seen in a sonnet of Shakespeare's.

'Yet this shall I not know, nor live in doubt,
Till my bad angels fire my good one out'

This instance shows that in the matter of the mother-tongue common to both countries, Yankees are even more conservative of the 'well of English' than Britishers themselves —*Rees, U S A*

Fire-box (*Passionate Pilgrims'*). A man of unceasing passion

Fire-new (*Prov Potteries'*) 'Brand-new', absolutely new—from drawing pottery from the oven or furnace

It seems an incongruity, an impossibility, for the sculptor and painter of such forms as those we owe to Watt's genius to become suddenly a 'fire-new' baronet —*D N*, 1st July 1885, referring to offer of baronetcy to Mr Watts

Fire-proof coffin (*Amer*) A last house which will resist the action of the nethermost region. Said of a bad man that he will need one

'My pa says that if your pa would stay at home from prayer meetin' to mix a little more sugar with the sand he sells for fourteen cents a pound, p'raps he might not need a fire-proof coffin when he dies'.—*Newsp Cutting.*

Fire the question (*Amer*) To propose marriage.

First on the top-sail and last in the beef-skid (*Navy*) Truly perfect able-bodied seaman More in praise could not be said of him.

Fish-bagger (*Suburban*) Suburban resident who working in the city, or in town, generally takes home food, especially cheap fish, in that respectable black bag which looks so very legal

The tradesman shook his head, and explained that 'fish-bagger' was a contumelious term applied to those who live in good suburbs without spending a penny there beyond rent —*Graphic*, 27th September 1884

Fishy about the gills (*Street*). Appearance of recent drunkenness Derived from very acute observation Drink produces a pull-down of the corners of the mouth, and a consequent squareness of the lower cheeks or gills, suggesting the gill-shields in fishes.

Fit in the arm (*Street*, 1897). A blow In June 1897 one Tom Kelly was given into custody by a woman for striking her His defence before the magistrate took the shape of the declaration that 'a fit had seized him in the arm', and for months afterwards back street frequenters called a blow a fit

Fit-up towns (*Theat*, 1880) Poor, behind-the-times places which cannot boast a theatre amongst them.

Perhaps you don't know what the 'fit-up towns' are Let me tell you They are the towns which do not possess a theatre, and which are therefore only visited by small companies carrying portable scenery, which can be fitted up in a hall or an assembly room —*Ref.*, 22nd July 1883

Fitz (*Peoples'*). Royal natural children—derivation obvious. Broadly applied amongst old theatrical people to the invasion of the stage by educated persons of position or fortune.

'I wish all the fitzes in the world were at the bottom of the sea.'—*Said by a young stage manager*, October 1883.

Five-barred gate (*London Streets*, 1886 on).—A policeman, from the force being chiefly recruited from the agricultural class.

The evidence against the defendant, given by Constable 308 A, was that whilst in company with a woman he abused him (the policeman) without reason, asking how long he had been away from a 'five-barred gate' (the country).—*D. N.*, 2nd July 1890.

Five o'clock tea (*Soc.*, 1879). Strictly tea, and nothing beyond, except a wafer biscuit, a little more wafery bread and butter, and perhaps a microscopic cake, if it is a society holiday. Came to be added first to the ordinary refreshmentless call between three and five P.M. Five o'clock tea has gradually stolen up to a four o'clock teapot, for people came in a crowd, and the old exclusive puritanic plan of one visitor retreating as another came, or retired, even if solus-visiting at the end of a quarter of an hour was abandoned.

Five or seven (*Police; London*, 1885). Drunk. From 'five shillings or seven days', the ordinary London magisterial decision upon 'drunks' unknown to the police, and reduced by Mr Hosack, a metropolitan magistrate, to five or seven.

Another is, 'Arthur Roberts in dress allegorical of five or seven, as Mr Hosack.' Mr Hosack, as many of my readers may not be aware, is a magistrate, and 'five or seven' means——but no matter.—*Ref.*, 17th January 1886.

Fiveoclocquer (*Paris-Eng.*, 1896). Afternoon tea.

Every one, we suppose, has heard of the delightful French phrase, 'five-oclocquer à quatre heures', which is, perhaps, the noblest achievement of the art of word-coining in sublime contempt of meaning.—*Newsp. Cutting*, 24th June 1898.

Five-pounders (*Jersey*). Not a piece of ordnance—but cheap excursionists, who fall upon Jersey in high summer-time, and who make a stay of three or four roaring days, having this sum when they start, and nothing by the time they reach London.

The five-pounders are usually of the genus 'Arry. They are not unwelcomed in Jersey, so long as their five pounds last.—*Graphic*, 31st March 1883.

Fiz (*Society*). Champagne.

Pat Feeney has sworn off fiz, and will never touch a drop for the rest of his life. Not even a drop of whisky. Another injustice to Oireland.—*Cutting*, 1883.

Pat was a patriotic singer of Irish songs, and constantly wailing over the 'green sod' of his native land.

Fizzle (out) (*Peoples'*). To fail, and a failure; from the noise made by the gas escaping from aerated waters when the corks fail, so that the water has no effervescent quality when opened.

Gale and Spader's 'Fizz-Bang-Boom' company has fizzled out in San Francisco. —*Newsp. Cutting*.

It is a foolish, highly-peppered story of love, intrigue and politics. It was little better than fizzle.—*N. Y. Tribune*.

Flabbergast (*Briv. Class*). To astound. Rejected of most lexicographers, but accepted of all men. Probably a proper-name word, possibly Phil Applegarth or Applegast.

The goings on of Cock-Eyed Sal flabbergasted him much, but he was spliced to her, and he couldn't help it.—*Cutting*.

Flag (*Printers'*). Woeful expression referring to an 'out'; that is to say, some missed words in setting up a piece of 'copy'. This may involve over-running a number of lines at a frightful expense of time. Taken from the aspect of the 'out' words written at the side of the proof and enclosed in a loop; a line leading from the nearer end of which concludes in the caret which marks the point in the copy where the missing words are wanting.

Flag of distress (*Street*). A boy's shirt through a too-open trousers-seat. From the flag of a distress on a ship being white—because more easily seen; though perhaps the flag in question is only more or less white.

Flag unfurled (*Rhyming*). A man of the world—passing into flag, after the mode of rhyming English of a passing character.

A cove who fancies himself a flag unfurled is very now or never we don't think.—*Cutting*.

Flam (*Soc* 18 *cent*) Fib—rather than lie Quite passed away from London, but still heard in the counties Probably from a proper name Johnson says, 'a cant word of no certain etymology' Words from proper names really have no etymology Butler (*Hudibras*) uses this word

A flam more senseless than the roguery.
Of old aruspicy and augury!

Miss Wilhelmina Skeggs (*Vicar of Wakefield*) is great in the use of this term May be from Flamborough Head, whence, in the 17th century, came false continental news, exactly as 'Humbug' came to be the term applied to continental false news from Hamburg.

Flannel-jacket (*Contractors'*) Familiar name for the gigantic navvy who, without exception, wears this garment. Generally pronounced 'flannin', *flannel* being a hard word from Wales. Tom Taylor used the term in a scene of the *Ticket of Leave Man*. 'Hey-sup (drink) thou dear flannin-jacket'

Flap-jack invalid (*Amer*) A victim of dissipation

'Reduce the nation to a vast hospital of flap-jack invalids'—*Texas Siftings.*

Flapper (*Lower Class*). Hand—sometimes flipper. Possibly from the slapping movement of the hand suggesting the striking tail or fins of a fish—when the word would be an onomatope—its sound being that of the flap of a fish on wet sand or stones. Said by some authorities to have a very disagreeable meaning

Flapper (*Society*) A very immoral young girl in her early 'teens'

A correspondent of *Notes and Queries* has been troubling his mind about the use of the slang word 'flapper' as applied to young girls Another correspondent points out that a 'flapper' is a young wild duck which is unable to fly, hence a little duck of any description, human or otherwise. The answer seems at first sight frivolous enough, but it is probably the correct solution of this interesting problem all the same —*E N*, 20th August 1892.

Flare-up (*Peoples'*, 19 *cent.*). A stir, riot, disturbance—obviously from a house on fire.

'Flare-up' at the present time is a purely jocular interjection. A noisy revel is very often spoken of by bacchanalians as 'a jolly flare-up', but sixty-three years ago 'flare-up' had another and a very sinister signification. To it was added the admonition 'to join the Union' 'Flare-up and join the Union!' The Union part of the cry is associated in my mind with processions of working men, yelling and cursing and bearing banners embellished with death's-heads and cross-bones, and inscriptions about 'Bread or Blood', while 'flare-up' had a direct bearing on incendiarism —G A Sala in *D T*, 28th July 1894.

Flash (*Thieves'*) Imitation gold coins—the name probably suggested by their glitter. Sometimes called 'Hanoverian' sovereigns — a term originating probably upon the accession of the House of Brunswick—looked upon by all true Jacobites as counterfeit. The last occasion where these terms were in transitory use was at the trial (1881) of one Lefroy, for murder The attorney-general, Sir Henry James (afterwards Lord James of Hereford), prosecuted. In his opening speech he said

'Precisely similar coins—the 'flash' or Hanoverian sovereigns found in the carriage, which Lefroy repudiated, etc' —*Newsp Cutting*

Flash (*Milit*) A ribbon decoration of the 23rd Royal Welsh Fusiliers

It is easy to imagine the indignation which would be displayed at any attempt to deprive the officers of the 23rd Royal Welsh Fusiliers of their right to wear what is called 'the Flash' This ornament consists of a black ribbon sewed on to the back of the tunic-collar, and allowed to flutter in the breeze in imitation of the tie of the old pig-tail —*D N*, July 1881

Flash (*Street*) Grand, splendid Evidently derived from strong flash of lightning

They're so flash that it's a blooming wonder they know themselves —*Cutting*, 1883

Flash dona (*Thieves'*) A high-class low-class lady.

'I was always a real lady, as much as any flash dona what gets her portrait took and then goes on the boards'—*Cutting*

Flash o' light (*New Cut*, *S. London*). Complimentary description of a woman dressed upon the model of the rainbow.

Flat as a frying-pan (*Peoples', old*). Flat indeed. Probably derived from the first implement of this kind which was level compared with the crocks of Elizabethan days.

'Egad—I'm struck as flat as a frying-pan'.—Farquhar, *The Inconstant.*

Flat chicken (*Lower Class*). Stewed tripe. All common foods have fine satirical names.

Flat-foot (*Navy*). A young sailor less than twenty-one. (*See* Shellback).

Flatty (*Thieves'*). A greenhorn. An endearing diminutive of flat, who would be more despised than the less contemned flatty.

Flaxation (*New Eng.*). One of the more remarkable American hypocritical evasions of actual swearing. Equal to damnation.

'Then, what in flaxation do you want of those things?'—*Newsp. Cutting.*

Fleet (*Old Eng.—gone to Nantucket, where it stays*). To trifle, idle. Heard sometimes in mid-counties, *e.g.*,

'He fleets his life away. Many young gentlemen flock to him every day, and fleet the time carelessly as they did in the golden age.'—*As You Like It.*

Fleshy part of the thigh (*Peoples'*, 1899). Evasive military hospital phraseology to describe a wound on that part of the human frame which 'goes over the hedge last'. Came into use upon the news from S. Africa of Lord Methuen having been wounded in this region.

Flier (*Sporting*, 19 *cent.*). A breeder of carrier and other homing pigeons.

'Fliers', a term given to the individuals whose sportsmanlike instincts induce them to spend considerable time and money on the training of homing pigeons. —*D. T.*, 17th December 1897.

Flight o' steps (*Coffee-house*). Thick slices of bread and butter. Royal order in relation to steps—at least four ridge and furrows.

He asks for a pint of mahogany juice, a flight of doorsteps, and a penny halligator.—*Mankind* (Surrey Theatre), 1883.

Flimsy (*Press*). Copy on very thin tracing paper. A dozen sheets of flimsy are interleaved with as many sheets of carbonized or charcoaled paper, when by writing heavily in pencil on the mass of flimsy, twelve copies are obtained. Passed into a verb—'Flimsy me that par', means 'make half a dozen copies on tracing paper'.

Had the questions to be copied out?—Yes; and the answers to be flimsied.—Sir C. Dilke, Crawford Divorce Suit, July 1886.

Fling out or flung away (*Peoples'*). Angry retreat.

Wardlaw whipped before him and flung out of the room. (Charles Reade.)

Theodore flung away and was rushing off. (Miss Yonge.)

Flip-flap (*Street boy*, 1898 on). Broad fringe of hair covering the young male forehead. This fashion, revived from the time of George IV., began with the quiff (*q.v.*), expanded to the guiver, and widened to the flip-flap, a name evidently gained from its motion in the winds.

Flop (*Low Lond.*, 1881). When the lower classes of women adopted the 'cretin' or 'poodle' style of wearing the hair low down over the forehead, they gave it this name.

Flounce (*Theatrical and Society*, 1854 on). The thick line of black paint put on the edge of the lower eyelid to enhance the effect of the eye itself. When under the second empire painting the face (*see* Mind the paint), became common, this term came to be heard in society.

Fluff in (*Lower Peoples'*). Deceive by smooth modes.

Fly cop (*Anglo-Amer.*). Detective (*see* Tec). Cop is abbreviation of copper (*q.v.*). Fly is quite an old word for adroit.

Fly donah (*Street*). Adroit lady—not perhaps too honest.

Fly loo (*Student*, 1850). Summer game. The players stand round a table, each having a lump of sugar or touch of honey well before him. The owner of the sweets upon which a fly first settles takes the stakes. (*See* Kentucky Loo.)

Fly me (*Ancient*). Exclamation against mistrust or doubt. From flay.

Fly member (*Com. Peo.*). Clever, adroit man—fly being used to give the idea of speed in apprehending, and lighting on what passes (*See* Hot member)

Fly rink (*Peoples'*, 1875). A polished bald head.

Flying the kite (*Soc*). Making public—in the 90's Earlier in the century it was issuing accommodation bills Now, however, it has the other meaning, as—

He would be very sorry to do entirely without the interview, and politicians were said to use it as a means of 'flying the kite'—Anthony Hope, April 1898

Foal and filly dance (*Soc*). Dance to which only very young people of both sexes are invited

Fog in (*Soc*). To see a place by chance, or to achieve by accident

Foot! foot! Now and again this expression is cast after the respectably dressed person who wanders into strange and doubtful bye-ways Phrase obtained much attention by its use by Emile Zola in *L'Assommoir*, where it is found even in the mouth of a priest It is difficult to say when this term passed into England The word is to be found as 'foutre' in Shakespeare (*Henry VI*) Probably reintroduced into England by the French court of Charles II

Foot-and-mouth disease (*Lancashire*) Swearing followed by kicking

Foot-bath (*European.*) Overflow from glass into saucer. Said in England of a full glass

It is customary throughout Spain for the waiters of cafés to fill a glass with wine or liquor so that it overflows upon the saucer This custom, in which it is desired to show an appearance of liberality, is called 'the foot-bath'—*People*, 28th July 1895

Foot-rot (*Public-house*). Contemptuous name given by the contemners of fourpenny ale (*See* Brown)

Footless stocking without a leg (*Irish*) Nothing—zero (*See* What the Connaught man shot at.)

Fopper (*Parvenus'*) Mistake. Perversion of 'faux pas' In its extreme application an 'event', if you accept the word's Latin meaning. Equivalent to what the French call *brise du soir*

Forcing the hand (*Soc*) Compel admissions. From whist, where to force the hand of an adversary is to play high in order to compel him to play higher Much used by lawyers—always great whist-players

Sir C Warren agreed with the assessor that it was hardly fair to put a question of this character.

Mr Wontner observed that it was forcing his hand—*Cass Case*, July 1887

Fore God (*American*). Shape of old English oath—'Before God, I swear'

Foreign line (*Railway*) Any line which is not that on which the speaker is employed.

Foreigneering coves (*Low London*, 1860). Most graphic description of dislike to others than British that has perhaps been invented.

We have no passion for ribbons, and orders, and all the tinsel trappings of aliens or 'foreigneering coves', as they are termed in the simple language of 'Those in the Know'.—*D N*, 1883

Foreigner (*Negro*) Elegant evasive title given by negroes to describe themselves, in order to avoid the hated word black

Forest of fools (*Literary*, 17 *cent*) The World.

Amongst all the wild men that run up and down in this wide Forest of Fools, etc—Decker's *Gull's Horn-Book*, 1609

Forever-gentleman (*Soc.*, 1870) A man in whom good breeding is ingrained (*See* Half Hour Gentleman)

Forrader (*Soc*, 1880 on). Forwarder—adopted from the gutter, one night, in the House of Commons Used in many jocular ways

Whether the Liberal Forwards will get any 'forrarder' over the light claret which we have no doubt is all that they can conscientiously allow themselves remains to be seen—*D. T.*, 15th December 1898.

Fortnum and Mason (*Soc*, 1850 on) Complete, luxurious hamper for picnic or races From the perfection of the eatables sent out by this firm of grocers in Piccadilly

49ers (*W-American*) Earliest Californian miners—from the year in which the movement to California commenced

Forum (*Birmingham*). The 'Forum' is the Town Hall, and known by that name through all Warwickshire.

Earl Granville, who was received with most enthusiastic cheers, said: I rise a stranger in this famous Town Hall—(cries of 'No')—known in Birmingham, I believe, by a still more classical name. —Bright Celebration (B'rgham), June 1883.

Forwards (*Polit.*, 1897). Radicals—last cry of the 19th century in discovering a new name for the advanced sections in the House of Commons.

Sir Charles Dilke leads a knot of Radical 'forwards' on questions of foreign affairs, whose views are, probably, at least as distasteful to the leader of the Opposition as the policy of Lord Salisbury.—*D. T.*, 21st June 1898.

Foundling temper (*London*). A very bad temper—proverbially said of the domestic servants poured upon London by the metropolitan Foundling Hospital.

The ladies who are conducting the Metropolitan Association for Befriending Young Servants are perpetually thwarted and discouraged by the singular incapacity for self-control of the girls who have been bred in the great pauper schools. Their chief characteristic is an ungovernable temper. This is popularly recognised as the 'Foundling temper'.—*D. N.*, 9th September 1885.

Foundry (*Peoples'*). Shop, but chiefly applied to a pork butcher's—probably because of the noisy vibration of the sausage machine.

Fountain temples (*London*, 90's). Places of convenience, sunk below the roadways. Remarkable for lavish marble, mosaic, and clear running water. (*See* Cottages.)

Four arf (*Costers'*). The costermonger's favourite beverage is a pot o' four arf.

Four-legged fortune (*Soc.*, 1880 on). Winning horse.

They talk Turf slang; they back 'four-legged fortunes', and his lordship owns a steed which brings him to utter grief. —*D.T.*, 22nd April 1898.

Four liner (*Soc.*). Very important. From 'whips' or messages to M.P.'s, which have from one to four lines drawn under them, according to importance.

Four-lined whips have been sent out on both sides of the House of Commons urging members to be in their places this evening.—*D. N.*, March 1890.

Four thick (*Public-house*). Fourpence per quart beer—the commonest there is (in London), and generally the muddiest.

Fourpenny cannon (*London Slums*). Beef-steak pudding—price, a groat. Named possibly from its shape, that of a cannon-ball (cut down to cannon), but possibly referring to the cast-iron character not only of the beef, but its integument.

Fourpenny pit (*Rhyming*). Fourpenny bit—now antiquarian phrase—since this silver coin has been absolutely withdrawn in favour of the threepenny bit.

Foxes (*American*). People of Maine—probably owing to the foxes which prevail there.

Frame (*Artists'*, 1890). Picture.

Franc-fileur (*French*, 1870). A cur, a freebolter—in contradistinction from franc-tireur, the volunteer light infantry of the defence. Used now and again in England in society for a man who gets away quietly and won't dance.

Freak (*Theatrical*, 1885). Actors who lose professional cast by aiding in eccentric shows. From New York.

Actors who play in dime museums are now called 'freaks'.—*Ref.*, 18th April 1906.

Freakeries (*London*, 1898). Barnum's freak and acrobat shows at Olympia.

Free (*Peoples' and School*). To make free. Process never of a very elegant kind—especially amongst school-boys. Expectoration enters into the process as a rule. (*See* 'Lynch'.)

Free hand (*Political*, about 1880). Plenary powers, *carte blanche*.

General Gordon has been given, if we must use a detestable piece of slang a 'free hand'. In plainer and better English he has been allowed to do as he pleased.—*D. N.*, 5th May 1884.

French (*S. of N. Amer. Soc.*). Term used in Maryland and Virginia for any fashion that is disliked. Probably from 18th century when the people of these states very much disliked the French population of Louisiana

Frenchman (*Soc.*, 19 *cent*). Bottle of brandy—from this spirit being French

Frenchy (*Street*, 19 *cent*, to 1854) A term of contempt addressed to any man with a foreign air in the streets

Fresh-whites (*Peoples'*, 19 *cent*). Pallor.

Freshers and toshers (*Oxford*, 1896). Freshers despised as freshmen, and toshers being men who have no sympathy with the Church Combined term of contempt.

Fretted (*American*) Vexed to do a thing

Friars (*L. C. and D. Railway passengers'*, 1860) Hurried short for 'Blackfriars'

Friction (*Polit.*, 1885) New satirical term for political or international quarrel

The letter from Lord Granville which Lord Edmund Fitzmaurice read in the House of Commons contained an expression of Lord Granville's hope that the 'friction' with Germany may now be considered a thing of the past.—*D N*, 10th March 1885.

Fried carpets (*London Theatrical*, 1878 82) Given to the exceedingly short ballet skirt, then especially seen at the old 'Gaiety'

Friendly pannikin (*Australian gold-fields*) An amicable drink together out of the small tin pot—one which serves the outlying Australian for most purposes

Fright hair (*Theatrical*) A wig or portion of a wig which by a string can be made to stand on end and express fright

Frisk at the tables (*London*) A moderate touch at gaming

My object is fulfilled if I have made it clear that 'a frisk at the tables' is now rendered easy to Londoners, and that those wishing to enjoy one have but to attend the first well-managed sporting meeting, to receive encouragement and respectful protection at the hands of the police —G A Sala

Frisky (*Com. London*, 1880) Bad-tempered, and a euphemism for the same

Frivoller (*Soc*, 1879 on) Person with no serious aim in life. Substantive derived from Lord Beaconsfield's celebrated phrase 'hair-brained frivolity'.

'Junius' contains plenty of fine stirring lines, even if they awake no more than an occasional echo in the bosoms of the cynical 'frivollers' who exclusively occupy 'the best parts' at all our theatres —*Ref*, 1st March 1885

Frochard (*Theatrical*, about 1870) Savage old woman part—from the demon-hag in *Les Deux Orphelines.*

Augustin Daly's *Under the Gaslight* was more or less a 'bobtail' piece, and thoroughly American in tone We had a New York blood, a low-comedy character called Bermudas, a 'side-walk merchant prince, with a banjo swarry', a Wall Street dealer, a judge of the Tombs Police Court, and a vile Frochard sort of person called Old Judas.—*D T*, 9th June 1899.

Froncey (*Low Lond*, 19 *cent.*). Français—protest in the interests of things English and of England.

Front (*Soc*, 1888) Audacity—from the forehead, pushing forward Equals affront

There is another rendering of the word 'front' in use among some clever folk, but I wouldn't for the world suggest that the promoters have any of that—to say nothing of 420 ft. of it —*Ref*, 9th March 1890

Front name (*Universal Street*, 19 *cent*). Christian name, and always considered as *the* cognomen

Front piece (*Theatrical*, 1880) Dramatic trifle which precedes the *pièce de resistance.*

The new front piece, *Written in Sand*, turned out to be a pretty little idyllic affair —*Ref*, 31st August 1884.

Frosy (*Devonshire*) A delicacy in food eaten quietly by not more than two, after the children are in bed—the couple generally man and wife

Froze out (*Amer-Eng*, 1880-96) Conquered, made the other a nonentity.

Fruit of a gibbet (*Peoples'*, 18 *cent*) Hanged felon The gibbet, as distinct from the gallows, was the frame upon which the hanged man was swung in chains.

I found thee a complete emblem of poverty, resembling the fruit of a gibbet seven years exposed to wind and weather —Gay's *Beggars' Opera*

Frump (*Soc.*, 1871 on). High cut bodice. When the second French Empire fell (1870), the low-cut bodice, which the Court of the Tuileries had maintained for eighteen years, was swept away. London society led with the high, and afterwards the square cut bodice, which still very generally prevails. Young men in society at once dubbed the high bodice patroness a 'frump'—a badly dressed woman.

Full as a goat (*Tavern*, 18 *cent.*). Drunk. This phrase is evidently 'Full as a goitre', the word often used for the huge throat wen which, common in the last century, is now rarely seen. The word having no distinct modern meaning, has been naturally changed to goat. The idea of fulness is complete in contemplating a huge goitre, which always looks upon the point of bursting.

. . . New Arrival—'I want a bed.' Clerk: 'Can't have one, sir; they're all full.' N. A.: 'Then I'll sleep with the landlord.' Clerk: 'Can't do it, sir. He's full, too; fuller than a goat, and has been for three days.'—*N. Y. Mercury*, 1888.

Function (*Soc.*, 1880 on). First used for grave musical performances; but the æsthetes began to apply the word to all kinds of meetings—even afternoon teas.

The drenching showers of Thursday night in no way damped the ardour of Haymarket reopeners. The ceremony was, in its way, almost a function.—*Ref.*, 18th September 1887.

Fury (*Navy*). Crew's name for the *Furious*.

Fuss (*Anglo-American*, 19 *cent.*). Dispute, row, wrangle, without any serious consequences.

Fuss and feathers (*Amer.-Eng.*, 1880). Bosh, pretence, froth. Probably from 18th century English; and referring to cock-fighting where the birds only pulled feather and threatened.

Well, as an American critic says of the notions of the solar mythologists, this was 'all fuss and feathers'.—*D. N.*, 10th February 1898.

Fuz-chats (*Beggars'*). The people who camp out on commons amongst the 'furze'. Generally show-people, and gipsy cheap-jacks, also gipsies proper.

G

G. O. M. (*Political Popular*, 1882). Grand Old Man. In this year Mr W. E. Gladstone, when Premier, was described in this way. The satirical journals took up the phrase, and reduced it to initials.

I knocked the G. O. M. down, Northcote sat on his head, and he gave in.—*Ref.*, 7th December 1884.

G. T. T. (*New York*). Gone to Texas. Confession of flight put on office door.

Gads O' (*Hist.*). Evaded swearing. Equals God's oath—probably refers to the promises made to the patriarchs.

Gadsbud (*Queen Anne*). God's blood, or God's bud, meaning the Infant Saviour. Another shape is Od's Bud (*q.v.*), 'Gadsbud! I am provoked into a fermentation.'—Congreve, *The Double Dealer*.

Gaelically utter (*Soc.*). The Scotch accent when trying to produce English.

'*West* of England!' cried a supporter of the majority, in an accent too Gaelically utter for London ink to reproduce. 'I don't believe there are any solicitors in the *West* of England. Only a set of clerks.'—*S. T.*, 1st February 1883.

Gaiety girls (*Stage*, 1890 on). Dashing singing and dancing comedians in variety pieces—from their first gaining attention at the Gaiety Theatre.

One of the most interesting features of the Nellie Farren benefit is the promised re-appearance of Miss Marion Hood, one of the brightest and most graceful of 'Gaiety' girls.—*People*, 27th February 1898.

Gaiety step (*Theat.*, 1888-92). A quick, high dancing pas, made popular at the Gaiety Theatre. Term spread to America.

Galbe (*Thieves'*). Profile of a violent character, and even applied to any eccentricity of shape above the knees. This is from the French, and doubtlessly came into fashion at the Court of Charles II. The word is one of the proper-name series, and comes from the Emperor Galba, who lived long in Gaul, where his pronounced profile and terrific nose begot the word. Galbe is used daily all over France, but especially in Paris —"*Quel Galbe*"

Gallersgood (*Thieves'*, 18 *cent*) Corruption of gallows' good. So bad that it is worthy of the gallows

Gally-pot baronet (*Soc*, 19 *cent*) Ennobled physician—outcome of the scorn of birth for even the scientific parvenu.

Gal-sneaker (*Common Lond*, 1870) A man devoted to seduction

Gambetter (*International*, 1879) To humbug—'Don't you try to Gam Better *me!*' From Gambetta, of Italian and Jewish origin, who was very popular in France from 1870 to about 1876, when politicians began to suspect his sincerity. In 1879 his popularity was rapidly waning In this year the verb in question was invented It is still used in French politics when accusing an opponent of double-dealing.

Gamblous (*Soc*, 1885). Gambling —invented by Mr J Chamberlain. (29th April 1885 Speech at dinner of the Eighty Club)

I suppose Lord Salisbury thinks that if this country only blustered enough we might attain all that we desired from the fears of foreign Powers There is something to be said for the game of brag, but in this case the stakes are so high, the risk so great, that I do not believe that any sensible men will commit their fortunes to a party or a statesman who would run such tremendous hazards in such a gamblous spirit

Gander (*London*, 1815-40). Fop It is a perversion of Gandin, the Parisian description of a fop from the Restoration to the '40's

Ganymede (*University*). Freshman, or man in his second or even third year, of an effeminate tendency

Gaperies, The (*London*, 1902) The very last outcome of entertainments ending in 'ies' (*see* Colindries, etc) It is simply a rendering of 'Gay Paris'

Garbage (*Naval*) Clothes, etc —probably from the appearance of a box of clothes waiting the wash

Garbed (*American*, *passing to Eng*) Full-dressed Would appear to be an intensification of the ordinary use of the word dressed.

Garret (*Hatters'*, 19 *cent*) A consultation of the members of a shop in relation to some trade or social difficulty of the moment

Garret (*Street*, 19 *cent*). Mouth—probably suggested by the mouth being high up in relation to all the body

Gas-pipes (*Street*). Name given to trousers when tight In France when fashion causes the hem of the trouser to widen out, this style is called *pied d'elephant*, to which it has a fair resemblance.

Gaul darned (*American*) Modern opposition to too plain bad language—'God damned'

Gawblimy (*Street*, 1870) Ceaseless apostrophe by the lower orders to heaven, in reference to some declaration This is 'Gaw Bli Me'. Gaw from the street shape of the word 'God'—this shape being Gawd, 'bli' an ellipsis, and 'me'

Gawd forgive him the prayers he said (*Peoples'*) Evasion of saying the sinner swore consummately

Gaze at the melody (*American*). Look a thing in the face. Another form of 'Face the music'

Gee-gees (*Infantry*) Cavalry This term, from the nursery, for a horse is directed at the cavalry by the infants (*See* Coldcreams, Porridge pots, Grinning dears, Muck)

Gee-ru (*American*, 1880) Extension of amazement. The 'Ge' is for Je'rusalem, a word once much used, accent on first syllable and on second. Often used, 'Je—you don't say so!'

General (*Com Life*) Chandler's shop — where everything may be obtained.

General (*Mid-class*, 1880 on). Maid of all work

That the race of generals threatens to become extinct is a proposition which is not really so startling as it sounds at first —*D T*, 18th January 1898

General (*Middle-class*, 19 *cent.*) Shilling 'Can you generalise?' A delicate mode of saying 'Can you loan me a shilling?'

General Backacher (*Military*, 1899) General Gatacher — modulation of his name to designate this soldier's love of hard-working his men (*See* Bobs.)

Genitrave (*Peoples'*, *Hist.*) Farthing — or smallest coin. Was in use before maravedi, which probably came to England with Philip of Spain.

Gentleman (*Liverpool*). There are no men in Liverpool; all are gentlemen.

Gentleman in blue (*London*, 1840). One of the satirical names for policeman.

Gentleman super (*Theatrical* — *about* 1884). A theatre-super of some position or standing — the ordinary super being a person of no standing whatever beyond earning about a shilling or two per evening. In 1884 Mr Wilson Barrett (Princess's Theatre) invented the gentleman super with a view to creating a school of actors, who began on the lowest rung of the ladder. Their price was about twelve to fifteen shillings per week.

Gentleman who pays the rent, The (*Irish peasantry*, 19 *cent.*). Pig —Milesian variety. Origin obvious.

The Irish pig, the gentleman who pays the Irish rent, if not exactly a willing immigrant into this country, has always proved a quiet one after his arrival. He has generally been *cured* before leaving home.—*D. T.*, 17th December 1897.

Gentlemen of the long robe (*Historical*). Term applied by warriors who wore short tunics, satirically to designate mere lawyers, who waged wars with but words.

George (*Military*, 1880-96). The Commander-in-Chief, George, Duke of Cambridge. Good evidence of the duke's popularity, which never waned to the moment he resigned the command.

Georgium Sidus (*Soc.*). The Netherlands — figuratively speaking. The Surrey side of the Styx.

Geranium (*Street*, 1882). Red nose.

German gospel (*Peoples'*, November 1897). Bounce, vain boasting, megalomania. From a phrase addressed in this month by Prince Henry of Prussia to his brother of Germany at a dinner: 'The gospel that emanates from your Majesty's sacred person, etc.'

Get away closer (*Coster*, *Hist.*). Invitation to yet more pronounced devotion.

Get curly (*Tailors'*). Troublesome.

Get fits (*Peoples'*). *Væ victis*— suffer rage from being conquered; impatient under defeat. Generally 'git fits'.

Get in (*Low London*, 19 *cent.*). Victoriously strike.

And then you goes and gets in both fists — one, two, three — afore I knew where I was. Then o' course I ups and gives you a one-er, and off I goes.—*D. T.*, 18th October 1897.

Get inside and pull the blinds down (*Low London*, 19 *cent.*). Gross verbal attack delivered on the highway at a poor rider.

Get it down the neck (*Lower Peoples'*). To swallow.

Get left (*Anglo-Amer.*). Abbreviation of 'in the lurch'.

Get outside (*Street*). Swallow.

Get religion (*Peoples'*). Become religious.

Get the drop (*Amer.-Eng.*). Outcome of the use of the revolver in U.S.A. The muzzle of the revolver is dropped down to the aim from a higher level—hence the term, which means to obtain victory.

Get the g. b. (*Amer.*). Dismissal —g. b. being 'go by'.

'Won't he feel cheap when he gets the g. b.?'

Get the heels on it (*Amer.-Eng.*). Victory, success—from the American habit (rapidly passing away) of resting the heels, when their proprietor is seated, on a level with his head, if not above it.

Get the shillings ready (*Street*, 1897). Be prepared to ladle out money. From the rush of charity which characterised the sixtieth year of Queen Victoria's reign, and especially referring to the *Daily Telegraph* shillings charity lists towards the fund for the payment of the debts of the London Hospitals.

Get the shoot (*Peoples'*). Dismissal —probably from the mill shoot turning out the flour.

Get the spike (*Low London*). Lose one's temper.

'O' course Chris git's the spike!'—*People*, 5th January 1895.

Get to onest (*Amer.*). Retire immediately.

Get up early (*Street*). Be clever.

Get up steam (*Peoples'*, 1840 on) Be energetic Outcome of the initiation of the railway system. Even George Eliot, who hated anything approaching slang, used this phrase so early as 1846

'I do not know whether I can get up any steam again on the subject of Quinet —but I will try '—George Eliot's *Life*, vol. i., p. 150

Get your eye in a sling (*Peoples'*) Warning that you may receive a sudden and early black eye, calling for a bandage—the sling in question

Getting a big boy now (*London*). Of age The line was the leading phrase of the refrain of a song made popular by Herbert Campbell It is applied satirically to strong lusty young fellows about whose manhood there can be little or no question

Getting all over a man (*L. Life*, 19 *cent*). Handling and examining him—not necessarily for theft, but in all probability feloniously

The only reason witness could give for the attack was that a few days previously he prevented Regan 'getting all over a strange man' whom he had brought into the lodging-house —*D T*, 8th October 1895

Getting before oneself (*Peoples'*) Personal emphasis of any kind — of vanity, boastfulness, threat, anger

Getting behind yourself (*Peoples'*, 19 *cent*) Lapse of memory in reference to events

Getting it down fine (*American*, 1880). Successful by adroitness.

Getting it down fine on burglars It is getting so that even burglars are seriously interfered with in the practice of their professions A recent invention, etc —*Albany Argus*, 1883

Getting ox-tail soup (1867-83) Refers to the maiming of cattle, exercised by Fenians and other disaffected Irish, against the property of cattle-owners who displeased them

In Ireland there have been no experiments at all, for the cutting off the tails of living cattle—'getting ox-tail soup', as some Irish facetiously styled this practice—is not a scientific experiment. *D N*, 7th June 1883

Good example of historical phrase

Giants (*Restaurant*) Huge asparagus

I was startled by hearing the player call the waiter and order, as he pointed to the carte, 'Two Giants' I arrived at a solution of the mystery when presently I saw the gourmands devouring 'giant' asparagus —*Ref*, 1882

Gibby (*Navy*) Spoon.

Giddy young whelp (*London*, 1896) Youth about town. Rather contemptuous Sometimes giddy young whelk — pronounced Wilk Giddy kipper was the first development—from probably giddy skipper

Gigglemug (*Street*) An habitually smiling face

Gigmanity (*Soc*) People who keep gigs — therefore respectable Took its rise from the trial of one Thurtell for the murder of a Mr Weare, as to whom it was asked by counsel of a witness—'Was Weare a respectable man?' the answer being 'Yes—he kept a gig'

Gilt on the gingerbread (*Peoples' —almost obsolete*) The past - away annual rural fairs were made ghastly gay with flat gingerbread cakes, covered with Dutch metal, which tried to look like gilt

Gin and fog (*Theatrical*). Peculiar hoarseness, generally believed to be caused by the abuse of alcohol

Dr Lennox Brown has been delivering an interesting lecture on the effects of alcohol on the voice There is a broken-down voice known in the profession as 'the gin and fog' —G R Sims, *Ref*, 11th January 1886

Gin bottle (*Street*). Dirty, abandoned, flabby, debased woman, generally over thirty, the victim of alcoholic abuse, within an ace of inevitable death

Gin crawl (*London, Fleet St and Strand*) Beaten street tracks haunted by drunken or broken down literary men, journalists, reporters, and inferior actors out of employ

Phil Benjamin was taking his daily constitutional, which consisted in what is called 'a gin crawl'—in this instance between Drury Lane and Covent Garden —*Bird o' Freedom*, 7th March 1883

Gin - sling (*Public-house*, 19 *cent*) Practically cold gin-punch Generally supposed to come from U S A., and named thus from slinging the mixture from glass to glass

Ginger blue (*Amer -Eng* , 1855) Exclamation protesting against caddishness Ginger was applied on the plantations of S. U.S.A. to over-eager negroes. Blue was added as a satirical reference to blue blood.

Girl of the period (*Soc.*, 1880 on). Term invented by Mrs Lynn Linton in a series of articles in *The Saturday Review*, attacking the self-emancipation of the young lady of this generation.

After Naseby, by Mr Briton Riviere. The reader, even if he has not visited the Academy, can imagine for himself the young lady of the period, bowed down with grief, and holding the fatal letter, below a tall window of the Royalist hall.—*D. N.*, Academy Crit.

Git a bit (*L. London*). May refer to woman, but generally means obtaining money.

On the day this 'ere job came off Chris comes around to me and says: 'I 'aint going to work to-day; you had better come out and see if we can't get a bit.—*People*, 6th January 1895.

Git the ambulance (*Street*, 1897). Declaration of incapacity, generally of a drunken character, cast at the sufferer. Took the place of 'git the stretcher'—which was (and is) maintained by the police. Took its rise from the introduction amongst civilians of ambulance service.

Git the sads (*Peoples'*). Vulgar synonym for 'to have the vapours'. (*See* Smokes).

Give a lift (*Amer.-Eng.*). A sharp quick kick.

Give it hot (*L. Life*). Severe castigation.

Remember, remember,
Next month of November,
The boycotting, treason, and plot—
For condoning this treason
(To win votes the reason)
We'll give it Lord Salisbury hot!
—*Ref.*, 18th October 1885.

Give the crock (*Peoples'*). Yielding victory—the crock must have been a jug.

I have been making a long calculation, and I find that this sum will only just cover ex.'s, so I am simply *giving* you the crock.—*Our Boys*, No. 2, December 1883.

Give away the racket (*American*). Unintentionally to reveal.

Give him rope enough (*Old English*). This phrase is abbreviated from the addition, 'and he'll hang himself'.

Give way to booze (*Street*). Mode of describing habits of drinking.

Give it a drink (*Theatre and Music-hall*, 1897). *Fin de siècle* shape of condemnation conferred upon a bad piece, or some poor turn at the music halls.

Give out (*American*). End—finish; from a mine giving out as to ore.

Give way (*Ladies'*, 19 *cent.*). Weep, break down, resolve in tears.

Unhappily the infection appeared to extend its influence even to Mr Barrymore, who, when Mr Forbes-Robertson was preparing to bring the scene to a close by 'taking the measure of an unmade grave', had begun to exhibit in his turn an alarming tendency to 'give way', as the ladies say.—*D. N.*, 11th November 1882.

Give the shake (*American*). Abbreviation of shaking hands upon departure.

Give us a rest (*American*, 1882). A figurative way of asking a long talker to curtail his sermon.

Give him a rolling for his all over (*Street*). Corruption of give him a Roland for his Oliver.

Giving one. The one here mentioned may be a kiss or a blow.

Glim (*Thieves'*). Candle.

Glory-oh (*Navy*). Name given by the crew to the *Glory*.

Glory hole (*Street*). One of the names found for the places of meeting of the salvationists—in their early days.

The 'Glory Hole' Disturbances at Maidstone:—The 'Glory Hole' disturbances were continued last night at Maidstone.—*D. N.*, 24th October 1887.

Glow (*Com. Class*). Blush.

Go and eat coke (*Back Street*). Direction implying contempt.

Go around (*American*). Drift; go with current in life; live thoughtlessly.

Go-away (*Soc.*, 1886). The dress into which a bride passes before she departs with her husband.

Go close (*Sporting Anglo-American*). To the winning post. Abbreviation.

Go down one (*Com. London*). To be vanquished.

Go in (*Peoples'*). Act with absolute vigour. 'Go in and win' is the best known of the applications of this phrase

The person who jumped on the communion table at St Paul's Cathedral the other day, pulling down the crucifix, knocking over the flowers and other adornments, may be said to have had a very inexpensive 'go in' He had been fined £5 —*Entr'acte*, April 1883

Go off (*Theatrical*) Go off—the stage

Go off (*Soc*) Not to take place

Mr Matthews 'There is something cut out of the diary?' 'That was an engagement that went off.' 'Whenever an engagement goes off you cut it out?' 'Yes' 'What do you mean by an engagement going off?' 'When a person says he will call and does not, I cut it out'—Sir C Dilke, *Crawford Divorce Suit*, July 1886

Go on the æger (*Oxford*) Signs the sick-list

If a man is ill, or thinks he is—the will often being father to the thought—he 'goes on the æger'—that is to say, he puts his name down on the sick-list and obtains the luxury of a hot dinner in his rooms.—*D T*, 14th August 1899

Go on tick (*Hist*), Credit—short for ticket. Fallen very low in the world

This phrase is derived from the French word 'Etiquet,' a little note, breviate or best—*i e.*, a ticket or note being made or taken instead of payment, consequently, to go on trust or credit. "We'll play on tick, and lose the Indies, I'll discharge it all to-morrow"—Dryden, *An Evening's Love*

Go on with the funeral (*American*) Continue the ceremony

Go out foreign (*Thieves'*) To emigrate under shady circumstances

Go one better (*American*) Superiority—from a term at 'poker', or 'brag'.

The merry Duchess can see the late Mrs Lydia Pinkham, and go her one better —*N York Puck*, September 1883

Go solid (*American-Eng.*, 1884) Thorough

The Irish Nationalist vote, whatever it may amount to, will, in American phraseology, 'go solid', against the Liberal party.—*D. N.*, 10th Sept. 1885.

Go to Hanover (*Jacobite, 18 cent.*) Paraphrase of 'Go to Hell'—Hanover being quite on a par with the hotter place in the opinion of the Jacobites

Go to bed (*Printers'*, 1860-80). Phrase used by printers in reference to printing a newspaper on the bed of the printing-press

Go to Hell or Connaught (*Hist.*) Be off From the time of Cromwell, but still heard, especially in Protestant Ireland Means utter repudiation of the person addressed The Parliament (1653-54) passed a law, driving away all the people of Ireland who owned any land, out of Ulster, Munster, and Leinster

Go to sleep (*American-English*) Fail, expire, come to an end, now generally accepted; but in the first place used as to wandering theatrical and other amusements companies about the U.S.A

Go up (*Oxford and Cambridge*). To go, academically, to one 'Varsity or the other

Wiclif went up to Oxford between 1335 and 1340 Balliol was his college naturally, as he was a North Countryman —*D N*, 30th December 1884.

(*See* Go down)

Go up (*Theatrical*) The action of going up—the stage—that is to the back boards of that platform. (*See* Go off, Come on)

Go up one (*Peoples'*) Applause Derived from the school class—the scholar going one nearer the top as he goes up one.

Go-aheaditiveness (*Amer*) Success.

Go between, The (*Holborn, W C*, 1897) St. Alban's Church, Holborn This high church used to be called 'Machonichie's'—from the name of its first spiritual director, who, dying in the snows of Scotland, was succeeded by Father Stanton, when the church came to be called 'Stanton's' It acquired the title here given from a police-court case

Mr Horace Smith What is your religion?

The Woman Well, my boy was christened at St Alban's, Holborn

Mr Carr (second clerk) · Is that Church of England?

The Woman I don't know You ought to know, you're more learned than me.

Mr H Smith Is it a Roman Catholic Church?

The Woman: Well, it's between the two. It ain't Roman Catholic, and yet it's very High. It's a go-between.—*D. T.*, 5th February 1897.

Go without passport (*Amer.* 1860). Commit suicide.

Go wrong (*Soc.*, 1870). Antithesis of prosper.

Goes Fanti (*Scientific*, 19 *cent.*). Tendency to return to primitive life—atavism.

Another sort of man simply 'goes Fanti,' like the Rev. John Creedy, M.A., Oxon, and reverts to savagery.—*D. N.*, 25th August 1887.

Going 'ome (*L. Class*). Dying.

Going into laager (*Colonial, passing to England*). Taking precautions against danger. From S. Africa, where the farmers in a given district, when fearing an attack from natives, assemble their waggons and form them into a zigzag circle or square, and pitch their tents within it. This is going into laager.

The news from Bechuanaland this morning is more serious. The magistrate and farmers at Kuruman have gone into laager.—*D. T.*, 9th January 1897.

Going ter keep a peanner-shop (*Street, London*). Evidence of complete grandeur, said aloud of and to a neighbour or other person passing in all the flaunting array adapted to holiday-making.

Going to Calabar (*Naval*). Dying—from Calabar being situated on the marshy estuary of Cross River, West Coast of Africa, and particularly one of the spots called white men's graves.

Going to buy anything? (*Streets*, 1896 on). Evasive request for a drink. One man who wants refreshment badly meets another, and puts this minute inquiry.

Going to see a dawg (*Sporting*). Meaning a woman, whose social position may be assumed by her association with 'dawg'—always thus spelt or pronounced.

Going to see a man (*Anglo-Amer.*, 1883). Going to get a drink.

A young fellow, who had a pretty young woman in tow, got up after each act and went out. When he came back the second time his companion asked: 'Did you see him?' 'See whom?' he demanded. 'The man you went to see.' 'I didn't go out to see a man; I wanted to get a drink,' was the candid rejoinder. The chronicler adds that the frankness of this admission so overpowered her that she could only squeeze his hand and say, 'Oh, George! and was it good?'—*Ref.*, 6th September 1885.

Gone coon (*Amer.-Eng.*). Raccoon, which has taken refuge in a tree, and thus offers a perfect aim to the sportsman. Conquered, trapped.

Gone over a goodish bit of grass (*Peoples'*). Tough—referring to a very hard leg of mutton, presumably old. Good example of evasive satire.

Gone through Hades with his hat off (*Amer.—just understood in England*). Bold.

Gone through the sieve (*Managers'*). Bankrupt—lost from sight.

Gone to Chicago (*Eng.-Amer.*). Vanished, levanted. Last outcome (1884) of G. T. T. (*q.v.*).

The spectacle of half a score of gold-laced and brass-buttoned generals in full uniform gravely discussing whether a fellow-officer was or was not wanting in proper respect for a civilian now shorn of official station and 'gone to Chicago' cannot fail to be inspiring.—*New York Mercury*, April 1885.

Gone to Rome (*Obscure*). Become silent.

Catholic Spain still keeps up her old traditions of Holy Week observances and religious ceremonies. When the clock strikes ten on the morning of Maundy Thursday all carriage, cart and tramway-car traffic ceases, even in the streets of Madrid; and the capital of Spain becomes a Silent City for forty-eight hours, until ten o'clock strikes on Saturday morning, and the bells of the churches 'return from Rome', as the popular saying has it, and announce High Mass.—*D. N.*, 4th April 1890.

(*See* Sent to Coventry.)

Godfer (*Peoples'*). Troublesome child. Short for God-forsaken.

God-forbids (*Rhyming*). Kids—a cynical mode of describing children, by poor men who dread a long family.

God-speed (*Nautical*). Hospitable meal given when a vessel is about to sail.

Mr Sutherland at a God-speed party on board the *Valetta* said, etc.—*D. N.*, 3rd March 1884.

Golblast (*Amer.*, 1883). A mild oath.

Gold hunters (*American*). Californians.

Gom (*Political*, 1883) G O M became a word Coined on the initials of Grand Old Man — Mr Gladstone, who in this year was quite the idol of the people

Gonnows (*Women of Lower Class*, 19 *cent*) God knows—with the 'd' elided 'Gonnows I'm innercent Mrs Biffley—gonnows that'

Gonoph (*E London*). Thief—this word being Hebrew for the same

Good curtain (*Theatrical*) Good ending to an act

Good hiding (*Peoples'*) The good refers to the hider, not the hided The second word refers to the hide, or skin of the victim

Good strange (*Queen Ann*) God's strings, that is, the cords which bound—string having possibly been pronounced strang, as it still is in some parts of England

Good strange — I swear I'm almost tipsy —Congreve, *The Double Dealer*

Good thing out of it (*Peoples' Hist*) Success—probably not wholly unaccompanied by smartness

Meantime it is as well to put in a word of warning against the notion that the British Government seeks — to use a common commercial phrase—to make a 'good thing out of it' from a financial point of view.—*D. T*, 18th January 1898.

Good young man (*L. Peoples'*, 1881) Catch phrase for hypocrite. Brought in by Mr Arthur Roberts in a song (*See* Bad young man)

Goose (*U S A.*) Practical joke Has nothing to do with goosing in theatres

Gooseberry-picker (*Soc —old*) A confidant in love matters, who shields the couple, and brings about interviews between them

Gorblimeries (*Police*) Seven Dials

Gorblimy (about 1875) A gutter phrase A corruption of 'God blind me'

Gord keep us (*London-Jewish*) A vulgar translation of one of the most beautiful Hebrew ejaculations

Gordelpus (*Street*) A 'starver,' or casual, who has obtained this name from his ordinary exclamation — 'Gordelpus (God help us)—what's a cove ter do?'

Gosh ding (*Anglo-Amer*). God damn

Gospel according to St Jeames (*Soc.*, 1847 on). Snobbery, abject devotion to persons of position. Derived from Thackeray's *Jeames de la Pluche*.

Gospel of gloom (*Anti-æsthetic*, 1880) Satirical description of æstheticism which tended to doleful colours, gloomy houses, sad limp dresses, and solemn, earnest behaviour

As what was called 'the artistic dress' was never adopted by acknowledged beauties or ladies of rank and fashion so did that theory of house decoration familiarly known as 'the gospel of gloom', completely fail to obtain any grip in Grosvenor, Berkeley, St James's, or Belgrave Square —*D N Workers, etc*, 17th September 1898.

Gospel of the tub (*Society*, 1845) The mania for the use of cold water.

A bath was, all over Europe, a luxury, or a remedy for illness, until what has been called the gospel of the tub was commenced in England. Athletics, tubbing, and the Broad Church seized on the English mind together, and cold water was preached as the great preserver of strength and beauty —*D N*, 9th February 1883

Got a clock (*Peoples'*, *Historical*) Carrying a handbag The creation of this phrase is quite historical The first serious explosion by dynamite in London (Victoria Terminus, 1883) was effected by dynamite in connection with an American clock whose hammer struck the trigger of a pistol whose charge fired the explosion (*See* Fenian)

Got a collar on (*Street*) Stuck up

Got a face on him (*Peoples'*) Evasion of ugly

Got the crop (*Military* — up to 1856) Short hair Until after the Crimean War, when the long beards the men brought home resulted in the hair being close cropped as a matter of natural taste, hair in the British army was worn somewhat long

Got the glow (*Com. London*). To blush

Got it (*General*, 19 *cent*) The 'it' here is very emphatic, and means punishment *in excelsis*

Got line (*Theatrical*, 1870 on) Shortly 'go', but the words mean more than this. They infer vigour, grace, strength and charm in movement, especially in dancing. Only applied to women.

Got right (*Sporting*, 19 *cent.*). Cured.

Mr C. Hibbert has, we understand, sent Kirkhill to Jesse Winfield to be got right. Jesse is a good trainer and rider, but he has theories.—*Ev. News*, 23rd January 1896.

Got swing (*Artistic generally*, 1880). Equivalent to 'go', vigour—or the French *avoir la ligne*.

Got thar (*Anglo-Amer.*, 1880). Got there—completion, triumph, victory.

Got the morbs (*Soc.*, 1880). Temporary melancholia. Abstract noun coined from adjective morbid.

Got the pants (*Common*). Panting from over-exertion. Figure of speech.

Got the perpetual (*Peoples'*). Chiefly confined to vigorous and go ahead young men.

Got the shutters up (*Peoples'*). Surly—from the silent appearance of a closed shop.

Got the woefuls (*Peoples'*). Miserable, wretched, in the dumps.

Got up and dusted (*Amer.-Eng.*). Escaped—from a man when running away throwing up the dust behind him.

Got up no end (*Peoples'*). Magnificent personal display, appertaining to all parts of the dress and person.

Götter-dam-merung (*Soc.* 1862). Grotesque swearing which was used after Wagner had allowed his *Ring* to be performed in London (1862).

Gowned (*L. Fashion*, 1890 on). Evening dressed.

The diamonds worn by Mrs Raleigh, exquisitely 'gowned'—we believed that is the word—would not bear the scrutiny of the experts of Hatton Garden.—*D. T.*, 26th September 1895.

Grab-bag (*Anglo-American*). Tombola, or lucky bag, filled with small and large prizes disguised in sawdust.

Grabber (*Thieves'*). Evasive term amongst the fraternity for a garotter.

Grabbies (*Country*). Infantry. Probably disguised grubbies, from the evident fact that the infantry are not out of the mud as are the cavalry.

Grace o' God (*Financial*). Term given to the copy of a writ issued upon a bill of exchange.

Grandfather Clock (*Peoples'*, 1868). High eight-day clock. Never had a name before this date. From an American song called 'My Grandfather's Clock,' which became popular and gave this title.

Grand Old Man (*Pol.*, 1880-90). Mr W. E. Gladstone. Mr Bradlaugh, although claiming no originality for this phrase, was the cause of its popularity, through introducing it, in reference to Mr Gladstone, in a speech at Northampton.

Five minutes later an almost painful silence, followed by a craning of necks and a general rising from chairs and benches, proclaimed the fact that the 'Grand Old Man' had been seen emerging from the central doorway at the back of the stage.—*D. T.*, September 1896. (*See* G.O.M.)

Grand Young Man (*Pol.*, 1885). Rt. Hon. Joseph Chamberlain — in contradiction to the Grand *Old* Man.

Granite-boys (*American*). People of New Hampshire, which is a granite-producing territory

Grass before breakfast (*Irish*, 18 *cent. and early* 19 *cent.*). Duel. May be a jocular derangement of grace before breakfast.

Dick Dawson had a message conveyed to him from O'Grady requesting the honour of his company the next morning to 'grass before breakfast'. — Lover, *Handy Andy*, ch. xix.

Grasses (*Printers'*). A cry directed at any one particularly polite; probably from French *gracieuse*. (*See* Bridges.)

Grave-digger (*Anglo-Ind.*, 19 *cent.*). Strong drink.

Too much 'route marching, pipe-claying, and starching' tends to dulness and apathy, whilst it leads the British soldier, when off duty, to make too free an acquaintance with the 'grave-digger', as it is termed in India.—*D. T.*, 21st August 1896.

Graved (*Sheer adopted American*). Buried. (*See* 'Nuptiated.')

Gray-mare the better horse (*Peoples'*). Praise of a wife, as more able than her husband.

Gray-mite (*American*). Vegetarian. From one Graham, who advocated severe vegetarianism. Grahamite offered an irresistible opening

Grease (*Westminster School*) — Struggle, contention, or scramble of any kind, short of actual fighting

Grease. *See* Bit o' Grease.

Grease-spot The imaginary result of a passage-at arms.

Greaser (*Navy*, 1860 82) A scornful way of describing naval engineers

Great bed of Ware (*Peoples'*). Anything very large in the furniture way The great bed of Ware was at Ware, in Hertfordshire, until near 1870. Shakespeare speaks of the Great Bed of Ware in *Twelfth Night*

Great bounce (*Am* , 1883) Death Everyday Americans, disgusted possibly with the sentimental fashion of describing death for some years (*see* Rocked to sleep, Joins the angels, Sweet bye and bye, etc., etc.) invented several grotesque paraphrases of death — (*see* Set to music) This was one of the attempts

Experience has shown that iron steamships are very dangerous in case of collisions, so the only plan now to increase ocean travel will be to build vessels entirely of india-rubber A collision between vessels would hardly do more than give the passengers the grand bounce.—*Detroit Free Press*, 1883

Great horn-spoon (*American—probably from the Dutch*) The Deity

Great Seizer (*Amer satirical*) The Sheriff

Greater Britain (*Polit*) Annexation Term seriously invented by Sir C Dilke (1885) to include all colonies.

Greater London (*Soc*) Popular, well-known 'He belongs to Greater London'—meaning that he is more than known to a mere division of society Originally invented to describe the vast modern increase in suburbs

Grecian Bend (1865-70) A satirical description of a stoop forward in walking noticed amongst women of extreme fashion during the last years of the Second French Empire, and which was due to the use of enormously high-heeled French boots The fashion fell with the Empire (*See* "Roman Fall," "Alexandra Limp," "Buxton Limp ")

Greedy Scene (*Theatrical*) An acting scene in which a principal actor or actress clears the stage in order to have it for himself or herself, and bring down the curtain upon himself.

Green mountain boys (*American*) People of Vermont—a droll translation)

Green, To be (*Railway*, not yet come to people) Be cautious, from green through the railway world being the colour signal for caution Good example of changed meaning—green still in one sense meaning foolish, inexperienced (*See* All over Red)

Greenery - yallery (*Soc* , 1880-84). Distinctive term applied to the æsthetes who affected this peculia. 'colour-tone'. Derived from W S. Gilbert's *Patience*

When we all admired maidens clad, like the Goddess Venus in an obscure minor poem, 'in mourning raiment of green and grey', when, in fact, the 'greenery yallery' view of life prevailed, then blood was at a discount, and albumen ceased to be firm in the market.—*D. N.*, 11th June 1885

Greens (*Hist Pre-reform*) Corruption of groans, no longer comprehensible after the reformation This word has got coalesced with 'agreeings'—these referring to domesticity, and thus the inexplicable 'greens' become comprehensible.

S'elp me greens, yer washup, I don't know what booze is I'm a most ill-used bloke

Grey (*Thieves'*) Evasive name for silver—from its colour presumably, and figuratively, money.

Griminess (*Literature*). Eroticism in literature, especially French

Attempt to write a novel in which the characters are 'all good' was no doubt a spirited reaction against the prevalent 'griminess' of French fiction.—*D. N.*, 19th January 1895

Grin like a Cheshire cat (*Peoples'*). Fearfullest grin of all.

Grinning at the daisy roots (*Anglo-Indian*). Dead—singular reminiscence of home fields, daisies being absent from the Hindustanee flora.

For thin potations are fortunately in favour, and the old-fashioned gormandizers of twenty dozen of oysters and unlimited stout are like the beer-swilling 'nabobs' or 'old Indians', all, in Calcutta language, 'grinning at the daisy-roots' now — *D N*, 25th September 1884.

Grinning dears (*Military*). Linesman's nick-name for 'Grenadiers'.

Groceries sundries (*Trade*). Wine and bottled spirits sold furtively on credit to women—the bills sent in to their husbands including the cost of these liquids, itemed as (groceries sundries).

Grogging (*Peoples'*). Adulteration. Took its rise from making false grog by pouring boiling water into empty whisky barrels, impregnated with the spirit. Thence passed as a well-understood word to represent adulteration in general.

Groping for Jesus (*Peoples'*, 1882). Public prayer. Derived from one of the imitative military orders of General Booth, the creator of the Salvation Army. They did actually use the cry 'Grope for Jesus—grope for Jesus', when the followers fell upon their knees.

Groundling (*Theatre*, 16 *cent.*). Occupier of the pit, probably came out of the bear-pit.

Grouse (*Army*). Grumble and growl. This is a provincial word still in extensive use for worrying and scratching.

Growler-shovers (*Peoples'*). Cabmen.

Grub-hamper (*Public Schools'*). Consignment of sweet edibles from home.

Gruel (*American*). Sloppy poetical effort.

Guanoing the mind (*Soc.*, 1847). Reading French novels. Invention of Disraeli, published in *Tancred*. Accepted by Geo. Eliot. "This is a piece of impiety which you may expect from a lady who has been guanoing her mind with French novels. This is the impertinent expression of Disraeli, who, writing himself much more detestable stuff than ever came from a French pen, can do nothing better to bamboozle the unfortunates who are seduced into reading his *Tancred*, than speaking superciliously of all other men and things."—*Life*, vol. i., p. 163.

Guess (*American-English*). Think; as 'I guess not'. Supposed to have come from U.S.A. to England, but it seems in the first place to have gone there from here. Escalus, in Shakespeare's *Measure for Measure*, replies to a question, 'I guess not'.

Guffoon (*Irish*). An awkward, shambling fellow. From Italian.

Gugusse (*French—used by certain English Catholics*). An effeminate youth who frequents the private company of priests. In Paris (1880) the word was taken from the name of one of the novels specially directed about this time at the French priesthood.

Guinea gold (*Peoples'*, 18 *cent.*). Sincere—perfect. The gold coin of the whole eighteenth century was made of gold from the coast of Guinea. It was of a magnificent yellow and gave the name to the new twenty-one shilling coin.

Guiver (*Street Boy Swells*, 1890 on). The tignasse or sweep of hair worn down on the forehead, lower and lower as the '90's proceeded. (*See* Quiff.)

Gum (*Lower Peoples'*). Said to be abbreviation of 'God Almighty'.

Gummed (*American-English Boys'*). American boys' ways of referring to age. 'He's gummed'—meaning that he has no teeth left—that he is only fit to die.

Gummed (*Amer.-Eng.*). Equal to damned. Disguised swearing. Term very common in U.S.A.

Gum-suckers. A native of Tasmania, where gum-trees abound; a fool.

Gummy (*Sporting*, 1870). Swell, a grandee. Imported by English racing book-makers who infested and infest Paris. A translation of 'gommeux'.

Gummy composer (*Musical*). Old and insipid.

Gun-flints (*Amer.*). People of Rhode Island.

Gunnery Jack (*Naval*). Gunnery lieutenant—very popular in the Navy during the Boer War, and especially after the relief of Ladysmith.

Gunning (*Amer.-Eng.*). Shooting,

Gyle (*Fast Life*, 1850-78). Shortened familiar, and secretive title for Argyle Rooms, Windmill Street.

H

H O G (*American*) Satire upon titles of honour—High Old Genius

H. Q (*Volunteers'*, 1860, etc) Abbreviation of Head Quarters

Had enough (*Street*, 19 *cent.*). Way of saying a man is drunk.

Haggis debate (*Parliamentary*) Referring to Scotland and Scotch affairs.

Hail up (*Australian*). Put up, as at an inn Also an order by a bush-ranger—an intimation to throw up the hands, so that no weapon shall be used

Haines (*American-Eng*) Intimation of sudden retreat Heard in Liverpool, whence it arrived from New York.

Hair raised (*American - Eng*). Feminine quarrelling.

Hairpin (*American Soc* , 1882) A simpleton.

Hake (*Cornish Local*) Offensive description of a man of St Ives—probably because hake is a very common fish, or possibly because it and St Ives smell equally fishy

It is an unpardonable sin to describe a gentleman of St Ives as a 'hake'—*D T*, 20th August 1896

Half-a-brewer (*Low Street*, 1850) Drunk.

Half a-doz (*Theatrical*) Short for half-a-dozen

Half-a-foot o' port (*Strand*, 19 *cent*) Glass of that wine at 'Short's'—opposite Somerset House From the height of the glass, its shape being that of the champagne beaker of the '40's

In the front department we have the 'ladies' who are the life-long companions of hard work, and enjoy their port of uncertain date, at 3½d the half foot, for the size of the long glasses warrants this description. —*People*, 20th November 1898

Halfalfanalf *See* Arfarfanarf

Half-and half *See* Arf an-arf

Half a pint of mild and bitter (*Tavern*) Intimated by a whistled phrase, well known to bar tenders, and quite as readily accepted as a spoken order throughout London—except the West district.

Half a ton of bones done up in horsehair (*Sporting*). A thin ill-conditioned young horse

Half - a - yennork (*Com London*) Half a-crown

Half-crown ball (*Mid.-Cl* , 1880) A respectable, commonplace hop

Half - go Three pennyworth of spirits, for mixing with hot or cold water

Half hour gentleman (*Soc* , 1870) A man whose breeding is only superficial (*See* For-ever gentleman).

Half - past nines (*Lond. Streets*) Very large feminine boots and shoes—nines being a large size even for men of moderate feet

Halfpenny howling swell (1870-79) An imitation howling swell—a pretender (*See* Brown)

Halfpenny-lot day (*See* 'Apenny-lot day)

Half-rats (*Peoples'*, 1897) Partially intoxicated

Half up the pole (*Street*). Half drunk (*See* Up the pole)

Hallelujah galop (*Salvationists'*) A quick hymn in $\frac{2}{4}$ or $\frac{6}{8}$ time, to which they marched—invented by General Booth to attract the multitude.

Hallelujah lass. (*See* Ally Luja Lass)

Halligator (*Coffee-house*) One of the variety of names for herring

Hamburg (*Anglo-Indian*) Bazaar rumour

Hamlets (*Theatrical*, 1885) Omelettes—started on Ash Wednesday by the actors of the Princess's Theatre, where Mr Wilson Barrett was then playing *Hamlet* These gay souls dined and supped at the Swiss Hotel, Compton Street, and necessarily therefore found themselves before omelettes They were dubbed 'Hamlets'—and they have kept the name in 'the profession'

Hammered (*N. Country Iron Trade*). Married—very local word

Hampshire hog (*Sussex*). Hampshire man. (*See* Sussex Sow.)

Hand - me - down shop (*Poor*) Illegal pawnbroker's—where halfpence are advanced upon property which the Lombardians will not look at. Used to designate the shop. (*See* Ammedown.)

Hand of Trumps (*Mid. - Class*), Bound to win. Victory.

Handful (*Mid. - Class*). Trouble, difficulty. Much to contend with.

Handy Jack (*Peoples'*). Contemptuous form of 'Jack of all trades'.

Handy man, The (*Boer War*, 1899-1900). Sailor. When the Boers (October 1899) overran Natal, the sailors who went to the front with cannon showed themselves very active.

The handy man. High praise for the naval brigade.—*People*, 1st April 1900.

Hang up (*Amer.*). Hold your tongue.

Hang up the ladle (*Soc.*, 18 *cent.*). To marry.

Hanover jacks (*Peoples'*). Imitation sovereigns. Probably originally false coins bearing the effigy of Jacobus, or James II., sent over from Germany, and passed as genuine in William III.'s reign. It may be doubted if the issuers could have been prosecuted—for their coins were not imitations of really current coin.

On searching the prisoner I found twenty-five 'To Hanover' sovereigns usually carried by magsmen, several 'Bank of Engraving' notes, and two duplicates relating to coats. — *Police Report*, 1888.

Happen on (*People's, Old*). Discover.

Happy dosser. (*See* 'Appy dosser.)

Hard and fast line (*Parliamentary*). Equal to obstinacy, argument which refuses to hear reason.

Mr Henley did not after 1870 take any prominent part in the debates. Some of his sayings will probably be always recollected in Parliament. The 'hard and fast line' and the 'ugly rush' are destined apparently to become stock phrases in our Parliamentary controversy.—*D. N.*, 10th December 1884.

Hard on the setting sun (*Anglo-Saxon Hist.*, 19 *cent.*). Phrase indicating utter scorn of the Red Indian.

'Hard on the setting sun' is a characteristic bye-word with which to signalise his humiliation.—*People*, 13th June 1897.

Hard Simpson (*Milk-sellers'*). Ice. Simpson was the general name for water up to the time when the introduction of the system of market inspectors put an end, or almost an end, to adulterated milk. This phrase came out in a police court—1865.

Hard tack (*Sailors'*). A sea biscuit. In passed-away times it *was* hard. Tack is the diminutive of tackle, to encounter. (*See* Soft tack.)

Hard up (*All Classes*). Impecunious.

Harder (*Anglo-Amer.*). Higher, in reference to betting.

Hardware (*Army and Navy*, 1880). Ammunition in general, and shells in particular. Jocular description.

If King Theebaw has had the precaution to lay in a supply of torpedoes, he may be able to give the expedition some trouble, but the chances are that the authorities at Rangoon may have had an eye on such kind of 'hardware'.—*D. N.*, 12th November 1885.

Harlequin Jack (*Low Class*). A man who shows off equally in manner and in dress; *e.g.*, 'What is 'e?—on'y a 'arlequin Jack.'

Haro. To yell. (*See* Cry haro.)

Harrico veins. (*See* 'Arrico veins.)

Harriet Lane (*Peoples'*, 1875). Australian canned meat—because it had the appearance of chopped-up meat; and Harriet Lane was chopped up by one Wainwright.

Harvested (*Amer.*). Guarded, watched over.

Hash dispensary (*Amer.*). Boarding house.

Hash-slingers (*Amer.*, 1880). College-student waiters in up-mountain hotels.

Hasty pudding (*Peoples'*). Literal—for it is flour and water boiled and completed in five minutes. (*See* Stirabout; Turn-round pudding.)

Hatter? Who's your (*See* Bad hat.)

Haussmannisation (1860-70 on). Imperious action in relation to the improvement of cities—without reference to the liberty of the subject. From Haussman, the minister of Napoleon III., under whose administration half Paris, for political purposes, was pulled down and rebuilt.

But, after all, the possibilities of improvement in this direction are strictly limited; land is too valuable, and the imperial process known as 'Haussmannisation' would not in all cases be popular. —*D T*, 12th July 1898

Have a cab (*London*). Paraphrase for admission or reproach of intoxication

Have a down (*Australian*) Bear a grudge. Very significant Saxon

Also, the handicapper would 'have a down'—as the phrase goes in Sydney—on that owner for all forthcoming races —*Ref*, 26th September 1886

Have a turn (*Pug*, 19 *cent*) A bout of fisticuffs, a pugilistic skirmish.

Ansburgh even told one of the officers that he would have liked to 'have a turn with him', placing himself at the time in a sparring attitude —*D N*, 10th April 1885

Have out (*Peoples'*, 1860) To hold a frank discussion, verging upon personalities

But she cannot forego the satisfaction of 'having it out' with her husband.—*D. N.*, 2nd April 1883

Have to rights (*Lower Peoples'*, 1880) To vanquish—frequently used in the passive voice.

Have to wait for the honey (*Devonshire*) Wait until hungry

Havelock's saints (*Military—Indian Mutiny*) Teetotallers, abstainers.

Having (*Leicestershire*). Greedy.

Mrs Deane was proud and having enough—she wouldn't let her husband stand still for want of spurring —George Eliot, *Mill on the Floss.*

Haw-haw toff (*Street*) Swell, aristocrat—'haw-haw' being an expression very common as to the opening words of upper class men, while toff is almost the sound caused by haughtily drawing in the breath with the lower lip on the edge of the upper teeth

Hawk and pigeon (*Soc.*, 19 *cent.*) Villain and victim

The station-sergeant on duty, not knowing the detective, supposed him to be the accused 'But I am the officer in the case' It was not until the real captive intervened with an explanation that hawk and pigeon were sorted out properly for the occasion'—*D T*, 17th June 1897

Hawking (*Amer*). Pouncing Derived from the action of birds of prey crashing on their quarry

Hawkins, Sir Frederic (*See* 'Awkins)

Haymaking (*College and Army*). Practical joking

A number of men go into a friend's room, find him absent, and testify to their chagrin by disturbing the arrangements of his furniture But haymaking of this sort is comparatively harmless and inoffensive —*D N*, 1882

He lies at the Pool of Bethesda (*St Beghs ?*) This comes from the German *To lie at the Pool of Bethesda* is used proverbially in Germany, in speaking of the theological candidates who are waiting for a benefice

He never does anything wrong (*Music Hall*, 1883) Satirical mode of describing a man who never does anything right 'What—bankrupt again? Oh, impossible—he never does anything wrong'

He worships his creator (*Soc*) Said of a *self-made* man who has a good opinion of himself

Heap o' coke (*Thieves', Rhyming*) Bloke—which means a comrade.

Some heaps o' coke haven't got an ounce of cheek in them until they're flatch kennurd, but they ain't worth calling into account

Heap o' saucepan lids (*Rhyming*, 1880) Rhyming with dibs—money This is one of the trade titles for money, and comes out of the hard ware trades

Heaping in (*Amer Agri*) Accumulating an argument, or debt From heaping in produce

Heapy (*Rhyming*) Bloke (a chum). Short for heap o' coke

Heated term (*Amer*) Name for the short but fierce American summer.

Hearthstone (*Coffee Palace*) Butter It results out of the term 'door-steps', as a description of the flight of three or four thick slices of bread and butter on a small plate The action of rubbing hearthstone over house-steps, and of spreading butter thinly on the slices of bread yielded this grotesque figure of speech

Heaves (*Com Class*) Spasms. Graphic description of the complaint.

Heavy hand (*Com Peoples'*) Deep trouble

Heavy merchant (*Theatr*) Man who plays the villain

Heckling (*N B*, 18-19 *cent*) Mild bullying—from cock-fighting, heckling being the process of pecking out the neck-feathers.

Heckling (*Polit.*, 1850 on). Searching enquiry by way of questions asked of political candidates. From passing hanks of raw hemp through carding machines.

There was some timid heckling, to which Mr Gladstone good-humouredly replied.—*D. N.*, 11th November 1885.

Hell and Tommy (*Old English*). Said to be Hal and Tommy, *i.e.*, Henry VIII. and Thomas Cromwell—this couple, after the fall of Woolsey, playing havoc with church property. 'I'll play hell and tommy with you!' In all probability this phrase is a corruption of 'hell and torment'.

Helter-skelter (*Historic*). Full speed. Reid says: 'Helter-skelter is a contraction of the Latin, Hilareter celerter—cheerfully and quickly.' Probably an onomatope—very fortunately applied when Van Tromp's fleet fled before the English—some ships north towards the Helder, others south towards the Scheldt (Dutch Skelder).

And helter-skelter have
I rode to thee,
And tidings do I bring.
Shakespeare, *Henry IV.*,
2 part, Act 5, Sc. 3.

He-male (*Com. London*, 1880). A full shape of male, and resulting from calling female she-male (*q.v.*).

Hemp's grown for you (*Peoples'*, 17 *cent.*). Periphrastic prognostication of the gallows—flax coming from hemp and rope from flax. Meaning that already the executioner's cord is in existence for the beneficiary referred to. (*See* 'Dance upon nothing', 'Mount the cart'.)

Henri Clark (*Drury Lane*, 1883). Flatter. From the flattering stage-mode of a singer of this name.

Her Majesty's naval police (19 *cent.*). Sharks—whose presence all over the world prevents sailors from deserting by way of harbour water.

Hercules pillars (*Lit. and Soc.—from Latin*). Limit of belief. Gibraltar and the corresponding rock on the African coast, were, for the Roman, the limits of the world of waters, and, colloquially, of any extreme statement.

Hero-hotic (*Bohemia*, 1897). Grotesque pronunciation of 'erotic' and applied to the more eccentric novels of the day.

He's saving them all for 'Lisa (*Peoples'*). Said of a good young man who will not use oaths or strike blows. This phrase arose in consequence of a row between a violent beggar and a frank young man of the people. The mendicant asked for a copper, the frank youth intimated he was saving them all for 'Lisa. A fight followed.

Hess-u-hen (*Lower Middle Class*). A way of asking for a copy of *The Sun* newspaper.

Hey lass—let's be hammered for life on Sunday! Probably, in the first place, from the work of the blacksmith at Gretna Green. It was said of him jocularly that he hammered couples together rather than married them.

Heye-glass weather (*Street*, 1860 on). Foggy—requiring the help of an eye, or rather eye-glass. Attack upon young men wearing single eye-glasses, which became common in this year.

Hidgeot (*Street*). Gutter translation of idiot.

High (*Oxford*). High Street.

Why, Oxford has laid out more than £100,000 in adding a barrack for purposes of examinations to the 'High', already sufficiently modernised by the tramway.—*D. N.*, February 1885.

High collar and short shirts (*Music Hall*, 1882). This was an attack upon the cheap swells of the period.

High time, or (intensified), **High old time** (*American*). Jovial period, enjoyment without much control.

'Look to your safes—the burglars are having a high old time of it.—G. A. Sala, *I. L. News*, 10th February 1883.

High part (*Dublin Theatrical*). Satirical phrase for the gallery.

High shelf (*Peoples'*). The ground.

Highflyer (*Nautical*). Slave-ship.

High-grade (*American-Eng.*, 1895). Superior. From railway world—meaning steep—above the general level.

High-toned coloured society (*American*, 1882). Negro-astheticism.

Higher culture (*Soc.*, 1885 on). Catch word of enthusiastic society people interested in education, who assume that all persons are capable of advanced education

Moreover, even if we neglect to organise in this way the force which appears to be thus mysteriously making for 'the higher culture,' its mere appearance among us is a highly encouraging sign —*D T*, 11th February 1897

Highland fling (*Political*, 1881) Series of speeches in Scotland When Gladstone (1879-80) delivered his famous Midlothian speeches, this term was applied to the statesman's efforts, and has since been accepted as representing a political speech delivered in Scotland

Hill-top literature Solid advice. Derived from danger-board warnings to cyclists on the summits of steep hills.

The attention which is now being given to that form of 'hill top literature', known as 'danger-boards', has resuscitated some stories concerning them It is said that in Ireland a tourist went down a steep and dangerous hill and was astonished to observe that it seemed to be without the necessary warning However, when he got to the foot of the descent he found the notice, 'This hill is dangerous to cyclists' —*D T*, 14th July 1898

Hinchinarfer (*Streets*, 1880 on) Gruff-voiced woman, with shrieking sisterhood tendencies Obscure erotic

His hand was out (*Peoples'*) Ready to take all and everything at all times

Histed (*American, outlying*). Vigilance committee evasion for hanged Corruption of hoisted — pronounced high-sted

Historical (*Society*, 1882) Old fashioned—said of a costume or bonnet which has been seen more than three times

Now, though dinner-dresses are rich, costly, and elaborate, if a lady appears at a fourth dinner or even a third in the same gown, it is immediately dubbed historical —*Fashion as it was and is*, *D N*, 26th December 1882

Hitch up (*Anglo-American*) Start From harnessing two horses to run abreast.

Ho—he's got the white coat (*Provincial*) Meaning he is drunk

Hold a candle (*Peoples'*). Be humble Serve abjectly, as seen in the proverb Took its rise from the habit of a host receiving an honoured guest by holding a candle in each hand and walking backwards before the arrival

Hold stock (*Eng -American*, 1879) Assertion of possession. From the money brokering operations in New York

I do not come as a grievance monger or complainant I do not ask for your pity, and have not the faintest feeling of revenge. Those were the passions of youth—a delightful period in which, as our American friends phrase it, no longer 'held any stock' —Mr E Yates, at Dinner given to him, London, 31st May 1885

Hold up (*Society*, 1860 on). To be cheated or turned to account. From the American highway-man's habit of calling upon his victim to 'hold up' his hands, that he may not fire

Holding up the corner (*Anglo-American*) Satirical description of a leaning idler

Hollanders (*S. London*, 1875-85) Pointed waxed moustache When Napoleon III became popular in England (1854) many adopted the chin-tuft or goatee he wore—a tuft to which the necessary name imperial was given. During the first half of the 19th century no face hair in England was possible below the mutton-chop whisker—probably from national horror of the over-bearded faces of the French revolutionaries A Mr W Holland became a popular lessee—he at last reaching Covent Garden Theatre Throughout his public life he grew, and always had on hand, or rather on upper lip, the finest pair of black waxed sheeny moustaches ever beheld.

Holler Cuss (*London*, 1899) From Holocauste—a French horse in the Derby of 1899 There is here also a little satire, for the horse in question showed several faults in form.

Holocauste, colloquially 'Holler Cuss', excited some ribald remarks by reason of his peculiar hue —*D T*, 1st June 1899

Holloway Castle (*Peoples'*) Prison at Holloway (chiefly for debt), in the north of London, hence, sometimes called North Castle, as more evasive than Holloway

It may be taken as highly improbable that Her Grace (of Sutherland) will be subjected to the indignities which are

[illegible]

[illegible]

Hug centre (*Amer.—passing to England*). Head-quarters of public love-making.

Central Park as a hug centre. The amount of love made visible in Central Park is simply appalling. — *N. Y. Mercury*, December 1882.

The word was soon taken up in London, Hyde Park doing duty as a 'hug centre'.

Hullabaloo (*Peoples'*). Noise, disturbance. It would appear to be a corruption of the French *hurluberlu*—the accent on the two 'lu's'.

Hullo, features! (*Com. Peoples'*). Friendly salute upon meeting an acquaintance.

Hullo, my Buck! (*Peoples'*). Exclamation of approbation. Possibly from Villiers, Duke of Buckingham, or from the idea of a fine deer. Or it may be from buckram, the first stiffening used in making men's clothes. In that case it is a metaphor from the man to his fashion.

Hum (*Navy*). Crew's name for the *Hermes*.

Hum (*Lower Classes*, 19 *cent.*). Smell evilly. This is an application from the humming of fermentation in an active manure heap.

Hum (*Peoples'*, *Hist.*). Attract attention.

Mr Douglas Sladen has given new life to an old and somewhat decrepit annual; a new life that makes it 'hum' in the very direction the reading world desires. —*People*, 4th April 1897.

Hunder-hand (*Street Boys*, 1880). Sudden blow given with advantage.

Hung (*Artists'*, 19 *cent.*). Picture accepted and hung at an Exhibition. "I'm hung at the Ac." (*See* Walled.)

Hung up (*Soc.*, 1879). Said where in lower classes stuck up would be used. From the American — where personal catastrophe is referred to by this phrase. (*See* Screwed up.)

Hunkered down (*American prairie*). Stooped, anchored down.

Hunter (*Soc.*, 1880). Hunting watch.

Jennings was on Friday presented with a gold hunter and chain, by a few of his kind friends in front, who took this opportunity of expressing their opinion of his form as man and manager.—*Ref.*, 9th August 1885.

Hupper sukkles (*Soc.*, 1846-70). Upper circles. Introduced by Thackeray in the *De la Pluche Papers.*

Hurry up (*Anglo-Indian*, 1850). Be quick—originated in the river steamer navigation of U.S.A.

Hustler (*Amer. Circus*). Name invented for flaming advertisements.

Hyde Park railings (*Streets of W. London*). Breast of mutton—from the parallel bones suggesting the parallel railings.

Hyking (*Peoples'*). Calling out at or after any one.

I

I. T. A. (*Peoples'*). Euphemism for Irish toothache (*q.v.*).

I believe you, my boy (*L. Class*). Certainly. Accepted by middle-class about 1850—from the drama of *The Green Bushes*, in which Paul Bedford, then a most popular actor, used the phrase as a catch line.

'Tis forty years since Buckstone's drama *The Green Bushes*, was first played at the Adelphi, and since Paul Bedford's 'I believe yer, my boy!' found its way on to tongues of the multitude. —*Ref.*, 18th October 1885.

I refer you to Smith (1897). Synonym of Ananias—champion long bowyer, etc. From a character named Smith with an affliction of lying in *The Prodigal Father* (Strand Theatre, 1897).

'I refer you to Smith.' This will be the new London catchword. Whenever anyone has been drawing the long bow, as Harry Paulton does in the new play, whenever a boaster has been telling tarradiddles or lying with extra vivacity, he will be met with the quick rejoinder, 'I refer you to Smith'.—*D. T.*, 2nd February 1897.

I say (*Peoples'*, 19 *cent.*). Protest.

Ichabod (*Nonconformist*). Lamentation. From Biblical source. 'Ichabod—Ichabod—I have lost my wealth. The Lord be praised.'

Idle fellowships (*Oxford and Cambridge*). The old as distinct from the new fellowships. Parliamentary action swept away towards the end of the

19th century most of these fatal sinecures

Much has been said against what are called idle Fellowships.—*D N*, November 1884

Ietqui (*C L —Sporting*) A remarkable shape of phrasing, where the first letter or so is removed from the beginning of the word and added at the end The word is 'quiet'

Ile (*Complicated rhyming*) Dance—Isle of France—dance 'Can't he ile?'

I'll give you Jim Smith (*Street*, 1887) Thrashing Sudden adoption of the name of a prize fighter to designate fighting

Imperial pop (*Street*, 1854) Pop is ginger beer, derived of course from the sound made when drawing the cork The adjective was added by street sellers of this refreshment when Napoleon III passed in state through London

Imperialists (*Polit*, 1888 on) Name found by the Radicals (who were in favour of the abandoning of the colonies) for the Conservatives, who wished the Empire to remain intact

Impressionist (*Soc*, 1884) Intensely appealing directly to the emotions

Of late years we are accustomed to take our notions of French dramatic art from something more 'impressionist', more vivid and rapid and startling, depending more on sudden effects and bold splashes of light and shade —*D. N*, 29th April 1885

Improve the occasion (*American*) Take advantage of it

In (*Peoples'*) Gain 'I'm nothing in by that deal' (*See* Out)

In and out (*Common*) Pauper who gives notice frequently to leave the poor-house, and who returns after a short holiday, say a day, or from Saturday to Monday.

There are considerable numbers of paupers, it seems who find the workhouse a convenient retreat on emergency, but have a strong aversion to permanent residence there They are known familiarly as 'the ins-and-outs' —*D N.*, 10th December 1884

In for a bad thing (*Peoples'*, 1880 on) To have ill luck

'You are in for a bad thing, Phil, my boy'—*E N*, 23rd February 1896

In Paris (*Soc.*, 19 *cent*). Eloped

In the drag (*Tailors'*) Behindhand.

Incident (*Amer —accepted in England*) An illegitimate child.

Indorse (*Amer*). To sanction

Inferior portion (*Polit*, 1885) Eighties party of younger Tories From a letter written by Mr W E Gladstone, which commenced

My Dear Sir,—In 1879 and 1880 the inferior portion of the Tory party circulated a multitude of untruths concerning me, etc

The phrase took at once, and was satirically used.

Ink-bottle (*Artisans'*). A clerk

Inkslinger (*Navy*) Purser's clerk Term of sovereign contempt

Innocent (*Thieves', Hist.*) Referring to a term of undeserved condemnation

An ex-convict, who admitted having undergone long terms of penal servitude, applied to Mr Denman, at Westminster, complaining that his worship gave him three months' 'innocent' in May 1893 at South-Western Police Court.—*D T*, 16th October 1896.

Inquiry note (*Theat*, 1860) Term came into use when provincial companies were replaced by travelling ones It is a letter asking for information as to what nights a theatre may be had for performance.

Ins (*Political*, 19 *cent*) The Ministerial side of the House of Commons (*See* Outs)

Inside (*Thieves'*) Abbreviation of 'inside a prison'

Beaufort's duke trots by, and then dashes past a once member of the dangerous classes, who has been 'inside' many a time and oft, but who, having run into a bit of ready, will now go straight while straightness pays.—*Ref*, 14th October 1888

Inside of (*American*) A very emphatic synonym for 'within'.

Inside the mark (*Anglo-Amer*) Moderate

Inside the probable (*American—reaching England*) Within probability

Introduce shoemaker to tailor (*Peoples'*) Evasive metaphor for fundamental kicking.

Inventories (*Soc*, 1885) Play upon the word inventions In the previous year a series of industrial exhibitions had been started in the then gardens of the S. Kensington Museum. This initial display was the 'Fisheries', and from that time the successive exhibitions had their titles changed into plurals in 'ries'. Hence the 'Inventions' became the Inventories.

As all the world knows by now, London was very near losing its 'Inventories' on Friday, for about noon a fire broke out there, and for some time threatened to be a big thing.—*Ref.*, 14th June 1885.

This is the close of the season. I suppose the Kensington Inventories has had the best of it, and owing to this fact I imagine many of the managers may be deprived of that great pleasure—paying income-tax.—Mr J. L. Toole's closing speech, Toole's Theatre, 7th August 1885.

Inveterate Cockney (*Political*, 1885). Ignorant of country life—a mere townsman.

. . . Now, gentlemen, there are three assumptions in this calculation, every one of which I, an 'inveterate Cockney', can see at a single glance to be totally inaccurate.—Mr Joseph Chamberlain, 14th October 1885.

Invincibles (*Fenian*, 1883). Short for Invincible Brotherhood.

Irish draperies (*Peoples'*, *England*). Cobwebs.

Irish toothache (*Peoples'*). *Enceinte.* (*See* I. T. A.)

Irishman's rest (*Peoples'*). Going up a friend's ladder with a hod of bricks.

Irons (*American*). Pistols.

Irvingism (*Lond. Soc.*, 1880 on). Imitation on or off the stage of the mode of speaking and bearing of Sir Henry Irving.

Mr William Felton may also be heard of again. The 'Irvingism' of his voice was obviously natural and in no way assumed.—*D. T.*, 12th October 1896.

Islands (*London*). Refuges (*q.v.*) or raised pavements in centre of roads, to facilitate road-crossing by pedestrians.

The statue (Charles I., Charing Cross) being situated on an 'island,' a certain amount of skirmishing was necessary in order to reach it.—*D. T.*, 31st January 1899.

It snowed (*Peoples'—from America*). Catastrophe, misery.

Italian quarrel (*Soc.*). Death, poison, treachery, remorselessness.

It's doggéd as does it (*Pugilistic*). Perseverance.

Mr Benjamin's race and nation have generally shown themselves perfectly alive to the truth of the principle that 'it's dogged as does it', and they are not as a rule devoid of wits.—*D. N.*, 10th February 1883.

J

J. (*Peoples'*). Lost reduction of Juggins (*q.v.*)—which in 1884 was quite exceptionally popular.

By means of this knowledge we find the greatest of all differences between the raid on betting men in 1869 and the raid on professional gamblers and their J.'s twenty years after.—*Ref.*, 19th April 1889.

J.A.Y. (*Peoples'*, 1880 on). Fool, over-trustful person, one of easy belief.

Our business is not, however, with them or their intentions; what we have to do is to think of the jays who offered about ten times the market price for a ten-round spar.—*Ref.*, 17th November 1889.

J. S. or N. or D. (*Divorce Court*). The initials of the three forms of disturbance amongst married folk.

Whether it was an application for a divorce, a judicial separation, or for nullity of marriage, no one outside the parties interested will, probably, ever be any the wiser, since the letter indicating this (either 'J. S.', or 'N.', or 'D.', as the case may be) was not added in this instance, for some inscrutable reason.—*People*, 16th August 1896.

Jack (*Lambeth*, 1865-72). A policeman—quite local.

Jack-a-dandy (*Rhyming*). Brandy. This evolution has something probably to do with brandy, as being the most expensive of the ordinary spirits.

Jack ashore (*Peoples'*). Jack elevated — practically drunk, and larky.

Jack up (*Street*). To quit — especially in love affairs.

Jacked it (*Obscure*). Died.

Jacket (*Military*). A soldier who wears a jacket (chiefly cavalry or horse artillery).

Jacket, To (*Peoples'*). Threat to have you locked up as a madman.

Jag (*Spanish - American - Eng*) Desire to use a knife against somebody —to jag him

Jaggers (*Oxford*) Men of Jesus College

Jesus College men were called 'Jaggers', long before a certain messenger - boy played the part of Mercury across the Atlantic.—*D T*, 14th August 1899

Jailed (*Peoples'*, 1879) Sent to prison From America, through Liverpool, over England

Jakkitch (*Provincial*) Term of opprobrium. Probably corruption of Jack Ketch

Jam (*Lower Class*, 1880 on) Pretty girl—presumably of easy habits The history of this word is very interesting A girl of notoriety in Piccadilly was named 'Tart' She, in compliment to her sweetness, came to be styled jam tart, and the knowing ones would ask— 'Would you like a bit of jam tart?' Then the tyranny of brevity asserting itself, the phrase became 'jam', which lasted twenty years.

Here's a timely warning for all burlesque writers The Examiner of Plays, which his name is Pigott, has determined that he will not give his sanction to the production of any piece in which the word 'tart' occurs It is not yet known whether orders have been issued from headquarters to all dictionary publishers to wipe the word out of the English language, but the order has been sent, or will be, first to the burlesque makers, and to the dictionary-makers it may be sent tart-er —*Ref*, 27th October 1889

Jam-pot (*Political*, 1883-84) One of the opprobrious names cast at Mr Gladstone—*apropos* to his recommending to Englishmen the cultivation of fruit and the exportation of jam

Mr Gladstone is insulted day after day and week after week in Tory prints. He is a jam pot, a wood cutter, a hopeless lunatic, a Jesuit, an Atheist, a windbag, a storyteller, an idiot, and a humbug — G R Sims, 28th September 1884

Jammiest bits of jam (*Com Lon.*, 1883) Absolutely perfect young females

Jane Shore's fate (*Provincial—very ancient*) Death in penury and shame.

Jap crock (*Soc*, 1860 on) Any piece of Japanese porcelain of a value from £10,000 to a mere 10d

Japanned (*Soc*, 1897-98) Dressed or furnished in Japanese fashion. Play upon the old word for lacquering

The play is 'japanned' by Mr Arthur Diósy of the Japan Society — From Daly's Theatre, London, play - bill, 1897-98.

Jarbee (*Navy*) Able seaman.

Jaundy (*Navy*) Master-at-arms Supposed to be from 'gendarme'

Jaunty (*Peoples'*) Self-sufficient in appearance or words

Jawkins (*Club*, 1846). A club bore. Name-word derived from Thackeray's 'Book of Snobs'

Jay town (*Anglo - Amer*, 1889) Valueless.

A brother-journalist who has spent some years in the United States has written explaining to me the meaning of a '*jay* town'—term alleged to have been used by Mrs Kendal in describing San Francisco A *jay* town is a *country* town A 'jay' or a 'yapp' is the American equivalent of an English yokel or country bumpkin —*Ref*, 25th November 1894

Jayhawkers (*American*) People of Kansas

Jee (*American*) Oath-like expression First syllable of Jerusalem. 'Jee! You don't dare to do it!'

Jeff (*Anglo - American*, 1862 - 83). Master, superintendent, director, manufacturer

Jenny, To (*Thieves'*) Comprehend

Jeremiah, To (*Peoples'*) To complain — from the character of that prophet.

Jeremiah-mongering (*Soc*, 1885) Deplorable and needless lamentation Invented to describe the social behaviour of those who after the fall of Khartoum went around maintaining that England had indeed come to a finality

Jerking a wheeze (*Theatrical*, 1860) Telling a wheeze (*q v*) with brilliant effect.

Jersey hop (1883) An unceremonious assembly of persons with a common taste for valsing, from Jersey, U S A

Jesus'-eyes (*Papal*) Forget - me - nots.

Jettisonise (*Col*, 19 *cent*) Imported—placed on a jetty

Jeune siècle (*Soc.*, 20 *cent.*). Conversion of *fin de siècle*, and describing people equally of the same social behaviour. Of course from Paris.

Jib (*Soc.*, 1848-80). Flat-folding, 'chimney-pot' hat, closed by springs set in centre of vertical ribs. Name from that of the French inventor 'Gibus'.

Jib, Big (*Navy*). Good wishes—'Long may your big jib draw' ostensibly refers to a valuable sail, but furtively has an erotic meaning. Practically it is wishing a man, who has served his time and is leaving the service, health and happiness.

Jiggot o' mutton (*Thieves'*). French—gigot.

Jimmies (*Hist.*, 17 *cent.*). Guineas—in the reign of James II. Remains to this day.

Jimmy Bungs (*Navy*). Coopers.

Jimmy Rounds (*Nelsonic Period*). Frenchmen—according to the Jack Tar of the wars with France in Nelson's time. From the cry of the French sailor when face to face with the English mariner—*je me rends*.

Joburg (*Military*, 1900 on). Johannesburg.

Jinks the Barber (*M. Class*, 1850). Secret informant. Idea suggested by the general barber being such a gossiper. Jinks is a familiar name for an easy-going man. Invented by Pierce Egan.

Job (*Peoples'*, *Hist.*). Hen-pecked husband. Patient origin obvious. Douglas Jerrold gave this Biblical name to Mr Caudle.

Jobanjeramiah (*Peoples'*). Maunderer—combination of the two doleful patriarchs.

Jockies, By (*American-Provincial*). Said to be survival of early English; 'By Jesus' cries.

Jockeying (*London Streets*, 19 *cent.*). Vehicular racing.

Joey (*Theatrical*). To mug, or attract the attention of the public, while the 'mugger' is up the stage, and should be quiet, letting actors "down the stage" have their chance.

John Fortnight (*Workmen's London*). The tallyman—from his calling every other week.

The tallyman, or 'John Fortnight', as the humorists call him, and the caller for the club-money secure varying receptions.

Johnny Crapose (*Peoples'*). Frenchmen. The second word is 'crapaud', but how comes it that this word has been accepted in conjunction with Johnny to describe a Frenchman?

Johnny Horner (*Rhyming*). Round the corner—meaning a public-house.

Joined the angels (*Amer.*, 1880). One of the ways of mentioning death. 'Do not ask me after my dear John Thomas—he has joined the angels.'

Joint (*Street*). Wife.

Jolly (*Middle Class*). Rally, a shout, a chevy. This word is evidently very old.

> He chanced to come where was a jolly Knight.—*Spenser.*
> Those were jolly days.—*Dryden.*
> While the jolly horns lead on propitious day.—*Milton.*
> The jolly hunting band convene.
> —*Beattie.*

Jolly utter (*London*, 1881). One of the phrases resulting out of Punch's attack (1881) upon the Æsthetic School. This is to be found in Sir W. S. Gilbert's piece *Patience.*

Broken Hearts is rather a ticklish piece to tackle. Badly or even carelessly played, the love-sickness and the moon-struckness would be quite too jolly utter for the ordinary Philistine mind to stand.—*Ref.*, 18th February 1883.

Jonah (*Theatrical*, 1883). An actor who brings bad luck to a theatre. Suggests the superstition of the evil eye. From Jonah's supposed ill-luck—bringing catastrophe, when at sea. Apt antithesis to Mascotte.

Joseph and Jesse (*Polit.*, 1886). Political satiric cry against Mr Joseph Chamberlain and Mr Jesse Collings, raised immediately after the latter took office (February 1886).

The amendment did not expressly contain the principle of compulsion, and the speech of Mr Collings is not binding upon the House of Commons or the Government. But, as Mr Chaplin rather neatly put it on the night of his last appearance as Chancellor of the Duchy, 'the voice is the voice of Jesse, the hand is the hand of Joseph.—*D. N.*, 26th February 1886.

Josser (*Hong-Kong*). A swell, a grandee. From joss, the name of the figures of Chinese gods, with the personal 'er' added. Suggested by observation of the request paid by the Chinese to the 'joss'

Jubilee (*Mid Class*, 1887) The Jubilee (1887) came to be applied in many ways — but one, satirically descriptive of supremacy chiefly survived

Judaic superbacey (*C. Garden and vicinity*, 1897) Jew in all the glory of his best clothes—generally a young Joseph, or a young old David.

Judy - slayer (*London, Jewish*) Lady-killer.

Juggins's boy (*L. Lond*, 1882) The sharp and impudent son of a stupid and easily ridiculed father

Juggins-hunting (*Tavern*). Looking for a man who will pay for liquor

Jumbo (*London*, 1882) Anything particularly large and striking became a 'jumbo'—there being at this time a large elephant of that name in the Zoo

The vulgar assert that Epsom is a very hotbed of training theories, and it must be admitted that it has its peculiarities in this direction Nay, did it not produce the genial Mr Ellis, whom the wicked called 'Jumbo'?—*E N*, 23rd January 1896

Mr Ellis was a big, heavy, solemn official. Some months after Jumbo's expatriation, a very tall man appeared in Drury Lane Theatre, and all the boys on hand yelled 'Jumbo', an amiable Bavarian eight-foot giantess was trotted out at a music hall—she was at once baptised Jumba by the very press itself

Jumbo (*Tavern*, 1882). The Elephant and Castle Tavern, S. London (*See* Animal)

Jumboism (*Polit*, 1882) The Liberals having invented Jingoism to describe the warlike tendency of the Conservative party, this latter took advantage of the Jumbo craze to dub the hesitative policy of the Liberal Whigs jumboism

Jump bail (*Anglo-American*) To run away from it Both jumped their bail.

Jumped up swell (*Street*) Sudden leap from rags to royal raiment; also a toff in a hurry

Jumping Moses (*Amer. - Eng.*) Exclamation equivalent to Great Heaven

June too-too (*Peoples'*, 1897). June 22 in 1897—the celebration of the sixtieth anniversary of the Queen's reign Survival, or rather resuscitation of the phrase 'too too', satirically directed against æstheticism in the '80's — meaning (satirically) too, too good Here used as a comic variation of '22'—two two

Jupiter Scapin (*Parisian*, 1810) Napoleon I Used in England now and again to indicate a tricky minister.

Just ached (*American*) Longed.

Just too sweet for anything (*American*) Highest form of praise.

K

K A B G N A L S. (*Mystic*) The letters of back slang (less the needless 'c'), and uttered rapidly to indicate that this mode of conversation will be agreeable to speaker Another form is Kabac genals.

Kangaroo (*Nautical in origin*). A tall, thin man, especially ill-shaped and round-shouldered.

Kansas neck - blister (*American*). Bowie-knife

The same with a knife Horsemen, when travelling, carry it in the boot, and footmen down the neck, hence a bowie-knife is popularly known as a 'Kansas neck-blister'. — *All Year Round*, 31st October 1883

Kapswalla (*N American-Indian*). To steal—adopted from the original by American thieves

Katterzem (*Scotland*). Quartorsième A man willing to go out dining at a moment's notice—a parasite.

Kee gee (*E London*, 1860). Go, vigour.

Keep off the grass (*Peoples'*). Be cautious

Keep the boiler clear (*Engineers'*, 1840) Watch your stomach — in reference to health.

Keep the devil out of one's clothes (*American — probably from Dutch*). To fight against poverty.

Keep up, old queen (*Street*). Valediction addressed by common women to a sister being escorted into a prison van.

Keep yer 'air on (*L. Class*, 1800 on). A favourite monitory proverb recommending patience as distinct from impatience, and tearing the 'air off.

Keep your nose clean (*Army*). Avoid drink.

Keep yourself good all through (*Soc.*, 1882). Modern paraphrase of Keep yourself unspotted from the world.

Keeping Dovercourt (*E. Anglia*). Making a great noise. Dovercourt (Essex) was once celebrated for its scolds—this we have on the authority of Halliwell. On the other hand the term may come from the great noise made by a local insect called the Dovercourt beetle.

Kemble pipe (*Hereford*). Last pipe of the evening. An ancestor of John Kemble, a Catholic priest, suffered martyrdom at Hereford, in the seventeenth century. On his way to execution he smoked his pipe and conversed with his friends.

Kenealyism (*Soc.*, 1874). Social method composed of alternate profound humility and complete rebuke — supposed to have been invented from Dr Kenealy, who in this year defended Arthur Orton, called 'the claimant', upon a charge of perjury. Orton claimed to be Sir Roger Tichborne.

Kentucky loo (*Students'*). Summer gaming operation. (*See* Fly loo.)

Kepple's snob (*Naval*, 1870). Expression of scorn by superfine naval young officers. 'The Kepple's Head', named after the admiral. The naval clubmen have converted knob into snob. 'Cut him—he puts up at the "Kepple's snob".'

Kerwollop (*Amer.*, 19 *cent.*). To beat, or wallop. 'Ker' is also frequently used before words implying movement, as kersmash, kerbang, kerash (crash), kerflummux, kerslap. (*See* Artemus Ward—'I went kerwallop over the fence.')

Kew (*Reverse Slang*). Week—spelt with one 'e'.

Key-vee (*Peoples'*, 1862). Alert, on the key-vee — of course a corruption of 'qui vive,' the French sentry challenge.

Khaki is a tint once called Devonshire grey. It was recommended by a military convention (1882) to replace the scarlet cloth of the British army—this scarlet being condemned in consequence of its offering a ready mark for the distant bullet.

Khaki (*Military*, February 1900). Volunteer—especially yeomanry volunteer for the Boer war, 1899-1900. Applied in all ways—to pease-pudding amongst many, from the colour. Hence resulted in common eating-houses the order, 'Cannon and Khaki,' *i.e.*, round beef-steak pudding and a dump of pease-pudding.

Kibe? (*University*). To whose benefit? Abbreviation of 'cui bono'.

Kick (*Anglo-American*). To succeed in pleasing audience.

Kick (*Costermongers'*). Trousers—short for kicksies, probably from the garment being that in which the wearer uses his boots at angles. Or it may be from 'quelques choses'.

'That dona's dotty,' said Obadiah, as he gazed upon his half-a-dollar, and put it carefully away in his only kick; 'and now for a jolly spree.'

If the burick (wife) wears the kicksies, that's your luck, not ours.

Kick is also used by thieves for 'pocket', probably because the kicksies or trousers have pockets. Fine example of application of the title of a whole to a portion.

When your kick is empty, and your mouth is dry, your blooming pals will not give you a yannep to get a drop of four thick.

Kick (*Trade-tailors'*). To seek for work — probably suggested by a barbarous mode of kicking at a door, before knocker or bell was invented.

Kick a lung out (*Anglo-Amer.*). Severe castigation.

Kick into dry goods (*American*). To dress—clothes being dry goods.

Kick up my dust in the park (*Soc.*). Promenade there. From French 'Faire ma poussière aux Champs Elysées'.

Kick out (*Anglo-American*). Die—from the frequent nervous movement of the legs as death approaches.

Kicked the cat (*L. Class*). Shown signs of domestic dissatisfaction.

Kid-catcher (*L. School Board*, 1869 on) L S B official who beat up school tenants.

Coroner. How did you escape the school board officers?—Witness I don't know how I managed to escape the 'kid-catcher', sir, but I did it.—*People*, 30th August 1896

Kill who? (*Peoples'*, 1870 on). Satirical protest against a threat, and an assertion of quiet bravery

Kill with kindness (*Peoples'*) This phrase is not generally understood, supposed to be literal. Really means to cause shame by overwhelming with satirical attentions a person who has misbehaved himself It is not forgiveness, but retaliation.

Killing the canary (*Bricklayers'*). Shirking work.

Kilmainham (*Political*, 1882) Compromise Said of an arrangement in which each of two parties concedes something to the other in order that a third party may be defeated. Took its rise early in 1882, when the Con servative opposition unintentionally brought about the Kilmainham Treaty

Kin'd (*Soc*, 1884) Satirical pronunciation of kind Result of Barrett's production of *Hamlet* (October 1884) wherein he made this reading 'A little more than kin and less than kin'd.'

Kingsman of the rortiest (*Sporting*, early 19 *cent*). Square, folded necktie of high colours

Kippers (*Navy*) Stokers Very probably because they are so smoke dried, and dark of complexion.

Kiss-curl (*Peoples'*, 1854 60) Flat temple curl, abandoned by middle-class in 1860 or about. Still seen in S E London, where it is patronised by the street belles of that locality

Kite (*American*, 19 *cent*) The face

Kite, Blow out the (*Com Lond*) To have a full stomach—suggested either by an inflated bladder, or a soldier's full 'kit'.

Klobber (*E London*) Jewish for best or state clothes generally

Kate Vaughan was perhaps a trifle too dainty, and I fancy any Kitty so circumstanced, on the sudden return of master in the midst of unlawful revelry, would have taken some pains to cover up the resplendent and unaccustomed 'klobber'—I believe that is the aristocratic term, Kate ought to know, now—donned for the occasion —*Ref*, 17th May 1885

'And belted knight
Isn't such a sight
As Becky Moss in her klobr.'

'So I klobbered myself up as well as circs would permit.'

K' mither (*Provincial*). Corruption of "Come hither"—a woman of the town

Klondyke (*Peoples'*, 1897 on) Mad—not fit to be trusted From the craze that set in August 1897 around the Klondyke gold-bearing district

Klondyke fever (*July*, 1897) Rush for gold in British Columbia Began in this month, increased as the year waned.

Klondike gold fever has 'caught on' in the City . . .—*D T.*, 31st July 1897

Knapsack descent (*Peoples'*). Soldiers in a family, either on the father's or mother's side, and very possibly both

Knee-drill (*Peoples'*, 1882). Hypocritical praying. Derived from the military terms introduced into prayer meetings by the Salvation Army.

Knickerbocker (*N. York*). Man or woman in best society in New York. Accepted from opponents and made a class word.

Knife (*Lowest Lond*, 19 *cent*). A shrew—suggestive of being 'into you' in a moment

Knife (*Theatrical*, 1880 on). Condense a piece Knife is now modified into blue pencil.

Knife and fork tea (*Middle Class*, 1874) Vulgarisation of high tea (*see*)

Knights of the Jemmy (*Soc.*, 19 *cent*) Burglars—the arms of the cavaliers in question being jemmies, the modern name for short crow-bars

Some seasons ago the place was overrun by knights of the jemmy, who committed their depredations on other people's property in the coolest manner possible, and yet contrived to evade capture —*D T*, 8th August 1896.

Knock about drolls (*See* Athletic drolls.)

Knock along (*Austral*). To idle.

There is an Australian phrase, isn't there, with reference to an idle fellow? they say he goes 'knocking along'.—I am not aware that it is an Australian phrase. We get our bad language from England.

The Lord Chief Justice: 'Knocking along' is not an English phrase. It is 'knocking about'.

Dr Kenealy: Well, it is 'knocking along'. I don't think it an improvement on the English phrase.—Tichborne Case, 1874.

Knock fairly silly (*Lower Class*) Almost, if not quite annihilated.

Capt. Thatcher said that when they first came in touch with the Boers they expected to be attacked, and they were. But they 'knocked the Boers fairly silly' and then made for Krugersdorp at a hand-gallop all the way.—*People*, 16th February 1896.

Knock in (*Costermongers'*). To make money—into the pocket understood.

Knock in (*Club*). Make one at a card table.

Knock off corners (*Music Hall*, 1880). Be successful.

Just as Arthur Williams had commenced to 'knock corners off' at the music hall, he is once more summoned to the Gaiety. More study!—*Entr'acte*, 16th April 1885.

Knock-upable (*Soc.*). Open to being knocked up.

For some time I have been weak and knock-upable.—G. Eliot's *Life*, vol. i., p. 440.

Knocker on the front door (*Peoples'*). Achieve respectibility.

Knows how many go to a dozen (*Hist.*). Sharp. Even to this day many things are sold thirteen to the dozen—especially books and newspapers. 'Thirteen' is generally called a baker's dozen from thirteen loaves being sold as a dozen, exactly as thirteen rolls in our days go to the dozen.

Knuckle end (*Cornwall*). The extreme west of the duchy—the Land's End, so named from its shape.

Kodak (*Soc.*, 1890 on). To surreptitiously obtain shape-information. From the snap-shot photographic camera—named after its inventor.

We are watching him (Sir Henry Irving, *Richard III.*), our eyes are riveted on his face, we are interested in the workings of his mind, we are secretly kodaking every expression, however slight.—*D. T.*, 21st December 1896.

Kollah (*Hebr.-Yiddish*). A bride. Often spelled calloh (*q.v.*).

Kop-gee (*Peoples'*, 1899). Last discovery of the century for head—from the Transvaal kopje or mound.

Kosal Kasa (*Hebrew—Trade*). 1s. 6d.—the Hebrew words for '1' and '6'.

Kosher (*E. Lond.*, *Judaic*). Pure—undefiled. Word used by the Jews in reference to eatables, and especially alcoholic drinks at certain feasts of the year, especially Passover and Pentecost. The word is here written phonetically, but in actuality the vowels are omitted K SH R, or rather R SH K, to be very precise. The antithesis of this word is Trifer—unclean, unholy, written T R F R.

Kruger-spoof (*Peoples'*, 1896). Lying. From the promises of fair dealing forwarded in January 1896, made by the President of the Transvaal republic, and not kept.

Kwy (*Fast Life*, 1800-40). First syllable of 'quietus'—death.

Kyacting (*Navy*). Jocularity during work.

'Here, knock off that "kyacting", will you?' an irate P.O. will say if he sees a youngster playing the fool instead of attending to his work.—Rev. G. Goodenough, R.N.

Kypher (*L. Class*). To dress hair—from the French 'coiffer'.

L

L., The (*N. York*, 1880 on). The Elevated Railway.

We have in New York a rich man who is almost the counterpart of Hetty Green. I refer to Mr Russell Sage. He was once associated with Jay Gould, and between them they engineered the 'L,' or Elevated Railroad of New York, much to their advantage, as most people imagine.—*D. T.*, 18th February 1897.

L. L. (*Dublin Tavern*). Best whisky. Initials of Lord Lieutenant.

L. L. (*Financial*, 1870 on). Initials of Limited Liability, and used satirically to suggest fraud.

La! (*Suburban London*). Nimminypimminy for the vulgar 'lor!' which is an abbreviation of the exclamation 'Lord!'

La-di-da (*Street*). Elegant leisure, and liberal expenditure

Laagered (*S African*) Waggon-defence. The waggons are zig-zagged in line or in square, so that the head of one waggon is half way down the side of the next—thus giving an extended firing line, while the length of the waggon is used to offer its fullest protection as compared with its width.

For several hours after we were laagered in position on Monday to receive the attack, concealed behind trees and tall grass, their sharp shooters kept up a scathing fire —*D N*, 29th January 1885

Lady from the ground up (*American*). (*See* Perfect Lady.)

Lady in the straw (*Hist*) 'Our Lady in the Straw'—referring to the stable in which the Redeemer was born An old popular oath

Lady Jane (*Soc*, 1882) A stout, handsome, cheery woman

Lally-gagging (*American Peoples'*). Flirting—origin probably Dutch

You see, Pa has been in a habit lately of going to the store a good deal and lally-gagging with the girl clerks —*Bad Boy*, 1883

Lamartinism (*Literary*) Goody-goody. Lamartine introduced the novelty, in historical writing, of maintaining that everybody has always acted for the best, whatever his action, in the best of possible worlds Term used scornfully since 1848 in French literature Now sometimes exercised deprecatingly at Oxford, and in London.

Lambeth (*Peoples'*, *S L*) Wash. From the popular cleansing place in S London being the Lambeth baths

Lambies (*Navy*) Mizzen-top men.

Lame as St Giles Cripplegate, As (*Peoples' Hist*). Very lame — applied to a badly-told untruth St Giles was the patron saint of cripples, as distinct from St Martin, who was the patron of all beggars. Cripples, therefore, had two saintly patrons. St Giles's, London, was just under London Wall at its most northern point, and was St Giles's Without—that is, outside the city. It abutted on the great north gate, and the church being frequented (in Roman Catholic times) by cripples in great numbers — many of them being fraudulent limpers — the gate came to be called Cripplegate; and this phrase suggested a lame excuse. The great bastion near the north gate is still represented by about half of it.

Land Navy (*Cadgers'*). Imitation sailors.

Land o' Cakes (*Historical*) Scotland.

It was my firm intention when I returned from my little Scotch tour to write glowing accounts of the scenery of 'the land of cakes'—G. R Sims, *Ref*, 5th October 1884

Land o' Scots (*Eng - American*, 1884) Heaven

'Lane (*Theatrical*) Classic term—became popular for Drury Lane Theatre.

Langtries (*Society*, 1880) Fine eyes Mrs Langtry, whose portraits as a celebrated beauty had been seen for years in shop windows, suddenly became popular (1882) by appearing on the stage in England and America, where immense crowds were attracted

Language (*Peoples'*), Sheer swearing Satire upon violent expressions

Meanwhile a scramble has been taking place between two omnibuses behind for the lead of the road, illustrated by a free use of what is called 'language.'—*D N*, 1st August 1890

Language of flowers (*Bow Street Police Court*, 1860-83). Ten shillings —or seven days; the favourite sentence of Mr Flowers, a very popular and amiable magistrate at this court for many years

Lap (*Coffee-house*) Tea

Lapsy lingo (*Peoples'*). Corruption of *lapsus linguæ*

Lard - king (*Anglo - American*) Typical Cincinnati millionaire, whose fortune is based upon pig

Lardy - dardy (*Peoples'*, 1862) Affected

Large - heads (*Anglo - Amer*) Drunkards.

Large-sized scare (*Amer.*). Wild panic

Lassitudinarian (*Soc*, 1894 on) Satirical evolution from valetudinarian.

Evasive term for a constitutionally lazy man.

. . . an occupation, by the way, exactly suiting a 'lassitudinarian' temperament. —*D. T.*, 4th February 1897.

Last bit o' family plate (*Artisans'*). Final silver coin.

Last shake o' the bag (*Peoples'—old*). Youngest child.

Latch - key (*Irish Constabulary*, 1881-82). Crowbar—name given by the Irish Constabulary to the crowbar, as the too frequent key with which they had to open house doors when in the process of eviction.

Law (*Police*). Advantage, start, privilege. Invented by the police.

The defendants were placed in the police van and driven off under the very noses of their would-be persecutors, who were quite unaware that their prey had escaped them. Having given the van a good extent of 'law', the crowd were allowed to go where they wished, but only in time to find that they had been out-witted.—*D. N.*, 15th September 1885.

Law's - a - me (*Hist. — now chiefly used in U.S.A.*). Lord save me.

He's full of the Old Scratch, but laws-a-me—he's my own dead sister's boy!—Mark Twain, *Tom Sawyer*, p. 19.

Lay (lie) on the face (*Peoples'*). Dissipate exorbitantly.

Lea toff (*Local Lond.*). A youth of social aspirations, chiefly in relation to Sunday; one who displays his distinction, in a hired boat, rowing up and down the River Lea.

Lead poisoning (*W. America*). Active bullets.

Very recently a gentleman who was at once editor of a local newspaper and town constable found it necessary to relinquish the latter post in consequence of a disease which he euphemistically termed 'lead-poisoning', the result of being shot through part of the lungs by a desperado of the township under his care.—*D. N.*, 27th March 1883.

Leaden pill — sometimes **Leaden favour** (*Anglo-American*). Bullet.

Leadenhall market sportsman (*Sporting*, 1870). Landowner who sells his game to Leadenhall market poulterers.

The true foxhunter loathes the preserver of pheasants as 'an old woman', or 'a Leadenhall-market sportsman'; while the latter rages at the wholesale destruction of his costly game by the fox.—*D. N.*, 11th November 1885.

Leaderette (*Press*, 1875). When, probably borrowing from the French, the idea of lightening journalism, short pithy 'leaders' were introduced, a technical name was to be found for them, and 'leaderette' was the result.

Leading article (*Trade*, 1870). A term used to denote the best bargain in the shop—one that should lead to other purchases.

Leading heavies (*Theat.*). Middle-aged women's serious rôles.

I am an actress. I was in Mr O'Connor's company during his engagement at the Star Theatre, playing the 'leading heavies' throughout that engagement. I was to receive 12 dollars a week and expenses.—*N. Y. Mercury*, 9th June 1888.

Leak (*Anglo-American*, 1880). To lie.

Leaky (*Peoples'*). Talkative when drunk.

Learn by rote (*Scholastic*). Learn by the road, route, or rut—that is to say, without intelligence, perfunctorily.

Learning shover (*Com. London*, 1869 on). Schoolmaster—took its rise at the institution of the London School Board.

Leather and prunella (*Middle-Class—ancient*). Expresses flimsiness. A corruption of 'All lather and prunella'—the 'lather' being whipped cream, the 'prunella' probably damson *purée* or plum jelly. Sometimes used to express humbug.

Then who shall say so good a fellow,
Was only leather and prunella.—*Don Juan*.

The Foreign Office regards all the organised cheerfulness of the last few days' Chinese diplomatic blandishments and promises, edicts and telegrams, alike, as so much leather and prunella. —*D. T.*, 24th July 1900.

Leave them to fry in their own fat (*Plantagenet English*). This phrase is equal to—Give him rope enough and he'll hang himself. The phrase was brought into fashion again by Prince Bismarck, who (1871) after the partial retirement of the German forces, applied it to Parisians and their politics.

Leave yer 'omer (*L. Class—Women's*). A handsome, dashing man This is derived, very satirically, from 'That's the man I'm goin' to leave me 'ome for'. Good example of street sentiment

Leccers (*Oxford 'er'*). Lectures—both 'c's' hard

Each man attends as cheerfully as he can his 'leccers'.—*D. T*, 14th August 1899.

Left centre (*Polit*, 1885) Whig. Bestowed by advanced Liberals on cautious Liberal party

Thiers used to say that France was essentially Left Centre, and that power would come to the party of the most prudent —*D N*, 20th October 1885

Left her purse on her piano (*Peoples'*, 19 *cent*) Satirical hit at self sufficiency.

Left the minority (*Soc*, 1879). No longer with the living.

Poor 'Benefit Thompson' has left the minority —*Entr'acte*, 30th April 1885

Leg (*Fast Society*, 1860) Footman —from the display of the lower limbs

Leg maniac (*Stage*, 1880 on) Eccentric, rapid dancer.

Mr Fred Storey holds a unique position as a 'leg maniac'—horrible term!—*D. T*, 3rd December 1896.

Leg up (*Peoples'*) Help

Legit (*Theatrical*). Shortening of legitimate, in its turn the curtailing of the legitimate drama

Leisure hours (*Rhyming*) Flowers

Leisured rich (*Soc*, 1885). Invented by Mr Gladstone

Lemon squash party (*Soc*, 1882). A meeting of young men, initially at Oxford, when nothing was drunk but this preparation.

Lemoncholy (*Transposition — London*). Melancholy

Lend us your breath to kill Jumbo (*Low London*) Protest against the odour of bad breath.

Length of the foot (*Irish*) Comprehend and manipulate the victim.

Does the enterprising tradesman who thus shields himself behind magisterial patronage undertake to teach the district the length of Mr Bushby's foot?—*D N.*, 18th August 1884.

Lengthy (*Parl*, 1875) Used by both houses for 'long'.

The fine people who think it elegant to say 'lengthy' when they mean 'long', though they have not yet come to say 'strengthy' when they mean 'strong', are fond of saying 'utilise' when they mean use —*D N*, April 1883

Let, To (*Art*) Sparsely - filled canvas

Let 'em all come (*Peoples'*, 1896) Cheery defiance Outcome of the plucky way in which the British, in the first days in the new year, accepted the message of congratulation by the Emperor of Germany to President Kruger on the repulse of the Jameson raid, followed next day by the imperial message sent by President of the U S A, *apropos* to the English boundary dispute with Venezuela; both followed by some defiant comments in the French press

Let her rip (*English-American*, 1840 onwards) Let her go as she wants. This phrase has a very striking history. When rival river steam-boats were fully established on the Mississippi and other American rivers, the rival captains would put on every ounce of steam in order to keep ahead Too frequently the boiler would burst, or 'rip', as emphatically it would when bursting 'Let her rip' came to be a common expression amongst these captains when more timid passengers or sensible sub-officers urged him to lower the steam pressure.

Let out (*American*) Releases—very emphatic

'Well, sah, I wanted to ax how many kinds of religun you had up dat way?'

'Oh, about a dozen, I guess'

'Cracky, golly!' he whispered, 'but dat lets me out!'—*Detroit Free Press*, 1883

Let out your back - band (*American*) Be more familiar and friendly in your statement

I ax you let out your back band a little on that last statement

Let through (*Peoples'*) (1) Escape; (2) Cause injury

Let up (*Anglo-American*) Make an end From 'letting' or lifting up the engine bar which, down, puts all steam on To end pressure.

Lethal (*Press*, 19 *cent*). Mortal. From the waters of Lethe Now applied by careless writers to any mode of violent death

It is always understood among the most distinguished members of the profession—the higher burglarious circles, as they are called—that nothing but the direst necessity shall ever make them use a revolver or other lethal weapon.—*Ref.*, 3rd February 1889.

Letter - fencers (*London*). Postmen.

Levenses (*E. Anglican*). Lunch—the meals of the elevens, whence this pleonastic plural has been evolved. (*See* Bever.)

Liberal forwards (*Political*, 1898). Modified Radicals—without fads.

'Liberal forwards'—as Mr George Russell's party styles itself—are notoriously suspicious of the reactionary designs which they attribute to Lord Salisbury.—*D. T.*, 2nd February 1899.

Lick into shape (*Com.*). To get ready. Obviously — from animals, especially bears, licking their young.

It had not been thought necessary to lick the piece into shape. The result was most laughable; the last act created more laughter than has done any farce for years.—*Stage*, 21st August 1885.

Lie down and die (*Anglo-American*). Despair.

Lie down to rest (*Amer.-Eng., Street*). Fail, come to an end, a dramatic company which has collapsed. Often seen, in the past tense, in American graveyards; finally it passed into a colloquialism. (*See* Climb the golden staircase.)

Henderson's *Uncle Tom* Company laid down to rest at Dunkirk, Ohio, on Tuesday.—*N. Y. Mercury*, December 1884.

Reached England about 1883.

Life and everlasting (*Peoples', Hist.*). Complete, final, without appeal—especially applied to sales.

His Honour: Why didn't you jib, and take the horse back then?

Defendant: I took it back the next morning. When he sold it he said 'it was for life and everlasting'.—*D. T.*, 23rd November 1897.

Lift up (*N. Eng. Methodists'*). To pray.

Lifter (*Stable*). Kicking horse, one which lifts.

Lifu (*Motor car*, 1897). Reduction of liquid fuel (paraffin or other oil).

Starting punctually to time, the Lifu, which takes its name from the liquid fuel (oil) which it uses, as the odour proclaims, arrived at London Bridge.—*D. T.*, 17th December 1897.

Light - comedy merchant (*Theatrical*). Comedian pure and simple.

Despite its title, *The Mormon* has no connection with the followers of Brigham Young, and the scene is laid not at Salt Lake City, but at Ramsgate; a very light-comedy merchant, the Hon. Charles Nugent, being heavily in debt.—*Ref.*, 13th March 1887.

Light - food (*Lower Peoples'*). Tobacco for chewing as a repast—very light.

Light-house (*Navy*). Pepper-castor.

Lightning curtain - taker (*Theatrical*, 1884). A curtain-taker (*q.v.*), who does not wait for much applause (which he may not receive), and who therefore rushes on upon the least approbation. (*See* Take a curtain, Fake a curtain.)

Lights up (*Theat.*, *circa*, 1900). Condemnation of a new piece on the first night of its production (*see* Boo). Chiefly the decision of the gallery.

Like to meet her in the dark (*L. Class*, 1884). Plain.

Lime - juice (*Theatrical*, 1875). Lime light.

Limerick (*Peoples'*). Queer and coarse rhymes, like 'There was a young lady of Lea,' etc. Some say this style of rhyme was called Limericks because all the specimens go to a tune to the original words,

'Won't you come up—up—up
Won't you come up to Limerick?'

Lincoln & Bennett (*Soc.*, 1840 on). Superior hat. From makers' name. (*See* Dorsay, Nicholls, Poole, Redfern.)

Lined (*Low Life*). Passive voice of active verb to line, and derived from certificate of marriage.

Link and froom (*Street, Hebrew*).

'Dolly', who was a Jewess, but one who was link rather than froom, was about forty years old at the time of her death.—*Ref.*, 3rd February 1889.

Linkman (*W. London*). General man-servant about kitchen or yard.

Lion Chang (*Fugitive Ang.*, 1896). Jocular Anglicising of the name of Li Hung Chang — and referring to his fleeting popularity. He arrived in the beginning of the month, went to America before the end of it, and in the meantime was dubbed long Lion Chang. His *entourage* also obtained, in several instances, droll names. Lo Feng Luh became Loafing Loo, Viscount Li became Lud Lulliety, and Seng became S'eng-song.

Lion comique (*Music Hall*, 1880) This term was a way of describing a leading comic singer

Changes of fancy and taste have abolished the 'lion comique', as he was known to an antecedent generation, and the death of Mr Macdermott practically snaps the last link —*D. T*, 9th May 1901

Liqueur of four ale (*City, satirical*) Precisely as the common folk make fun of cheap food and give it impressive titles such as calling sheep's head broth turtle soup, so middle-class young city men chaff their drinks. The most expensive liqueur, green Chartreuse would be eighteenpence—while four ale (City sherry) is the cheapest. Phrase really means, 'a glass of bitter'—beer understood.

Liquor (*Public - house keepers'*) Euphemism for the water used in adulterating beer.

Listening to oneself (*Irish, old*). Thinking.

Little beg (*Pub. Sch.*) Abbreviation of little beggar—friendly term applied by upper form to lower form boys

Little bit o' keg (*L Class*) Keg-meg meat, that is, common meat—erotic.

Little bit of sugar for the bird (*Peoples'*, 1897) Premium, unexpected benefit, surprise, acquisition.

She applied for five Ordinary shares at £1 premium, paying £2, 10s with her application, and on allotment she paid up the balance, £7, 10s in full She held all the shares when the corporation was wound up, and received nothing for her money

You didn't get anything of Goodman's 'little bit of sugar'? (Laughter)—No —*D. T*, 24th December 1898.

Little deers (*Soc Anglo-American*). Young women—generally associated, or declaring themselves to be associated, with the stage New spelling of 'dears' to form a feminine to stags

Little go (*Thieves'*) First imprisonment, first invented by a fallen university man

Little Ireland (1879) The then Home Rule brigade in the House of Commons.

Little more Charley behind (*Theatrical*) More lumbar width—speaking of feminine dress or costume

Little season (*Society*, 1880 on) London season between 6th January and Shrove Tuesday The real season begins about 15th April and ends with July.

London has been during the last few years not only full of visitors after Easter, but has developed a pre-Lenten or 'little' season, as it is called.—*D N.*, 6th July 1884

Little whack (*Drinking men's*). Small quantity of spirits

You may choose for the moment of illustration either your going into or your coming out of the Carnarvon Arms, where you intend to have or where you have had your little whack —Besant & Rice, *Golden Butterfly*, vol i, ch xii

Live down (*Soc*, 1870) To overcome by strenuous patience

When it took six months to go from India to England they made the most of a bad situation, and tried to live down heat and care —(Indian Hospitality) *Graphic*, 17th March 1883.

Live messages (*Telegraphers'*, 1870) Messages in course of transition.

In the telegraph department dining accommodation has been provided, because it is thought undesirable that those who are engaged in the transmission of telegraph messages should leave the premises during their period of duty With what are called 'live messages' fresh in their minds, there is felt to be an objection to their adjourning to neighbouring restaurants —*D N*, 27th September 1883

Live on (*L. Peoples'*) Fine girl or woman. (*See* Leave yer 'ome)

Live up to (*Æsthetic*, 1878-83). Exist purely up to a pure standard Invented by Du Maurier (*Punch*) Phrase used quite seriously by the Burne Jones school (*See* Apostle of culture)

Living bache (*Soc*) Life in chambers—living like a bachelor.

Living with mother now (*Music Hall*, 1881) The refrain of a doubtful song, in which this answer is made by the young person to all the blandishments of her inamorato

Lizards (*American*). Men of Alabama

Loaferies, The (*E. London*). Whitechapel Workhouse — from the tenderness shown towards the inmates. In 1898 the guardians even wished to do away with the term workhouse.

No very luminous suggestions were forthcoming as to a new title, though one of the guardians thought 'Paradise' a fitting change. The others, however, seemed to consider this a little previous. Perhaps 'House of Repose' or 'The Loaferies' would be considered appropriate. Mr Perez remarked that whatever the new name, in a few years it would be as unpopular as the old one.—*D. T.*, 10th February 1898.

Loan (*American*). Lend, now becoming English. Has been accepted probably as a euphemism.

Such a term as 'I will loan you my dog Schneider' is hardly British.—*D. N.*, 1882.

Loathly (*London Club*, October 1897). Offensive.

This savage sacrificial feat, performed with horrible frequency by Bitchlieli and his reverend subordinates on the 'teocalli', or green stone, surmounting the shrines of the loathly idols that were eventually overthrown and destroyed by Hernan Cortes.—*D. T.*, 24th December 1898.

Lobby (*Amer.—coming to Eng.*). To corrupt by process. To attempt to exercise an influence on members of a legislative body by persons not members —who attend the session of a legislative body for the purpose of influencing the debates.

Lobby through (*Amer.—passing to Eng.*). Is to get a bill accepted by influence.

Loblifer (*Cornwall*). Luck-bringing mannikin. Probably a corruption of Lob-lie-by-the-fire—from this genius being fond of warmth after his damp cave abode.

'Lob-Lie-by-the-Fire,' is a pretty story of farm life and rustic folk, in which mysterious agrarian services rendered by an unseen benefactor awaken all the old country superstitions. — *D. N.*, 17th December 1885.

Local pot. (*See* Pot.)

Locate (*American*). To settle.

Locked up (*Street*). Arrested.

Locust (*Soc.*). Extravagant person who sweeps everything away.

Locum (*Doctors'*). Deputy—short for *locum tenens.* Sometimes 'loke' —a medical man who performs for another who is ill or away.

Lolliker (*Durham—old*). Tongue.

Lollipop dress (*Theatrical*, 1884). Stripy dress, generally red and white, suggestive of sticks of confectionery.

London, Best side towards (*Peoples'*). Making the best of everything. Good example of the national desire to battle through adversity. Derived from the desire of all country people to visit London for themselves, and make their fortunes, though its street are not paved with gold.

London ivy (*Colloquial*). Dust—sometimes used for fog.

London smoke (*Soc.*, 1860). A yellowish grey; became once a favourite colour because it hid dirt.

Long last (*Eng. Prov.*). Time or period spaciously waited for.

At long last Sir George White and his gallant garrison are free. Lord Dundonald rode into Ladysmith on Wednesday night.—*D. T.*, 2nd March 1900.

Long pull (*Public-house*). Overmeasure, either as a custom, or to induce trade.

Long-shore (*Maritime*). Landlubber; coast people who have the misfortune not to be sailors.

But what would have been the alarm of those timid 'long-shore' races if they could have imagined the present dangers of the deep.—*D. N.*, 6th January 1886.

Long stale drunk (*American-Eng.*, 1884). State of depression owing to physical inability to throw off the effects of intoxication.

. . . recovery from what our American cousins describe as a 'long stale drunk'.—*Ref.*, 9th April 1885.

Long-tailed bear (*Peoples'*, *Hist.*). One of the evasions of saying 'you lie'. From the fact that bears have *no* tails.

Long 'un (*Poachers'*). Pheasant—referring to the length of the tail. (*See* Short-'un.)

Long's (*Strand*, 19 *cent.*). Short's wine-house opposite Somerset House.

Look into the whites (*Peoples'*)—'Of each other's eyes' understood. To be about to fight—from the fact that the eyes protrude, or the lids recede more than usual when a set-to is about to commence.

It would be absolutely impossible for any adjustment of the boundary question to be made if the Russians and Afghans kept advancing until they could look into the whites of each other's eyes —*D N.*, 14th March 1885.

Look old (*Street*). Severe. Very fine eulogy of the wisdom of age, as compared with the carelessness of youth

Look slippery (*Naval*) Hurry up, be quick — from the association of slipperiness and speed.

Look through the fingers (*Irish*). To evade, to pretend not to observe and see

Looking as if he hadn't got his right change (*London*) Appearing mad or wild.

Looking round the clock (*American*) Getting appearance of age—parallel between life and completion of the orbit of the hands of a clock.

Looking seven ways for Sunday (*Lower Middle London*) Squinting.

Looks like a widder woman (*Amer*, 1883) Appears old

Loose bit o' goods (*Street*, 1870 on) Young woman who has abandoned the proprieties (*See* Straight bit o' goods)

Loosing a fiver (*Peoples'*) Having to pay extravagantly for any pleasure or purchase.

Loosing French (*Street*) Violent language in English

Lord Blarney (*Irish*, 1885) Aristocratic flatterer. First given to Lord Carnarvon, who after his appointment as Lord Lieutenant of Ireland (1885) made many flattering speeches.

Lord Carnarvon's plausible and soothing, or to adopt the Irish expression 'soothering', speeches appear only to have won for him the nickname of Lord Blarney —*D N*, 14th November 1885.

Lordy me (*Prov. Hist.*) Exclamation Corruption of Lord have me! One of the sacred ejaculations of early reform days.

Lost a cartful and found a waggon-load (*Peoples'*). Getting stout

Lot's wife's back-bone (*Peoples'*) To suggest extreme saltness, as 'Salt as Lot's wife's back-bone'

Lottermy (*Mid Counties — rarely used*) Corruption of Lord take me!

Lotties and Totties (*Theatrical*) Ladies at large

If time and space permitted I should like to tell you all about the Lotties and the Totties and the other out-of-work pets who pervaded the stalls, and showed a liberal proportion of their backs—backs and bosoms, too—as bare as they were born —*Ref*, 15th November 1885

Lotus (*L Class*, 1885) Rhyme to hocuss

Love curls (*Society*, 1880) This term came in when women began to cut their hair short and wear it low over the forehead

For the defence the respondent, Mr Robert Nathaniel Latham, was called. He gave a positive denial to the charge of cruelty He had objected to his wife wearing what she called 'love curls' — Latham *v* Latham, Probate and Divorce Division, 9th February 1883

Lovely as she can be and live, As (*American*, 1882) Superlative praise of beauty That is to say—she could only be more lovely when raised to the condition of an angel

Lovey dovey (*Low London*). Example of nonsense rhyming.

Low comedy merchant (*Theat*, 1883) Farcical actor

The success of *Indiana* mainly depends upon the extravagant humours of the chief low-comedy merchant. — *Ref*, October 1886

He won't be able to box Mr Fred J Stimson, the low comedy merchant, for some weeks to come.

(*See* 'Shop'.)

Lully (*L. Class*) Shirt.

Lumberer (*Soc*) Lying adventurer —obscure

Mr Gill felt instinctively that there was something wrong with this man's appearance, and when this man came, in cross-examination, to give an account of himself, it accorded with the well-known expression 'lumberer'. — Lord Dunlo's Divorce, July 1890

Lump of ice (*Rhyming*). Advice—in common use.

Lump of school (*Rhyming*) Fool.

Lump o' jaw on (*Street*) Talkative.

Lump o' stone (*Thieves'*) County jail

Lumpy-roar (*Low London*, 1855). A grandee, a swell of the first water. Said to be an anglicization of 'l'Empereur' — Napoleon III., who became popular in 1885 by his visit to England, owing to the excitement produced by the Crimean War, and his encouragement of English trade.

M

M. D. (*Bridgewater*, 1857). Money down — referring to electioneering bribery.

McKinleyism — McKinleyise (*American-Eng.*, 1897). Protection. From President Mackinley, U.S.A., the great apostle of protection.

Meanwhile Congress is hearing from the people in no uncertain tones as to certain schedules which Mr Dingley proposes to 'McKinleyise'.—*D. T.*, 23rd March 1897.

Macing (*Peoples'*, 19 *cent.*). Severe, but regulated thrashing by fists. Early in the '19th century Mace was for an exceptional time a leading prize-fighter.

Mackinaw (*American Hunters'*). A very strong and ingeniously-woven blanket, said to have been first made and sold by a Scotch wool-stapler called MacInor.

Mad as hops (*American*). Excitable.

Made in Germany (*London*, 1890 on). Bad, valueless. Outcome of the vast quantity of inferior goods imported from Germany. Term increased in force from the date when this phrase had, legally, to be printed on the object.

Maffickers, Early.

Japanese merchants in New York met at dinner last night 'to celebrate the Japanese victory'. — *Star*, 10th February 1904.

Several days after the first naval success of the Japanese.

Mafficking (*Street*, 1900). Street rowdyism. April 1, 1900, added this word to the English language. It is quite as likely to stay as boycott. On the evening of that day the news of the relief of Mafeking arrived at about 9 P.M.—by eleven o'clock the streets were absolutely riotous.

Magdalen Marm (*Southwark*, 19 *cent.*). A servant from the Magdalen, a refuge for fallen women in the Blackfriars Road, which existed there until about the middle of the century. The women who went out as servants from that place had been too often pampered there, and gave little satisfaction — hence the Surrey side found this satirical term.

Mailed fist (*Peoples'*, 1897). Needless threats, boasting. From a send-off dinner speech by the Emperor of Germany when sending forth his only brother, Henry, to conquer China with a fleet of two sail—all of which ended in leasing a coaling-station by China to Germany.

Mailing (*Anglo - American*). To post for the mail.

After mailing, I returned to the Capitol, and rejoined Agneni on the balcony of the Senator's hall.—*D. N.*, 1870.

Maintenon (*Soc.*, *Hist.*). Mistress who affects piety. From the position and life of Madame de Maintenon, the last favourite of Louis XIV.

Major MacFluffer — or Fluffy (*Theatrical*, 19 *cent.*). Sudden lapse of memory, and use of words to call the attention of the inattentive prompter. It is said to have arisen from an actor, in this strait, yelling half a dozen times as he looked off on the prompt side—'Major MacFluffer —where the devil is Major MacFluffer.'

More than one of the principals were foggy with the text, and were reduced to fluffing or to waiting for 'the word' from the wings.—*Ref.*, 13th November 1887.

Major Methodist (*Soc.*, '80's on). Extremely precise person. Intensification of Methodist.

Make a fun (*Irish*). Exercise fuss.

The villagers make a fun over every sister leaving, but we don't like it in any instance. Being externs, they might express their gratitude that way, but we wish to avoid it. It was done in the case of Sister Mary Clare. — *Miss Saurin's 'Nunnery' Case.*

Make a stuffed bird laugh (*American*). Absolutely preposterous.

Make all right (*Election*, 19 *cent*). Promise to pay for vote

Make - it (*London Poor*) Corruption of make-weight, the piece of bread added by bakers when weighing a loaf, to make up the weight — few loaves being baked of the correct weight

Make it warm (*London*, 1880). Punish

Mr Firth remarked that he himself was engaged in the icy latitude of the north endeavouring, as some one had said, to make it warm for their good friends on the other side, and to help to carry the flag of progress once more to victory.—*D N*, 7th October 1885.

Make leg (*Com. Lond.*). To become prosperous

Make up (*Soc and Peoples'*, 1860 on). To make love to.

Make up my leg (*Costermongers'*). To make money From the time of smalls, stockings and buckled shoes, when making up the leg was a necessary prelude to going into society. (*See* Pull up my boot.)

Making your coffin (*Tailors'*) Charging too highly for an article Said when a tailor charges a heavy price for a first job, and so probably loses a second

Male impersonator (*Music Hall*) A misnomer—for the performer is a female who personates a man — and sings like one

Mall (*Metal Trades'*) Credit

Man of Sedan (*Political*). Last nickname given for Napoleon III — from his fall at that city

Man-killer (*Abstainers'*) Porter, stout, cooper—the black beers

Manchester school of nutrition (*Soc*, 1860) High-feeding, emphatically introduced by certain medical men of that city

Mandamus (*Legal*) Verb invented from a writ of mandamus

The court was not dispensed from considering this part of the case, as it would have been if Mr Bradlaugh had been trying to 'mandamus' the Speaker or the Serjeant-at-Arms —*D. N*, 28th January 1885

Mange, letty, bevy and clobber Italian — through the organ-grinders' lodging-houses. Eating, bed, drink, clothes—this last word being Hebrew.

Manny (*Jewish E London*). Term of endearment or admiration prefixed to Jewish name, as 'Manny Lyons'. Apparently a muscular Hebrewism.

Mantalini (*Mid Class*, 1840 on) A man-milliner—from the milliner's husband in Dickens's *Nicholas Nickleby*

A famous Mantalini, one who will very shortly open a palatial branch establishment in London town, has draped and adorned the feminine form divine of handsome Jane Hading —*D T.*, 2nd January 1897

From about 1860-90 this name was superseded by that of 'Worth', the English man-milliner of the second empire, and afterwards of the third republic.

Marcus Superbus (*Theat*, 1896). Grandee. This was the name given to himself by Mr Wilson Barrett in his play, *The Sign of the Cross* (1896). Soon after the success of this morality, a variety piece called *The Gay Parisienne* was produced; therein Miss Louie Freear made an immediate success as a burlesque actress, who invented a grotesque name—Marcus Superfluous.

Margery (*L. London*, 19 *cent*) Effeminate.

Mark time (*Mil*, 19 *cent*) Wait, hold on, be patient, don't be in a hurry. From the military order when soldiers are halted for a short time on march, or drill, and which is done that step may not be lost.

Marking M (*Irish Peoples'*) Rapidity The M. is the initial of the Virgin Mary, still a very sacred symbol in Ireland. Usually used in describing rapidity of action.

Marksman (*Old*) Legal term for a man who cannot write, and who makes his mark

Marm - poosey or **Marm - puss** (*Public-house*, 1863). Applied to a showily-dressed landlady.

Marmalade country (*Scotland*) Music hall reference to the orange marmalade made in Dundee and other Scotch places.

Marriage face (*Middle Class*) Sad one—because generally a bride cries a good deal, and so temporarily spoils her looks

Married the widow (*French — known in England*, 19 *cent*). Made a mess of things Derived from a man going to the guillotine, which makes widows, while the idea of marriage is suggested by the momentary association with the guillotine, which is called in French slang 'the widow'.

Married to Brown Bess (*Mil.*, 18-19 *cent.*). To serve as a soldier. Brown Bess was of course the musket.

You can tell her that you are safe and married to Brown Bess (that is to say enlisted). Thackeray, *Barry Linden*, ch. v.

Martialist (*Soc.*, 1885). Soldier holding a commission.

The marvel was 'that the colonel stood it'. He was, indeed, a long-suffering martialist.—*D. N.*, 31st December 1885.

Marwooded (*Peoples'*). Hanged. This term prevailed while Executioner Marwood held office. He died in 1883.

Mary Ann (*L. London*, 19 *cent.*). An effeminate man.

Mash, Made a (*Soc.*, 1883). Effected a conquest—struck somebody all of a heap.

Mash that (*Com. Lond.*). Hold your tongue. Probably from macher to chew, or figuratively—keep to yourself in your mouth.

Mashers' corners (*Soc.*, 1882). The O.P. and P.S. entrances to the stalls of the old Gaiety Theatre.

Masonics (*Soc.*, *Hist.*). Secrets—from the secret rites of Freemasonry. Not that there are either secrets or rites in Freemasonry—at all events in England—where combined secrets are neither wanted nor expected.

Massites (*Soc.*, 1897). Members of the Anglican Church who believe in transubstantiation. These believers accept the term gravely; but it was invented by the representative, or Low Church, party.

Masterpiece o' night work (*Street*). Admiringly said of a handsome unfortunate.

Match (*Soc.*, 19 *cent.*). Society classic for marriage throughout the reign—giving rise to the compound matchmaker, a woman who brings about marriages.

Mrs Gerard did her best to make the match, and although she afterwards conceived doubts as to whether her sister really loved him, she said nothing to Lord Durham to that effect. — Lord Herschel, *Lord Durham's Nullity Suit*, March 1885.

Materials (*Irish*). Evasive term for whisky-punch.

Matinée (*Theatrical*, 1870). Morning theatrical performance. This entertainment came from New York, and was speedily adopted not only in England, but in France, which accepted the word.

Matinée dog (*Theatrical*). Sufferer experimented upon. From vivisection of canines, or testing food for poison by submitting it to tykes. Of course a figure of speech in relation to the frequent dramatic rubbish which is submitted at matinées, as distinct from evening performances.

Arrangements have been made by Irvine Bacon and Charles Groves to try it ere long on the matinée dog—probably at the Haymarket.—*Ref.*, 3rd February 1889.

Matineers (*Soc.*, 1885). Frequenters of matinées. Outcome of the rage for matinées, 1884-85. They are composed of quite 80 per cent. of ladies.

Matineers on the look out for a really excellent and varied show will thank me for calling their attention to a matinée to be given in compliment to Mrs Robert Reece.

Maty (*London Workmen's*). Mate.

Maungo (*N. Country*, 1869). Shoddy. This word is said to come from the term 'it maun go'—that is to say it must sell from its cheapness.

Maw-sang (*Northumbrian*). Blood—a corrupted oath — probably mort saint, holy death.

Mawther (*E. Anglican*). Not only mother, but applied to even a girl baby, girl, maid, wife, and childless widow.

Mawwormy (*Peoples'*). Fault-finding, dismally anticipating wretchedness. From the character Mawworm.

Augustus Harris insisting on Carl Rosa accepting the wreath thrown on the stage last Saturday night was a delicious and touching spectacle. Here is a glorious subject for one of our figure-painters. Without being mawwormy, I fail to see why a wreath should be presented to any man who makes a business of giving opera.—*Entr'acte*, 6th June 1885.

(*See* Pecksniffian.)

May God blind me (*Street*). The original invocation of the gutterling, reduced to 'Gaw blin' me', 'bly me', 'blyme', 'bly'.

Mayhap (*Peoples*). Abbreviation of may happen.

'Your widow? Mayhap not.'—Garrick, *Abel Drugger*

Mean to do without 'em (*Music Hall*, 1882) The ''em' infers to women The phrase was first made popular by the singer Arthur Roberts.

Mean white (*Anglo-Indian*). A poor Englishman.

Meater (*Street*) Coward. Said of a dog who only bites meat, that is to say, one who will not fight Thence applied to cowardly men

Meddle and muddle (*Political*, 1879) Came in during contest between Beaconsfield and Gladstone—unmasterly policy which harries and does nothing

The Board is pursuing a policy of meddle and muddle, and is getting itself most cordially hated all round,—*Ref*, 26th April 1885

Meddling duchess (*Peoples'*, 1880) Intensification of duchess (*q v*) Ageing, pompous woman who fusses about and achieves nothing

Melt (*Financial*) To discount a bill

Melton hot day (*Sporting and Club*, 1885) Equivalent to melting hot day Created Derby Day (3rd June), which was very sultry, and *apropos* to the winner of the day—'Melton'.

Several who came near me after the big race remarked that it was a Melton hot day, and seemed to think they were saying something original and something funny—*Ref*, 7th June 1885

Memugger (*Oxford*) Martyrs' memorial A satirical and even profane application of 'er'.

The triumph of this jargon was reached when some one christened the Martyrs' Memorial the 'Martyrs' Memugger'—*D T*, 14th August 1899.

Mended (*Street*, 19 *cent*) Bandaged

Menkind (*Soc*, '90's) Male relatives simply.

The great pull which Pekin had, over other Eastern or over South American Legations was that it is the traditional custom that the ladies of the Corps Diplomatique, who can rarely be prevailed upon to venture so far from Paris as Chili and Peru, accompany their menkind forth to the Celestial City—*D T*, 4th July 1900

Mentisental (*Syllable traversion—E of London only*) Sentimental

Merchant (*Theatrical*, 1882). The theatre coming to be called the 'shop', actors dubbed themselves 'merchants', qualified by their line.

Merely moral man (*Soc*, 1890) Started by Ritualistic incumbents. Attack upon men who are moral without expressed Christian belief.

Mervousness (*Polit*, 1885) Satirical synonym for nervousness invented about 1876 by the political party who did not believe in the advance of Russia towards India

Messengers (*Country*) The small dark, rapidly drifting cloudlets which foretell a storm.

Micky. *See* Bob, Harry and Dick

Microbe of sectionalism (*Soc*, *and Parl*, *circa* 1896) Social fad in the House of Commons As gradually the 'microbe' was discovered to be the cause of all disease, or the effect of all tendency to disease, the phrase was used figuratively In this case it is applied to the total break up of the Liberal party in the '90's, by the divided feeling upon most extreme points Such as total abstinence, local veto, vaccination, voluntary schools, etc.

The abdication by the Radical party of its proper functions has an unfortunate tendency to foster what we have called the microbe of sectionalism.—*D T.*, 21st June 1890

Mid vire (*Sporting*, *Paris*) Midday wires, giving last prices in the coming-on races Heard in London.

Middle cuts (*Slums'*) These are the prime cuts of fried fish at fried fish shops.

Midge (*Devon*, *old*) A tell-tale.

Mighty roarer (*Yankee*). Niagara cataract.

Mikey (*Corrupt Rhyming*) Sick after drink. (*See* Bob, Harry and Dick)

Milikers (*Com. London*, 1870) Militia—probably a corruption of the true word, upon the basis that public-house is idiotically called shuvly-cowss

Military (*Tavern*, 1885) Porter. One of the later baptisms

Milk-bottle (*Com. Peoples'*). Baby.

Milken (*Thieves'*, 18 *cent.*). House-breaker. (*See* Fielding's *Jonathan Wild.*)

Million to a bit of dirt (*Sporting*, 1860). A sure bet requiring no caution. 'It's a million to a bit o' dirt the Plunger pulls it off.' (*See* Dollars to buttons.)

Mimodrama (*Theatrical*, 1897). Drama of dumb show, as distinct from melodrama, wherein the more noise the better.

He had found the argument of this minodrama in an artic e of criticism written by Theophile Gautier.—*D. T.*, 3rd March 1897.

Minchin Malacho (*Peoples'*, 18 *cent.* on). Whatever this may mean it is evidently still understood by the vulgar. In April 1895 the present writer heard a man in the gallery of the Palace of Varieties (London), after several scornful phrases, say derisively, 'Oh—ah—minchin maleego.'

Mind the grease (*Peoples'*). Let me pass, please.

Mind the paint (*Peoples'*). Said of passing girls who have painted their faces. Adopted from the ordinary phrase used by house-painters who flourish this legend on floor, pavement, and wall. (*See* Aristocratic veins.)

Mind the step (*Peoples'*). Veiled or satiric suggestion that the victim addressed is drunk.

Mine (*Low Life*). Husband—of a kind. Sometimes really applied to a husband.

Mine-jobber (*City*, 1880 on). Cheat. When English copper mining became comparatively valueless by reason of the import of Australian and other ore as ballast, all the rascals on change floated mine companies, which had not a chance of success.

Minnie P. play (*Stage*, 1885 on). Drama in which a little maid variety actress is the chief motive. She must sing, dance, play tricks, and never wear a long dress. From Miss Minnie Palmer's creations, chiefly in *My Sweetheart*. Now obsolete.

Misery (*Old Eng. and American*). Pain.

Misery bowl (*Tourists'*). Relief-basin—at sea.

Misery junction (*Music Hall Singers'*). The angle forming the south-west corner of the York and Waterloo Roads. So named from the daily meeting here of music hall 'pros' who are out of engagements, and who are in this neighbourhood for the purpose of calling on their agents, half a dozen of whom live within hail. (*See* Pro's Avenue.)

Misleading paper (1876 on). Name given to *Times* newspaper when it began to lose its distinctive feature as the 'leading paper' in Liberal policy.

Probably the critic of the leading—I should say the misleading—morning paper did not see the show.

Miss (*American*). To be unlucky.

Mistaken (*Birmingham*, 1885). Lie. From a satirical paragraph by Mr Chamberlain (9th November), at Birmingham.

Mitching (*Canadian*). Common term for playing the truant. Comes from Devonshire, where the term is still in use.

Mitten (*Amer.*, *Hist.*). Refusal of marriage by a lady. 'She gave him the mitten.'

Mixologist (*American Saloon*). Outcome of the complicated nature of American drinks—a learned mixer.

Mo'. (*See* **'Arf a mo'.**)

Mock litany men (*Irish mendicants'*). Sing-song beggars who utter plaints or requests in a chanting manner.

Modernity (*Soc.*, '90's). Obvious. This word was invented early in the '90's — first as a satire, then as a perspicacious descriptive.

Nothing seems to be wanting to the perfect 'modernity' of the process by which Clerkenwell is endeavouring to discover its most fitting 'shepherd of souls' save the presence of a few book-makers and a daily report of the state of the odds against the various competing candidates.—*D. T.*, 16th June 1898.

Moll-hunters (*Street*). Men, of all ages, who are always lurking after women.

Monaker (*Com. Lond.*, 1870). Title or name. From Italian lingo for name, Monaco being the Italian for monk.

Monday mice (*L. Str.*, *Hist.*). The processions of black eyes, in both sexes, and in back streets—as the result of the week-end closing at 11 P.M. on

Sunday nights — a black eye getting this name from its ordinary size and rounded shape suggesting a huddled up mouse

Monday pops (*Soc*) Abbreviation of popular and put in plural. Refers to celebrated long established concerts at St James's Hall, London

We have been to a Monday pop this week. — Geo Eliot, *Letters*, 26th November, 1862

Money bag lord (*Soc.*, 19 *cent*) Ennobled banker (*See* Paint brush baronet and Gally pot baronet)

Money bugs (*Amer - Eng.*). Millionaires Beetles are called bugs, or were, in the U S A The golden bug is a beetle that has the appearance of a lump of dead gold

It is estimated, I see, that the Vanderbilt family of millionaires control among them 20,000 miles of American railways, which in one way and another afford employment for three millions of human beings The happiness or the misery of three millions of people wholly dependent on the whims and caprices of, say, half a dozen 'money bugs'.— *People*, 20th March 1898

Monkey (*Mechanics'*) Clerk

Monkey and parrot time (*American*). Equivalent to cat and dog life

Monkey motions (*Military*). Extension drill. Used satirically by the men in reference to the manœuvres of this really droll drill

Monkey on the house (*Soc*). Expression current in Cambridgeshire. It means that the owner of the house has raised money on it The natives also say, 'A monkey on the land', the word 'monkey' being exactly equivalent to 'mortgage'.

Monkey, To (*American - Eng*). Prance and carry on effusively — especially towards a pretty girl

Monks Sickly parrots. They hold their heads down and in

Monos (*Westminster School*). King's scholar who at 4 P M announces, in Latin, the finish of the day's work

Moo (*L. Class*) Common woman.

Moocheries (*Peoples'*, 1885) One of the names given to The Inventions (*See* Muckeries)

Moony cove (*Peoples'*) The word is derived from the tendency of persons suffering from incipient insanity to keep the eyes raised when walking Moon-struck is another form of the word

Moorgate - rattler (*Clare Market*, 1899) Startlingly - dressed passer - by — a swell of that district, or in it Perhaps a corruption of Moorgate, or possibly Margate

Mops and brooms (*Peoples'*) Drunk — probably suggested by the hair getting disordered and like a mop From a time when hair was worn long.

'Mops and brooms' doubtless express a sense of confusion.—*Daily News*.

Moral Cremorne (*Soc*, 1883) Fisheries Exhibition, Royal Horticultural Gardens, 1883. So named because there had been no illumination fêtes since the closing of immoral Cremorne Gardens

The Fisheries Exhibition is over The lights of the moral Cremorne are out.— *Ref*, 3rd November 1883

More blue (*Devon, old*). Exclamation. Absolute pronunciation of 'mort bleue', and coming down probably from the Frenchified court of Charles II, when Exeter was a western metropolis (*See* Big beck, Zounds, Zooks, Odd's fish, Please the pigs, Maw sang)

More war (*Street*, 1898). Street quarrel or wrangle, especially amongst women Outcome of the somewhat discussive warfare carried on between U S.A and Spain in this year Satirical to some degree

Mother (*Complicated Rhyming*, 1868) Water Abbreviation of 'mother and daughter' — rhyming with 'water'.

Mother of the modern drama (*Theatrical*). An actress who took up high matronly ground in a lecture delivered (1884) at Birmingham The lady, successful early in life, and married to a rich, prosperous and devoted husband, spoke very *ex cathedra*, and during her oration pitied the strugglers, and announced her intention of quitting the stage when '40'. Calculating people arrived at the conclusion that the lady never therefore intended to leave the stage, as no one can be '40' twice.

Mother's help (*Mid. Class*, 1883 on). Nursery governess. Term invented for the accommodation of people who want a governess, and do not want to pay for one.

Motor (*London Soc.*, 1896). Fast, hard-living; said of a man about town.

Motor (*Oxford*, 1897). Coach, cram tutor for exams. Origin obvious. Simply the conversion of the old-time coach into the new-time motor—without the car.

Motor (*Soc.*, 1896). The motor-car, immediately shortened to motor, was first shown in London streets on 10th November 1896. Before the end of the year a score of phrases were built up around it.

Byron had shown the true origin of the Motor long before the gentlemen who thought they invented it were born. Did he not say in his famous riddle:

'Twas whispered in Heaven, 'twas Motor'd in Hell. — *D. T.*, 19th November 1896.

Motter (*Street*, 1896). Name given to the motor carriage on its very first official appearance in London on Lord Mayor's Day, 1896.

Mount the cart (*Peoples'*, 18 *cent.*). Be hanged—from the then habit of carting culprits from Newgate to Tyburn tree, or gallows — the cart being drawn from under the wretch when the rope had been attached to the beam.

Mourning coach horse (*Middle Class London*, 1850). A tall, solemn woman, dressed in black and many inky feathers. (*See* Sala's B.)

Mouth-pie (*Street*). Emphatic name for feminine scolding.

Move the previous question (*Soc., from Parliamentary Life*). To evade; to object to explain.

To 'move the previous question' is in Parliamentary phraseology simply to say that the present is not the most convenient moment for discussing any particular motion. Another time, it says—another time, by all means; but not just now.

Move the procession (*American Mining*). To incite a crowd against some unpopular person.

Mowrowsky (*Anglo-American*). Interchange of initial consonants of two adjacent words, by accident or intention, as bin and gitters for 'gin and bitters'. Very common, 1840-56. Brought into fashion by Albert Smith from hospital life. Now chiefly patronised in America.

A mowrowsky is often a transfer of two words, as in the *Taming of the Shrew*, where Grumio cries, in pretended fright, 'The oats have eaten the horses'. During the Donnelly discussion (1888) wherein it was contended that the plays of Shakespeare had been written by Lord Bacon, an intended satirical mowrowsky was invented by an interchange of initials between the two names, Bakespeare and Shacon.

Muck (*Military*). Scornful appellation bestowed upon all infantry by all cavalry.

Muck and halfpenny afters (*Middle Class*). Bad, pretentious dinner—spotted at the corners with custard powder preparations, and half-dozens of stewed prunes, etc., etc.

Muckeries (*Youths*, 1885). Name given to the 'Inventories' (Inventions Exhibition at S. Kensington) as the season went on, by the youthful frequenters.

Mucking (*Westminster School*). Idling, hanging round.

Mud island (*E. London*). Southend—watering-place on the mouth of the Thames, whose estuary still produces a deal of mud.

Mud show (*Soc.*). An agricultural, or other out-door show.

Mud-hovel argument (*Political*, 1879-84). Term given to Tory argument against extension of political liberty in Ireland.

A great part of his speech, however, consisted only of what we may call the 'mud-hovel' argument, an argument which he applied to Ireland, and on which it will be remembered he had recently an opportunity of expatiating in Ireland.—*D. N.*, 4th March 1884.

Mud-pusher (*Street*, 1870). Crossing sweeper.

Muff (*Soc.*, 1840 on). A stupid, dilatory, inactive, and generally amiable young man.

Muffin-puncher (*Street*). Muffin-baker.

Muffin-wallopers (*Middle Class London*, 1880). Scandal-loving women, chiefly spinsters, who meet over a cup of tea

Mug (*Theatrical*) To show variety of comic expression in the features

Multa bona fakement (*Tavern*, 1800-35) Very good trick — from the Italian molto bono, and abstract noun made from fake—to manipulate adroitly if dishonestly

A hand truck was procured, and drugged Charley (watchman) and his box were then transferred to another locality, so that when Charley awoke he found himself and box ready for doing duty in another parish This trick was estimated to be a multa bona fakement. —Diprose's Clement Danes, Pierce Egan, *Life in London*, vol i, p 101

Mumchance (*Peop*, *Hist*) Dolefully silent

The man or woman who can sit 'mumchance', and with faces as long as a yard measure, over a well-acted farce do not deserve to be ranked in the noble army of all-embracing playgoers —*D T*, 11th March 1897

Mumming booth (*Lower Stage*) A wandering marquee in which short plays are produced.

Munching house (*City*, 1850). Onomatope for Mansion House—from the lusty-feeding going on there

The distinguished artists who repeated *The Masque of Painters* at the Munching House the other day do not seem to have been quite satisfied with their treatment —*Ref*, 5th July 1885

Mundane (*Franco-Eng*, 1890 on) Person of fashion

The Comtesse de Maupeou, a mundane who has recently risen upon the musical horizon, rendered several songs —*D N*, 12th April 1897

Murder an' Irish (*Peoples'*, 19 *cent.*) Exclamation intimating that things are at a climax Sometimes more emphatically used as 'murderin' Irish'.

Museum headache (*Authors'*, 1857)

Many a student avers, whether candidly or not, that it costs him less to buy rare books than to hang about the Museum, waiting the leisure of the attendants, and struggling against a 'Museum headache'.—*D N.*, 11th December 1882.

Mush, gush, and lush (*Amer.-Eng*, 1884) Mean interested criticism —critiques paid for either in money or feastings

Mushroom (*Public-house*) Name given by frequenters (presumably in contempt), to the great clock to be seen in most taverns, and which gives warning as to closing time

Music Hall howl (*Musicians'*). The peculiar mode of singing in music-halls, the result of endeavouring rather to make the words of a song heard than to create musical effect

Music Hall public (*Soc*, 1884). Satirical description of public who do not care for high-class compositions

Next time M Rivière organises a benefit let him make up his mind whether he will seek the suffrages of the musical or the music hall public He might be happy with either, but he will never get both at once —*Ref*, 3rd May 1885.

Musk-rats (*American*) People of Delaware—given because those animals prevail in this division

Must know Mrs Kelley? You (London, 1898 on). Joking exclamation with no particular meaning, generally shot at a long-winded talker Phrase used for two years at all times and places by Dan Leno.

Mustard plaster (*Peoples'*) Dismal young man. Put a mustard plaster on his chest Said of a doleful and dismal pallid young man Derived from a comic song, in association with Colman's mustard, written by the celebrated pantomime writer, E. L Blanchard, and sung in one of his pantomimes at Drury Lane

Mustard pot (*Peoples'*) Carriage with a light yellow body Obvious outcome of mere relation of colours.

Mutton shunter (*Policemen*, 1883). Policeman.

My elm is grown (*Peoples'*, 18 *cent*). Prognostication of one's own death—figure of speech depending upon the practical fact that elm is used throughout the land for coffins.

N

N.—A.—D. (*Military Hospital*). Shamming in any way. Initials of No Appreciable Disease.

N. D. (*Soc.*, 19 *cent.*). Initials of No Date, used by librarians in making their lists. Applied to a woman who tries to look young.

N. F. (*Artisans'*, *masked*). Initials of No Fool.

N. G. (*Peoples'*, 19 *cent.*). Emphatic initials of No Go—which in its turn implies failure.

N. N. (*Soc.*). Necessary Nuisance —generally applied to husband.

N. Y. D. (*Military Hospital*). Evasive for drunk. Initials of Not Yet Diagnosed—found on military hospital bed-cards as a direction to visiting medical men and to nurses. In this case the true diagnosis would lead to a confinement to barracks.

Nail a goss (*Thieves'*). To steal a hat—industry gone out since hats became so cheap. The silk plush hat which succeeded and killed the beaver was so comparatively light that it was called a gossamer, soon naturally reduced to goss.

Nail a strike (*Thieves'*). To steal a watch.

Nailed up drama (*Theat.*, 1881). Satirical title found for the drama which depends upon elaborate scenery. Said first in relation to *The World*, produced at Drury Lane about this time.

Nana, Nanaish (*Club*, 1882). Outrageous, overstepping decency—from the French romance *Nana*, by Zola.

Theodora would be an unpresentable being to a London or a New York audience, and is almost too 'high' in the sense poulterers attach to the word for even a Boulevardier public. In the name of history, Zola's *Nana* is out-Nana-ed.—*D. N.* (criticism on *Theodora*), 29th December 1884.

Nancy (*Low London*, 19 *cent.*). Effeminate in a slight degree. Also used in the U.S.A.

Nancy tales (*Lit.*, 1890). Humbug, bosh.

The negroes of the West Indies call an old wife's fable 'a Nancy story', derived from Ananzi, the African spider who told tales.—*D. N.*, 17th January 1891.

Nanny (*Street boys'*). Banana. (*See* Tommy Rabbit.)

Nanty (*Italian organ-grinders'*). Nothing—corruption of *niente*.

''E's a nanty cove.'

Nanty narking (*Tavern*, 1800 on to 1840). Great fun. (*See* Egan's *Life in London*.)

Nanty worster (*Common London*). Nanty (Italian) here means 'no'; worster an intensification of 'worst'. The phrase means therefore a 'no-worse'.

Nark the titter (*Dangerous Classes*). Watch the woman. 'Nark' is probably a rhyming word to 'mark'. Titter is the very lowest mode of describing a woman—one who has teats.

Nap (*London*, 1855-70). A very pointed moustache—the two points forming a long line which 'cut' the face. It was re-introduced by Napoleon III., and is still worn by Napoleonists in Paris.

Nap or nothing (*Club*, 1868). All or naught.

Nap (knap) the regulars (*Thieves'*). Receive or grab the customary portion of the money resulting from the sale of stolen property.

Narrative (*Middle-class*). Dog's tail. A tale is a narrative—tale = tail in pronunciation.

Nathaniel, Below (*Old English*). Even lower than Hades—Nathaniel (like Samuel, or Zamiel in Germany) and Old Nick, or Nicholas, being familiar synonyms for Satan.

Throughout my life I have always had a burning desire and a dogged determination to get below the surface of things, and Eugène Sue's masterpiece took you, as the saying is, 'down below Nathaniel', as regards the basements and the subterraneans of society.—G. A. Sala, *D. T.*, 18th July 1895.

Nattermy (*Peoples'*). Word for a thin human being. From anatomy.

Natural, All your (*Peoples'*). Ellipsis of all your natural born days. Natural probably here meant as 'ordinary', which phrase would exclude your 'extraordinary' days.

Nautical triumvisetta (*Music Hall*) A singing and dancing nautical scene by three persons, of whom two are generally women

Near and far (*Public-house Rhyming*) The bar.

Neat (*Low Peoples'*) Unadulterated, unmixed—in relation to drink e g,

Two o' gin neat is quite an improvement upon a similar quantity of 'raw'.

Nec Ultra (*Soc.*, 17-19 *cent*) West side of Temple Bar

To the Countess Blushrose, Nature herself had written *Nec Ultra* on the west side of Temple Bar—D Jerrold's *The Story of a Feather*, chap ix

Neck oil (*E. London*) Beer generally

Ned Skinner (*Rhyming*) Dinner

Neddyvaul (*Street boys'*) 'Ned of all' Chief, commander, conqueror

Neecee peeress (*Soc.*) An E. C or city bride of little or no family, and an immense fortune, both of which are wedded to some poor lord or baronet.

Needful (*Peoples'*, 19 *cent*). Money—and one of the most urgent terms for it. In use by all classes.

Needle (*Tailors'*) Got the needle, *i.e.*, irritated, as when the needle runs into a finger Has spread generally over working classes, who have accepted the graphic nature of the phrase

Needles and pins (*Peoples'*) Warning against marriage. The rhyming runs—

Pins and needles—needles and pins
When a man marries his trouble begins

Common also to America, to which land it passed from Devonshire, where the phrase is still very common

Neetrith gen (*Backspeech*) Thirteen shillings The first word is thirteen spelt backwards—the 'th' very properly being taken as one letter 'Gen' is the short for general (a shilling)

Negus (*Queen Ann's reign*) Port wine and hot water, heightened by grated nutmeg One of the name words—from a Colonel Negus who invented the beverage

Never fear (*Peoples'*) Don't be anxious.

Never squedge (*Low London*) A poor pulseless, passionless youth—a duffer

Neversweat (*Common English*, 19 *cent.*). A graphic, one-word description of a lazy, or even a slow individual, used only towards men and boys.

New (*Britannia training ship*) Fresh arrival, last addition Used in the plural

New (*American*). News 'Oh, is that the new?'

New cut warrior (*S London*, 1830). An inhabitant fighter, in or near the New Cut, a road made only in the 19th century through the Lambeth Marshes from Blackfriars to Lambeth

New departure (*Soc*, 1880) Synonym for change of any kind.

We have often pointed out that the electoral changes which have just been accomplished must produce a new era—or, as the Americans would call it, a new departure—in legislation—*D. N.*, 9th August 1885

New pair of boots (*Mid class*) Another question altogether—later shape of another pair of shoes.

Once they have the concession made to them, then it becomes a 'new pair of boots' altogether—*Entr'acte*, 17th March 1883

Newcastle programme (1894 on) Extreme promises, difficult of execution From a speech of extreme Radical promise made by Mr John Morley at Newcastle

Next parish to America (*Irish*). Arran Island—most western land of Ireland

Just sixteen miles beyond Barna, and at the mouth of the Bay of Galway, is Arran island, which the people here call the 'Next Parish to America'.—*D N.*, December 1887.

Next thing to the judgment day (*wholly American*) Absolute social shock.

Nice as nasty (*Lower Peoples'*) Evasive way of declaring the opponent objectionable

Nice blackberry (*American*). Satirical phrase, intimating that the other is a bitter weed or fruit

Nice joint (*Street*). Charming, if over-pronounced, young person.

Nice place to live out of (*Peoples'*). Evasive way of condemning a locality

Without corresponding to the idea of 'a nice place to live out of', Harrogate is assuredly one of those spots which owe much to their surroundings.

(*See* Do without it.)

Nice thin job (*Peoples'*, 1895). Mean evasion of a promise. 'Thin'—to be seen through, comes from America—and in England antithetically suggested thick—now very prevalent for ill-usage and misbehaviour in general.

Nicholls (*Soc.*, 1860 on). Complete riding habit. From the splendid habits made by Nicholls, of Regent Street.

Nickel-plate (*American*). An equivalent to our German silver—a swindle, a social fraud.

The name 'nickel plate', as applied to the New York, Chicago & St Louis Railway, came into use in this way: speaking of the road by its initial letters—a common practice among railroad men—N. Y. C. L. suggested nickel, and from that to 'nickel plate' was an easy transition.—*Detroit Free Press*, 1882.

Niggers' duel (*Anglo-American*). A never-intended encounter. Each behind a mile-stone, therefore a mile apart.

Night flea (*Essex School*). Boarder—in contradistinction from Day-bug (*q.v.*).

Niminy-piminy (*Soc.*, 19 *cent.*). Effeminately affected.

Mr Beckford wrote in Leigh Hunt's *Story of Rimini*:

Nimmini Pimmini
The Story of Rimmini.
—*D. N.*, 11th December 1882.

Nimshes (*American Federal*, 1860-65). One of the contemptuous names describing the Secessionists. Origin not known.

Nine mile nuts (*Japanese pigeon*). Anything to eat or drink very sustaining. From the nutritive qualities of chestnuts—especially in Japan.

Nine tailors make a man (*Old Eng.*). Said derisively of a small man, whether tailor or not.

Nines, Up to the (*Common*). Perfect.

90 dog (*Street*). Pug. Referring to aspect of tail.

97 champion frost (*Peoples'*). First motor cars. The expectations raised on 10th November, 1896, by the procession of motor cars from the Embankment to Brighton, were disappointed by the immediate results.

No. I. (*New York*, 1883). When the U.S.A. were interested, early in this year, as to whether the 'No I.' of the Invincible Brotherhood (Fenian) was or was not in America, the term No. I. was often applied to noisy, or even merely evident, Irishmen.

No. I. (*Political*, 1883). Mysterious. This phrase took its rise early this year, consequent upon the collapse of 'The Brotherhood of Invincibles'.

No better than they ought to be (*Peoples'*). Worse than many.

There are fireworks on certain nights now at the Crystal Palace, and they are about the most successful of the displays given here; though it may be said they attract very many persons whom Mrs Grundy says are no better than they ought to be.—*Entr'acte*, 6th June 1885.

No beyond jammer (*Street*). Perfectly beautiful woman.

No church (*Peoples'*). When the great wrangle took place between the High Church party and the Low Church party, this phrase, which at once took, and has remained popular, was deftly discovered by Douglas Jerrold to represent the religious condition of the utterly outcast. The phrase was first published by the wit in a page of *Punch*.

No class (*Street*, 1893 on). Commonplace.

He proposed to Sal and she knew he was gone on her a bit—
Although I knew quite well it couldn't last;
But when she said, 'I love him, Bill,' it fairly knocked me sick,
Cos I seemed to know 'e wasn't any class.

'Soldiers! Why, soldiers ain't no class.'—*D. T.*, June 1897.

No earthly (*London*, 1899). Abbreviation of 'no earthly chance'.

The actors who have not booked their seats *viâ* Mr Henry Dana, are hereby notified that they have now no earthly, as all seats have been allotted.—*Ref.*, 22nd October 1899.

No grease (*Engineers'*). Absence of behaviour, of politeness.

No rats (*Peoples'*). Scotchman. Evasive reference to that native, it being supposed that a Scot is always associated with bagpipes, and that no rat can bear the neighbourhood of that musical instrument.

No return ticket (*Common, London*). Abbreviation of 'He's going to Hanwell and no return ticket'—said of a man who shows signs of madness.

Nobby (*Navy*). Anglicization of the 'Niobe'.

Nolled (*American*) Form of *nolle prosequi* Used by lawyers.

Non compos *See* Compos, Non.

Non me (*Peoples'*, 1820-30). Lie. 'That's a non me for one.' Took its rise from the trial of Queen Caroline, wherein the Italian witnesses observed 'non mi ricordo' (I do not remember) to every important question put to them in cross-examination

Nonsensational (*Critical*, 1897) Sensational nonsense

With a piece of nonsensational extravagance entitled *The MacHaggis*, Mr Penley on Thursday night re-opened his theatre —*People*, 28th February 1897.

Norfolk Howard (*Popular*). A bed-bug. Due to a man named Buggey advertising a change of name to this phrase, a combination of the family name and title of the Duke of Norfolk Produced much press comment and even sympathy for all persons with objectionable names. The following list of vexatious names was compiled and published in the *Times*.

Asse, Bub, Belly, Boots, Cripple, Cheese, Cockles, Dunce, Dam, Drinkmilke, Def, Flashman, Fatt, Ginger, Goose, Beaste, Barehead, Bungler, Bugg, Buggey, Bones, Cheeke, Clodd, Cod, Demon, Fiend, Funck, Frogge, Ghost, Gready, Hagg, Humpe, Holdwater, Headach, Jugs, Jelly, Idle, Kneebone, Kidney, Licie, Lame, Lazy, Leakey, Maypole, Mule, Monkey, Milksop, Mudd, Honeybum, Maydenhead, Mug, Piddle, Paswater, Pisse, Pricksmall, Pricke, Phisicke, Pighead, Pot, Poker, Poopy, Prigge, Pigge, Punch, Proverbs, Quicklove, Quash, Radish, Rumpe, Rawbone, Rottengoose, Swette, Shish, Sprat, Sheartlifte, Stiffe, Squibb, Sponge, Stubborne, Swine, Shittel, Shave, Shrimps, Shirt, Skim, Squalsh, Silly, Shoe, Smelt, Skull, Spattel, Shadow, Snaggs, Spittle, Teate, Taylecoate, Villain, Vittels, Vile, Whale

North Castle (*Slang of the impecunious*, 1880). Holloway Jail, in the north of London.

Nose (*Boating*) The extreme tip of the bow of a boat

Nose and chin (*Rhyming*) One of the modes of referring to gin.

Nose-bag (*Mid -class*, 19 *cent.*). A hospitable house

'These gulls', remarked the keeper before referred to, 'come now in larger numbers from year to year. The fact is they are like a good many of the people you see walking about—if they once find out where there's a good nose-bag they take care to be near it.'—*D. T*, 22nd December 1898

Nose-bagger (*Seaside Soc.*) A day visitor to the seaside, who brings his own provisions, presumably in a bag—one who is of no monetary value to the resort visited. Contemptuous comparison to the cab horse, or even the shore-donkey

'Last season was a bad one; there were plenty of visitors, but nearly all "nose-baggers"—people who come for the day and bring their own provisions,' said a Southend butcher in his examination at the Chelmsford Bankruptcy Court. —*Lloyds'*, 24th November 1807

Noser (*Covent Garden*) Said of visitors to the market who inspect the flowers and fruits, sometimes quite closely, and who do not buy

Nosper (*Low London back*). Common word for stranger. It is 'person'

Not a feather to fly with (*Colloquial —from Universities*). When the word 'plucked' was used to designate failure to pass an examination, the figure of speech was carried out by describing a very doleful failure as being plucked 'without a feather to fly with'—meaning that no success whatever was obtained. Applied in many ways.

Not dead yet (*Theatrical*, 1883). Ancient—generally said of an antique fairy

Not enough written (*Authors'*, 1870) Not sufficiently corrected for style

Not in it (*Sporting*) Failure—referring to a horse in a race as having no chance.

The gentleman who declared that gold mining was not in it was strictly correct. The gold production in the United States is worth between nine and ten millions, but the profit upon it is nothing like that on sugar.—*D T.*, 26th February 1897

Not on borrowing terms (*American*, 1882). Not in friendly relations—said of next-door neighbours.

The families of the two young souls were not on 'borrowing terms'.—*Texas Siftings*, 1883.

Not the cheese (*Peoples'*, *Hist.*). Not satisfactory. Dr Brewer absolutely refers this word back to the Persian and the Hindoo—cheez, thing; though he says nothing of the journey. May be from the French, 'Ce n'est pas la chose'—chose being used a great deal for thing in the sixties.

Not to-day, Baker (*Peoples'*, 1885). Said at a youth who is paying attentions which are obviously unwelcome. Term used by housewives refusing bread when the morning baker calls. But satirically applied in reference to a military man of this name who was given into custody for pressing his attentions upon a young lady travelling by accident alone with him.

The gentleman signs himself 'Baker', and wants to try an experiment on my family. In the words of the poet, I reply, 'Not to-day, Baker!'—*Ref.*, 8th March 1885.

Not too nice (*Soc.*, 1870 on). First degree of condemnation—equals bad. Outcome of the frequent use of nice.

Not up to Dick (*Common Respectable Life*). Not well; ill and wretched.

Not worth a rap (*Irish*, *Hist.*). Worth nothing. In the early years of the 18th century, from 1721, notwithstanding the savage Drapier Letters, copper money was so rare in Ireland that a quantity of base metal was in circulation in the shape of small coins. They came to be called raps—probably the short of *rapparee*, a good-for-nothing fellow—hence the word came to be applied to describe valuelessness.

Note (*Soc.*, 1860 on). Intellectual signature, polite war-cry.

Culture is the 'note' of Boston.—*D. N.*, 18th November 1884.

Notergal Wash, or N. Wash (*L. Class*, 1857 on). No wash at all—grubbiness. Very interesting if from Nightingale. Miss Nightingale, the creator (1855-56) of rational nursing, had the misfortune to incur the lower public satire for stating that a person could keep himself clean on a pint of washing water per day. She did not say he was preferably to do this.

Nothing to do with the case (*Peoples'*, *Hist.*). Elegant evasion of 'you lie!' Made very popular by Mr W. S. Gilbert's *The Mikado*, wherein Mr G. Grossmith had a capital song which began:

'The flowers that bloom in the spring
Have nothing to do with the case.'

Nottub (*Back phrasing*). Button.

Now or never (*Rhyming*). Clever.

Well, these Tommy Rotters kid the poor judy they're very rich, and if they're now and never they get carefully carried (married) to her.—*Biography of Cheap Heiress Hunters*, 1882.

Now we're busy (*Peoples'*, 1868). To suggest action. Also an evasive intimation that the person spoken of is no better for his liquor, and is about to be destructive.

Now we shan't be long (*Peoples'*, 1895 on). Intimation of finality. Origin obscure. Probably from railway travellers' phrase when near the end of a journey.

'Now we shan't be long', said Henry Martin to Thomas Hiom, as the couple equipped themselves with a pair of double-barrelled catapults and a copious supply of indiarubber pellets, and started off on a partridge-shooting expedition to the Finchley Road.—*D. T.*, 8th September 1896.

Now we shall be shan't (*Dec.* 1896). Another jocular shape of 'Now we shan't be long'—and purposely having no meaning.

Nudities (*Critics*, 1890 on). New shape of 'nude studies' or 'nudes'.

The nudities, though of the usual class, are fewer and less fragrant than usual, the horrors less horrible, and what may be called the medical pictures less repulsive.—*D. N.*, 19th April 1898.

Nuf ced (*From America*). Contraction of 'enough said'—absurdly spelt. Warning to say no more. Used in Liverpool chiefly.

Number one (*Navy*). Strictly naval for first lieutenant.

Nuptiated (*Wilful American*). Married.

Nurse the hoe-handle (*Agricultural American*). Lazy.

Nursery noodles (*Literary*). Critics who are very fastidious.

O

O (*Peoples', Hist.*) Most emphatic form of liking and satisfaction—always used as a suffix. "What O!"

O (*Printers'*) Emphatic, and abbreviation of overseer.

O B (*Criminal*). Old Bailey, City Criminal Court

O P. H (*Polit*, 1886) Old Parliamentary Hand—meaning Gladstone Invented by *Times* (February 1886)

O T (*Street, Satirical*, 1880). One way of observing that the weather is warm

O V. (*Booth*) Abbreviation of oven—the name given to the open space below the stage in which the Pepper's ghost illusion is worked This apparatus, which is at an angle of 35, and upon which the phantomised comedians lie, is surrounded by lamps, and is very hot—hence the title. (*See* Phant.)

OVO (*Low Class, Hist*) Quite inexplicable. No solution ever obtained from the initiates

O Bergami, or O Begga me (*London Peoples'*, 1820). Still used in the streets as intimating that the person addressed is a liar, or worse. From one Ber'gami—a lying witness at the trial of Queen Caroline—whose denial of everything brought about this phrase, with his eternal 'non mi ricordo'. (*See* Non me)

O chase me (*Streets*, 1898 on) Satiric invitation, or pretended satiric, by a maiden to a youth to run after her and hug and kiss her

O Cheese and Crust (*Lower Peoples'*) O, Jesus Christ!

O cricum jiminy (*Peoples', Hist*). An exclamation of pretended fear.

O! cry! (*Peoples'*) Exclamation of satiric surprise, confounded with cry, but probably nothing to do with it. 'O! crickey!' may be another shape of the expression May be an evasion of 'O! Christ!'

O dear me! (*Peoples'*) Exclamation of regret Probably from the Court of Katharine of Arragon (Henry VIII.), or perhaps from that of Catherine of Braganza (Charles II.)

'Ay di mi!' as the Spaniards say, we shall have no Pomard this year! The storms of yesterday and of Monday have devastated the vineyards.—*D N*, 1874.

O Gomorrah to you! (*Com. Life*). Play of a word upon 'to-morrow', and said either savagely or jocularly.

O—good night! (*Low English*) Meaning, 'This is too much—I think I must be going'

O! la! (*European—almost historical*) O! law! The influence of the Crusades upon European society was notoriously immense. Surely some expressions were imported! What more likely than that of 'Allah!'—which is in the mouth of every Mahomedan at all times, and always at the beginning of a sentence? 'Hullo!' may be from the same source

O my eye (*Peoples'—Old Catholic*) Corruption of 'Ah mihi'—the opening words of the prayer to St Martin, the patron of beggars Implies doubt, and a suggestion of deceptive utterance.

O P H (*Street*, 19 *cent.*) Off

O Pollaky! (*Peoples'*, 1870). Exclamation of protest against too urgent enquiries From an independent, self-constituted, foreign detective, who resided on Paddington Green, and became famous for his mysterious and varied advertisements, which invariably ended with his name (accent on the second syllable), and his address

O soldiers! (*Peoples'*). Exclamation—not now often heard

O Smith! (*Peoples'*, 1835-50). Cavernous laugh, very popular, for nearly a score of years 'What an O Smith' would be the comment upon hearing a grim 'Ha ha' O Smith always did the frequent Adelphi villains of that day, also the unscrupulous villains

O the language! (*Peoples'*) Generally said to a drunken woman using violent or spluttering English

O Willie, Willie (*Peoples'*, 1898) Term of satiric reproach addressed to a taradiddler rather than a flat liar

Oak (*Rhyming*) Joke—very common Now passed into chestnut

Oaky-pokeys (*Devonshire*) Cockchafers

Oat-stealer (*Country Tavern*). Ostler. A play upon the original word.

Obvious (*Soc.*, 1897). Fat, stout. Origin evident.

'Mary, you are becoming too obvious.'

Obviously severe (*Soc.*, 1890 on). Hopelessly rude of speech.

Occifer (*Colloquial imbecile*, 19 *cent.*). Officer.

Ochorboc (*Italian organ-grinders'*). Beer. The word is here found by taking the first letter of the word 'bochor' and adding it to the end, also adding 'oc'. The original word is 'Bocca' (mouth).

Odd job man (*Trade*). Modified description of the Shyster, who professes to do anything and only does his employer.

Odd-fellows (*Peoples'*). Name of a mutual benefit society. Corruption of God-fellows.

Odd's Bobs (*Peoples'*). *God's Babe* (the Redeemer). May be found in *Roderick Random*.

Od's death. The Crucifixion—His death; long since passed into 'Sdeath.

Od's fish (*Peoples'*, *Hist.*). Scotch exclamation, probably brought south by James I. 'Od' is an evasion of 'God', while fish is a Scotticism for fash, which in its turn is from *fâché*, one of the French terms brought into Scotland through French influence.

Od's my life (*Lower Class*). One of the religious adjurations—'God's my life.'

Know Lieutenant Bowling—odd's my life! and that I do.—*Roderick Random*, ch. xxiv.

Odsbud (*Peoples'*). Is probably God's Bud—and meaning the Redeemer, or it may be God's Blood. (See *Tom Jones*, bk. xvi., ch. viii.)

Odso (*Provincial*). Now only heard in country places. One of the evasive religious ejaculations of 17th century —'God's oath'.

Young Mirabel: 'Odso—the relics, madam, from Rome!'—Farquhar, *The Inconstant*.

Off chump (*Stable*). No appetite—onomatope of the noise made by horses in eating.

Off the rails (line) (*Peoples'*, 1840 on). Unsteady.

Officers of the 52nds (*Irish—City of Cork*). Known generally in Irish garrison towns. Young men, chiefly clerks and shopkeepers, who make a rigid official appearance on Sundays. There are fifty-two Sundays in a year.

Officers' wives (*Army*, 19 *cent.*). Prosperity.

The bugle sang out 'Officers' wives have puddings and pies, while soldiers' wives have skilly', that is the soldiers' translation of the call to mess.—*Ref.*, 10th April 1885.

Ofters (*Sporting*, 1884). Frequenters.

We may almost assume that the principle of heredity has once again asserted itself, and that the youthful 'ofters' whom I saw in the Haymarket the other night, all shirt front and fur collar, are the offspring of the very same sort of springalds who exploited themselves thirty years ago in the very selfsame neighbourhood.—*Ref.*, 23rd December 1888.

Og-rattin (*Lond. Restaurant*). *Au gratin*—anglicization.

Ogotaspuotas (*Street*, *S. L.*, 1897). Bosh, nonsense. At once dubbed 'Oh, go to spue'. Legend upon a Radical flag carried on Sunday, 7th March 1897, to Hyde Park and to a meeting in favour of the Cretans.

Old boots, To fight like. Fight like Marlborough—the first English general to wear immense jack boots. William III. preceded him in this display—but the Orange's were lighter boots. For several generations Marlborough was the people's hero. Indeed he was only displaced first by Nelson, and then by Wellington. The heroes have given several boots to society—Wellington and Blucher amongst others. 'My dawg can fet like old boots, and shoon too.'

Old boys (*Soc.*, 1880). Old schoolfellows.

An 'Old Boy's' Dinner.—An 'Old Boy's' dinner of Amersham and Amersham Hall School was held last night at the Freemasons' Tavern, when about 130 were present.—*D. N.*, 9th April 1885.

Old Ebenezer (*American-Sport*). Grizzly and grisly bear. Probably applied from its appearance.

The hunter on the lonely heights of the Rocky Mountains is far too well armed to-day to fear either a 'mountain lion', as the panther is locally called, or 'Old Ebenezer', the renowned grizzly bear himself —*D. N*, 2nd February 1883

Old gal (*Peoples'*) General term of affection describing a wife

Old gang)*Parliamentary*, 1870-1900) Ancient Tory party—uncompromising Tories, generally old men.

Lord Randolph Churchill has probably not gained all the points on which he was disposed to insist. But, in deference to his opinion, there will no doubt be a clearance out of some of those whom the Fourth Party is in the habit of politely designating as the 'Old Gang'—Mr J Chamberlain, 17th June 1885

Old geyser (*Street*) Elderly man.

Old hat (*Old English and new Australian*) Modern anatomical reference—very cogent, but not explainable.

I shall conclude this note with remarking that the term 'old hat' is at present used by the vulgar in no very honourable sense—Fielding, *Jonathan Wild*

Old Mother Hubbard (*Common English*, 1880). Fictional—said of a story which is past belief

Old moustache (*Street*, 1880) Elderly vigorous man with grey moustache.

'Prisoners of War', two English middies, one of them with his arm in a sling, on a bench in a French seaport An old moustache guards them.—*D. N*, 9th April 1885

Old put (*Soc*, *early* 19 *cent*—*now Peoples'*). A pretentious, stupid, aged gentlemanly man Derived probably from a proper name

It is quite credible that such a man, meeting in an omnibus an elderly gentleman of antiquated air and costume, should consider it funny to insult the 'old put' by pretending to be an intimate acquaintance, and accosting him with a familiar 'How's Maria?'—*St James' Gazette*, 7th August 1883

Old Shake (*Amer Press*, 1870) Shakespeare.

Old shoes Rum (*See* Old boots)

Old Shovel-penny (*Military*). The pay-master, who is generally an ancient

Old slop (*London*, 19 *cent*) A corruption of 'saloop', derived from the French 'salope' Applied to the *Times* newspaper from 1840 50, to intimate that it was bowing and smiling on all sides, and trying to attract, while having no will of its own

Old splendid (*American*, 19 *cent*). Splendid in the highest

Old Whiskers (*Street*, 19 *cent.*). Cheeky boys' salute to a working-man whose whiskers are a little wild and iron-grey

Old Wigsby (*Middle-class*) Crotchety, narrow-minded, elderly man, who snappishly can see no good in any modern thing Same in French—equivalent *perruque*

M Halévy, whom he welcomed at the Academy, is also no *perruque*, or solemn big wig, and it may be said, with some emphasis, that he is no prude—*D. N.*, February 1886.

Olds, middles, and youngs (*Provincial*). Scotch, English, and Irish

Some one who had studied the idiosyncrasies of the three chief component parts of the United Kingdom, summed up his experiences of them by comparing the Scotch to old people, the English to middle-aged, and the Irish to children—*D N*, 5th March 1885

Oldster (*Slang, Clubs*, 1884) Ageing man Gift from U S A

You mustn't trust the oldsters too implicitly when they endeavour to persuade you, as they always will, that there never was such a time as their time—*Ref*, 7th March 1886

Olive oil (*Music Hall*, 1884) English pronunciation of *Au revoir*.

Oliver (*Compound Rhyming*) Fist. As thus. Oliver Twist Derived from Dickens

Omnes (*Wine Merchants'*) Word for the mixtures of odds and ends of various wines

On dig (*School*) Abbreviation of 'on his dignity'

On for a tatur (*Peoples'*). Fascinated, enraptured. Said of a man talking to a barmaid, and making eyes at her Evidently from *tête-à-tête*.

On his ear (*Amer-Eng*). In disgrace—from American handy mothers grabbing their boys' ears while battling in the streets with other boys.

On his feet (*American*) Ruined.

On ice (*Amer.-Eng*) Dead From placing body on ice to aid in 'faking it'.

On (a bit o') toast 'He had me on (a bit o') toast'; figuratively to say he absorbed or swallowed me so readily that the act was no more trouble to him than swallowing anything that will lie on a fragment of the toast in question.

On the back seam (*Tailors'*). Another elegant evasion. Flat on the floor.

On the beer (*Peoples'*). Evident.

On the bias (*Dressmakers'*). Illegitimate. On the cross.

On the deck (*Costers' local*). Living in Seven Dials. (*See* Deck.)

On the marry (*American*). Looking out for a wife or husband.

On the nail (*Peoples'*). Immediate payment—no trust. From the habit of ancient shop-keepers having a square-headed, large nail driven through the counter. Upon its head the money in payment was laid.

On the pig's back (*Irish*). In luck's way. Comes from Rome. During the reigns of the Twelve a golden amulet in the shape of a pig was supposed to bring good luck.

On the pounce (*Irish*). Preparing to spring, verbally. Brought into sudden fashion by Mr E. Harrington, H.R., M.P. (13th September 1887). Upon his being suspended he observed, 'You, Mr Speaker, have been on the pounce for me since I rose—you have been on the pounce waiting for me all the evening, and I claim my right to speak.

Mr Smith has the further function of keeping ready—'on the pounce', as the irreverent phrase goes—to clap on the closure whenever he and his colleagues think they have had enough of a debate. —*D. N.*, 10th October 1890.

On the run (*Anglo-American*). Escaping.

On the slate (*Lower Peoples'*). Written up against you—from the credit-slate kept in chandlers' shops.

On the square (*Peoples'*). Totally honest and straightforward. From Freemasonry, where the square is typical of everything that is good.

On the tapis (*Diplomatic*). Rumour, equivalent to 'on dit'.

On velvet (*Mid.-class* 1860), Luxurious success.

Once (*Street*). Vigour, go, cheek—the substantivizing of 'on'—most emphatic.

I like Shine—I cannot help admiring the large amount he possesses of what is vulgarly called 'once'. — *Ref.*, 24th October 1886.

Once a week man or **Sunday promenader** (*London*, 1830-40). Man in debt. Could only go out on Sunday, because on that day no arrests for debt could be made. (*See* Egan's *Real Life in London.*)

Onces (*Artisans'*). Wages — abbreviation of 'once a week'.

One and a peppermint drop (*Com. London*). One-eyed person.

One bites (*Lond. Costers*, 1870 on). Small, acrid apples — which, being tested with one bite, are thrown away.

One consecutive night (*Soc. and Stage*). Enough.

The second lecture is almost invariably a dismal failure. 'One consecutive night' is the limit of the funny man's course.—*D. N.*, 15th August 1890.

One drink house (*Common London*, 19 *cent.*). Where only one serving is permitted. If the customer desire a second helping, he has to take a walk 'round the houses' after the first.

One leg trouser (*Soc.*, 1882). Tight, feminine skirt of the period.

. . . and ladies in the latest 'one-leg-trouser' fashion from Paris. — *D. N.*, 18th April 1883.

(*See* Eel-skin.)

One of them (*Streets*). A shilling.

One of those (*Peoples'* 1880). An obscure phrase, coming probably from a comic song entitled, 'I really must have one of those'. No ascertained meaning above the class in which it originated—but evidently quite understood by its patrons. Remained in gutter fashion for about four years, when it fell from its high intent.

1.30 (*Tavern*). That is to say, 'one hour and a half'—derived from railway mode of counting time.

One-eyed city (*American*). A poor, inactive place.

One-light-undershirt-and-no-suspenders weather (*American*). Very hot.

One-two (*Peoples'*). Familiar figure of speech for rapidity.

Oner over the gash (*Peoples'*). A blow over the mouth.

Oolfoo (*Low. Class*) Fool

He'll make the judy think that you're the biggest oolfoo that ever was started on the blessed earth

Oons (*Provincial — Romanesque*) Evasion of 'God's wounds' Once pronounced 'ouns'. (*See* 'Tare an' ouns', 'Hounds')

'No—hang it 'Twill never do—oons' —Farquhar, *The Inconstant.*

Op (*Soc.*, 1870). Opera.

Open-airs (*Salvationist*) Meetings beyond roofs

We have had some blessed heart-rejoicing times Last week three sinners wept their way to Calvary, and enlisted to fight under the blood-stained banner Our open-airs are glorious —*War Cry*, 1884

Open door (*Polit.*, 1898) Colonial free trade Heard long before this year, but took form in the autumn of this, due to the discord in China—when England urged that Chinese commerce should be equally free to all nations—hence the term, which at once passed over Europe

Open eye (*Trade*, 1899) Correlative and completion of open door—meaning that though the foreigner may trade with the whole empire, a sharp eye must be kept on him Invention of Mr Stuart Wortley (at Stoke-upon-Trent, December 1899), who said in a dinner-speech 'For our commercial prosperity we needed the open eye as well as the open door.'

Open to (*L. London*) To tell—confess

I knew then that Selby had got a bit more (money) than he opened to (told) me —*People*, 6th January 1895.

Opera (*Amer*, 1880) Perversion of 'uproar'

Operation (*Tailors'*) Patch, especially in relation to the rear of trousers.

Opportunism (*Polit*, 1860 on) Shaping ways to most available means Used rather in contempt, as subserving conscience to convenience, or to personal advantage

Opt (*American—passing to England*, 1882). Abbreviation of verb 'optate'.

Food and treatment are much better at lunatic asylums than at gaols, or in casual wards, therefore Mr Wickham 'opts' for lunatic asylums. —*D N*, February 1882

Order (*Theat*) Free pass.

Order dead-head (*Theat*, 1880). Patron of the theatre—the dead-head —who passes on with an order 'Dead-head' (*q v*) comes from America, and is there unqualified by the word 'order' (*q.v*).

On Monday the house was quite full of what looked like money, leavened by a faint sprinkling of the order dead-head. —*Ref*, 17th April 1885.

Order of the Boot (*M Class*) A species of violent assault. The order of knighthood is bestowed by a tap with a sword on the shoulder The Order of the Boot is conferred by the toe of the boot—farther down

Orf chump (*Peoples'*) No appetite 'Orf' is a variation of 'off'. Derived from stablemen's tongues in reference to their horses—'I'm orf chump altogether'

Orf his chump (*Peoples'*) Mad, cranky It has nothing to do with 'orf chump' Means 'off his head' —his brain not in order.

Ornary (*American*) Expression for contemptible. Corruption of 'ordinary'

But I was roused by a fiendish laugh
That might have raised the dead—
Them ornary sneaks had sot the clocks
A half an hour ahead!

Ornin' (*L Class*) Boasting, praising oneself. Probably from the bombastic self assertion of the hunter's horn Chiefly provincial

Otamies (*Lower Peoples'*). Surgical operations of all kinds. Probable corruption of anatomies.

And now, poor man, he is among the otamies, at Surgeons' Hall.—Gay, *Beggars' Opera.*

Other arrangements (*Theatrical*) Defeat—retreat

Wherefore Hartt, though still by no means bowed down by weight of woe or otherwise, thinks it now time to make other arrangements. —*Ref.*, 5th July 1885

Other side (*Anglo American*). In U.S A it is G Britain In G B. it is U S A

Ouah (*Erotic, Peoples'*, 1882). Exclamation of delight

Ought to know (*Soc.*) Expression of belief in capability of person spoken of

Out (*Peoples'*). Loss. Sometimes used in the plural.

Out (*Soc. and Peoples'*, 19 *cent.*). Quarrelled.

Nor is Russian statesmanship our only trouble at the present moment. Prince Bismarck is or has been 'out with us', as the children say.—*D. N.*, 6th March 1885.

Out of commission (*Clerks'*). Requiring an appointment.

Out of the cupboard (*Peoples'*, *Boys'*). Turn out in the world.

Out of mess (*Military, Hist.*). Dead—he eats no more.

In the Eastern Soudan, in 1884, at El Teb, many of our men were wounded—indeed, I believe, some killed—by the wounded, wily enemy; and it became necessary, as we searched the field for our own dead and wounded, to put some of these treacherous foes out of mess; but there was no unnecessary butchery. —*D. T.*, 7th January 1899.

Out of sorts (*Printers'*). Literally, out of sorts of types—some of the composing compartments empty. This term is quite obsolete—now that composing machines are universal.

Out of the tail of the eye (*Irish*). Furtive observation.

Out of the whole cloth (*Amer.*). Untruth in the deepest degree. Equivalent to 'Whole hog' (*q.v.*).

Out of the wood (*American*). Out of the difficulty. Derived from pioneers and others in the West.

Outs (*Polit.*, 19 *cent.*). The Opposition.

While the Outs look upon this discovery as a tremendous blow to the Ins, while Tory newspapers insist that all this is the outcome of Liberal concessions, there is little or no chance of our getting the remedy that is so necessary.—*Ref.*, 25th February 1888.

Outs (*Anglo-Amer.*). Out of friendship. Probably old provincial English.

It is currently believed that Mrs Willie K. Vanderbilt, *née* Alva Smith, and the Baroness Fontenilliat, *née* Mimi Smith, are decidedly and emphatically on the outs.—*New York Mercury*, 1892.

Outside Eliza (*Low. London*). Drunk again, Eliza. Applied to intoxicated, reeling women. Derived from a police case where a barman stated that he said to the prisoner over and over again, 'Outside, Eliza'—but she would not go, and finally smashed a plate-glass window.

Outward man (*Devon*). A guzzler, one who does not stop at home.

Ovate (*American - English*, 90's). Verb derived from ovation.

An acute stage of the troubles in China seems to have been thoughtlessly ended by the Allies without their Commander-in-Chief, who was really very busy being received and ovated. — *N. Y. Times*, August 1900.

Over the bender (*Old English*). Implying that the statement made is untrue, *e.g.*, 'You'll pay me cock sure on Monday?' 'Yes—over the bender.' The bender is the elbow. It is historical in common English life that a declaration made over the elbow as distinct from not over it, need not be held sacred. Probably from early Christian if not from Pagan times. The bender is always the left elbow, and may therefore have something to do with 'over' the left.

Over the lefter (*Poachers'*). A partridge before 1st September, or a pheasant before 1st October.

Over the stile (*Rhyming*). Committed for trial.

Over-eye (*Peoples'*, *old*). To watch.

Owl, Biled (*Eng.-Amer.*, 1880 on). Bad complexion—signs facial of dissipation.

But Christmas scooped the sheriff,
  The egg-nogs gathered him in;
And Shelby's boy, Leviticus,
  Was, New Year's, tight as sin;
And along in March the Golyers
  Got so drunk that a fresh-biled owl
Would 'a' looked 'longside o' them two
    young men,
  Like a sober temperance fowl.
      —Col. Hay, U.S.A., Ambassador
        to Eng., 1897.

Oyster months (*Peoples'*, *Hist.*). All the months (8) in which there is an 'R'—oysters being quite 'out' in May, June, July, August.

Oysterics (*Mid.-class*, 1900-04 on). A coined word, suggesting hysterics, to satirize the panic in reference to oysters creating typhoid fever.

Once again the public is thrown into a state of what is grimly known in the trade as 'oysterics', owing to reports of deaths at Portsmouth from infected oysters. It is two years since the great oyster scare followed on the deaths following the mayoral banquet at Winchester.—*D. T.*, 11th November 1904.

P

P. C (*Soc*, 1880) Initials of 'poor classes'.

P P and C C (*Irish*) Parish priest, Catholic curate.

P P C (*Middle-class*) Snappish good-bye. Of course from departure card, *Pour prendre congé.*

P P C. (*Soc*, 19 *cent.*) *Pour prendre congé.* Used in two ways, when sending a card If without addition, it means good-bye—if with future date added, it means *au revoir.*

P P C., To (*Soc.*, 1880 on) To quarrel and cut

P P. M (*Soc*, 19 *cent*) Initials of *Pour P'tit Moment*, a modification of P. P C.

P R (*Sporting*). Initials of Prize Ring.

P R. B (*Soc.*, 1848 on). Pre-Raphaelite Brotherhood Sometimes ironically styled 'the Purby' In 1848 three artists, D G Rosetti, Holman Hunt and J E Millais, formed a brotherhood, with these letters following their names Several other painters joined them, together with T Woolner, the sculptor. Theirs was a revival of religion in art, religion which the brotherhood maintained had been swept out of Italian art by the materialistic force of the Renaissance.

The Pre-Raphaelite brethren, or 'P R B's,' as they are familiarly called, brought skill, earnestness, and thoroughness to the purpose of overturning established beliefs in matters artistic.—*D. N*, November 1885

P S (*Theatrical*). Prompt side—first entrance left hand of the stage, when facing the audience

P S's (*Hatter's term*). This secret trade phrase is called as here written, but is always described in the trade by 'x' It represents a sum of money which the master is willing to advance to a valuable workman in addition to his statement of weekly account, when he has made a short week, and which P. S. he will repay when a 'long' week arrives

P. W. Abney (*Streets'*, 1897) A high, feminine hat which first appeared in 1896, and grew The phrase is a reduction of Prince of Wales Abney Cemetery; it is got from three black, upright ostrich feathers, set up at the side of the hat in the fashion of the Prince of Wales's crest feathers. (*See* 'Catafalque')

P Y C (*Baltic Coffee-house*) Pale yellow candle—from this establishment persistently rejecting gas.

Pa (*Peoples'*) Relieving officer of a parish

Pack (*Navy*) Curtailment of 'Pactolus'.

Pack (*Texas*). To carry.

Packing (*Peoples'*). Food.

Packing-ken (*Low Class*) Eating-house—because you pack the food in your stomach then and there

Padder (*Oxford*) Short for Paddington Terminus

Paddington Station, dearest of all the London termini to the undergraduate heart during term, is Padder.—*D. T.*, 14th August 1899

Paid shot (*Old Scotch*). 'Shot' is a common mode of expression to denote a reckoning, etc 'I have paid my shot,' or rather 'scot', from 'scottum', a tax or contribution, a shot

Paint a proof (*Printers'*) To make a number of corrections on a proof, and so paint it with ink on both margins.

Paint the town red (*Amer.-Eng*, 1890) Originally to produce a sense of danger by night rioting From railway system, where red is the danger signal Now applied in a thousand ways.

The delegates from California are full of Chicago firewater, and are in the streets howling for Blaine and threatening to paint the town red

An effectual stop has been put to the last eccentricity of the facetious ex-Communist Maxime Lisbonne, who had lately, it will be remembered, endeavoured to 'paint the town red' by promenading the streets of Paris in a scarlet brougham —*D. T.*, 6th November 1894

After a time variety was gained by the use of vermilion

There are no dreary exhibitions of 'comic' drunkenness—as if drunkenness could ever be comical—nor any representation of 'racketty' young bloods painting the place vermilion.

Paint-brush baronets (*Soc.*, 1885). Title invented for ennobled artists.

The two paint-brush baronetcies are also sure to be popular. Mr Watts has his admirers in the circles of 'culture', and is a magnificent artist of the imaginative school. Mr Christmas Number Millais is, however, a household word, and popular with all classes. Now he is a bart. he will be more popular still, and his pictures will fetch bigger prices than ever.—*Ref.*, 28th June 1885.

Painter stainers (*Soc.*, 1883). Artists. At the Royal Academy Banquet, 1883, remarkable for much erratic observation, the Lord Mayor endeavoured to obtain a lift for the then threatened glories of the city by declaring that 'in earlier times the Corporation was the means whereby art was fostered in this country, and we have still amongst us a body which has devoted itself largely to the encouragement of Art — namely, the Painter Stainers' Company, which existed in the reign of Edward III., and is still in a flourishing condition. This company may really be described as having been the Royal Academy of England until the foundation of the present Academy in 1761'.

For the remainder of the season artists were in society jocularly called painter-stainers. Indeed the term lasted for many seasons.

Pair o' compasses (*London*, 1880). This term for a couple of human legs (in connection with a human body) came into vogue when the narrowness of the trousers brought out the stretched, compass-like effect of a pair of long legs. (*See* Gas-pipes.)

Pair o' round-mys (*Low Life*). Trousers.

Palpitate with actuality (*American-Eng.*, 1885). Intensely evident.

As no one of any influence is at present proposing a separation between Church and State, the vow does not, in the beautiful phrase which has been wafted to us across the Atlantic, 'palpitate with actuality'.—*D. N.*, 12th November 1885.

Pan out boss (*American Miners'*). Successful. Pan out is derived from the process of washing for gold.

Panic (*Stock Exchange*, 19 *cent.*). Sudden alarm, followed by fall in prices.

Pannum (*Thieves'*). Bread, dinner.

Panny (*Low Peoples'*). A familiar house.

Panny (*Low Peoples'*). Fight amongst women.

Panorama (*Lower Class*). Paraphrase of paramour.

Mr Branson, the bank forger, murders his wretched panorama, Mary Power, and departs for Australia.—*Ref.*, 17th November 1889.

Pantile Park (*London*). View of roofs and chimney pots. Used by Charles Dickens upon viewing the scene from Foster's back windows at 58 Lincoln's Inn Fields.

Panto (*Theatrical*). Brief for pantomime. Who would call a pantomime by any other name than this, would be voted an outsider at a blow. 'I now hear that this house is not to be altered until after the panto.'

Pantry Politics (*Soc.*, 1884). Servants' talk.

The case has laid bare one side of 'Society journalism', or, if we may suggest an amendment, 'pantry politics', and very curious the revelation is.—*Sat. Rev.*, 21st March 1885.

Pants-shoulder (*American*). The broadest part of a pair of trousers.

Paper house (*Theatrical*). No money—all free admissions.

Paper trunk and twine lock (*Figurative Anglo-American*). The least possible amount of luggage—packed in an old news sheet and stringed.

Paperer (*Theatrical*, 1879). The official who issues 'paper', or free passes, and so 'papers the house'.

Results showed that the 'paperer' understood his business. — *Ref.*, 14th June 1885.

Par-banging (*Street*). Tramping, seeking for work. Origin obscure—but probably French.

Par-leader (*Press*, 1875). A short, commenting article, in which no break occurs. A little essay of perhaps a score of sentences, but all in one paragraph.

Parable (*Amer.-Eng.*). Long, dreary egotistical statement.

Parish pick-axe (*Peoples'*). A prominent nose

Parker (*Local L*, 1850 and on) Street description of a very well-dressed man in the neighbourhood of the parks.

Parliament Whiskey (*Irish*). Satirical description of potheen which has paid inland revenue dues

If you are very ignorant, you must be told that poteen is the far famed liquor which the Irish, on the faith of the proverb, 'stolen bread is sweetest', prefer, in spite of law, and—no—not of law-givers, they drink it themselves, to its unsuccessful rival, parliament whiskey —*Mirror*, 1829

Parlour-jumper (*Police*, 1870 on). From jump, to thieve, to start property from you to him.

A constable explained that the prisoner was known as a 'parlour-jumper' This, in ordinary language, meant that he went in for robbing rooms —*D. T.*, 4th August 1898

Parnelliament (*Soc*, 1886) Invented and accepted name for 'Parliament'—from the astounding success of Parnell in throwing the Conservatives and Liberals into confusion.

Parrot and monkey time (*Amer-Eng*, 1885) Period of quarrelling. Started from a droll and salacious tale of a monkey and a parrot. Soon shortened to parroty.

There is no work to be had for them and the unfortunate creatures are likely to have what has graphically been called 'a parroty time' in their new home

Leonard and the chairs have had what Leonard's gay countrymen call 'a parroty time' —*D N*, 12th October 1886

Parsley bed (*Peoples'*, *Hist*) The supposed matrix of the new baby, as chronicled in nurseries (*See* Visit from the stork.)

Part that goes over the fence last (*American*) Evident

Parts his hair with a towel (*American*, 1882) Bald

Pas de Lafarge (*Soc*, '40's) Tabooed subject—as the result of its being over discussed Did or did not Madame Lafarge poison her husband? The dinner discussions became as great a bore as did, long after, the Tichborne case—which by the way, led to the yell at dinner tables—'No Tich'. In Paris, for years, when a man showed himself a bore, the protest ran 'Pas de Lafarge'. Now 'Pas de Dreyfus'.

Pass round the arm (*American*). To apply open-handed castigation to children—after the manner of applause.

Pass the Rubicon (*Classic*) Venture everything, no going back.

Pattern (*Irish*) Delightful, brilliant Abbreviation of 'pattern fair', which is a corruption of 'patron fair', which is short for 'patron saint'

Paul capstan (*Navy*). Expression of admission of excellency on the other side—as 'Well, you paul my capstan'.

Paulies (*Transvaal War*, 1899). Followers of Oom Paul Kruger—a pun between this word and 'poor lies'

'The writer calls the Boers 'Paulies' —*E N*, 9th December 1899.

Pawked up stuff (*Sporting*) False goods—bad horses, or dogs, or valueless sportsmen.

Pay out (*American miners'—passing to England*). Derived from a mine ceasing to be productive, when it was said to have paid out. Passed into general use amongst English-speaking people

Peabody (*L. Class*) Short for block of houses built under the Peabody Bequest to the poor of London.

Peacock (*Anglo-Indian*) Walk up and down in full fig while the band plays

Peacock and the ladies, Before the (*Old Eng*) A solemn promise—an appeal to knightly honour

In olden days the peacock was a favourite dish with lords and ladies of high degree It was customary to skin the bird without plucking, and send the roast bird to table with its natural envelop The peacock was considered in the days of chivalry not simply as an exquisite delicacy, but as a dish of peculiar solemnity When it was brought to the table, decorated with its plumage, its comb gilded, and a sponge in its bill, wet with spirits of wine and lighted, it was the signal for the gallant knights present to make vows to accomplish some deed of chivalry 'before the peacock and the ladies'.

Peacock horse (*Street*). Mourning coach horse—which generally has much parade in his movements

Pear (*Parisian*, 1830-48) Name given to Louis Philippe—from the shape of his head. (*See* Jupiter Scapin).

Peas in the pot (*Low London*). Rhyming phrase — meaning 'hot', erotic.

Big Tim says you are very peas.—*Peoples'*, 6th January 1895.

Pecksniffian (*Peoples'*). Hypocritical — from Dickens's *Martin Chuzzlewit*.

Peel off (*City*, 1860). To obtain money by a Stock Exchange transaction.

Peel the patch off the weak point (*American*). Expose a man's weakness.

Peep o' Day tree (*Theatrical*, 1862). In this Exhibition year, one Edmund Falconer produced a piece called *Peep o' Day*, at the Lyceum, and made out of it a great fortune, chiefly by the ingenuity displayed in a stage tree, on the edge of a quarry. Its chief branch moved on a pivot by the use of which the hero swung down on to the stage just in time to prevent the murder of the heroine. From that time forward this providential stage machinery has been thus called.

The hero and heroine escape by a *Peep o' Day* tree, which enables them to descend from the cliff, amidst the enthusiastic and unanimous applause of the audience.—*Era*, April 1883.

Peg (*Theatrical*, 1884). Sensation point or effect of a piece. Something upon which the actors, or more probably an actor, can build up a scene.

Pegging away (*American, Military*). Used by General Grant for heavy artillery attack. Previously known as a careless phrase, but after the Civil War accepted gravely.

Penances and leatherheads (*American*). People of Pennsylvania —probably from their early puritanic origin—still very marked.

Pencil, open, lost, and found (*Com. Lond.*, 19 *cent.*). Rhyming phrase, means £10.

Pencil dates (*Theatrical*, 1896 on). Make engagements to perform.

The fourth D'Artagnan is Mr Charles Warner, who, full of spirit and energy, intends to bombard Suburbia and the provinces with the already successful Hamilton version, and is, as the phrase goes, 'pencilling in dates' as fast as a manager can who knows his business.—*D. T.*, 6th August 1898.

Pennorth o' treacle (*L. London*, 1882). A charming girl—the final outcome of the use of 'jam'.

Pennorth o' treason (*Newsvendors'*). Copy of a notorious penny Sunday London paper, which attacks every party, and has no policy of its own.

Penny death-traps (*L. London* 1897). Penny glass paraffin lamps—made in Germany. Fragile and easily upset; they caused many deaths.

Penny gush (1880-82). Exaggerated mode of writing English frequently seen in a certain London daily paper.

This, published in an English paper would probably be described as penny gush.—G. A. Sala, *Illustrated London News*, 16th December 1882.

Penny loaf (*Thieves'*). Cur — one afraid to steal; a man who would rather live on a penny loaf than steal good beef.

Penny locket (*Rhyming*). Pocket.

While he's got his peepers on the penny locket, you know, perhaps, how to be a bit careful.

Penny pick (*London, circa* 1838). Cigar. From *Pickwick*, Dickens's first popular creation.

Penny puzzle (*Street*, 1883). Sausage—because it is never found out. (*See* Bag o' mystery.)

Penny starver (*Street*). Lowest description of cigar—commercial value three for twopence.

Penny toff (*London*, 1870 on). The lowest description of toff—the cad imitator of the follies of the *jeunesse dorée*.

Perfect lady (*Street*). Not at all one — anything but. Satirically applied to any woman drunk and misbehaving herself in the streets. The phrase took its rise from a police court case, in which a witness deposed that, though the prisoner did get her living in the streets and drank a little, she was otherwise a 'perfect lady'.

Perfumed talk (*Anglo-American*). Satirical synonym for vile language.

Perhaps (*Old Eng.*). Equivalent to most decidedly.

Permanent pug (*Printers' and Tavern*). Fighting man around the door of the premises. Originally applied to the door-porter of editorial offices.

Perpetual staircase (*Thieves'*). The tread-mill

Perpetuana (*Norfolk*, 18 *cent*) A very strong dress fabric, which lasted an immense time Still applied to describe old women in Norfolk

Norfolk folk want a little fresh impulse now, to restore the flourishing condition of their textile manufactures Beauty arrayed herself in bravery that *was* cheap and was *not* nasty *Perpetuana* lasted for ever —*Athenæum*, 1870

Perplexed and transient phantom (*Politics*) Politician who fails and vanishes

Lord Salisbury hopes to be something more than a 'perplexed and transient phantom'.—*D N*, 1st July 1885.

Perseus (*Soc.*, 1883). An editor From a phrase used by Professor Huxley at the Royal Academy Banquet, 1883

Petit bleu (*Franco-Eng.*, 1898) Forgery. From the colour of the French telegraphic paper.

Then, with regard to the *petit bleu* which Picquart is accused of forging It is true that the address on this telegraphic post card was scratched out, the name of the addressee being effaced, and that of Easterhazy written over it —*D T*, 28th November 1898

Peto (*Soc.*) Evasion of P T.O — initials of Please turn over

Petticoat interest (*Literature*, 1860 on) Those portions of fiction referring to womankind

Scott did not trouble himself much about Maid Marian He had enough of what is now called 'petticoat interest' in his story without her —*D. N.*, 29th March 1892

Phant (*Showmen's*) The sheet of plate-glass placed sloping, or diagonally, on the stage, to reflect from below or from the side the illusion known as Pepper's ghost. In order to keep the secret as far as possible, the word glass was never used, but the first syllable of phantom Sometimes 'fant', at other times, in the North, 'peeble'—a new evasive name

Pheasant (*Common London*) Dried herring (*See* Two-eyed steak)

Phil and Jim (*Oxford*, 1890 on) Church of S Philip and S James. This phrase is sometimes pronounced 'Fillin Jim'.

Philistine (*Soc*). Formerly an outsider, but with no offensive meaning; but now with an offensive meaning

In 1840 Liszt's reputation was at its highest, but he met with indifference here, and no doubt regarded us as given over to philistinism.—*Ref*, 11th April 1886

Physic-bottle (*Peoples'*). Doctor.

Piano (*Soc*, 1870). To sing small, to take a back seat

Piccadilly fringe (*Low Class*, 1884). Front hair of women cut short and brought down, and curled over the forehead Fashion originated in Paris about 1868.

By Mr Russell—When Jarrett talked about cutting my hair, she asked me if I wanted a 'Piccadilly fringe'.

What is the 'Piccadilly fringe'?—Cut your hair on your forehead

Is there anything objectionable about that?—It makes you look ugly —*Armstrong Abduction Case*, October 1885

Piccadilly window (*Street*, '90's) Single eye glass worn by some men of fashion—hence the Piccadilly

Pick of the basket (*Sporting*). Best—derived from market baskets

Some of Sir Watkin's horses are of extraordinary build and value Comet stands out foremost, and 'is the pick of the basket' —*World*, 1878

Picker-up (*Thieves'*, 19 *cent*). Woman of the town.

Picking its eyes (*Stock Exchange*, '90's) Getting the best, or top, of a good thing From S Africa mining, there applied to obtaining the immediate and easily obtained gold

It is to be feared that more attention would, naturally, be paid to extracting the richest ore from the mines ('picking its eyes', as the popular term is) than to proceeding with the regular course of development —*D T*, 26th July 1900.

Pickled dog (*Provincial*) Term of contempt—rarely now heard

Pickles (*Peoples'*) Exclamation of good tempered mistrust, or even want of belief.

The promoters say that benefit will accrue to our Indian fellow-subjects by bringing before the English people actual representations of the methods of manufactures, amusements, etc, of our vast Indian empire, and will thus serve imperial interests That, of course, is all pickles.—*Ref*, 5th July 1885.

Pickpocketienne (*Anglo-French*). Woman pickpocket.

Picnic (*American-English*). A treat—from the frequency of picnics in America, where there is always room for them.

Native dramatists for the past week have enjoyed what the street gamins would call a picnic.—*N. Y. Mercury*, January 1884.

Pidgin (*World's Sea-shore*). Simplified mixture of two or three languages, of which English is generally one. Lingua Franca, the common tongue of the Mediterranean, has Italian chiefly for its basis, mixed with French and Arabic. The word started in the Chinese waters. The chief English pidgin, sometimes erroneously called pigeon, is the mixture of English with Hindostanee, and of English with Chinese—but there must in all be scores of pidgin in the world, negro specimens being the more curious. Pidgin is a corruption of business.

According to Herr Leo Wigner, this mysterious Yiddish is not the mere barbarous trade-jargon, the 'pidgin-Hebrew', of the indigent alien of Whitechapel.—*D. T.*, 6th July 1899.

Pie (*Eng.-American*, 19 *cent.*). Delightful—very enjoyable.

At the depôt the light was dim, and so it was in the sleeper, as it generally is; but as she got into the car a neat leg in a white stocking showed plainly enough to make Jim murmur to himself, 'Well, this is pie'.—*N. Y. Mercury*, 3rd January 1885.

Piebald eye (*Peoples'*). Black one—black by a blow.

My! Bill—where was yer piebaldered?

(*See* Mouse, Eye in a sling.)

Piebald mucker sheeny (*E. Lond.*). Low old Jew.

Pie-pusher (*Streets*). Street pieman, who ceaselessly recommends, or pushes, his wares.

Pieces, All to (*Soc.*, *from Sporting*, 1880). Exhausted—generally said of horses.

She was as pale as death, and trembling from head to foot. He was perfectly satisfied that what she had described took place, for when she came in she was 'all to pieces'.—Statement by Sir Beaumont Dixie concerning an attack on his wife, Lady Florence Dixie, March 1883.

Pie-shop (*London*). Dog—from the supposition (1842), when one Blauchard first started a penny pie-shop, that the pies were made of dogs.

Pieuvre (*Anglo-French*, '60's). Prostitute. When Victor Hugo published his *Les Travailleurs de la Mer*, his terrible description of the octopus—the *pieuvre*—as a creature which overcame a man by embraces, was at once seized upon by the boulevardier-journalists as an apt description of the woman of the town.

Pig months (*Peoples'*, *Hist.*). All the months (eight) in which there is an 'R'. These pig months are those in which you may more safely eat fresh pork than in the others—the four summer months in fact.

Pig-bridge (*Trin. Col.*, *Cambridge*). The beautiful Venetian-like bridge over the Cam, where it passes St John's College, and connecting its quads. Thus called because the Johnians are styled pigs (*q.v.*).

Pigeon pair (*Familiar*). A boy born first, a girl following, within not more than two years. Probably from the known fidelity of winged pigeon pairs to each other.

Pigs (*Trin. Col.*, *Cambridge*, 19 *cent.*). Name given by the men of Trinity to their neighbours of St John's.

Pigs, An't please the (*Pre-Reformation, Eng.*). Corruption of 'Please the Pyx'. Still common in West England, where 'x' becomes 'gs'. (*See* Please the pigs.)

Pigot or Piggot (*Hist.*, 1888-89). Lie—unblushing, obvious lie. Passed into verb, generally passive—to be pigotted. From the forger Pigot.

I must print the verses, and leave the reader to judge if I have been Pigotted or not.—*Ref.*, 17th March 1889.

Pigtail (*Street, obsolete* about 1840). An old man, from the ancients clinging to the 18th century mode of wearing the hair.

Pill (*Street*). Dose, suffering, sentence, punishment. Endless in application.

Pill (*Sailors'*). Custom-house officer. Because both are so very searching.

Pill-pusher (*Peoples'*). Doctor. Fine example of the graphic in phraseology.

If the pill-pushers will only chuck it out now that diamond rings are poisonous, broughams pestilential, oysters and champagne deadly, and villas in Singin's Wood fatal in every case, many a man will be happy, many a pal will be saved

Pillow securities (*City*, 19 *cent.*) Safe scrip, shares that rarely vary in price.

The shares of the earliest cable companies did not enjoy their present character of 'safe', or, as Mr Draper, Secretary of the Eastern Telegraph Company, who was associated with Sir John Pender thirty years, aptly terms, 'pillow securities'—those which do not trouble an investor's dreams at night and which a man need not worry about —*D T*, 8th July 1896

Pin (*Peoples'*) To pawn clothes

When Lantier was doing up his bundle to send to the pawnbroker's, one intelligent pittite shouted out 'Pin!' Evidently that pittite knew something —*Ref*, 1882

Pin pricks (*Hist.*, 1898). Slight attacks—assaults

Our friendship with France is not to be obtained by a policy of pinpricks—a phrase, by the way, which is not, as some suppose, of English origin, but was first employed by a responsible French journal, *Le Matin*.—*D T*, 9th December 1898.

Ping (*Sportsman*, to 1854) To speak in a quick singing high voice. From the sharp ping of the old musket

Pink 'un (*Sporting Times*, 1880) Sporting life—from the tint of the paper, and to distinguish it from the Brown 'un, Sportsman

Before doing so, I took the advice of one John Corlett, who propriets a paper called the *Pink 'Un* —*Ref.*, 31st July 1887

Pink wine (*Military*) Champagne.

Pinnacles (*Peoples'*). A corruption of 'barnacles', eye-glasses, spectacles.

Pint o' mahogany (*Coffee-house*). Coffee.

Piou-piou (*Soc*) Tommy Atkins translated into French

Pip-pip (*Streets'*). Hue and cry after any one, but generally a youth in striking bicycle costumery Onomatope of the horn warning which sometimes replaces the bell of the bike.

Pipe-opener (*University*) First spurt in rowing practice—to open the lungs, and get that kind of pipe in working order.

Pirate (*Low London*). Emphatic person — man or woman — especially the latter, and in music halls, where the actresses and singers of great force obtain this distinction.

Pistol-pockets (*American-Eng*) Warning not to fool.

Pitch in (*Scotch*). Railway collision

Pith (*Hospital*). Sever the spinal cord

Pittite (*Theatrical*). Frequenter of the pit Took the place of groundling (*q v*), when seats destroyed the force of the Shakespearian term

A correspondent wishes me to ask Mr Irving if, when he has finished looking after the interests of Lyceum pittites, he will be kind enough to turn his attention to Lyceum dress circlers. —*Ref*, 10th May 1885

(See *Stall-pots*)

Pizen (*American*, *circa* 1875) Corruption of poison, and here describing alcohol—generally in its whiskey form (*See* Death promoter)

Plain as a pipe-stem (*Peoples'*, 17 *cent* on). Utterly plain — nothing could be plainer than the stem of the white clay pipe from the cutty of the time of Charles II., to the long churchwarden—*tempo* George III

Plank the knife in (*L. Class*, *Hist.*). Stab deeply.

Planter (*Anglo-Indian*). Bad-tempered horse

Plaster (*Peoples'*, 1890 on) A collar —a huge shirt or applied collar, said to be introduced by the late Duke of Clarence

Plasterer's trowel and seringapatam (*Rhyming*) It means 'fowl and ham'.

Plates o' meat (*Low London—Rhyming*) Feet. (*See* Barges)

Platform ticket (*Railway*) Phrase uttered by friend who has been to see a friend off by train, and is stopped as a passenger.

Play camels (*Anglo-Indian*) Get drunk, or drink too much Playful reference to the drinking habits of the camel, who stores his drink rather than drinks it.

Play consumption (*American — becoming English*). This is the equal of malingering, or shamming.

Play dirt (*American*). Deceive.

Play for paste (*Billiard - room*). For drink — probably from 'pasta' (Spanish)—a meal, or perhaps 'vino di pasta'—a light sherry.

Play low (*American-Eng.*). Act meanly.

Farewell banquets have lately been played a little low down, but the 'send-off' supper given to Wilson Barrett at the Criterion, on Thursday night, was an exception.—*Ref.*, 15th August 1886.

Play owings (*Sporting phrase*). Living on credit.

Play the bear (*Lancashire*). Damage.

Played out since '49 (*W. American*). Ancient untruth.

If he further informs you that 'this has been played out since '49', he means that since the first colonization of the Pacific coast by 'smart men', such a thing was never believed in: 1849 being the year of the commencement of the Californian gold digging.—*All the Year Round*, 31st October 1868.

Playing a big game (*Criminal*). Trying for a daring success.

Prior to his finally leaving her, he had often spoken about 'playing a big game'. —*D. T.*, 31st March 1897.

Playing for a sucker (*American*, 1880). Attack upon the innocence of a youth.

Please I want the cook - girl (*London*). Said of a youth haunting the head of area steps.

Please mother open the door (*Street*). Expressed admiration of a passing girl. Always said in a high monotone, except 'door', which is uttered in a falling minor third.

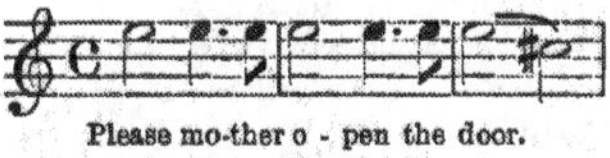
Please mo-ther o - pen the door.

Please the pigs (*Old Catholic*). *Deo volente*—God willing. Corruption of 'An it please the pyx' (Pyxis). A very interesting form of this phrase is to be found in Devonshire—'An it please the pixies.'

Pleinairists (*Art*, 1885 on). Open-air artists — the school of pleinair, which is utterly antagonistic to shadowed or claustral art.

These pretty illustrations, from the designs of the well - known French *pleinairiste* and figure painter, Raphaël Collin, are delicate and graceful even to the verge of effeminacy.—*D. T.*, 10th February 1897.

Plimsoll (*Nautical*). The 'cargo' line in merchant shipping. Plimsoll, in the House of Commons, forced the Bill for the better regulation of merchant shipping.

Plon-plon (*Parisian*, 1855). Name given to the despised Prince Jerome Napoleon after he hurried away from the Crimean War.

Pluck (*Peoples'*). Daring, as distinct from slow courage.

Plucking (*Peoples'*). Robbing.

Plug (*American*). To get into difficulties.

Ply (*Mid.-class*). Tendency, kink, inclination, leaning. Probably from the French 'pli'.

Pocket artist (*Critical*, '90's). Small actor or actress. Meant kindly, but not liked by the victims.

To the prettiness and grace of Miss Cutler *Florodora* owed not a little. She is quite a 'pocket' artist.—*D.T.*, 13th November 1899.

Pod (*Commercial*). Practical short for Post Office Directory.

Podsnap (*Soc.*, 1865 on). A Sir Oracle; whose word is sufficient—for himself. From Dickens.

Podsnappery. Wilful determination to ignore the objectionable or inconvenient, at the same time assuming airs of superior virtue and noble resignation.

Oppressed nationalities have not been accustomed to expect sympathy or assistance from Austria. But the question is a very grave one, and no amount of diplomatic Podsnappery can keep it any longer in the background.—*D. N.*, 8th July 1889.

Poet of the brush (*Art*, 1890 on). Artist. Outcome of the eternal search for new phrases.

Mr T. Hope M'Lachlan is the painter of night skies, through which the moon sails with an opalescent halo round her disc. He is in his truest conceptions a poet of the brush.—*D. T.*, 4th January 1896.

Poke (*Thieves'*) Purse This word for sack, pouch, satchel, is to be found in Shakespeare

Poked up (*Anglo-American*). Embarassed, inconvenienced

Poker (*American-Eng.*) Game of cards.

Polka, To (*Anglo-Amer.*). Another of the forms of expressing rapid retreat

'Boss, dis woman neber raise dat money in dis world,' and with a plaintive farewell, she polkaed from the office, and once more deep silence prevailed —*Providence Journal*

(*See* Balley, Skip, Valse.)

Pomatum pot (*Soc*, 1885) Small specimens of pot-shaped and covered china.

Mr Gladstone at twenty-five minutes to five was fairly embarked on his speech. The familiar throat mixture commonly known as the pomatum pot was at his side, only on this occasion there were two pots instead of one —*D. N*, 9th May 1886

'Pon my life (*Com. Lond Rhyming*, 19 *cent.*). Wife.

Pongelo (*Anglo-Indian Army*). Pale ale—but relatively any beer

Poole (*Soc*, 1840 on) Perfect clothing—from Poole, a leading tailor, in Saville Row (*See* Dorsay, Lincoln & Bennet, Redfern, Nicholls, etc)

Poor as a Connaught man (*Irish, Personal*). Poorest even amongst Irishmen

Marrying Mr Cecil Devereux, who is as poor they say as a Connaught man —Miss M Edgeworth, *Ennui*, ch xi

Poor man's goose (*Low. Classes*). Bullock's liver, baked with sage and onions and a bit of fat bacon.

Poot (*Hindostanee*). Shilling—use confined to E London where once E Indian beggars were common

Pop goes the weasel (*Street*, about 1870) Phrase—a great mystery of passing English. In the '70's every etymologist wrote about this phrase—and left it where it was. Activity is suggested by 'pop', and the little weasel is very active Probably erotic origin. Chiefly associated with these lines—

Up and down the City Road,
In and out the Eagle,
That's the way the money goes,
Pop goes the weasel!

Pop on (*Sporting*). Quick blow—generally on the face

Then big Tim popped it on Selby's face, and they had a bit of a spar round like —A Chivy Duel, *People*, 6th January 1895.

Pop visit (*Soc*, 18 *cent.*) Short ones

I have a dozen friendly pop visits to make in less than an hour, and would not miss one for the universe —Garrick's *Abel Drugger*

Pope (*Com Eng*) Abbreviation of pope o' Rome, the rhyming for 'home'

Poppa (*Amer.-Eng.*, 1890 on). Papa.

But even those who have never seen or read the American play can guess how an old Kansas millionaire, vulgar, bombastic, dictatorial, and good-hearted, the typical Yankee 'poppa', came to New York with his 'gals'.—*D. T.*, 15th February 1897

Popping crease (*Railway Officials'*). Junction station.

Popsy wopsy (*Low. Lond*). A smiling, doll-like, attractive girl

Pork pie hat and crinoline (*Street*, 1866-71). Satirical reference to women's appearance in the streets

Suppose my Œdipus should lurk at last
Under a pork-pie hat and crinoline
— R. Browning, *Prince Hohenstiel Schwangau*, 1871

Porky (*Low. Class*) Name for a pork-butcher, and sometimes satirically for a Jew

Porridge-hole (*Scotch*) The mouth.

Porridge-pots (*Military*) Linesmen's satirical mode of naming the Scotch guard. (*See* Cold creams, Grinning dears, Gee-gees, Muck)

Port wine don (*University*). Scornful description of the college professorial grandee, who leans to the Manchester school of nutrition.

Mr Mark Pattison was a very remarkable character . . He was extremely unlike the port wine don of fiction and caricature.—*D N*, 6th March 1885.

Portable property (*Doubtful Soc*). Easily stolen or pawned values—especially plate.

The testimonial consisted of a silver tea-pot, coffee pot, and chocolate-jug—all of which would doubtless have been considered by my friend Wemmick very fine specimens of portable property.—*Ref*, 7th June 1885.

Portuguese pumping (*Nautical*) Not to be learnt Ask sailors the meaning of this phrase, and they may laugh a good deal, but they give no etymology. It is probably nasty.

Possle (*Low. Class*). Earnest advocate. Corruption of apostle. Used satirically.

Post the blue (*Racing*). Gain the Derby.

Post haste (18 *cent. English—survival*). Rapid—from the post-chaise being the most rapid mode of travelling before 1840. (*See* Motor.)

Postage stamp (*Tavern*, 1837-85). Facetious name given to hotels and taverns signed the 'Queen's Head.'

Postern gate (*American*). Widest part of the trouser.

Postman's sister (*Mid.-class*, 1883). Secret informant.

For any little inaccuracy of detail which may have crept into the above paragraph I am in no way to blame. I tell the tale as 'twas told to me—by the postman's sister.—*Ref.*, 18th October 1885.

(*See* Jinks the barber, Boy Jones.)

Pot (*Naval*). Executive officer—as distinct from Greaser and Scratcher (*q.v.*).

Pot of all (*C. London*, 1883). Pot *in excelsis*, pot of exaltation, a perfect leader-hero, demigod.

Pot o' beer (*Abstainers'*). Bottle of ginger beer.

Pot o' bliss (*Public-house*, 1876). A fine tall woman.

Pot of O' (*Rhyming*, 1868). Short for 'Pot of O, my dear,' which is the rhyme for beer.

Potty (*Low Class*). Tinker.

Pot-au-feu (*Polit.*, 1885). Domestic policy. Due to Clémenceau, who invented it, and named it in antagonism to the Chauvinist principles of Ferry.

M. Clémenceau's rapidly-increasing influence is the most significant fact in the current politics of France. One might imagine that the *pot-au-feu* principle, as he himself has named it, would fail, as a cry, among a people like the French.—*D. N.*, 8th August 1885.

Pot-house (*Club Life*). Easy-go club. Suggestive of a licensed victualler's house.

Potching (*Hotel Waiters'*). Taking fees against rules. Probably from the French to 'pocher' or 'empocher'.

Good-natured customers may imagine that if they have given a fee to the waiter who presents the bill, they may hand another to the usual man who has attended upon them; but head-waiters are alive to the perils of this practice, which they call *potching*, and dismissal will be the punishment of the waiter who is caught taking vails on the sly.—*Graphic* (Restaurant Management), 17th March 1883).

Potentially (*Polit.*, 1883). To all intents and purposes.

This person considered that Russia was through her railway system practically, or as it is the fashion to say potentially, mistress of Herat.—*D. N.*, 29th April 1885.

Potsheen (*Irish*). Whiskey. Word varies in various districts—generally Potheen.

Potsheen, plase your honour—because it's the little whiskey that's made in the private still or pot; and *sheen*, because it's a fond word for whatsoever we'd like, and for what we have little of and would make much of.—Miss Edgeworth, *The Absentee*, chap. x.

Potter's field (*American*). Portion of graveyard appropriated to unpaid burials.

Poultice (*Soc.*, 1880). Fat woman.

Poultice (*Soc.*, 1882). Very high collar, suggestive of a neck poultice, ring-like in shape.

Poultice-mixer (*Navy*). Sick-bay man, or nurse.

Poultice over the peeper (*Peoples'*). A blow on the eye.

Pound to an olive (*Jewish*). This is a phrase resulting out of the Hebrews' love of olives, and is equivalent to the sporting term, 'It's a million pounds to a bit o' dirt.'

Powdering hair (*Tavern*, 18 *cent.*). Getting drunk—still heard in remote places. Euphemism invented by a polite landlord to account for lengths of time such as dressing and powdering hair required.

Pow-wow (*Anglo-American*). Convention or tentative meeting. From North American Indian — this word meaning in that language Congress.

Prairie. (*See* Bit o' prairie.)

Prairie comedians (*U.S.A.*). Poor, ranting, talentless actor.

Nothing can be more painful to a city summer audience than the wild rantings of barn-storming tragedians, or more aggravating than the inane drivel of prairie comedians.—*N. Y. Mercury*, 1883.

Prayer-book (*Sporting*, *circa* 1870). Ruff's *Guide to the Turf*.

Predeceased (*Legal—become satirical*) Used to ridicule the statement of some obvious fact, such as two and and two make four

Premiere (*Press*, 1884) Abbreviation of *premiere* representation, an ordinary Paris phrase First used in London press for first night in 1884

Prescot (*Rhyming*) Waistcoat

'Spot his blooming prescot'

Prester John (*Peoples'*). The unknown.

He's no more related to our family than Prester John — Farquhar, *The Inconstant*

Preterite (*Soc*, 19 *cent*) Ancient — especially applied to women. 'Young! She's quite a preterite—nevertheless, intense.' (*See* Has been)

Pretty-boy clip (*Soc*, 1880 on) Hair brought flat down over the forehead, and cut in a straight line from ear to ear.

We happen to know that the style termed by irreverent mashers the pretty-boy clip, the style sometimes called the upward drag, and the quiff which ranges from a delicate fringe to furze-bush proportions, at first amazed and amused the neat Japanese damsels —*D. N*, 26th January 1885

Pretty fellow (*Peoples'*). Fine, handsome, sometimes satirical

Polly thinks him a very pretty man.—Gay, *Beggars' Opera*

Pretty steep (*American*). Threatening

Previous. (*See* Behind yourself)

Price of a pint (*Workmen's*) Any sum below sixpence

Prince's points (*Soc and Club*, 1877). Shilling points at whist. Takes its origin from about this date. Very keen reasoning on the part of the then Prince of Wales, an eager whist-player. H.R H laid down the theory that the best whist players were not necessarily the richest of men, and therefore if he played high points he might deprive himself of the pleasure of meeting the best players. Prince's points became very rapidly fashionable

Printing House Square (*Club*, 19 *cent*, to 1880) Powerful—crushing, *ex cathedra*, from the *Times* being published in that locality.

Prize faggots (*Street*) Well developed breasts in women. Faggots are savoury preparations of minced bullocks or sheeps' viscera—or plucks, mixed with oatmeal, shaped into rounded lumps and baked until the outside forms a crust They are sold in all the busy lower parts of London at a penny Prize faggots would be those larger than usual

Problem novel (*Literary*, 1888 on). Title bestowed upon novels with a purpose—generally as affecting women, their aspirations and wrongs.

It was impossible to resist the question whether the 'problem novel' had had its day, and it appears 'not quite, but it is considerably less in demand than it was.' —*D. T*, 2nd October 1896.

Process-pusher (1880). Lawyer's clerk Satirical description.

Process server (*Artists'*, 1886 on) Photogravure printers

Perhaps many of our artists have not yet learned the technique which best suits processes, or perhaps our process-servers are not yet adepts in their business —*D N*, 9th December 1890

Procesh (*American-Eng.*) Abbreviation of procession — growing common in England (1884)

I was removed on a plank, escorted by a torchlight procesh of the local fire brigade —Besant & Rice, *Golden Butterfly*, vol i, ch xviii

Pro-donnas (*Music Hall*, 1880). Professional ladies—actresses

Professional beauty (*Fashionable slang*, 1879-82) This term arose in one of the Society papers, and was at once accepted by the best people, and even by the best of the Press It referred to women in society, sometimes the very highest, who 'professed' their beauty by permitting any number of their photographic portraits to be sold in infinite varities of poses.

Promoted (October 1890) Dead. From the public funeral of Mrs Booth, wife of General Booth, the originator of the Salvation Army.

Propers (*Low Class*) Meaning refused—but thoroughly comprehended by the coster classes Erotic.

Proper donas and rorty blokes (*L Peoples'*, 1880). Good and true men and women

Properties (*Theatrical*) Theatrical adjuncts

Propper bit of frock (*Com Lond*, 1878) Pretty and clever well-dressed girl.

Prospect (*American Miners'*). To search for new gold-fields

Prostituted (*Patent Law*). Made common. Said of a patent, so long on the market, waiting to be taken up by a capitalist or company, that it is common, and known to one and all.

Pros' Avenue (*Theatrical, circa* 1880). The Gaiety Bar (Strand). From this bar being the resort of gentlemen of 'the profession'.

Prosser (*Theatrical*, 1880). Pro passed into 'prosser'.

Protean entertainer (*Theatrical*). Artiste whose exceptional ability consists in rapid changes of dress.

Few will deny that Leopoldi Fregoli is an artist to the tips of his fingers, alert, versatile, neat in his business, quick as lightning in his changes, and, when all is said and done, the best 'protean' entertainer that the oldest playgoer has ever seen.—*D. T.*, 10th March 1897.

Proud nothing (*Provincial.*). Obvious.

Prudes on the prowl (*Soc.*, 1895 on). Hypersensitive women who haunted music halls to discover misbehaviour either on or off the stage.

Prudes on the prowl have long ceased to minimise the much too meagre fund of human enjoyment left in the world, and their place has been taken by a body who may be described as Guardians on the Growl.—*D. T.*, 16th December 1897.

Pschutt (*Parisian*, 1883). Ton, fashion, distinction. Reached America in 1884, and at once became ridiculous as pasha.

Psha (*Peoples'*). Exclamation. No derivation.

Psychological moment (*Soc. and Literary*, 1894 on). Opportunity. Nick of time. Became very popular in 1896.

I seized the p. m., and nailed him for a tenner.

It can afford to bide its time, and strike a decisive blow when the psychological moment has arrived.—*D. T.*, 6th March 1896.

Pub (*Theatrical*). The public—sometimes P. B.

Publican (1883). One of the names of General Booth after buying the Grecian Theatre and Tavern in the City Road (1883). (*See* Salvation Army.)

Publicaness (*Tavern*, 1880). The wife of a publican.

Puff-puff (*Children's*, 19 *cent.*). Railway engine. (*See* Gee-gee.)

Puffing billy (*N. Eng.*). Steam-engine, given contemptuously to Stephenson's first engine, still at Darlington, and accepted seriously by him.

Pull (*Peoples'*). Anxious moment. (*See* Extra pull.)

Pull-down (*Soc.*, 1870, etc.). Name given to the moustache which succeeded the nap. (*q.v.*).

Pull down the blind (*Low London*, 1880 on). This was addressed in the first place to spooney young couples who in public were making too great a display of their love.

Pull down your basque (*American—amongst women*). The 'basque' is the spine of the corset. The recommendation is a suggestion to behave properly.

Pull down your vest (*American*). Be well bred, behave yourself.

Pull leg (*Peoples'*). Satirize, humbug, mislead, ridicule.

Young Chinny hinted that they must be pulling his leg.—Rudyard Kipling, *The Tomb of his Ancestors.*

Pull oneself over (*Com. London*). To feed.

I took one for myself, and essayed to pull myself over it. But there, I will spare further recital, beyond that, burnt outside, the chops were raw inside, and like iron all over.—*Ref.*, 6th June 1886.

Pull the string proper (*Theatrical*). To know how to succeed with the public. Suggested by manipulating marionnettes.

Dressed in the uniform of the London Scottish Rifles, he hides from his mother-in-law in a shower-bath, and is swamped by that awful lady, who knows how and when to 'pull the strings'.—*Ref.*, 5th October 1884.

Pull-up (*American—becoming English*, 1870). Wave of prosperity following disaster; chiefly used in theatrical life.

Pull up my boot (*Costermongers'*). To make money. When a man prepares for his day's work, he pulls on and strings up his boots. (*See* Make up my leg.)

The Strand people are pulling the string with the *Comedy of Errors*, I am told (1883).

Pull your ear (*Peoples'*, *Hist.*). To produce memory.

Pulling a pop (*Anglo-American*). Firing a pistol.

Pulling the right string (*Cabinet-makers'*, 1863) Before calipers were in use by carpenters and others, small measurements were made with string Hence arose the term, 'Are you pulling the right string?' Some maintain it refers to the pulling of puppet show strings

Pumblechook (*American - Eng*) Human ass.

Pumpkin - face (*American*) A round face with no expression in it.

Puncheous Pilate (*Peoples'*) Corruption of Pontius Pilate, jocosely addressed to a person in protest of some small asserted authority.

Punkah one's face (*Anglo-Indian*). Fan the features From the Hindostanee

Push-buggy (*American—heard in Liverpool*) Perambulator

Pushing (*Peoples'*, 1885) Endeavouring to induce a man to propose marriage Early in 1885, in the suit brought by Lord Durham to obtain a nullity of marriage (Durham *v* Milner, otherwise Durham), the Hon Mrs Gerard, the sister of the defendant, said in evidence

Lord Durham joined my sister at Buxton.

What was her bearing towards him?—I thought she seemed shy, but I considered that was chiefly on account of there being only one sitting-room in the house I had a conversation with my sister as to the propriety of visiting Lambton She was nervous, and said it looked 'rather pushing' to go —28th February 1885.

Pusley (*American—heard in Liverpool*). Most mysterious — who *was* Pusley?

Pa is better, thanks to careful nursing You see, Pa began finding fault with me again because I didn't play more jokes on him I told him that people were getting an idea that I was mean as Pusley, because I played jokes on him, and I had quit Pa said 'never mind what people say I am your father, and it pleases me to have you practise on me' —*Peck's Bad Boy*, 1884

Pusserspock (*Naval*) Corruption of 'purser's pork'—bad, hard salt-meat, name being given to it because the purser was the purchaser.

Put a steam on the table (*Peoples'*) To earn enough money to obtain a hot Sunday dinner A figure of speech. Refers chiefly to boiled food, the phrase having been invented before domestic ovens

Put down (*Low London*). To eat.

Put it on (*L. London*) Extract money by threats, or whining lying, as the case may best be met

Arter all the brass was nearly all gone, Selby says, 'I'll go round to the Mug agin, and put it on him (make him pay) for another bit'—*People*, 6th January 1895

Put on (*Street*) Old woman mendicant who puts on a shivering and wretched look

Put on (*Theatrical*) To produce

Put on a boss (*Street*) Take a look—of a malevolent character, so that a squint is suggested—for squinting suggests malevolence.

Put on a cigar (*Peoples'*, 1850 on) Assertion of gentility, to the injurious exclusion of the pipe

Put on the flooence (*Peoples'*, 1850-83) Attract, subdue, overcome by mental force Corruption of 'fluence —from influence

Put on the pot (*All Classes*) Be grand

Put oneself outside (*American-English*, 1860) To eat or drink.

Put out (*Low Class, Hist*). Killed —abbreviation of 'Put out his lights' (*q v.*)

Brien, on the way to the station remarked to the officer, 'I am not in this, but I know they meant to put you out to-night.'—*D T.*, 14th May 1901.

Put the gloves on him (*Scotch Thieves'*, 1868) Ameliorate him

Put the light out (*Criminal and Street*), Kill.

In the days of Shakespeare wise men called 'stealing' conveying, now a malefactor does not murder, he pops a man off, or he puts his light out —*Graphic*, 24th September 1884.

Put the miller's eye out (*Peoples'*). To use too much water in making grog or tea

Put the windows in (*Street*). Smashing them

Put to bed (*Music Hall*) To conquer, to annihilate, figuratively

Put to find (*Low Class*) Prison.

Put you on your back seam (*Tailors'*). To seat a gentleman suddenly, not only on the ground, but on the seam which hemispheres the 'shoulder' of his trousers Very local

Put your hat up there (*Peoples'*). Friendly accusation of courting there—meaning you are resolved to make one of the family.

Put your clothes together when you come (*Provincial, Peoples'*). Shape of inviting for a long visit, stretching over time, requiring many changes of garments.

Puts a 'and in a pocket (*Lower Classes*). Hospitable, given to charity.

Putting a poor mouth (*Irish*). To complain moaningly.

The Irishman, putting a poor mouth on his position, declared that at his house 'whin they had a red herring it was Christmas Day wid 'um'.—*D. N.*, 1884.

Putting the value on it (*Artists'*). Signing a canvas. Satirical—meaning the work has no real value, and sells only by reason of the name attached.

Putty-medal (*Peoples'*, 1856). No medal at all. Satirical recommendation to reward for mischief or injury. A tailor makes a misfit; *e.g.*, 'Give him a putty medal.'

Pyrotechnic pleasantries (*Soc.*, 1897). Dynamite explosions of a feeble and harmless character. Probably the work of semi-idiots. Sign that destructive anarchy was abating.

There is, indeed, a growing impression that if he is found out, it will at once be perceived that he is a monomaniac, who has acted out of sheer silliness in indulging in these 'pyrotechnic pleasantries'.—*D. T.*, 17th June 1897.

Q

Q. B. (*Law*, '90's). Queen's Bench. Now King's Bench.

Q. S. (*Peoples'*). Initials of Queer Street—a figure of speech, even a metaphor, whereby a gentleman in difficulties relegates them to his district.

Quagger (*Oxford 'er'*). Queen's man—student of Queen's College. Also called 'gooser'. Quaggers is possibly goose, duck, quack—quaggers.

Quandary (*Peoples'*, 17 *cent.*). Difficulty, fix. Probably from the half-French court of Charles II., who was half French by his mother. Qu' en dirai-je? Skinner gives this derivation. Possibly a frequent expression of Louise Querouille (the Mother Carwell of the streets), who afterwards became Louise, Duchess of Portsmouth, when she built Portsmouth Place, S.W., corner of Lincoln's Inn Fields—some seven houses, those remaining still showing on the pilasters alternate roses of England, lilies of France, double flanked with torches of Hymen that look like rams' horns—which insignia would probably be more appropriate. Johnson calls 'quandary' a 'low word'. (*See* Curmudgeon.)

Quarter pound bird's eye (*Low. Class Smokers'*). Quarter of one ounce—a pennorth. Asked for quite seriously. Probably begun as a joke. (*See* Sherry.)

Quarter sessions (*Legal*). Jocose swearing.

Quarter stretch (*Thieves'*). Three months' imprisonment. 'Saucy Sall's got a quarter with hard.' (*See* Stretch.)

Quartern o' bliss (*Low London*, 1882). A taking small woman. Diminutive of 'Pot o' bliss'—a fine woman.

Quartern o' bry (*Complicated Rhyming*, 1868). Short for Bryan o' Lynn—which rhymes with gin.

Quartern o' finger (*Complicated Rhyming*), 1868). Short for finger and thumb, which rhymes with rum—the refreshment called for.

Queenie (*Street*). Mock endearing name called after a fat woman trying to walk young. 'Queenie, come back, sweet' (Drury Lane Panto., 1884). Addressed to Mr H. Campell, one of the heaviest men on the stage, and then playing 'Eliza', a cook. (*See* Poultice.)

Queen's bad bargain (*Military*). A recruit who turns out a bad soldier—from Queen's shilling.

Queen's weather (*Soc.*, 1837 to end of reign). Fine sunshine—from the singular fact that through her reign the Queen almost always had fine weather when she appeared in public.

Queer-bit makers (*Police*). Coiners.

Queer shovers (*Police*). Queer is bad money—shovers any kind of industrials; the whole—passers of bad money.

Queer the pitch (*Music Hall*, 1880). Spoil business, impede applause This phrase comes from the patter of street performers, whose 'pitch' for performance is 'queered' by a severe policeman In its application in music halls it means any act which injures a performance—the pitch For instance a jeer, a cough, a sneeze will queer the pitch, but it is chiefly applied to the band, when by a sudden stoppage, or error in accompaniment, the singer is, or might be, brought to grief

At home, if an actor or actress dared to act whilst some one else was speaking, he or she would be fined or dismissed as 'queering somebody's pitch', whereas every gesture, every animated movement assists the speaker instead of spoiling him —*D T*, 29th June 1897

Queue (*Theatrical*) Tail piece, last word, upon which another actor has to reply. Evidently from French, and quite clear from 'queu', as it is often lamentably spelt.

Quick-change artiste (*Theatrical*) Translation of protean entertainer

England has boasted a goodly supply of what were once called 'quick-change artists', from the days of the elder Charles Mathews until the more decadent and mechanical times of W S Woodin. —*D. T.*, 10th March 1897.

Quick curtain (*Theatrical*) Rapid descent of curtain

Quid-fishing (*Thieves'*) Skilled thieving—quid being a sovereign.

Quid to a bloater (*Street*). Sovereign to a herring — commonest shape of street cock-sure betting

Quiff (*Anglo-Indian*) Idea, fancy, movement, suggestion

Quiff (*Army*, 1890 on) The sweep of hair over the forehead.

Quifs (*Military*, 19 *cent.*) Manœuvres.

Quit off (*American*) To refrain

Quite a dizzy (*Mid.-class*) Very clever man—evidently from Disraeli

Quite the don (*Peoples' Hist*) Perfect, magnificent. Probably from the name given to the husband of Queen Mary Tudor—Philip being a very magnificent Spaniard

R

R. C. (*Catholic*, 1880 on). Roman Catholic

R M D (*London, Lower Financial*). Ready money down.

Racial atavism (*Society*, 1897). Atavism Came from Paris. It is a synonym for heredity

We prefer to believe that it is a case of what might be scientifically described as 'racial atavism'. It is simply that 'fault of the Dutch' which Canning discovered in the course of treaty negotiations at an early period of the century, and which has now broken out in a fresh place among their colonial descendants —*D. T*, 19th February 1897

Rad (*Political*) Abbreviation of Radical, and bestowed by the Conservatives probably from its suggestiveness of 'rat'.

Rag (*Oxford*, 19 *cent*) Disarrangement of another man's furniture, but with no damage

If you return and find your rooms in a state of chaos, your friends have been indulging in a 'rag' —*D. T*, 14th August 1899

Rag-stick (*Peoples'*) One of the names for umbrella, said of a loose and unreefed implement

Ragged edge (*Amer-Eng*, 1884). Deserted

It seems fair to assume that father, daughter and her child sailed yesterday for Paris, leaving poor Tom on the ragged edge —*N. Y. Mercury*, 10th January 1885

Raggies (*Navy*). Steady chums The term, however, seems to be generally one of disparagement.

Rags (*Art Jargon*, 1880) Old lace used for decorative purposes (*See* Crocks and Timbers.)

Rags, Daily (*Printers'*). London lower class daily newspapers

A man in the country wants to sell his old kicksies, Charley Prescotts and coats, and seeing the advertisements in the respectable daily rags, he sends them all up to the buyer, and gets five bob in return, which, he is told, is all they're worth

Rail-birds (*Racing*, 1890 on) Watchers of race-horses when exercising. From their perching on five-barred and other gates while on the wait.

The 'rail-birds', as certain people are called who closely watch the work of horses on the race tracks, would do well to keep an eye on Tommy Ryan.—*N. Y. Mercury*, December 1891.

Railroad Bible (*Amer. Travellers'*, 1880). Pack of cards.

Railways (*Railway Servants'*). Red stockings—of course worn by women, and resulting out of 'signal red'—used throughout the British dominions; *e.g.*, 'She's a pair of smart railways—ain't she?'

Rain-napper (*Street*). Umbrella—because it catches the rain. From 'knap'—to catch quickly.

Raise (*Amer.*, 1880). Kick—vigorous instance of replacing cause by effect.

Rajah, The (*Drury Lane*, 1850 on). Synonym for the Mogul.

Raked fore and aft (*Mariners'*). Desperately in love. Figure of speech from damage done to the whole of rigging by a well-directed shelling.

Raker (*Common Classes*, 1840-56). Comb.

'Ral (*Navy*). Strict naval for admiral.

Rampers (*London Street*). Noisy street-rangers, chiefly young men.

Randy-voo (*Army*). Tavern which is the headquarters of recruiting sergeants. Also synonymous with noise and wrangling—from Rendez-vous.

Rank and smell (*L. Peoples'*, 19 *cent.*). Common person.

Rare old water-bruiser (*Nautical*). A tough, hard-working old shore-man.

Rarified (*Soc.*, 1860 on). Tamed. Usually applied to tamed women—from one Rarey, a horse-tamer.

Rasher and doorstep (*L. Classes*). Coffee-house phrasing — the rasher speaks for itself. The doorstep is a thick slice of bread and butter.

Raspberry. (*See* Bit o' raspberry.)

Rat (*Artisans'*). A man who has not served his time, and therefore who has no indentures. He may, however, be a very fine workman; but he can enter no society or union.

Rat back clip (*Peoples'*, 1856). Short hair.

Rational costume (*Society*, 1895). Trousers for women. Early in the fifties these appendages were called Bloomers—from an American lady of that name. A generation passed, when they loomed up again as divided skirts and Bectives (probably from Lady Bective having approved the fashion). Next, about 1890, they took over the name for young boys' knee-trousers, and were styled knickerbockers—the name of which probably came from Washington Irving. Finally, in 1895, the female trouser was known as rational costume.

Rattle (*Sporting*). Good news of certain reliance, and in relation to a horse entered for a given race.

Rattle-belly-pop (*American Saloon*). Whiskey and lemonade. Changed, when speaking to the more elegant sex, to rattle-blank-pop.

Rattle, With a (*Racing*) Unexpected rapidity.

The only approach to a sensation was caused by Warrington and Kettleholder, the former coming 'with a rattle' in the morning to the price taken about him in the excitement caused by his forward running in the Cesarewitch. — *Newsp. Cutting*.

Raum method (*Anglo-Amer.*, 1890). Nepotism, corruption.

The 'Raum method' is simply the method by which Mr Commissioner Raum is said to determine the fitness of candidates for clerkships in the Pension Office. It consists in simply 'looking them in the face and giving a judgment'. He looked his own son, Green B. Raum, jun., in the face and formed a judgment of him.—*D. N.*, 17th July 1890.

Raven (*Public-house*). Small bit of bread and cheese—2d. From the idea that the ravens could only carry small quantities to Elisha.

Readied the rosser (*Lower Classes*). Bribed the police. Readied, past tense of to ready, from the 'ready'-money. *Rosseur*—French—one who harries and worries.

Ready-money betting (*Racing*). Where the backer at once pays his money to the bookmaker, and awaits the result.

Real healthy (*American—passing to England*). Well-brained.

Real Kate (*London Local, Clare Market*, 1882—*swept away*, 1900). Kind matron. In this year a charitable queen of the market, one Kate, died.

Real lady (*Music Hall*, 1881). A lady *in excelsis*.

Real Peacer (*Street Boys'*) Final shape of Charley Peace, a hero-murderer.

Real raspberry jam (*Street*, 1883). Climax of the use of 'jam' to describe lovely woman

Real razor (*Westminster School*, 1883). A defiant, quarrelsome, or bad-tempered scholar

Real Rugby (*Public school*). Cruel Derived from the Rugby rules of foot ball, which are more likely to lead to accident, it is generally held, than the more modified rules of the 'Soccer'.

Real scorcher (*Street*) Vigorous, active personality—but without vice

Real sweet (*Eng -Amer*) Perfect

Reb (*American Civil War*, 1862-65) Abbreviation of 'rebel', given in scorn by the Federals to the Confederates, and afterwards adopted by them

Reconstituting an epoch (*Lit*, 1875) Misrepresenting history De-vised when Mr Wills produced Charles I. at Lyceum Theatre.

M Sardou lays the scene of his story in a historic period, introducing more or less authentic historic personages, or, as the phrase goes, reconstituting an epoch —*D N's* Criticism of M Sardou's *Theodora*, 13th July 1885

Receipt of fernseed (*Proverbial superstition*) Ability to be present invisibly. The statement that if you held fernseed you were invisible was based upon the supposition that you could not do so, because fernseed had no existence—ferns showing no flowers

Rifle green, the dark artillery blue, and the dark grey of the service great-coat were as bad, or nearly as bad, as black, so that at present the British soldier of all arms must be admitted to be singularly destitute of the 'receipt of fernseed' —*D N*, March 1883.

Recently struck it (*Amer. Eng*). *Nouveau riche*—man of sudden wealth. That is—he has recently struck gold Common to U S A —growing in England.

Re dayboo (*Music Hall*, 1899). Re-débût Absurdity, of course—being a first appearance a second time

This welcome 're-dayboo', as Dan Leno would doubtless call it, was made, etc —*Sun*, 29th November 1899

Red (*See* Bit o' red)

Red, All over (*See* All over red.)

Red heart (*London Tavern*—about 1870. Short for 'redheart—rum'.

Red herring (*Soc.*). Intended deceit. From dragging a red herring, at the end of a string, over the track of a fox — whereby the hounds are thrown out.

The Conservative candidate gravely stated that if Home Rule is granted, Irishmen will come over in such numbers that instead of the labourers' wages being 12s or 13s a week, they will be reduced to 6s. and 7s, and this red herring has been implicitly believed — *D N*, 17th July 1886

Red-handed (*Hist.*). In the fact—*flagrante delicto*

George Wallis, 30, was charged on remand with stealing some cloth from a shop in Whitechapel —The prisoner was caught almost redhanded —*People*, 27th December 1896

Red-hot miracle (*Sporting*, 1882). Startling paradox of the very day

Red-hot treat (*Lower Peoples'*). Extremely dangerous person.

Red peppers (*American*) Form of swearing

Red-shirts (*Colonial and American Mining World*) The name given to gold and silver miners, all of whom wear red flannel shirts. Garibaldi while in America adopted the red shirt for life, introduced it upon the continent of Europe, and made it historically famous

Red-tie (*Univ., Oxford*, 1876) Synonym for vulgarity.

Redding up (*N Country, Hist.*). Tidying, putting the house in order From the habit of rubbing red ochre over the cleaned doorsteps, side-posts, and hearth-stones Passing away rapidly

Reddings (*Thieves'*) One of the words for watches. Probably from the name of a receiver of that name, who gave the best prices

Redfern (*Soc*, 1879) Perfectly-fitting lady's coat or jacket. From the vogue obtained, 1879 on, by Redfern, Maddox, W. Regent Street, whose lady's tailoring became celebrated over the whole world.

Redundant (*City*, 1898) Impudent Arose from the invention of Mr H. Bottomly in a speech.

Personally, and speaking entirely for myself, I regard the attitude taken up by Dr Alexander as a little redundant, having regard to the appointment of the committee.—*D. T*, 2nd June 1898

Reelings (*Rhyme*). Feelings.

Ref. (*Political*). Abbreviation of Reformer. Invented by the Tories as a term of brief contempt.

Refuges (*London Mid.-class*). The lamp-islands centred at wide crossings as half-way oases in the desert of London roads.

Reg. duck egg! (*Sporting*). A cypher of no value. From cricket—when a batter going out on nothing at all is marked 'O' — playfully described as a 'duck egg'. The 'reg' is a common abbreviation of 'regular'.

Regenerate. (*See* Degenerate.)

Regionalism (*Political*, 1880 on). Sub-nationality. Word to describe differences of political and social feeling between differing races or sub-races under one government—as N. and S. of North America, Hungary and Austria, Poland and Russia. Adopted in England during the Home Rule struggle in House of Commons.

As platinum and silver do not melt at the same degree of heat, so, too, diversity of disposition, which in Italy is more marked than elsewhere, will not allow of the Southerners being educated by the same method as the Piedmontese. The twenty-six years which have elapsed since our unification have proved this abundantly. Regionalism is still a profound sore.—Signor Fazzari, *D. N.*, 21st April 1886.

Regular oner (*Peoples'*). Individual past praying for—a scapegrace. Sometimes used in satirical praise.

Reign of Queen Dick (*Peoples'*). Never—a quibble.

Removal (*Political*, 1883). Assassination. When the exposure of the Phœnix Park and other assassinations (1882) took place Carey, one of the chief informants, in his evidence, always referred to a political murder as a removal. The word at once took.

Umbrellas as Weapons.—In reading the evidence which Town Councillor Carey gave as to the Phœnix Park murders—or 'removals', as the Irish Invincibles call them—it is impossible to avoid wishing that the heroic victims of hired stabbers had been armed.—*Graphic*, 24th February 1883.

Reparty (*Soc.*, 1874). Satirical pronunciation of *repartee*.

Just as the young Gaiety lady favoured by royalty who had a speaking part presented to her on that account was not good at reparty, so artists are not, as a body, good at spelling.—*Ref.*, 7th March 1886.

Repentance curl (*Soc.*, 1863). It was a solitary, heavy curl made of a portion of the back hair, and brought over the left shoulder and allowed to fall over the left breast. The Princess of Wales brought this fashion into England (1863), where it held good for many years. (*See* Zarndrer.)

Repetitious (*Literary*). Repetitional. First applied by the *Daily Telegraph*.

It was just as well, for the scheme of 'Self and Lady' had a tendency to become monotonous and to be repetitious in its effects.—*D. T.*, 20th September 1900.

Reprint (*Printers'*). Printed matter for putting in type, as opposed to manuscript.

Resistance-piece (*Press*). Chief dish, or leading stage-piece. From the French—*pièce de resistance*.

The Christmas treat was a great success. About sixty sat down to the banquet. After this, the resistance-piece, was over, etc.—*Ref.*, 10th January 1886.

Responsible (*Theatrical*). Fee'd to lead. He is an actor more of common sense than parts, who steadily obeys the lead—and takes that leader's place when not acting.

Wanted, for a first-class portable, Entire Co., including Gent. for Entire Lead, Juveniles, Responsibles, etc.

Resting (*Theatrical*, 1890 on). Obvious—but it has another satirical meaning — that of 'out of an engagement'.

This is the period of the year when the actor casts off his stage-mantle, and settles down to that easy, indefinite, unemployed time which comes under the description of 'Resting'.—*D. T.*, 11th August 1898.

Resurrection pie (*Peoples'*). All sorts pasty.

Revolveress (*Soc*, 1885). A woman who uses a pistol.

The details of the career of the charming Lucille, the latest revolveress, are romantic, though slightly mixed.—*Ref.*, 8th February 1885.

'Ria (*Maria*). Passing to 'Aryet (Harriet). The typical name of the costermonger's young lady—a coster herself.

Rib-shirts (*Street*, 1880). Fronts, or dickeys, worn over a grubby shirt to give the air of a fresh one.

Rice Christians (*Soc*, 19 *cent*) Natives in rice-bearing countries, who accept the missionaries in order to gain rice or food Now used generally of people who make of religion a business

It is extremely doubtful, in these circumstances, whether such converts as the missions boast are ever more than the dregs of Chinese society, coolies without family, home, or pedigree, 'rice-Christians' as they are scornfully named.—*Ref.*, 11th August 1895

Rich as crazes (*Irish*). Of course—Crœsus

Rich-one (*Upper Hetairia*) A wealthy wife. Said of the luckless spouse of a man who finds home not to his liking

Richmonds in the field (*Peoples'*) Satirical description of rivals in active work—no matter of what kind. From Shakespeare's *Richard III*

I think there be six Richmonds in the field

There were so many Richmonds in the field, so many pretenders to the throne, that it was quite impossible to discover the real king I cannot tell you how it is going to end Wars of disputed succession are proverbially long and bloody—Sir W. Harcourt (June 1885) in House of Commons

Ricing (*Mid.-class*) Throwing rice over the bride when in her go-away carriage From the East Indies, where this custom intimates the hope of children—rice being a prolific growth.

Ride square (*Racing*) Square here means 'fair'.

Riding (*Sporting*, 19 *cent*) Adroitness, ability—from racing, where a jockey's riding is a great factor in working out success Applied in every possible way.

Nobody questions the guilt of William Palmer. But there was some truth in his remark that 'the riding had done it', and if Mrs Bartlett were acquainted with the language of the turf, she might pay the same compliment to Mr Clarke as Palmer paid to Sir Alexander Cockburn.—*D N.*, 19th April 1886.

Rig sale (*London*, 19 *cent*). Swindle—a false sale

Right, About (*Peoples'*) Modest self-depreciation, or depreciation in general, not absolutely right, but nearly so, *e g.*, 'I thrashed him about right'. (*See* To rights)

Right gee-gee (*Sporting*, 1880). The horse certain to win

Right off (*Peoples'*, 1897) Rejection, failure, determination.

Right racket (*Amer - Eng*). Successful public declaration. Chiefly refers to entertainments and publishing

Right tenpenny on the cranium (*Peoples'*) Good phrasing A new rendering of 'Right nail on the head'.

Messrs Robertson and Bruce, at Toole's Theatre, with 'M P', seem to have hit the right tenpenny on the cranium.

Rights (*Thieves'*, 1860) Perfection.

Ring dropping (*Peoples'*) Equivalent to 'Tell your grandmother to suck eggs'. Said in scorn of weak attempts at deception From the stale cheat of the operator pretending to pick up a ring in the street in front of the intended victim

Rip (*Anglo-American*). Creation of a word from the initials of *Requiescat in pace*—in Catholic cemeteries, the pious wish being declared by these initials

Ripper (*Thieves'*). Daring murderer of women Very common noun devised from rip, the ripper making his wound with a knife in the human body In 1888-91 a number (ten) of murders of women were perpetrated, presumably by the same man, as the ripping treatment of the victims was common to all or almost all the cases

Ripping slum (*Tavern*, 1800-30). Capital trick. (*See* Egan's *Life in London*)

Rise bristles (*Anglo - American*) Excite to resentment.

Risky (*Soc*, '90's) Adulterous—but not openly so.

There are plenty of ladies living, as all their world knows, lives which are generally called 'risky', who are personally most scrupulous in observing all the minor conventionalities—John Strange Winter, *D T*, 5th August 1899

Rit (*University, passing to Peoples'*). A ritualistic clergyman. (*See* Tec, Cad, Pot.)

Ritualistic knee (*Doctors'*, 1840-50). When genuflection came in, with the success of Dr Pusey's church theories, the ritualistic knee really became known to medical men. It was caused by severe untrained momentary kneeling—when passing the altar, etc

Road combination (*Anglo - American Theatrical*). Congregation of variety artists moving rapidly from town to town.

Road-starver (*Mendicants*, 1881). Long coat made without pockets, especially without a fob for money. Road meaning generally the mass of beggars — the starver is that which deprives the road of food.

Roader (*Local London*). Sunday splendour of the youthful persuasion, who displays himself in the Mile End Road. Superior to Whitechapel streeter (*q.v.*).

Roast 'and an' noo (*Eating-house waiters'*). Short for 'roast shoulder (of mutton) and new potatoes'. 'And, or hand used for shoulder shortens the word by more than one-half, while 'noo' is quite a reasonable reduction.

Robbing the barber (*Peoples'*, 19 *cent.*). Wearing long hair.

Robin (*Street*, 19 *cent.*). Little boy or girl beggar standing about like a starving robin.

'Robin Dinners' are due to the kindly suggestion of the Rev. Charles Bullock, editor of *Home Words* whose appeals to the generosity of his readers to enable him to entertain 25,000 or 30,000 London children every year.—*D. T.*, 7th January 1899.

Robin Goodfellow (*Peoples'*, *Hist.*). In Shakespeare's time he was a merry urchin boy. See *A Midsummer Night's Dream*. Previously he was associated with the dusius, and even with Satan —for in the drawings of the 15th century frequently he had horns and hoofs added to his peculiar qualifications. Descendant of the fauns. Probably his pre-Shakespearian title was Good-Filler. This term Robin Goodfellow would result out of the national tendency, as Puritanism spread over the land, to veil the erotic by Anglicized euphemism.

Robustious (*Peoples'*). Pompous.

Mr Barnes's unfortunate tendency on this occasion was to a rather 'robustious periwig-pated' style that sits ill upon the shoulders of so sentimental a personage as Lord Lytton's Claude Melnotte.—*D. N.*, 29th October 1883.

Rocked to sleep (1880). One of the sentimental American modes of describing death, one which began to prevail about this time.

Rockiness (*Low. Class*, 1887 on). Want of foundation, unsteadiness. Used chiefly of a drunken man.

Rogers (*Soc.*, 1830-50). A ghastly countenance — probably from Rogers the banker-poet, who in his age looked very old; or from the pirate flag, the Jolly Roger, which showed a skull.

Rogues' walk (*Soc.*, 1882). The 'Walk' in the '90's was the north of Piccadilly—from the Circus to Bond Street.

Roman Fall (1865-70). A droop in the back produced by throwing the shoulders well behind. A fashion of the last years of the French Empire, borrowed from French military officers, who were compelled to accept this attitude as the result of tight lacing, one of the more ominous excesses of French life in those terrible days. The fashion being accepted in England, it was dubbed the Roman Fall, as a counterpoise to the Grecian Bend (*q.v.*). Said to have been invented by Mr F. C. Burnaud, in *Punch*. 'Proud? Not proud? Spot his Roman fall.' (*See* Two inches beyond upright.)

Roof scrapers (*Theatrical*). Gallery boys—especially those standing behind the highest row of seats—and therefore nearest the roof.

Rooster (*Parliamentary*, 1860). M.P. who makes himself heard, who is not a silent member.

Whether the returned member be a rooster or not time will tell.—*Bird o' Freedom*, March 1883.

Roosters (*River Lea Anglers'*). Followers of the gentle craft, who do not move from one spot — probably because they ground-bated it the night before.

Rope-yarn Sunday (*Mercantile Marine*). Thursday. On Sunday the food being at its best, Sunday and feasting well are synonymous. Thursday, as the half-way day, is distinguished by duff, or pudding, which is always made long, roly-poly shape, which suggests rope-yarn hanks — hence Rope-yarn Sunday.

Rorty bloke (*Costers'*). Vigorous, strong.

Rorty toff (*Costers'*). Variation of rorty bloke—an inferior rorty bloke.

Rortyness (*Street*). Vitality.

Before that she reminded me a little too much, in her rortyness, of the serio-comic lady who sings 'What cheer "Ria", Ria's on the job!'—*Ref.*, 23rd August 1885.

Rose, Under the. (*See* Sub rosa.)

Rose-coloured spectacles (*Soc.*). Optimism Free translation of *couleur de rose*

In these days, when the mind's eye is less apt to observe things through rose-coloured spectacles, a good many of the grand old crusted adages have broken down badly —G. R Sims, *Ref*, 1st February 1885

Roses and raptures (*Lit*, 1830 on) Satire of the Book of Beauty style of literature, the precursor of æstheticism. Attributed to Dr Maginn.

The social and religious life of Hellas was by no means what a vain people supposes. It was no more all roses and raptures than our modern existence is all beer and skittles —*D. N*, June 1885

Rossacrucians (*Press*, 1885). Followers of O'Donovan Rossa. Satirical term invented by Mr G R Sims.—*Ref.*, 8th February 1885

Rot-funks (*Cricket*) Panics.

Rothschild (*Soc*) A rich man (*See* Vanderbilt)

Rotten orange (*Lower Peoples'*, 1686). Term of contempt. Historical —from the name given by the Jacobites to William III —Prince of Orange.

Rotten-apple (*American, Theatrical*) To condemn an actor by hissing him. Figurative expression.

The last new American verb is 'To rotten-apple' Actors, it seems, in some of the minor New York theatres, are not infrequently rotten appled, much in the same way as our legislative candidates in the old hustings days used to be 'rotten-egged' —*London Figaro*, March 1883

Rotten row (*Rhyming*) Bow

Rotter (*Theatrical and Street*) Failure in any way, especially on the stage. Presumably from rot.

Rotting about (*Soc of a kind*) Wasting time from place to place.

Roughs and toughs (*Peoples'*) Beautiful rhyming coalescing, for 'rough' is English and 'tough' is the New York equivalent observation

All the way down, whenever there was a stop, they were insulted by Boers, and we in the truck had to mix with sixty or more of the 'roughs' and 'toughs' of a score of nations —*Sun*, 7th November 1899

Round (*Ball-room*). A valse, galop, or polka. (*See* Square.)

Round the corner (*Street*) Drink Figurative expression—not as the high road.

The barmaid replied 'It's good enough for you, go into the other bar, where the men are' Mrs Montgomery retorted 'You're wrong all round the corner,' meaning that she had had something to drink.—*D T*, 16th July 1898

Rovers (*American*) People of Colorado — given in consequence of their prospecting habits

Row in (*Peoples'*) Unfair conspiracy From Thames life through centuries. A man 'rowed in' in a river robbery, or even a murder

It's very likely the sellers and the general public concerned in auction sales are anything but satisfied with the results of sales by auction where a 'knock out' is arranged, and especially where the auctioneer 'rows in' with the crew —*D T*, 12th February 1897

Row de-dow (*Irish*, 19 *cent.*). Riot —term applied scornfully by Irish to a disturbance. From a chief portion of the chorus of 'British Grenadiers'.

With regard to the Prince and Princess's visit to Ireland, the 'row-de-dow'—that is, we believe, the Hibernian term for it—which took place, etc —*Ref*, 9th March 1885

Rubbing it in well (*Police*). Giving fatal evidence

Rubbish (*Military Anglo-Indian, early* 19 *cent.*) Luggage of any kind, and especially furniture, which was frequently very shabby (*See* Garbage.)

Ruck down (*West Provincial*, 19 *cent.*) To courtesy very low.

Ruckerky (*Soc*, 90's). Grotesque pronunciation of *recherché*

It was a security which a member of the Asylums Board had described, in a glowing adjective, as 'ruckerky'. —*D T*, 4th April 1898

Rudders (*Oxford*) Rudiments of Faith and Religion (now abolished)—irreverent statement in 'er'

Ruffer (*Peoples'*) One who is rough

Rugger (*Oxford Football*, 1880 on). Rugby rules. (*See* Soccer.)

Rule the roast (*Old Eng*) To govern noisily

Rule was granted (*Lawyers'*). Another chance.

Rum bottle (*Navy*, 1860) Sailor—from the liquor affected by mariners.

Rumbo (*Middle-class*, 1860) This is an exclamation of congratulation, probably obtained from the gipsies, as amongst them 'Rumbo' is a common cry upon the meeting of two men. Women never interchange this cry. It is a corruption of the Spanish carambo, the accent of which is upon the second, the word becoming almost k'rambo.

Rumourmongers (*City*, 1897). New coinage. Hitherto there have been iron, fish and cheesemongers. Newsmonger was the first modern discovery in this direction, and now the debased 'rumour' follows suit.

It would almost seem as if the once ingenious class of rumourmongers were losing its power of skilful imagination, and the method of the new school is to cover one blunder by a still greater blunder.—*D. T.*, 19th November 1897.

Run amok (*Asia*). Amok means homicidal mania — accompanied by running blindly forward. Passing from India to England it has got Anglicized into 'Running a muck', probably from the fleeting destroyer showing himself in a muck sweat. This corrupted phrase is now applied in England in a score of ways—all of which imply a good deal of action. In Malacca, Siam, Java and adjacent places the mental state which leads to amok is equally well known and dreaded. The perpetrator shows signs of moroseness for days, more or less in number, before he is seized with amok, when he dashes up, with a drawn knife, and lays about him amidst the scudding people until he himself is killed by a general onslaught. In the more civilised spots where this custom prevails, especially in Batavia, precautions are taken which prevent the destruction either of the victim to 'amok', or those near him when the murderous moment arrives. Every policeman is armed with a catch-fork. Directly a patient starts upon amok, supposing the police are not ready for him, as, being warned of the symptoms, they generally are, the spearing of this strange fish commences. Overtaken, the springed points of the amok-spear are pushed round the neck, which passed, the incurved articulations once more expand, and the victim is held at spear's length, when all the damage he can do is to himself. Thus hooked he is 'run in', where, if he has not wounded himself fatally, he is treated for 'D.T.'s'—the origin of most amok—when he either recovers or is passed into an asylum.

Run home on the ear (*American*). Entirely defeated.

Run through (*Parliamentary*). Rapid in action—especially official.

Runner (*Thieves'*). Technical name for dog-stealer.

Rushing business (*Thieves' and Public-house*). Robbery by adroitness, cheating under the semblance of fair treatment.

They go out on the rushing business, and a very profitable cmag they find it.—*Rag.*, 1882.

Rushlight (*Peoples'*). Very thin man. Derived from use of candles—of which the forgotten rushlight was the slimmist.

Rusted in (*American*). Settled down. Suggested by rust fixing in a nail or screw.

Ruttat-pusher (1882). Keeper of a potato car.

S

S. A. These are the initials and sign of the Salvation Army.

S. D. (*Theatrical*). Stage door.

S. M. (*Theatrical*). Stage manager.

S. P. (*Press*, 1870 on). Letters equalling special correspondent, being first two letters of first word.

S. S. (*Street*, 1883). These initials originally stood for sinner saved. The letters were revived, with a similar meaning by some of General Booth's enthusiasts (1882) in the Salvation Army.

Sacred lamp (*Theatrical*, 1883). Ballet-girl burlesque. The origin of this term is quite historical. Mr John Hollingshead, lessee for many years of the Gaiety Theatre, Strand, London, issued one of a series of remarkable lessee's ukases, in which he cynically referred to the burlesques he had produced as keeping alight the sacred lamp of burlesque.

Sad, and bad, and mad (*Soc.*, 1880). Fashionable Jeremiah-mongering.

Philosophers and sages, and people who speak of the 'fatal gift of beauty' would say, with Mr Browning's half-repentant lover, this was all very 'sad, and bad, and mad'.—*D. N.*, 10th March 1885.

Sad vulgar (*Soc*, 18 *cent and earlier* 19 *cent.*) Synonym for cad, snob.

He is a 'sad vulgar', as the ladies' expression was in the days of George III, and there is something very droll about the poetical retribution he meets with —*St James' Gazette*, 17th August 1883

Saddling - paddock (*Australian*) Place of amusement or rather place of assignation

Saffron Walden God - help - ye (*Provincial*). Beggars, outcasts, mendicants of that place. (*See* Gordelpus)

The triumph of scornful nomenclature was reached in the case of Saffron Walden, nicknamed 'Saffron Walden God-help-ye', from the presumed wretchedness of its inhabitants. . . . In the heart of the New Forest occurs a similar instance of nomenclature to that of Saffron Walden, with the difference only that it is accepted by the inhabitants instead of being thrust upon them by the surrounding population The village of Burley is always spoken of by the native as 'Burley God-help us'.—*D N.*, August 1884

Sag (*Amer -Eng*) Sinking, cessation, non success—from mining, where a sinking of the bed, or roof, of a mine, has this term applied

Still more when Mr Matthew Arnold or Mr Irving appears in the States, then there is 'no sag in the popular boom', which, being interpreted, means that there is no lull in the general excitement —*D N*, 5th October 1886.

Sage hens (*American*) People of Nevada — probably from the multiplicity of prairie fowl which frequent the sage bushes which cover the prairie in that state.

Sail in (*American - Eng*) Equivalent to 'Go it', and taking its place in England

Sailor's champagne (*Peoples'*). Champagne on the *do ut des* principle —an easy-go sailor shoots all his pay in a day, and then reminds you all the rest of his run on shore that you only exhibit beer—and mere board and lodging

St Alban's clean shave (*Church*). Appearance of the ritualistic or high church clergymen's face

St Alban's doves (*Electioneering*, 1869). Two active political canvassers, so called from attending a certain church of which they were shining lights

St Giles' carpet (*Seven Dials—old*). A sprinkling of sand

St John's Wood donas (*Public-house*, 1882). Immoral women of the better class, living at St John's Wood generally

St Lubbock (*Lower London*, 1880 on) An orgy, a drunken riot From the August Bank Holiday, the first Monday in the month, chiefly invented, in the parliamentary sense, by Sir John Lubbock The tendency on the part of the more violent holiday-makers produced the satirical 'St', and its accompanying meaning.

St Lubbock, Feasts of (*Public*, 1871 on) Bank holidays as established by law — Easter Monday, Whit Monday, first Monday in August and Boxing Day, 26th December. From Sir John Lubbock's Act, 1871, by which the first, second, and fourth were made legal, and the third created.

The feasts of St Lubbock—*i e*, Bank Holidays—established in consequence of the exertions of Sir John Lubbock, M P (afterwards Lord Avebury), in 1871, are regarded with the highest favour. Their influences upon the commercial world and whole community have been remarkable —*D T*, July 1899

St Peter's the beast (*Oxford*, 1890 on). St Peter's in the East.

All who have dwelt near St Peter's-in-the-East and been tortured by its fearsome bell will understand why, despite its pleasant situation and curious crypt, it should be referred to as 'St Peter's the Beast' —*D T*, 14th August 1899

St Stephen's hell (*Parliamentary*) No. 15 Committee Room, House of Commons When the Parnellite 'split' took place, the Irish Nationalist members 'discussed' in this chamber for many days—the noise resulting in the bestowal by the lower officials of this title upon the room in question

Sal hatch (*Peoples'*) Umbrella—origin quite obscure, but probably salacious

Sal hatch (*Prob Hist*, 17 *cent*) Dirty wench Probably one of the court of Charles II. French phrases of a certain fashion Of course a corruption—from 'Sale Ange', which is itself a French corruption of Sallanches, a town in Savoy whence spread over France, as from all other Swiss towns, women servants The French have historically always considered the

Swiss less cleanly than themselves; they still use the phrase to worry servant girls from Savoy, now, of course, part of France. Sal Hatch is applied in exactly the same way to dirty-looking young English girls. This word, however, may come from the Italian—Salaccia—a dirty, ugly, big woman. If so, it reaches us from the Hatton Garden division of London.

Sal slappers (*Costers'*). Modification of a vigorous name for a common woman.

Salad march (*Ballet*, 19 *cent.*). March of ballet girls in green, white, and pale amber—from the usual colours of salads.

A 'salad' march, with the *coryphées* dressed as lettuces and spring cabbages, is an admirably harmonious arrangement.—*D. T.*, 7th May 1899.

Sally B. (*American*, 1880 on). A very thin, tall woman in evening dress. This phrase, which fleetingly passed through London, is quite historical. Derived from Madame Bernhardt, who, though at the end of the Victorian era, she became a well-developed comedian, was for many years the most absolutely thin woman on the stage.

Sally Lunn (*Peoples'*). Bun, invented in the 18th century by a Chelsea industrial of that name. (*See* Simnel.)

Saloon (*Amer.-Eng.*). Tavern—applied to a brilliant establishment.

Salt, Barrel of. (*See* Barrel.)

Salt-cellars (*Peoples'*). The cavities behind the feminine collar-bones.

Salt-horse squires (*Naval*, 19 *cent.*). Warrant, as distinct from commissioned, officers. Name used to suggest the parvenu grandeurs of the warrant officer, who was dined upon salt beef—the salt horse in question.

Salt-pen (*Lit.*, 1860 on). Nautical. Figurative description of the pen of a writer of sea-stories.

Salt junk (*Music Hall*, 1897). Last rhyming cry for drunk—passing into 'salt'.

Salt's pricker (*Naval*). Thick roll of compressed Cavendish tobacco. Used sometimes very figuratively.

Salvation Army (*Street*, 1882). Drunk.

Salvation Army of politics (*Polit.*, 1885). Radicals. Invented by Mr Goschen in this year.

For us Radicals, the Salvation Army of politics, as Mr Goschen denominated us, the keen desire for social improvement, the great and healthy efforts for actual and immediate reforms, the enthusiasm of social progress; but for him the better part, for the educated and thinking men the nobler mission of the candid friend, the duty of criticising the work in which his culture and refinement prevent him from taking any part.—Mr J. Chamberlain's Speech: Dinner of the Eighty Club, 28th April 1885.

Salvation jugginses (*Com. London*, 1882). The early aversion exhibited towards the more violent members of the Salvation Army led to the addition of the word juggins.

Salvation rotters (1883). Final term of scorn levelled at the early Salvationists.

Salvation-soul-sneakers (1883). This was one of the last terms applied, before General Booth (February) yielded to circumstances and with almost papal authority forebade outdoor processions in London. (*See* Skeleton Army.)

Sam (*Peoples'*). Abbreviation of Stand Sam—pay for a drink.

Sam Hill (*American*). Some hell, replacing the name of a notoriously wild-tongued man.

Same o. b. (*Peoples'*, 1880). Abbreviation of 'old bob'—this standing for shilling. Phrase has reference to the universal shilling entrance-fee to most ordinary places of information or amusement.

Same old 3 and 4 (*Workmen's*). 3 shillings and 4 pence—which, multiplied by six working days, gives £1 per week.

Sampan (*Navy*). Historical name, from Nelson's time, of the *Sans Pareil*.

Sandford and Merton (*Press*). Didacticism—from the lofty tone of the speakers in this once celebrated boys' book.

It would, we think, have been more attractive but for an occasional tendency to fall into the *Sandford and Mertoun* or directly didactic vein, as when we are reminded that 'an undue concession to narrow prejudice or cowardly convention should be unsparingly denounced, because it is insidiously and subtly destructive'.—*D. N.*, 2nd February 1885.

Sandwich board (*Street*, 19 *cent.*). Police station stretcher, used chiefly for conveying drunken persons.

Sandwich men (*Street*, 1860 on) The doleful, broken-down men employed at one shilling per day to carry pairs of advertisement boards, tabard-fashion, one on the unambitious chest, the other on the broken back

Sangster (*London*, 1850) Umbrella. A Mr Sangster, of Fleet Street, invented a light and elegant steel-ribbed umbrella, which he called Sangster's patent umbrella

Sanguinary muddle (*Polit.*, 1884) Policy of Europe—which seemed always destructive Invented by Lord Derby

Lord Derby used a very strong expression the other day about the diplomacy of Europe He called it a 'sanguinary muddle', and recommended that England should keep out of it —*D. N.*, 17th October 1885.

Sans-culottes (*Peoples'*, 1793 1830) San skillets—such was the translation by the people for the people in the loyal later times of George III. This phrase came to be immediately applied to the most wretchedly-clad men in the revolutionary streets of Paris

Sapheadism (*Agricultural, Amer*). When the sap is rising, the bark is soft—hence this term for weak-headedness

Sapper (*Music Hall*, 2nd French Empire). Gay, irresistible dog From 'Rien est sacré pour un sssapeur !'—the chorus of a song by Theresa, a great Paris music hall cantatrice, 1860-70. She came to London about 1866

Mr Clement-Smith, the well-known theatrical bill printer, being captured the other day by another of those evening paper sappers to whom nothing is sacred, was irreverently christened by his tormentor 'the Bill-poster King'—*Ref*, 3rd February 1899

Sappy (*Low London*). Weak-headed. Origin obscure

Saratoga (*American - English*). Anything large, huge. Saratoga is an example of new word-growth Saratoga Springs being the most fashionable inland station for New Yorkers, necessarily the largest amount of personal luggage accompanied the fashionable frequenters, while size was required that ladies' costumes might not be crushed in travelling But the most remarkable development of Sarotoga was that of being used to describe anything of unusual size.

Sarcasm (*Soc* , 19 *cent.*). Satirical assumption of the meaning of a stupidly-said thing.

Sardine-box (*Peoples'*). A jocular name given to the prison-van, in which the prisoners were stowed away or packed, as it were. (*See* V R , Black Maria, Virtue Rewarded, Vagabonds Removed, etc)

Sarey Gamp (*London*, '40's). Huge market umbrella. Now not seen out of museums, and mostly bought up for their mines of valuable whalebone.

Sargentlemanly (*Peoples'*, 19 *cent*) Satirical perversion of 'so gentlemanly', and importing that the person has taken rank above a mere private.

Sarkaster (*Press*, 1880) Invented word, synonym for satirist—derived from sarcastic

Sarken News (*London*, 1860-83). The common term for *Clerkenwell News*—a journal which was begun in a small way in Clerkenwell, and became one of the chief metropolitan mediums for advertising

Sashay (*Anglo-American*) Slide, skip, dance, skirt, walkingly haunt, etc From term used by French and other dancing-masters—*chasser*—to glissade from one side to the other

Sat (*Univer.*, 1860) Satisfaction.

Satellite (*Public-school*). Modern synonym for 'fag'—a boy who revolves round a bigger one, whom he has set up as his model and hero. Sometimes 'Sat'

Saturday middles (*Soc* , 1875) The article on the left of the middle of the *Saturday Review*—where it opened in the centre

Saturday pie (*Peoples'*). Pasty, within which is interred all the disjecta membra of the week.

Sauce-box (*Peoples'*) The mouth.

Sausanmash (*Jun Clerks'*). Lowest common denomination of 'one sausage and mashed potatoes'

Saveloy Square (*E London*). Duke Place, Aldgate—so named satirically on the *lucus a non lucendo* principle—because, being wholly inhabited by Jews, no ordinary sausages are ever found there

Say (*American colloquial*) Commonest form of 'listen' Probably descended from the Plymouth Brethren who crossed to the States. 'Say', equivalent to 'do', is a common form of expression in Devonshire to this day.

Say howdy for me (*Amer.-Eng.*). Remember me to, etc. (*See* Howdy). Passing rapidly into English every-day expression.

Say soldi (*Italian—through organ-grinders'*) Six shillings.

'Sblood (*Cath. Exclamatory*). His blood. Will be found in *Tom Jones*, bk. xviii. ch. 10; where also will be found Od zookers—God's hooks, or hooker, which equals 'nails'—the three used in the Crucifixion.

'S'bodlikins (*Cath. Exclamatory*). His bodily-kins! Meaning obscure. Some say it refers to the earthly kin of Jesus—His brothers and sisters on Joseph's side. Others, extremists say the word is His body leakings—meaning the blood flowing from the side.

Scaffold-pole (*Common London*). Is the fried potato chip sold with fried fish.

Scaling down (*American-English*). Repudiation of debt.

Scalp (*American-Eng.*, 19 *cent*). Victories.

After securing all the amateur scalps in San Francisco, Corbett became a professional pugilist.—*D. T.*, 18th March 1897.

Scalper (*American-English*). A savage horse, suggested by the Indian habit of achieving the scalp, and the tendency of the scalper to snap at the head of his groom. Now extended to describe briefly any human being of merciless tendencies, especially in his financial dealings.

Scalps (*Soc.*, 1896). Jewel chain charms worn upon bangles, and given by young men to young girls.

Scandal village (*Sussex*). London Super Mare or Brighton, where the virtuous natives assume their London patrons to be all libellous.

Scare (*American-English*, 1880). Grow frightened.

Scare-crown (*American, Boys'*). Intensification of scare-crow, and adapted to a woolless old man. (*See* Bald head, Bottle nose.)

Scent of the hay (*Theatrical*). Sneer at false pastoral writing for the stage. From the protest of Mr Pinero upon being accused, in *The Squire* (a pastoral comedy), of plagiarising a book of Mr Hardy's. Pinero urged that his chief desire had been to waft a scent of the hay across the footlights.

M. Mayer's company have been engaged in wafting the scent of the hay across the footlights. It is French hay, but good of the sort.—*Ref.*, 21st February 1886.

Schlemozzle (*E. London, Jews'*). Riot, quarrel, noise of any kind. Colloquial Hebrew.

I had espied W. A. P., sitting not far off, and partly with a desire to prevent bloodshed, partly in the hope of promoting a schlemozzle, I notified Jones accordingly.—*Ref.*, 1st December 1889.

School Board 'ull be after you (*London Streets*, 1881). Practically meaning—'Look out—or the police will have you.'

School-marm (*Soc.*, 1886). Schoolmistress. (From U.S.A.)

Celibacy of the clergy is a familiar doctrine, both for banning and for blessing. But the celibacy of the 'school marm' is a heresy which as yet only exists in the pious dream of school managers and school boards, by whom marriage is regarded as an even more ruthless enemy than death.—*Pall Mall Gazette*, 12th January 1888.

Schoolmaster is abroad (*Peoples'*). In other times the country may have heard with dismay that 'the soldier was abroad'. It will not be so now. Let the soldier be abroad if he will; he can do nothing in this age. There is another personage abroad—a personage less imposing—in the eyes of some, perhaps, insignificant. The schoolmaster is abroad; and I trust to him, armed with his primer, against the soldier in full military array.

Schooners, frigates, and full-masters (*Naval*). Degrees of comparison as to the capabilities of apprentices in the Navy—the least accomplished being the schooner, the frigate the youth who is handy at his business, and the full-master the achieved youngster who can learn no more of the art—of navigation understood.

Scoop (*Military*, 1880). One of the modes of wearing the hair when the mode of bringing it down flat upon the forehead came in. (*See* Curtain.)

Scooped (*Amer.-Eng.*, 1880). Swindled—money being scooped out of the pocket.

Score (*Peoples'*). Reckoning—figuratively used 'I've got a score against you, and some day you'll pay'—from the custom in old times of drawing lines upon a board with a bit of chalk—the number of marks in a line being a score. (*See* Chalking against.)

Scorpions (*Theatrical*) Babies—whose observations do not help the performance

Scorpions (*Army, Hist*) Scornful reference by officers to the civil inhabitants of Gibraltar Originally referred to the natural children of English soldiers by Spanish mothers Sometimes 'Rock scorpions', the 'Rock' being Gibraltar.

A military correspondent writes from Gibraltar complaining of want of houses for officers attached to the garrison The 'Scorpions', as the inhabitants are facetiously called, have all the best houses in their hands. — *D. T.*, 5th November 1897.

Scotch (*Rhyming*). Abbreviation of Scotch-pegs, the catch-rhyme for 'leg'

Scrag-hole (*Theatrical*) Gallery. Probably suggested by the stretching of the scrag or neck, and the resemblance of the gallery to a dark hole.

Scrape along (*Poor Peoples'*). To live somehow from day to day, to scrape off a living

Scraper (*Soc.*, 1880) Short one to two-inch whisker, slightly curved, and therefore differing from the square inch.

Scratch down (*Street*) The public scolding of a man by a woman

Scratch me (*L. Lond*, 19 *cent.*). Lucifer match

Scratch-rash (*Artisans'*) Face scratched—presumably by wife

Scratchers (*Lower Class*) Lucifer matches Splendid example of peoples' onomatope—always going on The lower classes never took to the absurdly pompous word—lucifer, and even the middles added matches, from the old sulphur matches, probably a corruption of 'meche'.

Scratchers (*Naval*). Pay-masters and their subordinates Comes down from the noisy times of quill pens.

Scratching poll (*Peoples'*) Pole for cattle to rub their sides against A reference to a skin disease erroneously said to be prevalent amongst Scotchmen

An exhibition of Scotchmen's knees took place at the Castle, and was attended with great success Mr Sandy M'Alister MacDonoughloch took the first prize and a cold in the nose The prize consists of a scratching poll.

Screamer (*Press*). Alarmist article or leader.

Screaming gin and ignorance (*Sporting Reporters*, 1868). Bad newspaper writing

Screed (*American-English*) A pelt, or muck running Widely applied.

Side by side with these garrulous 'screeds' about what took place six or seven weeks ago comes news of what is doing to day —*Ref*, 9th March 1885.

Screw your nut (*L London*) Dodge a blow aimed at the head.

When we gets there, the Mug says, 'How did he get that?' looking at Selby's eye, and I says, 'He got it because he could not screw his nut.'—*Peoples'*, 6th January 1895

Screwed up (*Oxford and Cambridge Universities*) To be vanquished. The term takes its rise from the ancient habit of screwing up an offender's door, generally a don's. The action was only complete by breaking off the heads of the very thin screws.

Screwed up (*Artisans'*). Without money—can't move More emphatically—screwed up in a corner. (*See* Hung up, Stuck up.)

Scribe (*Press*, 1870 on) A poor writer.

Scribley (*Provincial*) Screw-belly, *i.e*, sourish small beer.

Script (*Authors'*, 1897) Short for manuscript—especially in the theatre.

Scripturience (*Literary*, 1900). Rage for writing, *cacoëthes scribendi*. Presumably invented by Mr William Archer, who wrote—

It is true that Mr Stedman's net is one of very small meshes, which hauls in the minnows as well as the Tritons, but what an amazing harvest, even of mediocrity! There is a serious danger, it seems to me, in this universal scripturience. — *M Leader*, 27th October 1900

Scrummage (*Youths'*, 1860). Struggle Derived from foot-ball term

Scrunging (*Country Boys'*). Stealing unripe apples and pears—probably from the noise made in masticating.

Scug, or Smug (*Schools'*). A new—that is new boy.

In regard to the general charge, it is well known that everywhere bullying has been reduced to the smallest proportion. In our fathers' time every new boy, 'scug', or 'smug', or whatever the generic name may have been, was kicked and knocked about as a matter of course for the first part of his curriculum.—*D. T.*, 12th June 1897.

Sculps (*American*). Convenient abbreviations of pieces of sculpture.

Perhaps no statue, except the unfortunates in Trafalgar Square, and the melancholy meeting of 'sculps' in Parliament Square, was more sharply criticised at the time of its erection, or more heartily laughed at afterwards than the gigantic equestrian effigy of the late Duke of Wellington.—*D. N.*, 18th January 1883.

Sculpt (*American Artists'*). Verb from sculptor—as writer—to write; dancer—to dance; singer—to sing; sculptor—to sculpt.

Sculptor's ghost (*Art*). Sculptor whose name is not associated with the marble upon which he works. May be the actual creator of a work which goes in another's name, or may be engaged only for his speciality which may be hair, or bust, or legs, or hands, or drapery.

Scurry around (*American*, 1876). Be active.

If you care to lynch him there are barrels of tar, and one of us might scurry around and get some feathers.—*Detroit Free Press*, 1883.

Scuttler (*Manchester*, 1870 on). Young street rough.

Might it not be possible to teach manners, and to enforce their observance, even by means of the rod and the cane, at the Board schools? It is in those expensive seminaries, we apprehend, that the majority of the juvenile 'scuttlers' are educated.—*D. T.*, October 1893.

'Sdeath (*Poetical*). Abbreviation of His death—meaning the Crucifixion. (*See* 'Sflesh.)

Se Tannhauser (*French-Eng.*, 90's). Bore oneself—as 'Que je me tannhause'.

Sea William (*Naval—early* 19 *cent*). Civilian.

'For d'ye see—I'm a Sea William, and not in no ways under martial law,' said the pilot.—Marryat, *Rattlin the Reefer*, ch. lviii.

Sea-side moths (*Mid.-class*). Bed vermin.

Seats Bill (*Political*, 1884). Short name suddenly given to the Redistribution of Parliamentary seats. Due to Mr Gladstone, and instantly accepted as a brevity, clear in meaning.

Further progress was made in the settlement of the main outlines of the Redistribution scheme, or the Seats Bill as it has now become the fashion to call it.—*D. N.*, 27th November 1884.

Sec. (*Commercial*, 1860). Abbreviation for second.

Second - hand sun (*Poor Folk*). Nothing much to be proud of—suggested where sunlight is only reflected into a given room from a neighbouring wall.

Second-hand woman (*Anglo-Indian Army*, 1859). Widow.

Second liker (*Tavern*, 1884 on). Repetition drink — another like the first. Now applied generally to repetition.

Second picture (*Theatrical*, 1885). Tableau upon the rising of the curtain to applause, after it has fallen at the end of an act, or a play.

Secrets of the alcove (*Soc.*, 1890 on). Most intimate influence of the wife over the husband. Outcome of analytical fiction. Phrase invented by Dumas *fils*.

It may be what Dumas called 'the secret of the alcove', but when perfectly represented, and with absolute purity, on the stage, it is very delightful to witness. Here we see a married woman using every feminine art and charm to tempt her husband back to companionship and love.—*D. T.*, 29th June 1897.

Sedition - mongers (*Polit.*, 1886). Name given to supporters of Home Rule. Started by Lord R. Churchill, 22nd February 1886, at Belfast.

See (*American*). To 'bet'. In the card game of poker each player 'sees' an opponent for so much—that is, bets so much upon cards which he holds, but has not yet shown. It is a word which now may often be heard in Liverpool commercial cotton circles.

Stearn Carpenter, the Heracles of the *Troy Times*, would have 'seen' Achilles, 'and gone ten dollars more', to employ the language understood by the countrymen of Mr Charles Dudley Warner.—*D. N.*, 13th February 1883.

See the breeze (*Cockney*, 1877). Expression of summer enjoyment at escaping from London to an open common (*See* Taste the sun.)

Seek a clove (*American*). Take a drink

Seen better days (*Middle-class*) Euphemism for saying a person is poor

Seen the elephant (*American-English*, 1880 on). Climax—witnessed the finish From the universal American circus—whose chief attraction in country places *is* the elephant. Therefore the phrase means proud exultation, and is applied to boastful persons.

Selah (*American-English*) The Hebrew 'vale', 'God be with you' Probably the origin of the London artisan phrase, 'So long' (*See*)

Happy, happy England! Everybody has got plenty of work to do except the judges of the Divorce Court. Selah!—*D T*. 29th October 1896.

Senal pervitude (*Com. Street Satire*). Penal servitude

Send for Gulliver (*Soc*, 1887 on). Depreciatory comment upon some affair not worth discussion. From a cascadescent incident in the first part of Dr Lemuel Gulliver's travels

Send off (*Anglo-American Lit.*). Poem, tale, or article written specially to attract attention—direct opposite to pot boiler

Mr English, then a journalist in active harness, promised the firm a 'send-of' poem —*N Y. Mercury*, 1888.

Sensation scene (*Theatrical*, 1862). Exciting scene of action in a play Title invented by Edward Falconer. (*See* Nailed up drama, Peep o' day tree)

Sensation-mongering (*Polit*, 1888). Searching for effect

Mr Chamberlain has resolved to take no part in a controversy raised and maintained either for party purposes or in pursuit of sensation-mongering.—*D N*, 26th February 1886.

Sensational (*American Press, passed to Eng about* 1870) Omniscient adjective used wherever extraordinary might be a possible equivalent.

Sensational writing (*Lit*) Crude, frank, banal description, or dialogue, intended to excite or dismay.

Sent (*Peoples'*) Evasion and contraction of 'sent to prison'

At Northwich William Flynn was sent for seven days for begging —*People*, 20th March 1898

Sent across the Herring-pond (*Lower Class*) Transported to Botany Bay

Sent to Coventry (*Rural*) Cut—not spoken to Origin so obscure as not to be within view of any known etymologist

Sent to the skies (*L Mid-class*) Killed—evasive accusation of murder

Sent up (*American Eng*) Exposed, publicized From the New York Police Court term for imprisonment 'Sent up for a month'—up to the prison that is

Sentimental hairpin (*Soc*, 1880). An affected, insignificant girl

Sentry go (*Military*) Mounting guard

The Volunteer billets himself now preferentially in forts and in barracks, enjoys compliance with the stern regulations enforced in such places, and would rather be on 'sentry go' than in a public-house carouse —*D N*, 28th April 1886

Sepulchre (*Middle-class, London*) Name given to the flat cravats covering the shirt front between the coat and throat Satire upon their effect in covering over and burying the shirt-front, when no longer immaculate. Afterwards called chest plasters (*See* Doggie, Poultice, Shakespeare-navels)

Serio-comic (*Music Hall*, 1860-82). The title given only to lady-singers of a lively turn, and in distinction from 'comics', who are always men

Serve (*Thieves Soc*). Euphemism for passing through a term of imprisonment.

Sessions (*Peoples'*). Noise, quarrelling, disturbance, from the fact that at sessions there are conditions not peculiar to quietude.

Set (*Street*, 1880) Conquered, put down.

Set about (*Peoples'*) To assault.

The present assault was committed on the 20th ult. As frequently happened, they 'had words' about money matters, and because she would not accede to his demands he 'set about her'—*People*, 4th April 1897

Set the Hudson on fire (*New York*, 1884) Instance of imitation, of 'Set the Thames on fire'

'Mme Boniface' is not likely to set

the Hudson on fire, as it is original in neither plot nor music.—*N. Y. Mercury*, 1884.

Seven Dials raker (*Costers'—local*). A girl of the town who never smiles out of the Dials. (*See* Deck.)

Seven times seven man (*Peoples'—Satirical*). Hypocritical religionist.

Seventy-five cent. word (*Amer.-Eng.*, 1884). Sesquipedalian.

'Sflesh (*Provincial*). His flesh—a very rare Catholic exclamation, descended from before the Reformation. (*See* 'Sdeath.)

Shack-per-swaw (*Sporting*). Every man for himself. French—*chaque pour soi*. Introduced in England by a French gentleman rider.

Shadder (*Work.-class*, 19 *cent.*). A thin, worn person.

Shadow of a shade (*Polit.*, 1886). More than immaculate, when used in the negative, as it always was. Invented by Lord R. Churchill.

But of confiscation, of taking away a man's property without paying him for it, there is not, as Lord Randolph Churchill would say, the shadow of a shade of a hint or suggestion or implication or inference.—*D. N.*, 26th February 1886.

Shadow of the owl (*Athenæum Club*). Cellar smoking-room (until 1899, when the Council added a floor, part of which was the new *fumoir* of the Athenæum), where the visitor was at once met by the topaz eyes of the high-perched owl, raised in honour of the tutelary goddess of that ilk, Minerva.

Shadwoking (*Soc.*). Grotesque rendering of shadowing.

Shake a flannin (*Navvies'*, 19 *cent.*). To fight. (*See* Flannel-jacket.)

Shake fleas (*Old Eng.*). To thrash.

Shake leg (*Peoples'*). Remove.

Shake old fel (*American*). Greeting—'Shake hands, old fellow.'

Shake-out (*Stock Exchange*, 19 *cent.*). Sudden revulsion and following clearance—due to panic, the result of discovery of fraud, or of stupendous bankruptcy, or even the death of a powerful financier of known speculative turn of mind.

After Saturday's heavy shake-out in New York, occasioned by the news of Mr Flower's death, the market has settled down a little in consequence of the evidences afforded that the big financial houses were fully prepared to grapple with the situation.—*D. T.*, 16th May 1899.

Shake-up (*Peoples'*). Start, beginning, spurring.

The first French Revolution, with all its attendant horrors, was entirely due to the fact that in a little preliminary shake-up the Paris masses found themselves, to nobody's surprise more than their own, fully equal to cope with the gendarmerie.—*Ref.*, 27th November 1887.

Shake yer toe-rag (*Beggars'*). Show a clean pair of heels—run away.

Shakespeare-navels (*Lond. Youths'*, 1870). Long-pointed, turned-down collar.

Sham-abram (*Peoples'*). Pretend illness. Very common use still in the Navy. The captain is shamabraming again—he wants a day on shore, to see—a doctor.

Sham-ateurs (*Sporting*). People who are not even amateurs.

The amateurs of Pancras Road showed themselves distinctly different from the sham-ateurs of Her Majesty's Theatre.—*Ref.*, 16th December 1888.

Shamrock (*Military*, 19 *cent.*). A bayonet prick.

Shan von Voght (*Irish Peoples'*). The Pasquinado, Mrs Harris, or Paul Pry of Irish life.

Can anything as spirited and stirring as the 'Shan von Voght' be rhymed in favour of declining to pay rent?—*D. N.*, 5th November 1883.

Shanghai gentleman (*Naval*). The very reverse of a gentleman.

Shank (*American*). Centre or heart. From the shank or grip of a button.

Why, you ain't going home already? It's right in the shank of the evening.—*Texas Siftings*, 1883.

Shank yersels awa (*Scotch*). Take yourselves off—move your shanks.

Shant of bivvy (*Hatton Garden*). Pint of beer.

Shan't take salt (*Theatrical*). Small returns. Good example of an elision creating obscurity. Means, 'We shall not take enough money to pay for salt, let alone bread.'

Shape up (*Peoples'*, 18 *cent.*). Show fight—from the aspect of a prize-fighter when prepared to kill.

When Fred called him an all-round ass—he shaped up!

Shapes and shirts (*Theat.*, 1883). Satirical name given by young comedians of the present day to distinguish old actors, who swear by the legitimate Elizabethan drama, which involves either the 'shape' or the 'shirt'—the first being the cut-in tunic, the other, or shirt, being independent of shape (*See* Chest-plaster)

Shave (*Peoples'*, 1884) Drink.

Shaves (*Services*). False news—sometimes mere jokes.

Belgrade is getting livelier because of the influx of miscellaneous foreigners It still maintains its pre-eminence for 'shaves'—*D. N.*, 1876.

Shawl (*Mid.-class*) Symptom of engagement

Lady Clonbrony was delighted to see that her son assisted Grace Nugent in shawling Miss Broadhurst.—Miss Edgeworth, *The Absentee*, 1809.

She (*Soc.*, 1887). Queen Victoria. From *She*, the African romance by Mr Rider Haggard—produced early in this year

She didn't seem to mind it very much (*Peoples'*, 1885). Cant phrase, intimating jealousy on 'her' part.

Sheckles (*Peoples'*) Money From the Hebrew

Shed a tear (*Peoples'*, 1860). Take a short drink—not a draught

Shedduff (*Mid.-class*) Corruption of *chef d'œuvre*

Sheet o' tripe (*Streets'*) Plate of this dish

She'll go off in an aromatic faint (*Soc*, 1883). Said of a fantastical woman, meaning that her delicate nerves will surely be the death of her

Shellback (*Navy*) Sailor of full age (*See* Flatfoot)

She-male (*Common London*, 1880). Synonym for female, and pairing with he-male (*See* He-male)

I love the she-male sex.

Sheol (*E. London*). Evasion of 'Hell'—the word being Hebrew for this place.

In our own channels or in the great Australian bight we who would go to sea for pleasure would go to Sheol for pastime.—*Ref*, 4th October 1887

Shepherd, To (*Boer War*, October 1899-1900) To surround, to drive into a crowd—from surrounding the enemy

Since Cronje was shepherded with his army into the bed of the Modder by a turning movement, the remaining Boer commanders have been very nervous lest a similar manœuvre should be tried against them.—*D T*, 2nd April 1900.

Sherry (*Tavern*). Four ale—that is, ale at fourpence per quart

She's been a good wife to him (*Streets'*) Satire cast at a drunken woman rolling in the streets

Shet down (*Engineers'*, *American*). Thoroughly commenced, suggested by 'shetting' or 'shutting' down a safety valve

Shet up, Sossidge (*Peoples'*, 1896). Recommendation to a German, noisy in public, to be quiet—really, 'Shut up, Sausage'

Shettered (*Low Life*) Complete ignominy. Word derived from shop-shutter

Shevvle chap (*Sheffield*) A man of that city.

Shift (*Irish*, 1800) Blow up

Shiftmonger (*Tavern*, 1882). Very remarkable expression. When the chappies and Johnnies became notorious for frequenting the old Gaiety Theatre stalls (1879-82), they were remarkable for the display of very large, rigid shirt-fronts Indeed, this shirt became a specialty—hence the word.

The shiftmonger rolled into the Roman's (Romano's—an Italian restaurant in the Strand) blind, speechless, paralytic Staggering up to the well-known slate, he wrote thereon, in trembling characters, 'Coffee and soda for one Wake me in time to bress for Baiety Gurlesque'—*Bird o' Freedom*, 7th March 1886

Shillelagh (*Irish*, *Hist*) Knobbed stick carried for fighting

What did he hit you with? Witness: An Irish shillelagh—a crinkled and thick stick—a kind of Irishman's truncheon.—*D T.*, 31st December 1895

Shilling tabernacle (*Peoples'*) Wesleyan or Baptist tea meeting—at twenty-four halfpence per head

Shin stage (*Peoples'*, 18 *cent*). Journey on foot—or by propelling the shins.

Shine (*American*). Smiling look.

Shingle (*American*) Close-cropped hair—ridge and furrow. When (1880) following a London fashion, the hair of American men of fashion was cut close, this term came to be applied It is derived from the name of thin wooden tiles—shingles, which, of course, lie flat and close to the roof-rafters

'There will be no more parting there',

said the man when he looked into the mirror after having his hair shingled.—*Texas Siftings*.

Shipwrecked (*E. London*). Drunk. (*See* Floored.)

Shirtsleeves and shirt-sleeves (*Peoples'*). Poor and rich, work and luxury. The first are rolled up to the shoulders. 'I do *my* work in my shirtsleeves.' The shirt-sleeves are fair, white, smooth, and only displayed, as a rule, at the cuff.

Shoe's on the mast (*Sailors' and Peoples'*, *Hist.*). 'If you like to be liberal, now's your time.' Originally typical of homeward-bound and pay-off. In the 18th century, when near the end of a long voyage, the sailors nailed a shoe to the mast, the toes downward, that passengers might delicately bestow a parting gift.

Shofel (*E. London*). Hansom cab. Said to be derived from the peaked bonnets in use about 1850-53, which Jewesses dubbed by this name. Shofel, it seems, is a common word for hood, peak, or eave—even a hook nose.

Shool (*E. London*). Church or chapel—from this Hebrew word representing synagogue.

The beadle's eye was all over the shool at once.—Zangwill, *Children of the Ghetto*.

Shoot (*S. Exchange*). To give a man a close price in a stock without knowing whether there will be a profit or loss on the transaction.

Shoot (*S. London*, 1868). Walworth Road Station, L. C. & D. Railway. Because of the immense number of persons 'shot' out there.

A recent writer on the condition of Italy adduces the wretched character of most of the railway stations as evidence of the poverty of the country. I would give something to know his opinion of Walworth, as evidenced by the condition of the 'Shoot!'—*South London Press*, November 1882.

Shoot, Blooming (*Common London*, 1880). Cursed crowd.

Here's bad luck to the whole blooming shoot.—*Cutting*.

Shoot into the brown (*Volunteers'*, *circa* 1860). Figuratively—to fail. The phrase takes its rise from rifle practice, where the queer shot misses the black and white target altogether, and shoots into the brown—*i.e.*, the earth butt.

Shoot the chimney (*American*). Chimney is figurative for talking, and derived from movement of chin. Shoot here means stop.

Shoot t' wood to t' hole (*Yorks.*). Be secret. Let no one hear you. Translated thus: 'Shut the wood to the hole;' or, in other words, 'Shut the door'.

Shoot your cuff (*Peoples'*, 1875 on). Make the best personal appearance you can and come along—from the habit of wearing wide cuffs. (*See* Cuff-shooter.)

Shooter (*American-Eng.*, 1870). Pistol.

Shooting at sight (*American*). Instantaneous homicide — without warning.

Shop (*Theat.*, 1880). Theatre. One of the mock-modest affectations of actors, putting themselves and their work on a trade basis. (*See* Low comedy merchant.)

Shop, To (*Low. London*). To be instrumental in sending an individual to prison. Generally used to describe imprisonment.

Sullivan shopped him — real landed him.—*People*, 6th January 1895.

Shop-constable (*Workshop*). He represents the first principle of justice, the most primitive type of the magistrate. He is appointed for a day; he takes his turn with the rest of his shop companions, and commands one day, only to obey the next. When there is a trade or a personal quarrel, an appeal is made to the 'constable', who has the case tried.

Shopped (*Theatrical*). Verb derived from shop. Engaged for piece.

Short (*Bankers'*). A cheque paid in as few notes as possible.

Short (*Public-house*). Raw spirits —to distinguish it from spirits and water.

Short turn (*Hatters' men*). A particular ring at the warehouse bell requires that the boy shall answer it. Upon his return he gives to the shop constable (*see*), of the day the message he has heard at the gate. 'Gentlemen, a short turn', he may say, or 'a long turn'. In the first case, the applicant is presumably a well-authenticated 'Unionist'.

Short 'uns (*Poachers'*). Partridges —referring to the almost complete absence of tail feathers. (*See* Long 'un.)

Short week (*Artisans'*). Not a full six days' wages to take.

Shortage (*Anglo-American*, 1880 on). Abbreviation of defalcation

Sho's (*American*). Abbreviation of 'sure as'

Shot (*Peoples'*, *Hist*) Freed—from past tense of a verb rarely used in the singular in police society.

It was a horse that didn't mean work, and witness was very glad to 'get shot of him'.—*D T*, 14th December 1897

Shoulder-dab (*London*, 1800) A warrant officer or bailiff, who tapped the debtor on the shoulder as a legal arrest

Shouldering (*Undertakers'*). Carrying corpse in coffin.

It appeared that at a late hour on Monday night the prosecutors were 'shouldering' a coffin, containing a corpse which they had just brought away from the Westminster Hospital.—*D. N*, 20th August 1890.

Shov (*Thieves'*). Knife, or rather dagger or dirk Said by some to be an application of 'shove'—the movement made with the knife; by others a corruption, very cogent, of 'chiv'—the Romany for knife

Shove (*Street*, 1880—*adopted generally*) Bounce, gas, self glorification, preposterous patriotic yell

You only get to know what a nice place England is by going abroad, and finding what a lot of 'shove' there is about the glorification of most other places —*Ref*, 24th July 1887

Shove in (*Common Class*) Pawn —requires no elucidation

Shove off (*Navy*) To quit, go, flee, depart—from shoving off a boat from land or ship

Show drink, To (*Amer - Eng.*). Obvious

Show-houses (*Soc.*, 18 and 19 *cent.*) Mansions containing valuable works of art

Show-houses is a very appropriate term for such of the mansions of our nobility and gentry as are open to public inspection.—*Mirror*, 1829

Show the hand (*Peoples'*). To reveal unintentionally From card-playing, where showing the hand is sure to lose the game

Showy (*Society*, 1880). This word for overdressed and over 'made up' began to be common in this year.

Shulleg-day (*Street*, 1880) Corruption of show-leg day—referring to muddy day in London when the ladies carry their skirts high and expose their ankles

Shunt (*Railway Officials'*) To kill or move out of the way—from shunting carriages and engines.

Shut down (*Amer -Eng*). Ceased —from closing the lid of the cash-box.

But Coghill didn't want any more of the lands at any price. Then Lafayette tried to get the balance of the money due in honour to Coghill from Barin' by selling Baring some more of the lands. But Baring by this time had got enough of the lands himself, and shut down.—*N. Y. Mercury*, 23rd May 1885.

Shut down (*Anglo - American*) Forbidden — very emphatic form of opposition.

Dr Oliver and Dr Myrtle—what pretty names!—have 'shut down' on 'monopole' and 'extra dry'—*Harrowgate D N.*, 31st August 1886

Shut up your garret (*Street*) Hold your tongue

Shuvly kouse (*Street*) Perversion of public-house. This phrase spread through London from a police-court case, in which a half-witted girl used this phrase.

Sick in 14 languages (*American Marine*). Very ill indeed.

Sick man of Europe (*Polit.*, 1853 on) Any reigning sultan of Turkey. The phrase, as applied to Turkey, is said to have been given currency by the Emperor Nicholas I. of Russia Conversing in 1853 with Sir George Hamilton Seymour, the English Ambassador at St Petersburg, he used the words —'We have on our hands a sick man—a very sick man It will be a great misfortune if, one of these days, he should slip away from us before the necessary arrangements have been made'

Side-scrapers (*Middle-class London*, 1879-82). This was the name given to the square inch or two of whisker parallel with the ear which came in about this time

Sieve-memory (*Peoples'—old*). Bad memory.

I pray you, sir, write down these charms, for I have but a sieve-memory. All runs through. — Garrick, *Abel Drugger*.

Signed all over (*Artists'*). Said of a good picture which instantly reveals its creator in every inch.

Silence-yelper (*Thieves'*). Usher in a court of law—this word being his chief shape of speech.

Silly dinner (*Soc., Anglo-American*, 1897). Free and easy feasts. Took its rise in an evasive paraphrase of the name Seeley. Mr Herbert Barnum Seeley gave (20th December 1896) a dinner in New York which was concluded by a femimine music-hall entertainment.

Instantly the news of the Seeley dinner got into the newspapers, Mr Oscar Hammerstein put a clever burlesque of the whole business on the stage of Olympia—a music hall in Broadway.—*D. T.*, 28th January 1897.

From this time a doubtful dinner was spoken of as a Silly one. Became quite colloquial. 'There will be a silly snack on Sunday, 11.30, T. W. B. F.

Silly moo! (*Provincial, Rural*). Evasion of silly cow. Said generally of a stupid woman.

Silver streak (*Patriotic*). English Channel.

The silver streak shelters England from those direct consequences of a great war on the Continent which might be expected to overtake France.—*D. N.*, 14th October 1885.

Simnel (*Scarborough*). Cake of two kinds set one on the other, and so baked. The result of an accidental baking. There is a legend in Scarborough, however, that this name refers to the pretender Simnel, and that this cake was first baked by him in Henry VII.'s kitchen.

The day was termed 'Mothering Sunday', because all children in service repaired to their homes, taking with them a spiced cake, called a simnel, to which quaint ceremony, still observed in many rural districts, Herrick alludes in the lines—

A simnel also will I bring
'Gainst thou goest a-mothering.

—*D. T.*, 16th March 1901.

Simpson *v.* **Hard Simpson.**

Singing drolls (*Music Hall*). Comic male duettists who invented this title to distinguish themselves from comic singers, who were not droll, and who rarely wore costume. (*See* Athletic drolls.)

Singing Spanish (*Old Eng.*). Making a wild, crooning noise—probably suggested by the church services of Queen Mary Tudor's husband.

Sinjin's Wood (*Streets'*, 1882). Satirical way of announcing St John's Wood.

You have tasted the bad lush called wines from the wood. Well, there is worse tipple than that, cully—the wines of Sinjin's Wood. They generally run you in about a dick a bottle.

Sip (*Com. Lond.*, 19 *cent.*). Synonym for kiss.

Sissies (*Soc.*, 1890 on). Effeminate men in society.

Sissy men in Society.—Powdered, painted and laced. They swarm at afternoon teas. Of late, says a London writer, a certain type of man has become protuberant—a languid, weak-kneed, vain, and lazy specimen of humanity who has literally no redeeming points that can be discovered, and who yet gives himself all the airs of one to whom the universe ought to do unquestioning homage.—*N. Y. Mercury*, May 1893.

Sit down supper (*Soc.*, 1860). When about this date the medical press began to agitate against high feeding, one of the economical results was the invention of the 'stand up' supper, a necessarily thinner meal than the old ball-banquet. Old-fashioned people thereupon adopted this term.

Sitter (*Cricket*, 1898). Easy catch.

Sivvy, Upon my (*Common London*). A polite way of taking or making oath—possibly a corruption of asseveration.

I'll not disgrace your toffish lot. I'll be a great man, upon my sivvy.—*Cutting*, 1882.

(*See* Thuzzy-muzzy.)

Six buses through Temple Bar (*Peoples'*, 1840-50). Impossibility. Originated by the celebrated M.P., General Thompson.

Everybody who asks the Government to go on with the Suffrage Bill and the Seats Bill as one measure, and at one time, will be committing that great mistake which our old friend General Thompson used to describe as being made by the man who insisted on driving six omnibuses abreast through Temple Bar.—John Bright, Leeds, 18th October 1883.

Six-cornered oath (*Anglo-American*). Complicated swearing.

Since we are going to have German opera this season, it is high time to explain that *Die Gotterdammerung* is not a six-cornered German oath, but an opera.—*N. Y. Mercury*, September 1883.

Six feet above contradiction (*American*) Completely imperious

Six feet and itches (*Peoples'*) Over six feet Corruption of inches, usually written 'ichs'—hence the word.

Six mile bridge assassins (*Tipperary*) Soldiers—from the fact that once upon a time certain rioters were shot at this spot, not far from Mallow.

Six of everything (*Workwomen's*). Said by workwomen and workmen's wives in praise of a girl who marries with a trousseau meeting the respectable requirements of this phrase

Six-monthser (*Police*). A stipendiary magistrate of a savage nature who always gives, where he can, the full term (six months) allowed him by law.

Six-quarter men (*Cloth Drapers'*) There are two widths of cloth—six quarter and three quarter. The superior employés are called 'six-quarter men'—the inferior 'three-quarter men'—a term of contempt

Sixes, Put on the (*Military*, 1879). Small hook curls, hence 'sixes' gummed by some privates on their foreheads, and composed of their forehead hair.

'Ain't the 3rd putting on the sixes,' said by a private at Dover of another regiment in reference to the 3rd, whose colonel allowed this style of hair-dressing.

Skalbanker (*Paper makers'*) An outsider paper-maker, one who has not served seven years to the trade.

Skeleton Army (*Street*, 1882). Street fighting The origin of this term for fighting in public took its rise about the end of 1882, when the Skeleton Army was formed to oppose the extreme vigour of the early Salvation Army.

Serious Affray between the Skeleton and Salvation Armies—A man named Timothy M'Cartney is at present lying in the London Hospital suffering from a severe wound in the back, which he received from one of the members of the Skeleton Army—*D. N*, 10th January 1883.

Skettling (*Naval Officers'*) Full dressing.

Ski (*Westminster School*) Street Arab, road boy

Skilamalink (*L. London*) Secret, shady, doubtful If not brought in by Robson, it was re-introduced by him at the Olympic Theatre, and in a burlesque

Skin-changers (*Peoples'*) Appertaining to metamorphosis. It referred, and refers generally, to the wehr-wolf throughout Europe

Lycanthropy (a charming subject) is by the late Mr J F M'Lennan The wolf is the animal, as Mr M'Lennan says, into which European 'skin-changers' commonly turn themselves.—*D. N.*, 7th August 1883.

Skinners (*Street*). Mental torture—figure of speech From the agony endured by being flayed alive

Skins a wicked eye (*American*) Evil-looking eye—the skinning referring to the wide opening of the lid.

Skip (*Anglo-American*, 1870). A rapid retreat, quick march to avoid consequences Also to run away meanly. (*See* Balley, Polka, Valse)

Skippable (*Soc.*, 1882). To be avoided—from skipping in reading.

Mrs Oliphant's contessa is not so odious nor quite such a bore as some contessas we have known, but she is 'skippable, too.—*D. N*, 26th December 1884

Skipper (*Criminal*, 1870) One retreating

Skipper (*Military*) Naval way of describing a military captain.

Skivvy (*Navy*) Japanese—equivalent to rumbo

Sky-pilot (*Naval*) Chaplain—brought in about the time of Dibdin and Tom Bowline. (*See* Holy Joe, Devil-dodger.)

While some of the members of the Congregational Union were enquiring the way to the hall where refreshments were served, the doorkeeper shouted in a stentorian voice 'Sky-pilots' beanfeast!'—*D T.*, 4th October 1895.

Skying a copper (*Peoples'*, 1830 on) Making a disturbance—upsetting the apple-cart From Hood's poem, *A Report from Below*, to which this title was popularly given until it absolutely dispossessed the true one.

Slagger (*Low Life*). Fellow who keeps a house of accommodation

Slam (*American—passing to England*). To skurry or chevy, probably from the vigour displayed in slamming a door.

Slam-slam (*Anglo-Indian*). To salute—taken from Eastern salaam.

Slanging (*Music Hall*, 1880). This is a term for singing, and is due to the quantity of spoken slang between the verses.

Slap (*Theatrical*). Paint used in creating a stage complexion. Probably from its being liberally and literally slapped on.

Slated (*London Hospital*, 19 *cent.*). To die. Visitors to their relations and friends in hospital are only admitted on certain days—until a patient is doomed, when he is 'slated'—that is to say, his name is placed on the door-porter's slate, in order that his relations and friends may mention his name, and obtain entrance to the hospital at any reasonable hour.

Slaughter-house (*Thieves'*). Name for the Surrey Sessions-house. (*See* Steel, X.'s hall, jug.)

Sleeps like a top (*Old English*). From taupe—a mole, which is practically always in bed.

Slice off (*Military*). Paying part of an old score.

'Slife (*Ancient*). Catholic exclamation—His life. (*See* Odd's my life.)

Slightly tightly (*Fast Life*). Bemused with beer; not drunk.

Sling a slobber (*Low Life*). To kiss, or rather sling a kiss—the salute itself being the slobber.

Sling hook (*Peoples'*). Dismissal. From the mining districts. Refers to a hooked bag which is hung up in dressing-room, and contains such things as the miner does not require down the shaft. When dismissed the miner removes his hooked bag, and takes it away.

Sling in (*American—now English*, 1860). Very common American verb to recommend action.

'Sling in your feet', said to a break-down dancer.

'Sling us in something hot in your rag', said to a newspaper critic.

Sling joints (*American*). Gain a living rather by physical than mental effort.

Sling over (*Soc., from Amer.*). To embrace emphatically.

Sling your body (*Low. London*). Dance with vigour.

Slipper (*Tailors'*). Sixpence.

Slippery or slippy (*Marine*). Active.

Sloan, To (*Peoples'*, 1899). Hamper, baulk, cut. A word that lasted only as long as a summer's leaves. From an American jockey (Archer), who, riding a French horse (Holocaust) in the Derby this year, attempted to slant him across the course inside Tottenham corner and hamper the race. It was a fearless trick, invented by Archer at the risk of his life—one that Sloan imitated at the expense of his horse's life.

When the rider of a mare named Nursemaid finished *à la* Sloan, the Devonshire labourer expressed his mingled surprise and admiration at the daring of the feat. —*D. T.*, 12th August 1899.

Slop-made (*Australian*). Disjointed.

Slosh the burick (*Common London Life*). Beating the wife.

Slosh the old gooseberry (*Low. London*). Beat the wife.

Sloshiety paper (*Press*, 1883). A satiric imitative, equivalent to Society paper—invented to attack the 'sloshy' gushing tendency of these prints.

Sloshing around (*American*). Hitting out indiscriminately.

Slow (*Cricketting*). Slow ball.

Slow curtain (*Theatrical*). Curtain lowered gradually.

Slug (*Thieves'*). Hard drive of the fist into a face. Probably an onomatope.

Slumming (*Soc.*, 1883). Visiting the poorest parts or slums of a city with a view to self-improvement.

The results of a little experiment, which has been tried with the kindly consent of the Benchers of the Inner Temple, are well worth the attention of people who interest themselves in what is cynically called 'slumming'.—*D. N.*, August 1884.

Slung (*Art Students'*). Rejected—probably derived from rhyme to hung.

Slush (*Com. People*). Coffee and tea served in common coffee-house.

Small and early (*Soc.*, 1877). A carpet dance to which only a few intimates are invited. It is begun about eight and ends about eleven.

The Earl of Northbrook had a dinner-party at his official residence yesterday.

A small and early party assembled after dinner.—*D. N.*, 6th March 1884.

Smash a brandy peg (*Military*, 1880). Drink the spirit in question.

Abdullah Bey would smash a brandy peg with any one of us, and on the present occasion quaffed his laager beer like a stolid old Dutchman.—*D. N.*, 7th May 1884.

Smash the teapot (*Street*). Break the abstinence pledge.

Smash-up (*Military*, 1854 on). Defeat.

Every one who was present at the 'smash-up' and victory at Tamai used to say that no battle like it would again be witnessed in the Soudan.—*D. N.*, 28th January 1885.

Smashed (*Navy*). Reduced in rank.

Smell hell through a gridiron (*American*). Reference to drink-madness.

Smell the foot-lamps (*Historic survival*). Stage-struck, but in many ways referring to the stage. Of course referring to the whale oil lamps used as the foot-lamps, where candles could not be conveniently snuffed.

Smilence (*Peoples'*). Word-disguising—with a suggested point.

Smilence, ladies, if you please.

Smithereens, Smither's ruins (*Irish*). Destruction. 'Faith, I was smashed entirely into smithereens.' May be an Irish word, but probably corruption of 'Smither's ruins'—as typical of complete smash. Though who Smithers may have been seems not to be known.

Smoke-waggons (*W. American-English*, 1890). Revolvers—pistols. They certainly do carry condensed smoke.

Smoker (*Social*, 1878). Club or corps concert, where the members sing, play, and smoke, and, as a rule, recite.

Upon Mr A. D. Sturley and Mr M. G. Dearin devolved the pleasant duty of presiding at the 'smoker'.—*D. T.*, February 1894.

Smoking (*School*). Blushing.

Smole (*Word disguise*). A grotesque variation of smile.

S'mother evening (*Music Hall* 1884). Cynical refusal.

Among the items was Roberts's song, 'S'mother evening'.—*Ref.*, 7th June 1885.

Smothering a parrot (*French*). Draining a glass of absinthe neat. Derived from the green colour of the absinthe.

Smouge (*American-English*, 1880). To steal—probably Dutch.

While grace is being said at the table, children should know that it is a breach of good breeding to smouge fruit-cakes just because their parents' heads are bowed down.—*American Comic Etiquette for Children*, 1882.)

Snaggle-tooth (*Street*). Woman of lower order, generally a shrew, who, lifting her upper lip when scolding, shows an irregular row of teeth.

Snake out (*Amer.-Eng.*, 1835-40). Hunt down. From rattle-snake hunting. Now dead in U.S.A. cities, where the force of the verb is lost. Comes from early settlers. Heard sometimes in rural England.

The present is a fair opportunity to snake Thompson out.—Proclamation, Boston 1835, against the English Abolitionist, Mr George Thompson, then visiting America.

Snakes (*Anglo-American*). Drink-madness—*delirium tremens*.

Snakes (*Eng.-American*, 19 *cent.*). Danger.

Mr Cluer asked if anybody was chasing the prisoner when he cried out, 'They're after me'?

The witness replied in the negative.

Mr Cluer. Then I suppose he saw snakes.—*D. T.*, 2nd January 1900.

Snakes alive (*American*). Much worse than snakes.

Snaky (*American Backwoods*). Evidently suggested by the backwoodsman associating untruth with the doubtful and uncertain behaviour of the serpent.

Snakes also have the vice of developing mendacity in the human race so conspicuously that in the Far West 'snaky' is the term applied to a tale more vivid than probable.—*D. N.*, 19th February 1883.

Snap-manager (*Anglo-American*). One who hurries a company together.

A snap manager in Canada lately exemplified the ultimate of check by asking James Herne to loan him his lithographs to advertise the playing of a filched copy of Herne's 'Heart of Oak'.

Snapping your head off (*Society*, 19 *cent.*) Brusqueness of manner.

Anthony Trollope seemed a singularly gruff and ponderous personage, rather blundering in converse, and slightly addicted to 'snapping your head off' if you differed from him. — *Illustrated London News* (G. A. Sala), 16th December 1882.

Snapping (*Colliers'*). Eating—very good suggestion of hungry man devouring.

Snappy (*Soc.*, 1893 on). Attractive. Applied in all ways.

I must send you a few lines to tell you to take care of yourself, and be a good little boy, and keep out of mischief. I am going to keep the spotted jersey, and it looks quite snappy.—*D. T.*, 4th July 1895.

Sneaking-budge (*Thieves'*). Shop-lifting. (*See* Fielding, Jonathan Wild.)

Snide and shine (*E. London*). General description of the common Jews of the East of London by their Christian brethren. Both words bear the same meaning, but taken together are most emphatic.

Snide-sparkler (*Trade — Jewish Jewellers'*). False diamond.

Snippety (*Literature*, 1890 on). Journals made up of snippings from other and generally ancient journals. Used satirically. From the noise made by scissors in the operation of editing.

Men-folk may buy the 'snippety' publications, but this fact never appears to deter women from getting copies for themselves.—*D. T.*, 2nd October 1896.

Snossidge (*Commonest London*, 1880). A nonsense mode of pronouncing 'sausage'.

Snubber (*Public - school*). Reprimand.

Snuff a bloke's candle (*Thieves' English*, 18 *cent.*). To murder a man.

S'elp me, Bob (*Pre-reformation*). Corruption of 'So help me, Babe'. An appeal to the mediation of the infant Saviour. Following the rule of peoples' colloquial, which always finds a new meaning for an exploded word, Bob has here been substituted. Some writers insist upon Bob being the diminutive of Robert, a policeman—as though the classes using such a phrase as this would ask assistance from the nearest constituted authority?

The City coppers can't leave the poor costers alone. It riles the coppers, *s'elp me bob*, to see a cove trying to get an honest living.—*Cutting*, 1883.

S'elp me greens (*Pre-reformation*). 'So help me, groans'—groans being aids to repentance after the manner of Jeremiah. To-day the word has a very remarkable meaning—'may I lose the attributes of masculine vigour if I am diverging from the line of rectitude.' A close study of Balzac's *Vautrin* will throw much probable light upon phrases of this kind.

Here's a nice little story, and it's all true, s'elp me greens.—1883.

S'elp me never (*Modern Low London*). Meaning, probably, 'May God never help me if I lie now' 'Never', however, may be a corruption of a distinct word.

So and so (*Military*). Short for Senior Ordnance Store Officer.

So'brien (*Mariners'*). Corruption of *Sobraon*, a well-known favourite Australian steam-ship, named after one of Wellington's victories. Good example of anglicizing.

So glad (*London*, 1867 on). Catch word from William Brough's *Field of the Cloth of Gold.*

His song is as likely to take the town as the French King's catch phrase, 'So glad', which was all over London twenty years ago.—*D. T.*, June 1867.

So long *v.* Aspect.

So very human (*Soc.*, 1880). Apology, originally for conduct, but applied finally in so many ways that it fell into disuse 1884.

An attempt to exclude foreign material would in all probability be met by retaliatory measures. This would not be a wise policy on the part of other countries, but then it would be, in the slang of the day, 'so very human'.—*D. N.*, 27th October 1884.

Soaked the mill (*American*). Sold all his property through drink.

Soap. Girls. (*See* Bits o' soap.)

Soccer (*Oxford Football*, 1880 on). Association football — saves three syllables.

'Soccer', however, is an excellent example of Oxford minting, whether or not she can claim the credit of its invention. For the rule is as follows: Take any word in common use; knock the end off and add 'er'. If it should sound acceptable, it suffers no further mult a-tion. If it is still harsh and cacophonous, see what it will look like by striking off its head and the casual removal of an intermediate syllable. All these processes appear to have been gone through in order to produce 'Soccer' from Association Rugby was more fortunate. It had only a tail to lose —*D T.*, 14th August 1899. (*See* Rugger)

Social E. (*Mid.-class*, 19 *cent.*) Evasion of social evil.

Society (*Artisans'*) A synonym for workhouse.

Society journal (*Soc.*, 1878). Evasive name for a scandal-publishing newspaper

It seems that Mr Legge is the proud inventor of the phrase *Society Journal*, and he may further plume himself on having rendered it much the same service as Hyperbolus performed for ostracism Probably no paper will be ambitious of the title *Society Journal* after the account which Mr Legge gave in the witness-box of the way in which the business is conducted. — *Sat. Rev.*, 21st March 1885.

Society journalist (*Press*, 1875) A contributor to the *Society Journal*.

Society maddists (*Soc.*, 1881). Term to describe people not born in society, who devote their whole lives, and often fortunes, to get into society

Sodgeries (*London*, 1890) Latest outcome of fisheries, colindries, etc Started by *Punch* (April 1880) A Military Exhibition, Chelsea Barracks.

Soft sawder to order (*Anglo-Amer.*) Tailor's clothes ordered and not ready made

There is a fine opportunity for any bishop who will fearlessly get in the pulpit, and tell a few truths to those eminent personages whose preachers supply them regularly with soft-sawder to order.—*Entr'acte*, 7th April 1883

Soldier's farewell (*Garrison*) 'Go to bed', with noisy additions.

Soldier's supper (*Garrison*). Nothing at all—tea being the final meal of the day

Some (*Anglo-American*). Is this word or not a pun? The question put 'Are you an American?' he will reply 'Some, sir'. Is this sum, Sam, or some, used with satire for out and out?

Some pumpkins (*American farmers'*) Considerable importance.

Some when (*Soc.*, 1860 70) Some time

Some one has blundered (*Soc.*, 1860 on) Emphatic yet evasive mode of complaint From Tennyson's *Charge of the Light Brigade*

I am sure the Lord Mayor will be very sorry to learn that on this occasion some one has blundered.—*Ref*, 5th July 1885.

Something in the city (*Peoples'*) Evasive suggestion of doubtfulness as to the person spoken of

(Something) please (*Amer.-Eng.*) Substitution of 'dam-well' please.

We cannot all go to learn English accent and style in Boston or New York, and must try to be intelligible without hoping to be accurate or elegant We are told not to say 'above his strength', but 'beyond his strength'. We shall do as we (something) please, to quote another Transatlantic authority.—*D. N*, 16th April 1885.

Sooper (*Theatrical*). Common pronunciation of 'super', contraction of supernumerary, the name given to the rank and file of a theatrical company.

Sossidge - slump (*Polit.*, 1896). Failure — derived from sossidge (a German), and slump (failure or pay-out of a mine-vein), and referred to the telegram of the Emperor of Germany in January, to President Kruger, congratulating him on repulsing Dr Jameson's raid This telegram made the Germans unpopular, and caused German trade in England to fall off woefully.

Soul-faker (*Peoples'*, 1883) One of the early names given to the Salvationists before their value was in any way recognized.

Souper and slang (*Thieves'*). Watch and chain Probably the first word is soup-plate from the once huge size of the watch, while the second may be a wilful corruption of sling, because the old long chain, worn round the neck would habitually sling about a great deal.

Soupy (*Low Peoples'*) Drunk to sickness.

Soured on, To be (*Anglo-American*) To dislike thoroughly.

South Chicago rough (*U S.A.*). Typical rough of American cities.

Souvenir egg (*American*). Ancient specimen—hence cogency of 'souvenir' always associated with time—which an egg should never possess

Souvenir'd (*Theatrical*). Gratis picture or pamphlet, celebrating a centenary, or bicentenary, or even a tercentenary of a new piece or variety show

First anniversary of *The New Boy* at

the Vaudeville next Thursday, when all the audience will be magnificently 'souvenired', as the Americans now say. —*Ref.*, 17th February 1895.

Sovereign not in it (*Nautical*). Jaundiced—said of a man whose complexion has suffered from yellow fever or other illness which leaves the skin chromy.

Spangle (*Theatrical*, 19 *cent.*). A sovereign.

Spank the kids (*Common London*). Figurative way of describing bad temper. (*See* On his ear.)

Spark (*Peoples'*). Man of fashion. Now and again heard in country places. Still very common in U.S.A., where it comes from Carolian times. Then chiefly used as a verb — 'to spark about'—equal to our once common, 'To beau about'. Evidently a figure of speech derived from the brilliancy and movement of a fire spark. Used as verb by Spenser, 'In her eyes the fire of love doth spark.' In Prior's time it was quite commonly used in place of beau. He says 'The finest sparks, and cleanest beaux.' Dryden has 'A spark like thee, of the man-killing trade, fell sick.' Farquhar (*The Inconstant*) says: 'Then the ideas wherewith the mind is preoccupate—but this subject is not agreeable to you sparks, that profess the vanity of the times.

Sparrer (*Dustman's*) (Sparrow). Finds in dust-bins—generally silver spoons, thimbles, etc.

I give you my word, sir, that I had never stole—in a regler sort of way, I mean—as much as a sixpence in my life. Course I had took plenty o' sparrers, but that you'll own is different.—James Greenwood, *D. T.*, 19th October 1895.

Speak (*Lower People*). To court, or make love.

Speak a piece (*American*). Recite. This phrase was taken, especially by Artemus Ward, from the schoolboy's way of referring to his own oratory.

Speak brown to-morrow (*Pure Cockney*, 1877). To get sunburnt. (*See* Can't you feel the shrimps, Taste the sun, See the breeze.)

Spellken (*Thieves'*, 18 *and early* 19 *cent.*). Cock-pit.

Booze in the ken, or at the spellken hustle. —Byron, *Don Juan*, canto xi., stanza xix.

Sperrib (*Middle-class, Lond.*). Wife of his bosom. Corruption of spare-rib, and derived from the legend of the creation of Eve.

Speshul! (*Street*, 1884-85). Lie. During the Soudan War the afternoon and evening papers were perpetually issuing special editions with extravagant news, rarely repeated in the next morning's editions.

Sphere of influence (*Diplomatic*, 1898). Nascent colony, range of country under a foreign eye, which so far has no real *locus standi*. Came out of the abortive scramble for China (1897-1900).

A rumour is current that France has offered the Pekin Government to suppress the revolt, considering the southern provinces within her sphere of influence. —*D. T.*, 14th July 1898.

Spieler (*Australasia*, 1890 on). Swindler.

Spieler, it would appear, is the Antipodean synonym for the professional swindler, whose business—and pleasure—it is to take in his fellow-man, to whom he contemptuously applies the generic term 'mug'.—*D. T.*, 14th July 1897.

Spierpon orchestra (*Soc.*, 1885 on). Public restaurant musical. This is Spiers and Pond, and the transmutation was due to a French musical conductor, who converted his employers' names into *Spière et Pon.*

Criterion.—Grand Hall, 3s. 6d. Dinner, at separate tables, 6 to 9, accompanied by the celebrated Spierpon Orchestra.—*D. T.*, 8th October 1894.

Spill (*Jovial*). Drink.

Spill and pelt (*Theatrical*, 1830, etc.). The name given to the practical fun at the end of each scene in the comic portion of a pantomime. Supers rush on with mock vegetables, meat, poultry, fish, etc., spill them all, and then pelt them at each other and altogether off the stage.

Spill milk against posts (*Lowest Class*). Extreme condemnation of the habits of the man spoken of.

Spilled in the big drink (*American-English*). Drowned in the Atlantic. (*See* Ditch.)

Zeus threw a thunderbolt at the rock, and, as the American says, Ajax was 'spilled in the drink'. — *D. N.* 8th August 1884.

Spin (*Anglo - Indian,* 1800 - 50) Short for spinster—the brigades of unmarried and poor young ladies who once went out habitually to India for husbands

Spin a cuff (*Navy*). Bore a mess with a long, pointless story, which the narrator is finally, as a rule, recommended to cut

Spin the bat (*Anglo-Indian,* 19 *cent*). Used figuratively for remarkable military language.

Spit amber (*Amer*, 1870). To expectorate while chewing tobacco

Spits on his hands (*American*) Goes to work with a will—suggested by this habit on the part of energetic workmen when about to start work

Splinters fly (*American Pastoral*). Riot—derived from the kicking experiments of the mule.

Split (*Low London*) Souteneur.

Split soda (*Tavern,* 1860 on) A bottle of soda water divided between two guests The 'baby' soda is for 'one' client

Sponge it out (*Anglo-Amer*, 1883) Forget it.

A new phrase is destined to become popular, viz. 'Sponge it out'—*N Y. Mercury*, November 1883

Spoof—oof (*Theat*, 1896) Money.

Mr Shine sings of Mashonaland, the land of British spoof, where the niggers do the digging and the white men get the 'oof'—*People*, 16th February 1896

Spooferies (*L Peoples'*, 1888 on). Sporting clubs of an inferior kind

About half-past one this morning I was in the 'Spooferies'—Where? In the 'Spooferies' in Maiden Lane—*People*, 6th January 1895.

Spoon, Big (*Amer.*) An oath—the origin of which is lost. Sometimes 'By the great horn spoon'. Probably Biblical

Rolling—roll—hold on! By the big spoon you've hit it!

Spooning the burick (*Thieves'*). Making love to a friend's wife

Spoony stuff (*London Theatres'*, 1882) Weak, sentimental work, below contempt

Sport (*Anglo-American,* 19 *cent*) Eccentric, physical aberration, chiefly relating to human beings

It is still undeniable that a child who is not interested in animals, especially of the larger and wilder species, must be wanting in some of the most graceful and endearing instincts of the childish nature Such infantile 'sports', however, are happily rare.—*D T*, 29th December 1896

Sportsman for liquor (*Sporting*, 1882) A fine toper

We never knew what a sportsman Algernon Charles Swinburne was for his liquor till we took up his last volume of poems—*Sporting Times*, 1882

Spot winner (*Sport and People*). Lucky, or capable—perhaps both. From racing—spotting meaning judgment

Some of them may have 'spotted winners', and were perhaps reflecting pleasurably on a success which they felt to be much more due to their own sound judgment than to mere good luck—*D. T*, 14th June 1898

Spotted dog (*Street Boys'*) Plain plum-pudding—spotted dough The dog here is one of the pronunciations of dough—the 'h' being removed and the 'g' made hard.

Spotted duff (*Street,* 19 *cent*) Another shape of spotted dog Duff has always been a street pronunciation of 'dough'.

Spotted leopard (*Street Boys'*). Another variety of spotted dog

A penny's worth of spotted leopard is not a bad way of filling up the space of the internals, though spotted leopard may make you have to squander some rhino in pongelow—1883

Spout (*Peoples'*) Large mouth—ever open (*See* Boko)

Spread (*Anglo - American*). Take great, self-satisfied aims in doing anything

Spring like a ha'penny knife (*Peoples'*). Floppy, dumpy, no resilience—from the absolute want of Sheffield perfection in the make of pen-knives at sixpence the dozen.

Sprung up (*Middle - class*) A parvenu—in the nature of a ready-made or self-made man

Spurrings (*Yorkshire—Old*) Marriage banns Origin vague, but ominously suggestive of the bridegroom being goaded to the church-door

Square (*Ball-room*). A quadrille or lancers (*See* Round)

Square up-and-down man (*Amer*). Square-shouldered, upright, tall man, with no fat or superfluous flesh about him

Squash (*Club and Hotel*, 1877). A temperance drink of lemon, soda-water, ice, and sugar—came into fashion during a panic against spirits and, in modified form, against wine. Onomatope, from the noise made by pressing the lemon.

By ten P.M., at the latest, you may be in the smoking-room of your club sipping lemon 'squash'.—*Illus. London News* (G. A. Sala), 17th February 1883.

Squash ballads (*Peace Party*). Ballads prompting war and personal devotion.

The new laureate has started off on a squash ballad *apropos* to Jameson's stir-up.—London Correspondent of *N. Y. Clipper*, January 1896.

Squasho (*American—passing into England*). Negro—a title probably resulting from the negro's love of melons, pumpkins, squashes, etc.

Squat (*Com. London*). A seat—probably derived from squatter.

Squat on (*American*). To oppose.

Squeaker, The (*Press*, '90's). Burlesque name given to the paper called *The Speaker*—a journal of representative Radicalism.

Squealer (*Fenian*, 1867, etc.). Informer.

Squeejee (*Streets'*). Mud-clearer; plate of vulcanized india-rubber fixed at right angles to a long handle. Onomatope—the cleaner in question actually saying the word now and again.

We were more than once awakened by the avalanche of the deck bucket and the noise of sandpaper and 'squeejee'.—*D. N.*, 27th April 1897.

Squeezability (*Polit.*, 1884). Political pressure. Word invented long since, but only accepted politically about 1884.

They could not realise the change which the Franchise Act had made in the counties; or they believed too implicitly in the squeezability of the newly-enfranchized electors.—*D. N.*, 3rd December 1885.

Squeeze-box (*Navy*). The ship harmonium—used in the hasty Sunday service. From the action of the feet.

Squilde (*L. Class*, 1895-96). Term of street chaff. Word designed from a Christian name and a surname coalesced.

Squint (*S. Exchange*). Man who hangs about the market with a paltry order, and who will not deal fairly.

Squirt (*L. Class*, 18 *cent.*). Doctor. Very suggestive of Molière in general, and of *Le Malade Imaginaire* in particular.

Squirt (*Doubtful Soc.*, 1870). One of the onomatopoetic titles of champagne suggested by its uppishness.

Stable Jack (*Infantry*). Cavalry—a scornful description, as intimating that the miserable man has incessantly to be the slave of his horse, an oppression from which the happier infantry man is free. (*See* Jack Tar, Jack in the water, Jack of all trades, Hulking Jack, Dona Jack.)

Stable mind (*Soc.*). Devoted to horses.

Stage, To (*American*, 1860). To stage a piece is to put a piece on the stage.

Stagger (*American*, 1883). Effort.

Staked out (*Mining*, 1880 on). Divided, measured.

When the first discovery of gold was made at Klondyke, in August 1896, the creek was staked off from end to end in claims—*D. T.*, 21st July 1897.

Stalked unchecked (*American origin*). Freed from the attentions of the criminal classes. Satirically said to have been invented by a West U.S.A. criminal upon being about to be lynched, and in reference to the villain public, who moved around him without being ordered by him to hold up their hands.

The thieving and ruffianism of Moscow took its country holiday; and at the Coronation and its attendant festivities respectability, in the bitter words of the Western American desperado, 'stalked unchecked'.—*D. T.*, 29th April 1897.

Stall off (*Peoples'*). Damp, impede, hinder, warn.

Stall-pots (*Theatrical*). Occupants of the stalls. Applied by the gods derisively to these well-dressed patrons of the drama.

Stalwarts (*Conservatives'*, 1886). Satirical name for Radicals, used by Mr Chamberlain seriously; accepted satirically by Conservative party.

Stamps (*Thieves'*). Boots—a sort of onomatope.

Stand (*Colloquial—all Classes*). Pay for—only used in a general way for drink or eatables.

Stand pat (*American*, 1860) Satisfied. Taken from a game of cards called poker 'Stand pat' means, 'I have got sufficient cards—go ahead !'

Stand-up supper (*Society*, 1860). About this date the 'stand-up' ball supper came into vogue—probably as the result of modern medical condemnation of late feeding. Necessarily more economical than its antithesis—the sit-down supper It took immensely, so that very rapidly the term came to suggest anything of a mean and paltry character.

Star company (*Theatrical*) A wandering dramatic company, composed of one well-known person and a number of nobodies, all of whom appear in but one piece, as a rule, with which they travel

A popular local leading lady writes for information regarding a Mr Henry C Warren, of Troy, N Y., who is alleged to load recognized actresses with propositions to take them starring next season. —*N Y Mercury*, February 1884

Stars and stripes (*New York*) Contemptuous phrase applied by the younger New York society to the Puritanic habits still clinging to New England, and above all to Boston. It refers to the solemn Sunday cold dinner of the 'hub' of the universe, which distinctively consists—or *did* consist—of cold boiled belly of pork (stripes) and Boston beans (stars).

New Englanders are proud of their national dish of pork and beans, eaten cold on Sundays in Boston, and derisively called 'stars and stripes' in New York —*D N*, 13th July 1883

Start a jolly (*Theatre and Music Hall*) To lead the applause, and effect a diversion in favour of a given performer

State tea (*Soc.*, 1870). Tea at which every atom of the family plate is exhibited Name probably suggested by State ball (*See* Five o'clock tea)

States can be saved without it (*Pol.*, 1880) Condemnation. Origin not known.

In short, Mr Stephenson may be advised to take away *Séverine* States can be saved without it.—*Ref*, 10th May 1885.

Stay and be hanged (*Peoples'*). Still heard amongst lower middle-class Probably started by Captain Macheath (*Beggars' Opera*) 'If you doubt it, let me stay and be hanged '

Steal thunder (*Soc*, *Hist*). Annexing another man's idea, or work, without remunerating him, and to your own advantage. Said to be derived from—

John Dennis, a play-writer in the 17th century, who invented stage thunder for a piece of his own which failed But the manager translated Dennis's thunder into another piece It was highly applauded, when Dennis started up in the pit, and cried out to the audience 'They won't act my piece, but they steal my thunder. Hence the origin of the phrase.

Steam on the table (*Workmen's*, 18 *cent* on) Boiled joint—generally steaming, on Sunday

Steel v. Bastile

Steeple Jack (*Builders'*) Climber of steeples and shafts for fixing scaffolding when repairs are required

Steeplechase (*Sporting and Soc*) Direct line, defying and overcoming all obstructions.

Mr Fowler was one of the oldest inhabitants of Aylesbury, not forgetful of the historic cross-country ride to Aylesbury church-steeple from Waddesdon Windmill, which gave the name to the very modern sport called steeplechasing I apprehend that the name of steeplechase arose from Aylesbury Church steeple being the goal of the famous race, in which Mr Peyton acted as starter, the Marquis of Waterford, of facetious memory was nearly drowned, Jem Mason finished third with Prospero, and Captain Beecher won on Vivian —*D N.*, 13th July 1885

Steever's worth of copper (*Streets'*, *E. Lond*) One penny—from Stuyver

Stellar (*American-Eng*, 1884 on). Leading Latin shape of 'starring' in relation to acting

William Terriss and Miss Millward, of London, and their company made their stellar *debût* at Niblo's garden to a tolerably good attendance —*N. Y. Mercury*, October 1889.

Stellardom (*Anglo-American—Theatrical*) The condition of being a star, or leading actor or actress.

Impossible to form a company of actors and actresses who have not sought the divorce courts, and who do not aspire to stellardom.—*N Y. Mercury*, November 1883

Stem-winder (*American — Liverpool*) Keyless watch.

Steps (*Low. London*, 19 *cent.*). Thick slices of bread and butter, overlaying each other on a plate—thus suggesting the idea of a flight of steps.

Stern ambition (*City*, 1898). Determination. Brought in by Mr H. Bottomley in speech (1st June 1889):

I will invite you to pass the necessary resolutions for getting the Market Trust out of the trouble into which it has got, and out of which it will be my own very stern ambition, as well as that of my colleagues, to extricate you at the very earliest possible moment.

Stick a bust (*Thieves'*, 19 *cent.*). Commit a burglary.

Mr Paul Taylor: What were his exact words?

Witness: I am going to 'stick a bust.'

Mr Paul Taylor: What does that mean?

Detective-sergeant Fitzgerald: Commit a burglary.—*D. T.*, 28th December 1899.

Stick and bangers (*Sporting*). Billiard cue and balls. A phrase having also an erotic meaning.

Stickings (*Lower Peoples'*). Butchers' cuttings laid on a board, to which they clammily cling. (*See* Door and hinge, Hyde Park railings.)

Sticks (*Navy and Army*). Drummer.

Still (*Anglo - American*). Quiet drunkard.

Still as a mouse (*Peoples'*, 18 *cent.*). Quite still. But a mouse is never still! Good example of a bad translation. No doubt from the half-Dutch Court of William III. Mr Rees (U.S.A.) says very keenly:

Expressive of noiseless action. The Dutch phrase is evidently its origin: *Als stille als in mee hose, i.e.*, as still as one in his stockings—a listener.

Or it may be, 'Still as Amos'—though what Amos is beyond ken.

Still he is not happy (*London*, 1870 on). Satire shot at a man whom nothing pleases or satisfies.

In 1870, a catch phrase used by Mr J. L. Toole in a burlesque at the Gaiety Theatre, 'Still I am not happy', enjoyed for some months considerable acceptance among sportive youths in the metropolitan thoroughfares.—*D. T.*, 28th July 1894.

Stilton (*Peoples'*, 1850 on). Distinction. Synonym for cheese (*see*).

She was the real Stilton, I can tell yer.

(*See* Cheshire.)

Stinker (*Working Boys'*). Penny cigars. Frequently so named in taverns. Also the most emphatic term for the high - smelling dried herring.

Stir-about (*Peoples'*). Pudding or porridge made by stirring the ingredients—generally oatmeal or wheat-flour — when cooking. (*See* Hasty pudding and Turn-round pudding.)

Stir up (*Peoples'*). Equivalent to beat up in society. To visit on the spur of the moment.

Stolypin's necktie (*Europ. Politics*, 1897). The final halter. This term was brought into fashion in 1907 (Nov.-Dec.), at a Duma then recently assembled in St Petersburg. One Rodicheff, an extreme Radical, brought in the term on 30th November 1907.

Stone and a beating (*Sporting*, 18 *cent.*). The speaker offers to weight himself with 14 lbs. avoirdupois, and then outrun his opponent.

Canis vulpis is, as a rule, able to give, intellectually speaking, and in language germane to the matter, 'a stone and a beating' to the majority of his pursuers. —*D. N.*, 4th February 1885.

Stop-gap (*Theatr.*). Piece rushed on between a failure and the production of a carefully-prepared new piece or new arrival.

After the first act *The Denhams* was well received, the adaptor receiving a call; but, except as a stop-gap, we do not think it will prove of much service to the management.—*Ref.*, 21st February 1885.

Stop - gap administration (*Polit.*, 1885). The Conservative Government formed June 1885. Name given by Mr J. Chamberlain (17th June 1885).

Stork, Visit from the (*Soc.*, 1880 on). Arrival of a baby. From the German.

She was in the habit of receiving visits from the Stork—as the Germans put it to the children—by which it is meant that she occasionally presented her husband with an infant.—*D. T.*, 15th February 1897.

Stote-an'-bottle (*N. York Theatre*). Audience who neither applaud nor laugh. Probably corruption from Dutch.

We had but a stote-an'-bottlish crowd last night.

Stow (*Streets'*). Abbreviation of bestow

Strad (*Musicians'*) Abbreviation of Stradivarius violin

Straight (*Theatr*).

In the United States the expression 'straight' is very generally used in theatrical circles to signify a part in which the actor or actress has but to be him or herself upon the stage

Straight as they make 'em (*London Streets, from America*) Upright and honest

Straight bit o' goods (*Streets'*, 1870 on) A young woman of good character (*See* Loose bit o' goods)

Straight drinking (*Low London*, 19 *cent*) Drinking without sitting down—bar-drinking

Straight up and down the mast (*Irish*) Calm An Irish sailor's way of describing a calm—when the mast is fairly perpendicular

Strapped (*Amer*) Without money—possibly suggested by the impossibility of removing when without money, as when strapped and bound

Straps (*Streets'*) Sprats One of the rhyming shapes of passing English.

Street yelp (*Low Class*, 1884) Evolution of passing street cry, such as 'Walker', 'Does your mother know you're out?' Every few weeks some new street yelp is invented, and eagerly taken up as a substitute for wit by the class that enjoys these things

Stretch (*Navy*). Outstay leave

Stretch his breeches (*Peoples'*) Said of a boy who has been thrashed. It comes down from the time when the tight leather breech might be fairly said to be stretched when flattened

Stretcher, The (*Irish*) Layer out of dead men.

Stretching (*Anglo-American*, 1895) Helping oneself at table without the help of servants

Strict Q T (*Peoples'*, 1870) The letters being the first and last of 'quiet'. The phrase is an invocation to secrecy

Strike (*Anglo-Amer*). To come across a person, or thing

Strike a bargain (*Sporting*, 18 *cent*) To conclude it by the act of striking the butt ends of the riding whips of the seller and buyer as a mutual agreement — equal to the stipulation of the Roman buyer and seller, who exchanged straws

In the end I agreed to charge him 26s per week, and we then struck the bargain.

Strike a bright (*Peoples'*). Have a happy thought.

Strike legislation (*Amer.-Eng*, 1897). Enforced bribery of legislators—the pressure being applied by the legislators themselves — to burke enquiries 'Sir, this is not fair trading, it is nothing less than strike legislation.' Known slightly in England.

Strike me pink (*Soc*, 18 *cent* on) Literally an exclamation to declare truthfulness Cover me with my own blood Sometimes God, etc. From duelling times—when to pink was not so much to pierce as to draw blood

Strike oil (*American — becoming English*) To be successful 'I've struck oil at last' This expression comes from the paraffin districts of North America, where sometimes numerous expensive artesian borings are made without the least success

Strike us up a gum tree (*Low. London*) Bring to grief.

Yes, and strike us up a gum tree, she says, if you won't give her sardines and bloaters for her tea instead of winkles she'll go back to her old man —1850

Australian — probably meaning 'terrible' The gum tree is enormously high, 100 feet of clear, smooth trunk without a branch, so that a man up a gum tree could not descend without help

Stricken field (*Soc*, 1898). Field where lie the vanquished Term found in several poets Re-introduced upon the fall of Omdurman in the autumn of this year.

Colonel Holden's happy idea of organizing in the museum of the Royal United Service Institution an exhibition of the trophies brought home from 'the stricken field' of Omdurman has brought a vast number of visitors to see the collection.—*D T*, 25th November 1898

Struguel (*Peoples'*) Struggle

Stuck up (*American-English*) Moneyless—very figurative expression derived from being 'stuck up' by highwayman, after which you have no money left in your pocket.

Stuff Girl. (*See* Bit o' stuff.)

Stuffed monkey (*Jewish Lond.*). A very pleasant close almond biscuit

Now the confectioner exchanges his

stuffed monkeys, and his bolas . . . for unleavened palavas, etc. — Zangwill, *Children of the Ghetto.*

Stun (*Reversed word*). Nuts.

Sub (*Editorially*). Abbreviation of subject. Very common in U.S.A.

With Captain Williams, her namesake, as chairman, would be the judges here. The Mercury will be pleased to hear from Mrs Williams on this sub.—*N. Y. Mercury*, May 1885.

Sub rosa (*Soc.*). In secret. Sometimes 'under the rose'. Used by the author of Junius's *Letters* as his motto, the rose being above. Confounded with 'under the rows'—a sort of rebus. When houses were built floor out above floor, so that the ground floor was some feet within the front of the garrets, talkers, say lovers, could not be seen from the floors above—therefore 'under the rows' (rows of superposed jutting floors) implied 'secretly'. There still exists (1907) in London, a group of 'rows', forming the north side of Staple Inn (Holborn)—where it can be seen that a maiden on the first floor might almost shake hands, from the window, with a grenadier on the pavement, while from the second floor, an observer could not catch a glimpse of the military heels 'under the rows'.

The rose, a symbol of silence, gave rise to the phrase, 'under the rose', from the circumstance of the Pope's presenting consecrated roses, which were placed over confessionals to denote secrecy, whilst others contend that the old Greek custom of suspending a rose over the guest table was employed as an emblem that the conversation should not be repeated elsewhere.—*Cutting.*

Sub rosa look (*Anglo-Amer.*). Doubtful aspect. Perversion of the Latin proverb.

The business had a sub rosa look throughout.—*Newsp. Cutting.*

Submerged tenth (*Soc.*, 1890 on). Tenth of London, which is always in utter poverty. Originated by General Booth. First accepted satirically but now quite received as a serious phrase.

If the population of London is reckoned roughly at 4,000,000 and 'the submerged tenth'—as the phrase goes—is taken as the basis of the calculation of recipients, 400,000 meals will have to be given, and at a shilling a head £20,000 at least will be required.—*World*, May 1897.

Such a dawg (*Theatrical*, 1888). Tremendous masher. First used by E. Terry in a Gaiety burlesque.

The next time Mr Biggar thinks fit to leave these shores, perhaps he will try to be less fascinating, bearing in mind that women are weak and not always able to wrestle successfully with the blandishments of such a Lothario. 'Such a dawg!'—*Entr'acte*, 17th March 1883.

Suck the mop (*Cabmens'*). To wait on the cab-rank for a job.

The man who gives his horse a rest on the rank is, in cabmen's phraseology, 'sucking the mop'.—*D. N.*, 10th June 1889.

Sucker (*American*). A young and confiding youth.

Suffolk punches (*Provincial*). Descriptive name for Suffolk folk, much on all fours with Norfolk dumplings. A punch is a comfortable kind of cob-like horse. This is rather a complimentary term.

Sugar (*Low. Class*). Grocer.

Sugar-shop (*Electioneering*). Money shop, literally; but figuratively a head centre of bribery.

Suggestionize (*Legal*, 1889 on). To prompt.

Many witnesses were called to establish his identity, and for the defence it was alleged that these people might have been 'suggestionized' by the influence of the crime on their minds.—*D. T.*, 16th October 1896.

Suitable for electioneering purposes (*Polit.*, *Historic.*). Bad eggs. From the exercise of projecting them at antagonistic candidates.

Leather Lane supplies the greater proportion of the eggs, and if not to be classified as 'suitable for electioneering purposes', would probably be of that order curtly set forth as 'eggs', without any subtle grading as 'Fresh laid', 'Breakfast', or 'Cooking'.—*D. T.*, 27th June 1898.

Sum. (*See* Some.)

Summer, Another (*Devonshire chiefly*). Butterfly — generally the first-seen 'Oh! — here's another summer!' Very poetic. Remarkable that Devonshire offers most of the poetic phrases. (*See* Any birds can build in my bonnet.)

Sun, Been in the (*Peoples'*). Drunk. Fine figure of speech. Drink and hot sun both produce red face. Good example of *double entendre*, or rather perhaps of direct satire by indirect means.

'I see you've been in the sun, Tom!'

Sun over the fore-yard (*Navy*). Evasive mode of observing that So-and-so is pretty well dead drunk

Sunclear (*Lit*, 1885) Very clear.

What there is in Royal subjects to paralyze the genius of a painter we fail to divine, but it is sunclear that Mr Haag could no more resist this unfortunate influence than the greater Landseer—*D N*, 10th November 1885.

Sunday (*Soc.*). To pass Sabbath with a given person

Sunday face (*Irish*). Holiday countenance.

Sunday - flash - togs (*Street*) Sabbath garments

A Sunday-flash-togs young man,
A pocket of hogs young man,
A save-all-his-rhino,
To cut-a-big-shine, oh,
Will soon-have a-pub young man

—Parody of a song in *Patience*, 1880

Sunrise London (*London*) East London

And, indeed, it cannot be denied that what has been spoken of as the 'sunrise' division of the great metropolis has of late years been greatly favoured. Thanks mainly to the advocacy of the most influential of the newspaper press, the aspect of the whole poverty-stricken area, in its length and breadth, from the Minories to Mile End, and from Spitalfields to Shadwell, has been vastly improved.—*D T*, 30th July 1896.

Surrey side (*London, exclusive*). Transpontine portion of London The northern portion of London bounded by the Thames, and especially the more western quarters, have always spoken of this division of the metropolis (Southwark and Lambeth) to the south of the Thames, as the 'Surrey side'.

Susanside (*Idiot Phrasing*). Suicide

Sussex sow (*Hampshire*) Probably a return compliment for the name of Hampshire hog (*q v*)

Swagger man (*Soc*, 1880) Person of position. Used rather with praise than not

Swaller a sailor (*Port and Harbour*). Get drunk upon rum

'Swallered the anchor (*Marine*). Said of a sailor who comes home, loafs, and does not show signs of going to sea again.

Swank (*Printers'*) Small talk, lying.

Swanny (*American Provincial*) Corruption of 'swear now'.

Swear off (*American—passing to Eng*) To abandon, in relation to drinking habits.

Swearing apartment (*Tavern*). The street.

Sweat (*Thieves'*) To unsolder a tin box by applying fire, or a blow-pipe.

Sweater (*Work-peoples'*) One who 'middles' between the manufacturer, or tradesman, and the worker He is answerable for the value of the work, and is therefore preferred to the worker himself The middle levies a heavy blackmail upon the worker Probably he pays no more than 50 per cent to the worker of the money he receives from the tradesman

In the second number of the *Charity Organisation Review* there is a short account of a co-operative needlework experiment, the object of it being to emancipate poor workwomen from the 'sweaters'—*D N*, 21st February 1885

Sweeping up (*Boer War*, 1899-1900). Grew out of the end of the war, when the dispersed Boers harassed the English very much

Though the time has come when Volunteers, Yeomen, and Guards should be sent home, there is still a good deal of sweeping up to be done in the Transvaal—*D T.*, 2nd October 1900.

(*See* Dusting.)

Sweeps and saints (*City*, 19 *cent.*). Stockbrokers and their surrounders, from the First of May (Sweeps' Day) and the First of November (All Saints' Day) being holidays on the Exchange

Sweet waters (*W. England*) Illicit spirit made from the residue of the cider press. Fearfulest drink in the world Term well known in all the apple counties

Swell donas (*Low Life*) Great ladies—in their way.

Swell donas lushes up on port wine, and that sort of pizon

Swig Day (*Jesus College, Oxford*) St David's Day—so called because a drink called swig, composed of spiced ale, wine, toast, etc, is dispensed out of an immense silver gilt bowl holding ten gallons, and served by a ladle of half-pint capacity—presented to the college in 1732 by the then Sir Watkin Williams Wynn.

Swipe (*Thieves'*, 18 *cent*) Stealing When silk pocket handkerchiefs (Indian bandannas) were used by all men of position and were worth stealing (*see* Dickens's 'Oliver Twist')—they were called 'Wipes'—hence to 'Swipe a Wipe' was to steal a bandanna.

Sworn at Highgate (*Peoples'*). Convenient asseveration whereby the declarant undertakes never to accept anything offered while he can obtain a better. The phrase took the shape of a coloured cartoon in 1796, when it was published (12th September) by Laurie and Whittle of 53 Fleet Street. A good impression of this print is now to be found at the Old Gate House, at the top of Highgate Hill—the locale of the toll-gate—where the swearing at Highgate was held to be only properly administered. The oath-taker is accompanied by a herald who holds aloof the significant horns, which are reproduced in letter-form on the front of the tavern before which the operation is completed. The 'maid' pins meanwhile a ragged clout to his coat-tail, while the mistress waits with a foaming pot of beer, or rather gallon measure, for the garnishing of everybody after the oath is complete. This declaration runs as follows:—

'Pray, sir—lay your right hand on this Book, and attend to the Oath—you swear by the Rules of Sound Judgment that you will not eat Brown Bread when you can have White, except you like the Brown the better; that you will not drink Small Beer when you can get Strong, except you like the Small Beer better—but you will kiss the *Maid* in preference to the *Mistress*, if you like the Maid better—*so help you Billy Bodkin.* Turn round and fulfil your oath.'

Sympathetic truth (*Art,* 1890 on). True, but not too true—some concession to the artistic ideal.

Mr James S. Hill has less experience, less power, perhaps, of making or seeing a picture, than some of his friendly rivals; but few, if any, of them surpass him in the sympathetic truth with which he renders some of the less obvious, the less showy aspects of nature. — *D. T.*, 4th January 1896.

Synagogue (*Covent Garden,* 1890 on). Shed in the north-east corner of 'the Garden'. So called from this place (erected 1890) being wholly 'run' by Jews.

Synthetic breadth (*Art,* 1890 on). Probably means 'harmony of treatment'.

Syrup (*Druggists'*). A trade word amongst dispensing chemists for money.

T

T. O. (*Printers'*). Turn-over, short for a turn-over apprentice from one master to another.

T. and O. (*Sporting,* 1880). New form of 2 to 1.

The betting to-night (Saturday) against the Empire's chance of getting the music hall licence is two and one (t & o).—*Ref.*, 4th August 1887.

T. W. B. F., also **C. W. D.** (*New York*). Mystic initials understood in certain New York society, but quite beyond the outer world. Placed at the foot of invitations, only one of these two series is used. When the recipient is a gentleman the arcana are T. W. B. F.; while the lady's masonics are C. W. D.

T. W. K. (*Military, Anglo-Indian,* 1840 on). Condemnatory initials of 'Too well-known'.

Tab (*L. C.*). *The ear,* amongst tailors and other workmen.

Tabby meeting (*London*). May meeting of the evangelical party at Exeter Hall (Strand, London — now turned to other uses). Probably contraction of Tabitha—generic name for quakerly persons.

Table beer (*Peoples'*). Poor beer. Commonly applied to any ordinary thing or proceeding.

The Spartan hosts entertained the visitor with cold beef, table beer, cheese, and pickles.—*D. N.*, 6th November 1884.

Table companions (*Oxford*). Men of the same College are called 'table companions' in one of the reports, which we take to be analogous to the 'stable companions' of our sporting contemporaries, and in certain cases are said, somewhat unintelligibly, to make the running for one another.

Table part (*Theatrical*). Rôle which is played only from the waist upwards, and therefore behind a table. Term in association with the protean entertainer, and the quick change artiste.

The whole of the 'table parts', as they were called, were, as usual, by Charles Mathews himself, but he was relieved in the dramatic acts by Yates, who undertook a series of rapid changes of dress and character then originally introduced —*D T*, 10th March 1897

Table-talk (*Soc*, 1883) Talk bordering on the unkind

In summer we have the new pictures, and some critics will say 'the old are better' But they are not better stuff to table-talk, because spite can get little pleasure out of condemning Sir Joshua or Rubens.—*D N*, 1st February 1884

Tabled (*American Legislation*). Short for placed on the table

Mr Forster spoke the other day of the amendments on the English Education Bill which he had just 'tabled', meaning which he had just laid on the table —*D. N*, 1st February 1884

Taboo (*Soc*, 19 *cent*) Prohibited, forbidden. Sacred, not to be touched.

The King of Dahomi is not allowed so much as to see the gold in the Fetish House where the remains of his dead forefathers lie That gold is taboo —*D N*, 22nd July 1887.

Tabs (*Theatrical*) Ageing women Abbreviation of Tabby, one of the common names for the cat, always associated with ancient women

Tacking (*Peoples'—from Seamens'*) Obtaining end by roundabout means, from the mode of sailing against wind by zigzag courses May be from tact

Tacks (*Art*) Artist's apparatus From tackle, taken from angling

Tadpoles (*American*). People of Mississippi—probably from the superabundance of water there.

Tail out (*Amer-Eng*, 1880) To run away, scuttle, bolt. From the tail of birds and animals being last seen as they retreat.

Next I made out a brown thing, seated on the table in the centre, and in another moment when my eyes grew accustomed to the light, and I saw what these things were—I was tailing out of it as hard as my legs could carry me.—Haggard, *King Solomon's Mines*

Tail tea (*Soc*, 1880 to death of Victoria) The afternoon tea following royal drawing-rooms, at which ladies who had been to court that afternoon, appeared in their trains—hence tail teas The King relegated drawing-rooms to the late evening

Tail-twisting (*American*, 19 *cent*). Worrying England — figuratively, twisting the tail of the British lion Generally a political process in order to deflect the conviction of the voter

We must, of course, be prepared for a little 'tail-twisting' from time to time whenever the domestic concerns in the States are turning out uncomfortably for the party in power —17th October 1896

Taits (*Church*). Moderate clergymen—from their following in the footsteps of Dr Tait, Archbishop of Canterbury, who sought, vainly, to assimilate all parties (*See* Anglican inch, St Alban's clean shave, No church.)

Taj (*Boys'*) Lucious, ripping

Take (*Printers'*) The bit of copy the printer's compositor 'takes' at one time

Take a curtain (*Theatrical*, 1880) Appear before the curtain in answer to sufficient applause.

Written in Sand was well received, and Broughton had to 'take a curtain'.—*Ref*, 31st August 1884.

(*See* Curtain - taker, Lightning curtain-taker, Fake a curtain)

Take a squint (*Low Class*) Look 'Take a squint at the donah, now!' (*See* Cast an optic)

Take a trip (*Trade*) To discharge oneself from a situation—which act would be followed by movement searching for a new situation.

Take and give (*C. L*, *rhyming*) 'Live', generally referring to man and wife

Take care of (*Police*). To arrest.

Take care of dowb (*Political*, 1855) New reading of Take care of No. I

Take gruel (*Low Classes*). To die —from the fact that gruel general accompanies any long illness which ends in death

Take gruel together (*Low Life*, 1884) To live together as man and wife. Derived from a case where a housekeeper to an eccentric clergyman was 'inquested' as the result of death from want of medical attendance The police newsmonger put a severe construction upon the case

'They took their gruel together!' This is a charming euphemism perpetrated by an old clergyman to explain his relations with an elderly female who lived alone in his house with him. 'We take our gruel together!' is likely to become a fashionable expression.—*Ref.*, 14th December 1884.

Take in (*Anglo-American*, 1882). Patronize—from taking in papers.

Take it fighting (*American-Eng.*, 1880). Be courageous, antithesis of take it lying down.

But if we intend 'to take it fighting', then the most ordinary economy and plain sense demand that the construction and supply of the proper depôts be commenced without an hour's delay.—*D. N.*, 5th March 1885.

Take it lying down (*American-Eng.*, 1880). To be cowardly—on the basis that a self-respecting fighter will not strike a prostrate enemy.

If we mean to 'take it lying down', like the preacher threatened by Colonel Quagg—then every penny we spend on the volunteers, and every hour they give to drill, is so much wanton waste.—*D. N.*, 5th March 1885.

Take my Bradlaugh (*Peoples'*, 1883). New phrase for 'take my oath'. Humorously, or perhaps satirically adopted at the time when Mr Charles Bradlaugh's name was intimately associated with the Affirmation Bill.

Take off corner pieces (*Com. Classes*). To beat another, generally one's wife. (*See* Knock off corners.)

Take off my coat (*Street*). Challenge to fight. (*See* Blood or Beer.)

Take soles off your shoes (*Anglo-American*). To surprise utterly.

'But ah, my dear sir,' with another engaging smile which took the soles off the shoes of the interviewer, 'I did not know what was coming. I did not know what that initiation really was.'—*N. Y. Mercury*, 1884.

Take the egg (*American*). To win.

Take the flour (*American.-Eng.*, 1885). Outcome of Take the cake, which was followed by Take the bun.

There is a woman in Fargo who takes the flour.—*N. Y. Mercury*, 1885.

Take the kettle (*Com.*). Obtain the prize. It is said at one time a kettle was the reward (U.S.A.), of village spelling bees.

Take the number off the door (*Peoples'*). Said of a domestic establishment where the wife is a shrew, and by scolding draws attention to the domus. The removal of the number would make the cottage less discoverable.

Take the pastry (*Amer.*). Lead.

Take the tiles off (*Soc.*). Extreme extravagance.

He flings his money about with a lavish recklessness, sufficient to take, as they say, the tiles off the roof of a house.—*Truth*, May 1878.

Taken in and done for (*Peoples'*, 1880 on). Absorbed.

As it is, they are literally 'taken in and done for'. They visit a theatre, where they have no notion that the presence of tobacco-smoke will be felt, and find themselves only separated by a curtain from a saloon where noxious cigarettes poison the atmosphere.—*Entr'acte*, 1883.

Take time by the forelock (*Peoples'*). Be in time — probably suggested by long forehead tuft of hair, now and again worn by old men. Certainly time is always represented with one tuft on the head.

Taken stripes (*U.S.A.*). Equivalent to our 'wears the broad arrow'. Evasion in reference to an U.S.A. state prisoner.

After 4th July the convicts with a good record in the Kansas State Penitentiary will wear suits of cadet grey instead of striped suits.—*D. T.*, 4th June 1897.

Taken to the stump (*Polit.*). Public oratory. From the tree stump on which the wandering puritans preached. Good example of freedom of opinion, existing long since in England, when wayside stumps could be used as points for public speaking.

According to our correspondent at Sofia, General Kaulbars has now taken to the stump.—*D. N.*, 4th October 1886.

Talk by a bow (*Com. London*, 1860-82). Periphrase of quarrel.

Talk to his picture (*Suffolk Peoples'*). Admonish so gravely that the admonished one will be no more able to speak than could his portrait.

Tall 'un (*Com. Life*). Pint of coffee, half a pint being a short 'un.

Tall weeping (*Amer.*, 1883). Deep grief.

Tamarinds (*Chemists'*). Sometimes used by chemists for 'money'. Not general.

Tamaroo (*Irish*). Noisy.

Tammany (*American - Eng*, 19 *cent*) Bribery—from Tammany Hall, a place where for forty years the corrupt manipulators of the municipality of New York have held their meetings

Not long ago there was an election on the other side of the water, and we were all full of contemptuous denunciation of Tammany. What was this but Tammany? This was a Tammany Government —*D. T*, 14th December 1897.

Tandem (*Cambridge*, 1870 on) Long Used in speaking of a tall man.

Tangle - leg (*Anglo - Amer*). Whisky Derivation obvious.

Tangle - monger (*Soc*, 19 *cent.*). Application of word 'monger'. Speaks for itself—an individual, generally a woman, who fogs and implies everything

Tanky (*Navy*) Foreman or captain of the hold—which looks like a tank

Tannery (*Anglo-American*, 1880). Large boots—also absolute reference to feet almost as capacious

Tanter go (*Provincial, Mid. Hist*). End, finish, departure. May be from Catholic times, and the 'Tantum Ergo'—the last division of a mass.

Tap (*Peoples'*). Draw blood, by a blow, from the nose Derived from the beer barrel

Before the magistrate one of them explained that they were simply engaged in a friendly, good-humoured contest, the one whose nose got 'tapped' first paying for a round of beer for the company —*D T*, 19th July 1897.

Taper (*Polit*) Seeker after profitable office. Abbreviation of Red Taper—from the colour of official tape.

We have our Tadpoles and our Tapers, it is true, and our greedy party-men clamouring for rewards, but our disappointed seekers after job, place and pay do not snarl and fight for their prey in public like hungry dogs over a bone —*D. T.*, 27th April 1897

Tare an' ouns (*Irish - English*) Corruption of 'Tear and wounds'—created when wounds rhymed with pounds (*See* Oons, Zounds!)

Tart (*Street*, 1884) A common girl — the outcome of 'Bit of jam' (*q v.*) Also a rhyming phrase — agreeing with 'sweet heart'. (*See* Banbury.)

I have to do my needlework
To make myself look smart,
But yesterday I'm glad to say
I found a little tart.

Taste of his quality (*Peoples'*, 19 *cent*) Obvious From the prize ring. Widely applied

A fair 'taste of his quality' is afforded by a comparison between pp 40 and 43. John Storm, who has become curate to a Canon of an outrageously caricatured type of worldliness, is being taken by him to call upon one of his lady parishioners, etc. — *D. T* (Crit. *The Christian*), 1898.

Taste the sun (*Cockney*, 1877) Used as an intensifier by Londoners out in the country for the day (*See* Speak brown to-morrow, Can't you feel the shrimps, See the breeze.)

Tatur-trap (*Irish*, 19 *cent*) The mouth, tatur being short for potato

Tax - fencer (*Com. Lond*, 1878). Disreputable shopkeeper — as distinct from the honest pusher

Tea and toast struggle (*Peoples'*) Said of Wesleyan tea-meetings where the supply is rarely adequate to the demand

Tea and turn out (*Peoples'*, 19 *cent.*). A roundabout way of saying there is no supper.

Tea in a mug (*Irish*). Suggestive of bad breeding.

Tea - bottle (*Mid.-class*). An old maid — from the ordinary drink of spinsters

Tea-kettle purgers (*L London*). Total abstainers 'Purgers' would appear to be a reminiscence of attacks upon Puritanism

Tea-pot (*Peoples'*) Total abstainer. This phrase is a reduction of tea-pot sucker.

Tea - pot (*'Varsities*, 1880) Tea party — antithesis of wine (*q.v*) About this year the more earnest life at the universities then commencing took as one shape that of temperance

Tea-room party (*Parliament*, 1866). A Radical party in the House of Commons, whose members first foregathered in the tea-room Gladstone and Bright were in favour of some limitation of the franchise, one which would exclude the so-called residuum, and it was proposed to draw a line somewhere above household suffrage pure and simple Hereupon forty-eight Radicals held a meeting in the tea-room of the House of Commons

Teatchgir (*Coster*). Right.

Tec, Teck (*Peoples'*) Detective—cut down after an ordinary fashion.

I'm told that Jack Shaw, the smartest and best tec in London or anywhere else, thinks of retiring from the force.—*Cutting*.

Teeth-drawing (*Med. Students'*, 19 *cent.* to 1860). Wrenching off door-knockers with club-like sticks. Head-quarters, Lant Street, Southwark—street now cleared away, but until 1860 the bowers of St Thomas's and Guy's students.

Teetotically (*Peoples'*, '90's). Comic intensification of teetotally.

Tekram (*Inverted word*). Market; very common usage.

Telescope (*American Railway*). To collide and close in like a telescope—applied to the running into each other of railway carriages in collision. Now applied in various ways.

The excursion train, of twenty cars, came into collision with a goods car. The shock was so severe that five crowded cars were completely 'telescoped'.—*D. N.*, 1878.

Temporiser (*Polit.*). Shiftless uncertain man. From a speech by Mr Gladstone (17th November 1885) in Scotland.

Ten bob squats (*Theatrical*). Stalls in a theatre. About 1880 going to the theatre had become so fashionable, owing possibly to the steady patronage of the Prince of Wales, that the price of stalls in most of the best houses was raised.

Ten stroke (*Billiard-players'*). Complete victory—from the fact that ten is the highest stroke at billiards that can be made; cannon off the red, all three balls in.

10 wedding (*Peoples'*, 1897). '1' the wife, and '0' the husband=10 wedding.

Tenderfeet (*American mining*, 1849 on). Doubtful roving industrials. Given to the mining rabble in California, during the gold-rush (1849), and now classic in U.S.A., and all Colonial mining districts. Applied in all ways.

Numbers of prospectors and tenderfeet started for the then unknown gold-fields, and when a steamer reached San Francisco with some of these miners who had 'struck it rich' aboard, the fact that gold had been found in abundance along the Klondike again excited public interest in the matter.—*D. T.*, 21st July 1897.

Tenip (*Public-house, inverted word*). Pint. As suggesting natural euphony.

Terrier (*American*). Troublesome boy.

A policeman came along and the dude told him I was a terrier, and the policeman jerked my coat collar off.—1883.

Terror to cats (*American—passing to England*). Most troublesome—chiefly applied to over-active and mischievous boys.

Pa says I am a terror to cats. Every time pa says anything it gives me a new idea. I tell you pa has got a great brain, but sometimes he don't have it with him. —*Detroit Free Press*, 1883.

Testril (*Hist.*). Sixpenny piece, and another shape of tester. Shakespeare proves that the testril was of the value of sixpence in the poet's time.

Sir Toby (to clown): Come on, there is sixpence for you. Let's have a song.
Sir Andrew: There is a testril of me too!—Shakespeare, *Twelfth Night*, Act ii., scene ii.

Testugger (*Oxford*). Testamur—a certificate.

Thames butter (*Poor London*, 1870). Very bad butter. A Mr W. Sawyer, then editor of *South London Press*, published a paragraph to the effect that a Frenchman was making butter out of Thames mud at Battersea. In truth this chemist was extracting yellow grease from Thames mud-worms.

Thank the mussies (*Peoples*, 1870). Equivalent to 'Thank the gods'.

Thank you for the next (*Hist.*) Lancashire expression of gratitude for something given.

That gets me (*Amer.*). Defeat—from the game of poker, the other side getting the stakes.

That kind of thing will not answer (*Peoples'*, 1885). Poverty — from a fragment of evidence given by the Hon. Mrs Gerard, sister of the defendant in the case 'Durham *versus* Milner (otherwise Durham)'—the celebrated suit brought by Lord Durham (1885), against his wife for nullity of marriage, on the ground that the lady was insane at the time of the ceremony. Mrs Gerard said—

In the season of 1881 Lord Burghersh paid her a great deal of attention. I did not think it would be a suitable marriage. It was one that would be distasteful to her family. That was made pretty plain to my sister. I don't think she was very much attached to Lord Burghersh. My sister, in reference to Lord Burghersh's attentions, said that kind of thing would not answer, as he was poor

That moan's soon made (*Scotch and Peoples'*, 19 *cent*) Grief easily consoled

There is no more to be said on the subject, as the Scottish saying has it 'that moan's soon made' —*D. N*, 10th March 1885.

That won't pay the old woman her ninepence (*Bow Street Police Court*) Condemnation of an evasive act

That's a cough lozenge for him (*Peoples'*, 1850 on) Punishment. Arose from an advertisement, 'Cough no more lozenges' It was to be inferred that they might kill the patient, who would then certainly cough no more.

That's gone to Pimlico (*W. London, Streets'*, 1888) Smashed—ruined Derived from the fact that Pimlico became a favourite residential centre of women who fell.

That's the ticket (*Peoples'*, 18 *cent.*). Proper thing to do — corruption of 'etiquette' — that's the etiquette. Diprose in his *St Clement Danes* says '—This term arose in 1717 when Spiller, a comedian, used the expression upon seeing the card of admission designed by Hogarth, then a very young man, for a benefit at Drury Lane Theatre, in favour of the celebrated Joe Miller. However, a good authority says — 'Ticket' is from Norman French The rules of 'etiquette' were written upon cards—hence the name 'ticket' The 'etiquette' or pass - card was also affixed to a bag or bundle, to show it was not to be examined.

That's up against your shirt (*Street*) Significant of victory

That's where you spoil yourself (*Peoples'*, 1880-81) A very popular catch - sentence applied to smart individuals who went a little too far.

Theatre Royal amen (*Low Class*). Church (*See* Holy Ghost shop.)

Theatricality (*Soc*, 1888 on) Anything generically theatrical Arose when theatres ceased to be a luxury.

And as if this 'terrible acting', these 'terrible frowns', and these 'terrific impressions', were not enough, as if the tinfoil, and the tinsel, and the theatricality were not sufficient, they must needs call in good old Colley Cibber to improve on Shakespeare, and enable the gifted actors to rant and storm the more —*D. T.*, 21st December 1896.

Then comes a pig to be killed (*Peoples'*) Expression of misbelief—based upon the lines of Mrs Bond who would call to her poultry — 'Come chicks, come! Come to Mrs Bond and be killed'

Then the band played (*Parliamentary*). Climax, finality. Derived from the use of brass bands on the nomination day, which immediately sounded when the opponent of their employer attempted to address the people

There, All (*Street*, 1860 on) Exclamation, declaring perfection. 'I'm all there, completely happy'. 'She *is* an all there bit o' jam'.

Mrs Saker has done great things at the Liverpool Alexandra with 'Aladdin', the scenery and company being alike excellent Miss Jenny Hill is all there, as she ever was, and I suppose ever will be —*Ref*, 18th January 1885.

There's 'air (*London Streets*, 1900). Shortened 'there is hair!'—meaning a quantity, and shaping out of the pulled up side hair, and fringe being about this time deserted in favour of packed masses, coming down over the forehead.

Thick (*Peoples'*) Severe, also too daring in cheating

Selby says. 'I've got it thick this time. So I looks at his leg, and sees he was ableeding' —*People*, 6th January 1895.

Thick ear (*Street*, 19 *cent*) One swelled by a blow.

Thick end of a hundred years (*Yorks.*) Nearly a century.

Thick starch double blue (*Common Soc*) Rustling holiday dress for summer — white dress very severely laundried

Thick tea (*N. England*) A tea as solid as a dinner Long known in the Ridings before high tea was thought of.

Thick 'un (*Peoples'*). Sovereign.

Thieves' kitchen (*London Street*, 1882), The name satirically given to the then new Law Courts.

Thin as a rasher of wind (*Com. London*) Complete skeleton of a man.

Thingembobs (*Com. Peoples'*). One of the idiotic names for trousers—like inexpressibles, unmentionables, etc

Think and thank (*English-Jewish*) Translated from the first words of the ordinary Hebrew morning prayer. Implies gratitude.

Think some (*American*). Mature consideration.

Thinking part (*Theatrical*). That of a supernumerary who has nothing to say. Satirical.

Thinks he holds it (*Sporting, becoming general* 1875). Said of a vain man. As obscure as emphatic. It refers to any sort of championship in athletics.

Thirteenth juryman (*Legal*, 19 *cent.*). A judge who, in addressing a jury, shows leaning or prejudice.

No English Judge would have so far forgotten the impartiality of the Bench, prone as one here and there may be to convert himself into a 'thirteenth juryman'.—*D. T.*, 10th October 1895.

This is all right (*Peoples'*, 1896 on). With accent on the *all*. Satirical—meaning everything is wrong.

Mrs Harris was not there, and Harris remarked: 'This is *all* right, nothing to eat or drink, and no one to speak to'.—*People*, 7th November 1897.

Thistle down (*Irish*). Children of a wandering nature generally, but more particularly in open breezy places, describing the children who gather thistle down in autumn—the down with which the Irish peasant, especially in Donegal, makes pillows.

Thistle seed (*Peoples'*). Devonshire for gipsies, because they drift carelessly—like winged thistle seed.

Thorough-handed man (*American*). Candid, open specimen of the genus.

Thou (*Society*, 1860, etc.). Abbreviation for thousand.

Three acres and a cow (*Peoples'*, 1887). Satirical exclamation directed at illogical optimism. This was the panacea suggested for the renascence of agriculture in England. Every peasant was to have these blessings—but no one discovered where the money was to come from to meet the expenditure. Mr George Smith of Coalville claimed the invention of this phrase in a letter to the *Daily News* (27th August 1887), wherein he says:—

I also brought the subject before the Select Committee on Canals in 1883, and about which Lord Wemyss good-humouredly made some fun in the House of Lords in 1884, which fun gave new life to the phrase living to-day.

Three and sixpenny thoughtful (*Soc.*, 1890 on). Satire upon the feminine theory novel, which became dominant, 1890-96. Antithesis of the shilling shocker, which was so full of action that it had no time to think.

Fielding, according to the theory which has apparently suggested this undertaking, is so constantly in the hands of his countrymen of mature years, they show so marked a preference for him as a novelist over the author of the latest 'shilling dreadful' or 'three and sixpenny thoughtful', that they long to admit the younger generation to a share in their enjoyment.—*D. T.*, 27th May 1896.

Three a'porth o' gordepus (*Streets'*). A street Arab.

Three B's, The (*Clerical*). Bright, brief, and brotherly—the modern protest against the sleepy nature of a majority of the 19th century church services.

Three cold Irish (*Tavern*). Threepenny-worth of Irish whiskey with cold water. Because (1867) of a passing pun between this order and three hanged Fenians. The three cold Irish were Allen, Larkin, and Gould, who were executed at Manchester (1867), for the murder of Sergeant Brett in the attempt to rescue from him certain Fenian prisoners.

Three cornered constituency (*Soc.*). House where an only child or mutual friend throws in the domestic casting vote, and so gives victory to husband or wife. From the parliamentary arrangement (1867), whereby certain boroughs returned three members while the voter was only allowed to vote for two members.

Three d. masher (*Peoples'*, 1883). Young men of limited means and more or less superficial gentlemanly externals.

Three is an awkward number (*Soc. and Peoples'*, 1885). Paraphrase of 'three are company, two are not', and brought in with surprising rapidity from a line of evidence given by the Hon. Mrs Gerard in the celebrated Lord Durham's nullity of marriage suit.

On the ride to Raby in the pony carriage did not your sister get as far away from Lord Durham as she could?—I did not notice.

But you said that Lord Durham was

very nice while your sister was very silent?—Three is an awkward number under the circumstances of the case (Laughter.)

Three out brush (*Public-house*). A glass shaped like an inverted cone, and therefore something like a house-painter's brush, especially when dry. The glass holds one-third of a quartern—a quartern being just half of half a pint

Three planks (*Com English*). A coffin

In France the coffin is spoken of as—la machine à quatre planches et quatre clous.

Three-quarter man (*Cloth-drapers'*) An inferior employé. (*See* Six quarter men)

Three wise men of Gotham (*Peoples'*). Meaning that they were not wise. Generally applied to a trio of male fools In the twenty-fourth year of the reign of Henry VIII, 3rd October, a law was passed by the magistracy of Westham, for the purpose of preventing unauthorised persons from setting '*nettes, pottes, and annoyances*', or in anywise taking fish within the privilege of the march of Pevensey The King's commission was directed to John Moor, of Lewes; Richard, Abbot of Begeham; John, Prior of Myehillym; Thomas, Lord Dacre, and others Upon the proceedings of this meeting, which was held at Gotham, near Pevensey, the facetious Andrew Borde, a native of that town, founded his *Merrie Tales of the Wise Men of Gotham*

Threepenny shot (*Artizans'*) Beef-steak globular pudding at that price, sold in common cook- and coffee-shops

Throat-latch (*American*). The larynx, as outwardly developed

Throw it up (*Theatrical*). Don't repeat it, figuratively Really means reject it, as something not fit to be retained.

If Miss Hodson ever revises and compresses the piece, she must take heed that she removes the 'throw it up' lines, and the references to Somebody's virgin vinegar and Somebody else's soap —*Ref*, 20th December 1885

Throw mud at the clock (*Peoples'*) Despair—even to suicide. Means defy time and die. Mostly used figuratively

Throwing the hammer (*Low Military*). Erotic. Obtaining money under false pretences. (*See* Catch cocks.)

Thumper (*American*). Man who steals by misrepresentation—thumper being 'a big lie'

Thusly (*American*) In this manner The word was the invention of Artemus Ward (about 1860)

Thuzzy-muzzy (*Low London*). Wilful corruption of enthusiasm Said to come down from the tenor Brahan, who either invented the term or thought he was using the true word His English was not great, as witness—

'Twas in Trafalgar Bay
We saw the Frenchman lay

Ticket o' leave (*Peoples'*, '70's). Holiday, vacation, outing

The expression, 'Ticket o' leave', is probably the invention of the criminal intellect, which, as everybody knows, delights in giving utterance to its own ideas in its own peculiar way —*D N.*, 27th October 1886

Ticket-skinner (*New York*). Opera and theatre ticket speculator, who buys for a rise Sometimes sells a 2-dollar ticket for 5 or even 10 dollars.

Innocent people regard the high rates announced by the managers as final, and only discover at the entrance that the advertised price for seats is a ruse to lure them to the merciful treatment of middle men, called ticket-skinners, who, having temporary possession of nearly all the tickets, exact just what they please for a seat.—*N Y. Mercury*, October 1883.

Tickle one's innards (*Anglo-American*) Indulge in a drink.

Thankee, mister, that war well thought of It's Sunday, but come, let's steer for a side door, and tickle our innards, ye know —*N Y Mercury*, 16th January 1885

Tickle to death (*U S*). Delight in the extreme

Ticklers (*Transvaal War*, 1900). Peacock feathers, which were sold to the youth of both sexes on 'Mafeking Night' for the first time, at one penny a piece, and so named by the vendors

It appears that the peacock feathers—'ticklers', for short—which were such an important feature in the popular rejoicings of the last few days, come from France The cheaper kind of Union Jacks come from Germany, the better kind from Scotland.—*D. T.*, 28th May 1900.

Street genius immediately raised the word to an endearment by changing it into tiddler.

Ticklish (*Peoples'*). Easily excited, or spurred to resistance.

Tiddle-a-wink (*Rhyming*). A drink.

Tie o' mutton (*Irish, London Tailors'*). Thigh of—meaning leg; and refers to the hopes of a hot Sunday dinner.

Tie up your stocking (*Oxford Univer.*). Finish your tumbler of champagne—don't leave any. No heel-taps.

Tie up with a curly one (*Cricketing*, 1890). Bowl out with a screwed or rifled projection of the ball, sent from the shoulder on a parabolic curve produced by simultaneous swing of the arm and turn of the wrist.

Tied down (*American*). Crushed by the force of circumstances.

Tiger (*American*). Prostitute. Never tigress. Shadwell, London, was called by sailors Tiger Bay—long since swept away.

Tiger (*Boys'*, 19 *cent.*). Tough-crusted bread. Probably from both offering a deal of fight.

Tiger (*San Francisco*). The guardian—inside the inner door of a gaming-house—equivalent to the chucker-out of a London tavern.

Tiger (*Political*, 1895). Hon. J. Chamberlain. Bestowed by the Radical party. Sir J. Kitson quoted this verse in a political speech:—

> There was a young lady of Riga
> Who went for a ride on a tiger;
> They finished the ride with the lady inside,
> And a smile on the face of the tiger.

The young lady was presumably Britannia.

Tiger bit him hard (*American gamester*). Meaning that he had lost a good deal of money at a sitting.

Tight as a biled (or boiled) owl (*American*). Completely drunk.

Tiled (*Masonic*). Closed—from the tiler closing in a house by way of the tiles. The outer-door paid officer of a masonic lodge is the tiler.

What is a 'tiled lodge of the Antediluvian Order of Buffaloes?' One of the Bristol lodges saw fit to meet together in a room in a public-house, and at this gathering there was singing and playing. Thereupon a constable entered and knocked at the door whence the sounds of revelry were proceeding. Here we get our first glimpse of the mystery attaching to the word 'tiled'. In one of the panels of the door there was a slide. Somebody looked through this aperture, shook his head, and the slide was closed again. Was the somebody a 'tiler'?—a term derived, like that of 'mason', from the old trade guilds.—*D. T.*, 2nd July 1896.

Timbers (*Art jargon*, 1880). Cabinets, bookcases, escritoires, elaborate tables—worked wood in general. (*See* Crocks and rags).

Timbers (*Gutter commerce*). Lucifer matches.

Timothy grass (*American*). Cat's tail grass.

Tin hat (*Anglo-Port Said*). Drunk—two tin hats very drunk—three, incapable, and to be carried on board.

Tinman (*Sporting*, 1880). Millionaire; from man possessing tin.

Too many of the big swells found profit in the Tinman to allow him to pass into retirement while able to earn winnings for them if conditions were modified for his benefit.—*Ref.*, 14th November 1886.

(Referring to F. Archer, a popular and rich jockey, who had some days before committed suicide.)

Tin-shin-off (*American*). Tin is money; shin is to walk; and together with the third word means—abscond with money.

Tinder-tempered (*Peoples'*, *old*). Hot-tempered—from the tinder sometimes taking fire in a moment from the flash of the flint and steel.

'Tis both your faults, you tinder-tempered knaves.—Garrick, *Abel Drugger*.

Tintamarre (*Devon*). Noise, hubbub. One of the French phrases common, and only common, to Devon.

Tip the velvet (*Crim. Classes*). Kiss with the point of the tongue.

Tipping the office (*Soc.*, 18 *cent.*). Revealing a secret—frequently in connection with some doubtful proceeding.

Titotular bosh (*Music Hall*, 1897). Absolute nonsense—made up by an absurd play upon the word teetotal, and one of the terms for 'humbug'.

Tittimatorterin (*E. Anglican*). See-saw.

Tius (*East London—reversed word*). Suit of clothes.

To away (*Theatrical*). Creation of a verb from the dramatic exclamation 'away'.

To Christmas (*Soc.*, 1880). To make high holiday with plenty of feasting.

The associations of Christmas for the young and for the people are almost wholly of a festive character. They conjugate actively the verb 'to Christmas'.—*D. N.*, 25th December 1884.

Toast v. On (a bit of) toast.

Toast your blooming eyebrows (*Peoples'*). Probably a delicate way of telling a man to go to blazes.

Toby (*Soc.*, 1882). Lady's collar—from the wide frill worn round the neck by Mr Punch's dog.

Toe-path (*Cavalry*). Regiment of infantry. Eminently suggestive of the contempt in which the cavalry hold the infantry, who as a rule are much smaller men than the gee-gees (*q.v.*).

Toe-rag (*Peoples', Prov.*). Beggar. Most country people ride or drive, hence the contempt enclosed in 'toe', with which the possessor walks. Another term (Devon) is footpad—without reference to robbery. Rags speak for themselves.

Toff bundle-carrier (*Music Hall*, 1870 on). He is the gentleman in attendance upon a serio-comic, and see her from hall to hall—a prosperous serio-comic often having to sing at three or four music halls in the course of one evening. Her changes of dress, etc., call for a large assortment of flying luggage, to which the devoted one gives all his attention—hence the term.

Toff-omee (*Thieves'*). Superlative of toff.

Toff-shoving (*London Rough*, 1882). Pushing about well-dressed men in a crowd.

Tog-bound (*Peoples'*). No good clothes to wear.

Tog-fencer (*Com. Lond.*, 1870). A tailor.

Toga-play (*Theatrical*). Classical play.

Togies (*Public-school*). Knotted ropes' ends carried about hidden by elder boys to beat their fags with—once-called 'colts'.

Toileted (*American-Eng.*, 1884). Dressed. Conjugated throughout.

Pretty Martha Springsteen brings suit against her husband for separation. The lady is young and good-looking and is exquisitely toileted.—*N. Y. Mercury*, January 1885.

Tom (*Street*, 19 *cent.*). A masculine woman of the town. In higher ranks one who does not care for the society of others than those of her own sex.

Tom and funny (*Rhyming*). Figurative description of money.

Tom o' Bedlam (*Provincial*). A wild, maddish fellow—from the name once given to inoffensive imbeciles who were licensed to go about begging.

Abram-men, otherwise called Tom o' Bedlams, are very strangely and antickly garbed, with several coloured ribbons or tape in their hat, it may be; instead of a feather, a fox-tail hanging down a long stick with ribbons streaming and the like. Yet for all their seeming madness they have wit enough to steal as they go.—*The Canting Academy*, 1674.

Tomahawk (*Street*). Policeman's staff.

Tomasso di rotto (*Middle-class Youths'*). Italian shape of Tommy rot.

Tomb-stone (*Com. Lond.*, 19 *cent.*). A pawn-ticket—the shape and printed heading of which do give the idea of a doll's tombstone.

Tommy (Bobby) Atkins (*Popular*, 1882). The friendly name found about this year for a soldier of the line—presumably invented amongst line soldiers, and certainly adopted by them. Tommy Atkins first appeared in print in the correspondence sent home during the Egyptian campaign (1882).

This time it was some other member of the family of Thomas Atkins who resumed the colloquy of which our friend Bill had dropped the thread.—*D. N.*, 28th September 1882.

Tommy and exes (*Workmen's*). Bread—beer, and 'bacca.

Tommy make room for your uncle (*Music Hall*). Suggestive of the uncle being a better man than the nephew, and accepted very willingly by the less juvenile of music-hall patrons. Adopted as the leading line of a chorus to a comic song. Said, however, to have a recondite meaning.

Tommy pipes (*Navy*, 19 *cent.*). Boatswain — because he pipes or whistles all hands.

Tommy rabbit (*Street Boys'*). Pomegranate. (*See* Nanny.)

Tomtug (*Rhyming*). Bed insect.

Tone - painting (*Soc.*, 1890 on). Referring to programme music.

Mr Silas points out that even great musicians do not appear at their best in tone-painting.—*D. T.*, 31st March 1897.

Tony (*American — coming to England*, 1890). Adjective, formed upon the abstract noun.

As for fashionable matters, there was less 'society', of course, in point of numbers in Hone's time than in ours, but it was just as 'tony' of its kind, if anything a little more so.—*N. Y. Mercury*, 18th May 1890.

(*See* No class.)

Too all but (*London*, 1881). One of the phrases resulting out of *Punch's* trouvaille 'too-too' (1881), and to be found in Mr W. S. Gilbert's extravaganza, *Patience.*

Too cheap (*Peoples'*). Under valued. Used in every possible way.

Too damned good (*Military*). Second Dragoon Guards. From the regimental indication on the shoulder-straps.

2
D.G.

Too full of holes to skin (*W. America*). Very much riddled with bullets.

Too mean to raise (*American*). Utterly contemptible.

Too much with us! (*Soc.*, 1897). Boredom, incubus.

Klondyke is 'too much with us' just now. It has long been dragged into conversation with the persistency of a pantomime gag.—*D. T.*, 14th January 1897.

Too numerous to mention (*London*, 1882). Angrily drunk.

Too too (*Soc.*, 1881). More than perfect. Too-too was first found in *Punch* in the height of the æsthetic craze (1881).

Too utterly too (*Society*, 1883). Final phrase resulting from the satirical use of 'too-too'.

Tooled (*Soc.*, 19 *cent.*). Murdered. Satirical metaphor. Invented by De Quincey.

Sir Edward Reed's suspected assassin is thought to have 'tooled', as De Quincey says, with a Japanese dagger. —*D. N.*, 12th February 1885.

Tooleries (*Theatrical*, 1885). Toole's Theatre—now swept away.

Toothpick (*American-Eng.*). Clasp knife—or bowie knife. Satirical description of its formidable appearance.

Toothpicks (*American*). People of Arkansas.

Top-drawing-room (*Low. London*). A garret.

Topical allusion (*Political—Music Hall*). Direct or indirect reference to passing events.

When Miss Victor, exclaiming, 'Noble nation, the Russians!' a faint laugh, broken by a faint hiss, indicated that a perception had somewhere dawned upon somebody of what burlesque writers call a 'topical allusion'.—*D. N.*, 27th April 1885.

Topical vocalist (*Music Hall*).' One who sings concerning the events or topics of the day.

Tora - loorals (*Theatrical*). Feminine bust. Generally used in reference to a dress very *decolletée.*

Torch-light procession (*American*, 1883). One of the more fiery American drinks.

Tory democracy (*Polit.*, 1885). Impossibility, absurdity.

Lord R. Churchill had given a new combination in the words 'Tory Democracy'. A Tory could not be a Democrat, and a Democrat could not be a Tory.—Mr H. Labouchere, Finsbury, 13th October 1885.

Tory rory (*London*, 18 *cent.* to 1845). Name given to those who wore their hats fiercely cocked.

Tosh (*Cricket*, 1898). Fatally easy bowling.

Tosh (*Thieves' — old*). Pocket—probably a corruption from the French *poche.*

Tot - hunter (*Low Life*). Bone-collector — generally used offensively in quarrels, and in reference to parents.

Tot-hunting (*Low. Class*). Scouring the streets in search of pretty girls.

Totty all colours (*London Streets'*). Young person who has contrived to get most of the colours of the rainbow into her costume.

Totty one lung (*Street*, 1885). An asthmatic, or consumptive young person who, whether good or bad, thinks herself somebody.

Tough as tacker (*Peoples'*). Tough in excelsis.

Tourney (*Pugilistic*). Mill or encounter of two fighters. Word coined after the Eglintoun tournament.

Concerning the present tourney — I think that's the word — arrangements for a special train were attempted to be made.—*Morning Star*, 1862.

Tournure (*Dressmakers'*, 1882). Happily invented name for the dress-improver of that year.

Town (*Rhyming*). Halfpenny. Thus—town—brown—so named from colour.

Tra la la (*Peoples'*, 1880). Parting benediction—not too civil; possibly contemptuous. Died out about 1890. The phrase took its rise with a comic singer named Henri Clarke, whose speciality was imitating Parisians. Whether he invented 'tra la la', or heard it in Paris, or uttered by a Frenchman in London—he made a great hit with it as the burden of a chorus.

Thanks. I hate personalities. Good-morning. So tra, la, la !—*Funny Folk*, No. 519.

Traffy (*Navy*). Portsmouth's seafaring reduction of the *Trafalgar* (once Nelson's ship), and long since anchored for life at Portsmouth.

Trailing coat (*Irish — spread to England in* 19 *cent.*). Defiance. In Irish village fights the man trailed his coat by way of challenge — he who took up the cartel trod on it, and the fight began.

Irishmen in the postal service may say that in introducing his 'blacklegs' Mr Raikes was 'trailing his coat'.—*D. N.*, 10th July 1890.

Train too fine (*Soc. and Sport*, 1890 on). Push things too oppressively —from sporting life, where men with too much training overdo the training.

There is undoubted ground for the belief that our bishops as a body are beginning to 'train too fine'.—*D. T.*, 10th June 1898.

Tram-fare (*London Streets'*, 1882). Twopence. Until the toll over Waterloo Bridge (London)—one halfpenny—was abolished, the lower women of the streets used to ask for coin to go over the bridge.

Transfer (*Society*). To steal.

Translate the truth (*Soc.*, 1899). Lie evasively. In general use during this year.

The resources of the French language for putting a polish of politeness on ugly facts are infinite. When M. Delcassé's mendacity in connection with the Muscat incident was exposed, a leading Paris paper extenuated his offence by the ingenious excuse that, after all, he merely 'translated the truth'.—*People*, 19th March 1899.

Translated (*Soc.*, 80's). Emphatically — intoxicated. Probably a reminiscence of Shakespeare — 'Bless thee, Bottom, thou art translated' (*Midsummer Night's Dream*).

Trap (*Australian*, 1870). Mounted trooper.

Travelling tinkers (*Inter-regimental*). 30th Regiment—Lancashire regiment.

Treacle-man (*Thieves'*). Beautiful male decoy who is the pretended young man of the housemaid and the real forerunner of the burglar. (*See* Leave-yer-homer.)

Often used to designate the commercial traveller who has to make sales of type-writers, sewing machines, etc. to young girls and old women. Sometimes bitterly applied by drapers' assistants to any one of their number who makes the smartest sales.

Treason-mongers (*Polit.*, 1885). Contemptuous name found for dynamiters as their great schemes for the destruction of London faded into nothingness.

None but treason-mongers will dispute the applicability of the inscription on the pedestal, which, in the familiar words from *Henry VIII.*, represents him as having fallen a martyr for his country.—*Globe*, 1st July 1885.

Trelawny (*West Cornwall*). War-cry of the Cornish men; derived from one of the three leading septs of Cornwall—

> By Tre, Pol, and Pen
> Ye shall know the Cornish men.

Used as a defiance.

Trifa (*Jewish*). Unclean — clean things may become trifa; others, such as pork and shell-fish, are always trifa. Applied widely in E. London.

Tripha, ritually unclean.—I. Zangwill, *Children of the Ghetto*.

The slaughterer must be a man of high moral character. In opening the animal, he must make a thorough inspection of it, and if he finds it in any way diseased, he pronounces 'trefa'—that it is unfit for the food of Jews.

(*See* Kosher.)

Trilby (*Soc.*, 1894). Woman's exquisite foot. American - English. From Du Maurier's book (1894) *Trilby*—the name of the book, and of the heroine, whose beautifully rare foot is insisted on.

Having exhausted palmistry an American paper has spent its energy of psychological investigation on the foot (I beg pardon, the trilby), but a rival comes out with a page of illustrated description of the mouth.—*People*, 7th July 1895.

Trimming (*Polit.*, 18 *cent.* on). Not sailing straight.

'He's a trimmer of trimmers, and he lies by heredity.'

Trimming was the name which the 18th century politician gave to what we now call opportunism.—Ouida, *An Altruist* (1896).

Trimmings (*Trade*, 1897). Masked alcohol. When, by the contrivance of Mr Gladstone, it was attempted to modify the attraction of the public-house by giving licenses to sell alcoholic drinks to various tradesmen, some linen-drapers and silk-mercers who gave credit, opened liberal refreshment rooms at their establishments, and put down their lady-customers' wine-lunches as 'trimmings' in the bills sent to the husbands. Hence the word became synonymous with secret drinking by women.

The *Drapers' World* declares 'alcoholic trimmings' to be fiction.—*D. T.*, 18th January 1897.

Trinity kiss (*Soc.*, about 1870). A triple kiss — generally given by daughters and very young sons, when going to bed, to father and mother.

Tripe (*Journalistic*). Rubbish, 'rot'.

Yet she puts in six or seven pages of her own tripe, and limits me to three columns. — T. Le Breton, *The Modern Christian* (1902), ch. 8.

Tripe, Blooming six foot o' (*Street*, 1880). A giant policeman. 'Yer blooming six foot o' tripe, how's yer fat old head?'—attack upon a tall policeman.

Triper (*Streets'*, *E. London*). Trifa (?) — this being the Jewish for unclean.

Tripos pup (*Cambridge Univ.*) Undergrad cantabs.

Every year the coaches exact more and more work out of their 'Tripos pups'.—*D. N.*, 14th June 1887.

Triumphant toast (*Soc.*, 18 *cent.*). Toast in excelsis.

Miss Chudleigh next was the triumphant toast: a lively, sweet-tempered, gay, self-admired, and not altogether without reason, generally-admired lady—she moved not, without crowds after her. She smiled at every one.—Richardson, *Letters from Tunbridge Wells*, 1748.

Trot (*Com. Lond.*, 1875). A walk—probably suggested by the ordinary quick movement of most young Englishmen.

Trot the udyju Pope o' Rome (*Street*). This is very enigmatic English, composed of rhyming and transposition styles, and is generally used by one man to another when he wants the wife, or other feminine person, out of the way. Udyju is judy (wife) transposed — judy being very common word for wife or mistress equally. Pope o' Rome is rhyming for home.

Trots (*Common London*). Feet — derived from 'trotting'.

Trots (*Peoples'*, 1846). Policemen. Refers to these officers being always on the go—or beat.

Trotter-cases (*Com. London*, 1860). Boots.

Trotting away from the pole (*American*). In error — wandering from subject. From horse-trotting sport; the pole being the winning post.

Trouble (*American*, 1870). Distinct American for 'anxiety'.

Troubled with the slows (*Aquatics*). Observed of the losing boat or swimmer.

Trouting (*Piscatorial*). Catching trout.

April and May are the best months for trouting on the Thames.—*People*, 3rd April 1898.

Trowser (*E. London*, 1895 on). Jack of all trades and master of none.

Sir Reginald Hanson: What is a 'trowser'. Sweeting: Vy, a man as does any hod jobs. Anythin'.—*D. T.*, 4th November 1897.

True bill, judgment, execution (*Anglo-American*). Medical analysis of the course of paralysis.

True inwardness (*Literary*, 1890 on). Reality. One of the principal shapes of literary jargon produced in the '90's. Probably the only serious survival of the æsthetic craze of the '80's.

Trying it on the dog (*Theatrical*). Abbreviation of 'the matinée dog'. Derived from the amiable habit, in the good old times of testing a present of eatables by giving a portion to the dog. In the present relation it is a contemptuous reference to the lower judging capacities of afternoon theatrical audiences. Testing the value of a new piece by an afternoon audience is trying it on the matinée dog—who is below consideration, but may be useful.

If any enterprising person desires to make money from a play or a composition of music he does not boldly attempt the experiment upon the public His shrewd suspicion that they would avenge the torture induces him to adopt the preliminary precaution of 'trying it on the dog —*D T*, 4th February 1897.

Tub practice (*Boating*). Unskilled efforts in broad-bottomed boats

During the intervals of racing in the eight they should have been taken out for 'tub' practice in convenient gig pairs —*D T*, 17th June 1897

Tubbichon (*Peoples'*, '60's) Corruption of *tire-buchon* (corkscrew) which was the Paris argot in the '60's for the long solitary ringlet of a portion of the back hair worn in front of the left shoulder, a fashion created by the Empress Eugenie, and accepted in London by the middle-classes immediately after that lady visited London (1855), when for a time everything French was very popular.

Miss Spong's fair hair is all pushed into a gold net, save for one long *tire-bouchon* hanging over the left shoulder. —*D T*, 21st January 1898.

Tug of war (*Peoples'*). Contest final and settling Now applied to two sets of boys or men pulling from the two ends of one rope—the tug being to get one side a mere inch over the dividing chalk line

Tumbling down to grass (*Peoples'*, 1884) Equivalent to going to the bad Breaking up, failing From the fact of land going out of cultivation 1875-85.

Tunnels (*Theat*, 1885) Opera Comique Theatre (swept away by Strand improvements) — Strand. From the several subterranean passages leading to this underground theatre.

These same 'coarse bullies' have often enough been Mr W S Gilbert's staunchest supporters at the Savoy, and at the Royalty and the Tunnels —*Ref*, 10th January 1886.

(Mr Gilbert had been complaining of the angry reception, by the gallery, of a play by him.)

Tup (*Streets' — especially in Woolwich*). Arrested. It is derived from 'locked up', the 't' of locked being prefixed to up

Tuppenny 'apenny ones (*Street*) Very poor and common sort

Tupper (*Soc.*, 1850 on). A commonplace honest bore who talks or writes A B C Takes its rise from Mr Martin Tupper who wrote a phenomenally successful book called *Proverbial Philosophy*—composed entirely of self-evident propositions

Turf (*Street*, 19 *cent.*). Prostitution From loose women being on parade. Thence came turfer.

Turn down your cup (*Soc*, 19 *cent*, 1785-1890). Die—from the once existing provincial habit of reversing one's cup in one's saucer when no more tea or coffee was required Finish—hence the figure of speech

This last word cost Mr Palmer half his breakfast; on hearing it he turned down his cup with a profound sigh —Miss M. Edgeworth, *Manœuvring*

Turn over (*Press*, 1860 on) Last column on the right of the front page of a newspaper, especially an evening one. So called from the social article which fills that column turning a few lines, for the sake of effect, over on to top of first column on second page

Turn paper collars (*American*) Figurative for poverty. (*See* Out o' collar)

Turn round pudding (*Peoples'*) Any slop pudding or porridge made by turning round the ingredients with a spoon, in a saucepan (*See* Stir about, Hasty pudding.)

Turn the best side to London (*Peoples'*) Shrewd way of recommending the hearer to make the best of everything.

Turn the tap on (*Common London*). To be ready with tears.

'You noticed, perhaps', said my companion, 'that when she had finished her song she fell a crying? That's what she's strong in. She can turn the taps on at a moment's notice, and that in a way you'd never think was any other than natural.' —*D. T*, 8th February 1883

Turn turtle (*Naval*). Tumble down drunk—from the over-turning of a vessel—which is to turn turtle.

Turn up (*Universal*). Appear unexpectedly.

Turn up friendly lead (*Coster*, 1870). Final jovial co-operation. A public-house sing-song to pay the burial expenses of a dead friend, or a pal who has turned up life.

Turnover (*Cornish mining*). Capital. Alas — it is generally the shareholders in these toils who are turned over.

Turn-over (*Lit.*, 1880). A work to dip into rather than read.

The book has as a 'turn over' much of the character of a good volume of *Punch*, and it has the merits (both rare in French comic drawing) of bringing no blush on the cheek of the young person, and of having its work finished and not merely indicated in outline.—*Sat. Rev.*, 26th December 1885.

Turn-up (*Thieves'*). Acquittal—the prosecution being turned up, or abandoned. 'This will be only a turn up.' Also used socially. 'Ginger May's turned me up', does not mean that this yellow-haired Circe has committed an assault upon the speaker, but has abandoned him.

Dear Parnell,—For heaven's sake stop the boycotting and the Moonlighting and the outrages. I have promised you Home Rule, and you shall have it; but if you let your lads play old gooseberry with law and order as they are doing now, I shall have to turn it up.—Salisbury, *Ref.*, 18th October 1885.

Turnups (*Lower Peoples'*). Rejection of a suitor. She dismisses him—or turns him up—said to be from hospital practice of turning up the ordinary joint bedstead when a patient left it for the grave. Corrupted into an idea of turnips — generally pronounced turnups by the vulgar.

Turkey-buyer (*Leadenhall market*). Swell, toff, dude, person of consequence, banker. Because it requires more than two-pence to buy gobblers.

Turkey merchant (*City*). Extensive financier in scrip — a city plunger. supposed to have some reference to the gaming traffic in Turkish bonds which continued until 1878. More probably a name-word, a corruption of 'T. K.' — the initials of some past away speculator, whose only legacy to the world was this phrase.

Turtle soup (*Workmen's*). Sheep's head broth. (*See* Clare market duck, City sherry.)

Tweedle-dum sirs (*Soc.*). Baronets or knights who gain their titles by way of music. Started when Sir Michael Costa obtained his title. Almost forgotten when Sir Arthur Sullivan was knighted. (*See* Gally-pot baronet.)

Twelve o'clock (*Artizans'*). Action—time to be moving. Derived from the fact that this is (or rather was), the dinner hour, and that the diners move rapidly towards home.

Twelve pound actor (*Theatrical*). A well-weighted newly-born baby—a child born in 'the profession' of course.

Mrs James O'Neill has added a twelve-pound actor to Jimmy's board account.

20 in the pounder (*Peoples'*). Gentleman who, owing a sovereign, does not make a composition, but pays his 240 pence in full.

Twicers (*Lower Class*, 19 *cent.*). Twins.

Twisting the lion's tail. (*See* Tail-twisting.)

Twixter (*L. London*). Either a lady-like young man, or a man-like young woman—as the case may be.

Two 'arts in a pond (*Lower Class*). Two hearts (*bullocks'*), in a pond-dish, this receptacle being a baking dish divided in two parts by a transverse wall — hence the ponds. Used on Sunday morning at the bake-houses to describe dinner baked there — and called for.

Two brothers alive, and one married (*Music Hall*, 1897). The one married being as bad as dead.

Two buckle horses (*Stables'*). Tuberculosis.

Two ends and the middle of a bad lot (*Middle-class*). Evasive method of utter condemnation.

Two F's (*Mid.-class*, 1880). Fringe and followers—of lady servants.

As for the two F's—fringes (forehead hair) and followers—surely they should be permitted in moderation. The fringe need not become a fuzz, the followers need not degenerate into polyandry.—*D. N.*, 20th October 1886.

Two inches beyond upright (*Peoples'*). Hypocritical liar. Perversion of description of upright-standing man, who throws his back backwards beyond upright.

Two L's, The (*American-Eng*, 1880) In England means certain destruction. In America — lead or liquor Comes from the Wild West, and chiefly Arizona, where between taking eternal pulls at Bourbon whiskey, and for ever drawing lead at sight upon the next door neighbour, or being drawn upon—a man of thirty was a phenomenon of old age

Two to one against you (*Peoples'*) Very much against you. Refers to the pawnbroker's golden sign 'the three balls'—two above one, implying that it is two to one that you will never get your pledge back

Two upon ten (*Tradesmen's*) 'Two' eyes upon 'ten' fingers—warning that a thief is in the neighbourhood, generally given out by one shopman for the benefit of the others

Two white, two red, and after you with the blacking brush—usually cut down—**two white, two red, and the brush** (*London Street*, 1860-70). This phrase is absolutely a legacy from the second French empire Under Napoleon III., the use of colour cosmetics became very marked. Like most French fashions this came to London, and even penetrated for a short time into fairly respectable society, whence it rapidly reached the streets, with much exaggeration—hence the phrase which thus satirizes the vulgarity of the use of colours It means 'two dabs of red, two of white, and the use of blacking brush to make up the eyebrows'. 'After you, miss, with the two two's and the two b's' (*i e*, blacking brush).

Two with you (*Tavern Life*). Suggesting a twopenny drink

Arthur Roberts may be congratulated. At the finish his friends crowded around, and challenged him with a 'Two with you'—*Ref*, 12th June 1887

Twopenny tube (*C London*, 1900) The Central London Underground Electric Railway (opened in the first week in August 1900), gained this shortened designation within ten days. At once it became a phrase to stay From the then one and only fare—twopence

We have already, it is true, the omnibus, the hansom, the four-wheeler, the tramcar, the underground railway, and the 'two penny tube'.—*D T* (Sir E. Arnold), 13th October 1900

U

U.K (*London*, 1870). Emphatic initials of United Kingdom

Minnie Palmer is on all call nightly, and may be pronounced the finest anti-dyspeptic dose in the U K—U bet!—*Sunday Times*, 14th October 1883

U P (*Lower Social*). 'Up' spelt, to make the word more forcible. Usually used with all—as 'It's all U P with him', which may mean that he is about to die, or fail in business, or his winnings, or his power of work of any kind.

Still the box did not come down, and I thought certainly it was 'U P' with all of us By this time some of the men who felt better had climbed up, but most of us were not strong enough to do so—*D T*, 17th May 1897

See N G and G T T.

Ud's my life (*Peoples'*, 18 *cent.*) One of the evasive forms of religious swearing, 'God's my life' (*See* Zounds, etc)

Ugger, The (*Oxford*). The Union.

Marvels have been done with the most unpromising material For example, one would have thought that 'the Union' defied corruption But not so Some ingenious wit had an inspiration and called it 'the Ugger', and his friends bowed low before him —*D T.*, 14th August 1899.

Ugly (*Common Coffee-house*, 19 *cent*) Thick (*See* Ungryome.)

Ugly (*Soc*, 50's) Bonnet shade.

'Ugly' The passing name bestowed by common consent upon the hideous shades worn upon the front of the bonnet, and made of silk drawn in gathers upon wires.

Ugly rush (*Parliamentary*) Speed to prevent enquiry—forcing a bill (*See* Hard and fast line)

Uhlan (*Parliamentary*, 1883) Free lance—or perhaps free-booter. Lord Randolph Churchill. The Uhlans were first familiarly known in England during the Franco-German War (1870-71)—but only by report. They were the *avant-courriers* of the German advance into France, their appearance presaging the arrival of a numerous body. The word soon came to represent a daring, headstrong skirmisher. Lord Randolph in politics answering this description, ultimately acquired this title.

Such an idea had long been in the mind of Lord Randolph Churchill, the Uhlan of the Conservative army.—*D. N.*, 17th February 1883.

Ulster (*Anglo-Amer.*). Skin of anything. Jocosely suggested by the long ulster coat covering the whole body.

Ultra-crepidation (*Soc.*, 19 *cent.*). Plunging, vaulting ambition. From *Ne sutor ultra crepidam.*

But be that as it may, the man whom proverbial wisdom exhorts to 'stick to his last' is the very man who most often sets that advice at nought. He has been 'ultra-crepidating', to use a word of Coleridgian coinage, throughout all history.—*D. T.*, 14th May 1895.

Ululation (*Press*, about 1875). First night condemnation by all the gallery and the back of the pit. (*See* Damned, Hornpipe.)

Umble-cum-stumble (*Low. Class*). Thoroughly understood.

Unattached (*Parliamentary*, 1850, on). A member of the legislation whose vote is never quite to be counted upon by any party.

Unavoidable circumstances (*American Satirical*). Court knee-breeches.

Unbounded assortment of gratuitous untruths (*Polit.*, 1885). Extensive systematic lying. From speech (11th November 1885) of Mr Gladstone's at Edinburgh, wherein may be found:—

It has become the fashion with a portion of the Tory party to circulate in reference to myself personally and individually an unbounded assortment of the most gratuitous untruths.

Unconscious self (*Soc.*, 1885). Genius—the quality of exceptional and inexplicable production of intellectual work.

Dore's very best drawings look like the work of an inspired 'unconscious self', to borrow the latest terminology of psychical research.—*D. N.*, 25th June 1885.

Uncrowned king (*Political*, 1881). Satirical name for C. S. Parnell, M.P. for Cork, the leader of the Irish movement. The crown referred to that of Ireland, from one of whose kings, like most Irish leaders, C. S. Parnell was descended.

Under or over (*American-English*, 1860 on). Contraction of under the grass or over the grass—this phrase being a metaphor of death (under the grass) and of life (over the grass). Applied to widows—meaning either a husband who is dead, or a husband in divorce, who of course is over and above the grass.

This widow of 'Under the grass' and 'Over the grass', the dead husband and the divorced one, is very fascinating, very brilliant, and certainly cynical.—*D. T.*, 9th August 1899.

Under the rose v. Sub rosa.

Underdone (*Colloquial*). Pale complexion. Took the place of doughy.

Underground Russia (*Socialistic*). Nihilistic Russia.

André Frangoli has himself played an important part in the Russian revolutionary movement; nobody is better acquainted than he with 'Underground Russia', and his name is not unknown in England. I give the story, word for word, as he gave it to me.—*D. N.*, 15th September 1883.

Understudy (*Theatrical*). Presumed inferior actor or actress, who learns a part played by a presumedly superior actor or actress, and who only gets a chance of appearing as the result of illness or other indisposition on the part of the superior being.

In the theatrical profession it is always understood to be a perfectly legitimate proceeding, and occasionally in the interests of art, for an 'understudy' to pray for the collapse of a principal.—*D. T.*, 20th May 1897.

Undigested Ananias (*Peoples'*, 1895). Triumphant liar.

'Just listen to him!' exclaimed Mrs Quick; 'look at his impudence. Hear how he cheeks the Court. Why, it's as bad as when he once called my husband an "undigested Ananias"'. — *D. T.*, 24th June 1896.

Unfair done by (*Peoples'*, *Hist.*). Ill-treated.

Ungryome (*Common Coffee-house*, 1880). Unaspirated and collided condition of the two words, 'hungry' and 'home'. (*See* Ugly.)

Unhitched (*Liverpool—spreading*) Let go, released, separated

When all the arrangements were made and the pair stood up the 'Squire gazed at them over his spectacles and unhitched on them in the most solemn and impressive tones —*N Y. Mercury*, April 1886

Unicorn carman (*L. Streets'*, 19 *cent*) Driver of three horses harnessed tandem

Unkinned (*Soc*, 1884) Satirical pronunciation of 'unkind'—the result of the production (1884) of *Hamlet* at the Princess's Theatre, where Mr Wilson Barrett in the title-rôle, acting under advice, used kin instead of kind in the great soliloquy.

Unrelieved holocaust (*Society*, 1883) In 1882 the destruction of the Ring Theatre (Vienna), and of a circus at Berditscheff (Russia), both accompanied by terrible loss of life, led a writer in the *Times* to use the above odd phrase in reference to these catastrophes—whereupon the satirical spirits of society adopted it to ridicule the most absurd incidents.

Up (*Sporting*). In the saddle 'Archer up'—favourite cry meaning success—in 1880-83

That most enterprising of picture publishers, Mr George Rees, of Russell Street, Covent Garden, has issued a splendidly got up coloured lithograph of St Blaise (a horse), 'with Charlie Wood up'

Up (*Theatrical*) Up—the stage Under this condition as a rule the up'd one has only to look on. (*See* Come down)

Up a tree for tenpence (*Peoples'*, 1850 on) Moneyless, stone-broke.

Up fields (*Westminster School*) Enclosure of Vincent Square, Westminster, practically the private property of St Peter's It is historically the field where the Westminsters played, and play—especially football

Up my sleeve (*Ancient English*) This phrase is very obscure, but it is certainly used in the sense of being intoxicated.

It was six pots up my sleeve when we reached port, and Sarah asked me to her next Sunday tea fight.

Up or down (*Peoples'*) Heaven or Hades

Up School (*Westminster School*) Short for 'Upper School'—the great school-room

Up the pole (*Peoples'*, 1896 on). Drunk

Plaintiff. I did not; but your little girl was frequently saying that you were 'up the poll'

The Judge. Up the what?—Up the poll, sir

What is that?—You know, sir. Up the poll.

The Judge · I don't know

The High Bailiff explained that the term was a slang one for being intoxicated —*D T*, 11th December 1897

The approach to drunkenness is 'getting on the pole'.

Up to date (*Soc. and Peoples'*, 1873 on). Total modernity

The two principals were made up like Corbett and Fitzsimmons, and the entertainment was a triumph of 'the up to-date' —*Peoples'*, 4th April 1897.

Up to the scratch (*Peoples'*, 19 *cent*). Fit, sufficient, allowable. Said to be from the lady committee of Almacks approving of names submitted to them by scratching some cabalistic mark intimating that the owner of the name might be allowed to enter Almacks 'Not up to the scratch' referred to the fact that all who applied for entrance were not found worthy. Said to have been started by Beau Brummel

The picture-destroyer pays his polite attentions to Mr Herbert as well as to Mr Alma Tadema. Who can say after this that Mr Herbert's pictures are not up to the scratch?—*Entr'acte*, 30th May 1885

Up-end (*Street*, 1880 on). Fling down heavily, so that the heels fly up. Used figuratively for amazement—as 'I was fair-upended!'

Up-keep (*Soc.*, 1897). Maintenance, keeping up, keeping as a going concern First noticed in print in this year

The Council has now resolved to relieve local authorities of the cost of the up-keep of those places which they at present defray —*D T*, 1st December 1897

Upper and downer (*Lower People*). Wrestling struggle, in which combatants upset, but rarely if ever strike, each other. Generally for a bet.

Upper ten set (*Servants'*) Ladies and gentlemen employed by the upper ten thousand Phrase found by themselves for themselves

Uppertendom (*New York*) Word coined from upper ten.

Use (*High Church*, 1890 on). Function.

On Palm Sunday the benediction of palms carried in procession was more than ever the 'use', not merely in very advanced Anglican churches, and in more than one case a bishop was the chief officiator.—*World*, April 1897.

Usher of the hall (*Soc.*, 1883). Odd kitchen man—male. Equivalent of char or chore woman.

Mr M'Coan asked as to the sentence upon George Gardiner, described as a tutor, charged with stealing a jug of beer and sentenced to six weeks' imprisonment. Sir W. Harcourt, amid much laughter, explained that owing to the custom in large establishments of the odd man being called 'the Usher of the Hall', a position held by Gardiner, the writer of the newspaper paragraph had converted him into a tutor.—*House of Commons*, 19th April 1883.

Util (*Theatrical*). Utility. The util actor in a company. He is the odd man—ready to do anything. Generally a clever man who has missed his mark.

V

V.C. (*London*, about 1882). Plucky. The initials of Victoria Cross.

V.C. (*American-Eng.*, 19 *cent.*). Abbreviation of Vigilance Committee. A body of American neighbours bound together to punish an evil-doer, murderer, highwayman, horse-stealer, or unscrupulous sensualist who contrives to evade the law. Chiefly operates in out-lying and southern districts. 'Take care, or you'll be V.C.'d' (veeceed). (*See* Burke, Wainwright).

V.R. (*Peoples'*). Evasive reference to the prison van, which, in the reign of Victoria, bore these initials on each side. (*See* Black Maria, Virtue rewarded, Vagabonds removed, Sardine box).

V.R., V.R., V.R. (*Jubilee*, 1897). Ve are, ve are, ve are=we are, we are, we are. One of the jocular readings of 'V.R.' during the Diamond Jubilee. Applied to a placard in Kensington when the Queen visited that suburb (28th June 1897).

Vagabonds removed (*Peoples'*). Droll application of the initials V.R. —the letters standing, of course, for Victoria Regina, which appeared on the outside of the prison van to the end of the reign of Victoria.

Vales (*Soc.*, 18 *cent.*). Presents to servants. Still used in old houses.

Valse (*Anglo-Amer.*). Synonym for airy walking, especially in quitting a room. (*See* Balley, Polka, Skip).

Vanderbilt (*American*). The U.S.A. synonym for Rothschild (*q.v.*). To describe a very rich man—the Vanderbilts of New York being historical millionaires.—1884.

Vapourage (*American*). Medical vapour bathing.

Vardy the carsey (*Criminal*). Italian. Look at the house. One of the Italian organ-men's expressions—passed on. From 'vedere' and 'casa'.

Variant (*Lit.*, '90's). Variation, divergency.

He piloted *Florodora* into the harbour of safety by his diverting variant of John Wellington Wells.—*D. T.*, 13th November 1899.

Variety stage (*Music Hall*, 1880). As distinct from the dramatic. Outgrowth of the prosperity of music halls.

Varnish (*Soc.*, 19 *cent.*). Bad champagne.

Vary means (*Polit.*, 18 *cent.*). Contradict, turn-coat, prevaricate. Introduced by Burke. Held its ground until 1840.

The contradiction between his methods is due, he pleads, to the identity of the object at which he aimed then, and at which he aims now. He varies his means, as Burke expressed it, to secure the essential unity of his end.—W. E. Gladstone (Edinburgh, 11th November 1885).

Venture girl (*Anglo-Indian*). Early Victorian. Poor young lady sent out to India to obtain a husband.

Verandah (*S. London*). The gallery of the old Victoria theatre.

Very familionaire (*Soc.*, 1870). Referring to the shape of patronage displayed by rich men. Derived from the satirist Heine.

Very froncey (*Soc.*, 19 *cent.*). Too pronounced. Shape of Très Français. Supposed to be an elegant evasion of saying a given thing is vulgar.

Very well (*Soc.*, 1860 on). Second degree of approval—Not Bad being the first.

Vestrify (*Parliamentary*, 1884) To minimise; to reduce in dignity.

Mr Chaplin has enriched the English dictionary with the verb 'vestrify', which is perhaps destined to a longer life than the somewhat uncouth verb 'boycott'.—*D. N.*, 31st December 1884

Vic (*Theatrical*) When the first theatre was built in the New Cut (Lambeth) it was called the Brunswick, in honour of the Princess Charlotte It was burnt down before it was opened, and by the time it was rebuilt the poor Princess Charlotte was dead, and the eyes of the nation turned to the Princess Victoria The new theatre was baptized the Royal Victoria, cut down by the New Cut warriors to Vic, before the first dramatic week was out Strangely enough, the Princess Royal came to be called by this prompt diminutive She is often thus named in the Queen's Diary. (*See* Bird, Brit, 'Delphi, Eff, Lane).

Viewy (*Political*, 1860-70) Mistrustedly theoretical, *dilletante*, lacking breadth Invented in opposition to the philosophy of J S Mill Remained as a condemnatory adjective

Village blacksmith (*Music Hall—passing to theatres*) An artiste who never has a longer engagement than a week. Euphemism for a failure Figuratively derived from a verse in Longfellow's poem

'*Week in, week out*, from noon till night
You can hear his bellows roar'

Vintage (*Anglo-American*). Year of birth.

'I want to sue a man for breach of promise,' said a maiden of the vintage of 1842, coming into a lawyer's office—*N Y. Mercury*, 1883

Virgins' bus (*Peoples'*, 1870) The last bus from Piccadilly Corner westward. So named satirically in reference to the character of the chief patronesses at that late hour. No longer runs—the tubes bowled over this vehicle (*See* Covered brougham)

Virtue rewarded (*Peoples'*). Prison van—ironical reference to the moral nature of its occupants, and based upon the initials V R, which used to be seen on each side

Vogue (*Soc.*, 1897) Fashion This word was markedly used only early in 1897

A remarkable instance of the commercial value of 'vogue' in art occurred at Christie's on Saturday.—*D T*, 8th March 1897

Voice, To (*Soc*, 1897 on). Assert, declare loudly This use of a noun as a verb is very significant of public life

London yesterday voiced the very spirit of the country—*D T*, 17th October 1899.

Volunteer knee drill. Abject adulation Outcome of volunteer movement.

Vote khaki, To (*Peoples'*, 1900). Opting for the Conservatives, plumping for the Liberal Unionist First heard in the May of 1900

One would give something to hear Mr Hosea Biglow's opinion upon 'voting khaki'—*M Leader*, W Archer, 27th October 1900

Voulez-vous squatty-vous? (*Theatre gods'*). Will you sit down? One of the half French nonsense phrases which began with the frequency of French *emigrés* and prisoners in England Started by Grimaldi

W

W 2. (*Peoples'*, 1896) Double-u Two—satirical description of the Emperor William II, following on his telegram to President Kruger on New Year's Day 1896. Said of any military-looking man stalking town

W P B (*Press*) Waste paper basket. Ominous initials—generally referring to communications

If the criticism or remark is nice, I read and enjoy it, if it is nasty, it is thrown into the W P B, and it troubles me not'—*Ref*, 2nd March 1884

I should say the printer's devil picked up the pieces from the editor's W.P B, and handed them in for copy

Wabbler (*Sporting*) Pedestrian.

Mr Edward Payson Weston, the well-known long-distance pedestrian, illustrated 'endurance without alcohol' by walking 50 miles in ten hours, or rather in nine hours fifty minutes, for the 'wabbler' saved ten minutes of his advertised time

Wad (*Navy*). Gunner—interesting as a survival from the days of muzzle-loading cannon.

Wade in (*American*). To begin a fight. This expression was begun during the Civil War, and was probably started by some farmer recruits who obtained the figure of speech from the memory of the courage with which ducklings take to the water almost as soon as born.

Waggernery, O (*Lower Soc.*, '80's). New shape of 'O agony', based upon the ignorant contempt for the great German, Wagner, through this decade.

Waistcoat piece (*Tailors'*). Breast and neck of mutton—from its resemblance to the shape of half the front of a waistcoat not made up. (*See* Hyde Park railings.)

Waistrel (*Lancashire and the North generally—old*). A wretched, half-starved wanderer.

Wait (*Theatrical*). Time between the acts; the time between the appearances of an actor in the same piece.

Wait till the clouds roll by (*Peoples'*, 1884). Catch line used to induce hopefulness—from an American ballad, in which this phrase formed the chief feature of the chorus.

Wherever I have been lately and found the people festively inclined I have gathered that they intend to 'wait till the crowds roll by'.—*Ref.*, August 1884.

Wait a quarter of a sec! (*Society*). Intensification of 'Half a sec!' Protest against being over-hurried.

Wake snakes (*American - Eng.*). Provoke to the uttermost.

Walk out (*American - Eng.*, *Theatrical*, 1890 on). Failure—from the American habit of condemning a bad play before it is over by going home. Reached England by way of Liverpool.

I am delighted to find, on the assurance of the author, that though New York 'walked out', Washington 'walked in' and received it warmly, and the Boston audience gave it a most enthusiastic reception also.—*D. T.*, 24th February 1897.

Walk out with the bat (*Soc.*, 1880). Victory—from the last cricketer in an innings taking his bat out, the last player but one having 'gone out'.

Walk turkey (*American - Eng.*). Promenade with constrained effort, like the movement of the turkey.

Walking round (*Peoples' — old*). Preparing for assault. From dogs walking round each other to look for the safest attack.

Walled (*Artists'*, 1882). Picture accepted—took the place of hung.

Wallop down (*Com. Lond.*). To fall with a crash.

Waltzing off on the ear (*American*). A person who acts upon the first word to which he happens to listen.

Wander (*Street*, 19 *cent.*). Satirical expression and meaning 'Be off'.

Want of proportion (*Criticism*, 1883). Term providing a new shape of attack upon the inductive process. Attributed to Mr Theodore Watts Dunton.

Want to score (*Peoples'*). Desire to succeed. From scoring, or marking in all athletic and many other exercises.

He was engaged in the most difficult scenes of a risky play. And he helped it, not because he 'wanted to score', but because he is a thorough artist, and knows the responsibility of his business.—*D. T.*, 6th January 1896.

Wants a apron (*Workman's*). Out of work—the apron off.

Wants salt (*American - English*, 1880 on). Wants grit.

Oh, thunder, you want salt on you. A super is an adjunct to the stage.—*Bad Boy's Diary*, 1883.

War Cry (*Salvation Army*, 1882-83). The 'huzza' of this body and of religious, and a title to their peculiar newspaper.

That's a very pretty dona, though, I came across in Regent Street the other evening who sold me a *War Cry*.—1883.

War-cry (*Public-house*, 1882). Mixture of stout and mild—ale understood. Applied satirically by 'topers' because the Salvation Army spoke stoutly and ever used mild terms. (*See* Brighton bitter, Cold four, Baby and nurse.)

War-paint (*Soc.*, 1875). Court, state, and evening dress in general—jewels, white gloves, etc., etc. Derived from North American Indians who always painted themselves when going into battle. (*See* Full fig.)

Wardour Street woods (*Cabinet-makers'*). Imitation old furniture, knocked together yesterday. Name obtained from Wardour Street (Soho,

London), because that place is or was supposed to be the headquarters of this business. (*See* Worm eater)

Warm as they make them (*Street*) Immoral.

Warm bit (*Com London*, 1880). Vigorous woman

Warm corner (*Soc*, *Sporting*) A nook where birds are found in plenty

Warm with (*London Taverns*). Refers to orders for spirits and water, the 'with' refers to sugar.

Warrocks (*American — passing to Eng*) Beware! This seems to be a corruption of war-hawks — meaning tomahawks Certainly it is menacing and comes originally from the vocabulary of the North American Indians.

Warwick weed (*Warwickshire*) Warwick *elm*. Disguised self-glorification of the splendour of the county elms.

Passing through the ridge and furrow country where the elm, the 'Warwickshire weed', rises straight out of the corn, etc —*D N*, August 1885

Warwickshire Will Name given to Shakespeare in his county

Washer-dona (*Com Lond.*, 19 *cent*) Washer woman.

Watch him like a hawk (*Hist*) Watch to the very death

Hawks were tamed by watching Shakespeare has several allusions to this Desdemona in assuring Cassio how she will urge his suit with Othello, says

'I'll watch him tame, and talk him out of patience'

Selden, in his *Table Talk*, says 'Lecturers get a great deal of money, because they preach the people tame, as a man watches a hawk'

Watchers (*Election*). Euphemism for spies on the look out for bribery

Water-bottle (*Street*) Total abstainer. (*See* Rum-bottle, Milk-bottle, Ink-bottle, etc , etc)

Water down (*Political*) Weaken —minimise results

It is no use increasing the number of voters if you water down and minimise the political influence which the vote confers —Mr J Chamberlain, 13th June 1883.

Water dona (*Lower Class*) Washer-woman—a lady who disports herself in water, together with soap and suds.

Waterloo (*Streets*, 19 *cent* to about 1870). Half-penny—as thus There was a half-penny toll over Waterloo Bridge, on the Surrey side of which lived most of the poorer common women who harassed the Strand As midnight arrived, these moneyless women who hung about Wellington Street at the Strand end of the bridge begged for a 'Waterloo' to pay their toll over the bridge

Wauns (*Peoples'*, *provincial*). Wounds — God's wounds Another shape of zounds

Wauns — so sound that they never wake? I wish my wife lay there — Farquhar, *The Recruiting Officer*

Way of all flesh (*Peoples'*) Dead —probably from Puritanic phrase

Weak in the arm (*Public-house*) Caustic euphemism for a short pull of beer, as compared with the long pull Chiefly refers to half-pint drawn in a pint pot

Weaken (*Amer.*, 1880) Soften.

Wears a revolver-pocket (*Doubtful Soc*, 1880 on) Evasive statement to the effect that the speaker carries a revolver.

The hateful and barbarous custom of carrying these deadly weapons has risen to an incredible height, it has long been known to the Home Office, who need only to have asked the tailors how many revolver pockets they now make — Mitchell Henry, *Times*, 23rd January 1885

Wears the broad arrow (*Thieves'*) Elegant evasion of a reference to convict life (*See* Taken stripes)

Wears the head large (*Low. Mid-class*) Recovering from alcoholic excess

It was half-past six before all was over, and during the day heads were worn large —*Ref*, 15th August 1886

Wears the leek (*Popular*) Is a Welshman It seems likely that the wearing of the leek actually came into usage when Henry VII conquered at Bosworth by the aid of his Welsh followers under the Tudor colours, white and green, suggestive of the leek itself. To this view a Harleian MS, written by a Welshman, in the time of James I., gives some grounds

Weasel (*East Anglia*) Bribe—probably from this animal slimly introducing himself into pocket-like rabbit holes.

Weases (*Amer.*). People of S. Carolina.

Weather peeper (*Nautical*). Best eye.

Web-foots (*Provincial*). People of Lincolnshire, probably bestowed upon them by their higher county neighbours, who did not live in the wretched fens of Lincolnshire. Also called yellow-bellies. Taken together suggestive of fen-game, such as wild ducks and geese, widgeon, all common to the fens. In the States, most of the state nicknames are derived from the flora, fauna, or prevailing geology of the district.

Why English people give each other comical names is a question fitter for a learned essay than a descriptive sketch: but the fact remains that we have besides Yorkshire 'tykes', Norfolk 'dumplings', Cheshire 'cats', Essex 'calves', and Suffolk 'punches', as well as Lincolnshire folk, who are web-foots.—*D. N.*, August 1884.

This term web-foot is applied to the people of Oregon—but as an alternative to web-foot they are often called hard-cases.

Wedge (*Thieves'*). Jew. A wedge fixes objects or breaks them up. So a Jew-fence, in relation with thieves, or a Jew ordinary, in his everyday business, is supposed to 'wedge' the other.

Wee-wees (*Peoples'—Hogarth period*). Frenchmen—from the habit of Frenchmen, common to this day, of repeating the ordinary affirmative *oui*.

This looks very much as if the English race were dwindling into a people of town-loafers, afraid to risk themselves in new enterprises in rude lands, and as incapable of being genuine colonists as the despised 'men of Wee Wee'—the French.—*D. N.*, 20th October 1886.

Weed out (*Polit.*, 1870). Change politics.

The Chairman had said that he had no hesitation in saying that if Mr Goschen did not weed himself out of the Liberal party, the Liberal party would not attempt to weed him out.—Mr J. Morley, Nottingham, October 1885.

Weeper (*Soc.*, 1884). Long sweeping moustache. Probably adapted from the long ends of crape worn at funerals until burial reform (1866-67) swept them away.

Weg (*Polit.*, 1885). Initials of William Ewart Gladstone. Given in memory of Mr Wegg (*Our Mutual Friend*), who was a great sayer of words.

It seems that in 1857 a speech was delivered by a Mr James Hall who called Weg a great political coward. This speech is now reprinted in the *Globe* nearly thirty years afterwards.—*Ref.*, 17th May 1885.

(*See* G. O. M.)

Welcher or welsher (*Racing*). A cheat. When a book-maker does not pay his debts after a race he is often fallen upon with cries of 'welcher', and his clothes almost as often are torn off his back. It is said the word takes its rise from the name of a man who, after repeated warnings, was the first to suffer from this adaptation of Lynch law.

Weigh in (*American-Eng.*). Assert oneself—from weighing, in horse-racing.

The journal 'weighs in' with a prismatic Christmas number.—*D. N.*, November 1885.

Weigh out (*L. London*). Give one his fair share. Fine idea of the distribution of stolen plate melted down to avoid identification.

'I made Criss weigh out my share!'—*Peoples'*, 6th January 1895.

Weighing the thumb (*L. Class*, 19 *cent.*). Cheating in weight by sticking down the scale with the thumb, so as to give the idea of full weight, and then seizing the scale before the rebound occurs.

For practising the old trick of 'weighing his thumb' to the disadvantage of the customer, a City coster, named James Martin, who said he thought it 'a light affair', was directed to pay a fine of 20s. and costs.—*D. T.*, 25th August 1896.

Well (*Soc.*, 1860). Capital, very good, satisfactory. Used as an adjective instead of an adverb.

Well certainly (*American Soc.*). This phrase is very common in U.S.A.—now and again used in England.

Well-groomed (*Peoples'*, 1881). Perfectly dressed. From the stables, when the highest praise is to speak of a horse as well-groomed.

Well-sinking (*Anglo-Indian*, 18 *cent.* on). Digging for treasure. Generally—making money.

Questioned as to why he had no pension for his wounds, Fraser stated that after the relief of Lucknow he bought his discharge, he had then upwards of £200 He got the money by 'well sinking', i e, the discovery of buried treasure —*People*, 22nd September 1895.

Well shod (*Anglo-American*). Well off. Specimen of figurative slang—a horse only going prosperously when well shod

Well sot up (*Provincial American*) Well-dowried Only said of middle-class brides, chiefly agriculturally.

Wellingtons (*Mid-class*, 1812 on). Plural of Wellington, and referring to boots named after the Iron Duke 'Where are my Wellingtons?' (*See* Von Blucher)

Wen, The (*Middle-class*) London —from its shape, and figuratively from its absorbing quality.

Cobbett called the London of his day 'The Wen'. The movement of the rural population townwards was only then beginning —*D. N*, 26th June 1885

Wet a line (*Anglers'*) Go fishing

Year by year the communications with the lovely Thames Valley have been increased until there is no difficulty in the way of the Thames angler 'wetting a line'

Wet-bobs (*Eaton*) Bobs means boys—the phrase designates boating Etonians, as distinct from dry-bobs, or cricketers

Wet canteen (*Military*) Where liquors are sold. Antithesis of dry canteen — which is the stores-centre of the barracks, where all things but beer may be obtained—on payment

Wet ship (*Nautical*) Ship in which captain and company drink deeply.

Wet 'uns (*Low Class*, 19 *cent*) Wet ones—meaning tears.

Whack up (*American, from Irish*) To subscribe

Whales (*American—passing to England*) Desperately devoted

'The Red Lamp' belongs to the Princess Claudia Morakoff, who is whales on Nihilist-hunting —*Ref*, 24th April 1887.

What a bean feast! (*Peoples'*). Satirical exclamation in reference to a riot, quarrel, or wretched meal; or other entertainment (*See* Bean feast)

What a Collins! (*Exeter*, 19 *cent*) Greedy person—evidently from name of a gourmand who has long since been forgotten

What a tale our cat's got (*Peoples' proverbial—old*). Figure of speech to describe a woman or girl flaunting in a new dress, and swinging the hind part of the skirt from side to side with a haughty motion of the hips.

What do you think? (*Mid-class*, 1882) What is your general opinion of things? Introduced in this year by a comic singer, who interpolated the enquiry at various strong points in his song, accent on '*you*'

What ho! she bumps! (*London* 1899) Satirical cry upon any display of vigour—especially feminine. Said to be derived from a report of a boating adventure, where this term was used as 'she' fetched land A popular song made this term more popular.

To see Willie Edouin dance a hornpipe is a liberal education, and his official proclamation, 'I trade in bumps Oblige me by not saying, "What ho!"' almost tempted an Ibsenite to smile —*D. T*, 13th November 1899

What next, and next? (*Peoples'*, 19 *cent.*). Exclamation signifying contempt for audacious assertion A favourite phrase of William Cobbett's

The Tories must be hard up for a stick to bang Gladstone with when the *Globe* actually has to reprint an attack upon him from the *Oswestry Observer* of 1857 Ye gods! what next, and next?—*Ref*, 17th May 1885.

What Paddy gave the drum (*Irish Military*, 1845) Elegant euphemism for a sound thrashing, as 'I'll give you what Paddy gave the drum'.

What the Connaught man shot at (*Irish*) Roundabout for 'nothing at all'

'What the Connaught man shot at' has been of late far from 'nothing'.—*D N*, 1888

(*See* Footless stocking without a leg.)

What the hell! (*Peoples'*) Exclamation of anger. Is it one of the Catholic corruptions? 'What the hail!'—from 'Hail, Mary'?

What will you liq.? (*Middle-class*). What will you drink?

What would Mrs Boston say? (*American-Eng*, 1850 on) Equivalent to—What would Mrs Grundy say? Sometimes heard in England The people of Boston hold Boston to be the most superior city in the U.S.A.

Whatchir! (*Sailors'*). Shape of 'What cheer?'

What-er, A (*Street*). Shape of 'what'—thus formed in answer to some reply as to what the speaker is. He may say I'm a chimbler (chimney-sweep)—to which the reply, always in response to a noun ending in 'er'—'A what-er?'

What's the dynamite now? (*Soc.*, 1890 on). Protest against a burst of ill-temper, as suggestive of blowing people up.

What's the hullaballoo? (*Peoples'*, 18 *cent.* and 19 *cent.*). Riot, noise, contention. Is this one of the Catholic corruptions—is it 'What's the holy belly'—'Ventre Saint Gris'—the nickname of Henri IV. of Navarre—and referring to the dead, therefore grey, body of Christ. On the other hand, 'Hurliberlieu' is a French term.

What's the lyddite? (*Boer War*, 1899-1900). Latest shape of 'What's the row?'

What's the mat? (*Public-school*, 1880). Abbreviation of 'matter'.

What's yer fighting weight? (*Street*, 1883). 'At what weight do you fight, and are you fit? I'm your man!'

What's yer Gladstone weight? (*Street*, 1885). Satirical shape of 'What's your fighting weight?' Means that the speaker doubts if you will fight if invited. From the disrepute into which Mr Gladstone passed with the Jingoes, or war party, for his alleged unwillingness to carry on the war in the Soudan with eagerness.

What's your poll to-day? (*Printers'*, 19 *cent.*). Amount of piece wages—from numbers on a statement of votes.

Whaty?, A (*Peoples'*, 18 *cent.*). An enquiry made when any strange statement is made: *e.g.*, 'He's a jimjack'—'A whaty?'—'A jimjack.' This diminutive is probably of court descent; for all the familiar memoirs of George III. give an anecdote of his defiance to some peeress to fog him with Scotch, and his immediate defeat, when he cried 'A whaty, my lady—a whaty?' The popular interchange of 'v' and 'w', which has now utterly passed away, was a singular evidence of even the lowest of the people accepting and adopting the early royal Georgian modes of pronouncing English. Sam Weller made this mode classic. Old puns reek with it. 'Oh—it's a wherry is it?—werry good, etc., etc.'

Wheel-house, Abaft the (*Amer.*). Below the small of the back.

The next instant a huge bull charged out of the door, and, catching the hero of Valley Forge abaft the wheelhouse, incontinently slammed him into a big apple tree.—*Newsp. Cutting.*

Wheeled (*Low Life*). Moved upon wheels, as distinct from wheel, which is 'barrered' (*q.v.*). Instance of expressed awe in the contemplation of unaccustomed luxury. That is wheeled—in a cab.

Wheeze (*Theatr.*). Gag, *i.e.*, lines (usually comic) interpolated in the text by the player.

Wheezer (*Music Hall*, 1897). Phonograph.

Whelps (*American*). People of Tennessee.

When at Rome do as Rome does (*Proverbial*). Recommendation to fall in with the arrangements of those about you. Counsel to be not too conscientious.

Where are you a-going to—can't yer! (*Low. London*, 1880). Really meaning, Take care who you're shoving against.

Where did you get the Rossa? (*Peoples'*, 1885). Enquiry as to borrowed plumes. Arose from the trial of a Mrs Dudley (New York, July 1885) for shooting at O'Donovan Rossa.

When Rossa said his name was Jeremiah O'Donovan Rossa, Mrs Dudley asked, 'Where did you get the Rossa?'—*D. N.*, 1st July 1885.

It was supposed that the Rossa was a flight of fancy. This phrase commenced in New York, thence went to Liverpool and over all England.

Where do I come in? (*Peoples'*, '90's). Personal protest. From a police-court case in which a shrew put this question until she was turned out.

'Where', to use a phrase which Mr Labouchere has made Parliamentary, 'do we come in?' Unfortunately, we do not come in at all.—*D. T.*, 5th August 1899.

Where the flies won't get it (*American*). To swallow 'it'—generally drink.

Where's the war? (*Peoples'*, 1900). Applied to some scattered and divided street wrangle From the Boer War after June 1900—when both sides seemed to be distributed over creation, and never appeared to get really face to face.

Whig (*Mid-class*, 1860-99). Irresolute person—even a turncoat From the Whig, in parliament, being generally a temporiser.

Whipped out of one's boots (*American*). Completely conquered.

Whirl (*Anglo-American*). A stormy turn, a general challenge

Whisht (*Provincial*). Dangerous—to be avoided. Probably an onomatope from the catching of the breath in fear

Companionship offered to such beings (Protestant nuns) in a remote rural neighbourhood in England was not all kindly They were 'whisht' women, even witches, to the rustics—*D. N.*, 29th December 1884

Whiskbroom 'with' (*American-Eng.*, 1897) Cry describing drunkenness This phrase came from U S.A on 8th of July 1897

Prohibition (U S A) has always been followed by a remarkable display of ingenuity in evasion, but, according to Miss Kate Field, no State ever evaded the prohibitory law so neatly as Kansas Desiring to purchase a whiskbroom when on a lecture tour out there, Miss Field went into a druggist's where they were displayed in the window. 'Will you have one with or without?' asked the man behind the counter 'I do not understand your meaning,' she replied Holding up two whiskbrooms apparently exactly alike, he parted the wisps of one, disclosing a small flask, and with a little whirl of his thumb and finger the top of the broom came off, like the cork out of a bottle Miss Field bought the two whiskbrooms, one for ordinary use, the other to exhibit to audiences as an argument in her lecture, 'Does Prohibition Prohibit?'—*D T.*, 8th July 1897

The whiskbroom is a small coir brush about a foot long

Whisker-fake (*Theatrical*). Cosmetic for facial hair

Whiskeries (*London*, 1888) Irish Exhibition in London.

Early on Monday morning I arose and donned my caubeen, my brogues and other things, and lighting my dhudeen, and selecting my finest shillelagh, went off to Olympia to assist at the opening of the Whiskyries, otherwise the Irish Exhibition.—*Ref*, 10th June 1888

Whisky-bottle (*Scotch*) A Scotch drunkard

Whisky stalls (*Press*, 1883). End stalls, or near the end, so that an occupier can adjourn to the refreshment bar without much inconvenience to himself, or a long line of neighbours.

Whisky straight (*American Saloon*) Whisky—with no water about it

Whispering gallery (*Theatrical*, 1883) The then Gaiety Bar—long since razed, and its site aiding in the formation of the front of Aldwych. Derived from the Whispering Gallery of St Paul's Cathedral. Said in satire of the poorer actors 'out of a ship', who frequented that hostelry, and whispered to any one of their more fortunate brethren—as, 'Could you lend me half a dollar?' (*See* Pros' Avenue)

Whist drive (*Soc.* 1895) Whist—where the players are shifted, at the end of a rubber, to other tables and other players.

Whistle for wind (*Peoples'*, 19 *cent.*). Description of a fool

The reef-points clatter upon your fair white mainsail and the helmsman whistles softly for the wind which will not come—Sir E Arnold, *D T*, 31st March 1897

Whistler (*E London*). Chance labourer at docks—from the poor fellow whistling for work

Only fifty men were wanted beyond the 'royals', or regular hands. So a hundred and fifty needy 'whistlers'—the dock term for chance labourers—had to turn with heavy hearts away—*Ref*, 29th March 1885

Whistler (*Soc*, 1880). Misty, dreamy, milky, softly opalescent atmosphere—from many peculiarly exceptional pictures painted by the artist of this name Came to be applied to ethics, æsthetics, and even conversation, where the doctrines enunciated were foggy

The river, too, never looks better than on one of these 'Whistler' evenings Symphonies in silver and gold and blue and purple and cold grey are to be found on the embankments, notably on the south of the river, for the trouble of going there. — *D. N.*, 11th November 1884.

Whistlers (*Scotland*). Bag-pipers.

In their native wilds, the people of Fife are known as 'whistlers', not on account of their musical proclivities, but because their country take its name from a very highly-pitched musical instrument, between which and a 'whistle' the Caledonian ear distinguishes little difference. —*D. T.*, 4th March 1898.

White Army, The (*Street*, 1883). A band of men who formed themselves together to combat social evil.

Another 'army' has been formed. This time it is a band of youths and men who are to wear a white cross, and battle against the social evil. The White Army may be very earnest, but if it is to parade the streets like the other armies it will be just what it is formed to put down.—*Ref.*, 18th February 1883.

White Brahmins (*Anglo-Indian*, 19 *cent.*). Excessively exclusive persons. Invented by Hindoo satire to describe the Brahminic-like exclusiveness of those of the English in India, who wished to prevent the native Indian from obtaining any power.

When Indians mean to be sarcastic, they denominate the English in India White Brahmins.—*D. N.*, 9th December 1884.

White elephant (*Soc.*, 18 *cent.* and on). An article (generally large and expensive), for which you have no use. Again, a present which entails more expense than advantage, one generally bestowed by a donor who wishes to relieve himself of a burden. Derived from a habit of the remoter Kings of Siam, who, when they wished to ruin a courtier, made him a present of a white elephant, whose sacred nature made his keep and that of his attendants so expensive that the owner was necessarily reduced to beggary.

White horse (*Irish*). Cowardice. Derived from the tradition that James II. fled from the battle of the Boyne on a white horse.

White light (*Railway—now spread to Peoples'*). All right, correct, safe. From a white light throughout the railway world representing safety, and freedom from danger. (*See* All over red, Be green.)

White magic (*Soc.*, 19 *cent.*). In general, innocent legerdemain, but figuratively applied to very beautiful fair women. Also applied by Protestant writers to the Roman Catholic ritual.

White nigger (*Negro*). Term of contempt and offence used by blacks against white folk.

The emancipated blacks of Sierra Leone not only address each other as 'niggers', but salute as 'white niggers' all Europeans with whom they are not on friendly terms.—*D. N.*, 20th June 1883.

White soup (*Thieves'*). Melted silver—run down from stolen plate, to avoid identification.

One or two colleges at Oxford have a crozier or so of the fourteenth century, or a platter of the time of Edward IV. But most of the college plate made 'white soup' at the time of the Civil War, and went unavailingly to buy horses and feed men for the King.—*D. N.*, 5th May 1887.

Whitechapel (*Peoples'*, 1888). Woman murder. In and about 1888 a number of women of the town in the East of London were murdered and mutilated. Before the year was out a woman murder came to be called a Whitechapel.

When charged prisoner said he knew nothing about the murder; he was very drunk. A witness who worked with him said he had heard Nicholson say, 'I shall do a Whitechapel on my wife yet'.

Whitechapel oner (*Local London*). A leader of light and youth in the Aldgate district—chiefly in the high coster interests. (*See* Roader.)

Whitechapel warriors (*E. London*). Militia of the Aldgate district.

Whitechokery (*Peoples'*, 1870). Figure of speech for the general scheme of life maintained by the various classes who wear white neckties habitually—or only in the evening.

Whitehall (*Military*, 19 *cent.*). Metaphor of cheerfulness. When a soldier has leave of absence to London, his sergeant probably says to him, 'Don't go near Whitehall, or we shan't see you to time'. This refers to the fact that a soldier can generally get an extension of leave of absence if he makes personal application for it at the Horse Guards, which is the very heart of Whitehall. It is popularly supposed in the army that if a soldier on leave goes near Whitehall he cannot resist the temptation to apply for extra leave. Hence when a soldier looks particularly cheerful, it is said of him, 'He's been to Whitehall'.

White-washed (*Builders'*) Compounded with creditors or passed through the bankruptcy court

Whittington Priory (*Debtors'*) Holloway prison for debt—from its propinquity to Highgate, and the associations of Highgate with Whittington

Whittling (*Polit*) Niggling and reducing things by fragments. From the ancient and past away habit of agricultural Americans, shaving away a stick with a clasp-knife, while talking Is now used for petty, wasteful action, as distinct from sheer evident work

Lord Salisbury put forward with great ingenuity and ability what he called the Tory programme at Newport. He has since been engaged in whittling it away until what was little before has become small by degrees and beautifully less, until there is hardly any of it left for your consideration — Mr Chamberlain (Birmingham), 3rd November 1885

Who are yer? (*Street*, 1883) Enquiry in an offensive tone, made in the street, and which, when answered, usually receives the counter-enquiry, 'who are *you*?'

Who did you say? (*L. Streets'*, '90's) Satire levelled at a passing person of evident, or self-asserting importance, and uttered by one friend to another, without any preliminary statement on any side.

Who pawned her sister's ship? (*Local London, Clare Market, Strand*). The meaning of the term is quite obscure, but during the last year of this historical ramshackle and labyrinthine spot, this sentence would always create a burst of laughter amongst the intimates of that doubtful locality. May have been an evasion of 'shift'

Who shot the dog? (*L. C.*, '60's) Term of contempt levelled at volunteers, who were not at their initiation popular with the masses, who had not got over the revulsion of feeling in favour of the real soldier The phrase arose from the rash shooting of a dog in the streets by a Surrey Volunteer.

'Who shot the dog?' was a very ill-natured cry prevalent in London streets in the early days of the Volunteer movement, and was supposed to refer to a misadventure of some rifleman who had inadvertently shot a dog —*D T* (G A Sala), 28th July 1894

Who stole the goose? (*Peoples' —provincial*). Interjection of contempt, which appears to have some hidden meaning, probably of an erotic nature

Who sups with the devil must have a long spoon (*Historical*) Brought into fashion again by Mr J Chamberlain (1898), meaning of course, that in dealings with rascals one must keep one's eye open—said in reference to Russia's action in China

Who took it out of you? (*Street*) Meaning wholly unknown to people not absolutely of lower class

Who? who? (*Soc*, 1852) Doubtful, to be mistrusted. From a parliamentary episode

The 'Who? who? Government' The story went that the Duke of Wellington, asking Lord Derby one evening in the House of Commons for the names of the new Ministers, and knowing nothing of many of them, had to call out 'Who? who?' so often in tones audible to the whole House, that the attention of friends and enemies was alike attracted, and the humour of the day found a title for the Ministry out of the Duke's astonished and repeated enquiry —*D N*, 10th December 1884

Whoa, bust me (*Low London*) Protest. A very common expression through the 19th century

Whoa, carry me out (*Common London*, 19 *cent*) Here we have the protecting 'Whoa' preceding a droll affectation of being shocked to death, which involves being effectually carried out.

Whoa, Emma! (*Street*, '80's). Entreaty to be modified—addressed to women with marked appearance or behaviour in the streets It came from an inquest on a woman who had died under astounding circumstances She was suffering from inflammation; she induced her husband to allay her pain by the use of a small Dutch clock weight Finding relief from the contact of the cold iron, she urged the husband to continue the operation—whereupon she died. At the inquest the husband had to defend himself He urged that he said to his wife 'Whoa Emma!' over and over again, but she would not listen to him. For years this phrase lasted as a street protest, too often shot at drunken women. (*See* Outside Eliza, Now we're busy.)

Whoa, Jameson! (*Peoples'*, 1896). An admiring warning against plucky rashness. When Dr Jameson invaded the Transvaal, with a handful of men, and lost, the people recognised his equal pluck and rashness.

Whole hog (*Anglo - American*). Thorough bare-faced lie—derived in the first place from a recommendation to a man of Connecticut (where pork affords the chief menu) to go the whole hog—the man having made a statement as to a quantity of pork he had eaten. As usual with popular phrases, it passed into a song—'The whole Hog or None.'

Whole souled time (*American*, 1882). Perfect delight.

It was a whole-souled time, as the Americans call it — now unknown. — *Graphic*, 17th March 1883.

Whole team (*American*, 1878). Perfect, absolute — from the agricultural states, where the 'whole team' does the work.

It is an Americanism. We cannot tell who invented it, but it means that a man is in possession of uncommon powers of mind. That he is a whole team when he is smart; when he is very smart he is a whole team and a horse to spare, and when the smartest, a whole team and a horse to spare and a pair of coach dogs under the waggon.—*N. Y. Mercury*, 2nd March 1878.

Whole team and a little dog under the waggon (*American*). Distinguished, liberal, proper—said of anything.

Wholeskin brigade (*Transvaal War*). Cautious cowards in its general application, but in actual war meaning a regiment, battalion or brigade which has not been in action. Does not necessarily mean that the brigade in question has shirked action.

. . . the 'wholeskin brigade', to borrow a phrase from the pungent vocabulary of the British private in South Africa, etc. —*D. T.*, 31st October 1901.

Whoop up (*American*). To tune a musical instrument.

Whooperups (*Theatrical and Entertainment generally*). Inferior, noisy singers.

Whoy-oi! (*Street*). Cry used by coster - class upon sight of a gaily-dressed girl passing near them. Also the cry of welcome amongst London costermongers.

Whyms (*Club*, 1882). Consolidation into a word of the initials 'Y.M.C.A.' (*q.v.*).

Widow, The (*Army*, 1863 on). Affectionate name for Queen Victoria. In no way disparaging.

Widow, The (*Soc.*, 1850 on). Clicquot champagne — brand of *la Veuve Cliquot*, hence the term. (*See* Squat, Dutchman, etc.)

Wielder of the willow (*Sporting*). Cricketer—from the bats being made of this wood.

Wife out of Westminster (*Old English*). Doubtful spouse — sometimes still heard in the East of London.

Wig-faker (*Low. London*, 18 *cent.* on). Hair-dresser.

Wigs on the green (*Irish*, 18 *cent.*). Fighting. The Irish Parliament House (1782-1800) was on the Green, Dublin, in days when wigs were worn. The Green was the constant scene of riots, and as constantly wigs would strew the roadway. Still used figuratively all over Ireland.

In taking leave of Bayreuth and the 'Ring', I can only counsel a continuance of that policy of peace which seems happily to have been adopted both by ardent Wagnerites and by those who choose to cleave to the older ways of music. Twenty years ago, if the chroniclers tell us truth, it was almost a case of 'wigs on the green' at Festival time, to such heights did party feeling run.—*D. T.*, 25th August 1896.

Wild - goose (*American mining*). Promise of fortune. A thin vein of ore, generally referring to silver, which presages the discovery of valuable veins.

Wilhelm II. much (*Soc.*, 1898). Wilhelm Too much. Obvious chaff suggesting the extremely busy activity of the Emperor of Germany.

Will you short? (*Australian Tavern*). Pay for a small dose of spirits.

Willie — we have missed you (*Peoples'*, 1899). Welcome. In the 'fifties a ballad with this title was very popular. Finally it became a march which is played to this day. On 20th November the Emperor of Germany arrived at Portsmouth, and this march was the first music to welcome him when he came on shore.

While the inspection was in progress the band of the Royal Marine Light Infantry played 'Willie, we have missed you', a playful attention which pleased the Emperor, who heartily shook the bandmaster, Lieutenant Miller, by the hand as he passed. — *D. T.*, 21st November 1899

Willie—Willie—wicked, wicked! (*Street*) Satiric street reproach addressed to a middle-aged woman talking to a youth From a county court case in which a middle-aged landlady sued for a week's rent from a young man lodger whose defence was that he left the house because the plaintiff would not only come into his room, but would proceed to sit on his bed

Windfall (*Hist*) Unexpected fortune

Window (*Street*, 1860) Eye-glass—invented to meet the requirements of the round, rimless, stringless eye-glass which so many young men still carry, as by a miracle, in the right eye

Wine (*'Varsities*, 19 *cent*) Abbreviation of wine-party.

His first 'wine', given in his own room, was an awful ordeal. — *D. N.*, 6th March 1885.

(*See* Tea pot.)

Wing (*Theatrical*) Perform with much help from the prompter—who stands at the wing

Let us take the slang verb 'to wing' It indicates the capacity to play a rôle without knowing the text, and the word itself came into use from the fact that the artiste frequently received the assistance of a special prompter, who often stood upon the stage, but screened from the audience by a piece of the scenery or a wing —*Stage*, 31st August 1885

Wingers—sometimes called **Flanges** (*Colloquial* — about 1865) After the Crimean beard, which meant all the hair growable on the face, had lasted in fashion about ten or twelve years, the chin came to be once more shown, and the whiskers were thrown back, or pulled away from the cheeks, and allowed to grow as long as nature decided The name was obtained from their streaming and waving character

Winifred, O (*Peoples'*, '90's) Exclamation importing disbelief — from St Winifred's Well, in Wales

St Winifred's Well, in Flintshire, whose miraculous cures are the envy of Lourdes and the wonder of the North of England, is not to be turned into a soda-water manufactory without a struggle —*D T*, 15th December 1898

Wink (*American Saloon*). Dumb mode of ordering liquor.

Winter campaign (*Peoples'*, 1884). Riot, shrewishness, drunken disturbance—from the name given by the dynamiters to their operations in the winter months, when general darkness threw but little light upon their proceedings.

After the explosion of 30th May there was a lull, and then there commenced what, on the other side of the Atlantic, they were pleased to call the 'winter campaign'. There was an attempt to blow up London Bridge, then there was the explosion in the railway tunnel near King's Cross, and afterwards the explosions at Westminster and the Tower. *D N*, 3rd March 1885

Wipe off your chin (*American*, 1860) To drink a liqour—probably suggested by the habit of a bearded man wiping the moustache and beard about the chin, with the hand, after a drink. Also used as a recommendation to be silent—from chin being used to mean speech

Wiping feet (*Hoppers'—Kent*). Asking for beer-money Mode of asking for money from visitors to hop-fields The boots are brushed with hop-bines, and the money is waited for

Wire in and get your name up (*Peoples'*, 1862) Recommendation to struggle for success, but originally very erotic

By-and-bye, when the white heat of excitement is over, no one will be able to say that anybody connected with this maladorous squabble missed a chance of 'wiring in and getting his name up' — *Ref*, 21st October 1888

Without any (*L. Class*, 1890 on). Abstinence from any shape of alcohol. One of the elegant evasions.

The old lady made a curtsey to the Bench as she entered the dock, and repeated her obeisance when asked what she had to say She said she had gone for years 'without any', and was afraid she had taken too much —*D. T*, 17th December 1897

Without authorial expenses (*Literary*) Cheating, piracy, theft.

From this phrase being used against the U.S.A. to explain that the original English author has been paid nothing for the reprinted work.

Witness-stand (*American*). Witness-box in court of law. Rather a misnomer, as the witnesses are seated. In the English witness-box no witness is allowed a seat while he can keep his feet.

Talk of volubility, why, a darkey lady on the witness-stand is irrepressible. They are all ladies, and I observed that each of them referred to the other as a lady, even when she was an opponent.—*D. T.*, 2nd April 1897.

Woffle (*Music Hall and Music generally*). To mask, evade, manipulate a note or even difficult passage.

Wollies (*E. London*). Well known term for olives, of which the great mass brought to London are consumed by the Jews and other East Londoners. Probably an abbreviation of the call, 'O! olives!' by the street vendors of these delicacies.

Wolverines (*American*). People of Michigan—probably from the territory being over-run with wolves.

Won't run to it, It (*Sporting Peoples'*). Too poor. Figure of speech from a horse not reaching the post; in other words—a horse with no stay. Very common expression.

Won't take off his coat (*Street*). Equal to a coward.

Won't wash (*Peoples'*). No permanent value—derived from the printed calico trade.

Wood-spoiler (*Navy*). Merely average ship's carpenter.

Woodbine (*L. London*). Name of the maker of a penny packet of five cigarettes.

Wooden nutmegs (*American*). People of Connecticut. Given in consequence of these traders having been the first to discover this spice, which, it has been said, they once palmed off upon the unwary.

Wooden spoon (*Soc.*, 19 *cent.*) Thick-head; idiot. From Cambridge University—a wooden spoon being until recently given as the lowest possible mathematical honour—but at least an honour—at the Tripos Examinations. (Now no longer given, Tripos being abolished.)

He will never do any good—he is too quite a wooden spoon.

This year a student from Caius College and another from St Catharine's were bracketed equal for the honour of the 'wooden spoon' in the Mathematical Tripos, and to each was presented a huge trophy in the form of a malt shovel, gaily adorned with his college arms and colours.—*D. T.*, 19th June 1894.

Wooden Ulster (*Street*). Coffin.

Word-mongering (*Press*, 1878). Redundancy of description. Used in critical scorn.

Work (*Theatrical and Music Hall*). Perform. Natural affected outcome of calling the theatre 'shop' (*q.v.*).

Work the steam off (*Soc.*, 1870 on). Get rid of superabundant energy.

Work up (*Peoples'*). To aggravate.

Worker (*Polit.*, *American*). A civil service placeman who politically works to bring in his candidate, so that this voter may not go out of office at the next presidential election.

Workus (*Church of England*). Methodist chapel — from its plain, white-washed appearance.

Worm-eater (*Trade—Cabinet-makers'*). A deft artisan who drills very diminutive holes in imitation old furniture, to give the effect of worm-holes to the wood. (*See* Wardour Street Woods.)

Worrab (*Costers' transposed word*). Barrow.

Worrocks (*Peoples'*). Beware. Probably a corruption of ''Ware hawks'—ware being short for beware. The phrase implies—look after your pockets; there are thieves about—a threat presaging attack.

Worry down (*American*). To swallow greedily, like a dog.

Worry the dog (*Peoples'*). Bully—said of a man who upsets even the welcome of the house-dog, which retreats at his approach.

Worth (*Soc.*, 1860-85). Most fashionable costume. From name of a man-milliner of the second French empire.

Wotchero! (*Peoples'*). Agglomeration of 'What cheer oh!'

Wotchero! another one.—*E. T.*, 11th April 1885.

Wreckers, First-night (*Theatr.*). In 1882 a small band of men, chiefly very young, but led by a man of fifty, who combined to wreck pieces on their first night, became very troublesome. They numbered about ten or a dozen, were chiefly superior journeymen, and combined only in relation to their behaviour in the theatres, rarely even drinking together. Injudicious approval of one or two of their remarks, published in one or two cheap Sunday papers, touched their vanity, and they proceeded from objection to objection until nothing pleased them. They received their first check at the Vaudeville on the first night of *The Guv'nor*, when they were 'rushed' from pit and gallery. But their great shock was experienced on the first appearance of Miss Lotta at the Opera Comique (1883), where they were attacked by friends of the management, in which it was said the son of a military duke took victorious part as against the wreckers. So powerful did these people become in the '80's, that managers, even including Irving, changed their first nights from Saturday to some other day in the week, in the belief that the wreckers were generally patrons who could only, as a rule, frequent the theatres on the last night of the week.

Happily there are good reasons for believing that the managerial belief in 'first-night wreckers', as they are called, is greatly exaggerated.—*D. N.*, 25th September 1884.

Wrecking (*Financial*, 1880). Destroying without mercy—and obviously adopted from the old Cornish custom of attracting vessels by false lights, and then destroying all who came ashore. About 1880, the immense height of consols encouraged speculation, and for some three years a vast number of limited liability companies were started, of which nine out of ten came to complete grief. A class of financial solicitors then sprang into existence, who gained doubtful incomes by 'wrecking' companies and grabbing what they could.

Wriggle off (*Lond.*, 1860). Take one's departure.

Wriggling in for a commish (*American*). Sneaking for the payment of a commission.

Writ-pushers (*Legal — vulgar*). Lawyers' clerks.

Write one's name across another's (*Sporting*). To strike in the face.

Mr John Coleman, having been accused of being the author of a certain book, writes to the papers demanding to know the originator of the 'slander'. Mr Coleman is anxious 'to write my signature across his'. This picturesque phrase will be a useful addition to the vocabulary of the ring.—*Globe*, 5th October 1885.

Wrong scent (*Hunting*, 19 *cent.*). Mistaken enquiry. From the phrase 'on a wrong scent'. Good parallel is Barking up a wrong tree (*q.v.*).

Wrong side of the hedge (*Coaching times*). A figurative way of describing a fling from a coach-top.

Wroth of reses (*Theatrical*, 1882). He wore a wrothe of reses—letter inversion of 'wreath of roses'. This treatment was started by Mr F. C. Burnaud (*Punch*, about 1877), who began with 'she smole a smile', etc., etc. Said of a male singer who vocalises too sentimentally.

Wrux (*Modern Public-school*, 1875). A rotter; a humbug.

X

X. S. (*Peoples'*, 1860, etc.). Abbreviation of expenses.

X. X. (*Tavern*). Double X—abbreviation of 'double excellent'.

X. X. X. (*Tavern*). Treble X—Treble excellent.

X's hall (*Thieves'*). Sessions House, Clerkenwell. X's is a corruption of Hicks—Hicks being a dreaded judge who sat for many years on the bench. In the time of imprisonment for debt, every county jail was called by its Governor's name with hotel added—as Chelmsford Jail was called MacGorrorey's Hotel. (*See* Slaughter house.)

Y

Y. M. C. A. (*Anglo-Amer.*). Goody-goody, pure in excelsis. Initials of 'Young Men's Christian Association'.

Yaller-bellies (*Lincoln*). People of Lincolnshire — from the quantity of geese which came from the county of Lincoln. The belly feathers of the goose are yellowish in the shade.

Yaller dog (*American*). Yellow is the tint of most dogs in America—hence it is the most searching term of ordinary contempt.

Yankee main tack (*Navy*). Direct line; is generally associated with a threat to knock a man down. 'I'll lay you along like a Yankee main tack.'

Yankee paradise (*England*). Paris. In the time of the Second Empire, it was said, 'All good Americans go to Paris when they die'. As, however, the century wore on, the excessive extortions of the Parisians drove the touring Americans to London, where they remain in peace and comparative economy.

Yankeeries (*London*, 1887). American and American-Indian display at Earl's Court Gardens.

Bill West's Wild Buffalo — I mean West Buffalo's Wild Bill—at any rate, you know what I *do* mean, though I can't get it quite right—has been the Jubilee boom up to the present. Her gracious Majesty has been to the Yankeeries.—*Ref.*, 15th May 1887.

Yard of satin (*Women's*). Glass of gin. Specimen of grim satire, comparing the colour and smoothness of the spirit with a material generally far distant from the fashions of the patronesses of gin.

Yardnarb (*Transposed word*, 1880). This is confused back-phrasing, being 'brandy'. Here the 'y' for ease in pronunciation is converted into 'yar' to collide with the 'd'.

Ye gods and little fishes! (*Peoples'*). Exclamation of contempt, mocking the theatrical appeal to the gods by an added invocation to finny small fry.

Miss Hilton was engaged—O, ye gods and little fishes!—at a salary of £15 a week.—*Ref.*, 1st March 1885.

Probably means that the lady would be receiving quite enough.

Yell (*Yale College, U.S.A.*). Classical war-cry.

Yell-play (*Theatr.*). A farcical piece in several acts where the laughter is required to be unceasing.

Yellow journalism (*Political*). Extreme jingoistic and overwhelming views.

America remains true to her British friendship, and the stories of American Fenians invading Canada are officially characterised as 'the latest outbreak of yellow journalism'. — *D. T.*, 27th December 1899.

Yellow-backs (*Middle-class*). They were cheap two-shilling editions of novels, which were generally bound in a yellow, glazed paper, printed in colours.

Yellow-bellies. (*See* Web-foots.)

Yelp (*Music Hall*, 1870, etc.). To sing in chorus. In all music halls the audience join in the choruses.

Yere they come smoking their pipes (*Billingsgate*, '70's). Always said by buyers of fish at the auctions when the bids were awfully rapid and high—it meant probably independence and determination. (*See* Now we're busy.)

Yo Tommy (*Minor Theatr. and Peoples'*). Exclamation of condemnation by the small actor. Amongst the lower classes it is a declaration of admiration addressed to the softer sex by the sterner.

Yon kipper (*Yiddish*). The Day of Atonement—New Year's Day amidst the Hebrews. The phrase is yon kippur — this final word being a spondee.

Yorkshire (*Peoples'*). Fair and square payments.

You musn't squeal (*Peoples', Anglo-American*, 1898). Exhortation to be brave. Often satirically used. From the first speech by Mr Roosevelt, New York, to volunteers formed in May 1898, upon outbreak of war between U.S.A. and Spain.

You make me tired (*Anglo-American*, '90's). 'You bore me'—exact synonym. Sometimes now heard in London—supposed to be introduced by the Duchess of Marlborough (1898)—a then leader of fashion.

You'll get yourself disliked (*Street*, 1878) A satirical protest against any one who is behaving abominably.

Young person, The (*Soc*, about 1880). Girl from fifteen to marriage.

To know 'Théo-Critt' is to like him It is true that his morality is rather lax even for a cavalry officer, and that he cannot be recommended to the young person. But then there is such plenty of literature for the young person —*Sat. Rev.*, 26th December 1885

Young thing (*Masculine Women's Society*). A youth between seventeen and twenty-one

You're off the grass (*Cricketing*). Without a chance

Yurup (*American Street*). Europe—accent on the 'rup'

Z

Zambo (*Merchant Marine*, 19 *cent*) Probably a perversion of Sambo (*see*).

A term on the Spanish main for a race produced by the union of the negro and the Indian — it literally means bow-legged — Smyth's *Sailors' Word Book.*

Zarndrer (*Street*, 1863-70). The long single curl brought from the back hair over the left shoulder, and allowed to lie on the breast 'From Alexandra, Princess of Wales, having brought over this fashion from Denmark

Zeb (*Shortened inverted word*, 1882) Best

The *zeb* way we know is to throw the crockery at her If you owe rent, toss the landlord double or quits, and if you know anything of tossing you're bound to come off first zeb.

Zeb taoc (*Curtailed inverted word*) Best coat

Zedding about (*Soc.*, 1883). Going zigzag, diverging

Zoodikers (*Catholic Survival*). God's hooks — hook sometimes being hooker.—*Tom Jones*, bk xviii, ch. 13

Zooks (*Catholic Survival*) God's hooks—hooks being old English for nails, here meaning the nails used upon the cross

'Zouks', said my father — Sterne, *Tristram Shandy.*

Zounds (*Catholic Survival*) God's wounds—this word here rhyming with 'sounds' This oath has survived even to our times It was common in the time of Latimer

Zounds and blood May be found in *Tom Jones*, bk xvi, ch 4

Zulu express (*Railway*). Name given to a Great Western afternoon express, at date of Zulu War.

CPSIA information can be obtained
at www.ICGtesting.com
Printed in the USA
BVHW092107240621
610373BV00002B/234